WHEN CAN WE GO BACK TO AMERICA?

WHEN CAN WE GO BACK TO AMERICA?

Voices of Japanese American Incarceration during World War II

Susan H. Kamei

Foreword by
Secretary Norman Y. Mineta

SIMON & SCHUSTER BFYR

NEW YORK LONDON TORONTO SYDNEY NEW DELHI

An imprint of Simon & Schuster Children's Publishing Division

1230 Avenue of the Americas, New York, New York 10020

Compilation and text © 2021 by Susan H. Kamei

Foreword © 2021 by Norman Y. Mineta

Front jacket photograph courtesy of the National Archives

Back jacket photograph courtesy of the Bancroft Library

Jacket design by Greg Stadnyk © 2021 by Simon & Schuster, Inc.

For information about special discounts for bulk purchases, please contact
Simon & Schuster Special Sales at 1-866-506-1949 or business@simonandschuster.com.

The Simon & Schuster Speakers Bureau can bring authors to your live event. For more
information or to book an event, contact the Simon & Schuster Speakers Bureau at
1-866-248-3049 or visit our website at www.simonspeakers.com.

Interior design by Hilary Zarycky

The text for this book was set in New Caledonia.

Manufactured in the United States of America

First Edition

2 4 6 8 10 9 7 5 3 1

Library of Congress Cataloging-in-Publication Data

Names: Kamei, Susan H., author. | Mineta, Norman Yoshio, 1931–
writer of foreword.

Title: When can we go back to America? : voices of Japanese American incarceration during
World War II / Susan H. Kamei ;
foreword by Secretary Norman Y. Mineta.

Description: First edition. | New York : Simon & Schuster BFYR, [2021] | Includes
bibliographical references and index. | Summary: "A narrative history of Japanese Americans
before, during, and after their World War II incarceration, including the voices and stories of
over 130 individuals who lived through this episode, most of them as young adults"— Provided
by publisher.

Identifiers: LCCN 2017052016 |
ISBN 9781481401449 (hardcover : alk. paper) | ISBN 9781481401463 (ebook)

Subjects: LCSH: Japanese Americans—Evacuation and relocation, 1942–1945—Children—
Biography. | World War, 1939–1945—Children—United States—Biography. | World War,
1939–1945—Japanese Americans—Children. | World War, 1939–1945—Personal narratives.

Classification: LCC D769.8.A6 K36 2021 | DDC 940.53/17730923956—dc23

LC record available at https://lccn.loc.gov/2017052016

In admiration and appreciation of all those of Japanese ancestry who suffered the consequences of the mass incarceration in the United States during World War II solely because of their race, and in hopes that my daughter, Akemi, and other descendants of the Issei and Nisei will remember their stories and will stand up for justice

CONTENTS

I'm always fearful that something like this might happen again. Not to me maybe, but just in the world. I see the neo-Nazis. That scares me to death. And these ultraconservatives . . . I think they could do something like this again. Not necessarily to me but to whoever will be vulnerable. I think I'm more fearful of racism since that whole experience.

—Emi "Amy" **Akiyama** (Berger), female, Sansei, Berkeley,
California, incarcerated age 8, Tanforan Assembly Center, Topaz
Relocation Center[1]

AUTHOR'S NOTE

Most of the voices you will encounter in this book are from persons of Japanese ancestry who shared their thoughts and feelings in previously published works, oral histories, congressional testimonies, or works in the public domain. For consistency, I have identified these individuals by their first names (with nicknames in quotations), last names in bold, and maiden or married names in parentheses. The name in bold is the name by which they were known during their incarceration.

Since the gender of Japanese names might not be obvious to all readers, I have also identified the gender as "male" or "female" on the basis of their names. I have also included their generation identifier of Issei, Nisei, or Sansei. For persons who were incarcerated, I have provided their location at the time of forced removal, the name of their assigned assembly center (if they were sent to one), and the place or places of their long-term detention. I have included their age at the time they received the government order to leave the West Coast military zones. For those persons who were not incarcerated, I have included their location and age at the time Pearl Harbor was bombed.

I acknowledge each of those whose voice is included in this book as a contributor. You'll find key pieces of information and personal stories about the contributors in the section called "Contributor Biographies." The Contributor Biography Sources are online under the "Resources and Downloads" tab at www.simonandschuster.net/books /When-Can-We-Go-Back-to-America/Susan-H-Kamei/9781481401449. I apologize in advance for any inaccuracies as a result of relying upon these sources, especially in those cases when I was not able to confirm the biographical information with the individual or a family member.

As you read this book, you will also come across direct quotes from certain articles and books. In those instances, a footnote is provided at the bottom of the page. More extensive information about the source, including page numbers, is included in the Chapter Sources at the back of the book.

•   •   •

For your reference, "Issei" (pronounced *EE-SAY*) refers to the first generation of immigrants who left Japan to make new lives in the United States. The Issei formed neighborhoods known as Little Tokyos and Nihonmachis, or Japantowns. Whether they were Buddhist or Christian, they celebrated traditional festivals and customs of Japan, their country of origin, and revered cultural values such as the primacy of family, social order, discipline, and honor. However, because of American naturalization laws against immigration on the basis of race, the Issei could not become US citizens, even though they might have been living in the United States, their adopted country, for decades. Of the approximately 120,000 persons of Japanese ancestry who were incarcerated, approximately 39,000 of them were Issei, or 33 percent.

The children of the Issei are called "Nisei" (pronounced *NEE-SAY*), which means "second generation." Under the Fourteenth Amendment, persons born in the United States are citizens, so by virtue of their birth in the United States, the Nisei were American citizens. The Nisei grew up with a complicated perspective of being Japanese Americans in a pre–World War II society. Unlike their parents, who spoke little or no English, the Nisei were native English speakers; most had rudimentary Japanese-language skills, sufficient enough to communicate only with their parents and other Issei. Although their Issei parents wanted them to appreciate their Japanese heritage and "be Japanese" at home, the Nisei identified with being "all-American." The Nisei constituted approximately 60 percent of those incarcerated, or about 72,000 of the 120,000 total. Almost half (45 percent) of the incarcerated Nisei were between five and nineteen years old; the majority were teenagers between the ages of fifteen and nineteen.

"Sansei" (pronounced *SAN-SAY*) means "third generation," or the grandchildren of the Issei; "Yonsei" (pronounced *YONE-SAY*) means "fourth generation," or the Issei's great-grandchildren. Today there are even "Gosei" (pronounced *GO-SAY*), or "fifth generation," representing the great-great-grandchildren of the Issei.

"Kibei" (pronounced *KEE-BAY*), which means "go home to America," refers to American-born children of Issei who were sent to Japan to be educated or for family considerations, and later "came home" to the United States.

"Nikkei" (pronounced *NEE-KAY*) refers to all persons of Japanese ancestry, regardless of citizenship; the term does not differentiate between those born in Japan, in the United States, or in other countries.

● ● ●

Some comments about terminology: The wartime experience of the Nikkei in the United States is commonly referred to as internment. However, "internment" specifically refers to the US government's legal authority during wartime—originating under the Alien Enemies Act of 1798—to detain, or "intern," individuals, or "internees" (as those terms are defined under the Alien Enemies Act), who are from other nations, known as "nationals," and who have come to this country to live and work. When the country of their nationality is at war with the United States, then those individuals are categorized as "enemy aliens." In the case of World War II, if you weren't an American citizen and you were a native of Japan, Germany, or Italy, you were characterized as an enemy alien no matter how long you had lived here. If the government thought you would be more loyal to the country of your citizenship than to the United States and that you might engage in subversive activity against US interests, you would most likely be arrested by agents of the Federal Bureau of Investigation. The FBI would confiscate anything you owned that was considered contraband and you could be sent to one of the "internment" camps designated for enemy aliens run by the US Department of Justice or the US Army for the duration of the war. And this did happen, especially during the first week after Pearl Harbor.

But the objective of President Franklin D. Roosevelt's Executive Order 9066 was to imprison all Japanese persons—every man, woman, and child (enemy aliens and US citizens alike)—living in California, Oregon, Washington State, and parts of Arizona. And after all was said and done, nearly *two thirds* of those people of Japanese ancestry who were uprooted, forcibly removed, and detained by the government during World War II had been born in the United States; they were Nisei American citizens. And so the term "internment" should not be applied to them, then or ever, because as US citizens, they were not "enemy aliens." Still, this episode has come to be known as "the Japanese American internment," and when you read other books and materials on this subject, you will often see the word "internment" used. In this book, instead of referring to this experience as the "internment," I call it the "incarceration" and refer to individuals who were imprisoned as "incarcerees."

"Incarceration" captures the notion of imprisonment, which is considered accurate when applied to the entirety of the population of persons of Japanese ancestry who were detained against their will. And this incarceration also applies to individuals of Japanese descent who were living as far away as Latin America, particularly in Peru. Over two thousand Latin American citizens of Japanese ancestry were rounded up in those countries in the same manner as Japanese Americans and brought to the United States for indefinite detention. And even though they were brought to America by force, after the war they were classified as illegal aliens.

What to call the camps has become even more controversial. The government's terminology of "assembly centers" and "relocation centers" imply benign processes, masking the harsh realities of armed guards, barbed wire fences, and indefinite confinement in desolate conditions. President Roosevelt himself as well as other government officials referred to these places as "concentration camps," which are prisons where masses of people are concentrated. This usage is consistent with the origins of the term dating back to the Anglo-Boer War of 1899–1902, or South African War, during which British officials established "concentration camps" to hold Boer families hostage. Sources such as the Japanese American National Museum, and Densho—the nonprofit organization that has assembled documents, oral histories, and digital archival material regarding the imprisonment of Japanese Americans during World War II—believe "concentration camps" to be the more precise term, noting that this usage is not meant to suggest any equivalency with the experiences of Holocaust victims in Nazi death camps. Recognizing this sensitivity, I use, but not exclusively, the term "concentration camp" in this book.

• • •

As this book is going to press, we are experiencing an alarming spike in discrimination and violence against the Asian American and Pacific Islander (AAPI) communities across our country. During this pandemic year, hateful and hostile racist rhetoric has escalated into— and has attempted to justify—attacks upon unsuspecting individuals of Asian descent, including the elderly.

On March 18, 2021, the House Judiciary Subcommittee on the Constitution, Civil Rights, and Civil Liberties convened a hearing in the wake of the murder of eight people, six of whom were women of Asian descent, in three spas outside of Atlanta, Georgia. In her testimony at that hearing, Congresswoman Doris Matsui said, "The fear of 'the other,' whether racial, religious, or tribal, . . . works to suppress the better angels of our nature." Born in the Poston War Relocation Authority camp, Congresswoman Matsui was reminded of the unchecked racism that her family endured before, during, and after World War II. She concluded, "We have seen the consequences when we go down this path. My family has lived through these consequences. This is what we are working to root out from the deepest place in our social conscience."

FOREWORD

I f you happen to catch me wearing a jacket these days, you'll see a pin of an American flag in my lapel. It's my way of reminding everyone I encounter that despite how they might judge me by my Japanese face, I am an American, and a proud one, at that.

On a grim spring day in 1942, my parents, three sisters, brother, and I boarded a train in San Jose, California, for the Santa Anita Race Track near Los Angeles and then, in November 1942, to the Heart Mountain detention camp in a desolate part of Wyoming, where we were incarcerated behind barbed wire for the duration of World War II. I was only ten years old, yet I knew that our government was wrong to deprive us of our constitutional rights simply because we were of Japanese ancestry. But I wanted to wear my Cub Scout uniform anyway to express my patriotism. I never lost faith in my country, despite the prejudicial actions of the US government.

You see, while my family endured the hardships of the incarceration along with 120,000 others of Japanese ancestry, my siblings and I learned from our parents to view life as a glass half-full instead of half-empty. Rather than dwell on the injustice of our imprisonment, I was raised to remain positive about the privilege of being an American citizen.

My way of turning the very difficult and challenging wartime episode into a path of hope was to see life in the United States as full of opportunity. After my family left the Heart Mountain camp, I grew up to serve in the Korean War, and when I came home, my father encouraged me to get involved in my community's local politics as a way of making a difference.

I became mayor of San Jose, California, the first Asian American mayor of a major American city. It was important to me to be the voice of the people who were either underrepresented—or not represented at all. I remembered when there were too few voices who spoke up for us way back in December 1941 after the attack on Pearl Harbor. This principle of representation motivated me to serve as a member of Congress for twenty-two years, the first Japanese American in the House of Representatives from the mainland.

As a congressional representative, I was able to speak up for the disenfranchised by working for the passage of the Civil Liberties Act of 1988. This legislative accomplishment was an impossible dream come true. It provided financial redress to the surviving former inmates of the camps whose constitutional rights had been trampled due to decades of racial discrimination. With a bipartisan coalition and a wide spectrum of support from across the country, we succeeded in getting our government to admit—what I already knew as a young boy—that it had made a tragic and terrible mistake. On behalf of the federal government, President Ronald Reagan gave the entire Japanese American population a meaningful apology. In that one act alone, we learned that our democracy is resilient enough to right a wrong.

Susan Kamei and her father, Hiroshi Kamei, were among the community leaders whose work on the legislative ground game helped us get the legislation passed. In the decades since its enactment, Susan, a daughter and granddaughter of incarcerees, has been deeply committed to helping people understand that the incarceration didn't happen simply as a reaction to wartime hysteria surrounding the attack on Pearl Harbor. We now know that, fundamentally, it was a breakdown in our constitutional system.

To that end, Susan has set forth in this landmark book not just *what* happened to us, but also *why* these events happened in the way that they did. And now, for the first time ever, you can learn in one place about the entire trajectory of the Japanese American experience, from the pioneer Issei facing "Yellow Peril" hostilities, to their grandchildren and great-grandchildren who stand today in solidarity with others facing similar racial hostilities. And their stories will come alive for you, as you read about their thoughts and feelings, in their own words, as the situation was unfolding.

I had hoped that after the passage of the Civil Liberties Act of 1988 what happened to us in 1942 would never happen again. But on September 11, 2001, terrorists hijacked US passenger airplanes to attack us on our soil. As secretary of transportation for President George W. Bush, I took the responsibility for grounding all flights in the aftermath of the attacks. Immediately I heard calls to keep Middle Easterners and Muslims off airplanes and even to remove them to detention facilities—another instance of assuming an entire group of innocent people are guilty of a crime simply because they look like the enemy. Fortunately, President George W. Bush resisted these calls, recognizing that his secretary of transportation had once been treated like the enemy on the basis of how he looked.

I encourage everyone reading this book to get involved in your student government or your town's or city's local civic affairs to get a taste of what you could accomplish when you are part of the political discourse. I hope you'll be inspired by the examples of citizen bravery and leadership in this book and then contribute in your own community. Our municipalities, cities, counties, states, and our whole country need you to be in the room where decisions are made on important policies and practices.

Where else but in the United States could I, as the son of immigrants, have had the opportunity to serve in the cabinets of both President George W. Bush and President Bill Clinton, two presidents of different political parties? I was able to be the public servant in the room to remind others of our constitutional responsibilities.

As you will read, Japanese Americans are not monolithic—no community is. It's our diversity that brings vitality to our society. This book will give you a broader understanding of what it means to be an American, and my fervent wish is that it will motivate you to make real the words we say when we salute the flag, "with liberty and justice for all."

Secretary Norman Y. Mineta
Edgewater, Maryland
October 26, 2020

INTRODUCTION

Growing up as a third-generation Japanese American Sansei in Orange County, California, I had a vague notion that my Japanese immigrant Issei grandparents and my American-born Nisei parents had spent the years of World War II in some kind of prison camp because they were presumed to be disloyal simply because of their race. Generally, the first- and second-generation Japanese Americans didn't talk about their World War II incarceration, let alone share their feelings about what had happened to them.

It's taken me years of listening and researching to better understand why it was so difficult for the incarcerees to tell their stories, to gain some appreciation for the hardships they endured, and to realize why their stories are so important today. The few stories that I heard from my parents took on more meaningful significance for me. And with this understanding of the wrongful actions of the US government, I became motivated to contribute to the cause of righting the constitutional wrongs that were done to them. Allow me to share with you a few examples of what I have learned, and why I think it is so important that you are reading this book.

One afternoon when I was in elementary school, I had finished practicing for my upcoming piano lesson. My mother said to me wistfully, "I wish I still had your aunt's piano music for you. We had to leave so many things behind when we left for camp." It wasn't until I was in high school that I learned more about the magnitude of what my parents had to face and what my family had to sacrifice when they, along with thousands of other persons of Japanese ancestry from the West Coast, were ordered to leave their homes, taking only the things they could carry, and relinquishing their possessions, their pets, their livelihoods, and their educations to board buses and trains without having any idea where they were going.

Once they arrived at the desolate places in our country's interior states called war relocation centers, they were confronted with the harsh reality of being detained indefinitely in hastily and poorly constructed barracks, behind barbed wire, under searchlights, with guns and bayonets pointed at them. My mother described the bitter winters in Heart Mountain, Wyoming—how icicles would form in her wet hair as she walked across camp from the cold showers to her barrack. My father told me about sleeping outside on the bare ground during work breaks as he and his family harvested sugar beets. He would do anything rather than be idle in camp. He eventually testified before a congressional commission about the economic losses his family had incurred and the irrevocable harm that the lack of adequate schooling had had on him and his whole generation.

I remember the look of resolve on my father's face during one conversation we had not long after I started college. He told me that on the night of December 7, 1941, the day of the Pearl Harbor bombing, two FBI agents searched my grandparents' home without a search warrant. Over the years he had thought about the confusion and fear he and his family experienced that night and how they continued to live with those debilitating feelings for the duration of the war and its aftermath. He described how powerless they felt being subjected to government order after government order.

He went on to tell me about the family's legal issues after the war was over. "After my family got out of camp," he said, "and returned to Orange County to pick up the pieces and start farming again, we didn't have anyone who could advise us on our rights. We couldn't afford an attorney, even if we knew one, and I thought then that we sure could have used an attorney in the family. You could be that attorney."

In that conversation, my father motivated me to set the goal of becoming a lawyer. I ended up using my legal education and training to work with him for over a decade in what is now called the redress movement. Redress volunteers throughout the country wanted acknowledgment from the federal government that the constitutional rights of the Japanese men, women, and children who were incarcerated had been violated, especially those of the second-generation Nisei, who had been born in America and were US citizens. Various redress groups sought restitution through legislative campaigns in Congress and in court. One of the greatest days of my life was August 10, 1988, when my father and I were among the redress volunteers invited to the White House to witness President Ronald Reagan sign the Civil Liberties Act of 1988, which expressed a national apology and pledged token restitution payments to the surviving incarcerees.

The combined legislative and judicial findings in the 1980s finally produced all the evidence we needed to reveal the real reason behind the Japanese American incarceration. By this time, we knew that it had not been a "military necessity," as the War Department had claimed over and over again; it did nothing for our national security. Rather, hundreds of thousands of pages of evidence were presented to Congress and in court cases to show that the government's orders had stemmed from baseless perceptions of disloyalty grounded in racial stereotypes and the long-standing, anti-immigrant "Yellow Peril" rhetoric. It was also rooted in greed. Private business interests wanted Japanese Americans permanently removed from agriculture, seafood canneries, and other industries because they were perceived as economic threats. In other words, they were too skilled at farming and fishing for their own good.

Why should we care today about events that happened nearly eighty years ago? We should care because there are those today who cite the Japanese American incarceration as "precedent" for "rounding up" others on the basis of race, national origin, and religion, for no justifiable reason. We should care when our government behaves in unconstitutional ways.

I created and now teach a history course at the University of Southern California titled War, Race, and the Constitution, using the Japanese American World War II incarceration as a lens through which we can examine our constitutional framework and what happens when our constitutional system of checks and balances among the executive, legislative, and judicial branches breaks down. We consider the actions our government must take in order to safeguard our national security while also protecting the civil liberties of individuals against detention without charges, unlawful searches and seizures, and the presumption of guilt instead of innocence until proven guilty. These are all questions that my students find to be piercingly relevant in today's heated discourse on nearly every issue of consequence.

As poet and philosopher George Santayana said, "Those who cannot remember the past are condemned to repeat it." To this, I would add a corollary: Those who don't know our past will find a way to reinvent it. The voices in this book speak over the passage of time and yet need to be heard urgently now. Can you catch the significance of the title, *When Can We Go Back to America?* The origin of this title is from a story that circulated among the incarcerees in the camps. It's said that a small girl was so startled to be in an environment surrounded by all Japanese faces that she assumed her family had taken her to Japan. She looked up at her mother and said, "Let's go back home to America."

The story has symbolic meaning: When the events of World War II unfolded, my parents and their fellow Nisei could not believe that this unconscionable experience was happening to citizens of the United States—the land of their birth. In the years since their wartime hardships, my parents often wondered if the day would ever come when their rights, and those of others similarly targeted, would be treated with equal protection under the law. During and after the war, they asked themselves, *When will the America promised in the Fourteenth Amendment to the Constitution come home again? When will its fundamental ideal of due process apply to us?*

To this end, I earnestly hope that as you read this book, you will want to learn more about the Japanese American incarceration so you can better appreciate the degree of vigilance with which we must fight injustice with the full measure of the Constitution's power.

PART ONE

CHAPTER ONE

Day of Infamy

All of a sudden, three aircraft flew right overhead. They were pearl grey with red dots on the wing—Japanese. I knew what was happening. And I thought my world had just come to an end.

—The Honorable Daniel "Dan" Ken **Inouye**, male, Nisei, Honolulu, Hawaii, age 17 when Pearl Harbor was attacked[2]

Sunday morning, December 7, 1941, just before 8:00 a.m. Hawaii time. A pearl-gray Mitsubishi A6M Zero "Reisen" carrier-borne naval fighter and a Nakajima B5N "Kate" carrier-borne torpedo bomber with red dots on the wings launched from one of six Imperial Japanese Navy aircraft carriers. As soon as they reached the US Navy's Pacific Fleet in Pearl Harbor—a natural lagoon on the island of Oahu—they began dropping bombs and torpedoes.

Minutes later Rear Admiral Husband E. Kimmel, commander in chief of the Pacific Fleet, sent out a radiogram to all navy ships in Hawaii: "AIRRAID ON PEARL HARBOR X THIS IS NO DRILL." But Kimmel's urgent alert could not stop the onslaught of approximately 360 Imperial Japanese bombers from raining down on Pearl Harbor and nearby army bases and airfields for almost two hours. Kimmell and the other commanders watched helplessly as the daring Japanese raid devastated the Pacific Fleet and crippled the defense of the naval base in a single attack.

President Franklin D. Roosevelt and his advisers had been anticipating imminent war because diplomatic relations between Japan and the United States had completely deteriorated. But no one had imagined Pearl Harbor to be Japan's likely first strike. Everyone had assumed that Japan would hit closer targets first, like the Philippines or the Malay Peninsula; they'd discounted Japan's capacity to carry out a long-range assault on Hawaii's fortified naval base. Believing that the US Navy's Pacific Fleet would be needed at full strength against the Japanese in the Pacific, the US military had amassed eight of the nation's battleships and other support ships together at Pearl Harbor. Likewise, Lieutenant General Walter C. Short, the local army commander, had ordered the planes at nearby Hickam and Wheeler airfields to be clustered together on the ground. He figured the planes could be more easily guarded against sabotage by local Japanese residents this way. But those fears were unfounded, and the battleships and aircraft in Hawaii were sitting ducks.

As a consequence, the Japanese forces were able to hit all eight battleships at once, destroying the USS *Arizona* and USS *Oklahoma*, along with 149 American airplanes. And the human toll was gruesome: 2,340 Americans killed and 1,178 others wounded. Among the American servicemen who gave their lives that day was Japanese American Private Torao Migita of Company D, 298th Infantry Battalion, killed tragically not by Japanese bombs, but by friendly fire as he was reporting for duty. Japanese American civilians were also among those killed in the attack, most by friendly fire. In contrast, Japan lost only 29 planes and 64 servicemen.

Around the same time on the mainland, ten-year-old Sam Yoshimura was riding his bicycle in his small hometown of Florin, California. Twenty-one-year-old Miyo Senzaki was working at her family's produce stand in Los Angeles. Twenty-two-year-old Fred Korematsu was relaxing in the Oakland hills with his girlfriend. And ten-year-old Norman Mineta had just come home with his family from services at their Methodist church in San Jose when they heard the radio blasting news of the attack on Pearl Harbor.

It was the first time Norm had ever seen his father cry.

"I can't understand why the land of my birth attacked the land of my heart," his father said.

Then Joyce Hirano, his neighbor and close friend, came running over, "yelling, screaming and crying that the FBI was there to take her father away."

Norm's father rushed over to the Hirano home next door, but by the time he got there, Joyce's father was gone.

• • •

I was attending St. Mary's Episcopal church on the Sunday morning that the war broke out. . . . When I reached home later that day, I found my mother in hysterics, crying and trying to pick up after the FBI had searched the house.

"They took Papa!" Mama shouted. "They chained him and numbered him like an animal!"

> —Mitsuo "Mits" **Usui**, male, Nisei, Los Angeles, California, incarcerated age 25, Santa Anita Assembly Center, Granada (Amache) Relocation Center[3]

On a peaceful Sunday morning, December 7, 1941, Henry, Sumi and I were at choir rehearsal singing ourselves hoarse in preparation for the annual Christmas recital of Handel's "Messiah." Suddenly Chuck Mizuno, a young University of Washington student, burst into the chapel, gasping as if he had sprinted all the way up the stairs.

"Listen, everybody!" he shouted. "Japan just bombed Pearl Harbor . . . in Hawaii! It's war!"

The terrible words hit like a blockbuster, paralyzing us. Then we smiled feebly at each other, hoping this was one of Chuck's practical jokes. Miss Hara, our music director, rapped her baton impatiently on the music stand and chided him, "Now Chuck, fun's fun, but we have work to do. Please take your place. You're already half an hour late."

But Chuck strode vehemently back to the door. "I mean it, folks, honest! I just heard the news over my car radio. Reporters are talking a blue streak. Come on down and hear it for yourselves."

With that, Chuck swept out of the room, a swirl of young men following in his wake. Henry was one of them. The rest of us stayed, rooted to our places like a row of marionettes. I felt as if a fist had smashed my pleasant little existence, breaking it into jigsaw puzzle pieces. An old wound opened up again, and I found myself shrinking inwardly from my Japanese blood, the blood of an enemy. I knew instinctively that the fact that I was an American by birthright was not going to help me escape the consequences of this unhappy war.

One girl mumbled over and over again, "It can't be, God, it can't be!"

Someone else was saying, ". . . Do you think we'll be considered Japanese or Americans?"

A boy replied quietly, "We'll be Japs, same as always. But our parents are enemy aliens now, you know."

A shocked silence followed.

—Monica Kazuko **Itoi** (Sone), female, Nisei, Seattle, Washington, incarcerated age 23, Puyallup Assembly Center, Minidoka Relocation Center[4]

I still remember turning on the radio Sunday morning [and] heard the announcer say, "We have been attacked by the Japanese at Pearl Harbor, we are at war." I thought, hold on, this must be another radio play. Have you ever heard of that Orson Welles "The War of the Worlds"? It was so realistic, people running all over, getting their guns ready to fight the Martians. Well, I thought it was one of those radio plays, so I didn't pay much attention to it.

—Frank Seishi **Emi**, male, Nisei, Los Angeles, California, incarcerated age 26, Pomona Assembly Center, Heart Mountain Relocation Center, Leavenworth Penitentiary[5]

The news hit us like a bomb.

—David Masao **Sakai**, male, Nisei, San Jose, California, incarcerated age 25, Santa Anita Assembly Center, Heart Mountain Relocation Center[6]

• • •

The wreckage in Pearl Harbor was still smoldering a few hours later when FBI agents fanned out all along the West Coast. The FBI had already targeted thousands of Japanese Issei men for arrest: prominent community and business leaders, members of the Japanese Chamber of Commerce, Buddhist and Shinto priests, newspaper editors and reporters, leaders of flower-arranging and bonsai societies, principals and teachers of Japanese-language schools, martial arts instructors, farmers, business executives, travel agents, donors to Japanese charities, those who had recently visited Japan, and those who'd been denounced as potential traitors by neighbors they might never have met. The agents knew exactly where these Issei men lived.

• • •

The full impact of this day was realized that night when my grandfather was taken away by the FBI without reason or cause. This gentle man was a scholar, poet, and educated as a librarian. . . . He had bookcases full of books. He was a master calligrapher, and I used to sit by his side and watch him paint with a [Japanese] paintbrush. . . . He won the Emperor's poetry contest. He could write beautiful poetry.
—Aiko Grace **Shinoda** (Nakamura), female, Nisei, Los Angeles, California, incarcerated age 15, Manzanar Reception Center, Manzanar Relocation Center[7]

They got [Papa]. . . . FBI deputies had been questioning everyone, ransacking houses for anything that could conceivably be used for signaling planes or ships or that indicated loyalty to the Emperor [of Japan]. Most of the houses had radios with a short-wave band and a high aerial on the roof so that wives could make contact with the fishing boats during those long cruises. To the FBI, every radio owner was a potential saboteur. The confiscators were often deputies sworn in hastily during the turbulent days right after Pearl Harbor, and these men seemed to be acting out the general panic, seeing sinister possibilities in the most ordinary household items: flashlights, kitchen knives, cameras, lanterns, toy swords. . . . Two FBI men in fedora hats and trench coats—like out of a thirties movie—knocked on [the] door and when they left, Papa was between them. He didn't struggle. There was no point to it. He had become a man without a country. . . . About all he had left at [that] point was his tremendous dignity.

—Jeanne Toyo **Wakatsuki** (Houston), female, Nisei, Santa Monica, California, incarcerated age 8, Manzanar Reception Center, Manzanar Relocation Center[8]

The FBI came to our house and searched everything. It was awful, just awful. They even ran their hands through our rice and sugar bowls looking for guns and radios or anything with Japanese writing.

—Hisaye **Yamamoto** (Desoto), female, Nisei, Oceanside, California, incarcerated age 20, Poston Relocation Center[9]

It made me positively hivey the way the FBI agents . . . continued their raids into Japanese homes and business places and marched the Issei men away into the old red brick immigration building, systematically and efficiently, as if they were stocking a cellarful of choice bottles of wine. . . . We wondered when Father's time would come. We expected momentarily to hear strange footsteps on the porch and the sudden, demanding ring of the front doorbell. Our ears became attuned like the sensitive antennas of moths, translating every soft swish of passing cars into the arrival of the FBI squad.

—Monica Kazuko **Itoi** (Sone), female, Nisei, Seattle, Washington, incarcerated age 23, Puyallup Assembly Center, Minidoka Relocation Center[10]

. . .

At Sumi Okamoto's wedding reception in Spokane, Washington, the FBI led away four Issei men who had gathered there for the celebration. Most of those arrested were husbands, fathers, and breadwinners who were forced to leave their wives, children, and elderly relatives to fend for themselves. In many cases, their family members would not know what happened to them after their arrest, and the families would not be reunited for months or years—or ever.

Donald Nakahata's father worked for the Japanese Association of San Francisco and San Jose. Nakahata remembers walking him to a bus stop on either December 7 or December 8, and that was the last time he saw his father. Later he would find out that his father died in a Department of Justice (DOJ) internment camp.

Also swept up in the first wave of arrests were nearly all of the Japanese fishermen on Terminal Island—an area just five miles long and largely man-made—in Los Angeles harbor. These fishermen were part of a thriving, close-knit community of approximately 3,500 Japanese residents whose fathers and grandfathers had grown a prosperous industry in canned tuna and sardines. Unfortunately for the Japanese Americans who had established their homes and livelihoods there, the small island was next to a naval shipyard where warships were under construction. Many fishermen were arrested as soon as they docked their vessels and were prevented from even saying good-bye to their families. They were treated like criminals, placed in temporary Immigration and Naturalization Service (INS) detention centers or county jails, then transferred to internment camps operated by the US Army or the DOJ.

In some cases, families were able to obtain permission to visit the men at the local detention centers before they were moved farther away. Yoshiko Uchida was lucky she could see her father, Takashi "Dwight" Uchida, before he was sent to an internment camp in Missoula, Montana, with ninety other men. From there he was able to write letters home that were censored, and send telegrams identified as "internee telegrams."

· · ·

Don't forget to lubricate the car. And be sure to prune the roses in January. Brush Laddie every day and give him a pat for me. Don't forget to send a monthly check to Grandma and take my Christmas offering to church.

—Takashi "Dwight" **Uchida**, male, Issei, Berkeley, California, incarcerated age 58, Fort Missoula Alien Detention Center, Tanforan Assembly Center, Topaz Relocation Center[11]

THINKING OF MY FAMILY FROM THIS PLACE OF EXILE

Leaving a city of everlasting spring.
  I am buried in the snow of Montana.
In the Northern Country.
  You in San Diego, I in Montana
The path of my dream
  is frozen.

—Kyuji **Aizumi**, male, Issei, San Diego, California, incarcerated age 56, Fort Missoula Alien Detention Center, Santa Anita Assembly Center, Poston Relocation Center[12]

• • •

In the wake of this dragnet, the West Coast Japanese Americans panicked that they might be caught with possessions that would cause the authorities to question their loyalty.

My mother told us to bring all the books out that were Japanese. She had a big bonfire. I saw all my children's books and records go up in flames. I was crying. She said, "We can't keep them here. The FBI may come, and we don't know what is going to happen."

—Dollie Kimiko **Nagai** (Fukawa), female, Nisei, Fresno, California, incarcerated age 15, Fresno Assembly Center, Jerome Relocation Center[13]

We knew it was impossible to destroy everything. The FBI would certainly think it strange if they found us sitting in a bare house, totally purged of things Japanese. But it was as if we could no longer stand the tension of waiting, and we just had to do something against the black day. We worked all night, feverishly combing through bookshelves, closets, drawers, and furtively creeping down to the basement furnace for the burning. . . . It was past midnight when we finally climbed upstairs to bed. Wearily we closed our eyes, filled with an indescribable sense of guilt for having destroyed the things we loved. . . . As I lay struggling to fall asleep I realized that we hadn't freed ourselves at all from fear. We still lay stiff in our beds, waiting.

—Monica Kazuko **Itoi** (Sone), female, Nisei, Seattle, Washington, incarcerated age 23, Puyallup Assembly Center, Minidoka Relocation Center[14]

I remember . . . yanking our pictures from our family album and burning them. We removed all Japanese calligraphy hangings from our walls, even though we could not read them. In short, we tried to deny our very culture and origins.

—Minoru "Min" **Tamaki**, male, Nisei, San Francisco, California, incarcerated age 24, Tanforan Assembly Center, Topaz Relocation Center[15]

• • •

On the day Pearl Harbor was bombed, President Franklin D. Roosevelt (FDR) issued Presidential Proclamation Nos. 2525, 2526, and 2527, which authorized the United States "to detain potentially dangerous enemy aliens" from Japan, Germany, and Italy:

> Whenever there is a declared war between the United States and any foreign nation or government, or any invasion or predatory incursion is perpetrated, attempted, or threatened against

the territory of the United States by any foreign nation or government, and the President makes public proclamation of the event, all natives, citizens, denizens, or subjects of the hostile nation or government, being of the age of fourteen years old and upward, who shall be within the United States and not actually naturalized, shall be liable to be apprehended, restrained, secured, and removed as alien enemies.

The next day FDR addressed a joint session of Congress and referred to December 7, 1941, as "a date which will live in infamy." Japan had not publicly declared war against the United States, so the words "Pearl Harbor" were now synonymous with a surprise or sneak attack. The president received from Congress a declaration of war on the Empire of Japan. As a result, all Issei residing in the United States were classified as enemy aliens. Two days later, on December 10, Italy and Germany declared war on the United States and became allies of Japan.

As news of the destruction at Pearl Harbor spread, Americans reacted with shock and anger. The White House was inundated with telegrams and phone calls from people everywhere demanding revenge. From then on, anyone with a Japanese face, no matter where they'd been born or whether they were US citizens, was viewed as the enemy: Their mail would be censored, their fishing boats grounded, their food markets closed, their Japanese-language press shut down, and all of their bank accounts frozen.

• • •

I felt like everybody and their uncle was looking at me, so I hurried home. When I got to Japantown the place looked as though it was deserted. No one was out in the streets and some of the stores were still open, and as soon as I got home my parents said, "Stay home, we don't want you to be wandering around," and as I looked out the window, I could see extra police cars in the area. And suddenly I began to see, I guess they could either have been detectives or FBI agents. . . . I suddenly felt insecure. I don't know quite how to describe it but it was a funny feeling, it was the funniest feeling I ever had.

— Katsumi Thomas "Tom" **Kawaguchi**, male, Nisei, San Francisco, California, incarcerated age 21, Tanforan Assembly Center, Topaz Relocation Center[16]

I went to [high] school on Monday. We used to eat lunch with other kids, but all of a sudden it just slammed down on us. None of the kids would associate with us. Before Pearl Harbor, I had good friends who were Caucasians—an Italian kid, a Jewish kid, an Okie, and a couple of Mexican kids. We all used to hang around together. I was the one Japanese. The day after Pearl Harbor, they were civil with me, you know, but they weren't that friendly. The son of the junior high school principal and I used to run around together. I had had dinner over at their house. Not after Pearl Harbor.

— Ben Toshihiro **Tagami**, male, Nisei, Los Angeles, California, incarcerated age 17, Fresno Assembly Center, Jerome Relocation Center[17]

My eldest brother was a practicing dentist in Gardena, having just graduated from USC [University of Southern California] Dental School in 1941. . . . He volunteered for the U.S. Army immediately after Pearl Harbor but was turned down. He was told that the U.S. Army did not need any Japanese American dentists.

— Mary **Sakaguchi** (Oda), female, Nisei, Los Angeles, California, incarcerated age 22, Manzanar Reception Center, Manzanar Relocation Center[18]

• • •

Meanwhile, Secretary of the Navy Frank Knox was on an airplane bound for Hawaii. He knew he'd be facing a congressional inquiry; one US senator was already calling for his resignation. He needed to find a way to deflect attention from the military's lack of preparation, so he falsely cast blame on the Japanese Americans living in Hawaii, further inciting the general public's growing paranoia. He claimed that Japan was enlisting agents and sympathizers from within the United States to engage in "fifth column" espionage in preparation for a second all-out attack on the California coast. Knox's term "fifth column" refers to Americans who are considered traitors because they engage in espionage or sabotage against the United States on behalf of US enemies acting within the country. In short, he was claiming that Japanese Americans were secretly plotting disloyal acts against the US government *on US soil*. He included his fifth column accusations in his December 14 report to the president and then announced them in a press conference to more than two hundred reporters the next day.

Even after the FBI and army intelligence concurred that there had been no such sabotage by Japanese Americans during or after the attack, Knox continued to repeat these false charges without ever offering any evidence. Intelligence officials in Washington and Hawaii disputed his claims in private but not in public. Before joining the Roosevelt administration, Knox had been an executive with the Hearst media empire, which was well known for spreading "Yellow Peril" rhetoric in its newspaper pages. He knew what would play in the headlines: SECRETARY OF NAVY BLAMES FIFTH COLUMN FOR THE RAID and FIFTH COLUMN TREACHERY TOLD.

Knox became the first official of the US government to put his weight and office behind a frenzy of baseless allegations against Americans of Japanese ancestry. He energized long-standing prejudice against them from some of California's most prominent industries, especially the large agricultural organizations that wanted to eliminate Japanese American farmers from the US market entirely. Charles M. Goethe, a member of the California Joint Immigration Committee, put it openly: "This is our time to get things done that we have been trying to get done for a quarter of a century."

Ironically, Japanese American farmers operated only 2 percent of all farms in California. In 1913, California had passed the first of its Alien Land Laws, which prohibited "aliens ineligible for citizenship"— meaning the Issei farmers—from owning land or holding long-term leases. In addition to California, other states, including Arizona, Idaho, New Mexico, Oregon, Utah, Washington, and Wyoming, had similar laws. The Issei worked around the restrictions of the Alien Land Laws by buying land in the names of their American-born Nisei children, or sometimes in partnership with Caucasian friends. But even with those work-around arrangements, by 1940 only 1,290 of the 5,135 Japanese American farmers in California were landowners, and 3,845 (roughly 75 percent) were managers and tenants.

In terms of scale, Japanese American farmers were in direct competition only with other small farmers, not the White growers who farmed wheat and potatoes on enormous tracts of land. Nevertheless, White farmers resented their productivity; Japanese Americans far excelled in growing labor-intensive crops by using high-yield techniques such as crop rotation. Issei farmers became especially adept with strawberries, which required backbreaking stoop labor. In California the Issei farmers were soon outproducing all other farmers in the state on a per-acre basis, causing a sizeable increase in the value of their land over the land of White farmers. In 1940 the average value per acre of all West Coast farms was $37.94 (with one out of every four acres planted in crops), while Japanese farmland averaged $279.96 per acre (with three out of every four acres actively producing crops).

In contrast, White agribusiness had a resource-intensive, low-yield approach. As a result, by the 1940s Japanese American farmers were producing an astounding 40 percent of California's commercial vegetable crops. They dominated the production of truck crops: 73 percent of the snow peas, 50 percent of the tomatoes, 75 percent of the celery, and 90 percent of the strawberries. Japanese American farmers were considered "the most important racial minority group engaged in agriculture in the Pacific Coast region." Consequently, White farmers saw them as serious economic rivals.

A constellation of agricultural groups, including the Grower-Shipper Vegetable Association, the California Farm Bureau Federation, the White American Nurserymen of Los Angeles, and the Western Growers Protective Association, joined up with the California department of the American Legion, the Native Sons of the Golden West, and the Native Daughters of the Golden West to lobby federal authorities to remove Japanese Americans from their farms. They saw the post–Pearl Harbor racial climate as a golden opportunity for a land grab, not only to eliminate this unwanted competition from the state's most productive family farms, but also to confiscate the land from Japanese American farmers as soon as they were removed.

Austin E. Anson, managing secretary of the Salinas district of the Grower-Shipper Vegetable Association, was quoted in the May 9, 1942, issue of the *Saturday Evening Post* as saying, "We're charged with wanting to get rid of the Japs for selfish reasons. We might as well be honest. We do. It's a question of whether the white man lives on the Pacific Coast or the brown men. They came into this valley to work, and they stayed to take over. . . . If all the Japs were removed tomorrow, we'd never miss them in two weeks, because the white farmers can take over and produce everything the Jap grows. And we don't want them back when the war ends, either."

• • •

Don't worry. Don't worry. This is America.

—Edward Kanta **Fujimoto**, male, Issei, San Francisco, California, incarcerated age 43, Fort Lincoln Internment Center, Camp Livingston Internment Camp, Topaz Relocation Center[19]

But the Nikkei—all persons of Japanese ancestry—had plenty of reasons to worry. In studies conducted on popular attitudes in the 1920s and 1930s, the majority of respondents described Japanese

Americans as "dishonest, tricky, treacherous," as being "ruinous, hard or unfair competitors," with principal traits of "sneakiness" and "intelligence."

Japan's aggressive invasion of China in 1937 had increased fears among senior US government and military leaders about the "Japanese problem" and potential disloyalty among the second-generation Nisei Americans as well as the first-generation Issei, particularly in Hawaii. In September 1939, President Roosevelt directed the army's G-2 division and the Office of Naval Intelligence (ONI) to coordinate the surveillance of Japanese Americans with the FBI. In an attempt to discourage Japan's plans for military expansion by way of the Greater East Asia Co-prosperity Sphere—a concept created by the Empire of Japan to control Indochina through puppet governments—FDR froze all Japanese assets in the United States and ceased exports of oil, which the small island country could not provide for itself.

However, in November 1940 the FBI prepared a lengthy report on national security in Hawaii that depicted the Nisei as loyal Americans. FBI director J. Edgar Hoover and other bureau officials, though, equated Issei political loyalty with their cultural attachment to Japan. As a result, those Issei who were community leaders were identified as individuals with the highest likelihood of becoming potential saboteurs and espionage agents.

In the months before the Pearl Harbor attack, FBI agents interviewed residents of Japanese neighborhoods and scanned record books from Japanese-owned businesses, newspapers, periodicals, and club notices, in order to compile a list of names categorized into A-B-C levels of threat. The A list consisted of individuals belonging to organizations classified as "dangerous." B list names were those in organizations considered "less dangerous" but believed to be directly or indirectly under the control of the Japanese government. Those on the C list belonged to organizations with ties to Japan that seemingly posed less danger than A or B list groups. Over two thousand Issei names were on the combined A-B-C lists, and these were the first men arrested within hours after the attack on Pearl Harbor.

The Office of Naval Intelligence took a more nuanced approach than the FBI. Lieutenant Commander Kenneth D. Ringle was only one of twelve intelligence attachés in the navy who spoke Japanese. Ringle developed his Japanese-language skills and familiarity with Japanese culture in an ONI immersion program in Japan from 1928 to 1931. In July 1940 he was asked to determine the security risk that disloyal Japanese Americans could pose to West Coast naval bases. So Ringle established himself as part of the Japanese American community in Southern California, and in particular with local Nisei leaders from the Japanese American Citizens League (JACL). Technically, he reported to ONI's San Diego district director, but he was given the freedom to run his own operations.

For the next eighteen months he worked mostly alone out of a YMCA office in San Pedro or in the field getting to know the first-generation Issei farmers, fishermen, and businessmen who were becoming Americanized and believed in the American way of life. They respected Ringle's position in the navy, and he respected the time they were willing to spend with him. Ringle had the background to recognize the tremendous differences between the Japanese he previously knew in Japan and the West Coast Japanese. He came to a keen understanding of the relationships between the generations of Issei and Nisei, as well as the contrast between Japanese Americans who had little or no contact with or attachment to Japan and those who did. Ringle wanted to keep support for Japan's militaristic agenda from taking root in the West Coast, and he turned to Issei and Nisei friends for help. At one point he put out the word that he was looking for the membership list of the Black Dragon Society in the San Joaquin valley, a group loyal to the Japanese emperor; three days later its books for the western half of the United States were put into his hands.

Then one night, in a dramatic midnight raid, Ringle broke up a spy network being run out of the Japanese consulate in Los Angeles. The operation, believed to have occurred in March 1941, resembled a scene from *Mission: Impossible*. With the aid of the FBI and a safecracker "checked out" from a local jail, Ringle accessed the consulate safe while police stood guard in the street and at the elevator bank below. After photographing the consulate's records in the embassy safe, they left quietly, undetected.

The clandestine operation produced lists of network informants, which, the FBI concluded, adequately identified the pool of likely suspects on its A-B-C lists. The raid also produced enough evidence to break up Japan's entire West Coast espionage ring and arrest its ringleader, Itaru Tachibana, a Japanese naval officer posing as an English-language student. The charges against him were later dropped at the request of Secretary of State Cordell Hull because "conversations with the Japanese were at a crucial stage." Tachibana was eventually deported to Japan for "attempting to purchase military secrets." But as far as Ringle was concerned, the most valuable evidence he had unearthed consisted of direct communications between the consulate and officials in Japan, in which Japanese agents referred to Japanese Americans as "cultural traitors" not to be trusted. Ringle considered this proof that Japanese Americans were being viewed with suspicion by the Japanese government—far from being recruited for espionage purposes.

Upon the attack on Pearl Harbor, Ringle became responsible for arresting the known Japanese agents on the enemy's own lists, which he had lifted in the raid, as well as on the lists already developed by the FBI and ONI. Forty-eight hours later Ringle and the FBI had arrested 450 known agents of Imperial Japan in Southern California.

In this time before the Central Intelligence Agency existed (the CIA would not be created until September 18, 1947), President Roosevelt was dissatisfied with the intelligence he was receiving from various government agencies. The president began commissioning his own agents using undisclosed White House funds. In February 1941 he hired his friend and journalist John Franklin Carter to assemble a political intelligence network on the West Coast and report directly to him.

Six months later—and four months before Pearl Harbor—New Deal congressman John D. Dingell Sr. of Michigan advised the president in private correspondence that the United States should prepare to place 10,000 alien Japanese in Hawaii in concentration camps and hold the remaining 150,000 Japanese Americans as a "reprisal reserve" against hostile acts by Japan. An act of reprisal is an action that a country takes when it believes another country has violated international law. On July 26, 1941, FDR froze all of Japan's assets in the United States in retaliation for Japan's occupation of French Indochina. Japan responded by detaining 100 American citizens as an act of reprisal. Congressman Dingell recommended that the president prepare for the next step in the "reprisal contest" by detaining Japanese aliens in the United States, who would be held in reserve in the event the US military needed to offer them to Japan in exchange for US prisoners of war (POWs).

Reprisals are supposed to be equal in proportion to the other country's offense. But Dingell had in mind something far beyond a one-for-one exchange—he proposed that the United States detain approximately 160,000 hostages in response to the 100 American citizens being held hostage by the Japanese government.

Dingell's idea apparently prompted Roosevelt to order Carter to secretly investigate "the Japanese situation" on the West Coast and in Hawaii. Carter in turn hired Curtis B. Munson, a wealthy midwestern businessman, to go out west and confer with FBI and ONI investigators, including Ringle, with whom Munson became friendly. Both Ringle and Munson believed—and in October and November 1941 Munson's reports conveyed—that Japanese Americans posed no security threat whatsoever.

In his first report to FDR on October 19, 1941, Munson wrote, "We do not want to throw a lot of American citizens into a concentration camp of course, and especially as the almost unanimous verdict is that in case of war they will be quiet, very quiet. There will probably be some sabotage by paid Japanese agents and the odd fanatical Jap, but the bulk of these people will be quiet because in addition to being quite contented with the American way of life, they know they are 'in a spot.' . . . 90 per cent like our way of life best" and are "straining every nerve to show their loyalty. . . . It is only because he is a stranger to us that we mistrust him."

On November 7, Carter forwarded Munson's second and final report to the president, attaching a cover memo of his own that summarized Munson's points. But Carter took them out of context, which made it seem as if Munson believed that Japanese Americans were more threatening than Munson actually wrote in the report.

MEMORANDUM ON C.B. MUNSON'S REPORT
"JAPANESE ON THE WEST COAST"

Attached herewith is the report, with supplementary reports on Lower California and British Columbia. The report, though lengthy, is worth reading in its entirety. Salient passages are:

1) "There are still Japanese in the United States who will tie dynamite around their waist and make a human bomb out of themselves . . . but today they are few."

2) "There is no Japanese 'problem' on the coast. There will be no armed uprising of Japanese. There will be undoubtedly some sabotage financed by Japan and executed largely by imported agents. There will be the odd case of fanatical sabotage by some Japanese 'crackpot.'"

3) "The dangerous part of their espionage is that they would be very effective as far as movement of supplies, movement of troops and movement of ships . . . is concerned."

4) "For the most part the local Japanese are loyal to the

United States or, at worst, hope that by remaining quiet they can avoid concentration camps or irresponsible mobs."

5) "Your reporter . . . is horrified to note that dams, bridges, harbors, power stations etc. are wholly unguarded everywhere. The harbor of San Pedro could be razed by fire completely by four men with hand grenades and a little study in one night. Dams could be blown and half of lower California might actually die of thirst. . . . One railway bridge at the exit from the mountains in some cases could tie up three or four main railroads."

J.F.C.

Ironically, Munson's report was intended to relieve concerns about Japanese American loyalty, but Carter's memo gave the impression that the potential for sabotage had increased rather than diminished. Unfortunately, FDR probably read just Carter's summary; if so, then he didn't read Munson's account of the remarkable degree of patriotism shown by Japanese Americans toward their country. Carter placed no emphasis there, so FDR dismissed the entire report as "nothing much new."

On the contrary, Munson reported:

The Nisei are pathetically eager to show [their] loyalty. They are not Japanese in culture. They are foreigners to Japan. Though American citizens they are not accepted by Americans, largely because they look differently and can be easily recognized. . . . The loyal Nisei hardly know where to turn. Some gesture of protection or wholehearted acceptance of this group would go a long way to swinging them away from any last romantic hankering after old Japan. They are not oriental or mysterious, they are very American and are of a proud, self-respecting race. . . .

The Issei or first generation is considerably weakened in their loyalty to Japan by the fact that they have chosen to make

this their home and have brought up their children here. They
expect to die here. They are quite fearful of being put in a concentration camp. Many would take out American citizenship
if allowed to do so. The haste of this report does not allow us
to go into this more fully. The Issei have to break with their
religion, their god and Emperor, their family, their ancestors
and their after-life in order to be loyal to the United States.
They are also still legally Japanese. Yet they do break, and send
their boys off to the Army with pride and tears. They are good
neighbors. They are old men fifty-five to sixty-five, for the most
part simple and dignified. Roughly they were Japanese lower
middle class about analogous to the pilgrim fathers. They were
largely farmers and fishermen. Today the Japanese is farmer,
fisherman and businessman. They get very attached to the land
they work or own (through the second generation), they like
their own business, they do not work at industrial jobs nor for
others except as a stepping stone to becoming independent.
The Kibei, educated [in Japan] from childhood to seventeen,
are still the element most to be watched.

Although officers of the War Department, the State Department,
and ONI also received copies of the Munson report, it ultimately did
nothing to change the minds of the three cabinet secretaries overseeing those departments, who would eventually support "mass evacuation."

The thinking within army leadership was that race alone determined
loyalty, without regard to any other factors. Two weeks prior to Pearl
Harbor, the prospect of war with Japan was looming; every department was preparing its wartime plans. In the event of war, the Justice
Department would assume responsibility for internal security measures, and the War Department would lead the national defense. The
attack on Pearl Harbor put those plans in motion, but a misinformed

and prejudiced conflation of race, culture, and loyalty was embedded in their thinking, which now can only be described as racist.

In early December, Carter reported to FDR: "Army intelligence poor or nonexistent on West Coast." He followed up with a plan for Roosevelt's "Japanese problem" in a memo dated December 19, 1941:

SUMMARY OF REPORT ON PROGRAM FOR LOYAL
WEST COAST JAPANESE.

Curtis Munson reports from Los Angeles that already five L.A. Japanese-Americans have committed suicide because their honor could not stand suspicion of their loyalty. He is rushing to Washington a program, which is based largely on the O.N.I. (Commander Ringle) proposals for maintaining the loyalty of Japanese-Americans and establishing wholesome race-relations. Its essence is to utilize Japanese filial piety as hostage for good behavior.

The chief points of this program are as follows:

1) Encourage the Nisei (American-born Japanese) by a statement from high authority;

2) Accept offers of patriotic cooperation from the Nisei through such agencies as a) Civilian Defense, b) Red Cross, c) United Service organizations;

3) Appoint an Alien Property Custodian to supervise Isei [sic] (Japanese-born residents ineligible for citizenship), under instructions to encourage the Nisei (U.S. Citizens of Japanese blood) to take over Isei [sic] property;

4) Accept INVESTIGATED Nisei as workers in defense industries such as ship-building plants, aircraft plants, etc.

5) Put responsibility for the behavior of the Isei [sic] and Nisei on the leaders of Nisei groups such as the Japanese-American Citizens League;

6) Put responsibility for the production of food (fish,

vegetables) on the Nisei leaders mentioned above. (Japanese produce is frozen by Treasury orders; Japanese fishing-boats are beached by the Navy; result is threat of starvation to loyal Japanese families and food shortage in Los Angeles).

J.F.C.

Roosevelt initially expressed interest in the Munson-Ringle plan that proposed an alternative to rounding up all persons of Japanese ancestry. In fact, he referred Munson's recommendations to FBI director J. Edgar Hoover and Attorney General Francis Biddle. Carter responded in another memo, dated December 23, 1941, that Hoover and Biddle were "enthusiastic and offered full cooperation." But unfortunately, their enthusiasm was followed by inertia and dead silence. Roosevelt never followed up or lent any further support. Lieutenant General John L. DeWitt of the US Army's Western Defense Command had nothing to say about it, and the plan effectively died in committee at the Justice Department.

As 1941 came to a close, the president was distracted by the holidays and a state visit by Prime Minister Winston Churchill to the White House. The military situation was getting dramatically worse in the Pacific: FDR as well as the American public heard the demoralizing news that Thailand, Guam, Wake Island, Hong Kong, and Manila had fallen in rapid succession to Japanese forces. General Douglas MacArthur, in charge of the Pacific Command, raised the concern that the Japanese were treating American and British civilians harshly in Japanese-occupied areas of the Philippines. And Congressman Dingell's proposal that the United States have a reprisal reserve of Japanese nationals who could be exchanged for American POWs had taken hold.

If there had ever been a chance the government would believe that Japanese Americans were loyal, the moment had passed. Instead, the political cards were stacking up against them.

CHAPTER TWO

Executive Order 9066

I didn't think it had that much to do with me. I said, "What's the big fuss about my being of Japanese heritage? We didn't bomb Pearl Harbor. We're Americans." . . . *I thought, this will all blow over. It's just a temporary hysterical overreaction. I never took any of it seriously.* . . . *I was so naive.*

> —Yoshito "Yosh" **Kuromiya**, male, Nisei, Pasadena, California, incarcerated age 19, Pomona Assembly Center, Heart Mountain Relocation Center, Cheyenne County Jail, McNeil Island Federal Penitentiary[20]

Three days after Secretary of the Navy Frank Knox delivered his self-serving report to the president, FDR appointed a fact-finding commission made up of both active and retired military officers to determine the military errors that led to the Pearl Harbor disaster. The commission, headed by Supreme Court Justice Owen J. Roberts, flew to Honolulu, where they interviewed 127 witnesses from December 22, 1941, to January 10, 1942. The thirteen-thousand-page report was delivered to the president on January 23, 1942, and released to the public on January 25, headlining the Sunday-morning papers.

The Roberts Commission focused on the failure of the army and navy commanders, Lieutenant General Walter C. Short and Rear Admiral Husband E. Kimmel, respectively, to adequately prepare for an attack. The report also included one vague reference to spies, which the media seized upon as evidence that all Japanese Americans, regardless of citizenship, were disloyal and untrustworthy. Even though the Roberts Commission report did not mention the local Japanese American population *at all*, the mere mention of spies further aggravated the fear plaguing Americans that the Japanese enemy was living in their midst. The release of the report may well have been the tipping point in turning public opinion against Japanese Americans.

In the three weeks following the release of the Roberts Commission report, a perfect storm of factors propelled the "Yellow Peril" characterizations of Japanese people as sinister and treacherous to permeate the newspapers and airwaves. Well aware that 1942 was an election year and that Japanese Americans made easy targets, a number of politicians perpetrated a full-scale propaganda campaign asserting that an invasion of the West Coast by Imperial Japan could be expected any day, together with a hidden rebellion of thousands of Japanese Americans ready to rise up and take over California, Oregon, and Washington. The media was whipping up anti-Japanese sentiments into a frenzy, and the steady stream of racist editorials and radio reports seemed unstoppable.

"I am for the immediate removal of every Japanese on the West Coast to a point deep in the interior. I don't mean a nice part of the interior, either. Herd 'em up, pack 'em off and give 'em the inside room of the badlands. Let 'em be pinched, hurt, hungry, and up against it. Personally, I hate the Japanese. And that goes for all of them," wrote columnist Harry McLemore in the *San Francisco Examiner* on January 29, 1942.

Even the highly respected journalist Edward R. Murrow went so far as to say, "I think it's probable that, if Seattle ever does get bombed, you will be able to look up and see some University of Washington sweaters on the boys doing the bombing."

· · ·

Under the door the following note was left: "This is a warning. Get out. We don't want you in our beautiful country. Go where your ancestors came from. Once a Jap, always one. Get out." As we became increasingly the target of blind hate, our government failed to come to our aid. Indeed, the government joined in the hysteria by overreacting, rounding up supposed enemy agents and, above all, keeping

silent about the increasing antagonism against all Japanese Americans.
　　—Minoru "Min" **Tamaki**, male, Nisei, San Francisco, California,
　　incarcerated age 24, Tanforan Assembly Center, Topaz Relocation
　　Center[21]

We couldn't open the doors of our houses because we were simply afraid. There were a lot of rumors going around that people were being beaten.
　　—Haruyuki "Jim" **Matsuoka**, male, Nisei, Los Angeles, California,
　　incarcerated age 7, Manzanar Reception Center, Manzanar
　　Relocation Center[22]

People stared suspiciously at us on the streets. I felt their resentment in a hundred ways—the way a saleswoman in a large department store never saw me waiting at the counter [and] after ten minutes I [would have] to walk quietly away as if nothing had happened.
　　—Monica Kazuko **Itoi** (Sone), female, Nisei, Seattle, Washington,
　　incarcerated age 23, Puyallup Assembly Center, Minidoka Relocation
　　Center[23]

I read in the paper that Chinese Americans were walking around with buttons saying "I'm an American Chinese" because they were mistaken for Japanese. There were all kinds of rumors like if you go [into] a Japanese restaurant they'll put poison in your food. [Barbers] would refuse to give [us] haircuts.
　　—Yukio **Tatsumi**, male, Nisei, Terminal Island, California,
　　incarcerated age 22, Manzanar Reception Center, Manzanar
　　Relocation Center[24]

· · ·

The madness of hatred was a gift to nativist organizations. That year at the sixty-fifth Grand Parlor convention of the Native Sons of the Golden West, its members voted "first to prosecute, then to carry through to the Supreme Court, if necessary, a suit challenging the United States citizenship of the Japanese; and second to draft and sponsor an amendment to the Constitution of the United States which shall have for its object the exclusion of all persons of Japanese ancestry from American citizenship."

Founded in 1875 with the mission "to preserve California history," the Native Sons of the Golden West ostensibly was an organization open to all California-born citizens. But as early as 1907, the Native Sons had called for a resolution to ban all "Orientals" from the state. Then in 1920 its grand president, William P. Canbu, made his position clear: "California was given by God to a white people, and with God's strength we want to keep it as He gave it to us."

The Native Sons teamed up with the California State Grange, the California State Federation of Labor, and the American Legion to become the California Joint Immigration Committee. This group was dedicated to prohibiting Asian immigration altogether, and its efforts were successful in getting the Immigration Act of 1924 enacted.

But that wasn't enough to satisfy the Native Sons. It took almost twenty years, but Pearl Harbor finally gave the nativists an opportunity to fight the Japanese in court in an attempt to revoke their constitutional access to American citizenship by birthright. The Native Sons was counting on its lobbying influence in Congress and some of its powerful members, like California Attorney General Earl Warren, to support its position against Japanese American birthright citizenship. Oddly enough, Warren's discrimination against the Japanese gave no indication that eventually he would become one of the most consequential liberal Supreme Court justices in our nation's history. Nevertheless, at the time Warren was already an influential politician, and his opinion may have swayed Roosevelt in favor of mass removal.

• • •

Cries began to sound up and down the coast that everyone of Japanese ancestry should be taken into custody. For years the professional guardians of the Golden West had wanted to rid their land of the Yellow Peril and the war provided an opportunity for them to push their programs through. As the chain of Pacific islands fell to the [Imperial] Japanese [military], patriots shrieked for protection. . . . A Californian sounded the alarm: "The Japanese are dangerous and they must leave. Remember the destruction and the sabotage perpetrated at Pearl Harbor. Notice how they have infiltrated into the harbor towns and taken our best land."

> —Monica Kazuko **Itoi** (Sone), female, Nisei, Seattle, Washington, incarcerated age 23, Puyallup Assembly Center, Minidoka Relocation Center[25]

I remember [my high school] had an oratorical contest sponsored by the Native Sons and Daughters, and I ended up one of the nine qualifying competitors. Then the principal and the teacher called me in and told me that I couldn't be in it because of my ancestry. . . . [My teacher] was upset and so discouraged that the Native Sons wouldn't change their position. . . . That they would discriminate made her very angry, but she couldn't do anything about it. She . . . was the one that was responsible in getting me to college because of that experience—to the College of the Pacific. That teacher was poor herself . . . but . . . before my dad knew anything about it, she had arranged to get me a $150 scholarship. . . . My dad was so deeply touched, of course, he let me go.

> —Mary Tsuruko (Dakuzaku) **Tsukamoto**, female, Nisei, Florin, California, incarcerated age 27, Fresno Assembly Center, Jerome Relocation Center[26]

• • •

Other groups contributing to the anti-Japanese campaigns—veterans associations, mayors of cities, local law enforcement, and the governors of western states—all backed the growing desire to remove Japanese Americans from the West Coast. It began with losing their jobs and livelihoods. The city of Portland, Oregon, revoked the licenses of all Japanese nationals to do business in the city. The California State Personnel Board issued an order that barred all "descendants" of Issei from civil service positions. And the Los Angeles County Board of Supervisors terminated all of its Nisei employees; on January 27, 1942, two days after the release of the Roberts Commission report, the board issued a resolution in support of the federal government removing all Japanese aliens from the West Coast to "inland points." Meanwhile, California Governor Culbert L. Olson personally made the same request for the removal of Japanese aliens to Lieutenant General John L. DeWitt, commander of the Western Defense Command and the Fourth Army at the Presidio of San Francisco.

The declaration of war had lit a match to the powder keg of pent-up prejudice against the Nikkei that had been cumulating over the previous 150 years, almost since our nation's founding. Under the Naturalization Act of 1790, only "free white persons" of good moral character were eligible to become naturalized citizens. The Chinese contract laborers who first arrived in the mid-1800s were among the first racial groups to challenge the legal definition of "white" in order to be eligible for citizenship in the eighteenth and nineteenth centuries.

These first Asian immigrants were accepted as suitable for back-breaking, low-paying physical labor in grueling conditions on mainland farms, Hawaiian sugar plantations, and the transcontinental railroad in the American West. But they were considered inferior to White people, incapable of assimilating into society as a whole, and unfit for citizenship.

Labor leaders, politicians, and sociologists of the time came to characterize the Chinese as a social and economic threat. These and other discriminatory forces converged in 1882, resulting in the passage of the first Chinese Exclusion Act, which barred any further immigration of laborers from China. The provisions of this act and other exclusionary legislation reinforced the notion that the Chinese should not and could not become American citizens.

And so the industries that had been relying upon Chinese labor turned to Japan to fill the void. There the labor contractors for the sugar and pineapple plantations found a Meiji government supportive of emigration and were able to acquire a supply of young men, especially from the rural areas of southwest Japan, eager for opportunities overseas. By 1900 an estimated 154,000 Japanese had immigrated to Hawaii, making up 22 percent of the population and surpassing the Chinese as the largest immigrant group in the islands.

When their labor contracts ended, some Issei migrated to the mainland to work as crop pickers, domestics, lumber mill workers, and cannery workers. They saved their money and became entrepreneurs. In San Francisco, Los Angeles, Seattle, Portland, Salt Lake City, and Denver, they opened boardinghouses, hotels, shops, restaurants, nurseries, and other small enterprises.

. . .

My parents came to America in the early 1900s. I think they would have become citizens if they were accepted. They had no plans to go back to Japan. Why would they come to a strange country . . . against all odds if they weren't coming here to better themselves and their children? But all the laws were made to keep them aliens in this society.

—Mitsuru "Mits" **Koshiyama**, male, Nisei, Santa Clara Valley, California, incarcerated age 18, Santa Anita Assembly Center, Heart Mountain Relocation Center, McNeil Island Federal Penitentiary[27]

. . .

Japan's conquest of Russia in the 1904–5 Russo-Japanese War further fueled "Yellow Peril" fears and reinforced the views of white supremacy that were prevalent at the time. The stereotypes of Chinese as heathen, unassimilable, treacherous, and unsuitable for citizenship were now being applied to the Japanese. Exclusionist groups like the Native Sons of the Golden West, the American Legion, and the California State Grange that had been working so hard to stop a Chinese labor force from immigrating into the

United States were now focusing their efforts on stopping the influx of laborers from Japan. Labor unions (whose membership consisted, ironically, of mostly immigrants and their descendants of European heritage) joined the exclusionist groups in the commitment to eliminate the Japanese as competition.

San Francisco was the first port of entry for immigrants of all origins and became a hotbed of anti-immigration sentiment. In May 1905 labor forces there mounted the first large-scale protests against the Japanese and all Asian immigration, an effort that resulted in the formation of the Asiatic Exclusion League. San Francisco area politicians like Democratic Congressman James George Maguire adopted an anti-Japanese platform. The exclusionists repurposed the populist anti-Chinese cry of "The Chinese must go!" as "The Japs must go!" Speaking in the proceedings of the Asiatic Exclusion League, Maguire said, "I believe . . . that 'All men are created equal, and endowed by their Creator with certain inalienable rights,' but I do not recognize the right of migration as one of those inalienable rights, because its unlimited exercise may, and frequently is, destructive of the equal rights of others."

And then he quoted from *Organized Labor*, the labor movement newspaper publishing extreme propaganda at the time:

> It is the old question between the Orient and the Occident— the conflict for supremacy, the struggle for self-preservation, the fight for existence. . . .
>
> . . . The Japanese are only the scouts—the vanguard of the vast Asiatic army. There are Koreans, Chinese, Manchurians, Manchus, Mongolians, Malays and Hindoos numbering over ONE BILLION.
>
> Allow them to secure a foothold in the United States, and they will, within a few generations, sweep like an avalanche of death from the Himalayas around the globe.

> **The Japanese, with all his politeness and pretenses,
> is only a corrupted Chinaman. He is a Malay-Mongolized
> mongrel** [emphasis added].

Facing such constant political pressure to halt Japanese immigration, President Theodore Roosevelt (FDR's fifth cousin) issued an executive order in 1907 to stop Japanese transmigration from Hawaii to the mainland and entered into a series of diplomatic understandings with Japan that became known as the Gentlemen's Agreement. Under these arrangements, the Japanese government voluntarily restricted emigration by not allowing manual laborers to have passports, even though the workers would be traveling from Japan to the United States to satisfy American labor contracts.

However, the others who were not laborers—merchants, ministers, leisure travelers, students, teachers, and families of Japanese immigrants already admitted to the United States—could still receive passports. Also, through the "family exception," thousands of young Japanese women were permitted to come over as "picture brides," an extension of the practice of arranged marriages in Japan. A picture bride was, literally, a woman in Japan whose photo was sent to a Japanese man in America as someone he could marry. After the man in America saw her photo and learned of her background from a *baishakunin* ("go-between") and agreed to marry her, and the woman in Japan saw his photo, learned of his background, and agreed to marry him, the *baishakunin* would arrange for the marriage to take place in Japan. But the groom would not be there; he was waiting for his wife in America. An estimated one in four Issei women, usually in their late teens or early twenties, were picture brides. When the young women arrived in the United States, they were often shocked and dismayed to discover that their new husbands were not nearly as handsome or as well off as they had been represented to be.

. . .

When my mother arrived [as a picture bride] in the US in 1917 at the age of twenty-nine, she discovered that the man she had married was just a railroad coach repairman who had little money—he was, in fact, living in a rented shack. Because she had no money with which to return to Japan, she had no choice but to stay with my father.

—Bruce Teruo **Kaji**, male, Nisei, Los Angeles, California, incarcerated age 16, Manzanar Reception Center, Manzanar Relocation Center[28]

In 1904, Father sailed for the United States. . . .

. . . About this time, the Reverend Yohachi Nagashima—[my] grandfather—brought his family to America. . . . He arrived in Seattle with his wife, Yuki, three daughters, Yasuko, my mother Benko, and Kikue, twenty-two, seventeen, and sixteen years of age respectively, and two little round-eyed sons, Shinichi and Yoshio, six and four years.

Mother and her sisters sailed into the port looking like exotic tropical butterflies. Mother told us she wore her best blue silk crepe kimono, Yasuko chose a deep royal purple robe, and Kikue, a soft rose one. Their kimonos had extravagantly long, graceful sleeves, with bright red silk linings. Over their kimonos, the girls donned long, plum-colored, pleated skirts, called the hakama, *to cover the kimono skirts that flipped open as they walked. Shod in spanking white* tabis—Japanese stockings—and *scarlet cork-soled slippers, the young women stood in tense excitement at the rails of the ship. Yasuko, the eldest, held a picture of a young man in her hand, and she could hardly bring herself to look down at the sea of faces below on the dock where her prospective husband, whom she had never met, stood waiting. Mother told us she and Kikue scanned the crowd boldly and saw hundreds of young, curious masculine faces turned upward, searching for their picture brides.*

—Monica Kazuko **Itoi** (Sone), female, Nisei, Seattle, Washington, incarcerated age 23, Puyallup Assembly Center, Minidoka Relocation Center[29]

• • •

Kane (pronounced *KA-NEH*) Watanabe was one of these picture brides. In April 1912 she was married in Japan by photograph to Kunisaku Mineta, in Salinas, California. Almost two years later, at the age of twenty, Kane left Yokohama, Japan, on the SS *Chiyo Maru*, traveling unaccompanied to San Francisco, California. Upon her arrival on January 20, 1914, at the Angel Island Immigration Station in San Francisco Bay, she was brought before the Board of Special Inquiry: two immigrant inspectors, a stenographer, and a translator. She presented a copy of her Japanese family register as confirmation of her marriage, her medical certificate of release from the US Public Health Service, and a letter from Yasutaro Numano, acting consul general of Japan, certifying that her husband, Kunisaku Mineta, was a farmer in Salinas, "a man of good character," and had the means to support his family.

Kunisaku Mineta was also interrogated. He testified that he was twenty-five years old, that he had the means to support a wife, and that after marrying her by photograph, he'd waited almost two years before bringing her to the United States, until he knew he could support her. He presented articles of co-partnership with Clarence Sherwood, an American citizen, that enabled him to lease 140 acres of land. He said he had personally invested about $1,700 in the farm, had $500 in the bank, and had brought with him a check for $500. He said he had a house ready for her. Nevertheless, the board took the position that the laws of the State of California did not recognize marriage by photograph, so Kane could be admitted to the United States only if the couple agreed to be married according to the laws of the State of California. They agreed, and the couple were remarried in San Francisco by Zenro Hirata, president of the Japanese Interdenominational Board of Missions.

• • •

Although the "family exception" provided a way for some Issei men to marry and have families in the United States, there were Americans who looked at the picture bride practice as nothing more than a ploy by Japanese men to take advantage of an immigration loophole. These individuals stoked fears that the children of Issei were incapable of being absorbed into mainstream American culture; they argued the Nisei would always be "alien" and would "overrun" the West Coast. They believed that US-born Japanese Americans should not be citizens, no matter what the Constitution said.

In the 1920s numerous states—particularly those in the West—continued to institute laws that limited the rights of the Issei and other Asians. The Immigration Act of 1924 was the first comprehensive immigration act to place limits on the number of foreigners entering the country and to impose a hierarchy that favored certain racial categories over others. The Japanese government interpreted the passage of the 1924 act as another example of anti-Japanese hostility and formally protested it as a political attack, inflaming already tense US-Japan relations. The act's impact ensured that all Japanese (as well as other Asians) were racially ineligible for citizenship by naturalization, a prohibition that would continue until the Immigration and Nationality Act of 1952. The law also prevented the Issei from voting and from testifying against White persons in court. In this prewar environment, even Issei who were in the US *legally* were being swept up by immigration officers and summarily deported or granted "voluntary" departures back to Japan.

In addition to being caught in the geopolitical crosshairs, the Nikkei were subject to the countless discriminatory practices of the time against other non-Whites or non-Christians. They could not buy homes in the more desirable areas of a city because of the discriminatory redlining practices of banks, real estate agents, and insurance companies, and in particular, because of the operation of racially restrictive covenants (RRCs). RRCs were contractual agreements between homeowners (often set forth in the deeds of ownership) that prohibited them from selling their land or their homes to minorities.

The Nikkei were caught in a catch-22: They could live only in certain areas, yet they were criticized for "sticking to themselves" and not assimilating. Nisei students could not attend schools for only White students, so they often attended schools that were de facto segregated with other non-White students. They were even blocked from entering most public parks and swimming pools. The ultimate segregation was that Nikkei could bury their dead only in cemeteries for non-White persons.

• • •

When I was in the Boy Scouts . . . I was about 11 or 12 years old. . . . Our whole troop went swimming to the San Fernando Plunge and they wouldn't let me in because I was the only non-White in that troop. So I sat on the bench, watching my fellow scouts swim. And that sort of ingrained a lot of hatred in me, I guess, for discriminatory things.

—Frank Seishi **Emi**, male, Nisei, Los Angeles, California, incarcerated age 26, Pomona Assembly Center, Heart Mountain Relocation Center, Leavenworth Penitentiary[30]

• • •

Intermarriage to White persons was fraught with legal peril, and mixed-race couples often faced public harassment and even physical violence. Namiko "Nami" Nakashima's parents experienced the challenges of being an interracial couple. Under the Expatriation Act of 1907 and the Cable Act of 1922, a woman would lose her US citizenship if she married a man who himself was ineligible for citizenship. So when Nami's mother, a Mexican American, married her father, an Issei, her mother lost her US citizenship. (The Cable Act was amended in 1931 to allow Nisei women to marry Issei men, and the law was repealed altogether in 1936.) When Nami, herself a Nisei, wanted to marry a Mexican American man, she had to get around the laws preventing interracial marriage that remained on the books in many states until the *Loving v. Virginia* Supreme Court decision ruled all such laws unconstitutional in 1967.

• • •

In 1939, my husband and I couldn't marry here. He's [an] American-born Mexican, and I'm half Japanese-American. We had to go across the border, down into Tijuana, Mexico. . . . An Oriental couldn't get a job in Long Beach. I couldn't get a job in Kress's. Japanese who were university-educated were still working in farm stalls, selling at the market downtown. My mother always said, "You're not going to sell vegetables." I guess you'd call it proud. She'd see all these kids who had gone to the University of California at Berkeley, and there was nothing here for them. They sold vegetables.

—Namiko "Nami" Aurora (Nakashima) **Diaz**, female, Nisei, Long Beach, California, incarcerated age 25, Santa Anita Assembly Center[31]

• • •

Community cohesion and cultural values were important to the Issei, so they formed and supported Japanese-language schools, social organizations, Buddhist and other religious groups, and regional associations stemming from the prefectures in Japan where they had come from originally. The Issei were willing to make great sacrifices so their children could have better lives, and even though they could not become American citizens themselves, they tried to show allegiance to the United States. They endeavored to raise their children to appreciate their Japanese heritage while also being "fully American." Their guiding principle was always *kodomo no tame ni*, meaning "for the sake of the children."

Even so, their Nisei children often found that they, like their parents, were excluded from professional and social organizations dominated by White civic leaders. Despite obtaining good grades and college degrees, the Nisei were frustrated to find that they could not make any headway in the job markets outside of the Japanese American community. To overcome the racial stigma they faced and to emphasize their American citizenship, a group of young Nisei professionals founded the Japanese American Citizens League (JACL) in 1929, with the motto "Better Americans in a Greater America."

. . .

My father cherished copies of the Declaration of Independence, the Bill of Rights, and the Constitution of the United States, and on national holidays he hung with great pride an enormous American flag on our front porch.

—Yoshiko **Uchida**, female, Nisei, Berkeley, California, incarcerated
age 21, Tanforan Assembly Center, Topaz Relocation Center[32]

My father had a philosophy about when you're in America: this is your country, you're growing up here. Don't speak Nihongo [Japanese]. He was against Japanese schools. He says you go to the school your neighbor does, and what they play, you play.

—Paul Yashiro **Shinoda**, male, Nisei, Gardena, California, age 28
when Pearl Harbor was attacked[33]

We wanted to be accepted as Americans. We had no ties with Japan. . . . Because of discrimination we hated everything Japanese. . . . I used to tell my mother, "Why can't we have bread like everybody else? Bacon, eggs in the morning. Why do we have to eat rice? Why do you have to read the Japanese paper? Why do I have to be foreign?"

—Mitsuru "Mits" **Koshiyama**, male, Nisei, Santa Clara Valley,
California, incarcerated age 18, Santa Anita Assembly Center, Heart
Mountain Relocation Center, McNeil Island Federal Penitentiary[34]

The first five years of my life I lived in amoebic bliss, not knowing whether I was plant or animal, at the old Carrollton Hotel on the waterfront of Seattle. One day when I was a happy six-year-old, I made the shocking discovery that I had Japanese blood. I was a Japanese.

Mother announced this fact of life to us in a quiet, deliberate manner one Sunday afternoon as we gathered around for dinner in the small kitchen, converted from one of our hotel rooms. . . .

Up to that moment, I had never thought of Father and Mother as

Japanese. True, they had almond eyes and they spoke Japanese to us, but I never felt that it was strange. It was like one person's being red-haired and another black.

Father had often told us stories about his early life. He had come from a small village in the prefecture of Tochigi-ken. A third son among five brothers and one sister, Father had gone to Tokyo to study law, and he practiced law for a few years before he succumbed to the fever which sent many young men streaming across the Pacific to a fabulous new country rich with promise and opportunities. . . .

For our family quarters, Mother chose three outside rooms looking south on Main Street, across an old and graying five-story warehouse, and as the family increased, a fourth room was added. . . .

At first glance, there was little about [our] simple, sparse furnishings to indicate that a Japanese family occupied the rooms. But there were telltale signs like the zori *or straw slippers placed neatly on the floor underneath the beds. On Mother's bed lay a beautiful red silk comforter patterned with turquoise, apple-green, yellow and purple Japanese parasols. And on the table beside the local daily paper were copies of the* North American Times, *Seattle's Japanese-community paper, its printing resembling rows of black multiple-legged insects. Then there was the Oriental abacus board which Father used once a month to keep his books.*

. . . In the kitchen were unmistakable Oriental traces and odors. A glass tumbler holding six pairs of red and yellow lacquered chopsticks, and a bottle of soy sauce. . . . The tall china cabinet bulged with bright hand-painted rice bowls, red lacquered soup bowls, and Mother's precious somayaki *tea set.*

. . . At the bottom of each teacup was the figure of a galloping, golden horse. When the cup was filled with tea, the golden horse seemed to rise to the surface and become animated. . . .

In the pantry, the sack of rice and gallon jug of shoyu *[soy sauce] stood. . . . A peculiar, pungent odor emanated from a five-gallon crock* which Mother kept filled with cucumbers, nappa (Chinese cabbage), daikon (large Japanese radishes), immersed in a pickling mixture of nuka, consisting of rice polishings, salt, rice and raisins. . . .

. . . A dark red stone mixing bowl inside of which were cut rows and rows of minute grooves . . . was used to grind poppy seeds and miso (soybeans) into soft paste for soups and for flavoring Japanese dishes. . . . For all the work that went into making miso shiru, soybean soup, I thought it tasted like sawdust boiled in sea brine. Mother told me nothing could be more nutritious. . . .

. . . And when I finally started grammar school . . . [at] Bailey Gatzert School . . . I felt like a princess walking through its bright, shiny corridors on smooth, shiny floors. I was mystified by a few of the little boys and girls. There were some pale-looking children who spoke a strange dialect of English, rapidly like gunfire. [My friend] Matsuko told me they were "hagu-jins," white people. Then there were children who looked very much like me with their black hair and black eyes, but they spoke in high, musical singing voices. Matsuko whispered to me that they were Chinese.

And now Mother was telling us we were Japanese. I had always thought I was a Yankee, because after all I had been born on Occidental and Main Street. Montana, a wall-shaking mountain of a man who lived at our hotel, called me a Yankee. I didn't see how I could be a Yankee and Japanese at the same time. It was like being born with two heads. It sounded freakish and a lot of trouble.

—Monica Kazuko **Itoi** (Sone), female, Nisei, Seattle, Washington, incarcerated age 23, Puyallup Assembly Center, Minidoka Relocation Center[35]

CHAPTER THREE

Betrayal

This is my country, the land that I love, doing this to us. . . . I was betrayed, not by individuals, but by our United States of America.
—Allan Minoru **Hida**, male, Nisei, Sacramento, California, incarcerated age 13, Sacramento Assembly Center, Tule Lake Relocation Center, Granada (Amache) Relocation Center[36]

On December 11, 1941, Army Chief of Staff General George C. Marshall declared that the Western Defense Command was a western theater of operations, thereby creating the legal fiction that the mainland was under attack by the Japanese. Lieutenant General John L. DeWitt was now responsible for managing a war zone that consisted of the coastal western states.

A "legal fiction" refers to a statement or position that is not based in fact, but is presented as if it were true because it is convenient for legal purposes for it to be considered a fact. In this case, the legal fiction being perpetrated on the public was that the entire 1,300-mile coastline of California, Oregon, and Washington and the 6,000-mile coastline of Alaska were theaters of war actively under attack by the Japanese, even though this was not true.

In the days after the bombing of Pearl Harbor, DeWitt had interceptor planes and patrol bombers scanning the coastline day and night. He ordered air support to sweep an ocean strip six hundred miles wide from Canada to Mexico, seeking enemy aircraft carriers. Civilian employees and families of officers stationed at McClellan Field, a military aircraft maintenance facility, were sent to Sacramento, seven miles away, where they would be less vulnerable to attack.

DeWitt's intelligence staff sent out reports of Japanese planes spotted over California—but they all proved to be false alarms. Regardless, DeWitt ordered a series of blackouts in several cities so they couldn't light the way for Japanese bombers at night. San Francisco, however, was unable to cut the power completely: Vivid neon lighting persisted in the business district through two alarms. Twenty-four hours later a furious DeWitt stood before the city's Civil Defense Council, including Mayor Angelo Rossi, and accused them of "criminal apathy" for the indifference with which they had responded to the two air raid alarms that DeWitt had called the night before.

"Japanese planes were over the city," he said, "and it might have been a good thing if they had dropped some bombs to awaken this city."

He warned them, "Death and destruction are likely to come to this city at any moment." But no evidence of Japanese planes invading the West Coast ever came to light. His second-in-command, Joseph Stilwell, who became known as Major General "Vinegar Joe" Stilwell, was one of the most respected military commanders in history. When Stilwell, then corps commander of Southern California, heard about DeWitt's blackouts, he wrote in his diary, "What jackass would send a general alarm under the circumstances?" Stilwell thought DeWitt's intelligence units were "amateur" and his public announcements of a looming attack on the West Coast by the Japanese, irresponsible.

• • •

Just before I evacuated from West Los Angeles, there was a blackout of that area. Searchlights crisscrossed the sky . . . to locate Japanese planes. This fake attack was instigated to further arouse the public's hatred for the Japanese people. There has been no authenticated proof that any planes had crossed the Pacific Ocean at that time.

—Elizabeth Aiko (Takahashi) **Nishikawa**, female, Nisei, Los Angeles, California, incarcerated age 31, Manzanar Reception Center, Manzanar Relocation Center[37]

• • •

DeWitt was motivated by a fear of failure, so this legal fiction suited him. He was afraid he'd suffer the fate of his colleagues Husband E. Kimmel and Walter C. Short; both were facing dereliction of duty charges in their commands at Pearl Harbor. He didn't want that to happen to him. Moreover, he seemed to have formed a deep-seated resentment against the Japanese during his four tours of duty in the Philippines. In words that have since become infamous, DeWitt's opinion was, "A Jap's a Jap. It makes no difference whether he is an American citizen or not. I have no confidence in their loyalty whatsoever." And yet, in contrast to General George Marshall—the army chief of staff and a seasoned combat officer—DeWitt was just a supply officer who specialized in logistics, an administrator with virtually no combat experience. Before his post at the Western Defense Command, his most significant work in the military was as quartermaster general, organizing a European pilgrimage of Gold Star mothers and widows to visit the graves of their dead men buried on foreign soil.

• • •

He was a weak man to whom circumstances had given enormous power. No doubt he believed there had been sabotage in the Hawaiian Islands during the Japanese attack and he feared the possibility of sabotage on the Pacific Coast. . . . DeWitt was a racist who . . . saw the war in the Pacific not as a conflict between governments or ideologies, but as a race war.

—Mike Masaru **Masaoka**, male, Nisei, North Platte, Nebraska, age 26 when Pearl Harbor was attacked[38]

• • •

DeWitt was susceptible to pressure, and over the course of three months—from December 1941 through February 1942—he was both motivated and influenced by others to take conflicting positions about the disposition of persons of Japanese ancestry. Initially, DeWitt recommended that Japanese aliens age fourteen and older be removed to the interior states along with German and Italian nonchild aliens.

Under a long line of Alien and Sedition Acts going back to 1798, presidents could arrest, intern, and deport foreign nationals without congressional approval if they were suspected of being potential subversives. Throughout the course of World War II, the government interned German and Italian enemy aliens, in addition to the Japanese.

But neither DeWitt's military superiors nor the White House ever considered taking collective action against German and Italian enemy aliens *and* their American-born children. There were just too many Germans and Italians living in the United States to even contemplate the mass removal of their entire populations. At the time, the German and Italian ethnic communities were the two largest foreign-born populations in the United States, numbering into the millions. And because German and Italian first-generation immigrants were not legally restricted from citizenship the way the Chinese and Japanese were, many German and Italian immigrants had become naturalized citizens. By 1941 the majority of Germans and Italians, as citizens, were able to vote, so they had become constituents, something the Issei were not. The military and political leaders agreed; they could not risk alienating a significant number of voters who were not perceived to be threats.

However, what DeWitt's superior, Army Provost Marshal General Allen W. Gullion, had in mind for the Japanese was something far beyond internment of potentially subversive Issei. Gullion wanted to remove all Issei now classified as enemy aliens from the West Coast *in addition to their American-born children*; in short, a wholesale removal of all persons of Japanese ancestry. At first DeWitt resisted the idea. Even he didn't see the common sense in adding Japanese American citizens to the number of enemy aliens to be interned. He was more obsessed with the possibility of an underground network of Japanese saboteurs.

While this was going on, General Marshall asked General Mark W. Clark (the youngest four-star general in the army during World

War II) to survey the West Coast conditions. When Clark heard from
DeWitt about the plans being hatched to implement a forced evacuation, he could not believe it and concluded that such a plan would be
ill-advised. Both he and Lieutenant General Delos E. Emmons (who
had succeeded Short as the commanding army general in Hawaii)
voiced their strong opposition to the West Coast "evacuation" plan.
Emmons dismissed all calls to remove persons of Japanese ancestry
from the islands of Hawaii and resisted any political pressure to do
so. Hawaii was under martial law (which had not been declared on
the West Coast). With this military authority, Emmons could selec-
tively detain Japanese persons, and he felt that was enough. Emmons
also recognized the massive impracticality and costs of moving more
than 35 percent of Hawaii's population into camps, as most of them
would have to be shipped to the mainland. Japanese Americans were
an essential part of the islands' workforce, and removing them would
cause significant harm to the local economy and the war effort.

General Clark estimated that if the Issei "enemy aliens" were
detained on the mainland, up to fifteen thousand soldiers would
be required just to guard them; it wasn't a practical use of military
resources to contemplate guarding the Issei, much less the whole Japanese American population along the Pacific coast. He sensibly suggested that rather than round up thousands of people and incarcerate
them in some remote facility, the government should increase the
security around all vulnerable military installations and remove only
enemy aliens from the island areas near defense facilities. Besides,
he, along with Chief of Naval Operations Harold Stark, agreed that
an invasion effort by Japan was "out of the question." In fact, later, on
February 4, 1942, they both testified to members of Congress from
the Pacific states that the chance of any sustained attack or an invasion
was—as General Clark put it—"nil." Even if Japan were capable of
having "a submarine throw a few shells into some city," it would be "a
futile operation from the standpoint of practical results."

Marshall's main concern was about protecting factories like Boeing in Seattle; he and other army leaders were satisfied that removing all Japanese Americans from the area was not a rational military precaution. But Gullion was single-minded and determined to bring DeWitt, at least, around to his way of thinking. And he had just the person to do it—his aide, Major Karl R. Bendetsen, an ambitious Stanford Law School graduate who'd only been on active service for less than a year.

Whereas DeWitt was indecisive, Bendetsen was a bold and cunning strategic thinker. After meeting with DeWitt at the Western Defense Command's San Francisco headquarters in January 1942, Bendetsen discovered that DeWitt "often seemed to be the creature of the last strong personality with whom he had contact." Indeed, DeWitt completely changed his mind after talking with California Attorney General Earl Warren, who voiced unqualified agreement with Culbert L. Olson, governor of California, that all Japanese should be removed from the state. In order for DeWitt to make this happen, however, the army needed to be in charge of it; at the moment, the Justice Department—which opposed mass removal—was still the controlling authority over the Japanese and all aliens in the United States. The bureaucratic battle that ensued would have dire consequences for Japanese Americans.

As with DeWitt, Gullion's qualifications didn't seem to match the job. He had commanded no troops, and as provost marshal general, he was responsible for civil affairs, the Army War College, and the military police. James H. Rowe Jr., who had come from the White House as FDR's administrative assistant to be deputy attorney general under Francis Biddle, said, "I never thought [Gullion] was very smart. I mean, as far as comparing him to a man like Bendetsen. He wasn't even in the major leagues." And Edward Ennis, director of the Alien Enemy Control Unit under Biddle, said that he never "felt Gullion was very important even with his superiors." All the same, Gullion was a master of military politics and managed to create a fully functional back chan-

nel of communications with DeWitt (by way of Bendetsen) throughout the period in which the mass incarceration of Japanese West Coast
residents, regardless of their citizenship, was being debated.

Eventually, Bendetsen was dividing his time between San Francisco
and Washington, DC, acting as a liaison between the two generals and
bypassing the army chain of command. More important, perhaps, is
how he positioned himself between two relatively weak leaders who
had conferred upon him the task of writing all the key position papers,
including the concept of how to incarcerate all persons of Japanese
ancestry so that it could be argued as constitutional.

In July 1941, five months *before* the bombing of Pearl Harbor, the
FBI and the War Department had agreed that, in the event of war, the
FBI would be responsible for all enemy aliens. But now that the war
had come to them, Bendetsen, with DeWitt, undertook a campaign to
wrest control over civilians from the Justice Department so that the
War Department could become the governing authority.

• • •

*On the West Coast, General J. L. DeWitt . . . did not think martial
law was necessary, but he favored mass evacuation of the Japanese. . . .
We suspected that pressures from economic and political interests who
would profit from such a wholesale evacuation influenced this decision.*
　—Monica Kazuko **Itoi** (Sone), female, Nisei, Seattle, Washington,
　　incarcerated age 23, Puyallup Assembly Center, Minidoka Relocation
　　Center[39]

• • •

In the president's cabinet, both Attorney General Biddle and Secretary of the Interior Harold Ickes opposed infringing on the civil
rights of the more than eighty thousand Nisei American citizens. They
considered any proposal to remove the Nisei against their will to be
a violation of constitutional rights guaranteed to citizens, specifically
the Fifth Amendment protection in the Bill of Rights, which provides that "no person shall be . . . deprived of life, liberty, or property,

without due process of law." In addition, Secretary of the Treasury Henry Morgenthau recognized that the Japanese American community would suffer devastating financial losses if the government did not provide secure storage for their belongings and serve as a custodian for their businesses and land holdings.

To this, Roosevelt coldly responded, "I am not concerned about that."

Secretary of War Henry L. Stimson shared the view that Japanese Americans could not be trusted as a group, nor did he think it was possible to distinguish loyal Nikkei from disloyal ones, which was an entirely racist point of view, since that belief was based only on their physical appearance. However, he also felt that absent specific charges, an evacuation solely based on race would "blow a tremendous hole in our Constitutional system."

Meanwhile, constituents in Washington, Oregon, and California were calling for the Japanese removal through their congressional representatives. On January 16, Congressman Leland Ford of Los Angeles County wrote identical letters to Secretary Stimson, Secretary of the Navy Frank Knox, and FBI Director J. Edgar Hoover to say that his mail was running heavily in favor of removal. In his letters, Congressman Ford urged that "all Japanese, whether citizens or not, be placed in inland concentration camps." He further promoted the idea that "truly loyal" Japanese Americans could prove their patriotism and show they were "working for us" by agreeing to be placed in concentration camps. Ford's argument in his letters and in his subsequent speech on the floor of the House of Representatives was repeated over and over and became effective in lumping Nisei citizens with the Issei aliens in the removal considerations.

Following Congressman Ford's lead, by January 29, 1942, a bipartisan congressional committee of the three Pacific coast states was strenuously lobbying the Justice Department to remove all persons of Japanese ancestry. Bendetsen, as part of his responsibilities, had been charged by

Gullion to design a mass evacuation plan and present it on Friday, January 30, to this West Coast congressional delegation, on Gullion's behalf. Bendetsen steered the committee into recommending to the president that the War Department be given the authority to establish exclusion zones on the West Coast, which would legally require the removal of all people, including American citizens, from restricted areas on the condition that they would be allowed reentry if they weren't thought to be a security risk. But without a timeline associated with any of it, the government would have the right to legally remove anyone, even if it meant from the whole state, for however long it was deemed necessary.

The congressmen endorsed Bendetsen's plan, which specifically called for removing the Issei Japanese aliens. However, with his penchant for clever drafting, Bendetsen included the Nisei citizens in the evacuation plan without directly saying so, by referring to them as "families" of the Issei and as "dual citizens" (whether or not they had exercised their rights as ethnic Japanese under Japanese law to claim dual citizenship).

In response to the growing pressure to remove all Japanese Americans from the West Coast, Congressman John H. Tolan, a Democrat representing the Oakland, California, area, announced in early February the formation of the Select Committee Investigating National Defense Migration, which would hold hearings later in the month. Mike Masaoka, the JACL national secretary and its only full-time employee, was the first Japanese American to testify. Masaoka thought the hearings would be the national platform where Japanese Americans could make their case that they were loyal. But by the time the Tolan Committee had started its hearings, the congressional and public pressure for mass removal had overwhelmed the constitutional objections of the Justice Department, and it was practically a fait accompli—a done deal.

Nevertheless, throughout January and February 1942, the Justice Department was pitted against the War Department in a battle of wills. Attorney General Biddle, Deputy Attorney General Rowe, FBI Director J. Edgar Hoover, and Alien Enemy Control Unit Director Edward Ennis were in direct conflict with Secretary Stimson, Assistant Secretary of War John J. McCloy, and the army personnel of Gullion, DeWitt, and Bendetsen. Bendetsen's attendance at these meetings between leaders of the War Department and top officials of the Justice Department was considered above his rank of major, and yet his forceful views of the "Japanese question" seemed to get him a seat at the table, where he significantly undercut the DOJ's civil rights defense.

Even Hoover said that his agents had already detained anyone suspected of illegal activity, so there was no longer the need for such a complicated, costly, and controversial undertaking as the evacuation of more than 100,000 Japanese Americans. In a letter to Biddle he attacked "the army's intelligence on the West Coast for exhibiting signs of hysteria and lack of judgment." Hoover recognized that the calls for "mass evacuation" were coming from public and political pressure, not facts. But he did not publicly voice his objections, nor did he criticize the mass removal plans on constitutional grounds.

And so Bendetsen continued to build his case for the "military necessity" of removing all persons of Japanese ancestry from designated military areas to get around the constitutional issues. He would later claim (and then subsequently deny) that he was "the architect of the internment," using the term that relates only to enemy aliens and disingenuously applying it to Nisei citizens as well. But he had an ally in McCloy, who said to the attorney general, "If it is a question of safety of the country, [or] the Constitution of the United States, why, the Constitution is just a scrap of paper to me."

And yet, as of February 11, Stimson still had serious misgivings about the "military necessity" argument. Even in the face of the intense advocacy from McCloy, Gullion, and various politicians, Stimson felt the need to put the question to the president and requested a personal meeting with him. That day Roosevelt was dealing with Japan's recent invasion of Singapore, and he replied to his secretary of war that he was too busy for a personal meeting.

When Stimson was finally able to reach FDR by phone later that afternoon, he asked the president if he was "willing to authorize [them] to move Japanese citizens as well as aliens from restricted [military] areas," and if so, whether to evacuate the Japanese from the entire West Coast, the larger cities, or the small areas around military installations. In his diary Stimson recorded, "I took up with him the West Coast matter first and told him the situation and fortunately found that he was very vigorous about it and told me to go ahead on the line that I myself thought the best." Stimson also understood that the president would sign an executive order to confer upon the War Department any authority that Biddle, overseeing the Justice Department, would have to relinquish.

McCloy relayed his own version of the telephone discussion between the president and his boss in a phone call to Bendetsen, who was in San Francisco at the Western Defense Command. The assistant secretary of war stated, "We have carte blanche to do what we want to as far as the president's concerned." Regarding the army's evacuation plan, McCloy added, "If it involves citizens, we will take care of them too." His spin on what he'd heard from Stimson was, "[The president] says there will probably be some repercussions, it has got to be dictated by military necessity, but as he puts it, 'Be as reasonable as you can.'" Bendetsen's interpretation of "reasonable" was to draft a memorandum called "final recommendations" authorizing the mass removal of approximately 120,000 persons, nearly two thirds of whom were American citizens.

On the following day, February 12, the famous syndicated columnist Walter Lippmann ran an article called "The Fifth Column on the Coast," which continued to stoke the public's collective panic. His piece, which was carried in the *New York Times*, the *Washington Post*, and more than 250 other newspapers, referred to material from DeWitt and Bendetsen (and reinforced in meetings with California Attorney General Earl Warren) that warned of the "imminent danger of a combined attack from within and from without." Lippmann criticized "the unwillingness of Washington to adopt a policy of mass evacuation and mass internment of all those who [were] technically enemy aliens."

Three days later columnist Westbrook Pegler quoted Lippmann's article in his own piece in the *Washington Post*. Pegler added editorial emphasis: "[Lippmann] is a high-grade fellow with a heavy sense of responsibility. . . . The Japanese in California should be under armed guard to the last man and woman right now—and to hell with habeas corpus until the danger is over."

On the same day that Lippmann's article ran, political cartoonists depicted Japanese Americans as apelike infiltrators aiding the Japanese military. Even the politically progressive editorial cartoonist Theodor Seuss Geisel—a man intensely opposed to anti-Semitism as well as the army's policy of segregating Black soldiers—held prejudicial views on Japanese Americans. In the liberal newspaper *PM*, Geisel's cartoon "Waiting for the Signal from Home . . ." showed a forever-long line of grinning, virtually identical, bucktoothed, bespectacled Japanese Americans queuing up from the Pacific coast states to get their allotment of TNT from a man in a shack. On the roof of the shack stands another man, eagerly looking out to sea through a telescope, presumably "waiting for the signal from home." "Home," we assume, is Japan, and the "signal" is for the Japanese Americans to commence their murderous activities. The cartoon was signed with Geisel's pen name, "Dr. Seuss."

• • •

In their efforts to create a public atmosphere of hate against this American minority, the . . . hate-mongers have relied on racist themes, echoing General DeWitt's "a Jap is a Jap" justification for his military evacuation order.

—Larry Taneyoshi **Tajiri**, male, Nisei, Los Angeles, California, age 27 when Pearl Harbor was attacked[40]

For us, the citizens, it hurt you inside.

—Mitsuru "Mits" **Koshiyama**, male, Nisei, Santa Clara Valley,
California, incarcerated age 18, Santa Anita Assembly Center, Heart
Mountain Relocation Center, McNeil Island Federal Penitentiary[41]

• • •

Biddle, in the meantime, did not know that Stimson and McCloy
already had the president's approval for a mass evacuation plan. The
attorney general was unaware that Stimson and McCloy were keeping
him and his chain of command in the dark. In response to the claims
dominating the press, Deputy Attorney General Rowe drafted a memorandum to the president for Biddle's signature, dated February 17,
1942, to dissuade him from mass evacuation, on the grounds that neither the army's general headquarters nor the FBI could produce any
evidence of absolute military necessity.

The memo stated, "It is extremely dangerous for the [newspaper]
columnists, acting as 'Armchair Strategists and Junior G-Men' to suggest that an attack on the West Coast and planned sabotage is imminent when the military authorities and the FBI have indicated that this
is not the fact. It comes close to shouting FIRE! in the theater; and if
the race riots occur, these writers will bear a heavy responsibility." The
memo concluded with Biddle's suggestion that the president make a
public statement in support of the loyalty of Japanese Americans.

It is believed that after receiving this memorandum, Roosevelt
surprised his attorney general by informing him that he had already
approved the War Department's plan to implement a mass evacuation
of all Nikkei from the western states.

Bendetsen had already laid out his plan in a document drafted for
DeWitt's signature titled "Evacuation of Japanese and Other Subversive
Persons from the Pacific Coast," dated February 14, 1942:

In the war in which we are now engaged, racial affinities are
not severed by migration. The Japanese race is an enemy race

and while many second and third generation Japanese born on United States soil, possessed of United States citizenship, have become Americanized, the racial strains are undiluted. . . . It, therefore, follows that along the vital Pacific Coastal Frontier over 112,000 potential enemies of Japanese extraction are at large today . . . organized and ready for concerted action at a favorable opportunity. The very fact that no sabotage has taken place to date is a disturbing and confirming indication that such action will be taken.

In other words, the fact that no evidence existed proving Japanese Americans had engaged in any espionage or sabotage whatsoever was a sign that such nefarious activity was still to come. This echoed DeWitt's earlier conversation with Gullion on January 24, when DeWitt had stated what became one of the principal arguments for mass evacuation: "The fact that nothing has happened so far is more or less . . . ominous . . . in view of the fact that we have had no sporadic attempts at sabotage that there is a control being exercised and when we have it, it will be on a mass basis." He actually saw the *lack* of any concrete evidence as suspect and the *lack* of any acts of destruction as proof that the Japanese Americans were guilty.

After FDR approved the plan, Bendetsen assisted Gullion in drafting an executive order. That Tuesday evening, February 17, Gullion brought the draft executive order with him to a meeting held in Attorney General Biddle's home. Rowe and Ennis joined Biddle in representing the Justice Department; McCloy and Stimson were also there from the War Department. The contrast between the two departments couldn't have been starker. Rowe and Ennis confronted the War Department directly: A mass evacuation of American citizens was unconstitutional. They preferred to develop a program of selective internment of enemy aliens instead.

In response, Gullion pulled the draft evacuation order out of his pocket and read it out loud. Rowe laughed in his face and told him he was crazy. Biddle said nothing. He had already given up, knowing that the president had decided it was a matter for the military. He couldn't fight the president when the president was fighting World War II. Bendetsen knew that the FBI couldn't possibly manage mass removal orders for over 100,000 Japanese people; the plan to adopt a policy of evacuating all Japanese Americans, regardless of citizenship, out of their homes meant the army had to take over. FDR had signed off on it; the fate of these Japanese Americans was sealed.

Ennis and Rowe were devastated. They'd thought they were still debating the terms of internment for enemy aliens, but clearly the plans had escalated without their knowledge. They saw that their government was making an irreversible and completely unjustified decision to destroy and cripple the lives of thousands upon thousands of American citizens because they happened to be Japanese. Rowe was so angry, he could barely speak. Ennis was so upset, he nearly wept.

Consequently, on Thursday, February 19, 1942, FDR signed without ceremony Executive Order 9066, which authorized the secretary of war and any of his military commanders to designate military zones and remove "any or all persons" from these zones—by force, if necessary—and place further restrictions on "the right of any person to enter, remain in, or leave" such areas at the discretion of the military. The executive order also authorized the secretary of war to provide food, transportation, and shelter for those being evacuated, and it allowed the military to circumvent civilian authorities, such as the Department of Justice, in order to take over the governance of these zones without declaring martial law. Decades would pass before this executive order was recognized as effectively incapacitating the Constitution and its guarantees of civil liberties.

The next day the task of announcing Executive Order 9066 to the press fell to Attorney General Biddle, who had consistently opposed the evacuation plan. Although the order did not specifically single out Japanese Americans, nor their removal, detention, or incarceration, there was no mistaking its intent; everyone knew it was aimed at the Japanese persons in the western states. In his remarks Biddle himself mentioned the Japanese when he disingenuously indicated the motivation behind the order as being "largely for the protection of the Japanese themselves." The general public, politicians, and the press reacted approvingly, even with joy and relief.

Although Roosevelt gave the broad direction to "be as reasonable as you can," Executive Order 9066 represented an unprecedented expansion of presidential power. Never before had military rule been imposed on civilians without a declaration of martial law. Moreover, under the Constitution, only Congress could suspend the writ of habeas corpus, which is the law that requires those arrested to be brought before a judge or have their day in court. Since Congress had not done this, the Nisei, as citizens, should have been entitled to individual hearings to determine whether there was a lawful basis to imprison each and every one of them.

Notwithstanding this constitutional right, FDR's executive order allowed the government to assume that the Nisei, along with their Issei parents, were disloyal, without having any charges or evidence brought against them. They could now be exiled from their homes and imprisoned under armed guard indefinitely. Most important, Executive Order 9066 stands as an ignoble example of revoking rights protected by the due process and equal protection clauses of the Constitution, solely on the basis of race. And given that the vast majority of the Japanese Americans were Buddhist (which contributed to the perception of their "foreignness"), the case could be made that the order and its execution discriminated against the Japanese on the basis of religion as well.

Roosevelt never made any comment about his decision to sign Executive Order 9066; it's possible that he did not consider its constitutional implications. But he was apparently unmoved by the impact his government's plan would have upon individuals who were innocent of any wrongdoing. Ultimately, he was morally indifferent to the consequences he was inflicting upon a minority group with whom he could not relate and that lacked any political clout.

• • •

I learned . . . we were a group of people who had no power because we had no representation in Congress or in any governmental agency, and that if we really wanted to get our voices heard, then we had to be an active participant in a democracy.

—Sueko "Sue" **Kunitomi** (Embrey), female, Nisei, Los Angeles, California, incarcerated age 19, Manzanar Reception Center, Manzanar Relocation Center[42]

• • •

Biddle later wrote, "I do not think [the president] was much concerned with the gravity or implications of this step. He was never theoretical about things." FDR had capitalized on racial fears to maintain and build support valuable to him in Congress. His advisers had their personal views, and they, in turn, received recommendations from the people reporting to them, who had their own agendas. Roosevelt held the social and cultural prejudices of his time, believing that Japanese persons were inherently inferior, racially unassimilable in American life, and untrustworthy. FDR's decision, and those made by his administration, would shape the incarceration experience to come, and in the process, invalidate the rights of American citizens guaranteed to them by the Constitution.

• • •

After the president signed Executive Order 9066, we had all these meetings in Little Tokyo [Los Angeles]. I went to one of them. There were some people who wanted to protest and others who wanted to wait and see what the government was going to do. There was a big debate over whether we should go quietly and cooperate with the government, or whether everybody should go on their own wherever they could.

—Sueko "Sue" **Kunitomi** (Embrey), female, Nisei, Los Angeles,

California, incarcerated age 19, Manzanar Reception Center, Manzanar Relocation Center[43]

• • •

DeWitt took the first step in carrying out the order by issuing Public Proclamation No. 1 on March 2, 1942. This proclamation created Military Area No. 1 (the western half of Washington, Oregon, and California and the southern half of Arizona) and Military Area No. 2 (the remaining portions of those states not included in Military Area No. 1). Nearly 120,000 citizens and aliens of Japanese descent would be forbidden from living and working in these areas inside these states, now called "military zones"—94,000 of them in California, with more than 35,000 in Los Angeles alone.

Public Proclamation No. 2, which DeWitt issued on March 16, designated four more military areas in the states of Idaho, Montana, Nevada, and Utah, and 933 more prohibited areas. DeWitt wanted to remove all Japanese persons from these areas as well, but those plans never came to pass. The proclamation also required all people of Japanese ancestry who changed their place of residence within the Western Defense Command area to obtain and sign a "change of residence notice" at a US post office.

Then on March 21, Congress passed and President Roosevelt signed enforcement legislation known as Public Law 503, which made it a crime not to obey the provisions of FDR's Executive Order 9066. Bendetsen, the author of Public Law 503, was successful in giving the order legal teeth. Violating Executive Order 9066 would now be punishable by a sentence of one year in prison.

DeWitt appointed Bendetsen to head two new divisions within the Western Defense Command to carry out the logistics of what DeWitt initially envisioned as a "voluntary" self-removal program. He further directed that those leaving Military Area No. 1 would go to one of two large euphemistically named "reception centers"—one at Manzanar, in eastern California's Owens Valley, and one in Parker, Arizona, on the Colorado River Indian Reservation.

At first DeWitt thought the Japanese Americans would be motivated to voluntarily leave the western states and move inland. But very few families could afford to do this. The government had frozen their bank accounts, and the idea of moving several hundred miles to a place unknown to them was about as appealing as flying to the moon. Those who attempted it could not buy gas on the road, were turned away from restaurants and lodging, and were even thrown into local jails for no reason. As some families approached the Arizona border, they were turned back by local sheriffs; those trying to enter Nevada were met by armed vigilantes. Others confronted NO JAPS WANTED signs.

By the end of March 1942, approximately five thousand Japanese Americans had moved from the Pacific coast states "voluntarily," most to Colorado and Utah. "Voluntary evacuation" was not going to work for the purposes of the Western Defense Command.

· · ·

Unfortunately we could not simply vanish into thin air, and we had no place to go. We had no relatives in the east. . . . All our relatives were sitting with us in the forbidden area, themselves wondering where to go. The neighboring states in the line of exit for the Japanese protested violently at the prospect of any mass invasion. They said, very sensibly, that if the Coast didn't want the Japanese hanging around, they didn't either.

A few hardy families in the community liquidated their property, tied suitcases all around their cars, and sallied eastward. They were greeted by signs in front of shop windows "Open season for Japs!" and "We kill rats and Japs here." On state lines, highway troopers swarmed around the objectionable migrants and turned them back on the governor's orders.

—Monica Kazuko **Itoi** (Sone), female, Nisei, Seattle, Washington, incarcerated age 23, Puyallup Assembly Center, Minidoka Relocation Center[44]

DeWitt's voluntary removal plan was in reality a tragic farce. Most Japanese Americans had never been east of the coastal states. Few had friends inland on whom to depend for . . . help. Moreover, the federal government and the Army guaranteed the failure of voluntary evacuation by doing nothing to explain to the residents of the interior areas why they should accept people considered too much of a security threat to be left on the West Coast. . . . Some had windshields smashed and tires slashed. Local law enforcement officials were getting calls that "Japs" were "escaping" from California and ought to be apprehended at the state line. It was only too obvious that unrestricted and unsupervised movement inland was fraught with danger.

> —Mike Masaru **Masaoka**, male, Nisei, North Platte, Nebraska, age 26 when Pearl Harbor was attacked[45]

• • •

Something had to change. FDR had supported an agreement between the War Department and the Justice Department that once the army had accomplished the initial evacuation, a civilian agency would be created to handle the relocation of Japanese Americans as a task of social welfare. And so on March 18, 1942, less than a month after signing the order, Roosevelt created the War Relocation Authority (WRA) to coordinate a program for "the removal, relocation, maintenance and supervision of persons designated under Executive Order 9066." Although the name of the new agency focused priority on the "relocation" aspect of its mission, adding "maintenance" and "supervision" to its description revealed the intention of the government to incarcerate the Japanese Americans for the foreseeable future.

The president then summoned one of his confidantes, Milton S. Eisenhower (whose older brother was future president Dwight D. Eisenhower), to the Oval Office and appointed him WRA director. The only direction FDR gave him was to complete his job at "the greatest possible speed."

• • •

Our first meeting with officials in Washington was with Milton Eisenhower. . . . I asked Eisenhower's aid . . . to let the nation know that our evacuation was a military decision not connected with any acts of disloyalty so that we could eliminate public suspicions about where our commitment lay. . . . Eisenhower, admitting he knew little about Japanese Americans, expressed some support for our objectives, and in turn asked our assistance in carrying out his difficult assignment.

—Mike Masaru **Masaoka**, male, Nisei, North Platte, Nebraska, age 26 when Pearl Harbor was attacked[46]

• • •

Eisenhower had opposed mass removal when the idea had first surfaced. Not long after his appointment, he wrote to his former boss, Secretary of Agriculture Claude R. Wickard, "I feel most deeply that when this War is over we consider calmly this unprecedented migration of 120,000 people. We are as Americans going to regret the avoidable injustices that may have occurred."

He thought that once the Nikkei had been moved out of the West Coast military areas, they should be "resettled" into communities to live as normally as possible. Eisenhower saw the intermountain states as the logical places where the Japanese Americans could resume farming and establish new communities.

Mike Masaoka, the national secretary of the JACL, along with the rest of the JACL leadership, encouraged cooperation, fearing that resistance would cause the government to use military force. Masaoka and the JACL saw no alternative but to obey the orders without objection as a way of proving that they were loyal, patriotic Americans. To this day, many in the Japanese American community remain bitter about the JACL's position of peaceful compliance.

• • •

I finally opened a JACL office near the end of March . . . to help the people who were asking questions and trying to get ready for this terrible ordeal ahead of them. . . .

I remember Mrs. Kuima, whose son was thirty-two years old and retarded. She took care of him. They had five other boys, but she took care of this boy at home. The welfare office said No, she couldn't take him, that the families have to institutionalize a child like that. . . . I remember going out to the field—she was hoeing strawberries—and I told her . . . that you can't take your son with you. And so she cried, and I cried with her. A few days before they were evacuated they came to take him away to an institution. . . . It was only about a month after we got to [the] Fresno Assembly Center that they sent us a wire saying he died.

—Mary Tsuruko (Dakuzaku) **Tsukamoto**, female, Nisei, Florin, California, incarcerated age 27, Fresno Assembly Center, Jerome Relocation Center[47]

We had been led to believe that if we cooperated with the Army in the projected mass movement, the government would make every effort to be as helpful and as humane as possible. Cooperation as an indisputable demonstration of loyalty might help to speed our return to our homes. Moreover, we feared the consequences if Japanese Americans resisted evacuation orders and the Army moved in with bayonets to eject the people forcibly. . . . At a time when Japan was still on the offensive, the American people could well consider us saboteurs if we forced the Army to take drastic action against us. This might place our future—and the future of our children and our children's children—as United States citizens in jeopardy. . . . I was determined that JACL must not give a doubting nation further cause to confuse the identity of Americans of Japanese origins with the Japanese enemy.

—Mike Masaru **Masaoka**, male, Nisei, North Platte, Nebraska, age 26 when Pearl Harbor was attacked[48]

. . .

Bendetsen, in the meantime, had been preparing for mandatory mass removal by identifying locations where "assembly centers" could be constructed or facilities adapted to serve as temporary housing for approximately 100,000 people. On March 24, less than a week after Eisenhower assumed his position, Bendetsen issued a proclamation of his own over DeWitt's signature. Public Proclamation No. 3 put into place an 8:00 p.m. to 6:00 a.m. curfew for all persons of Japanese ancestry in Military Area Nos. 1 and 2. This curfew meant that all Japanese persons living anywhere in Washington, Oregon, California, and Arizona could not be seen in public before 6:00 a.m. or after 8:00 p.m., and they couldn't travel outside of a five-mile radius from their homes. It was the initial step toward mandatory removal.

• • •

We had been restricted to traveling five miles from our homes; it was nine miles to Sacramento, and . . . everything was in Sacramento, like doctors, banks, and grocery stores. So it was just a terrible, fearful experience. Every time we went anywhere more than five miles away, we were supposed to go to the WCCA [Wartime Civil Control Administration] office in Sacramento, nine miles away, to get a permit. It was ridiculous. . . .

Every little rule and regulation was imposed only on the Japanese people. There were Italian and German people in the community, but it was just us that had travel restrictions and a curfew.

—Mary Tsuruko (Dakuzaku) **Tsukamoto**, female, Nisei, Florin, California, incarcerated age 27, Fresno Assembly Center, Jerome Relocation Center[49]

• • •

DeWitt also began issuing the first of 108 exclusion orders, which directed all persons of Japanese ancestry to take only what they could carry and report to their Civil Control Stations for transportation to assembly centers. When Bendetsen wrote the exclusion orders, he engaged in another bit of clever drafting by including the American-born Nisei as "non-aliens," a strategic reference to avoid acknowledging them as US citizens.

To address the question of where the Nikkei would go after they arrived at the assembly centers, Bendetsen convened a meeting on April 7 in Salt Lake City, where Eisenhower met with governors, attorneys general, and officials of ten western states—Arizona, Colorado, Idaho, Montana, Nevada, New Mexico, Oregon, Utah, Wyoming, and Washington. (California representatives did not attend.) Masaoka clearly hoped that by encouraging Japanese Americans to cooperate with the removal process, it would engender reciprocal cooperation from the government, so that the Japanese Americans could have as much freedom as possible while they were banned from the West Coast. But this needed the support of the government and the leaders of the intermountain states.

Eisenhower was hoping that seven of those states not classified as military zones—Colorado, Idaho, Montana, Nevada, New Mexico, Utah, and Wyoming—would embrace the idea of Japanese Americans entering their states to work, live, become part of the community, and settle down. Not only could they help harvest crops, like sugar beets, that were ripe and in danger of rotting in the fields, but they could also assist in other areas where there were wartime labor shortages. Eisenhower had in mind that the farm laborers and their families would rent places to live, become consumers, and in general contribute to the local economy.

Instead, Eisenhower soon ran into the buzz saw of Bendetsen's plans and the intense hostility that the American public had generated toward Japanese Americans. Six of those governors categorically refused to allow their states to be used as dumping grounds for potential traitors and wanted assurances that "all Japanese be put in concentration camps for the remainder of the war." Nels H. Smith, governor of Wyoming, shook his fist in Eisenhower's face and "growled through clenched teeth": "If you bring the Japanese into my state, I promise you they will be hanging from every tree!" Bert Miller, the attorney general of Idaho, was the most transparent: "We want to keep this a white man's country." The one exception was Colorado's governor,

Ralph Carr, who said he was opposed to racist thinking and he considered it his duty to cooperate with the federal government in wartime.

Eisenhower was shocked. He now realized that the so-called evacuees were not going to be housed temporarily but incarcerated instead. They would have to be indefinitely detained and segregated from the White communities. Moreover, Bendetsen had promised state officials that the displaced Japanese Americans would remain "under military police guard." The guard towers with armed soldiers—one of the defining features of the assembly centers and the camps to come—were a direct result of Bendetsen's promises. Eisenhower had the horrible feeling that his title as WRA director had just changed to prison warden.

• • •

Eisenhower made it clear . . . his idea was to establish scores of temporary havens . . . to shelter the evacuees. . . . But the hostility expressed by Western governors . . . caused Eisenhower to think in terms of detention.

—Mike Masaru **Masaoka**, male, Nisei, North Platte, Nebraska, age 26 when Pearl Harbor was attacked[50]

• • •

The term "evacuation" usually refers to the process of removing individuals for their own protection from an area in which they face imminent danger, such as a bomb threat or an approaching wildfire or hurricane. Given that the Japanese Americans were perceived as the threat to be removed, the reference to the government's plan as an evacuation, whether voluntary or mandatory, was bogus; it was actually the forced removal and imprisonment of persons, including American citizens.

Terminal Island and Bainbridge Island were the first communities where the Nikkei residents were removed by force—and the first to experience the government's cruel and uncoordinated process of evacuation. These evacuations were effectively serving as the army's dress rehearsal for the mass removal to come. Far from being detained for their well-being and supported by services in the interest of their welfare, the Terminal Island and Bainbridge Island residents were subjected to a contradictory series of military and executive orders delivered on such short notice that the orders had terrifying, devastating, and long-lasting impacts.

The FBI arrests of the Issei men on the A-B-C lists that had begun on the day of the attack on Pearl Harbor continued to occur in daily dawn raids through January 1942. By the end of January the War Department had declared Terminal Island to be a "restricted (critical) area" and suspended all traffic to and from the island. The Department of Justice put up posters throughout the fishing community on Tuesday, February 10, notifying all island residents that they had to depart by the following Monday, February 16. However, on the next day, February 11, without warning, FDR issued another executive order transferring control of Terminal Island to the navy. Secretary Knox then ordered that all Japanese Americans be informed by February 15 that they had to be off the island within thirty days, after which their homes would be condemned. But ten days later, the orders changed again, and on February 25, Knox demanded that all residents of Japanese ancestry get off the island in just forty-eight hours.

• • •

It was during these 48 hours that I witnessed unscrupulous vultures in the form of human beings taking advantage of bewildered housewives whose husbands had been rounded up by the FBI within 48 hours of Pearl Harbor. They were offered pittances for practically new furniture and appliances; refrigerators, radio consoles, etc., as well as cars, and many were falling prey to these people.

—Yoshihiko Fred **Fujikawa**, male, Nisei, Terminal Island, California, incarcerated age 32, Santa Anita Assembly Center, Jerome Relocation Center[51]

• • •

What the families could not sell, they simply had to abandon; in one fell swoop they lost the businesses they had built up for decades. The government provided no assistance for relocation, and very few residents owned motor vehicles. They were told to just pack up and go. After they were gone, the navy confiscated the fishing equipment they'd had no choice but to leave behind and demolished their homes, shops, and even their Shinto shrine.

Similarly, Bainbridge Island, approximately five miles wide and ten miles long, in Seattle's Puget Sound, was home to a vibrant Japanese American community located, like Terminal Island, near naval facilities. On March 24, 1942, DeWitt launched Civilian Exclusion Order No. 1, notifying the 227 Japanese residents of Bainbridge Island that they were being physically removed only six days later. The population received booklets telling them what to pack: clothes, toiletries, utensils, plates, bowls, blankets, and linens. Everyone was forced to make heartbreaking decisions to sell or store what they could, give away pets, take only what they were able to carry, and walk away from the rest. Thirteen residents were seniors at Bainbridge High School; they couldn't even attend their senior prom because of the 8:00 p.m. curfew. And just as on Terminal Island, the "vultures" were immediately on the scene.

Then, on March 30, all 227 Japanese Bainbridge Islanders—including elderly family members and mothers carrying infants and small children—solemnly walked between rows of bayoneted soldiers to the Eagledale dock to board the ferry *Keholoken* to Seattle. A young Nisei said that the long trudge onto the ferry was the most humiliating moment of his life. From the time they boarded the ferry, each family was assigned one soldier to watch them during the entire trip. Even as they made the familiar crossing through Puget Sound, they still had not been told of their final destination, nor how long they would be away from their homes.

The Bainbridge residents were the first to arrive at the not-yet-completed Owens Valley Reception Center in Manzanar, California (which also became known as the Manzanar Reception Center). As they surveyed the rows and rows of barracks, the awful realization dawned on them that they were at the vanguard of a massive process and that thousands of other "evacuees" would soon be joining them in this prison setting.

• • •

At the sight of the camp . . . our hearts sank to a new low. Even some of the soldiers who escorted us down couldn't believe what they saw. . . . Some had tears in their eyes as they left us.

—Paul Tsutomu **Ohtaki**, male, Nisei, Bainbridge Island, Washington, incarcerated age 18, Owens Valley Reception Center, Manzanar Relocation Center[52]

• • •

Shortly thereafter DeWitt issued Civilian Exclusion Order Nos. 2 and 3 for Los Angeles County. The pace of such orders shifted into high gear when one after another was posted over the next seven months, until a total of 108 exclusion orders had been completed by the end of October 1942.

The frightened Japanese Americans up and down the West Coast saw soldiers in their neighborhoods hammering the Civilian Exclusion Orders onto telephone poles, tacking them onto trees, taping them to shop windows, stapling them onto post office bulletin boards, and posting them in public places and government office buildings. The orders had the headline: INSTRUCTIONS TO ALL PERSONS OF **JAPANESE** ANCESTRY LIVING IN THE FOLLOWING AREA. The word "Japanese" was extra-large and bold-faced. The postings described the area being evacuated and announced a time and place for a "responsible adult member" or an individual living alone to report to one of the ninety-seven Civil Control Stations, all located in neighborhoods where people of Japanese descent lived in large numbers. The orders were also clear that it was a crime not to obey.

The army divided the exclusion areas into districts and produced plans for removing all of the Japanese people from those districts in groups of approximately one thousand persons at a time. The military planners were able to do this quickly because they had the cooperation of the US Census Bureau, which surveys the entire population of the United States every ten years. It is against the law for the bureau to reveal any data from its questionnaires that could be traced to an individual. However, this law was repealed temporarily under the Second War Powers Act of 1942 to aid in the army's herding of Japanese Americans into camps. Even so, the bureau was entitled to release only block-by-block information that pointed to Japanese American neighborhoods; now there is evidence to support that the bureau also released microdata (meaning name, address, sex, age, race, and marital status) that could be used for surveillance purposes. Certainly, the bureau provided the US Secret Service and Western Defense Command with information from the 1940 census that identified where the ethnic Japanese lived by city blocks and tracts, but it may have disclosed even more about them as individual citizens. The confidentiality of the census wasn't restored until 1947.

But no matter what they thought about the military orders, the vast majority of the targeted West Coast Nikkei complied without protest because the soldiers had guns, and they saw no other option.

. . .

My history teacher told me, don't worry, Yoshio, you are an American citizen, and the Constitution will protect you from being forcefully moved. The next week I told him I had orders to evacuate. He was stunned.

—Yoshio "Yosh" **Nakamura**, male, Nisei, El Monte, California, incarcerated age 17, Tulare Assembly Center, Gila River Relocation Center[53]

Henry went to the Control Station to register the family. He came home with twenty tags, all numbered 10710, tags to be attached to each piece of baggage, and one to hang from our coat lapels. From then on, we were known as Family #10710.

—Monica Kazuko **Itoi** (Sone), female, Nisei, Seattle, Washington, incarcerated age 23, Puyallup Assembly Center, Minidoka Relocation Center[54]

As an impressionable 12-year-old in 1942, I had learned about the US Constitution and what it meant. . . . I felt that I could count on our government. The remotest thing on the minds of our family was to be incarcerated under some emotional decision contrary to the Constitution. I could not believe at the time that this was happening to us.

—Allan Minoru **Hida**, male, Nisei, Sacramento, California, incarcerated age 13, Sacramento Assembly Center, Tule Lake Relocation Center, Granada (Amache) Relocation Center[55]

I . . . was [in] the seventh grade. I would be called by the other kids . . . "Jap." I resented it, so I kind of fought with them. First thing I knew . . . I was sent to detention class. I don't know if the teacher [was] trying to help me or . . . punish me. . . . I believe that she made me study all about the Constitution because that's the subject . . . kids didn't want to study. . . . I didn't want to be punished anymore, so I studied the Constitution pretty hard. Then the teacher [asked] me, . . . "What'd you learn? Don't you know that all Americans are supposed to fight for their constitutional rights?" And it'd kind of go through one ear and [out] the other. . . . "It protects all citizens," she told me. "Don't you understand? . . . It's for your own protection that the Constitution was written." . . . It finally sunk into my head. . . . I did realize that, like she said, the Constitution is the main law of the land. . . . Presidents come and go, teachers come and go . . . but she says, "The Constitution [will] be always there no matter what." She says, "You'd better learn all about the Constitution because sooner or later it's gonna help you."

—Mitsuru "Mits" **Koshiyama**, male, Nisei, Santa Clara Valley,

California, incarcerated age 18, Santa Anita Assembly Center, Heart Mountain Relocation Center, McNeil Island Federal Penitentiary[56]

• • •

At the control stations the family representatives were told where their families were to report to board a bus or train to a temporary assembly center within a week. But when asked where these assembly centers were, how long they would be living there, and where they would be going afterward, the soldiers said nothing.

All across the western states, Japanese Americans were experiencing what the Terminal and Bainbridge Islanders had already dealt with as they scrambled to decide what to pack, struggled to anticipate what they would need, and agonized over disposing of the rest of their belongings.

• • •

We were advised to pack warm, durable clothes. In my mind I saw our . . . camp sprawled out somewhere deep in a snow-bound forest, an American Siberia. I saw myself plunging chest deep in snow, hunting for small game to keep us alive. I decided that one of my suitcases was going to hold nothing but vitamins from A to Z. I thought of sewing fur-lined hoods and parkas for the family. I was certain this was going to be a case of sheer animal survival.

—Monica Kazuko **Itoi** (Sone), female, Nisei, Seattle, Washington, incarcerated age 23, Puyallup Assembly Center, Minidoka Relocation Center[57]

We surveyed with desperation the vast array of dishes, lacquerware, silverware, pots and pans, books, paintings, porcelain and pottery, furniture, linens, rugs, records, curtains, garden tools, cleaning equipment, and clothing that filled our house. We put up a sign in our window reading, "Living room sofa and chair for sale." . . . Without a sensible scheme in our heads, and lacking the practical judgment of my father, the three of us packed frantically and sold recklessly. . . . We felt desperate as the deadline approached. Our only thought was to get the house emptied in time, for we knew the Army would not wait.

—Yoshiko **Uchida**, female, Nisei, Berkeley, California, incarcerated age 21, Tanforan Assembly Center, Topaz Relocation Center[58]

I remember having to sell my most treasured possession—my bicycle—which I had bought with my earnings from selling newspapers. My two younger brothers also had to sacrifice their bicycles.

—Ernest Nobumaro **Uno**, male, Nisei, Los Angeles, California, incarcerated age 17, Santa Anita Assembly Center, Granada (Amache) Relocation Center[59]

Hey, you Japs! You're going to get kicked out of here tomorrow. I'll give you ten bucks for that refrigerator. I'll give you fifteen bucks for your piano. I'll give you two bucks and fifteen cents for that washing machine.

—William "Bill" Kumpai **Hosokawa**, male, Nisei, Seattle, Washington, incarcerated age 27, Puyallup Assembly Center, Heart Mountain Relocation Center[60]

What really hurts most is the constant reference to us as Japs. Japs are the guys we were fighting. We're on this side, and we want to help.

—Theodore "Ted" Katsuyoshi **Nakashima**, male, Nisei, Seattle, Washington, incarcerated age 30, Puyallup Assembly Center, Tule Lake Relocation Center[61]

On the day before the posted evacuation date, there was a line of cars in our driveway extending out about another 200 yards in both directions . . . waiting their turn to come to our house to see what they could get from us for a small fraction of its worth or nothing. Most of the people were strangers, but some were people we thought were our friends. One man wanted to buy our pick-up truck. My father had just *spent $125 for a new set of tires and tubes, and a brand new battery. Our friend bought, and I use the words "friend" and "bought" face-tiously . . . [the machine we used to spray crops] for $15. We had only a few weeks earlier purchased it for about $100. . . . The man told my father that he . . . might as well take the $15, otherwise he would be back the next day and pick it up for nothing.*

—Hiroshi **Kamei**, male, Nisei, Westminster, California, incarcerated age 14, Poston Relocation Center[62]

People would just come and take things off our porch. "You won't need this." And not pay for it or anything, they'd just take it. And one of the things my mother said for me to watch is to make sure nobody takes the vacuum cleaner, because we have to clean the house before we leave. But they would come and they would take chairs and couch, and my mother had this real nice . . . planter like thing, and it was very "Japanesey," and somebody . . . came up and they realized that [it] was a real nice thing and they just took it, table and all.

—Keiko "Kay" **Uno** (Kaneko), female, Nisei, Los Angeles, California, incarcerated age 10, Santa Anita Assembly Center, Granada (Amache) Relocation Center[63]

[My mother] Komika, showing an admirable fortitude, even man-aged to sell her plants. . . . [She] didn't want to negotiate, but [she] wasn't going to give anything away. . . . A friend had the sewing machine of his mother who had passed away. Nobody would give him a decent price for it, so he took it out to the backyard and broke it up.

—Sueko "Sue" **Kunitomi** (Embrey), female, Nisei, Los Angeles, California, incarcerated age 19, Manzanar Reception Center, Manzanar Relocation Center[64]

• • •

Jeanne Wakatsuki Houston's mother had reached her limit. When a secondhand dealer offered her mother an insulting pittance for her valuable and prized china, she threw plate after plate at his feet, tears streaming down her cheeks. After he went running off, her mother continued to smash the remaining pieces in rage and frustration until all that was left was a pile of blue-and-white porcelain shards on the wooden porch.

• • •

I heard some people were going to chain themselves to a telephone pole. They were dissuaded. We kept wondering whether anybody was going to protest. We sat around saying, "They can't do this to us. We're American citizens."
    —Sueko "Sue" **Kunitomi** (Embrey), female, Nisei, Los Angeles, California, incarcerated age 19, Manzanar Reception Center, Manzanar Relocation Center[65]

One Issei, Mr. Iwasa, committed suicide.
    —Mary Tsuruko (Dakuzaku) **Tsukamoto**, female, Nisei, Florin, California, incarcerated age 27, Fresno Assembly Center, Jerome Relocation Center[66]

• • •

Some families had time to take advantage of the offer by the Buddhist temples in Los Angeles to store their belongings, whether they were members of the temple or not. The Quakers and the Congregational churches helped too. Occasionally, neighbors offered to keep possessions safe for the evacuees until they returned. Some turned out to be steadfast friends who kept their promises, but sadly, few could be trusted.

• • •

We sold our car for eight hundred dollars, which was just about giving it away. . . . But some wonderful friends came to ask if they could take care of some things we couldn't store. Mr. Lernard, a principal of a high school, took my piano, and his daughter took our dining room set, which was a wedding gift. . . .

When we left we swept our house and left it clean, because that's the way Japanese people feel like leaving a place. . . .

I remember that sad morning, when we realized suddenly that we wouldn't be free. It was such a clear, beautiful day. . . . We saw the snow-clad Sierra Nevada mountains that we had loved to see so often and I thought about God.

— Mary Tsuruko (Dakuzaku) **Tsukamoto**, female, Nisei, Florin, California, incarcerated age 27, Fresno Assembly Center, Jerome Relocation Center[67]

• • •

In addition to disposing of their personal belongings, families had to leave pets behind to fend for themselves if the owners could not find anyone to care for them. Most Japanese American businesses on the West Coast had to be sold at prices that were a fraction of their worth. Some people had no choice but to simply walk away from their stores and restaurants. Farmers had to leave crops ready to harvest and sell their property to land vultures. Thieves would later vandalize the recently vacated homes and steal whatever had to be left behind. Some estimates of their total property losses run as high as three billion dollars (not adjusted for inflation). The land they'd once owned, valued at less than $200 an acre in 1942, increased in value to between $10,000 and $30,000 an acre by 1986. Their sudden emotional suffering is incomprehensible, but the full economic loss to these Japanese American families and their heirs is incalculable.

• • •

I had to leave my German Shepherd dog home. His name was Poochie. He was about two years old. It was over twenty-five years we lived on the farm. We had to get rid of the horses and the farm equipment. The day we evacuated, I saw my father talking to the horses. He was saying, "I hope the next person will take care of you real good." The tears came.

— Sumiko "Sumi" **Seo** (Seki), female, Nisei, Los Angeles, California, incarcerated age 18, Santa Anita Assembly Center, Jerome Relocation Center[68]

At the peak of the strawberry season, the military descended upon us. It was incredible. The all-important berry crop we had worked the entire year to produce was to be abandoned. Each year we were deep in debt merely to make it until harvest time. Every crate we sold now meant paying back the debts we had accumulated through the winter months to survive. . . . Reluctantly, we were now forced to leave with debts to dishonor our name. More serious was the fact that we were penniless as we began a frightful journey to destinations unknown. . . . Nearly 500 families were removed from the Florin area. Florin never recovered from this ordeal. The community we remembered died on May 29, 1942.

　　—Mary Tsuruko (Dakuzaku) **Tsukamoto**, female, Nisei, Florin,
　　California, incarcerated age 27, Fresno Assembly Center, Jerome
　　Relocation Center[69]

• • •

The hand-written sign left in the window of the drugstore in Los Angeles's Little Tokyo read: "Many thanks for your Patronage. Hope to Serve you in the Near future. God be with you till we meet again. Mr. and Mrs. K. Iseri."

• • •

So much was left behind, but the most valuable thing I lost was my freedom.

　　—Teru **Watanabe**, female, Nisei, Los Angeles, California,
　　incarcerated age 28, Manzanar Reception Center, Manzanar
　　Relocation Center[70]

• • •

Although most obeyed the exclusion orders, over one hundred individuals defied at least one of them. Those arrested were convicted, but they lacked the financial resources to appeal their cases. Three of the individuals who deliberately refused to accept some or all of the orders were Minoru Yasui of Portland, Oregon; Gordon Hirabayashi of Seattle, Washington; and Fred Korematsu of San Leandro, California, near San Francisco. Although they did not know one another and at the time were unaware of one another's actions, their names would become entwined as a result of their criminal convictions and their commitment to challenge the constitutionality of the government orders.

On Saturday, March 28, 1942, the first night of DeWitt's 6:00 p.m. curfew, twenty-five-year-old Minoru Yasui was walking along downtown Portland's Third Avenue, deliberately violating the curfew order. He didn't know it would be so hard to get arrested. Yasui went up to a policeman on the street, pointing out that he was a Japanese American in violation of a military curfew, but the officer just said, "Run along home, sonny boy, or you'll get in trouble."

Eventually Yasui got tired of walking the streets of Portland, so he went back to his office. There he had his secretary, Rei Shimojima, and Chiye Tomihiro (the sixteen-year-old daughter of Yasui's good friend Senichi Tomihiro) call the police to report his violation of the curfew. But the officers answering the phones thought the reports were crank calls and hung up. Frustrated, Yasui walked down to a nearby police station, and the desk sergeant obliged him by throwing him into the "drunk tank" at 11:20 p.m.

Yasui was an attorney who'd believed from the start that the Japanese American incarceration was unconstitutional and decided to create a test case in court by refusing to abide by one of the orders. He later explained, "Knowing the uncertainties, I could scarcely blame anyone for refusing to go ahead and deliberately violate the law. And it seemed to me that someone had to do it, and the ultimate choice became, since nobody else would do it, I did."

Although Yasui had carefully planned out how he would initiate his test case, he could not have known that the curfew order was just one component of a mass removal and detention program of all Japanese American citizens on the West Coast. He chose to break curfew because Public Proclamation No. 3 applied to all persons of Japanese ancestry. Yasui reasoned that while the curfew order could be applied to the Issei because they were considered enemy aliens, it could not be applied to American citizens because it was a violation of their constitutional rights.

• • •

I grew up in Oregon . . . and believed myself an American, equal to all other Americans. I loved the green hills of home, and believed that this magnificent land was my land and my country. I studied the history of our United States, her institutions, and our Constitution and our laws. I was brought up to be an American. . . .

If we believe in America, if we believe in equality and democracy, if we believe in law and justice, then each of us, when we see or believe errors are being made, has an obligation to make every effort to correct them.

—Minoru "Min" **Yasui**, male, Nisei, Portland, Oregon, incarcerated age 25, Portland Assembly Center, Minidoka Relocation Center, Multnomah County Jail[71]

• • •

On May 16, 1942, seven weeks after Yasui's arrest, twenty-four-year-old Gordon Hirabayashi turned himself in to the FBI in Seattle, Washington, instead of reporting to an assembly center. He went with his friend and attorney Arthur Barnett, carrying a four-page state-ment he had carefully prepared, in which he explained his religious beliefs. Hirabayashi was a Quaker; while he was a student at the Uni-versity of Washington, he had become a member of the Religious Society of Friends. As a pacifist, he did not believe that war solved any problems and had registered with the Selective Service as a conscien-tious objector. Hirabayashi did not think that the government should use military powers to protect national security and considered the curfew and exclusion orders to be expressions of military force, which were at odds with his pacifist views. Moreover, the discriminatory aspects of the military orders offended his sense of morality.

When he shared his decision to not report to the Puyallup Assembly Center as ordered with the local American Civil Liberties Union (ACLU), the organization pledged to support him. Hirabayashi also received the backing of the American Friends Service Committee and the Fellowship of Reconciliation, a progressive pacifist group.

Like Yasui, Hirabayashi surrendered to authorities with the intention of serving as a test case to challenge the constitutionality of the forced evacuation without due process of law. But when an FBI agent confiscated his diary and read his diary entries, the agent discovered that Hirabayashi had also disobeyed the curfew. As a result, he was charged with violating the curfew order, in addition to violating the exclusion order. He was then taken to King County Jail.

• • •

This order for the mass evacuation of all persons of Japanese descent denies them the right to live. It forces thousands of energetic, law-abiding individuals to exist in a miserable psychological and horrible physical atmosphere. This order limits to almost the full extent the creative expressions of those subjected. It kills the desire for a higher life. Hope for the future is exterminated. Human personalities are poisoned. . . .

I am objecting to the principle of this order, which denies the rights of human beings, including citizens.

—Gordon Kiyoshi **Hirabayashi**, male, Nisei, Seattle, Washington, age 24 when Pearl Harbor was attacked, King County Jail, Tucson Federal Prison/Catalina Federal Honor Camp, McNeil Island Federal Penitentiary[72]

I don't know very much about law. . . . I'm making a personal stand. . . . Each person should follow the will of God according to his own convictions. . . . [I] could not reconcile the will of God, a part of which was expressed in the Bill of Rights and the United States Constitution, with the order discriminating against Japanese aliens and American citizens of Japanese ancestry.

—Gordon Kiyoshi **Hirabayashi**[73]

• • •

And then, just two weeks after Hirabayashi's arrest, on the afternoon of Memorial Day, May 30, 1942, a police officer stopped twenty-three-year-old Fred Korematsu and his girlfriend on the street. Korematsu confessed to being Japanese and failing to obey the exclusion order. In contrast with Yasui and Hirabayashi, whose plans had always been purposeful, Korematsu did not start out thinking about constitutional issues. He was supposed to report for evacuation along with his family, but he didn't because he wanted to marry his Italian American girlfriend and work on the West Coast until he could earn enough money to move to the Midwest. Korematsu had even undergone plastic surgery on his face in an attempt to make his eyes look "less Japanese" and escape detection. But after he was arrested, Korematsu and his girlfriend broke up, and he never saw her again.

Korematsu was being held at the Presidio stockade in San Francisco when he was approached by Ernest Besig, an attorney from the ACLU. Besig was looking for someone willing to bring a test case to challenge the exclusion orders. Although his family had disapproved of his decision to disobey the exclusion order, and he was being characterized as a troublemaker by the Japanese community, Korematsu resolved that the government's actions were wrong and agreed to pursue his case with the ACLU. He was sent to the Tanforan Assembly Center, where he was reunited with his family and awaited trial.

• • •

My older brother arranged a meeting in Tanforan. . . . I asked whether I should go ahead and fight the case or not. Some people said, "We're in here now, why make it worse." And other people said, "It's up to you." They left everything up to me, because I'm fighting the case and they're not. So I decided to go ahead and see the thing through.

—Fred Toyosaburo **Korematsu**, male, Nisei, San Leandro,
California, age 22 when Pearl Harbor was attacked, Presidio,
Tanforan Assembly Center, Topaz Relocation Center[74]

· · ·

From the start, however, the national JACL was "unalterably
opposed" to these test cases. The organization thought that basing
legal challenges on criminal acts undermined the JACL's goal of full
cooperation with the government. More important, Masaoka feared
the men ran the risk of losing their cases, so the JACL refused to provide any of the three men with financial or moral support. In fact,
Masaoka had read in some Oregon newspaper accounts that Yasui was
being characterized as a "maverick publicity seeker." Masaoka accused
him of being a "self-styled martyr."

· · ·

*Completely in the dark and fearful that Yasui was endangering the
delicate unwritten understanding we had with federal authorities, I
issued a strong statement criticizing him.*
  —Mike Masaru **Masaoka**, male, Nisei, North Platte, Nebraska, age
  26 when Pearl Harbor was attacked[75]

· · ·

All three were convicted of criminal charges and appealed their
convictions to the Court of Appeals for the Ninth Circuit. Yasui,
Hirabayashi, and Korematsu were all serving their sentences while
their cases were on appeal. In the meantime, their families and friends
faced their own imprisonments.

PART TWO

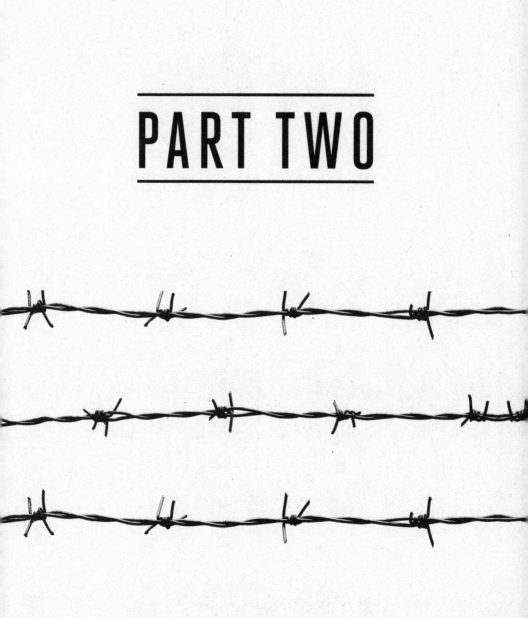

PART TWO

SAGA OF A PEOPLE

They have sprung from a race as old as Time,
Their backs are bent, their hands are wrinkled and brown,
For they have toiled long years under a harsh master—Life;
Each passing year has left its mark
Upon their seamed and weathered faces
That show as other faces do,
A heart-deep yearning for a far-off land;
A land of frail houses, stunted trees, a sacred volcano
Sleeping under a blanket of snow.
Traces of half-forgotten customs
A love for the life-giving sun, the freshening rain, the
     deep brown soil,
Still lingers in their hearts.
Deep scars of pain and grief are etched on their worn faces
And yet their wise twinkling eyes
Have looked on life and found it good.

They have come to a fabulous land,
While still dreaming the long thoughts of youth;
They have sowed their seeds, weeded furrows,
Hoed a sun-parched land, watered and nursed it,
Harvested their plentiful crops, built a home
And borne their children.
Lest they forget the islands of their fathers,
They have brought their little treasures with them—
A miniature chest of drawers, lacquered dragon-red;
Two dainty fans gay with dancing girls;
A bamboo screen with a tiny arched bridge
And fragile lilies reflected in still water;

Little dolls in bright kimonos of hand-painted silk;
Delicate tea cups set on a polished tray.

The seeds they sowed took root and sprouted,
Grew tall and straight with bursting pods;
Giving rich promise of fulfillment.
So grew their black-haired children
Straight and tall, drawing nourishment from the free soil
Of this, their native land.
Their lives were like a deep, peaceful river
The old familiar customs of their ancestors
Mixing with the new bewildering ones of their foster country
And slowly giving way before them
Eating a breakfast of crisp bacon and scrambled eggs
Instead of the hot soup and rice they had eaten
In the home of their fathers;
Raising a huge paper carp on Boys' Day;
Awkwardly tying a silver star to the tip of the family
    Christmas tree;
Reluctantly going to a movie with the children,
Leaving behind a friendly game of Go
And a cup of steaming, green tea;
Driving to the beach and learning to roast hot dogs
Over a driftwood fire,
And eating them with seed-covered rice cakes;
Passing on to their children the ceremonious courtesies
That they had learned so long ago.
And so they lived out their lives
Guided by their sons and daughters
Through this strange new world,
Slowly changing their deep-rooted ways.

They have come to a new home
Living in a single room
Behind barbed wire—
They know that peace has been shattered throughout the
    world
By heavily laden bombs of terror and destruction;
But they who love the deeply tranquil soil
Are stunned, bewildered by it all,
By the cold wall which their American friends
Have built about them.

Now they are standing on the beloved soil of their
    western mother,
Their wizened bodies huddled together
Against the bitter cold.
Rising they look toward the sea
Vainly striving through the mists of the past
To live again the dreams of their youth,
Thinking of a pleasant land where cherry blossoms
Warmed their hearts in spring,
Where placid goldfish lazily swam in sunny ponds,
Where all was contented and peaceful;
They turn towards the red glow of a sinking sun,
Seeing through the distant hills, seeing over all the
    land
The rolling hills and valleys of their western mother.
Then they turn towards each other with eyes full,
Unashamedly,
Understandingly;
For deep in their almond brown eyes,
Deep in the innermost depths of their souls

There shall always glow a hope,
A hope that peace shall come one day
A peace forging with understanding and friendship,
The islands of their long-lost youth
And the far stretching land of their children's birth.

by Ruth Tanaka, 16 years old
Fourth Prize (among 6,000 entries)
Scholastic Magazine Literary Contest
Parker Valley High School, Poston Relocation Center

—Ruth **Tanaka** (Gray), female, Nisei, Dinuba, California, incarcerated age 13, Poston Relocation Center[76]

CHAPTER FOUR

Only What They Could Carry

We left for camp at a bus stop in Burbank on a gray, cloudy day,
and just before we got on the bus, it began to rain. A mother of two,
standing next to me, said, "See, even God in heaven is crying for us."
    —Mary **Sakaguchi** (Oda), female, Nisei, Los Angeles, California,
    incarcerated age 22, Manzanar Reception Center, Manzanar
    Relocation Center[77]

In early April and May 1942, the "evacuees" (to use the government's term) were arriving in waves at their assigned Civil Control Stations—each with only what they could carry. In Los Angeles, the Nishi Hongwanji Buddhist Temple had been an important gathering place for the Little Tokyo community; now it was the departure point for residents who were being wrenched away from their homes. Families huddled together, sitting on suitcases, clustered around their belongings. Everyone was required to wear a dehumanizing identification tag with a five-digit number, which compounded the indignity of the situation. The tags hung from the buttons on their jackets and coats as they sat there like lost-and-found packages with no destination or return address.

• • •

I lost my identity. At that time, I didn't even have a Social Security
number, but the WRA gave me an I.D. number. That was my identifi-
cation. I lost my privacy and my dignity.
    —Masako "Betty" (Fujisaki) **Matsuo**, female, Nisei, Stockton,
    California, incarcerated age 16, Stockton Assembly Center, Rohwer
    Relocation Center[78]

• • •

There was confusion about whether non-Japanese people whose husbands or wives were of Japanese descent would be included in the mass removal. By and large, spouses who were not of Japanese descent did not have to be incarcerated, but many chose to accompany their families to camp in order to remain together.

Concerning individuals of mixed heritage, however, Bendetsen created his own definition of who met the requirement for incarceration.

"I am determined that if they have one drop of Japanese blood in them, they must go to camp," he said.

In less than three months Bendetsen had made such a strong impression on his superiors that the army gave him a double promotion, from major to lieutenant colonel to full colonel, in connection with his new role of supervising the evacuation plan. Now flush with authority, Bendetsen and his aides toured the orphanages to identify babies and young children who looked like they might have Japanese blood in them. He identified 61 young children from a few foster homes and three orphanages (the Maryknoll Home for Japanese Children, and the Shonien, both in Los Angeles, and the Salvation Army's Japanese Children's Home in San Francisco). May Ichida was alarmed. As a Salvation Army brigadier, she was in charge of 55 orphaned children in the Salvation Army's Japanese Children's Home. She "questioned the rights of parentless children who were American citizens, without parental rights, being placed in concentration camps arbitrarily."

Despite her objections, the orphans were all removed to the Children's Village at Manzanar. Bendetsen even took into custody Japanese infants and children from their Caucasian foster parents. Half of the orphans being detained were younger than seven, nearly a third were younger than four, and some were as young as six months old. By the end of the war, the number of children living at the Manzanar Children's Village had grown to 101.

• • •

The day was too early for the sun. . . . My heart pounded. My entire body suddenly felt weak with fright. The horror of the day dawned as I quickly arose. My throat was dry and my body sore from yet another night of weeping.

My angry tears were reserved [for] the privacy of my bed at night. But, fear and desperation multiplied. . . . I realized then how helpless we were and how hopeless it was. Afraid for the safety of our elderly Issei parents, now called "enemy aliens," there was nothing for us to do but follow the orders of the Army.

We only had a few hours left . . . before surrendering our freedom. We were gripped in a nightmare, a nightmare that clutched at the very soul of every person of Japanese ancestry. . . .

I kept pondering. Why? What had we done? Why was this happening to us? Why?

. . . We have broken no laws. . . . We are farmers, growers of strawberries. . . . We love our country and only ache to prove our loyalty if we could be given a chance. . . . We are criminals because we have Japanese faces.

How will we ever explain this to our children?

—Mary Tsuruko (Dakuzaku) **Tsukamoto**, female, Nisei, Florin, California, incarcerated age 27, Fresno Assembly Center, Jerome Relocation Center[79]

We were filled with fear. We weren't sure that they weren't going to just take us out into the desert and shoot us. We had no idea what to expect.

—Aiko **Yoshinaga** (Herzig), female, Nisei, Los Angeles, California, incarcerated age 17, Manzanar Relocation Center, Jerome Relocation Center, Rohwer Relocation Center[80]

Some people [were] actively stating that the government was going to make us all starve to death. There were thousands of wild rumors

going around, you know, sounding as if they were all true and authen-
tic stories.

—Riichi **Satow**, male, Issei, Sacramento, California, incarcerated age
47, Pinedale Assembly Center, Poston Relocation Center[81]

One strong rumor floating in the Japanese community is that we
would be sent to the desert, abandoned by the United States govern-
ment. . . . Our fantasy was that we would be made to wander around
aimlessly like American Indians in tribal reservations. As a conse-
quence, my mother purchased canteens for water containers, high
boots to protect us from rattlesnakes and heavy canvas to be made into
bags to carry our belongings.

—Bebe Toshiko **Horiuchi** (Reschke), female, Nisei, Los Angeles,
California, incarcerated age 10, Santa Anita Assembly Center,
Rohwer Relocation Center[82]

The entire city block around the Civil Control Station [in Berke-
ley, California] was guarded by military police. Baggage was piled on
the sidewalk the full length of the block. Greyhound buses were lined
alongside the curb.

—Miné **Okubo**, female, Nisei, Berkeley, California, incarcerated age
30, Tanforan Assembly Center, Topaz Relocation Center[83]

Before long, we were told to board the buses that lined the street
outside, and the people living nearby came out of their houses to
watch the beginning of our strange migration. Most of them probably
watched with curious and morbid fascination, some perhaps even with
a little sadness. But many may have been relieved and glad to see us go.

—Yoshiko **Uchida**, female, Nisei, Berkeley, California, incarcerated
age 21, Tanforan Assembly Center, Topaz Relocation Center[84]

• • •

As the long procession of families began to board buses and trains at San Diego's Santa Fe Depot, the silence was broken by the uncontrollable sobs of one elderly Issei woman.

Although they didn't know it, the displaced Nikkei were headed to assembly centers that had been hastily adapted into temporary housing under DeWitt's command. The WRA had identified existing sites large enough to house an approximate total of 80,000 people: racetracks, stockyards, fairgrounds, and other public spaces on expansive grounds connected to railways and roads, close to Japanese American neighborhoods, and equipped with running water and electricity.

In addition to the so-called Manzanar Reception Center in central California and the Parker Dam Reception Center (later known as Poston Relocation Center) then part of Yuma County, Arizona, there were fifteen other assembly centers: Fresno, Marysville (also known as Arboga), Merced, Pinedale, Pomona, Sacramento, Salinas, Santa Anita, Stockton, Tanforan, Tulare, and Turlock in California; Mayer in Arizona; Portland in Oregon; and Puyallup (also known as Camp Harmony) in Washington. The two largest assembly centers were at the Tanforan Racetrack in San Bruno, California, not far from San Francisco's Japantown, and the Santa Anita Race Track in Arcadia, California, only twelve miles from Los Angeles's Little Tokyo.

• • •

We had neighbors that worked for the LAPD [Los Angeles Police Department]; one was an investigator . . . the other was a regular police[man]. And when they heard that [the FBI] took my grandfather away, they said, "The Japanese are the most law-abiding people." They didn't ever remember booking a Japanese ever in the whole L.A. jail system. Ever. . . . [The FBI] took him away . . . to Fort Sill, Oklahoma, where it was below zero degrees.

They took him to nine places.

[A week later] they took us to Union Station. . . . Melvin [the

investigator] was the one that took us, and he was unprepared for what he saw. He saw the [soldiers] with bayonets shoving people, herding them onto the train. . . . And I saw something I will never forget as long as I will live. . . .

[There] was a young couple who had four children. The mother had twins that she was cradling in her arms. [The couple] were both dressed in their Sunday best . . . and there were two toddlers hanging on to her coat. All four babies were crying, and the poor young father had all these diapers [and] baby bottles strapped on his back, and then he had these two [oversized] suitcases for all six of them.

—Aiko Grace **Shinoda** (Nakamura), female, Nisei, Los Angeles, California, incarcerated age 15, Manzanar Reception Center, Manzanar Relocation Center[85]

. . .

Family members tried to stay together so they could be sent to the same destination. But in some cases extended families ended up getting separated. For those families whose husbands and fathers had been arrested, most of the women had no idea where the men had been taken, and they didn't know if they would be reunited with the rest of their family at the assembly center. Apprehensive and terrified but focused and vigilant, the Issei mothers tried their best with limited English to shepherd their children through this bewildering and disturbing process without their husbands. Many of them packed their children's clothing and daily necessities separately, in case the children had to care for themselves.

Sixteen-year-old Peter Ota and his thirteen-year-old sister had to manage without either parent. Their father had been taken away, and their mother was in a tuberculosis sanitorium.

Most of the adults, especially the older first-generation Issei, remained dignified and patient—at least on the outside. Many, of course, were embarrassed that they had to stand by while their families were humiliated by this gross injustice. Even the very little children and babies seemed to sense that this was a time to keep quiet. Smaller children, too young to understand what was happening, heard that they were going to "camp" and thought it would be a fun adventure. They watched carefully as their usually dependable parents became more and more downhearted with each passing hour. Aiko Kubo's sister tightly clutched a large stuffed teddy bear.

One of the rare journalists who presented the arguments for and against the government's actions was Ernest K. Lindley, Rhodes Scholar, public intellectual, and head of *Newsweek*'s Washington, DC, bureau. His article "Problems of the Japanese Migration" was published in *Newsweek* on March 30:

> For the first time since the Indians were put on reservations, a racial group within the United States is being forced to migrate. . . .
>
> The exodus has been ordered for two reasons: Federal and local officials feel incapable of distinguishing between loyal and disloyal persons of Japanese descent, and, in the event of attack, sabotage, or even further reverses in the Pacific, angry white people might wreak vengeance on the innocent as well as the guilty.
>
> Against the decision, many arguments have been presented. The first is that rights of American citizens are being violated. To this the answer given is that citizenship is not a dividing line between loyalty and disloyalty to the United States, especially among a people who have not been assimilated socially. The second is that no similar emigration has been ordered from a much more vulnerable area—the Hawaiian Islands. It is pointed out also that not a single instance of sabotage by persons of Japanese lineage has been established in Hawaii.
>
> The answer is twofold. The practical difficulties of such an exodus from Hawaii are almost insoluble; the absence of sabotage both in Hawaii and on the Pacific Coast is the surest sign that Japanese agents will go into action later. . . .

> A third argument bites deep. Loyal Japanese-Americans
> would be of great value in espionage and propaganda work in
> the Far East.

Sensible voices, like Lindley's, pointed out the inconsistent policy: On the one hand, Japanese Americans living in Hawaii were allowed to stay in their homes because of the "practical difficulties" of removing them; on the other, Japanese Americans living on the West Coast were on their way to concentration camps. It was impossible to know at the time that reasonable and rational minds had prevailed in Hawaii, but not on the West Coast. In the end, less than 1 percent of the 150,000 Japanese Americans living in Hawaii ended up in Department of Justice internment camps.

Meanwhile, newspapers, magazines, and radio broadcasts were all falsely reporting that the Japanese Americans were cheerful about being removed from their homes by force, as if it were happening for their benefit and for the benefit of the country at war. On April 4, 1942, the *Los Angeles Times* wrote about opening day at the Santa Anita facility under the headline SANTA ANITA GATES OPEN TO 1000 JAPS: "Most of the new arrivals loved the place at first glance, expressing open admiration of the beauty of the surroundings, their faces wreathed in smiles."

The *San Francisco News* announced on April 7, S.F. JAPANESE EXODUS STARTS, and described the evacuation of 664 Japanese Americans to the Santa Anita Race Track as "orderly, and generally, cheerful. Most of the evacuees seemed to feel they were going on a picnic."

• • •

Newspaper photographers with flash-bulb cameras pushed busily through the crowd. One of them rushed up and asked a young couple and their little boy to step out and stand by the door [of the Greyhound bus] for a shot. They were reluctant, but the photographers were persistent and at length they got out of the bus and posed, grinning widely to cover their embarrassment. We saw the picture in the newspaper shortly after and the caption underneath it read, "Japs good-natured about evacuation."

—Monica Kazuko **Itoi** (Sone), female, Nisei, Seattle, Washington, incarcerated age 23, Puyallup Assembly Center, Minidoka Relocation Center[86]

EVACUATION

*As we boarded the bus
bags on both sides
(I had never packed
two bags before
on a vacation
lasting forever)
the* Seattle Times
*photographer said
Smile!
so obediently I smiled
and the caption the next day read:*

*Note smiling faces
a lesson to Tokyo.*

—Mitsuye (Yasutake) **Yamada**, female, Nisei, Seattle, Washington, incarcerated age 19, Puyallup Assembly Center, Minidoka Relocation Center[87]

• • •

It was the second time young Norm Mineta had seen his father cry. The family was boarding the train for the Santa Anita Race Track, about three hundred and fifty miles away from their hometown of San Jose, California. The Minetas had just sold Skippy, their wirehaired terrier, to a complete stranger. Ten-year-old Norm was wearing his Cub Scout uniform. He'd brought along a special baseball mitt that he'd been given as an Easter gift less than a year before, but his baseball bat was confiscated in the loading area by the military police, who considered it a deadly weapon.

• • •

I looked at Santa Clara Street from the train over the subway. I thought this might be the last look at my loved home city. My heart almost broke, and suddenly hot tears just came pouring out, and the whole family cried out, could not stop, until we were out of our loved county.

—Kunisaku "Kay" **Mineta**, male, Issei, San Jose, California, incarcerated age 54, Santa Anita Assembly Center, Heart Mountain Relocation Center[88]

There were about a dozen Boy Scouts and half a dozen Cub Scouts in our uniforms and we were designated to be messengers. We could go from car to car, but others couldn't.

—The Honorable Norman "Norm" Yoshio **Mineta**, male, Nisei, San Jose, California, incarcerated age 10, Santa Anita Assembly Center, Heart Mountain Relocation Center[89]

I shall never forget how I spent the night of April 7th sleeping on the train. My sister and I stuck our heads out the window never peeling our eyes off the direction of our home.

—Louise Yoshiko **Ogawa** (Watanabe), female, Nisei, San Diego, California, incarcerated age 18, Santa Anita Assembly Center, Poston Relocation Center[90]

As the train began to move, armed Military Police came through the cars. They ordered everyone to pull the shades down so we could not see out. It was hot and cramped and people could hardly move.

—Ben Satoshi **Segawa**, male, Nisei, El Cajon, California,

incarcerated age 11, Santa Anita Assembly Center, Poston
Relocation Center[91]

I don't remember my mother being emotional. All she said was, "Well, we're going to go together." You had an uncertainty about where you were going and what was going to happen, but you knew you weren't going to be killed. . . . We went by train to Santa Anita about five o'clock in the afternoon. The train to Los Angeles goes down the coast by way of Monterey near the highway we had travelled so often. The sun was just going down. I remember looking out under the shade and saying to myself, "This is mine, my country. I don't care, I'm coming back."

—Fuji (Okamoto) **Takaichi**, female, Nisei, San Jose, California,
incarcerated age 29, Santa Anita Assembly Center, Heart Mountain
Relocation Center[92]

The journey—the trip itself was lousy. We didn't know where we were going. They never told us where we were going. They never told us—again, we didn't know what the charges were! Why were we going? We're American citizens.

—Chizuko "Chizu" **Kitano** (Iiyama), female, Nisei, Berkeley,
California, incarcerated age 21, Santa Anita Assembly Center, Topaz
Relocation Center[93]

To get to Camp Harmony [Puyallup Assembly Center], we were all herded like livestock onto Army trucks. The ride was cold, dirty, crowded, and humiliating. To be looked on by others as a group of people different and not worthy of being an American. Some of the red-necks in the crowd of onlookers hurled epitaphs [sic] or called us by using derogatory terms.

—Shuzo Chris **Kato**, male, Nisei, Seattle, Washington, incarcerated
age 16, Puyallup Assembly Center, Minidoka Relocation Center[94]

On the train, we were told not to look out the window, but people were peeking out. After a long time . . . somebody said, "Oh there's some Japanese standing over there." So we all took a peek, and we saw this dust, and rows and rows of barracks, and all these tan, brown Japanese people with their hair all bleached. They were standing in a huddle looking at us. . . . Then somebody on the train said, "Gee, that must be Japanese people in a camp." We didn't realize who they were before, but I saw how terrible it looked: the dust, no trees—just barracks and a bunch of people standing against the fence, looking out. Some children were hanging onto the fence like animals, and that was my first sight of the assembly center.

—Mary Tsuruko (Dakuzaku) **Tsukamoto**, female, Nisei, Florin, California, incarcerated age 27, Fresno Assembly Center, Jerome Relocation Center[95]

. . .

As they arrived at the assembly centers, the detainees were shocked to discover military police patrolling the perimeter fences covered with barbed wire. They could not believe that armed soldiers stood watch in tall guard towers. No one was fooled by what the government had told them—that the "evacuation" was for their own good, a necessary measure to protect them from harm by racist vigilante groups. The new arrivals could see plainly that the machine guns manned by the guards in those tall towers were pointing *in* at them, not out.

. . .

At the entrance . . . stood two lines of troops with rifles and fixed bayonets pointed at the evacuees as they walked between the soldiers to the prison compound. . . . Overwhelmed with bitterness and blind with rage, I screamed every obscenity I knew at the armed guards daring them to shoot me.

—William Masayoshi **Kochiyama**, male, Nisei, Alameda County, California, incarcerated age 21, Tanforan Assembly Center, Topaz Relocation Center[96]

All I remember is a mass of people—a great mass of Japanese people. . . . I had never seen so many Japanese people—until I got to Santa Anita. . . . There [were] no Caucasian or blacks or Hispanic among us. That's when I realized, maybe I am a little different. I thought I was American, but that's when it finally dawned on me that maybe people look at us differently—I was 11 years old then.

    —Ben Satoshi **Segawa**, male, Nisei, El Cajon, California, incarcerated age 11, Santa Anita Assembly Center, Poston Relocation Center[97]

• • •

After they got off the buses, everyone—even the children—stood in long lines for interrogation, fingerprinting, a quick medical exam, and inoculations. They were body-searched to make sure they hadn't brought any knives, razors, flashlights, binoculars, cameras, or short-wave radios. Many had no money because their bank accounts had been frozen, so they were issued monthly coupon books to purchase clothing and other necessities—$1.00 for evacuees under sixteen, $2.50 for evacuees over sixteen, and $4.50 for married couples, with a maximum of $7.50 for families. Finally, they were told to find their suitcases and duffel bags in a mountain of dumped luggage.

• • •

Baggage of all sizes and shapes was piled high along the driveway in back of the grandstand, and earlier arrivals were searching among the stacks for their possessions. . . . We collected our baggage and hailed a truck to have it delivered to our barrack. The truck was already bulging, but our belongings were tossed in, too, and we climbed on top and held on. On the long, bouncing ride back to the barrack we stopped to make several deliveries. At Barrack 16 we were unloaded with our goods.

    —Miné **Okubo**, female, Nisei, Berkeley, California, incarcerated age 30, Tanforan Assembly Center, Topaz Relocation Center[98]

We stumbled out [of the bus], stunned, dragging our bundles after us. . . . The receptionist, a white man, instructed us courteously, "Now,

*folks, please stay together as family units and line up. You'll be assigned
your apartment." We were standing in Area A, the mammoth parking
lot of the state fairgrounds. There were three other separate areas, B,
C and D, all built on the fairgrounds proper, near the baseball field and
the race tracks.*

> —Monica Kazuko **Itoi** (Sone), female, Nisei, Seattle, Washington,
> incarcerated age 23, Puyallup Assembly Center, Minidoka Relocation
> Center[99]

*Every one of us had a family number when we were evacuated. We
had to wear that number where it could be seen. Well, when we got to
Santa Anita I didn't have my tag on and there stands this soldier with
a bayonet and a helmet and he pointed at me and he said . . . "Where's
your tag?" and I didn't have it and he said, "Get out of the line!" . . . So
I was carrying my 6-year-old sister Florence . . . she had gone to sleep
and I couldn't find my tag! I looked in my coat pocket, I looked in my
sweater pocket and my purse. Finally, I found my tag. It was in my
sister's sweater pocket. So he says—"O.K. get back in line!"*

> —Margaret "Maggie" Tokuko **Ishino**, female, Nisei, San Diego,
> California, incarcerated age 17, Santa Anita Assembly Center, Poston
> Relocation Center[100]

· · ·

As the darkness descended on that first night, no one could escape
the bright searchlights that continually swept across the grounds. Words
like "exclusion," "evacuation," and "assembly center" were starting to
sound like mean jokes. These terms didn't come close to describing
the horror that the detainees felt was engulfing them. And then, when
they were confronted with the realities imposed by the army the next
day, such as daily roll calls and unannounced inspections, they realized
that "incarcerated," "convict," "prisoner," and "POW" were the best
words to describe their situation.

· · ·

I was too young to understand, but I do remember the barbed wire fence from which my parents warned me to stay away. I remember the sight of the high guard towers. I remember soldiers carrying rifles, and I remember being afraid. . . . I remember women weeping as our bundles were piled onto trucks. I remember armed guards herding us about, and I remember the fear that I felt. I could not understand, but I remember waking up in the middle of some nights and hearing my parents and a few of their friends in hushed discussions; sometimes my mother would be crying and my father always seemed deeply worried. I was too young to understand what they were talking about. . . . But my childhood memories of fear, anxiety and tension are vivid and very real.

—George Hosato **Takei**, male, Nisei, Los Angeles, California, incarcerated age 5, Santa Anita Assembly Center, Rohwer Relocation Center, Tule Lake Relocation Center[101]

• • •

In those centers where the army had thrown together wood-framed, tar-paper-covered barracks on parking lots and fairgrounds, everyone searched row upon monotonous row for their assigned quarters. Others arrived to discover that they'd be living in recently vacated horse stalls. When the humans first began moving into the Santa Anita horse stalls on March 27, 1942, they could see horsehair whitewashed onto the walls. The horses had been moved out only days before. Santa Anita's claim to fame was Seabiscuit; the legendary Thoroughbred racehorse had won his last race there just two years earlier. Some detainees who had to deal with the stench of horse urine and manure tried to make light of their circumstances by claiming they lived in Seabiscuit's stall. Others who were housed in livestock pens couldn't say the same. But it wasn't just a matter of putting up with the smell of horse urine and manure; according to local hospital records of the Santa Anita inmates, 75 percent of the illnesses were attributed to living in these unsanitary stalls.

• • •

The North Portland WCCA assembly center was a livestock exposition hall, surrounded by man-proof fences, topped with concertinas of barbed wire, and with guard towers equipped with searchlights at strategic intervals. Within the vast rambling building, where animals had been quartered, the footing underneath was asphalt; the stalls where animals had been stabled, the walls were calsomined [whitewashed]. Inasmuch as the quarters were intended to be only temporary, some mangers [long, open feeding boxes for horses and cattle] were still in place—and many a baby of Japanese ancestry—[who were] deemed by the Commanding General to pose a potential threat to the security of the United States—slept in such mangers . . . , which reminds me of another babe who similarly slept in a manger some 2,000 years ago, only to grow up to be crucified. Certainly, substantial numbers of the evacuee population were devout Christians, and this humbling parallel was not lost upon them.

. . . There were scary rumors, apprehensions and fears . . . , especially as large headlines in local newspapers clamored: "MAKE THE JAPS SUFFER!" "LET THEM HURT AND BE MISERABLE!" "CASTRATE 'EM, STERILIZE 'EM" "SHIP THEM OUT!" "GET RID OF THEM!"

—Minoru "Min" **Yasui**, male, Nisei, Portland, Oregon, incarcerated age 25, Portland Assembly Center, Minidoka Relocation Center, Multnomah County Jail[102]

• • •

On April 18, 1942, the *Fresno Bee* published a letter to the editor by "MS from Del Rey, California":

The history of this war will record one of the greatest mass evacuations in the life of the nation, the movement of more than 150,000 Japanese aliens and citizens from homes along the Pacific Coast. I have been told it was like a festival when the first group of Japanese left San Francisco last week. Everybody wore a grin, everybody had a wisecrack, nobody complained and nobody shed a tear. It was a "new experience in life." We never should forget that if such a mass evacuation of Japanese could take place in the United States, all races could face the same problem in time of war. The Constitution of the United States stresses definitely under the Bill of Rights, Fourteenth Amendment: "In time of peace none of the rights guaranteed by the Bill of Rights can be taken away by the Federal government from any citizen or alien living here." But now we are in war and anything can happen. We must win this war to preserve our rights.

• • •

We were assigned to apartment 2-1-A, right across from the bachelor quarters. The apartments resembled elongated, low stables about two blocks long. Our home was one room, about 18 x 20 feet, the size of a living room. . . . It was bare except for a small tinny wood-burning stove crouching in the center. The flooring consisted of two by fours laid directly on the earth and dandelions were already pushing their way up through the cracks.

—Monica Kazuko **Itoi** (Sone), female, Nisei, Seattle, Washington, incarcerated age 23, Puyallup Assembly Center, Minidoka Relocation Center[103]

The guide left us at the door of Stall 50. We walked in and dropped our things inside the entrance. The place was in semi-darkness; light barely came through the dirty windows on either side of the entrance. A swinging half-door divided the 20 by 9 ft. stall into two rooms. The roof sloped down from a height of twelve feet in the rear room to seven feet in the front room; below the rafters an open space extended the full length of the stable. The rear room had housed the horse and the front room the fodder. Both rooms showed signs of hurried whitewashing. Spider webs, horse hair, and hay had been whitewashed with the walls. Huge spikes

and nails stuck out all over the walls. A two-inch layer of dust covered
the floor, but on removing it we discovered that linoleum the color of
redwood had been placed over the rough manure-covered boards.

—Miné **Okubo**, female, Nisei, Berkeley, California, incarcerated age
30, Tanforan Assembly Center, Topaz Relocation Center[104]

• • •

Once the incarcerees found their living quarters, they were directed
to stuff canvas bags with hay for their mattresses. Sharon Tanagi, a
sixteen-year-old at the Puyallup Assembly Center in Seattle, Washington, went with her mother to the outdoor field where they were told to
prepare their family's mattresses. Her mother had not shown any emotion throughout the removal process, but suddenly she stopped her mat-
tress stuffing and started to cry.

"I think that was the last straw that broke her back," Tanagi recalled
with some irony.

The housing formula for new barracks concocted by the Wartime
Civil Control Administration (WCCA) allotted each couple a space of
two hundred square feet. But due to bad planning and miscalcula-
tions, not to mention wartime labor and material shortages, the living
quarters were vastly overcrowded. Some large families shared a single
room, and some young married couples had to live with other married couples. The interiors of the barrack apartments had no partitions
to provide any private spaces for family members and no furnishings
beyond the cots and bare lightbulbs hanging from the ceilings.

Immediately the search was on for any material that could possibly
serve as room dividers or made into furniture. The wood from discarded vegetable crates and scrap lumber left behind from the barrack
construction became valuable commodities as the residents scavenged
for ways to make their spaces habitable. They quickly started ordering curtains and other much-needed household supplies from Sears,
Roebuck and Montgomery Ward mail-order catalogs. The flimsy barracks had been built with spaces between the lumber framing and wall

partitions, so the walls did not go all the way up to the ceiling, which meant everyone could hear everything anyone was doing or saying. No one had any sense of privacy. At its peak, Santa Anita—the largest assembly center—housed 18,719 people; there was simply no place to go, if only for a moment, for any solitude.

• • •

Lots of fellows tell me that they have more petty arguments . . . but the thin walls help keep them in a low voice. One girl says that her mother gets her under the blankets to bawl her out. They are so conscious of what the neighbors may say or think.
    —Charles **Kikuchi**, male, Nisei, San Francisco, California, incarcerated age 26, Tanforan Assembly Center, Gila River Relocation Center[105]

We heard language from over the partitions, language I didn't want my daughter growing up hearing. There was talking back to parents, young people shouting, fathers shouting and angry. . . . It was a terrible, terrible time of adjustment.
    —Mary Tsuruko (Dakuzaku) **Tsukamoto**, female, Nisei, Florin, California, incarcerated age 27, Fresno Assembly Center, Jerome Relocation Center[106]

• • •

The living conditions within the centers varied as a result of the army's hurried conversion of existing facilities into short-term housing for thousands of displaced persons. For all of the differences in the assembly center circumstances, one commonly shared indignity was the intolerable toilet situation. At the Marysville, Sacramento, Salinas, and other smaller centers in rural central California, the latrines were nothing more than a line of pits in the ground. The ever-present stench from the overflowing holes was overwhelming. The detainees at the Merced, Tulare, Fresno, and Pinedale centers had it somewhat better: They sat on plywood planks above metal troughs. Maggots swimming in the tanks kept them company while they did their business. The larger Tanforan, Manzanar, and Santa Anita centers, in more urban locations, actually had flush toilets of some fashion, invariably located great distances from the living quarters. At Santa Anita the toilet run-off into the cesspool system would overflow into the barracks area.

No matter the camp location, none of the latrines had any partitions; the typical setup consisted of inmates sitting back-to-back, twelve people at a time. Toilet paper was in such short supply that most families rationed theirs.

The communal showers caused equal anguish, with their multiple heads (as many as eight) in one large room without partitions. Some brought towels or makeshift shower curtains and somehow held them up while they washed. Others showered in their underwear or enlisted devoted family members to form a protective circle around them. As if all of this weren't enough, the women complained that the men (and boys) were peeking through knotholes or over the tops of the shower building walls. People started going to the latrines and showers at dawn or midnight to avoid the long rush-hour lines and to hope for some privacy. But there were downsides to that approach. They'd risk arriving at the showers to find the water was cold. And with the constant rain in Puyallup, Washington, creating a perpetual state of mud, they'd get stuck in the muck while trying to navigate the distance to the showers or latrines in the darkness. A few claimed they would just stay dirty until the war ended.

• • •

We began to realize what it meant to stand in line . . . in front of the latrine. . . . For us, women and children, this was something which we just couldn't . . . it was just a shock. I remember we got sick . . . we couldn't go . . . we didn't want to go. [The latrine] was smelly, and it was dirty. . . . In the shower, the water was poured over you, and there were no partitions, and it was so cramped that we almost touched each other. It was very humiliating.

—Mary Tsuruko (Dakuzaku) **Tsukamoto**, female, Nisei, Florin,

California, incarcerated age 27, Fresno Assembly Center, Jerome
Relocation Center[107]

It took about two months before we lived halfway civilized.
—Misao "Sadie" Marietta (Nishitani) **Sakamoto**, female, Issei,
Seattle, Washington, incarcerated age 36, Puyallup Assembly Center,
Minidoka Relocation Center[108]

• • •

In the larger centers the laundry and ironing areas, similar to the
latrines and showers, were far from the barracks. This, of course, made
life even harder for the women. Some used their children's little red wag-
ons to haul their clothes and washing supplies back and forth between
their barrack and the laundry area, which could be half a mile away.

But the longest lines, sometimes three hours in duration, were for
meals, three times a day, seven days a week. The assembly centers
served food to thousands of people, and it wasn't unusual for detainees, particularly the elderly, to faint from having to wait in line for such
extended periods in the summer heat.

• • •

*I can still vividly recall my 85-year-old grandmother gravely stand-
ing in line with her tin cup and plate.*
—Haru Michida **Isaki**, female, Nisei, San Francisco, California,
incarcerated age 28, Tanforan Assembly Center, Topaz Relocation
Center[109]

*The heat of Fresno in the summer melted the tar from the roof onto
our beds. The asphalt floors of our crowded rooms melted, and our
beds and chairs sank. We became ill from lack of salt as we perspired
from morning till night. We ate in noisy mess halls, several hundred
waiting in line in three shifts. We ate hurriedly, perspiration dripping
from our elbows.*
—Mary Tsuruko (Dakuzaku) **Tsukamoto**, female, Nisei, Florin,

California, incarcerated age 27, Fresno Assembly Center, Jerome Relocation Center[110]

By this time it was four o'clock and suppertime in camp. We rushed back to the huge grandstand. The ground floor served as the mess hall for the 5,000 evacuees then in the center; later it would serve 8,000. When we arrived, four lines, each a block long, waited outside the mess-hall doors. It was very windy and cold. An hour passed and we finally reached the door only to learn that the line did not lead anywhere. The thought of starting over again left us when we saw the length of the other lines. We started to crowd ourselves in, as so many others were trying to do, but it was impossible. Everyone was hugging the person ahead. Fortunately we discovered a friend who made room for us. People glared at us as we squeezed into line.

—Miné **Okubo**, female, Nisei, Berkeley, California, incarcerated age 30, Tanforan Assembly Center, Topaz Relocation Center[111]

• • •

The inmates soon learned why it was called a *mess* hall. Japanese cuisine is carefully prepared and aesthetically served, so the Issei watched in horror as kitchen workers used shovels to dish out inedible meals. Farming families who were used to eating their homegrown fruits and vegetables were now eating canned sausages and boiled potatoes. To deflect anti-Japanese accusations that the government was "coddling" the detainees, the army's WCCA spent an average of only thirty-three to thirty-nine cents a day per inmate—a fraction of the cost to feed soldiers.

• • •

There was never any consideration for the oriental diet. Since the food was not refrigerated, or even prepared properly, most of the people in the Assembly Center were affected with ptomaine poisoning at one time or another.

—Emiko "Emi" (Yada) **Somekawa**, female, Nisei, Portland,

Oregon, incarcerated age 24, Portland Assembly Center, Tule Lake
Relocation Center[112]

*People got stomach upsets from the strong soap residue left on cook-
ing utensils and on plates, cups and dishes.*
—Minoru "Min" **Yasui**, male, Nisei, Portland, Oregon, incarcerated
age 25, Portland Assembly Center, Minidoka Relocation
Center, Multnomah County Jail[113]

· · ·

In the chaotic mess hall atmosphere, the Nisei children used meal-
times to be with friends, not family. For the first time, children were
seeing their parents as powerless and degraded by the evacuation process, and—combined with the lack of living space inside their units—
the Issei ability to maintain strong family ties was eroding. Some
parents gave up disciplining their children altogether.

· · ·

*The Assembly Center . . . [was] so crowded that all of us wanted
to kind of get away from each other. And so, we would be with our
friends most of the time. At the mess hall . . . my brothers would sit
clear over . . . with their buddies. My sisters would sit with their
friends and . . . I had to sit with my father because I was the youngest
and, and I really wasn't happy with that. . . . So we never ate as a
family, during the whole time.*
—Sato **Hashizume**, female, Nisei, Portland, Oregon, incarcerated
age 11, Portland Assembly Center, Minidoka Relocation Center[114]

· · ·

The assembly center administrators and the detainees began organizing activities to occupy the time. The young Nisei were more care-
free than their first-generation Issei parents, so they adjusted fairly
quickly and made the best of their newly restricted lives. They played
baseball, basketball, bridge, horseshoes, volleyball, tennis, badminton,
and Ping-Pong, and they practiced judo as well as Greco-Roman and

sumo wrestling. They formed and joined bands, orchestras, and social clubs; they went to movies, craft fairs, and Saturday-night dances.

• • •

Many of the young Nisei are quite Americanized and have nice personalities. They smile easily and are not inhibited in their actions. They have taken things in stride and their sole concern is to meet the other sex, have dances so that they can jitterbug, . . . and have fun in general. Many are using the evacuation to break away from the strict control of parental rule. . . .

Many of the parents who would never let their daughters go to dances before do not object so strenuously now. They are slowly accepting the fact that their children cannot stay home night after night doing nothing without some sort of recreational release. Books are still a rarity. Consequently, the Thursday night talent show and the Saturday dances are jammed to capacity.

—Charles **Kikuchi**, male, Nisei, San Francisco, California,
incarcerated age 26, Tanforan Assembly Center, Gila River
Relocation Center[115]

• • •

Some of the assembly centers managed to set up libraries. Kyoko Hoshiga, a college graduate, had one up and running only three days after the Tanforan Assembly Center opened. She began with sixty-five books donated by friends, churches, Buddhist temples, and nonprofit organizations, and thousands were added over the coming months. Many kids at Santa Anita received books in the mail from Clara Breed, the first children's librarian of the San Diego Public Library system. Breed had come to know many Japanese Americans as young library patrons at the main branch of the San Diego Public Library, near Japantown. And before they left, Breed gave her young friends stamped postcards so they could write to her and she could write back, which she did devotedly over the duration of their incarceration. Breed had also volunteered to store possessions of some of the San Diego Japanese American families and would mail her young correspondents the supplies they needed, using the small amounts of money they would send to her from their earnings in jobs at the assembly center.

· · ·

July 15, 1942

Dear Miss Breed,

Thank you a million times for the delicious candy, soap, and the most interesting book! I was most interested in the book because I have read, Peggy Covers Washington, London, and Peggy Covers News. I enjoy Emma Bughee's books very much. The books which you so kindly have sent are now scattered all over this camp and I won't at all be surprised if one of them has entered Seabiscuit's stable. . . .

The distribution of our second checks began today. It was, of course, my first check. I felt so proud to receive it because I really earned it all by myself. It makes me feel so independent. We receive about 37¢ a day. For 11 days work I received $3.04. I am going to take advantage of your generosity and ask you to go on a little shopping tour for me in your leisure time. Will you please send me the following:

1) 2 yards of printed seersucker (something that would look nice when made into a drindle. I already have 2 striped ones—green & white, red & white—so please do not send striped one.) Cost = not over 50¢ a yard.

2) 1 1/2 yd. of plain white seersucker. (About same price has [sic] printed one)

10) 2 Boys Coopers Jockey shorts—size: 28 waist, store: Walkers

3) 1/2 yd. of muslin (going to use it for stiffening)

11) 1 small face towel (cheap one is all right) .05

4) 1 card of snaps

5) 5 Hollywood curlers

6) 2 shower caps .29

7) 1 bottle of brown liquid shoe polish—10¢

8) 1 bottle of Skrip's royal blue ink—15¢

9) 1 mirror sold at Kress for 15¢ or 25¢

I have enclosed $4.50 in money order. I hope this amount will be sufficient—if not please let me know. I hope I'm not causing you too much trouble.

I want so much to repay you for all the nice books, candy, and soap but do not know how I can. In my spare-time I made this bookmarker. It is made very crudely but I hope you will be able to use it. . . .

Yours very sincerely,
Louise Ogawa

Ps. If there seems to be some money left after deducting the shipping expense, I would like to have some Butterscotch balls or Fruit balls or drops. Thank you again.

—Louise Yoshiko **Ogawa** (Watanabe), female, Nisei, San Diego, California, incarcerated age 18, Santa Anita Assembly Center, Poston Relocation Center[116]

• • •

Less than a month after arriving at the Tanforan Assembly Center, a group of Japanese American artists quickly launched the Tanforan Art School. Believing in the power of artistry and creativity to provide hope for this incarcerated community, artist and art professor Chiura Obata organized a comprehensive program for inmates of any age in topics such as still life, landscape, figure drawing, fashion design, architectural drafting, and commercial layout.

The official policy of the WCCA was not to discriminate "against any religious denomination which the Japanese constituency or group within the Center have requested," but the exceptions were notable—any observance of Shintoism was banned, and the practice of Buddhism, which was the predominant religion of choice, was severely limited. The WCCA had also implemented a ban on any materials written in Japanese. Christian Japanese-language materials such as Bibles and hymnals were permitted as exceptions under the ban, but Buddhist texts in Japanese were confiscated. Spoken Japanese in any assembly center gathering was forbidden, unless the purpose had prior approval and the proceedings were monitored by a member of the center's administration. For the principally Buddhist Issei and many Kibei (those Nisei who had spent some time in Japan and were more comfortable speaking Japanese), these policies made it difficult, if not impossible, to practice their faith.

Every assembly center printed an English-language newspaper (with some Japanese sections), such as the *Santa Anita Pacemaker* and the *Camp Harmony News-Letter*. They were written under the supervision of the army but edited and published by the incarcerees. Most had two or three editions per week that contained information about outside events and reported news within that particular assembly center, as well as official announcements from the WCCA.

• • •

About 20 of us met tonight to really get the Camp paper going because we really do need some source of information. . . . All the Nisei lads want to be postmen because they feel that it will be a good opportunity to get to know the girls.

—Charles **Kikuchi**, male, Nisei, San Francisco, California,
incarcerated age 26, Tanforan Assembly Center, Gila River
Relocation Center[117]

• • •

For high school seniors, being forcibly removed from their hometowns during their last semester meant they were unable to attend their graduation ceremonies. Some received their diplomas mailed to their camp address.

The WCCA did not anticipate having to provide schools, so students weren't sure if they'd be able to continue their education. The certified teachers among the detainees jumped into action. Anyone with a teaching degree, or even just a college education, offered or was asked to be a teacher overnight. They structured course curricula and obtained materials (pens, pencils, paintbrushes, crayons, paper, blackboards, and books) from state and county schools, many of which the students had attended prior to their removal. Donations also came in from charitable individuals and organizations. Unused space that could be turned into classrooms was in short supply; some students sat on the ground or worked on benches made by inmates with carpentry skills. The grandstand at Tanforan became the high school, with classes clustered so close to one another that teachers had to shout to be heard over the others.

• • •

We looked forward to school because that would kind of suck up the day.

—Emi "Amy" **Akiyama** (Berger), female, Sansei, Berkeley, California, incarcerated age 8, Tanforan Assembly Center, Topaz Relocation Center[118]

• • •

Although medical care was free, it took place in understaffed, inadequate, and ill-supplied hospitals. But the inmates at Tanforan and Santa Anita benefitted from having optometrists and dentists among them, which enabled many to get new eyeglasses and some long-neglected dental work.

The Issei women found a slight silver lining in the dark cloud they were forced to live under. No longer did they have to cook and clean dishes seven days a week for their (oftentimes large) families while also working to support them. Although the way they had to do laundry and ironing was labor intensive, they were able to find the time to take up flower arranging, knitting, sewing, gardening, and calisthenics classes. And some Issei decided this was a good time to learn how to read and write English.

• • •

June 13, 1942 . . .

Pop has finally broken down and . . . he will go and learn to speak English in the class with Mom. He is afraid that he will make many mistakes and be ashamed for showing his lack of education. . . .

June 21, 1942 . . .

The competition is getting keen and they eat up the praise that we lavish on their achievements. Patsy came in to compliment Pop and he said with such a pleased grin on his face, "Oh scram! I study now."

—Charles **Kikuchi**, male, Nisei, San Francisco, California, incarcerated age 26, Tanforan Assembly Center, Gila River Relocation Center[119]

• • •

For most of the Issei men, however, the captivity represented a new trial. They had just lost all the fruits of their labor over decades of hard work and sacrifice, and now they had nothing to do. Some got involved in tournaments of Japanese chesslike games of *go* and *shogi*; some played cards, gambled, and got drunk on their own version of homemade alcohol. Some were simply demoralized and disillusioned that the America they had once thought of as a land of opportunity was now a land of betrayal and misfortune. For those men who had tried to make it on their own, incarceration imposed on them a welfare state that many of them deeply opposed, and robbed them of the ability to be self-reliant.

• • •

Our financial situation was so bad it was almost a relief to go to camp and let the government take care of us for a while.

—Harry Katsuharu **Fukuhara**, male, Nisei, Los Angeles, California, incarcerated age 22, Tulare Assembly Center, Gila River Relocation Center[120]

· · ·

Visits from those who remained on the outside were complicated to arrange. Prospective visitors had to secure a permit, which wasn't easy. In some assembly centers, visitors could meet their family and friends at the barbed wire perimeters. In other centers, visitors were thoroughly searched before they could enter reception rooms, where they could sit on one side of a long table and incarcerees could sit on the other, just like in prisons. For some detainees visits only reminded them of their demeaning situation; they felt disgraced and ashamed by what the government was doing to them. But these visits brought greetings and news from the outside world, and often much-needed items like soap, deodorant, washboards, towels, electric cords, candy, and games.

· · ·

I shall never forget that day you [Clara Breed] visited us. At the sight of your smiling face a big lump formed at the pit of my throat never dreaming I would see you again.
    —Louise Yoshiko **Ogawa** (Watanabe), female, Nisei, San Diego, California, incarcerated age 18, Santa Anita Assembly Center, Poston Relocation Center[121]

At some of the centers, residents were allowed only to talk to visitors through a wire fence. At Tanforan a room on top of the grandstand was reserved for receiving visitors. Children under sixteen years of age were not allowed to visit the center. Pets that had to be left behind with friends were also barred.
    —Miné **Okubo**, female, Nisei, Berkeley, California, incarcerated age 30, Tanforan Assembly Center, Topaz Relocation Center[122]

· · ·

At first everyone was told the assembly centers were temporary— a brief but necessary stop on the way to more permanent housing until the end of the war. But the incarcerees were living their lives in limbo.

Transportation problems, the lack of foresight, and nonexistent communication between coordinators caused considerable delays with construction of the long-term detention facilities. And so the incarcerees' time at the assembly centers was not as short as they'd been led to believe. The average stay was three months, but at Santa Anita and Tanforan, the average stay was nearly twice as long. They'd been given the impression that they'd have "real" housing and the freedom to come and go as they pleased within the local communities. Just thinking they'd be moving on to a better place helped them create some semblance of home.

So they coped and cooperated, but soon worry and anxiety gave way to speculation and paranoia. Where were they going next and for how long? How far away was it? What were the conditions, the climate? When would they be able to resume their normal lives? There was even a rumor that they were being sent to America's version of Siberia—some remote, desolate wasteland in the vast interior of the United States where no one in their right mind would choose to live.

Of all the rumors, that one turned out to be true.

CHAPTER FIVE

Gaman *in the Wasteland*

The terrible emotional drain of camp life was responsible for more permanent damage than the harsh physical surroundings. Humiliation, anger, frustration, degradation, guilt, boredom, isolation, fear, anxiety and uncertainty were my constant companions. It was as though time had frozen and me with it. I had no future. We had no future.

> —Haru Michida **Isaki**, female, Nisei, San Francisco, California, incarcerated age 28, Tanforan Assembly Center, Topaz Relocation Center[123]

Two Japanese expressions have often been used to describe the core response of Japanese Americans toward their incarceration: *gaman* and *shikata ga nai*. *Gaman* stresses that the individual should not get angry or retaliate in the face of adversity. Coming from a Buddhist origin, *gaman* conveys the idea of enduring the seemingly unbearable with patience and dignity. *Shikata ga nai* teaches that some things cannot be helped; that is, nothing can be done about them. The Issei lived these principles as expressions of strength, not resignation.

• • •

I didn't become bitter. I guess we learned to roll with the punches. My parents were very stoic about it. You know, they never showed anger or bitterness, so I guess we sort of adopted their attitude.

> —Mabel Takako (Kawashima) **Ota**, female, Nisei, Holtville, California, incarcerated age 26, Poston Relocation Center[124]

We just didn't have the time [to get angry]; it was a shock and you didn't have the time to sit down and think about it. You just do what

*you're told and try to make the best of it. I think we were forced into a
situation and we weren't going to fight it.*

—George **Akimoto**, male, Nisei, Stockton, California, incarcerated
age 20, Stockton Assembly Center, Rohwer Relocation Center[125]

• • •

While the Japanese Americans were being ousted from their West
Coast homes and despairing for their futures, the US Army and the War
Relocation Authority were busy identifying potential relocation center
sites. Out of three hundred sites to choose from, the WRA selected
ten—all on remote and inhospitable lands. The criteria were accessi-
bility to rail, road, water, and electricity as well as space to accommodate housing for a minimum of five thousand people on unpopulated
public territories. The sites also had to be a safe distance away from
cities and strategic installations, including power lines and reservoirs.
By definition, the sites would be on land no one else wanted to inhabit.

The WRA took over the Owens Valley Reception Center from the
army. Since the facility was located in Manzanar at the foot of California's Sierra Nevada, the WRA renamed it the Manzanar Relocation
Center. The WRA also acquired land in the swamplands of Arkansas
from the Farm Security Administration to establish the Rohwer and
Jerome Relocation Centers. Arkansas Governor Homer Adkins was not
enthusiastic about having WRA camps in his state. A former Ku Klux
Klan member, Adkins wanted the War Department to make a formal
request of the State of Arkansas to "accept a number of these evacuees"
as its "patriotic duty." He insisted on a pledge from the army to "move
these Japs back to their original homes," assume "full responsibility for
keeping the Japs under control, be responsible for their whereabouts at
all times," and have the camps "guarded by white troops."

In the spring of 1942 construction was underway for the Rohwer and
Jerome camps and five more in the western desert: Tule Lake, on a dry lake
bed in northeastern California; Granada (which came to be known as Camp
Amache), in southeastern Colorado; Topaz, in Delta, Utah; Minidoka,

outside of Hunt, Idaho; and Heart Mountain, near Cody, Wyoming.

In addition, as a result of a problematic agreement between Milton Eisenhower and John Collier, commissioner of the Office of Indian Affairs (OIA), later known as the Bureau of Indian Affairs, two camps were built on Native American reservations over the objections of the local tribal councils. The Colorado River Indian Reservation in Arizona—three miles from the Colorado River in the Sonoran Desert—became the site of the Poston Relocation Center, and the Gila River Indian Reservation in southern Arizona became the site of the Gila River Relocation Center.

And so began the WRA's construction blitz to erect ten camps for tens of thousands of people, requiring resources that were already constrained by the demands of war.

"Just a moment, let me be sure I understand you," said one official of the War Production Board to a WRA staff member trying to order supplies. "Are you asking for these priorities on this scarce material for the benefit of *Japs*?"

The forced transfer of Japanese Americans from assembly centers to long-term concentration camps started at the end of May while the camps were still being erected, and continued for five months until the end of October 1942.

• • •

June 14, 1942. . . .

A lot of people would rather stay [in the assembly center] permanently as they are more or less settled down. . . . They dread to think that we will be sent all the way to Arkansas or Arizona. . . . The majority of the Japanese here still think in terms of returning to the Bay Area as soon as the war is over.

July 30, 1942. . . .

The radio announced this morning that General DeWitt had ordered the clearance of all assembly centers. . . . . Everyone got greatly excited and the news spread around camp like wildfire. . . . There is an increasing tension among the people.

—Charles **Kikuchi**, male, Nisei, San Francisco, California,
incarcerated age 26, Tanforan Assembly Center, Gila River
Relocation Center[126]

*We were anxious to complete our migration into a permanent camp
inland. The sultry heat took its toll on temper and patience, and everyone showed signs of restlessness. . . .*

*Within two weeks, we were told we were moving immediately to
our relocation camp. By then we knew we were headed for Idaho. . . .*

*We were excited at the thought of going to unknown territory. . . .
I knew it wasn't going to be a comfortable experience, but it would be
a change.*

—Monica Kazuko **Itoi** (Sone), female, Nisei, Seattle, Washington,
incarcerated age 23, Puyallup Assembly Center, Minidoka Relocation
Center[127]

*There were now administration bulletins on such matters as bag-
gage preparation, the approximate dates of the movement . . . and conduct on trains. No one knew exactly when and where the relocation
would begin, but it was not long before we received a notice telling us
to be packed and ready. . . . Everywhere there was a stir of final preparation, of packing and crating. Scrap-lumber furniture and shelves
had to come down and the precious tags bearing the family identification number had to be brought out of safekeeping. Two days before the
date of departure everything had to be packed and tagged and ready
for inspection [after which] . . . each box, crate and duffel bag was
closed and taken away. . . . At the gate, a Caucasian worker checked
our names and family number and told us to open our luggage for
inspection. Thousands of people, most of them friends of the departing
residents, were gathered around the wire fence to bid us good-bye.*

—Miné **Okubo**, female, Nisei, Berkeley, California, incarcerated age
30, Tanforan Assembly Center, Topaz Relocation Center[128]

• • •

Given the remoteness of the WRA centers, the logistics of getting thousands of people there was far more nightmarish than the process had been to move them to the assembly centers. Some journeys would take as long as four days by rail. Many detainees had never been on a train before, and they were filled with trepidation.

First the incarcerees were divided into groups of approximately five hundred people. At their designated departure time, they were made to walk single file through a double row of armed military police, who were counting them as they boarded the trains. Those who were sick or disabled were placed in the rear sleeping cars. Most people spent the whole trip sitting up. Toilets leaked; people vomited.

The trains transporting the Japanese Americans were left over from World War I—unreliable, slow-moving, and either too hot or too cold. The journeys, which would have taken days under the best of circumstances, took even longer because the passenger trains were routinely sidetracked to give the right of way to trains carrying cargo essential to the war effort. The US armed military on board did not want the White population to be able to see inside the cars, so the guards ordered the shades to be pulled down, causing poor ventilation and plunging the interior into darkness. Despite this precaution, the townspeople already knew who were on the trains, and sometimes when the cars filled with Japanese Americans passed through a station, the townspeople would shout, "Don't stop! Keep going!"

• • •

The trip was a nightmare that lasted two nights and a day. The train creaked with age. It was covered with dust, and as the gaslights failed to function properly we travelled in complete darkness most of the night, reminding me of the blackout trains in Europe. All shades were drawn and we were not allowed to look out the windows. . . . The first night was a novelty after four and a half months of internment. However, I could not sleep and I spent the entire night taking the chair apart and readjusting it. Many became train sick. . . . The children cried from restlessness. At one point on the way, a brick was thrown into one of the cars.

—Miné **Okubo**, female, Nisei, Berkeley, California, incarcerated age 30, Tanforan Assembly Center, Topaz Relocation Center[129]

By noon we were traveling through Nevada sagebrush country, and when we reached a properly isolated area, the train came to a stop. Our car captain then announced that we could get off for a half hour break in the fresh air. As we stepped down from the car, we found that armed MPs had stationed themselves in a row parallel to the train. Only if we remained in the narrow corridor between them and the train were we allowed to stay outside. Some people ran back and forth, some did calisthenics, and others just breathed in the dry desert air.

—Yoshiko **Uchida**, female, Nisei, Berkeley, California, incarcerated age 21, Tanforan Assembly Center, Topaz Relocation Center[130]

• • •

Guyo Okagaki was living in Salt Lake City, outside of the designated West Coast military areas that were being cleared of persons of Japanese ancestry by the exclusion orders. Although Guyo was not ordered into incarceration, her father was on a train headed to the Heart Mountain concentration camp. Guyo learned that her father's train would be stopping in Salt Lake City en route to Heart Mountain, so she was hoping to see him when his train reached the Salt Lake City station. She waited at the station all day, not knowing when it would arrive, all the while holding a box of his favorite cigars to give him to take to camp. The train finally pulled in, but a string of armed guards blocked her from getting any closer than two platforms away. Guyo asked a guard to give the cigar box to her father, but he gave the box to an officer instead. The officer opened up the box and proceeded to break each cigar in half in full view of everyone on the platform. The officer's cruelty was long remembered by the eyewitnesses that day.

The journeys were arduous. The incarcerees later reported harassment by the military guards, as well as babies dying along the way. The two-and-a-half-day train ride made thirteen-year-old George Taketa so ill that he passed out upon arrival.

Any hope that the incarcerees were going to more pleasing environments was extinguished when they finally disembarked from the trains and boarded the buses to their assigned relocation centers. Throughout the twenty-five-mile drive from the train station in Parker, Arizona, to the Poston Relocation Center, the bus delivering the incarcerees kept getting stuck in the deep, soft dust covering the dirt road from the sudden, monstrous dust storms.

• • •

September 7, 1942

> *Dear Miss Breed,*
> *This is ole prodigal writing to you amid the heat and dust of this h—hole called The Colorado River War Relocation Project—Poston, Arizona. . . . At 2:00 Mountain Time we arrived in Parker, Arizona. What a jerkwater town, nothing but shanties. . . . The natives . . . told us that we were lucky to have come on a cool day . . . only 104 degrees and not dusty at all!!!! Wait 'til it gets really hot and dusty. . . .*
>
> *Sincerely yours, Tetsuzo*

—Tetsuzo "Ted" or "Tets" **Hirasaki**, male, Nisei, San Diego, California, incarcerated age 22, Santa Anita Assembly Center, Poston Relocation Center[131]

We disembarked in the middle of the desert, and many an evacuee sat on their belongings dumped along the side of the railroad tracks and wept. It was a desolate feeling, no trees or greenness about—only sage brush, rocks, and shimmering heat of the desert. We were trans-ported by Army trucks to yet uncompleted barracks, over raw dirt roads, choking in the dust kicked up by trucks in front of us. And dust permeated everything; it got into our nostrils, our eyes, our clothes, our bedding, our foods, our shoes—and as we perspired, we became mud dolls, with rivulets of sweat streaking our faces, arms and bodies.

—Minoru "Min" **Yasui**, male, Nisei, Portland, Oregon, incarcerated
age 25, Portland Assembly Center, Minidoka Relocation
Center, Multnomah County Jail[132]

Our exodus and arrival in the desert was in caravans of 30 or 40 buses. Each was filled with humanity from babes in arms to the elderly.

—Elizabeth Aiko (Takahashi) **Nishikawa**, female, Nisei, Los Angeles,
California, incarcerated age 31, Manzanar Reception Center,
Manzanar Relocation Center[133]

The bus trip to Poston III was long and dusty. So dusty that the sky was blotted out completely. At first we tried to keep the windows of the school bus that was transporting us closed, but it was so hot— over 110 degrees that people, especially the older people, and the kids, were getting sick. So we opened the windows. Immediately, everyone was covered by dust. I know you won't believe this, but it's really true, friends couldn't recognize each other.

—Masami **Honda**, male, Nisei, San Diego, California, incarcerated
age 25, Santa Anita Assembly Center, Poston Relocation Center[134]

We rode through seventeen miles of alfalfa fields and greasewood-covered desert. Half of the distance was over rough, newly con-structed dirt roads. We were all eyes, hoping to spot something interesting in this flat, dry land that extended for miles in all direc-tions. Suddenly the [camp] was stretched out before us in a cloud of dust. It was a desolate scene. Hundreds of low black barracks

covered with tarred paper were lined up row after row. A few
telephone poles stood out like sentinels, and soldiers could be seen
patrolling the grounds.

—Miné **Okubo**, female, Nisei, Berkeley, California, incarcerated age
30, Tanforan Assembly Center, Topaz Relocation Center[135]

As the bus drew up to one of the barracks I was surprised to hear
band music. Marching toward us down the dusty road was the drum
and bugle corps of the young Boy Scouts who had come with the
advance contingent, carrying signs that read, "Welcome to Topaz—
Your Camp." . . . The instruction sheet [we were given] advised us . . .
about words. "You are now in Topaz, Utah." . . . "Here we say Dining
Hall, not Mess Hall; Safety Council, not Internal Police; Residents, not
Evacuees; and last, but not least, Mental Climate, not Morale." After
our long and exhausting ordeal, a patronizing sheet of instructions was
the last thing we needed.

—Yoshiko **Uchida**, female, Nisei, Berkeley, California, incarcerated
age 21, Tanforan Assembly Center, Topaz Relocation Center[136]

When we got to Jerome, we were shocked because we had never
seen an area like it. That's where they put us—in swamplands, sur-
rounded by forests. It was nothing like California.

—Mary Yuriko "Yuri" **Nakahara** (Kochiyama), female, Nisei, San
Pedro, California, incarcerated age 21, Santa Anita Assembly Center,
Jerome Relocation Center[137]

I stood bewildered, glaring at the hot dusty desert, wondering how
we could survive.

—Chiyoko **Morita**, female, Nisei, Santa Clara County, California,
incarcerated age 14, Salinas Assembly Center, Poston Relocation
Center[138]

August 27, 1942

Dear Miss Breed,
. . . This camp is so far away from civilization that it
makes me feel as if I was a convict who is not allowed to see
anyone. . . .

Most sincerely,
Louise Ogawa

—Louise Yoshiko **Ogawa** (Watanabe), female, Nisei, San Diego,
California, incarcerated age 18, Santa Anita Assembly Center, Poston
Relocation Center[139]

I could see . . . the first rows of black [tar-papered] barracks, and
beyond them . . . rows and rows of barracks that seemed to spread for
miles across this plain.
   —Jeanne Toyo **Wakatsuki** (Houston), female, Nisei, Santa Monica,
   California, incarcerated age 8, Manzanar Reception Center,
   Manzanar Relocation Center[140]

How . . . did they ever find places like this to put us in?
   —Sumiko "Sumi" **Seo** (Seki), female, Nisei, Los Angeles, California,
   incarcerated age 18, Santa Anita Assembly Center, Jerome Relocation
   Center[141]

Psychologically, it was a concentration camp.
   —Michio "Mich" **Kunitani**, male, Nisei, Alameda County, California,
   incarcerated age 24, Tanforan Assembly Center, Poston Relocation
   Center[142]

• • •

Some new arrivals, such as the family of Toranosuke Kamei and others from Orange County, California, came straight from their homes to the relocation centers. As they arrived at their places of detention, they went through the "intake" process of questioning, instructions, fingerprinting, and physical exams. For those who had been transported directly from the assembly centers, the experience of having to repeat the intake process seemed not only unnecessary, but galling.

Afterward they received their housing assignments and made their way to their new barrack "homes."

. . .

As we passed through the laundry, a Caucasian nurse peered into our throats with a flashlight and gave us the "okay" slips. We were now free to go in search of our room.
—Miné **Okubo**, female, Nisei, Berkeley, California, incarcerated age 30, Tanforan Assembly Center, Topaz Relocation Center[143]

They put as many people as possible on a truck to take us to our barracks. . . . They shoved us, pushed us, rammed us all in like cattle. I felt like an animal.
—Dollie Kimiko **Nagai** (Fukawa), female, Nisei, Fresno, California, incarcerated age 15, Fresno Assembly Center, Jerome Relocation Center[144]

Hammering, tarring, and roofing were still in progress, and one unfortunate woman received second degree burns on her face when boiling tar seeped through the roof onto the bed where she was asleep.
—Yoshiko **Uchida**, female, Nisei, Berkeley, California, incarcerated age 21, Tanforan Assembly Center, Topaz Relocation Center[145]

We were taken to . . . a cluster of fifteen barracks that had just been finished a day or so earlier—although "finished" was hardly the word for it. The shacks were built of one thickness of pine planking covered with tarpaper.

    —Jeanne Toyo **Wakatsuki** (Houston), female, Nisei, Santa Monica, California, incarcerated age 8, Manzanar Reception Center, Manzanar Relocation Center[146]

The first week in Topaz was a series of adjustments—becoming acquainted with new neighbors, coping with the weather, following the mess hall schedules, resigning ourselves to the inconvenient location of the laundry and the latrine. Inwardly, we appreciated the fact that we were no longer in flimsy horse stalls, but at the same time, we realized how deep was the feeling of isolation. This separation from our home state and the outside world was difficult for most of us. We kept talking about remembered places in Berkeley and of friends there who still wrote to us. Struck by the barrenness of the place, we spoke wistfully about California; we experienced natsukashi-mi, the Japanese term for this emotional state of yearning, of longing.

    —Toyo **Suyemoto** (Kawakami), female, Nisei, Alameda County, California, incarcerated age 26, Tanforan Assembly Center, Topaz Relocation Center[147]

I missed my friends. . . . When I got to camp, I wrote to everybody I could think of. We were so hungry for people to write to us, for some kind of news from the outside.

    —Sumiko "Sumi" **Seo** (Seki), female, Nisei, Los Angeles, California, incarcerated age 18, Santa Anita Assembly Center, Jerome Relocation Center[148]

Everyone was forced to use out-houses since the sewer system had not been built. For about a year, the residents had to brave the cold and stench of these accommodations.

    —Shuzo Chris **Kato**, male, Nisei, Seattle, Washington, incarcerated age 16, Puyallup Assembly Center, Minidoka Relocation Center[149]

. . .

At Topaz the water was turned on and off on an unpredictable schedule. When it came on, people would shout, "It's on!" They had to hope they could finish their showers without getting caught all soapy before the water ran out.

. . .

August 27, 1942

> *Dear Miss Breed, . . .*
>   *. . . I'd much rather sleep in the Santa Anita horse stables—this has made me realize how fortunate I was to be able to live in Santa Anita. The nearest town which is a very tiny one is about 20 miles away. . . .*
>
>   *Most sincerely,*
>   *Louise Ogawa*
>
>   *Ps. There is no water on Sundays. The electricity is also turned off. Sunday morning everyone eats before 6:00 A.M. Water and electricity turned off between 6:00 A.M. to 6:00 P.M. on Sundays. Very very inconvenient. Never realized how valuable water is. This place looked deserted all the time because of the sandiness. Every[one] stays inside and no one is outside— not even the children so it looks as if no one lives in the barracks. If American soldiers can endure hardships so can we!*
>
>   *My new address is:*
>   *Louise Y. Ogawa*
>   *Camp No. 3*
>   *Block 330 Bldg. 12 Apt B*
>   *Poston, Arizona*

—Louise Yoshiko **Ogawa** (Watanabe), female, Nisei, San Diego,
California, incarcerated age 18, Santa Anita Assembly Center, Poston
Relocation Center[150]

. . .

New arrivals at Poston learned quickly how to cover their faces
with bandanas or towels so that the sand and dust didn't get into their
eyes and mouths. By the time they walked back from the showers,
their eyebrows and hair were white with dust, and they were ready for
another shower. The sand could get so deep on the ground that they
would sink into it up to their ankles. It didn't take long for them to
realize that no matter how diligent they were in sweeping and stuffing
the crevices, their living quarters would never be clean.

. . .

*On our first day in camp, we were given a rousing welcome by
a dust storm. It caught up with us while we were still wandering
around looking for our room. We felt as if we were standing in a
gigantic sand-mixing machine as the sixty-mile gale lifted the loose
earth up into the sky, obliterating everything. Sand filled our mouths
and nostrils and stung our faces and hands like a thousand dart-
ing needles. Henry and Father pushed on ahead while Mother, Sumi
and I followed, hanging onto their jackets and banging suitcases into
each other. At last we staggered into our room, gasping and blinded.
We sat on our suitcases to rest, peeling off our jackets and scarves.
The windowpanes rattled madly, and the dust poured in through
the cracks like smoke. Now and then when the wind subsided, I saw
other evacuees, hanging on to their suitcases, heads bent against the
stinging dust. The wind whipped the scarves and towels from their
heads and zipped them out of sight.*

—Monica Kazuko **Itoi** (Sone), female, Nisei, Seattle, Washington,
incarcerated age 23, Puyallup Assembly Center, Minidoka Relocation
Center[151]

There was such a terrible dust storm that we couldn't see where we were going, and we couldn't tell which block because. . . they hadn't put the numbers on the blocks yet. And so we struggled back and tried to locate where our room was, and we all, I think a lot of us ended up in the wrong place. And that was the first sight of the very dusty, very strong wind, and we saw all kinds of things flying around. . . . There was no protection because they had bulldozed all, you know, all the trees and brushes and shrubs . . . in order to build the barracks, with no protection from the wind. . . . We stood at the window and [looked] out at the tumbleweeds and branches flying by.

—Sueko "Sue" **Kunitomi** (Embrey), female, Nisei, Los Angeles, California, incarcerated age 19, Manzanar Reception Center, Manzanar Relocation Center[152]

DESERT STORM

Near the mess hall
along the latrines
by the laundry
between the rows of
black tar papered barracks
the block captain galloped by.
Take cover everyone he said
here comes a twister.

Hundreds of windows
slammed shut.
Five pairs of hands
in our room
with mess hall
butter knives
stuffed

newspapers and rags
between the cracks.
But the Idaho dust
persistent and seeping
found us crouched
under the covers.
This was not
im
prison
ment.
This was
re
location.

—Mitsuye (Yasutake) **Yamada**, female, Nisei, Seattle, Washington, incarcerated age 19, Puyallup Assembly Center, Minidoka Relocation Center[153]

• • •

The relocation center facilities were built according to an army base model, with twelve to fourteen barracks forming the basic housing unit of a block. For example, Topaz had thirty-four residential blocks with twelve barracks per block—seemingly endless rows of identical one-story, military-style barracks blanketing the otherwise featureless landscape.

• • •

In the [Sacramento] Japanese community where we grew up, the family had been the identifying unit. Whenever we were introduced to others, we would give our surname and often [where] in Japan . . . Mother and Father came from. Now, in Topaz, the block was the unit to which we belonged. In exchanging greetings with someone from another location within the camp, we usually mentioned the block where we lived. The family entity we had known before had become decentralized.

Now, even the family surname had been replaced by an identification number.

—Toyo **Suyemoto** (Kawakami), female, Nisei, Alameda County, California, incarcerated age 26, Tanforan Assembly Center, Topaz Relocation Center[154]

All residential blocks looked alike. People were lost all the time.

—Miné **Okubo**, female, Nisei, Berkeley, California, incarcerated age 30, Tanforan Assembly Center, Topaz Relocation Center[155]

• • •

Each block had its own mess hall, recreation hall, laundry rooms (with tubs and ironing boards), and communal latrines and showers. Approximately two hundred to four hundred people lived in each block. Typically, each barrack was approximately 20 feet by 100 to 120 feet, divided into four to six rooms, each room (or apartment) housing at least one family.

Besides a bare lightbulb, each room contained only cots and an oil-, coal-, or wood-burning stove. And—just as in the assembly centers—the new residents threw themselves into making furniture, room partitions, screens, and home furnishings out of meager supplies. Yet again, single adults shared rooms with strangers. Some of the concentration camps were so crowded that people were forced to sleep in the communal mess halls and recreation halls, and at times as many as twenty-five people were crammed into an apartment meant for six or eight.

• • •

How would you like to live in one room with your father and mother, your sisters and brothers all around, your aunts in the next room . . . all knowing exactly what you do every minute of the time?

—Chizuko "Chizu" **Kitano** (Iiyama), female, Nisei, Berkeley, California, incarcerated age 21, Santa Anita Assembly Center, Topaz Relocation Center[156]

. . .

At all the camps, the incarcerees were subjected to extreme weather conditions. For the Japanese Americans who were accustomed to the moderate climates on the West Coast, the drastic temperature ranges were among their greatest challenges. When they arrived, they confronted the intense summer heat. If people at the Gila River Relocation Center wanted to take a bath, they simply left a bucket of water outside to heat up in the noonday sun. They carried umbrellas during the day and frequently suffered heat prostration and nosebleeds. Cots were provided for anyone who fainted from the 110-degree early-morning temperatures. At Poston, heatstroke was considered a large-scale issue.

. . .

The first day here was so hot I should not know how I should express how I felt then. Whoever I met carried wet towels on their heads. Even in the mess hall people ate with wet towels on their heads. . . . That night, as I tumbled into bed, I kept thinking how we could ever survive in such a place.

—Chiyoko **Morita**, female, Nisei, Santa Clara County, California, incarcerated age 14, Salinas Assembly Center, Poston Relocation Center[157]

Extreme heat that can melt iron. No trees, no flowers, no singing birds, not even the sound of an insect. All at once a strong wind began to blow, sandy dust whirled into the sky, completely taking the sunshine and light from us. That night a full moon shone in the wilderness.

—Kyuji **Aizumi**, male, Issei, San Diego, California, incarcerated age 56, Fort Missoula Alien Detention Center, Santa Anita Assembly Center, Poston Relocation Center[158]

. . .

Then came the harsh winters, particularly in Idaho at Minidoka (with approximately seven thousand incarcerees), where temperatures fell to 21 degrees below zero, and in Wyoming at Heart Mountain (with approximately ten thousand incarcerees), where in winter 30 degrees below zero was not uncommon.

• • •

Naturally, I wondered what kind of place Wyoming was. People from California never realized . . . especially in a state in the Rocky Mountain area, how harsh the climate was . . . when we went to Heart Mountain. I think it was one of the coldest winters in Wyoming history. We were really out of our environment, so to say. And [we] really suffered there.

—Mitsuru "Mits" **Koshiyama**, male, Nisei, Santa Clara Valley, California, incarcerated age 18, Santa Anita Assembly Center, Heart Mountain Relocation Center, McNeil Island Federal Penitentiary[159]

As a native Californian, I was ill-equipped to deal with the biting winds, sub-zero temperatures, and knee-deep snows. The snow did not fall gently in Heart Mountain. It came horizontally like icy spears across the barren plains to crash into the tar-papered barrack walls as if to obliterate this abomination, euphemistically called a "relocation center," at the foot of the majestic mountain it was named after.

The wind was incessant. Even in the heat of summer, the dust storms would coat our faces and hair with a fine white powder as if to make us look more like our oppressors, in a vain attempt to mask the damning evidence of our ethnicity; the apparent root of our woes and persecution.

The mountain took little note of the insanity occurring at its feet. It had, no doubt, witnessed in passed eras, the massacre of others of dark skin, brutally stripped of their land, their culture, their livelihood and their power of self-determination. It had, no doubt, witnessed the butchering of herds of buffalo for their hides and horns, leaving their bloody naked carcasses to bake and rot under the blazing desert sun, while their young calves stood about, bewildered and abandoned. . . .

The winters are still cold in Heart Mountain—but not as cold as the winters in the hearts of men.

—Yoshito "Yosh" **Kuromiya**, male, Nisei, Pasadena, California, incarcerated age 19, Pomona Assembly Center, Heart Mountain Relocation Center, Cheyenne County Jail, McNeil Island Federal Penitentiary[160]

• • •

People reported outbreaks of pneumonia, influenza, chicken pox, dysentery, polio, and tuberculosis, and experienced untold heartbreaks over deaths and disabilities resulting from inadequate health care. The seven doctors at Jerome were expected to care for more than eight thousand incarcerees.

• • •

The camp-based hospitals were not furnished with a sufficient number of bedpans, urinals, or washbasins. We never had enough linens, and we'd run around looking for blankets and pillows. The facilities were not there to take care of a hospital full of patients, and . . . our base hospital in Tule Lake always had about eighty or ninety patients.

—Emiko "Emi" (Yada) **Somekawa**, female, Nisei, Portland, Oregon, incarcerated age 24, Portland Assembly Center, Tule Lake Relocation Center[161]

When I arrived at the hospital [in labor], a nurse checked me in. She stated the doctor had delivered three babies [that day] and had collapsed, so he had returned to his barracks for a much needed rest. There was only one "ob" doctor for the entire camp [of nearly twenty thousand people].

—Mabel Takako (Kawashima) **Ota**, female, Nisei, Holtville, California, incarcerated age 26, Poston Relocation Center[162]

• • •

At camps such as Poston, Gila River, and Manzanar, Japanese Americans fended off centipedes, black widow spiders, tarantulas, scorpions, venomous Gila monsters, and deadly rattlesnakes. Some of the more intrepid incarcerees would trap rattlesnakes and display them in cages so that everyone could admire the creature (up to seven feet long) and the number of its rattles, or they'd just keep them as pets. Gengoro Tonai hunted rattlesnakes at the Granada (Amache) Relocation Center. He'd kill the rattlesnakes and cut off the rattles. Years later Tonai gave his grandson, John Tonai, a whole rattlesnake skin, a bunch of rattles, and a couple of fangs he had kept from his camp days.

The area surrounding the Jerome Relocation Center in Arkansas had copperheads and water moccasins as well. The tall barbed wire fences and Jerome's manned guard towers seemed superfluous for keeping inmates inside the camp when the surrounding swamps were infested with such poisonous snakes. Jerome and the other Arkansas camp, Rohwer, also had to deal with malaria-carrying mosquitoes.

• • •

When the rains came in Rohwer, we could not leave our quarters. The water stagnated at the front steps. . . . The mosquitos that festered there were horrible, and the authorities never had enough quinine for sickness. . . . Rohwer was a living nightmare.

—Masako "Betty" (Fujisaki) **Matsuo**, female, Nisei, Stockton, California, incarcerated age 16, Stockton Assembly Center, Rohwer Relocation Center[163]

• • •

Much to their dismay, parents quickly realized that they could no more get their families to eat together at dinnertime in the relocation centers than they could at the assembly centers. The deterioration of the family unit that had begun in the assembly centers accelerated in the relocation centers. Issei parents feared that the close-knit dynamic of their Japanese culture, which they had carefully nurtured in the real world, would not survive incarceration.

• • •

Sitting down at the table is a kind of celebration. In camp it was a down experience. You finish something because you are hungry, but there's no pleasure in it.

—John Sohei **Hohri**, male, Nisei, Los Angeles, California, incarcerated age 17, Manzanar Reception Center, Manzanar Relocation Center[164]

About a week after we got there, we said, We're not going to eat with our parents. All the kids would meet and we would sit at our own table. That's where this terrible breakdown of the family happened. You're not with your family at mealtime or the rest of the time.

—Lillian Reiko **Sugita** (Nakano), female, Sansei, Honolulu, Hawaii, incarcerated age 14, Jerome Relocation Center, Heart Mountain Relocation Center[165]

I insisted that my two brothers and I eat together in the mess hall as a family unit. I insisted that we have grace before meals. And I insisted that they be in our room at eight o'clock at night. Not because I wanted to see them but because I thought that's what we should do as a family—we should be together, spend our time together, and live as a family group—and I tried in all the really childish ways to maintain us that way.

—Helen Matsue **Yamahiro** (Murao), female, Nisei, Portland, Oregon, incarcerated age 16, Portland Assembly Center, Minidoka Relocation Center[166]

We stopped eating as a family. Mama tried to hold us together for a while, but it was hopeless. Granny was too feeble to walk across the block three times a day, especially during heavy weather, so Mama brought food to her in the barracks. My older brothers and sisters, meanwhile, began eating with their friends, or eating somewhere blocks away in the hope of finding better food. The word would get around that the cook over in Block 22, say, really knew his stuff, and they would eat a few meals over there. . . . Camp authorities frowned on mess hall hopping and tried to stop it, but the good cooks liked . . . to see long lines outside their kitchens. . . .

Younger boys . . . would make a game of seeing how many mess halls they could hit in one meal period. . . .

Not only did we stop eating at home, there was no longer a home to eat in.

—Jeanne Toyo **Wakatsuki** (Houston), female, Nisei, Santa Monica, California, incarcerated age 8, Manzanar Reception Center, Manzanar Relocation Center[167]

• • •

Food supplies were rationed in accordance with policies that applied to all other Americans during wartime, although the press falsely claimed the camps were exempt.

• • •

When we read reports in the papers of our luxurious quarters and lavish food, we resented deeply these untruths by ignorant politicians. When several Senators proposed [an] investigation of conditions we encouraged just that.

—Robert Ritsuro **Hosokawa**, male, Nisei, Seattle, Washington, incarcerated age 24, Puyallup Assembly Center, Minidoka Relocation Center[168]

• • •

The mess hall wasn't the only place where the family's traditional ways were falling apart. Communication between family members had eroded in the assembly centers and continued to worsen in the relocation centers due to the lack of privacy. The role of husband and father—crucial in Japanese American culture—had been undermined when so many of the Issei men had been taken away by the FBI. Eventually, when some men were released to join their families in the

WRA camps weeks, months, or sometimes years after their arrests, the reunion was strained and sad. Many men appeared to have been severely damaged, mentally and physically, by their imprisonment. Some would never fully recover.

• • •

[Papa] arrived at Manzanar on a Greyhound bus. We all went down to the main gate to meet him. . . . The door whished open, and the first thing we saw was the cane—I will never forget it—poking from the shaded interior into the sunlight, a straight, polished maple limb spotted with dark, lidded eyes where small knotholes had been stained and polished. Then Papa stepped out, wearing a fedora hat and a wilted white shirt. This was September 1942. He had been gone nine months. He had aged ten years. He looked over sixty, gaunt, and as wilted as his shirt, underweight, leaning on that cane and favoring his right leg. He stood there surveying the clan, and nobody moved, not even Mama, waiting to see what he would do or say, waiting for some kind of cue from him as to how we should deal with this.

—Jeanne Toyo **Wakatsuki** (Houston), female, Nisei, Santa Monica, California, incarcerated age 8, Manzanar Reception Center, Manzanar Relocation Center[169]

• • •

Some of the young Nisei became embarrassed by their too "Japanesey" parents, whom they felt were hopelessly clinging to preferences for tea ceremonies and classical Japanese art forms, such as Kabuki theater and music performed on the koto (a floor harp), shamisen (a three-stringed instrument), and shakuhachi (a bamboo flute). From the Issei point of view, their children not only lacked appreciation for Japanese values and customs, but were becoming selfish and trivial, overly concerned with going to dances, drinking sodas, and meeting the opposite sex.

• • •

The student body president was . . . asked which he liked better, chocolate, candy, or Coke. He happened to like a girl nicknamed

"Coke" and replied "Coke." So they brought out a bottle of Coca-Cola. Everyone screamed with surprise and hunger at the sight of a bottle of Coca-Cola. He had to get down on his knees and propose to the bottle of coke. . . . How we all envied him!!

— Louise Yoshiko **Ogawa** (Watanabe), female, Nisei, San Diego, California, incarcerated age 18, Santa Anita Assembly Center, Poston Relocation Center[170]

• • •

And then, when you least expected it, a dog changed everything.

The Hashimotos' canine pet had come into their lives as a result of a trade: The family exchanged some canaries that they had raised in an aviary behind their Watsonville home for a puppy with a winning personality. When the Hashimotos had to depart for the Salinas Assembly Center on April 17, 1942, they left behind the keys to their boarded-up house on Union Street and their beloved dog with a trusted friend. Six-year-old Mas Hashimoto was especially heartbroken to part with their pet.

• • •

Her name was Sunny and she was a little white dog that you couldn't tell one end from the other. She was so cute. [Our friend] later wrote to me saying that the dog isn't eating very well and she was afraid the dog might die. So, she asked if she could send the dog to Poston, Arizona, our second camp. And, of course, you know, yes!

But how do you send a dog [575 miles] from Watsonville, California to Poston, Arizona near Parker, Arizona, near the Colorado River— Greyhound bus. Greyhound bus! And the thing was the drivers made sure she got food and water.

I had the only dog in the Poston II camp and she was the petting zoo. Everybody loved her. She was my constant companion. So I was one very happy six-, seven-year-old.

One day she disappeared. I had the family and my friends go out looking for her. We couldn't find her, all over camp. . . . So I concluded that the coyotes must have eaten her. Because there were wild coyotes nearby.

But miraculously she reappeared and I was the happiest eight-year-old. You want to ask, "Where were you? What happened?" But she couldn't tell me.

Are pets important? And the answer is absolutely! I mean, sometimes they're just as important as family members.

—Masaru "Mas" **Hashimoto**, male, Nisei, Watsonville, California, incarcerated age 6, Salinas Assembly Center, Poston Relocation Center[171]

After the camp closed, Mas brought his best and loyal friend home with him.

• • •

The inmates honored the cycle of life, celebrating births and marriages and supporting those who mourned the death of a family member. Without access to fresh flowers, they fashioned artificial flowers out of tissue and crepe paper for funeral and casket wreaths. They set about beautifying the campgrounds with gardens and walkways and transformed into art the materials they scavenged from their local landscapes. They decorated their apartments with carvings from scrap wood and made dresses out of rice bags. Shells and gemstones at Tule Lake and Topaz became mosaics and jewelry, ironwood turned into polished carvings at Gila, and desert sand formed the bases of miniature tray landscapes at Camp Amache. Heart Mountain residents became known for their exquisite embroidery, thanks to the volunteer instruction by a former teacher of this traditional Japanese art form.

• • •

MARY

Against the black hood of night twinkled the stars
Like the lights in Mary's dark brown eyes.
Jupiter, Saturn and lovely Venus
Watched over our quiet world.

A bubble of joy seemed to swell within me
As I thought of the halo of happiness that surrounded
    her
And gathered others into its warmth.

Wispy clouds trailed across the face of a troubled
    moon.
A thin mist seemed to envelop the stars.
It grew blacker, denser;
The bubble broke!
My soul grew heavy and grey
As I thought of the heart-shaped face and laughing
    eyes
Now gone forever. . .

—Ruth **Tanaka** (Gray), female, Nisei, Dinuba, California,
incarcerated age 13, Poston Relocation Center; written at the age
of 16 in memory of her high school classmate Mary Nagata on the
occasion of Mary's death at Poston[172]

• • •

Over time a handful of photographers captured the incarceree
experience. The WRA hired Dorothea Lange, known for her por-
trait *Migrant Mother* and other photos of the Great Depression, to
photograph the forced removal process and incarceration life. Her
photos capturing the hardships were so unflinching, however, that the
government impounded them until 1972. Ralph Merritt, the project
director at Manzanar, arranged for his friend, nature photographer
Ansel Adams, to take photos there. Not surprisingly, Adams's photos
focused on the drama of the desert landscape. In contrast, the photos
taken by amateur photographer Bill Manbo at Heart Mountain and by
Manzanar incarceree Toyo Miyatake (who in 1923 had founded Toyo
Miyatake Studio in the Little Tokyo section of Los Angeles) captured

the rhythm of camp existence and the people's commitment to creating good times with joy and exuberance despite their imprisonment.

In these ways Japanese Americans carved a vision of community out of the massive scale of the relocation centers. Tule Lake became the largest WRA concentration camp, with a peak population of 18,789 inmates. Gila River had a population of over 13,000, divided into two camps, known as Canal Camp and Butte Camp. Poston, consisting of seventy-one thousand acres and a peak population of 17,814, was divided into three separate camps three miles apart—nicknamed Roasten, Toasten, and Dustin. All together the Poston population was so large that it was considered the third-largest city in Arizona.

Poston was also the only relocation center run by both the Office of Indian Affairs (OIA) and the WRA, until the WRA took over sole responsibility in 1943. But Poston wasn't just a concentration camp; it had been built on the Colorado River Indian Reservation in large part due to the role of John Collier, once a social service worker on Manhattan's Lower East Side, who had been selected to be OIA commissioner by Secretary of the Interior Harold Ickes. After Collier took over the position in 1933, he became architect of the Indian New Deal, which was intended to restore to Native Americans some civil rights as well as political and social independence. He supported the growth of traditional cultures, including their arts and crafts, just as much as he supported the application of social science and psychiatry to the plight of minority groups.

Collier didn't believe in assimilating tribes into White society; he believed in self-government, so that native people could be in a position to sustain their own culture and beliefs. But in order for the tribal community to be self-supporting, he needed a way to get water to the desert land for growing crops. To that end, Collier had a grand vision of developing an irrigation system for twenty-five thousand acres. This would mean digging irrigation ditches and canals, and leveling and preparing the land to receive water.

All this, Collier believed, would carry with it the ultimate goal of colonizing the reservation by attracting the Hopi and Navajo tribes along the Colorado River with the promise of water, electricity, and fertile farmland. Collier, like his predecessors, wanted to consolidate the tribes from smaller, overgrazed, and barren reservations onto one that would significantly improve their quality of life. The problem was, there weren't enough people occupying the Colorado River Indian Reservation for the government to justify funding its irrigation. But if the government wouldn't pay for it, Collier realized, he could make do with a massive incarcerated workforce.

In March 1942 when the WRA was looking for places to build concentration camps, Collier suggested to Harold Ickes and Milton Eisenhower that they use Native American lands. Collier recognized that having Japanese Americans live on land that needed their agricultural expertise could rebound the entire reservation. In addition to doing most of the work to support themselves, the inmates could provide, in essence, free labor for the US government.

Unbeknownst to the Japanese Americans, however, they'd be working at the behest of the OIA, not the WRA. By creating livable conditions for themselves, they'd be doing the government's work for the reservation that it otherwise refused to support—bringing power deep into the reservation, manufacturing their own adobe bricks for building schools, and irrigating the land into farms and fields.

Eisenhower agreed, in writing, and Poston was born.

Then Eisenhower became disillusioned with the job.

On April 23, 1942, Eisenhower wrote to Utah Senator Elbert D. Thomas, "Frankly, I would not have become identified with this War task had I realized in advance all that was involved."

Troubled by the responsibility of imprisoning people he considered to be innocent, Eisenhower resigned as WRA director after only ninety days in office. He was replaced by Dillon S. Myer on June 17, 1942, a little over two weeks after Poston had opened its doors to seventeen thousand incarcerees. Myer's policies would govern the agency and the lives of the incarcerees for the duration of their detention.

• • •

Myer . . . had nothing to do with the evacuation itself. He was an unwilling jail-keeper, and within a week or two of taking the WRA job, he made the restoration of freedom his top priority. . . . A soft-spoken, gentle manner concealed an inner toughness and dedication to justice and humanitarian principles.

—Mike Masaru **Masaoka**, male, Nisei, North Platte, Nebraska, age 26 when Pearl Harbor was attacked[173]

• • •

Myer insisted that the staff treat the incarcerees respectfully; each staff member was given a manual of terminology. The camps were not to be called "concentration camps" (although the term was commonly used during that period and lacked the connotation it acquired after the Holocaust). Those incarcerated were supposed to be called "residents" or "colonists"; most frequently they were referred to as "evacuees." Myer intended that "Jap" was not to be used by the camp personnel, but the administrative staff were known to use the derogatory term among themselves, and Myer himself was known to slip up. At one camp a White teacher used the word "Jap," and the entire class walked out. She was subsequently fired.

• • •

Myer and his staff labored diligently . . . [to] make camp life less disagreeable.

—William "Bill" Kumpai **Hosokawa**, male, Nisei, Seattle, Washington, incarcerated age 27, Puyallup Assembly Center, Heart Mountain Relocation Center[174]

I'm quite aware that among [the WRA staff] some were reactionaries. But they didn't have much to do with the evacuees. The staff as a whole was very humane, with . . . people who gave us a great deal of support and encouragement. They deserve credit for the fact that so many of us emerged from the experience with a minimum of damage to our egos.

—Sada Hasegawa **Murayama**, female, Issei, San Francisco,
California, incarcerated age 41, Tule Lake Relocation Center[175]

• • •

And yet despite the good intentions, relations between the WRA staff and incarcerees were strained. The staff had separate and much nicer living quarters. They were forbidden to fraternize with the "colonists." They didn't have to stand in line to eat three times a day, and in an attempt to create some class distinctions, some project directors instituted a policy that WRA staff and incarcerees could not eat in the same mess hall.

• • •

A Jim Crow system existed in the camp. The Caucasians lived on the south side of the administration building. They were housed in white painted structures. They had the cooling system for the terrible heat of the desert summers. They had the heating system which made their life comfortable. . . . The Caucasians went to a dining hall. They were served by the inmates who waited on them. Sumptuous meals were served to them compared to what we were fed.

—Elizabeth Aiko (Takahashi) **Nishikawa**, female, Nisei, Los Angeles,
California, incarcerated age 31, Manzanar Reception Center,
Manzanar Relocation Center[176]

• • •

Perhaps most troubling of all were the accusations of corruption occurring within the staff itself, notably that they were stealing food and selling it on the wartime black market. Angry over their living conditions, some inmates began questioning Myer's authority. They pointed out times when he had announced plans that didn't come to pass or made promises that were slow to be fulfilled. For example, the incarcerees were frustrated when Myer represented that they would receive household goods, but months went by before any arrived.

Friction also arose over how the camp community was governed. Project directors appointed certain incarcerees to serve as block managers on the basis of their leadership potential. Many Issei who had bilingual ability were chosen because of their prewar status as elders among the population. The block managers were responsible for acting as liaisons between the project director and the incarcerees in their block and for handling various tasks within their section of the barracks. They settled internal disputes, distributed supplies and materials, handled incoming and outgoing mail, and performed general maintenance.

In some camps, block councils were formed. They consisted of representatives elected from each section of the barracks, in addition to the block manager. But Issei were not allowed to hold elected offices, and their exclusion from the block councils only made their relationships with the younger Nisei worse. Ultimately, though, neither the block managers nor the community councils had any substantive authority or policy-making powers, since the relocation center's project director could veto any decision for any reason at any time.

• • •

The Project Director . . . held virtual dictatorial powers . . . over the evacuees in his charge. He was surrounded by a staff of aides, all Caucasians.

—William "Bill" Kumpai **Hosokawa**, male, Nisei, Seattle, Washington, incarcerated age 27, Puyallup Assembly Center, Heart Mountain Relocation Center[177]

• • •

Among the thorniest issues Myer inherited from Eisenhower was the question of employment for the incarcerees in the camps. The WRA needed their help to run the camps as cooks, dishwashers, bakers, gardeners, teachers, typists, secretaries, and firefighters. Being confined, however, meant the Japanese Americans had no real career opportunities. But Myer made good on his representations that they would contribute to the war effort while in camp. At Manzanar, Gila River, and Poston they made camouflage netting; at Heart Mountain they made silk-screen posters; at Gila River they built model warships that were used as training aids for the US Navy.

Myer arranged for the incarcerees to be paid according to a wage scale. However, the politics of the situation were such that the wage scale for Japanese Americans could not exceed the base pay of a soldier at $21 per month. As a result, the wage scale was set at $12 per month for unskilled labor, $16 for skilled labor, and $19 for professional work. Food, shelter, medical care, and school were free. Small unemployment payments would be made to employable incarcerees who were out of work through no fault of their own, along with each dependent.

Still, it wasn't enough, not even remotely. Under this system the incarcerees could not afford basic living expenses like shoes for their children, let alone meet financial obligations such as a mortgage left behind. They were insulted that a WRA librarian could be paid $167 per month but an incarceree librarian only $16 per month. Japanese doctors and nurses received $19 per month but sometimes reported to white doctors who were paid much more, even if those doctors were less skilled and not as well trained. Many of the older Issei claimed they were being discriminated against because of their age. The better jobs, they said, were going to the younger Nisei because the WRA staff were more comfortable working with people who spoke fluent English. The inequity of the pay scale and all issues relating to employment were never resolved to anyone's satisfaction.

The Japanese Americans worked constantly anyway, and soon the farmers were supplementing the mess hall fare with much-needed fresh vegetables. By the end of 1943 the incarcerees were producing 85 percent of their own vegetables. Gila River incarcerees ran a dairy, and eventually they were making their own tofu and soy sauce for distribution. They also raised poultry, cattle, and hogs.

• • •

The hogs ate everything we left and ultimately we ate the hogs.
—Miné **Okubo**, female, Nisei, Berkeley, California, incarcerated age 30, Tanforan Assembly Center, Topaz Relocation Center[178]

• • •

Meanwhile, Collier was still hoping to create a humanitarian project in which the Japanese Americans, with their agricultural expertise, would develop thousands of acres of barren reservation land in Arizona to grow surplus crops for American troops. Instead of a concentration camp, Collier envisioned the center as a showcase for community planning and local economic development. He wanted the Japanese Americans to live alongside the Native Americans long-term on lands they would cultivate as a collective. He was a scholar of communal life and believed that "the efficiency and splendor of the cooperative way of living" would raise the spirits and democratic ideals of the two populations. But Collier had made the mistake of pursuing the deal with Eisenhower before securing permission from the tribal councils, and once Myer replaced Eisenhower as WRA director, Myer broke all of Eisenhower's promises to Collier.

Myer insisted that Poston should operate like all other camps; the Japanese Americans would not stay long-term, and he authorized the cultivation of only five thousand acres out of the twenty-five thousand originally planned. Myer's philosophy about minority populations was diametrically opposed to Collier's. He believed in total assimilation of all cultures into one melting pot. He wanted the Japanese, and then the Native Americans, to abandon their culture and their way of life completely. He wanted them all to become part of a European American community so that eventually all distinctions among the Native American, Japanese American, and European American cultures would be

156 · SUSAN H. KAMEI

permanently erased—their languages, values, traditions, and beliefs. Harold Ickes called Myer a "Hitler and Mussolini rolled into one."

Nevertheless, by August 1942 over seven hundred incarcerees at the Poston camps were working on irrigation-related projects. They leveled over two thousand acres and designed and constructed an irrigation system that watered the fields, yielding produce from ground that had once been mere wasteland. The incarcerees set up power lines and built bridges over the irrigation canals. They constructed gravel-surface roads to the farms and a hard-surface highway to the town of Parker. They built and managed poultry and hog farms, a butcher shop, warehouses, an ice storage facility, and a plant nursery. Ironically, once the Japanese Americans were gone, Hopi and Navajo families moved into the same barracks that had just been vacated by the Japanese—one group of displaced people replacing another in accommodations that were actually an upgrade from the Native Americans' previous living conditions. In effect, Poston was a concentration camp inside a concentration camp.

• • •

The lights have been turned off
Here at the Relocation Center
And I'll sleep this evening
With the voices of migrating ducks
Passing through my heart.

—Kojin **Tahara**, male, San Francisco, California[179]

CHAPTER SIX

For the Sake of the Children

*Can we the graduating class of Amache Senior High School, still
believe that America means freedom, equality, security, and justice?
Do I believe this? Do my classmates believe this?*
  —Marion Tsuruko **Konishi** (Takehara), female, Nisei, Los Angeles,
  California, incarcerated age 16, Santa Anita Assembly Center,
  Granada (Amache) Relocation Center[180]

As families were getting settled into the WRA relocation centers,
high school students with college aspirations were getting worried. It didn't seem to them that the government, in its haste to
construct the detention facilities, had given much thought to their
education. For the most part, these students had lost their 1942
spring semester, dropping out after the Pearl Harbor attack in the
face of intensifying hostilities and the chaos of forced removal from
their homes. Taking in the bleakness of their isolation, they soon
realized that they could be spending the rest of their high school
years in these camp prisons. Now their hopes and dreams for a college degree were seriously at risk, as were the hopes and dreams
that their Issei parents had for them. In the spirit of *kodomo no tame
ni*—"for the sake of the children"—the Issei parents realized that,
just as they had done in the assembly centers, organizing schooling
for their kids would be up to them. It wasn't long before they found
out just what they were up against.

What no one knew was that the WRA intended for its prisoners to
build the schools *themselves*. Although the WRA said that education
would be a priority, its original construction plans for the relocation
centers did not include any school facilities. Under John Collier's work

plan in the three Poston camps, for example, the incarcerees were expected to build the schools from adobe bricks they would make using wooden molds. In fact, Charles A. Popkin, Poston's construction engineer, reported that the women made "better workers than men," and the women laid most of the adobe and applied a clay finish on the adobe walls. By September 30, 1943, the three Poston camps had made an estimated five hundred thousand adobe bricks to use in building schools on Poston grounds. A year and a half later, in March 1945, the Poston incarcerees had completed fifty-four adobe brick school buildings—just eight months before Poston officially closed.

• • •

When construction of the school began the whole community volunteered in making adobe bricks for the school buildings. Even school children helped so that school could open in time for the fall semester. . . . Yes, the students can rightfully be proud to say "It's my school" for they built it with sweat and toil.

—Tetsuzo "Ted" or "Tets" **Hirasaki**, male, Nisei, San Diego, California, incarcerated age 22, Santa Anita Assembly Center, Poston Relocation Center[181]

• • •

Without teachers, desks, or educational materials, camp volunteers and administrators rolled up their sleeves. Students sat on the floor until school furniture materialized out of scavenged wood, and for blackboards, teachers used plywood painted black.

• • •

We now have tables, twenty inches tall and homemade chairs eighteen and nineteen inches high, so children keep toppling over. Pulling slivers has become an avocation.

—Hatsune "Helen" **Aihara** (Kitaji), female, Nisei, Santa Clara Valley, California, incarcerated age 29, Salinas Assembly Center, Poston Relocation Center[182]

• • •

The WRA did try to hire qualified teachers to teach in the camps, but it was hard to get them. In addition to a wartime shortage of teachers, a significant number of women were taking higher-paying defense jobs that were available to them while the American men were serving overseas. The few Caucasian teachers who did sign up took one look at the camps' extreme locations and walked away. Of the ones who stayed, most did not stay for long. In the first year at Poston, for example, teachers averaged a tenure of less than five months. The majority of teachers were not certified to teach—they were young high school graduates called cadet teachers. They functioned as assistants but became responsible for much more than that.

• • •

I have a great deal of respect for these inexperienced youngsters who are courageously trying to give the children a chance to learn.

—Hatsune "Helen" **Aihara** (Kitaji), female, Nisei, Santa Clara Valley, California, incarcerated age 29, Salinas Assembly Center, Poston Relocation Center[183]

Hakujin (Caucasian) teachers who had credentials and experience were employed at prevailing salaries, but the schools still had to be partly staffed by Nisei who were educated, but untrained. The Nisei worked for the camp professional wage scale of nineteen dollars a month although they carried full teaching loads. . . . Other school employees—the assistant teachers, school library staff, secretaries and clerks—were all evacuees.

—Toyo **Suyemoto** (Kawakami), female, Nisei, Alameda County, California, incarcerated age 26, Tanforan Assembly Center, Topaz Relocation Center[184]

Our teachers and people in responsible positions were very caring people and did the best they could to provide us with the things we needed. For a student, life was pretty normal. We kept busy. We didn't realize the hardships the older people had to face.

—Rhoda Akiko **Nishimura** (Iyoya), female, Nisei, Berkeley, California, incarcerated age 15, Tanforan Assembly Center, Topaz Relocation Center[185]

Our education . . . was given a high priority by our parents, a value shared by most Issei parents. Because of their own educational background, my parents expected us to study hard and do well in school. Mother would say she had given us a sound mind and kept our bodies properly nourished, so we should not shirk our responsibility to study hard and earn top grades. A grade below an A was not acceptable. Mother would question us closely when we failed her expectations. She did not accept excuses.

—Toyo **Suyemoto** (Kawakami), female, Nisei, Alameda County, California, incarcerated age 26, Tanforan Assembly Center, Topaz Relocation Center[186]

• • •

Teachers improvised as best they could around the lack of teaching materials. As they had done when the assembly centers had been established, sympathetic church groups (such as the Quakers) and other community organizations donated books, drawing paper, pens, and pencils to the relocation centers. At Minidoka, book donations came from the city of Seattle, where most of the incarcerees at that camp had come from. The biology and chemistry classes started out without lab equipment; once those supplies were scrounged up, labs were set up in the washrooms. Students learning to type never had typewriters; they practiced on paper or blocks of wood with letters their teachers wrote within circles.

The University of Arizona repeatedly refused pleas from the Gila River camp for library books and faculty lectures. Alfred Atkinson, president of the university, took the position, "We are at war and these people are our enemies."

Despite all that the students had endured since December 7, 1941, their patriotism for their country was heartfelt. But the public did not believe them. To ameliorate the public's lack of trust, Myer instituted an "Americanization" program within the concentration camps to promote American values. (The program also included English and citizenship classes for the Issei, even though they remained barred from naturalization.) Myer thought, as Eisenhower had thought before him, that the Japanese Americans should be resettled into various parts of the country as soon as possible. He believed that Americanization would help the students integrate into new communities and would neutralize the cynicism, anger, and anti-American feelings bred by their being incarcerated in the camps. Aspects of the program included raising the flag, pledging allegiance, writing essays on democracy, and encouraging young people's participation in organizations such as the Camp Fire Girls, the Girl Scouts, and the Boy Scouts. Mike Masaoka of the JACL supported the Americanization program vigorously.

• • •

AMERICANIZATION: JACL should carry out a long-range Americanization program to help Japanese Americans become, as its motto states, "Better Americans in a Greater America."
—Mike Masaru **Masaoka**, male, Nisei, North Platte, Nebraska, age 26 when Pearl Harbor was attacked[187]

It made me a little teary-eyed 'cause I think of the irony of learning the Pledge of Allegiance while being behind barbed wire fences.
—May Kimiko **Nakamura** (Sasaki), female, Nisei, Seattle, Washington, incarcerated age 7, Puyallup Assembly Center, Minidoka Relocation Center[188]

• • •

Certainly Myer, in his wildest imagination, could not have anticipated one particular outcome of his Americanization program. Norm Mineta, the ten-year-old Cub Scout who had worn his uniform on the day his family left for the Santa Anita Assembly Center, was now a twelve-year-old Boy Scout at the Heart Mountain Relocation Center, diligently working toward his Eagle Scout rank. The leaders of Mineta's troop at Heart Mountain and the Boy Scout troop in nearby Cody, Wyoming, had organized an Americanization jamboree so the Scouts in the camp could meet the Scouts who lived locally. Mineta was paired up to share a pup tent with a White twelve-year-old named Alan Simpson from the Cody troop. They became close friends and continued to send each other Christmas cards throughout high school.

They lost touch for several years until Simpson read about Mineta's election as mayor of San Jose in the Cody newspaper. At that time Simpson was serving in the Wyoming legislature, and he gave Mineta a call, renewing their friendship. As life would have it, Mineta went on to become elected as a Democrat to the US House of Representatives in 1974; Simpson was elected as a Republican to the US Senate in 1978.

"When Alan came to the US Senate," Mineta said, "our friendship went back as if we were still sitting in that pup tent when we were 12 years old." The two share a deep and abiding friendship to this day and have worked together in bipartisan ways as fellow congressional leaders. After serving in Congress, Mineta served as secretary of commerce for President Bill Clinton and as secretary of transportation for President George W. Bush. Mineta continues to wear an American flag pin on his lapel to show the importance he places on the value of United States citizenship.

But there were other students, especially in the upper grades, who resented being subjected to the WRA's embedded Americanization agenda. They balked at essay topics like "American Democracy and What It Means to Me." Minidoka student Henry Miyatake was expelled after he refused to rewrite his frank opinions.

Heart Mountain student Katsuye Aiko Horiuchi (Tsuneishi) wrote in an essay, "Why then were citizens of Japanese ancestry removed from their homes and placed behind barbed wire?" Then she watched her teacher edit her words to read, "Why then were citizens of Japanese ancestry removed from their homes and placed in relocation centers?" The teacher wanted Katsuye to "rationalize and arrive at a conclusion whereby you can reconcile this seemingly undemocratic act as an act of Americanism."

While some laughed at the absurdity of Americanization, others failed to find it funny and expressed their true feelings in other ways. At Jerome the students got so tired of flag raising ceremonies that they toppled the flagpole. At Rohwer someone (presumably a student) scrawled the words "Jap Prison" in chalk on a school wall.

· · ·

Through imitation of my brothers, who attended grade school within the camp, I learned to salute the flag by the time I was five years old. I was learning, as best one could learn in Manzanar, what it meant to live in America. But I was also learning the sometimes bitter price one has to pay for it.

—John Yoshio **Tateishi**, male, Sansei, Los Angeles, California, incarcerated age 3, Manzanar Reception Center, Manzanar Relocation Center[189]

· · ·

Eventually the incarcerees settled in and by and large reconciled themselves to their circumstances. They were relieved to experience fewer of the oppressive, prisonlike aspects of daily life that had taken place at the assembly centers, such as roll calls and spot inspections. Issei and Nisei alike energetically expanded upon the kinds of activities they had previously organized at the assembly centers: arts and crafts, clubs of all kinds, concerts, plays, literary groups and productions, beauty pageants, religious services and events (including interfaith observances), and elaborate holiday celebrations, especially the August *obon* festivals, a Japanese Buddhist tradition that honors one's ancestors.

At Topaz and elsewhere, students were encouraged to join the YMCA and the YWCA, the American Red Cross, and Future Farmers of America. Some played cards, chess, checkers, or hopscotch, while others joined glee clubs or took dance classes—the choices at Topaz were tap and ballet. Sports included everything from Ping-Pong and judo to boxing and, of course, baseball. Baseball proved to be the national pastime inside the barbed wire as much as it was outside of it. Some centers had as many as 117 teams playing in different leagues, complete with uniforms, coaches, umpires, and hotly contested championships. Sometimes the guards were the players' biggest fans: They would put down their rifles and cheer when someone smacked a double to left field or pulled off a late-inning, rally-ending double play.

. . .

Kiyo and I and all the other children finally had a school. *During the first year, teachers had been volunteers; equipment had been make-shift; classes were scattered all over camp, in mess halls, recreation rooms, wherever we could be squeezed in. Now a teaching staff had been hired. Two blocks were turned into Manzanar High, and a third block of fifteen barracks was set up to house the elementary grades. We had blackboards, new desks, reference books, lab supplies.*

—Jeanne Toyo **Wakatsuki** (Houston), female, Nisei, Santa Monica, California, incarcerated age 8, Manzanar Reception Center, Manzanar Relocation Center[190]

In addition to the regular school sessions and the recreation pro-gram, classes of every kind were being offered all over camp: sing-ing, acting, trumpet-playing, tap-dancing, plus traditional Japanese arts like needlework, judo, and kendo. The first class I attended was in baton twirling, taught by a chubby girl about fourteen named Nancy. In the beginning I used a sawed-off broomstick with an old tennis ball stuck on one end. When it looked like I was going to keep at this, Mama ordered me one like Nancy's from the Sears, Roebuck catalogue. Nancy was a very good twirler and taught us younger kids all her tricks. For months I practiced, joined the baton club at school, and even entered contests. . . .

[My brother] Ray, a few years older, played in the six-man touch football league, sometimes against Caucasian teams who would come in from [nearby towns]. My sister Lillian was in high school and singing with a hillbilly band called The Sierra Stars—jeans, cowboy hats, two guitars, and a tub bass. And my oldest brother, Bill, led a dance band called the Jive Bombers. . . . Dances were held every weekend in one of the recreation halls.

—Jeanne Toyo **Wakatsuki** (Houston), female, Nisei, Santa Monica, California, incarcerated age 8, Manzanar Reception Center, Manzanar Relocation Center[191]

We had a large rhythm band of children. All these were nursery and kindergarten children, yet they put on shows for the whole center.

—June Hisaye (Abe) **Toshiyuki**, female, Nisei, Fresno, California, incarcerated age 28, Fresno Assembly Center, Jerome Relocation Center[192]

It was called Manzanar Secondary High School. I went from the ninth to the twelfth grade. My older sister and I were on the baseball team, the Fighting Nine.

—Mary Haruko **Matsuno** (Makino), female, Nisei, Terminal Island, California, incarcerated age 14, Manzanar Reception Center, Manzanar Relocation Center[193]

Sports were real important. We'd get up and play basketball, baseball. I was on the basketball team, and I helped coach football. I remember we had to buy our own baseballs and basketballs from [the] Sears [catalog], and our own uniforms and set up our own league. We had championship playoffs. It's funny but I think sports were one of

*the key factors that kept people from going astray or feeling dissatisfied
in camp. If it weren't for those athletic leagues, I think there would
have been more dissension.*

—Jack Shigeru **Matsuoka**, male, Nisei, Watsonville, California,
incarcerated age 17, Salinas Assembly Center, Poston Relocation
Center[194]

*In some ways, I suppose my life was not too different from a lot
of kids in America between the years 1942 and 1945. I spent a good
part of my time playing with my brothers and friends, learned to shoot
marbles, watched sandlot baseball and envied the older kids who wore
Boy Scout uniforms. We shared with the rest of America the same movies, screen heroes and listened to the same heartrending songs of the
forties. We imported much of America into the camps because, after
all, we were Americans.*

—John Yoshio **Tateishi**, male, Sansei, Los Angeles, California,
incarcerated age 3, Manzanar Reception Center, Manzanar
Relocation Center[195]

• • •

High school graduation ceremonies were a big deal, complete with
diplomas and stirring speeches by valedictorians. At Topaz, caps and
gowns were borrowed from the University of Utah. Thirty thousand
Japanese American students went to school in the camps, and seven
thousand graduated behind barbed wire.

• • •

*We, who are graduating tonight and all fellow Nisei and Sansei are
living proofs that the efforts and struggles of our immigrant parents
were not in vain. We represent all their labors, their sweat, their suf-
ferings, their tears, their dreams and prayers in this land. We are all
they have lived and worked for. And now, now that we have reached
young manhood and womanhood, we must individually prove to them
that . . . their faith in us is justified. Tonight, we are getting more than*

a diploma. We are getting an opportunity to prove our trust in our country. . . . With the past, the American heritage given us by right of birth, and with the past, the enviable past given us by our parents, we must continue their fight and our fight for not only existence but for a glorious future.

—Alice Natsuko **Nakamura** (Nishikawa), female, Nisei, Manteca, California, incarcerated age 17, Stockton Assembly Center, Rohwer Relocation Center[196]

• • •

It was June 1942. Only six months after Pearl Harbor, the US Navy had just defeated the Imperial Japanese Navy at the Battle of Midway in one of the greatest naval battles in history. The Midway Islands, a coral atoll in the central Pacific Ocean, were an unincorporated territory of the United States, with a total land mass of 2.4 square miles. Japan's loss at Midway meant that an attack by Japan on the American homeland could no longer be considered a threat, if it ever had been.

Back home, the Native Sons of the Golden West were about to bring a lawsuit before the federal district court. Ulysses Sigel Webb, a Republican lawyer who had served as the nineteenth attorney general of California for almost thirty-seven years, agreed to argue the case on behalf of John T. Regan, grand secretary of the Native Sons of the Golden West. With support from the American Legion, the Native Sons of the Golden West sued Cameron King, the registrar of voters in San Francisco County, demanding he remove ninety Nisei American citizens from the voter rolls for the August 1942 primaries. In court Webb said the case dealt with "the citizenship and right to citizenship of all peoples and all races who do not fall within the characterization or description of white people," and on the basis of White supremacist ideology, he believed the Declaration of Independence and the Constitution had been made entirely "by and for white people."

The judge ruled against the plea, citing the landmark 1898 Supreme Court case of Wong Kim Ark, a Chinese American who was born in

San Francisco in 1873. After his parents returned to China, Wong went to visit them. The first time, he had no problem coming back into the United States. However, the second time he visited them, he was denied reentry. Even though Wong had been born in the United States, the government reasoned that he was not an American citizen because his parents were aliens. In 1895, Wong, at the age of twenty-two, sued the federal government, and three years later he won. The Supreme Court ruled in a 6–2 majority opinion that under the Four-teenth Amendment, Wong Kim Ark was an American citizen by birth-right, regardless of the citizenship of his parents. Webb then appealed the Native Sons of the Golden West decision to the Ninth Circuit Court of Appeals.

JACL National President Saburo Kido and former JACL President Walter Tsukamoto, both lawyers, wanted to prepare an amicus brief in opposition to the appeal (in Latin *amicus curiae* means "friend of the court"). But Kido and Tsukamoto were incarcerated in concentration camps and had no access to files or law books to organize a proper case. So they reached out to Hugh MacBeth Sr., a Black attorney and leader of California's Race Relations Commission, as well as to Thomas L. Griffith, president of the Southern California branch of the National Association for the Advancement of Colored People (NAACP), and A. L. Wirin of the Southern California ACLU, who joined the brief as counsel. The brief argued that the lawsuit threatened all people of color in the United States, not just the Nisei.

Two days later Webb argued that the Wong Kim Ark case had been "erroneously decided." Wirin was just about to present the JACL's position when the judges broke to discuss the briefs among themselves and then ruled to sustain the lower court's ruling, declaring it "not necessary" for the JACL to present its argument at all. Webb made one last-ditch appeal to the Supreme Court, but the court officially declined to hear the case a few months later. One can only think what might have happened to the Native Sons' lawsuit if Wong Kim Ark had not acted on his courage to fight for his rights and won his Supreme Court case over forty years earlier.

At the same time, the government's lawyers for the WRA were coming to grips with the certain knowledge that the Western Defense Command's "military necessity" rationale for keeping the Japanese Americans indefinitely imprisoned was unsustainable. In fact, they understood that the indefinite detention of 120,000 persons without individually charging them with a specific crime was a constitutional violation, just as the Justice Department had argued, making the entire so-called relocation effort vulnerable to judicial attack. American Nisei had already started filing lawsuits against the government, seeking their release through writs of habeas corpus. By pursuing habeas petitions, the detainees were exercising the right of prisoners to get a ruling in the courts on the legality of their imprisonment. This Constitutional right is so important that habeas corpus has been suspended only four times since the Constitution was ratified in 1788: once throughout the entire country during the Civil War, in eleven South Carolina counties overrun by the Ku Klux Klan during Reconstruction, in two provinces of the Philippines during a 1905 insurrection, and in Hawaii after the bombing of Pearl Harbor.

• • •

If, in the judgment of the military and federal authorities, evacuation of Japanese residents from the West Coast is a primary step toward assuring the safety of this nation, we will have no hesitation in complying with the necessities implicit in this judgment. But if, on the other hand, such an evacuation is primarily a measure whose surface urgency cloaks the desires of political or other pressure groups who want us to leave merely for motives of self-interest, we feel we have every right to protect and to demand equitable judgment of our merits as American citizens.

—Mike Masaru **Masaoka**, male, Nisei, North Platte, Nebraska, age 26 when Pearl Harbor was attacked[197]

*One hundred thousand persons were sent to concentration camps
on a record that couldn't support a conviction for stealing a dog.*
—Eugene V. Rostow, dean of Yale Law School, 1955–65[198]

•   •   •

The WRA attorneys were especially worried about a lawsuit that
had been brought by Mitsuye Endo, a young Nisei woman from Sacramento. On April 2 the State Personnel Board notified sixty-three
Nisei California state employees, including Endo, that they were
immediately suspended from their jobs. Then on April 13 the secretary of the personnel board sent each of these Nisei state employees
a statement that dismissal proceedings against them were underway.
The statement of charges alleged that they were citizens of Japan loyal
to the Emperor of Japan, and that as persons of Japanese descent,
their exposure to the public in their state positions "created discord,
hostility, unfriendliness, opposition, antagonism, disharmony [and]
truculency." While politicians were calling for them to be fired, the
Nisei state employees were ordered to report to assembly centers
under DeWitt's exclusion orders.

Working with JACL's Saburo Kido, James Purcell, an ACLU attorney, contacted Endo while she was in the Sacramento Assembly Center with her family, to see if she would be willing to be a plaintiff in
a test case challenging the State of California's pending dismissal of
Nisei state employees. Purcell's strategy was for Endo, an American
citizen, to file a habeas corpus petition on the basis that the federal
government was unlawfully detaining her, depriving her of her right
to return to her job.

What made Endo such a strong plaintiff were factors that pointed
to her loyalty to the United States (or, to put it another way, factors that
gave no reason to suspect she would have any loyalty to Japan). She was
Christian, not a Buddhist; she did not speak or read Japanese; she had
never been to Japan; and she had a brother serving in the US Army. If
a court determined that there was no reason to suspect that Endo was

a dangerous person to the United States, and the government had no basis for the "military necessity" of indefinitely detaining such a person, then the entire evacuation-exclusion-detention program of the Western Defense Command and the WRA would be finished. The JACL also believed that a habeas corpus challenge represented the strongest legal basis for getting the Japanese Americans released from the camps.

To protect against cases like Endo's and others like hers, the WRA attorneys advised Myer and the WRA administration to have a process by which the Nisei could apply to leave the camps after there was some determination that they were not a security risk—exactly what DeWitt and Bendetsen had claimed the government did not have time to do. But now the government argued that by giving the incarcerees a pathway to leave the camps, the Japanese Americans could not claim that they were being detained against their will and that the government was violating their constitutional right to habeas corpus and due process.

Myer supported the leave concept. He saw the WRA relocation centers as "undesirable institutions" that invariably resulted in an unhealthy atmosphere; he was particularly concerned about the effect that incarceration was having on young people. He disagreed with the administration and military officials who wanted these Japanese Americans of all ages to remain in the camps "for the duration." He wanted to get them out as quickly as possible so they could resettle into communities where they could reenter mainstream American life. He had the support of outspoken First Lady Eleanor Roosevelt, who also advocated for finding ways that Nisei students could continue their educations. Even FDR himself—now that he was suddenly confronted with the growing and formidable costs and complications resulting from Executive Order 9066—was eager to have the Japanese Americans resettled away from the West Coast and get the issue behind him.

Needless to say, politicians, congressional committees, the American Legion, and the media strenuously objected to the leave clearance concept. DeWitt, New York City Mayor Fiorello La Guardia, and Earl

Warren, now governor of California, were among those who spoke out against the leave proposal. La Guardia asked why, if Japanese Americans were so dangerous that they had to be put into prison camps, it was now okay for the government to send them to New York. Myer was accused of nothing less than pampering potential terrorists.

Nevertheless, in July 1942, Myer announced a leave clearance plan that would give selected incarcerees options for leaving the camps, in some cases permanently, to areas outside the West Coast, which remained off-limits.

The able-bodied, who would rather do anything than sit idle inside the camps, took advantage of the various leave options. Others knew they should venture out of the camps—for their own good—but were still reluctant. Some feared random hostility or were just too daunted by the complicated requirements. Many couldn't understand why anyone would want to leave voluntarily. Still others, like the Issei, were afraid that the family unit could be permanently impaired if one member of the family left the camp for good, leaving the other family members behind. Of course, the vast majority of incarcerees had no choice but to stay put—especially the Issei, children, young teenagers, and the infirm. But at least by then many relocation centers had evolved into fully functioning communities.

• • •

By fall [1942], Camp Minidoka had bloomed into a full-grown town. Children went to school in the barracks, taught by professional teachers among the evacuees and people hired from the outside. Except for the members of the administration staff at the main building and the head of the hospital staff, the evacuees themselves supplied the entire labor pool in the camp, in the mess halls, in the hospital, on the farm, on roadwork, and in internal policing.

—Monica Kazuko **Itoi** (Sone), female, Nisei, Seattle, Washington, incarcerated age 23, Puyallup Assembly Center, Minidoka Relocation Center[199]

The Topaz Public Library . . . originated in October 1942, a time when the camp as a whole was not yet completed, and the library grew along with the camp. The library's official opening was delayed until December, after the transfer of approximately five thousand books, cartons of periodicals, and boxes of supplies from the Tanforan Assembly Center. The books, crated in boxes made from the dismantled shelves of the Tanforan Library for shipping to Topaz, were donated by California schools, colleges, and public libraries as well as by individuals.

—Toyo **Suyemoto** (Kawakami), female, Nisei, Alameda County, California, incarcerated age 26, Tanforan Assembly Center, Topaz Relocation Center[200]

When my youngest daughter and I left the camp people laughed at us. They said, "What are you going to do outside? If you stay in the camps, they will feed you. It is so comfortable here. Are you looking for trouble outside?"

—Kazuko (Ikeda) **Hayashi**, female, Issei, Salinas, California, incarcerated age 56, Salinas Assembly Center, Poston Relocation Center[201]

Life here has made me soft and indolent. . . . I'm clothed, sheltered, and I don't have to worry about where my next meal is coming from. . . . I want to prolong this sort of life but [if] I procrastinated I'll be here for the duration and I don't want to be here when the war ends. My better conscience tells me that the sooner I re-establish myself in a normal American community, the better I will be prepared to meet the postwar future.

—George "Jobo" Ryoji **Nakamura**, male, Nisei, Berkeley, California, incarcerated age 35, Tule Lake Relocation Center[202]

• • •

First came seasonal leaves given to those who could help White farmers in the Rocky Mountain states of Utah, Idaho, Montana, and Wyoming harvest their sugar beets—an essential contribution to the war effort. Sugar beets could be juiced and boiled to enable the extraction of sugar and create a liquid called mash. Mash could then be fermented and distilled to extract an industrial alcohol that could be used to make synthetic rubber and munitions. According to the US Beet Sugar Association, in 1943, "whenever a sixteen-inch gun was fired, one-fifth of an acre of sugar beets went up in smoke."

The very states that didn't want the Japanese to resettle in their towns now desperately wanted them as minimum-wage laborers to save their sugar beet harvest, as long as the workers remained under armed guard and faced criminal penalties for "escaping" or violating the terms of their leaves. Willing to do backbreaking labor under harsh conditions to escape the monotony of camp life, nearly ten thousand Japanese Americans—Nisei children and teenagers as well as Issei—were working in the beet fields by mid-October 1942.

• • •

After spending the summer months of '42 in Tule [Lake], we heard that workers were needed to harvest sugar beets in Idaho. Being 14, I felt this was my chance to leave the camp. . . . I was the youngest of three teenagers who decided to go to Caldwell, Idaho . . . housed in a Farm Security Administration (FSA) camp. The farmers would come with their trucks and pick out the number of workers they needed. I was shocked to see the signs around town that said, "No Japs Allowed." On the way to the farms, we were harassed and cursed. Here we were, helping out in the war effort, harvesting sugar beets, being paid a minimal wage, and being treated in this manner. The bitterness and frustration from that experience are still with me. . . . In the summer of '43, again, we heard that the farmers now in Burly, Idaho needed workers to hoe their sugar beets and onions. Again, I decided to leave camp and when we arrived there, we were met by a farm supervisor who led us to a large horse barn, one-third of which was filled with hay. He told us this was where we were going to sleep. . . . The most painful incident that happened while in Burly was when one evening twelve local punks made six [Minidoka] teens crawl about 250 feet on their hands and knees through the center of the city park and they returned to the barn horrified and crying.

—George **Taketa**, male, Nisei, King County, Washington, incarcerated age 13, Pinedale Assembly Center, Tule Lake Relocation Center, Heart Mountain Relocation Center[203]

• • •

Short-term leaves allowed incarcerees to make short trips to take care of personal affairs, such as medical appointments or family emergencies, or just to take a break from camp for the day.

• • •

Five of us girls from the block took passes to go to this little town, Cody [Wyoming]. We were around fifteen years old. We thought, Oh, this is great. We're going to go out there and have a soda. We got on the bus, and everybody is staring at us, I mean like something from Mars. We started giggling and laughing throughout the whole thing. We went into a drugstore and sat down, ready to order. Nobody would come. Finally they brought out this sign that says, "We don't serve Japs." We looked at that and we didn't know what to do. We said we didn't want anything anyway. We were devastated. All we did the rest of the day was wait for the bus so we could get back to camp. Even after we got back, we laughed. We made a big joke about it. We didn't know how to deal with it.

—Lillian Reiko **Sugita** (Nakano), female, Sansei, Honolulu, Hawaii, incarcerated age 14, Jerome Relocation Center, Heart Mountain Relocation Center[204]

• • •

Indefinite leaves could be granted for those who had identified a job outside of the West Coast. At first blush, the possibilities for Nisei young adults seemed promising. Thousands of jobs were available in factories, business offices, hotels, and restaurants, all of which were offering high wartime salaries. This was especially true in cities like

Chicago, where a large segment of the labor force had gone off to war.

But endless bureaucratic red tape was bogging down the approval process for granting leaves. First, the applicants had to supply paperwork proving that a job was available and that the prospective employer had agreed to be a sponsor. Next, they had to provide three recommendations from White people who had known them before their removal. Only then could they apply to the camp's project director for permission to leave. The project director would then petition the WRA's regional office, which would consult with the FBI. The FBI would then investigate the community where the job was located to make sure its residents would accept Japanese Americans. And finally, the FBI would check the applicant's extensive files for any derogatory information or reason to believe he or she was disloyal.

This incredibly cumbersome process could take as long as three months, by which time the job was most likely filled. As a result, by the end of December 1942, approximately 2,200 incarcerees had applied for leave clearance, but only about two hundred job leave applications had been approved. To Myer, these numbers were just a trickle. Moreover, many Nisei who wanted to apply for leave faced opposition from their parents and were even discouraged by fellow incarcerees.

For those Nisei who persevered through the application process, the job leave option was a lifeline for them to leave camp. The WRA opened branch offices in Cleveland, Chicago, Minneapolis, Salt Lake City, and other cities across the country to assist in their resettlement. As the Nisei left camp, the WRA offered them pamphlets titled *How to Make Friends* and *How to Behave in the Outside World*, and admonished them to keep a low profile. But there were some who could not withstand the loneliness on the outside.

• • •

I told my wife, "I don't want to be in camp more than one year." I left one day before the year was up.

—Kazuo **Masuda**, male, Nisei, Livingston, California, incarcerated

age 33, Merced Assembly Center, Granada (Amache) Relocation
Center[205]

*I got a sponsorship from the YWCA in Madison, Wisconsin. I
told my mother, "I'm leaving." She didn't want me to go because my
brothers were up for draft status. I said, "I can't stay here. I just cannot
stay. . . . You came from a country to another land where you didn't
speak the language. You didn't know the people. You didn't even know
the husband you were going to marry, and you've lived here for forty
years. I've lived here all my life. I can speak English. I know I can get
by all right." "They're going to beat you up," she said. I said, "I don't
think so, but I've got to go and see."*
    —Sueko "Sue" **Kunitomi** (Embrey), female, Nisei, Los Angeles,
    California, incarcerated age 19, Manzanar Reception Center,
    Manzanar Relocation Center[206]

*It is good to have somewhere to go in the morning, a place to work,
and in the evening, somewhere to return. That may sound strange; it is
so commonplace. But it is not so for me. Only three weeks ago we were
behind the barbed wire of a War Relocation Authority project, a drab,
desert city of tarpaper barracks.*
    —Robert Ritsuro **Hosokawa**, male, Nisei, Seattle, Washington,
    incarcerated age 24, Puyallup Assembly Center, Minidoka Relocation
    Center[207]

· · ·

Frank Bunya left camp, with his mother's grudging approval, to find
work in Salt Lake City. Work was difficult to find, so he subsisted on
water and half a hot dog a day (splitting one with his roommate). His
sister Emi had to send him rent money. He tried cleaning chickens at
a poultry house, but the working conditions were so bad that he didn't
last a day. He eventually found jobs as a dishwasher in two different
restaurants.

. . .

*My roommate worked at night. I worked during the day. I never
saw him. . . . So all I did was work, go back home, sleep and work the
next day. Every other week I would treat myself to a movie. I was only
seventeen and it was very lonesome all by myself. So after three months
I decided to go back to camp.*

—Frank Nobuo **Bunya**, male, Nisei, Seattle, Washington,
incarcerated age 16, Puyallup Assembly Center, Minidoka Relocation
Center[208]

*I graduated from high school in Jerome [Arkansas] in May or June
1943. They were asking young people to get out of camp, and I wanted
to go. The girls who lived in the same barracks with us were out
already. My girlfriend wrote from Chicago and said there were a lot
of jobs and they were having a lot of fun. The Edgewater Beach hotel
in Chicago, one of the biggest hotels there, said they needed "salad
girls." I got the permit to go out, but my dad said, "No. . . ." I obeyed
him and didn't go. I worked in the hospital for six months. But good
reports were coming back from Chicago. After six months, my father
said O.K., and my mother packed my suitcase. I . . . got an apartment
in Chicago with some girlfriends. One day when we went to do some
shopping, a bunch of women on the sidewalk started yelling. It was like
they thought Japan had invaded Chicago, and they were scared and
running away from us. It gave us a funny feeling.*

—Sumiko "Sumi" **Seo** (Seki), female, Nisei, Los Angeles, California,
incarcerated age 18, Santa Anita Assembly Center, Jerome Relocation
Center[209]

Sept. 3, 1943

Dear Miss Breed, . . .
    As I recall, you asked in your last letter if I applied for

leave. Well, I have not as yet. . . . At the present time, I am trying awfully hard to convince my father that I should go out, but he feels I should wait a little while. He believes I am too young, in mind if not in age. But at the rate I am pestering him, he'll give in sooner or later, unless his patience holds out! . . . But just you wait and see, I'll be writing soon saying, "I'm finally going out Miss Breed!" Oh what happy days that will be. But on the other hand, the thought of leaving my father leaves me hesitant. . . .

> *Most respectfully,*
> *Louise Ogawa*

—Louise Yoshiko **Ogawa** (Watanabe), female, Nisei, San Diego, California, incarcerated age 18, Santa Anita Assembly Center, Poston Relocation Center[210]

• • •

High school students, and Nisei who were in college at the time of Executive Order 9066 and were forced to withdraw from schools on the West Coast, could apply for admission to inland universities and, if admitted, could request permission to leave camp to continue their education.

The American Friends Service Committee (the Quakers) organized the National Japanese American Student Relocation Council (NJASRC), which created a process for identifying colleges that would accept Nisei high school graduates and transfer students and support their resettlement. The NJASRC worked with Japanese American leaders who were not in camp, philanthropic foundations, churches, and college administrators to help the Nisei students in the application process and review their applications.

The process of applying for student leave was not for the fainthearted. Some institutions refused to issue the transcripts of their former students of Japanese descent. All applicants had to submit evidence that they had sufficient financial resources for college expenses, which meant their parents had to make incredible sacrifices and students had to anticipate working long hours while in school to make ends meet. They also had to arrange for a statement from a public official in the college community that said they would "fit in" there.

Since the beginning of the war, the War Department had prohibited colleges or universities from accepting students of Japanese ancestry if the institutions or their home cities were engaged in defense-funded research or ongoing defense production. Because of this prohibition, most major universities outside California, Washington, Oregon, and Arizona—such as the Massachusetts Institute of Technology (MIT) and all Ivy League schools—were completely inaccessible to Nisei students. College applicants had to pass an FBI security check and confirm that their target institutions were not on the War Department's restricted list.

After the defense funding restriction was lifted in 1944, the Nisei applicants had to complete an additional "personal security" questionnaire. Generally, institutions in the Midwest—such as Wayne State University, Case Western Reserve University, and Washington University in St. Louis, as well as those with religious affiliations—were more open to having Japanese students. However, some Nisei applicants found that even after they were accepted and cleared for leave, their hopes could still be dashed. The University of Idaho admitted six Nisei students in the fall of 1942 but bowed to anti-Japanese community pressure and rescinded those admissions. As the tide of the war turned more favorably toward the United States, the University of Idaho resumed admitting Japanese American students the following year.

High school students in their final year before graduation were also able to apply for college leave. But standardized tests showed that incarcerated students had fallen more than a year behind their normal grade levels. Many students simply gave up on those dreams altogether. Of those who persevered, some found that colleges would not recognize their camp high school diplomas as being from an accredited institution, despite the WRA's claim that the camps' high school curriculum met accreditation standards. Sometimes the universities wouldn't admit the applicants just because they were Japanese students coming from a camp.

• • •

At my first opportunity, in March 1943, I left camp to attend school in Milwaukee, Wisconsin. On my way, I was harassed by MPs checking for my ID number and [Leave Clearance] pass many times. I even got spat upon by some of the passengers on the train. When I arrived in Milwaukee, I discovered that the engineering school had misrepresented themselves and only wanted my money. Then I moved to Chicago, Illinois, and with the help of the American Friends Service Committee, I found a job in a box factory. I worked there for three months. Then I tried to enroll in a school of engineering at the University of Illinois, but when I told them I was an evacuee from camp, they refused my admission. I told them of my WRA clearance, but my protests went unheeded. Finally, I was accepted at the University of Michigan in Ann Arbor, because I listed my Chicago address and did not mention internment.

—Richard "Dick" **Nishi**, male, Nisei, Yolo County, California, incarcerated age 21, Turlock Assembly Center, Gila River Relocation Center[211]

• • •

When the college student release option was reported to the public, letters flooded in to the press, legislators, and even First Lady Eleanor Roosevelt, objecting to "Japanese-American students being sent to college while our American boys are sent to war." One letter writer to the editor of the *Sacramento Bee* complained, "Our boys [are] giving up their schools and homes and all good and decent things to go and fight the yellow devils and in their absence, the Japanese are allowed to attend our very own schools . . . taking what rightfully belongs to our own boys."

The Daughters of the American Revolution wrote to the War Department, saying, "Jap students are being allowed to continue their studies and professions, but not our boys" and "our boys are being killed, but Japs are sitting cozy on the dole of Uncle Sam."

And yet even in the face of such hostility, approximately 4,300 Nisei students took advantage of the college leave option to attend more than six hundred institutions. For those students, the support of the NJASRC made their futures possible. But the government's harm to their education was one of the greatest losses suffered by the Nisei generation.

• • •

No matter what has happened in the past, America is still my country. This is where my children will be born and will grow up.

—George **Aki**, male, Nisei, Berkeley, California, incarcerated age 28, Tanforan Assembly Center, Topaz Relocation Center, Jerome Relocation Center[212]

PART THREE

THE YEARS BETWEEN

My name is Kaizo Kubo. I have a story to tell. It concerns three years of my past, years which will no doubt leave their marks on me to the end of my days. My name probably sounds strange, foreign; so will my story.

I am an American, although for the last three long years I have been so in name only. I am writing these very words behind the shadows of barbed wire. I've done no wrong. My only crime is that my hair is black, my skin yellow, my eyes slant; because I am of Japanese ancestry. This is my personal account of prejudice and of human blindness. This is a plea for future justice and tolerance.

I was born in a small town in California not far from the Pacific Ocean. If not for an unfortunate quirk of fate, I would in all probability have never stirred from the scene of so many happy memories. That black day I read the news in the daily papers left me momentarily paralyzed. I stared in mute incredulity at the words emblazoned in bold print: GOVERNMENT ORDERS MASS REMOVAL OF ALL JAPANESE FROM COAST HOMES TO INLAND WAR CENTERS.

I took it hard. It meant leaving the only life I knew, parting with my boyhood friends. It spelled goodbye to life. Was this what I had believed in? Was this democracy?

In the ensuing weeks I was spared little time to brood or to think. In the upheaval that followed, we lost our home. Our belongings were either discarded or at best sold at pitiful losses. Before my very eyes my world crumbled.

From the instant I stepped into the barbed wire enclosures of our destination, I felt that queer alienable presence within me. All the rash bravado I had saved for this precise moment vanished like a disembodied soul. I suddenly felt incredibly small and alone. So this was imprisonment.

The oppressive silhouette of the guard towers looming cold and dark in the distance affected me in only one way. They seemed to threaten, to challenge me. I hated their ugly hugeness, the power they symbolized. I hold only contempt for that for which they stand. They kept poignantly clear in my mind the unescapable truth that I was a prisoner.

Thus my life as an evacuee began, with a government granted broom, a bucket, and a twelve-by-twenty-foot room. We were quartered in converted horse stables which fairly reeked with evidence of recent occupation. Men, women, and children shared these discomforts alike. I learned to eat with strangers, to wash and bathe side by side with unfamiliar faces, and I learned that to hear and not be heard was the best or at least the most healthful policy to follow.

At first I was inclined to think my imagination was provoking the wall of silence that seemed to shroud my being, but it was real, as real as evacuation itself. An incomprehensible air of tension hung over the confines of the entire center. Twenty thousand souls brooding. It was not pleasant. The next abruptly discernable phase was a lifting of the silence and in a surprisingly short time, the atmosphere had changed to a noisy, equally unpredictable show of human emotions. Camp life is like that—uncertain.

Three years of a hard existence behind steel and armed guards, no matter what the conditions, cannot go without its ill effects. Our family, like most Japanese families prior to evacuation, was very close. Today, after these years of communal living, I find myself stumbling over words as I make vain attempts to talk to my father. I don't understand him; he doesn't understand me. It is a strange feeling to find such a barrier between my father and myself.

The fixed routine existence offers little incentive for progress; hence, a gradual loss of individual enterprise and initiative is in evidence. I have undergone a similar period of lethargy myself. It is like living in a realm of forgotten people. It was a strange and disturbing malady developed under unusual circumstances, but I overcame it, and with the restoration I won back my faculty of logical and clear thinking.

Here is what I say: there is no need to be bitter. We are situated thus through no fault of our own, but there is nothing to gain by eternally brooding for things that might have been. I have exacted lessons from my past which I hope to put to advantage in my future.

I shall be on my own. It will be no new experience for me. Evacuation was a pioneering project; re-establishing myself into the American stream of life can be looked upon as another such enterprise. Now I stand on the threshold of freedom. I face the future unafraid, proud of my ancestry, but even prouder of my heritage as an American.

by Kaizo George Kubo, 17 years old
Honorable Mention (among 6,000 entries)
Scholastic Magazine Literary Contest
Poston Relocation Center

—Kaizo "K" George **Kubo**, male, Nisei, San Diego, California, incarcerated age 14, Santa Anita Assembly Center, Poston Relocation Center[213]

CHAPTER SEVEN

The Loyalty Questionnaire

In the months before the riot, the bells rang often at our mess hall,
sending out the calls for public meetings. They rang for higher wages,
they rang for better food, they rang for open revolt, for patriotism, for
common sense. . . . Some meetings turned into shouting sessions. Some
led to beatings. One group tried to burn down the general store. Assas-
sination threats were commonplace.

— Jeanne Toyo **Wakatsuki** (Houston), female, Nisei, Santa Monica,
California, incarcerated age 8, Manzanar Reception Center,
Manzanar Relocation Center[214]

From December 7, 1941, to late fall 1942, Japanese Americans
had endured one crisis after another. Throughout it all they had
remained steadfastly focused on one thing: survival. The initial
shock that had characterized their first year of incarceration was
wearing off, and in its place had come the painful reality that they
were prisoners of the US government. They had no idea when, if
ever, they would be freed. What's more, the WRA's public relations campaign continued to characterize the incarceration as the
"opportunity" given to Japanese Americans to demonstrate their
patriotism.

Add to this Dillon Myer's relationship with JACL leadership,
especially Mike Masaoka, who'd been helping him form WRA policy
and identify "known agitators" so they would be separated from the
other incarcerees. Many were already suspicious of the JACL. James
Omura was among those who accused the JACL of having sold the
Japanese American community down the river, publishing editorials
critical of the JACL in his magazine, *Current Life.*

It wasn't long before frustrations among the inmates boiled over. JACL leaders and anyone suspected of being an "informer" or being too cozy with the administration was called *inu*, or "dog," in a derogatory way. Anti-administration gangs formed, including a pro-Imperial group at Manzanar called the Black Dragons, who took to beating up anyone they considered *inu*. And as far as the WRA was concerned, anyone who staged protests against its policies was considered disloyal.

Suspicion of the JACL leaders ran particularly deep among those in Manzanar, where most of the population had come from Little Tokyo in Los Angeles. In the months leading up to Pearl Harbor, many in the Little Tokyo community had suspected JACL leaders of acting as informants for the FBI and the Office of Naval Intelligence. Decades later, in 1989, the JACL commissioned an investigation into long-standing allegations that its wartime leaders had collaborated or "cooperated" with the government, and in particular, with the intelligence authorities. The report resulting from that investigation, which became known as *The Lim Report* (named after Deborah Lim, the attorney who was hired by the JACL to conduct the investigation), confirmed evidence of the JACL's wartime collaboration with the federal government. But the full report was never made public; instead a redacted version was distributed to the organization's membership. The revised report suppressed much of the critical material.

By late fall of 1942, a considerable amount of divisiveness had grown between the camp administration and the incarcerees, as well as among the incarcerees themselves. Teenagers, who tended to get caught up in any kind of action, were warned by their parents to keep their distance from any political unrest. Although the inmates mostly remained stoic on the surface, negative emotions were beginning to break through.

• • •

I don't understand those who say things like, if it hadn't been for the JACL we would never have been in camp. That's nonsense, but they

still believe it. . . . My response to them is, What would you have done?
How would you have stopped it? I don't see that there was anything
that could have stopped the evacuation from happening.

—Yoshiye **Togasaki**, female, Nisei, Los Angeles, California,
incarcerated age 38, Manzanar Reception Center, Manzanar
Relocation Center, Tule Lake Relocation Center[215]

When a human being is placed in captivity, survival is the key. We
developed a very negative attitude toward authority. We spent count-
less hours [trying] to defy or beat the system. Our minds started to
function like any POW or convicted criminal.

. . . For so many of our Issei parents, who were used to being active,
it was a slow process of deterioration, degeneration, and dying. It
could be seen on their faces, the hopelessness, uncertainty. Many with
only a few good years left lost their will to survive.

—Kinya **Noguchi**, male, Nisei, Kent, Washington, incarcerated age
14, Pinedale Assembly Center, Tule Lake Relocation Center[216]

• • •

Fred Tayama was one of those prominent JACL leaders who was
suspected of being a prewar informant. So when he and Mike Masaoka
decided to attend the November 1942 JACL national convention to
advocate for Nisei induction into combat units, Tayama knew he could
face hostility, even to the point of violence, when he returned to camp.
At the convention Masaoka argued persuasively that military service
was the only way Japanese American men could hope to be accepted
and treated equally after the war. Masaoka's goal was to win consensus
for a reinstatement of the mandatory draft for American-born Japanese so they could serve in the armed forces like any other male citizen. The appeal succeeded, and Masaoka returned to Washington,
DC, to build support on Capitol Hill. Tayama returned to Manzanar.

On the night of Saturday, December 5, 1942, two days before the
first anniversary of the attack on Pearl Harbor, six masked men beat up

Tayama in his barracks. From his hospital bed Tayama identified one of his attackers as Harry Ueno, a popular mess hall cook openly opposed to the WRA. Ueno had organized fifteen hundred incarcerees into the Mess Hall Workers Union, and he opposed any block leaders he believed were working too closely with the camp administration. Ueno had also publicly accused Manzanar's assistant project director, Ned Campbell, and the camp's chief project steward, Joseph Winchester, of black market profiteering on the sales of sugar and meat meant for the incarcerees. After the attack on Tayama, Ueno was arrested and jailed off the grounds of the concentration camp. Ueno denied participating in the attack, and many believed he was being framed by the administration in an effort to cover up the corruption activity by two of their own.

The next morning two hundred incarcerees gathered to protest Ueno's arrest. They were chanting Japanese slogans and waving Rising Sun flags, symbolic at the time of the Imperial Japanese military. Ralph Merritt, the Manzanar project director, appointed a committee of five to work with him, led by Joseph Yoshisuke Kurihara, an embittered Nisei World War I veteran. Merritt arranged for Ueno to be brought back to the Manzanar jail for trial. But later in the day an agitated crowd of more than two thousand reassembled, demanding Ueno's release. A group of over fifty men arrived at the Manzanar hospital to kill Tayama, but the female hospital workers had hidden him in blankets under a bed.

Meanwhile, a larger group of approximately five hundred had arrived at the Manzanar jail to free Ueno. Merritt declared martial law and called in the military police armed with machine guns. The MPs threw tear gas to disperse the crowd, which quickly reassembled when the strong winds blew the tear gas away.

• • •

There was some miscommunication between the director, Ralph Merritt, and the group that was demanding Ueno's release. They ended up in front of the camp entrance and the director called out the military police. And I guess the group started to chant and sing and the MPs became worried that they were going to be rushed. . . . Two young men who were just watching got pushed forward.

—Sueko "Sue" **Kunitomi** (Embrey), female, Nisei, Los Angeles, California, incarcerated age 19, Manzanar Reception Center, Manzanar Relocation Center[217]

• • •

Suddenly, without any orders to do so, the MPs opened fire, killing seventeen-year-old James H. Ito, known in the camp for raising pigeons, and shooting twenty-one-year-old Jim Kanagawa. Ten others were wounded, including an MP hit by a ricocheting bullet.

• • •

So that night, all the kitchen workers went out and rang the kitchen gongs, and they rang them all night long. Most people didn't really know what was going on because this affected only about 200 people of the entire camp, but Monday morning—it happened to be December 5th— . . . the newspapers played up that this was a group of pro-Japan people celebrating Pearl Harbor anniversary, which wasn't true at all. . . . It just happened to be a coincidence that it happened a year later.

—Sueko "Sue" **Kunitomi** (Embrey), female, Nisei, Los Angeles, California, incarcerated age 19, Manzanar Reception Center, Manzanar Relocation Center[218]

We were sixteen years old. What did we know about politics? Nothing. I didn't know why they were yelling. I didn't know why they were shooting. I didn't know what relations the JACL had with the community. Nothing. Didn't know what the JACL represented. But that was another phase of our growing up, finding that there were different elements in our community—antagonistic and some maybe more cooperative with the government. There's a lot that's been talked about, but I don't know . . . what really happened.

—Bruce Teruo **Kaji**, male, Nisei, Los Angeles, California, incarcerated age 16, Manzanar Reception Center, Manzanar Relocation Center[219]

• • •

Kanagawa died in the hospital five days later. Dr. James Goto, of Japanese ancestry, was chief of medical services at Manzanar, with six years of experience as a house surgeon at Los Angeles General Hospital before the mass removal. He examined all the shooting victims and found that all the bullets had entered them from the back or the side, proving that the victims were fleeing the scene when the shots were fired. During the inquest that followed, Dr. Goto was ordered to testify that the bullets had entered the bodies from the front, so that the military police could claim they were acting in self-defense. But Dr. Goto refused to give false testimony. Nevertheless, the board of officers from the army's Ninth Service Command found the MPs innocent. Dr. Goto was relieved of his position, and a White doctor took his place. Only one soldier attended James Ito's Buddhist burial service— his older brother, who was serving in the US Army at the time.

World War I veteran Joseph Kurihara, who, as one of the leaders of the Manzanar Riot, had tried to work with the camp administration, was transferred to and incarcerated at the Tule Lake Segregation Center. He renounced his American citizenship and, after his release from camp, lived the rest of his life in Japan. Kurihara followed through on his principles and later became recognized as a leading dissident and fighter against injustice. The Manzanar Riot and disturbances at Poston and elsewhere signaled to WRA Director Dillon Myer the seriousness of the situation evolving in the camps. He feared there would be similar blowups in the future, something he desperately wanted to prevent.

• • •

During that first summer and fall of sandy congestion and windblown boredom, the bitterness accumulated, the rage festered in hundreds of tarpapered cubicles like ours. Looking back, what they now call the December Riot seems to have been inevitable. . . . Some have called this an anniversary demonstration organized by militantly pro-Japan forces in the camp. It wasn't as simple as that. Everything just came boiling up at once.

    —Jeanne Toyo **Wakatsuki** (Houston), female, Nisei, Santa Monica, California, incarcerated age 8, Manzanar Reception Center, Manzanar Relocation Center[220]

• • •

"This was a period of my greatest anxiety," Myer said. "The month of December was a horrendous month. I didn't know what was going to happen in the other centers and whether this was a pattern that was going to develop in center after center, which some people were predicting. . . . We had not followed the recommendations of the Army when they turned the evacuees over to us to hire forty to fifty police at each of the centers from the outside, because we did not feel that it was necessary."

Myer was acutely aware of the factors that had contributed to the tensions at Manzanar. One was the high turnover of administrators—there had been five project directors in its first eight months. Promises made under one administration, like higher salaries, were broken by the next. He was also aware of the incarcerees becoming apathetic, and he feared that one of the consequences of incarceration was the emergence of a subculture in the population that would be permanently dependent on the federal government.

And then the weather turned bitterly cold.

• • •

They didn't have enough wood to heat the rooms. . . . We had to go into the woods to chop wood. All the men stopped everything; school, everything, was closed and the young people were told to go out and work. They brought the wood in, and the women helped to saw it. Then, of course, we can stoop so low as human beings; we get so greedy

and selfish. People started to hoard wood. There wouldn't be enough
for some people. . . . When we're unhappy and miserable, our sense of
values and our behavior changes. We can become hateful people.

—Mary Tsuruko (Dakuzaku) **Tsukamoto**, female, Nisei, Florin,
California, incarcerated age 27, Fresno Assembly Center, Jerome
Relocation Center[221]

The people were so wrapped up in their misery in camp, in their
own unhappiness, in their own problems, which is only to be expected,
that nobody had anything to give anybody else.

—Helen Matsue **Yamahiro** (Murao), female, Nisei, Portland,
Oregon, incarcerated age 16, Portland Assembly Center, Minidoka
Relocation Center[222]

• • •

Put simply, the leave program was not getting the incarcerees out
of the camps quickly enough; Myer had to find another way to achieve
faster resettlement. Much to his surprise, the plan materialized from a
most unexpected source—the US military.

At the time of the attack on Pearl Harbor, approximately five thousand Japanese American soldiers serving in uniform, mostly draftees,
had been instantly deemed to be disloyal. Commanders on the mainland had been given the option of discharging them honorably—or
not. Most of the soldiers had been sent to Camp Robinson in Arkansas, where their guns had been taken away, and they'd been assigned
to menial labor like collecting garbage.

On January 5, 1942, the War Department officially classified all
Japanese Americans 4-C, or "enemy aliens ineligible for the draft."
Two weeks later Lieutenant General Delos E. Emmons removed all
Japanese American soldiers from the Hawaii Territorial Guard, the
core of which consisted mostly of Japanese American students from
the Reserve Officers' Training Corps (ROTC) at the University of
Hawaii. The unit was dissolved right before target practice and then

reconstituted the next day—without the Japanese Americans.

The Japanese American ROTC students were devastated, but they decided to do something about it. With backing from the police department, the YMCA, the university, advisers to the military, and even FBI field office head Robert Shivers, they put together a petition, which they delivered to Lieutenant General Emmons. In it they declared:

> We, the undersigned, were members of the Hawaii Territorial Guard until its recent deactivation. We joined the guard voluntarily with the hope that this was one way to serve our country in her time of need. Needless to say, we were deeply disappointed when we were told that our services in the guard were no longer needed. Hawaii is our home; the United States our country. We know but one loyalty and that is to the Stars and Stripes. We wish to do our part as loyal Americans in every way possible and we hereby offer ourselves for whatever service you may see fit to use us.

Support for the young men was impressive enough that on February 25, Emmons agreed with their request. The group became known as the Varsity Victory Volunteers (VVV)—a battalion of 169 noncombat civilians (student volunteers as well as some amateur boxers off the streets of Honolulu) assigned to work with the Thirty-Fourth Combat Engineer Regiment at Schofield Barracks. It would be nearly a year before the army would lift their 4-C "enemy alien" status. In many ways, the initiative of the VVV laid the foundation for the ability of Japanese Americans to serve in the war.

Still, Lieutenant General Emmons and army chief of staff General George C. Marshall were concerned about potential warfare between Japanese Americans in Hawaii and Japanese soldiers from Japan, so they quietly shipped out all 1,432 Nisei soldiers off Oahu on the Matson liner SS *Maui* to San Francisco while the Battle of Midway was taking place. From there, cloaked in secrecy, they were transferred to Camp McCoy in Wisconsin in three different trains, to become part of a new battalion that would come to be known as the 100th Infantry Battalion (Separate), consisting of only Japanese American soldiers. The term "separate" signifies that it was an "orphan battalion," meaning it wasn't part of a larger army unit.

By the summer of 1942, as the Japanese Americans were being herded into camps, the US military was realizing that the war was going to grind on. As the battles for Guadalcanal and other strategic positions in the South Pacific were underway, the navy and marine corps leadership were beginning to estimate how many casualties the troops would likely suffer, as well as the number of deaths that might result from tropical diseases. The military leaders grimly concluded they were going to need more than a few good men; they wanted hundreds of thousands of them. Political decisions made in the overheated post–Pearl Harbor atmosphere—such as reclassifying the Nisei as ineligible for the draft—were being reconsidered. Moreover, the army's Military Intelligence Service (MIS) had determined well before the start of the war that it was going to require Japanese-language speakers for use as interpreters, translators, interrogators, propaganda writers, and radio announcers in order to fight Japan effectively.

On November 1, 1941, a little over a month before the Pearl Harbor attack, the Military Intelligence Service Language School was launched in an abandoned aircraft hangar on Crissy Field in the San Francisco Presidio. The first class included 58 Nisei soldiers who were fluent or deemed proficient in Japanese, or who were thought to have the capacity to learn Japanese quickly. A year later the MIS had quietly scouted out 167 young Japanese American men from the ten relocation centers to leave camp for MIS training. Ironically, the incarcerees with the strongest Japanese-language skills were the Kibei, the individuals who were presumably the most likely to be disloyal because of their time and education in Japan.

• • •

*I thought I [had] a fair speaking knowledge of the language, but
the interviewer quickly proved me completely inadequate. . . . First he
asked me to read a high school text [written in Japanese]. I would make
out perhaps two or three characters in a hundred.*

—William "Bill" Kumpai **Hosokawa**, male, Nisei, Seattle,
Washington, incarcerated age 27, Puyallup Assembly Center, Heart
Mountain Relocation Center[223]

*On the one hand, Japanese Americans were condemned for having
the linguistic and cultural knowledge of Japanese, and, on the other
hand, the knowledge they had was capitalized on and used as a secret
weapon by Army . . . intelligence.*

—Mark Yutaka **Murakami**, male, Nisei, Multnomah County, Oregon,
incarcerated age 32, Portland Assembly Center, Minidoka Relocation
Center[224]

• • •

Over the course of the war, the MIS trained six thousand linguists,
the majority of whom were Japanese Americans, who would go on
to interrogate more than ten thousand Japanese POWs; the language
specialists were also combatants in Guadalcanal, Papua New Guinea,
and Iwo Jima. Working individually or in small groups, the MIS linguists would parachute in with the troops and monitor communications between enemy fighter planes and control towers. They would
intercept, decipher, and translate messages and orders to ascertain
troop strength, weaponry, and future movements. The government of
Imperial Japan believed their language to be so complicated that they
didn't bother to code many of their commands and apparently hadn't
considered that Japanese Americans could be translating them.

In a war with Japan, however, the MIS Nisei faced dangers above
and beyond the possibility that they could be injured or killed—risks
assumed by all MIS men. Unlike their Caucasian comrades, the MIS

Nisei knew that if they were captured, the Japanese would execute them as traitors. At the same time, they were under constant threat of being mistaken for the enemy by American soldiers and getting killed by friendly fire.

Because the MIS served on classified and sometimes undocumented missions, the extent of the Nisei contributions was not known for decades after the war. When their records began to be declassified in the 1970s, the significance of their service was revealed. Nevertheless, Major General Charles Willoughby, chief of intelligence for General Douglas MacArthur, credited the work of the Nisei MIS interpreters with saving tens of thousands of American lives and shortening the war by as much as two years.

Meanwhile, the 100th Battalion was amassing a remarkable record during its training at Camp McCoy. Soldiers such as Spark Matsunaga, who went on to serve as one of Hawaii's US senators for thirteen years, were writing home about their great hope of proving their loyalty by serving in combat. Unbeknownst to the soldiers, their letters first went to the War Department, where they were read by censors who blacked out information that they thought was sensitive or inappropriate before sending the letters on to their intended recipients. The censors reported the contents of those letters up their chain of command, so Assistant Secretary of War John McCloy heard about the sincerity of the 100th Battalion members. This information, coupled with what he had also heard about their high caliber and exemplary performance, led McCloy to begin reconsidering DeWitt's position that Japanese Americans were inherently untrustworthy. He started pairing the idea of a Nisei combat unit with a strategy for releasing the Nikkei from detention—both of which would necessitate individual assessments of loyalty. In spite of this issue, the idea was growing within the administration that having the Nisei serve in battle would help rehabilitate Japanese American men in the public eye.

In October 1942 twenty-five soldiers were selected from the 100th at

Camp McCoy to participate in its first top secret mission on Cat Island, a subtropical barrier island at the mouth of the Mississippi in the Gulf of Mexico. War dogs were being trained to attack Japanese men by sight and smell on the premise that the Japanese had a distinctive odor. The soldiers were sent to act as bait to see if the war dogs could tell the difference between White and Asian men. The objective was for the dogs to identify and kill Japanese soldiers so White American soldiers would not have to engage in hand-to-hand combat. But the dogs were unable to differentiate between the races, so the mission failed.

At the same time, McCloy was receiving other field reports that helped solidify his thinking that the Nisei should be allowed to serve in the army. Lieutenant General Emmons in Hawaii was an especially strong advocate, saying the Nisei men would make "grand soldiers." Even the recruiters of military intelligence linguists were reporting that many Nisei men in the relocation centers resented being blocked from military roles that did not require Japanese-language skills. WRA Director Myer kept raising the issue with Assistant Secretary of War McCloy, who had just received a War Department study on the subject. Prepared by military careerists, the report recommended against the Nisei's military potential "because of the universal distrust in which they [were] held."

Then Elmer Davis, director of the newly created Office of War Information, along with his deputy, former WRA director Milton Eisenhower, took the issue to President Roosevelt, casting it as a matter of wartime propaganda. A Rhodes Scholar, Peabody Award recipient, and former editorial writer for the *New York Times*, Davis understood the importance of public relations. He wrote to the president, pointing out that Japan was using the existence of the US concentration camps to bolster its claims that the United States was conducting a race war. He argued that if Nisei men could be released from the camps to fight for their country—like any other American young man—it would combat Japanese claims of American racism. As Davis and Eisenhower had hoped, Roosevelt referred Davis's memo to Secretary of War Henry Stimson, the top War Department decision maker, which gave McCloy the opening he needed to make the case with his superior.

In his memorandum to Stimson dated October 15, 1942, McCloy recommended that the Nisei be allowed to volunteer for the army. He said the War Department study did not take into account three important considerations: Almost everyone agreed by then that most Nisei were loyal; a fundamental right of citizenship was the ability to serve one's country; and permitting the Nisei to serve would play well internationally.

Stimson dispatched a handwritten note to General Marshall that said, "I am inclined strongly to agree with the views of McCloy and Davis. I don't think you can permanently proscribe a lot of American citizens because of their racial origin. We have gone to the full limit in evacuating them. That's enough."

In the meantime, WRA Director Myer and colonels in the War Department were considering the formation of an all-Nisei combat unit, modeled after the segregated units that the military had created for Black soldiers. The idea percolated that a segregated unit under the command of White officers would increase the visibility of the service of Japanese Americans. The army commanders also thought that a segregated unit would prevent the racial tensions that could occur if the Japanese Americans were mixed in with White soldiers.

At first Myer was against the idea; both he and Mike Masaoka initially protested the concept of a *segregated* combat unit. In fact, Myer admitted that he thought the proposal was "wrong in principle." But both men came around to seeing the upside to having an all–Japanese American segregated combat team. And Masaoka was the first one to volunteer.

· · ·

Our thinking was that we [would be] inconspicuous scattered throughout the army. Individual records wouldn't prove much. The army had said that Nisei protestations of loyalty were so much hogwash. We had to have a demonstration in blood.

—Mike Masaru **Masaoka**, male, Nisei, North Platte, Nebraska, age 26 when Pearl Harbor was attacked[225]

• • •

Roosevelt tabled the army's proposal until after the November 1942 election. Two and a half months later, on January 1, 1943, General Marshall approved an all-Nisei combat team. And on January 28, 1943, just as the US Air Force was making its first air strikes on Germany, Stimson announced the organization of the 442nd Regimental Combat Team (RCT), an all–Japanese American volunteer unit of about six thousand men. The navy, led by Secretary Frank Knox, continued to bar Japanese Americans from its branch of service for the duration of the war.

• • •

I want to be able in the years to come to know that my children and their children after them will not be forced to suffer, as we have suffered, because I was not visionary enough, or courageous enough, to be baptized under the fire of enemy guns and to prove beyond all doubt that we who are Americans in spite of our Japanese faces are loyal to the land of our birth, even unto death. . . . I have a stake in America. I believe it is worth fighting for.

—Mike Masaru **Masaoka**, male, Nisei, North Platte, Nebraska, age 26 when Pearl Harbor was attacked[226]

• • •

Finally, on February 1, 1943, FDR issued a statement addressed to Secretary of War Stimson that said, in part:

The proposal of the War Department to organize a combat team consisting of the loyal American citizens of Japanese ancestry has my full approval. The new combat team will add to the nearly five thousand loyal Americans of Japanese ancestry serving in the armed forces of our country.

No loyal citizen of the United States should be denied the democratic right to exercise the responsibilities of citizenship, regardless of his ancestry. The principle on which this country was founded and by which it has always been governed is that Americanism is a matter of the mind and heart; Americanism is not, and never was, a matter of race or ancestry.

Not quite one year had passed since Roosevelt had signed Executive Order 9066, and yet the same president was now saying "Americanism is not, and never was, a matter of race or ancestry." The press responded with favorable editorials, but the Oregon senate passed a resolution opposing any Nisei serving in the military, and the Idaho legislature demanded that all Nisei be immediately discharged.

FDR's use of the word "loyal" was no accident; only *loyal* Japanese Americans would be permitted to enlist. So how would the military determine who was loyal and who was not?

• • •

President Roosevelt announced that volunteers would be accepted in a Japanese American combat unit. A recruiting team came to the center, and a printed form was submitted to all men of military age. . . . At the same time, the War Relocation Authority . . . decided to conduct a general registration of all persons in the camp seventeen years of age or older.

—Miné **Okubo**, female, Nisei, Berkeley, California, incarcerated age 30, Tanforan Assembly Center, Topaz Relocation Center[227]

• • •

On January 2, 1943, the day after General Marshall approved that Nisei could serve in the army, Joseph T. McNarney, Marshall's deputy chief of staff, convened a committee to determine "by what means Japanese-Americans of the Nisei class may be released from war relocation centers, and if released, what disposition may be made of them." One week later the committee proposed a process that they thought would create a path by which the incarcerees could leave the camps. Instead it was a path to a complete debacle.

The committee envisioned a questionnaire that would be filled out by all Nisei men over the age of seventeen. Its purpose was to filter out the men most likely to be disloyal.

Myer had not been involved in the War Department's initial planning, but once he learned of the military's intent to administer a questionnaire to draft-age Nisei men, he saw an opportunity to accelerate his leave clearance program. The WRA proceeded to piggyback the leave clearance process onto the military's loyalty clearance process. The army questionnaire was retitled "Application for Leave Clearance" and distributed to all persons in the camps age seventeen and up.

The whole procedure would be handled by a joint board, which would evaluate the questionnaire responses, conduct the loyalty hearings, and rule on whether the Japanese Americans in question could serve in the military or be allowed to leave the camps. The board would be chaired by a representative of the office of the assistant secretary of war, along with voting representatives from Office of Naval Intelligence, army intelligence, the provost marshal general's office, the War Department, the WRA, and the FBI. However, two months into the joint board process, J. Edgar Hoover withdrew the FBI from participating.

Not surprisingly, DeWitt and Bendetsen vehemently opposed the plan because it meant that the government would be making individual rulings of loyalty. After all, this was the same War Department that had incarcerated 120,000 people of Japanese ancestry partly on the principle that their loyalty was impossible to discern and trust. It had been less than a year since the War Department had spent eighty million dollars incarcerating Japanese Americans; now it was considering the very sort of screening that DeWitt and Bendetsen had refused to set up.

Bendetsen feared a public relations disaster, anticipating that the country would demand to know why, after spending millions, the government was doing what it had said could not be done. And suddenly everyone else who mattered in the War Department—including Major General Allen Gullion, McCloy, Stimson, and even FDR, the commander in chief—had decided that the loyalty of the Japanese *could* be assessed? And all the government had to do was ask them in a questionnaire? Apparently so, because after receiving General Marshall's approval to execute the loyalty plan, the committee overruled DeWitt's and Bendetsen's objections, and the War Department began working with the WRA to distribute the questionnaire.

Unfortunately, the four-page questionnaire was a total disaster. Most people were tired of filling out forms and were already suspicious of the WRA and any communications from the government. Not only was the questionnaire poorly and sloppily worded, but no one understood why it was called "Application for Leave Clearance" if it was being used for draft registration, or why they had to fill it out if they were neither eligible for the draft nor applying for leave clearance. Many suspected it was some kind of trick—if they didn't answer the questions *correctly*, then they would be *required* to leave the camp and resettle "outside," something many of them were still reluctant to do. The Nikkei were primarily concerned with keeping the families together. And nearly all of them resented being asked to prove, yet again, their undying loyalty to the US government under the pretense that their answers would remain confidential—another promise no one believed.

• • •

The registration form was long and complicated. The questions were difficult to understand and answer. Center-wide meetings were held, and the anti-administration rabble-rousers skillfully fanned the misunderstandings.

—Miné **Okubo**, female, Nisei, Berkeley, California, incarcerated age 30, Tanforan Assembly Center, Topaz Relocation Center[228]

• • •

Camp meetings about the ramifications of filling out the form were spontaneous and heated and often continued far into the night. Two questions in particular—numbers twenty-seven and twenty-eight—sparked a firestorm of reactions ranging from uncertainty and anxiety to anger and outrage.

27. Are you willing to serve in the armed forces of the United States on combat duty, wherever ordered?

28. Will you swear unqualified allegiance to the United States of America and faithfully defend the United States from any or all attack by foreign or domestic forces, and forswear any form of allegiance or obedience to the Japanese emperor, or any other foreign government, power, or organization?

Some incarcerees were afraid that by responding yes to number twenty-seven, they were agreeing to enlist. And since anyone over seventeen years old was *required* to answer these questions, many people concluded that the government was planning to send the women and old people off to war too. As if that prospect weren't frightening enough, families were worried that they all had to give the same answer in order to stay together.

Question number twenty-eight posed even deeper problems. The Issei, who were prevented by law from becoming American citizens, had no alternative but to retain their Japanese citizenship. They thought if they answered yes to question twenty-eight, they were renouncing their only nationality and they would be stateless. It could also be a trick question—if they agreed to "forswear any form of allegiance or obedience to the Japanese emperor," were they admitting that they had ever held an allegiance or obedience to the Japanese emperor in the first place? One Nisei later said the question was like "Have you stopped beating your wife?" The question itself implied guilt. Or was the question just another way of getting their agreement to serve in the military? To blindly pledge allegiance to a country that was incarcerating them was ludicrous, and the absurdity was not lost on anyone confined behind barbed wire.

Masaoka had never imagined that the method for allowing Nisei men to serve in the military would get tangled up with the WRA's leave clearance process. Calling the questionnaire a "dumb mistake,"

Masaoka saw the whole episode as "further evidence of the government's continued ignorance about Japanese Americans."

Myer and the WRA staff were shocked and caught flat-footed by the bitter reactions to the questionnaire, which became known as the "loyalty questionnaire." By the time he and others attempted to rephrase the questions and retitle the form, the damage had already been done. The episode had divided families, turned friends against friends, and undermined whatever enthusiasm or willingness there might have been for military service. There were rumors that if any of the boys answered no to both questions, they would be removed by force and sent to a special camp—which was, in fact, true.

· · ·

On the question pertaining to the loyalty oath all my family wrote yes/yes. There is a Japanese saying, "umi-no-oya yori mo sodate no oya" meaning, your adoptive parents are your real parents. America was the country of my parents' adoption and therefore was our family's country. . . . My husband was among the first 14 who volunteered from Manzanar as a special group destined to become the linguists so vital for America's final victory. One bigot on a TV show asked, "If you were so badly treated, why did you volunteer to fight for this country?" My answer is: our situation was analogous to that of battered children. We were the battered children of this country who in spite of unspeakable treatment by their parents, still love their motherland and fatherland and still strive to please them. Why? Because they know no other parents.

—Mary Sakaguchi (**Oda**), female, Nisei, Los Angeles, California, incarcerated age 22, Manzanar Reception Center, Manzanar Relocation Center[229]

In my case I registered "yes, yes" because I felt that this is the only country I have.

—Harold Norio **Ouye**, male, Nisei, Sacramento, California,

incarcerated age 35, Sacramento Assembly Center, Tule Lake
Relocation Center, Heart Mountain Relocation Center[230]

• • •

Myer and the WRA staff were just as perplexed in figuring out how
to interpret the incarcerees' answers. In the process of setting up the
questionnaire and loyalty hearing bureaucracy, no one had thought
to make a sociological assessment of what the incarceree meant by
answering no to either or both of the problematic questions. A WRA
report described the staff's dilemma:

> As WRA officials looked more carefully into the table of returns,
> the figures alone, without the aid of their real knowledge of what
> had taken place, began to reveal peculiarities that challenged
> any simple conclusion in terms of loyalty. From center to cen-
> ter there were striking differences. For instance, at Minidoka
> and Granada less than 3 percent of the young men were "No"
> answers while over 50 percent of the young men at Manzanar
> had answered "No." And so it ranged through the centers. The
> conclusion was inescapable that the motives behind the answers
> depended on many things that the questionnaire had not taken
> into account. The WRA staff in the centers knew what these
> factors were because they had seen the process and they had
> begun almost immediately to interview the young men to get at
> the meaning to them of a "No" answer.
>
> They learned in the course of interviewing to distinguish
> between the "No" of protest against discrimination, the "No" of
> protest against a father interned apart from his family, the "No"
> of bitter antagonism to subordinations in the relocation center,
> the "No" of a gang sticking together, the "No" of thoughtless
> defiance, the "No" of family duty, the "No" of hopeless confu-
> sion, the "No" of fear of military service, and the "No" of felt
> loyalty to Japan.

Of the approximately 75,000 Nisei who filled out the form, about 12 percent either answered no to question 28 or qualified a yes answer. Among male Nisei respondents, almost 22 percent answered question 28 with an unambiguous no. Those who answered no to both questions 27 and 28 became known as the No-No Boys.

Myer was facing a conundrum. He had hoped that the incarcerees would take advantage of the leave clearance program to depopulate the camps, but their resettlement was still going at a snail's pace. Myer realized that the incarcerees would not leave the camps in significant numbers—or at all—until they could return to their West Coast homes. In a letter dated March 11, 1943, he urged Stimson to rescind the exclusion orders that implemented Executive Order 9066, or at least to conduct individual hearings so that those who were determined to be loyal could leave the camps without restrictions and resume their lives in their hometowns. Myer reminded him that the WRA was carrying out its responsibilities under the assumption "that all American citizens and law-abiding alien residents of the United States should be treated by the government, insofar as possible under wartime conditions, without racial discrimination."

Myer's mission confrontation with Stimson triggered the War Department's own conundrum. McCloy admitted to Bendetsen in a phone call on April 19, 1943, that they had "never thought about" how to treat loyal Japanese persons after they were excluded; there was never a plan, let alone a consensus, for how to release the Nikkei from their incarceration. He recognized that the War Department could not maintain the deceit of "military necessity" for keeping the Japanese Americans off the West Coast, and the government couldn't very well take any actions that would expose that deception or allow the situation to look like the government was backtracking in any way. In a phone call with Captain John Hall, one of McCloy's assistants, Bendetsen repeated his earlier fears about a public affairs debacle, saying, "I'm scared to death principally because of the public relations part of it."

Secretary of the Interior Harold Ickes had alerted FDR that the morale inside the camps was deteriorating dramatically. He wrote, "I do not think that we can disregard the unnecessary creation of a hostile group right in our own territory."

In response, FDR dispatched his wife, Eleanor, to visit the Gila River concentration camp. The First Lady, who always had strenuously opposed the incarceration, reported back to the president that the Japanese Americans should be allowed to return to their homes. But FDR continued to believe that relocating the Japanese Americans "throughout the country" was the "best hope for the future." He still supported Stimson's call that before releasing the Japanese Americans from camp, any "agitators" or "troublemakers" (including the No-No Boys and their families) should be removed to a separate facility at Tule Lake. And so, as a direct result of the loyalty questionnaire, nearly five thousand No-No Boys and their families were moved to Tule Lake—the only relocation center converted by the WRA into a maximum-security prison, now referred to as a "segregation center," ruled under martial law and occupied by the US Army.

The No-No Boys and their families would be mixed in with so-called loyal incarcerees who refused to transfer out of Tule Lake for another camp. The tensions among the populations with different and strongly held perspectives, the oppressive atmosphere, and labor issues fueled protests and disturbances that got sensationalized in the press. Reports of rioting and militant pro-Japan activities by "disloyal" Japanese Americans played right into the hands of the anti-Japanese constituency, as vocal as ever in Congress. Mike Masaoka had to fend off calls on Capitol Hill to strip Japanese Americans of their citizenship.

At the same time, a growing number of Issei and Kibei were responding to the loyalty questionnaire by applying for repatriation to return to Japan. But most shocking was that the questionnaire prompted many Nisei to want to revoke their US citizenship and request expatriation to Japan, a place where most of them had never been. The groundswell of repatriation and expatriation requests ended up confirming the very suspicion of disloyalty that propelled their incarceration. In reality, those deciding to go to Japan were either protesting the whole registration process or despairing of having a future in the United States.

More than 6,000 Nisei applied to renounce their American citizenship, and the Department of Justice approved 5,589 of the renunciation applications, representing almost 8 percent of the 72,000 Nisei citizens incarcerated. In order to provide the political and constitutional cover to expel "disloyal" Nisei to Japan after the war, Congress passed the Denaturalization Act of 1944, the first ever of its kind. Even before the war was over, most of the "renunciants" regretted their decision and later tried to reverse their expatriation requests. Attorney Wayne Collins would undertake years of legal battles on their behalf to revoke their renunciations and restore their American citizenship status.

The story of Ernest Kinzo Wakayama is one heartbreaking example. Born in Kohala, Hawaii, in 1895, Wakayama was a World War I veteran; a member of the American Federation of Labor, the Republican Party, and the American Legion; and the secretary-treasurer of the fisherman's union in Los Angeles harbor. After the attack on Pearl Harbor, he was ordered to evacuate Terminal Island "under the point of a machine gun by armed sailors."

To determine if, as a World War I veteran, his detention was lawful, the ACLU filed a habeas corpus petition in his name and the name of his wife, Toki. Soon after, the US military arrested him for "knowingly and willingly attempting to overthrow the United States government," a charge made in apparent retaliation for bringing the case at all and seemingly invented in the moment by the US military. A photo of him being arrested and handcuffed at Santa Anita Assembly Center ran in the newspaper the next day. He was accused of being a traitor and incarcerated for seventy-two days in a Los Angeles jail, then held for two weeks at the Lone Pine prison near the Manzanar Relocation Center.

Wakayama was subsequently moved many times—to Pomona, Manzanar, Tule Lake, the Santa Fe Internment Camp, and the Crystal City Internment Center—as a way of punishing him for fighting for his rights, even though he had fought for his country in the First World War. He was physically assaulted and constantly threatened for pursuing the lawsuit and continuing to question his circumstances. Wakayama, who claimed to be a loyal American "regardless of race, creed or color," wrote a letter to General DeWitt, asking if a separate camp might be created for World War I veterans of Japanese ancestry—but he received no response.

And then, in another tragic turn of events, Rosalie Wax, a field worker from the Japanese American Evacuation and Resettlement Study, made a false allegation against him to the FBI, claiming he was a ruthless gang leader. Fearful that he would be wrongfully imprisoned again, Wakayama renounced his citizenship, whereupon he and his wife were deported to Japan. He never returned to the United States and remained deeply wounded by how he had been treated after having fought to defend democracy.

But perhaps the most divisive and shattering issue of the incarceration concerned the call to volunteer for the 442nd Regimental Combat Team. Many parents saw no point in having their sons (and daughters) risk their lives in defense of a democratic government that was holding them captive. Many young men were willing to enlist anyway but felt obliged to obey their parents, who forbade them from volunteering. Other sons were worried about their parents' well-being if the young men left their parents behind in camp.

• • •

The only thing I really recall thinking was, boy, I wonder what my parents would do in camp if I was—if I didn't come back.

—Kimitomo "Kim" **Muromoto**, male, Nisei, King County,

Washington, incarcerated age 19, Pinedale Assembly Center, Tule
Lake Relocation Center[231]

I didn't feel outraged. I felt that this was war, and war was an unrea-
sonable thing. . . . So when they asked for volunteers for the Army, I
volunteered.
　　—Wayne Masao **Kanemoto**, male, Nisei, San Jose, California,
　　incarcerated age 24, Santa Anita Assembly Center, Gila River
　　Relocation Center[232]

[My parents] just felt that I shouldn't be [joining the Women's Army
Corps] . . . and going so far away from home. But I told them that
I just couldn't stay home and do housework. I wasn't accomplishing
anything. . . . I said, "There is a war going on and [my brother] can't
do it alone." . . . I tried to talk my parents into letting me go, and finally
they released me and signed the consent [form].
　　—Grace **Harada**, female, Nisei, Pocatello, Idaho, age 20 when Pearl
　　Harbor was attacked[233]

There were friends fighting against friends . . . brothers fighting
against brothers . . . it was terrible. And people asked, "Why do you want
to volunteer?" I just said, "I don't understand what the argument is. Our
country is being attacked and I want to defend it. It's that simple." They
looked at me and said, "You must have holes in your head."
　　—Katsumi Thomas "Tom" **Kawaguchi**, male, Nisei, San Francisco,
　　California, incarcerated age 21, Tanforan Assembly Center, Topaz
　　Relocation Center[234]

When the Nisei combat battalion was being formed, I volunteered
and had my first fallout with my father. He thought that after all the
hardship created by the incarceration of our people, [how did I have]
the nerve even to think of joining up with the armed forces.

"We lose everything, the property, the business, our home," Papa said. "It's like kicking you in the pants and now they're saying, come in and shine my shoes."

But I explained that it was my duty to volunteer as a citizen of this country and as a citizen I must fight for our country and even die for it. He kicked me out of the barracks.

I slept in the furnace room that night because I dared not and feared going back to the barrack unit where we were staying.

It was my mother that came to me the next day and said, "If you feel that strongly about your country, then you volunteer and go. I will miss you. You may never come back. But go, I'll take care of Papa."

Strengthened by these words, I hurriedly rushed to volunteer.

—Mitsuo "Mits" **Usui**, male, Nisei, Los Angeles, California, incarcerated age 25, Santa Anita Assembly Center, Granada (Amache) Relocation Center[235]

• • •

The army had been hoping to enlist at least 3,500 Nisei out of about 10,000 eligible. But the registration in the camps on the mainland was so badly handled and the acrimony about their incarceration ran so deep that only 1,208 persons volunteered for combat. Of those who did, 805 passed their loyalty tests and physical examinations. The volunteer registration process was a stunning failure, which made the call for reinstating the mandatory draft of Nisei men even more urgent.

• • •

It was confusing that their loyalty to the United States should be questioned when the Army was asking them to volunteer.

—Miné **Okubo**, female, Nisei, Berkeley, California, incarcerated age 30, Tanforan Assembly Center, Topaz Relocation Center[236]

• • •

In contrast, Hawaii had no mass incarceration and more than 10,000 volunteered, including many men from the VVV. Of these, 2,686 were accepted.

• • •

[As soon as it was announced that Nisei men living in Hawaii were eligible to volunteer, young men] exploded into a fury of yells and motion . . . and ran—ran!—the three miles to the draft board, stringing back over the streets and sidewalks, jostling for position, like a bunch of marathoners gone berserk. And the scene was repeated all over Oahu and the other islands. Nearly 1,000 Niseis volunteered that first day alone, and maybe because I was in better shape than most of them and ran harder, I was among the first 75.

—The Honorable Daniel "Dan" Ken **Inouye**, male, Nisei, Honolulu, Hawaii, age 17 when Pearl Harbor was attacked[237]

• • •

In the meantime, political forces were now pushing to reinstate the mandatory draft of Nisei men under the Selective Training and Service Act of 1940. Myer and Masaoka continued to see military service as the key to restoring full rights to Japanese Americans after the war, and they lobbied strenuously to reopen the selective service to Japanese Americans, including those who were incarcerated. McCloy, from his vantage point as assistant secretary of war, knew that Nisei soldiers were desperately needed; the military was running short of manpower. When the number of Nisei volunteers from the camps fell far short of the expected target, army officials publicly threatened that they would simply reinstitute the draft of Japanese Americans. These factors converged to lead Secretary Stimson to announce on January 20, 1944, that Nisei males were now eligible for the draft. A new firestorm of protest and a new level of controversy erupted in the camps.

Issei parents were anguished. Stimson's announcement a year earlier had focused on the 442nd—an all-volunteer Nisei fighting force—but enlisting had not been required; the Nisei had faced no penalty if they decided not to volunteer. Now all those who deliberately refused a draft order could be charged with a federal crime, face fines, and go to prison because Stimson had lifted the Nisei ineligibility for the draft.

As the first wave of young Nisei men received orders to report for physical examinations in preparation for induction, they had to decide whether they were willing to comply. One Issei father of two draft-age Nisei sons said, "After being evacuated to this relocation center from the outside I have lost everything in worldly goods. All I have left is my family. . . . I'd rather have [my boys] go to prison and I know that they will come back alive someday."

• • •

I felt deep in my mind a turmoil, because I did not want my sons to take arms against my mother country and shed blood. I just could not bear the thought of it. On the other hand, I have received so much from this country and owe it a lot . . . [so] I had to take an absolutely neutral position. It was the only way out for me.

— Yoshisada **Kawai**, male, Issei, Seattle, Washington, incarcerated age 52, Puyallup Assembly Center, Minidoka Relocation Center[238]

• • •

Approximately three hundred Nisei in concentration camps—mostly from Poston and Heart Mountain—chose to resist the draft. Members of the Heart Mountain Fair Play Committee—the only organized draft resistance in the camps—took the position that they were not afraid to risk their lives for their country and would gladly serve in the military, but only if they could serve in nonsegregated units and only after their constitutional rights to freedom and justice had been restored. By June 1944 sixty-three members of the Heart Mountain Fair Play Committee had been arrested and were standing trial in federal court for draft evasion. They were convicted together in the largest mass trial in Wyoming history.

• • •

I was a resister as a matter of principle. After what my government did to us, I could not be in the military and kill others because they were in a different uniform. This was beyond my feelings of humanity. I couldn't do it. We lost our individual identities. We were given a fam-

ily number by our government. But the draft board put my personal name on my draft letter. I had to answer it. If nobody else agreed with my decision, so be it. I'm not willing to kill nor die until my government squared things with me. . . .

> —Yoshito "Yosh" **Kuromiya**, male, Nisei, Pasadena, California, incarcerated age 19, Pomona Assembly Center, Heart Mountain Relocation Center, Cheyenne County Jail, McNeil Island Federal Penitentiary[239]

President Roosevelt said many, many times that it was the duty of the citizens to preserve democracy. I often asked myself, "What citizens? What democracy?" At that time, we were part-time citizens and part-time aliens. . . .

To this day I can recall the event that took place at the first day of our trial. When the judge was informing us of the agenda for the following day, he referred to us as, "YOU JAP BOYS", and then quickly corrected himself[;] then and there we knew we were up against a stacked deck. Here is a man, supposedly a man of high esteem and integrity, sitting on the federal bench, [who] was nothing more than a racist and a bigot.

> —Jack Kiyoto **Tono**, male, Nisei, San Jose, California, incarcerated age 22, Santa Anita Assembly Center, Heart Mountain Relocation Center, McNeil Island Federal Penitentiary[240]

· · ·

Other Nisei draft resisters were tried in Arizona, Arkansas, California, Colorado, Idaho, and Utah. All resisters were convicted except the twenty-seven from Tule Lake. In that case, *United States v. Masaaki Kuwabara*, Judge Louis Goodman took a novel approach; he found the resisters not guilty on the basis that it was unconstitutional to imprison American citizens on the grounds of disloyalty while compelling them to serve in the military or face prosecution for not complying with orders to serve.

· · ·

And yet in the Northern California camp this group had the same format as ours from day one, and their case was dismissed because in the judge's opinion, they were deprived of their liberty without due process of the law. These men were released a free man. The "Rubber Band Justice" of the 1940's, "Damned if you do and Damned if you don't." . . .

Through all our adversities, we were able to endure the humiliations and hardships and upheld our dignity . . . because of what the Issei brought with them to this country, some of the most prized possessions of their rich, treasured philosophy and the doctrine of their heritage: dignity, honor, shame, gratitude, compassion. Otagai translates into mutual respect; okage, indebtedness. . . .

The restitution is way over due; let's clear the black clouds and the smear on the Constitution and make it work for everyone as it was written and observed.

—Jack Kiyoto **Tono**, male, Nisei, San Jose, California, incarcerated age 22, Santa Anita Assembly Center, Heart Mountain Relocation Center, McNeil Island Federal Penitentiary[241]

• • •

Those convicted received varying sentences, which they served in federal penitentiaries in Kansas, Washington, and Arizona. Jack Tono, Gordon Hirabayashi, and Yosh Kuromiya were all imprisoned at McNeil Island in Puget Sound, Washington. "McNeil Island is a federal penitentiary," Kuromiya recalled. "One does not normally go there to seek liberation. Strangely enough, that's where I discovered it—within myself."

Although President Harry S. Truman pardoned the convicted draft resisters in December 1947, they remained stigmatized by others in the Japanese American community who considered them cowards instead of patriots standing up for principles of conscience. When Tono received his presidential pardon, he tore it up and burned it.

CHAPTER EIGHT

Go for Broke

Grown men leaped with joy on learning that they were finally going to be given the chance on the field of battle to prove their loyalty to the land of their birth.

—The Honorable Spark Masayuki **Matsunaga**, male, Nisei, Kauai, Hawaii, age 25 when Pearl Harbor was attacked[242]

While army recruiters were signing up Nisei men for the 442nd Regimental Combat Team, the 100th Infantry Battalion moved from Camp McCoy to Camp Shelby in Hattiesburg, Mississippi. There, in the spring of 1943, the 100th came together with the newly formed 442nd, which had just arrived for basic training. A regimental combat team is an infantry unit, and in World War II the 442nd RCT consisted of 1,200 Japanese Americans from the mainland; 2,686 Hawaiian-born men of Japanese ancestry (which made up approximately two thirds of the regiment); and 1 Korean American named Young Oak Kim. The team as a whole was organized into three infantry battalions, the 522nd Field Artillery Battalion, the 232nd Combat Engineer Company, a cannon company, a service company, an anti-tank company, a medical detachment, and the 206th Army Ground Forces Band.

The 100th had already undergone several months of training in Wisconsin and had amassed an outstanding record; they were seasoned, tough, and proud. In comparison, the 442nd were green newcomers who had to get up to speed. But the level of warfare preparedness was not the only distinction between the units. The men in the two groups came from very different backgrounds and their cultures clashed. The nicknames each group developed for the other unit showed the divide between them. The soldiers from Hawaii were called Buddha-heads—a name deriving either from the Buddhist monks who shaved their heads or from *buta*, the Japanese word for "pig"—while the men from the mainland were called Kotonks, an onomatopoeia for the hollow sound of their heads when they hit the ground.

They also talked in different ways. The Buddhaheads spoke pidgin (a vernacular in Hawaii that combines words in English, Hawaiian, Japanese, Portuguese, and Chinese), which the Kotonks often struggled to understand. For example, in pidgin, "funny kine" means "strange."

The Buddhaheads had money to spend and gamble away. The Kotonks came with nothing and saved whatever money they earned so they could send it back to their families in the camps. The Kotonks felt the Buddhaheads were thoughtless and unrefined; the Buddhaheads thought the Kotonks were resentful and ill-tempered.

Most important, the two groups of soldiers came from vastly different backgrounds. The Buddhaheads came from Hawaii—a multicultural society—and they had never experienced incarceration. The Kotonks had grown up being discriminated against as a small racial minority and brought with them the humiliation of having camp identities. They fought the Buddhaheads constantly, often in drunken brawls. Finally, in an attempt to bring the two groups together, Colonel Charles W. Pence, commander of the 442nd, sent a contingent of Buddhaheads to visit the Jerome and Rohwer camps in Arkansas.

Arriving with their ukuleles and guitars, the fun-loving soldiers from Hawaii were expecting to have a good time when they entered the camps. Instead, they were immediately sobered by the camp environment of barbed wire, machine gun towers, and guards with rifles and bayonets. They began to regard the soldiers who had volunteered from these conditions with new respect.

* * *

Overnight the situation in Camp Shelby changed because the word went out like wildfire. The experiment worked. I went back and said,

"I got to tell you guys about these Mainlanders. You won't believe what I'm going to tell you." And this must have gone on in every hut throughout camp. The next day, you thought you were visiting a new regiment. We were blood brothers.

—The Honorable Daniel "Dan" Ken **Inouye**, male, Nisei, Honolulu, Hawaii, age 17 when Pearl Harbor was attacked[243]

• • •

The nicknames that had started out as terms of derision became expressions of camaraderie. Whether they were from a small village on a little island or the "big city" of Los Angeles, the soldiers came together with a sense of purpose they hadn't had before. They weren't just fighting to defend their country; they were proving their patriotism on behalf of all Japanese Americans. The now-unified 442nd even came up with a motto: Go for Broke—gambling slang from Hawaiian pidgin that referred to wagering everything on one roll of the dice. They would live this motto and carry this solidarity into the battlefield as they faced unspeakable horrors, protecting the backs of their comrades, even unto death.

Then in May 1943 the 100th was sent separately to Camp Livingston in Louisiana for war games against a mock enemy. It was the height of the Jim Crow South, and the Nisei men were told they would be treated as White people. They were advised to use White restrooms and drinking fountains, and to sit at the front of the bus. But Mike Tokunaga couldn't stand by when he saw an elderly Black woman get roughed up by a bus driver as she was trying to board the bus before White riders. Tokunaga later recalled that in a rage he "grabbed the bus driver by the shirt and dragged him out. . . . Six of us kicked the hell out of him."

Two months later the unit returned to Camp Shelby ready for war.

After fifteen months of training that had begun in Hawaii, the 100th traveled to Staten Island, New York, where, on August 21, 1943, the soldiers boarded the SS *James Parker*, bound for North Africa. They arrived in Oran, Algeria—southwest of Algiers—on September 2, 1943. Lieutenant Colonel Farrant Turner, a World War I veteran in his forties, was one of the White officers commanding the Nisei segregated units. In fact, Turner had pleaded with his commanders to let him lead the 100th into combat. He was devoted to his troops and fought any racism hurled their way. In turn, he was deeply respected by the entire battalion and affectionately called the Old Man. Every Monday morning he would gather them together for a kind of coaching session and ask, "Isn't this the most important time in your life? Every one of you is being watched. Don't forget that the future of your families rests on your shoulders. This is the chance you've been waiting for—the chance to go to the front."

But upon arriving in Algeria, Turner discovered that the battalion was meant to stay there and guard German POWs. He demanded that they be sent to join Allied forces in Italy. The army eventually gave in, and the 100th was attached to the 133rd Infantry Regiment, Thirty-Fourth "Red Bull" Division. The forces were sent to the Salerno beachhead, near Naples.

Entering combat on September 29, the 100th fought against strong German resistance to take the city of Benevento, a critical rail and road target. That fall the 100th fought fiercely at the city of La Croce to recapture the hills on the way to Monte Cassino. But pressing on to Monte Cassino meant having to ford the Volturno River, which the Germans were using as their line of defense. After crossing the river twice through water that was generally chest high and sometimes over their heads, many of the soldiers were unable to keep their feet dry and were suffering from trench foot.

And then on October 29, after having driven the enemy out of another stronghold on Castle Hill, the unit endured its first change of command. Lieutenant Colonel Turner was replaced because of concerns over his health and stamina; he also had difficulty withstanding the death of his troops. Saying good-bye to him was emotionally wrenching for everyone. He had commanded the 100th since the day it was activated. Fortunately, Major James L. Gillespie took over in time to prepare the battalion for the third and last crossing of the Volturno River, before they entered one of the most fiercely contested battles of the Allied campaign to retake Italy from Nazi control.

Then Major Gillespie fell ill, and the unit underwent another change in command when Major Caspar "Jim" Clough Jr. took over on Christmas Day 1943. Commencing in mid-January 1944, amidst torrential rains and blizzard conditions, the 100th set its sights on the fifteen-hundred-foot peak of Monte Cassino and the hilltop monastery of Saint Benedict. The Germans were well fortified behind the ten-foot-thick walls of the fortress. They were perfectly positioned to rain down artillery and machine gun fire on any attempt to approach it through the mine-filled mud lakes surrounding the nearby Rapido River and up through the mined slopes and barbed wire.

Colonel Carley L. Marshall, commander of the 133rd Infantry Regiment, then ordered Major Clough to have his men cross the mud-flats in broad daylight, completely exposed to German fire from above. Clough refused to give the order because he considered it a suicide mission. At midnight he was relieved of his command.

Lieutenant Colonel Moses, the First Battalion commander, was given the same orders for his reserve company and agreed with Clough. He refused to issue the order without sharing the risk by leading the company himself. And if he survived, he said, he'd support court-martial charges against Marshall. Major George Dewey, executive officer of the 133rd, arrived to take Clough's place and to make his own assessment—he agreed with Clough that Marshall should call off the attack. Dewey supported restoring Clough to his command. Instead Marshall dug in his heels.

Dewey decided to go across the flats that night on a personal reconnaissance mission, which was strongly opposed by Major Jack Johnson, the battalion executive officer. It was too dangerous, he said. Dewey went anyway and took with him Major Mitsuyoshi Fukuda and two radio operators. Major Johnson, who had grown up in Honolulu, also ended up going, along with his aide. By the end of the night, Johnson and his aide were dead, and Dewey was critically wounded. Johnson's death, in particular, hit everyone hard. Decades later the surviving 100th Battalion veterans of the battle at Monte Cassino would remember him: "There wasn't another white officer in the 100th Battalion who was liked as much as Jack Johnson."

The next morning Marshall still insisted on the order, and Lieutenant Colonel Moses was killed leading his own men into the mudflats. Major James Lovell took command. Just out of his own hospital bed and still not recovered from his injuries, Lovell was a man they all knew and trusted.

The 100th continued to try to carry out the order by going farther to the right of the fortress. They managed to cross the Rapido River and reach the castle walls—the closest anyone had come—but it wasn't a battle the regiment could win. After its first assault on the monastery, the 100th came away with only 14 out of 187 men still standing. The second assault was pulled back when it resulted in only 5 of 40 soldiers still standing. The attack was one of the most grueling and costly efforts in the European theater, wiping out nearly half of the 100th Battalion.

Then on February 15, 1944, 255 Allied planes dropped 576 tons of bombs on the mountaintop, obliterating the abbey that had been run by the Benedictine Order since the Middle Ages. But even that onslaught wasn't enough to defeat the Germans, who sent in their paratroopers to defend the ruins.

Ultimately, the battle to take Monte Cassino over the next three months would cost some 200,000 Allied lives and injuries and would require two more major Allied assaults and five fresh divisions to do what the 100th had attempted on its own. The 100th, which had started out with 1,432 soldiers, ended up with only 521 survivors.

Those injured were known to leave aid stations or hospitals to rejoin their unit, only to be wounded again.

Lyn Crost, one of the few female war correspondents during World War II, had been assigned by the *Honolulu Star-Bulletin* to cover the 100th/442nd exclusively. She wrote, "War correspondents had watched and admired and written about the 100th Battalion during this devastating campaign. . . . For their endurance and pluck and bravery in the face of insurmountable odds, they were hailed as 'the little iron men.'" In heartbreaking press reports the 100th became known as "the Purple Heart Battalion," amassing nine hundred Purple Hearts. Its ranks decimated, the 100th received replacements from the First Battalion of the 442nd RCT (with the full combat team still at Camp Shelby, preparing to come overseas). As soon as its numbers were replenished, the 100th headed for the beachhead of Anzio, Italy.

At the end of March 1944, the Allied objective in Anzio was to take out the German strongholds that were protecting their control of the road to Rome. In order to identify where the Germans were located, the 100th needed information they could get only by capturing and interrogating a German soldier. First Lieutenant Young Oak Kim, the only Korean American officer, and four Nisei soldiers volunteered for a daring overnight maneuver.

Starting at midnight on May 16, they crept past enemy outposts and waited in the predawn hours until the German fighting stopped. With three Nisei riflemen covering them, Kim and Private First Class Irving M. Akahoshi crawled on their stomachs more than six hundred yards through heavy briar and wheat stalks until they came upon German soldiers talking and cleaning a gun. Without firing a shot, Kim and Akahoshi captured the two German guards and crawled away with them as prisoners. The Allied forces got the critical information they needed, and they regained control of eleven towns and villages and two major hills. The result was no less than the liberation of Rome.

Lieutenant Marshall Haines wrote to Vernon McCann of the *Auburn Journal* about the 100th battalion of Japanese American soldiers:

> The liaison officers from my battalion say that this Japanese American infantry outfit is the best damn infantry they have ever worked with. . . .
>
> See where there is a lot of controversy about the Japanese returning to California. Also that proper respect has not been shown the Japanese American soldier. Things like that sure go against the grain with me. . . .
>
> We had been sitting and living in foxholes at Anzio some 63 days. Then the big push out and the capture of Rome. They (the Japanese-American infantrymen) wiped out the last heavy German resistance we met some 12 miles south of Rome and then it was practically a walk into the city. . . .
>
> I know that all of the combat men here in Italy think the world of the Japanese American soldiers. . . .
>
> They have never failed to take an objective since I have been fighting with them. They have shown as much bravery as the American dough boy, and in some cases more. I have never heard them speak the Japanese language at any time.

Meanwhile, the entire 442nd RCT finally arrived in Italy, traveled from Naples through Anzio and Rome, and met up with the 100th in the middle of June. Although the 442nd's First Battalion had been sending replacements to the 100th as a result of the tremendous losses sustained at Monte Cassino, the 100th had fought in Italy as a battalion for more than seven months before the 442nd even left the States.

Now here at last, the 442nd was officially attached to the 100th. In recognition of its unparalleled bravery and combat record, the 100th would be allowed to keep its name, identity, and numerical distinction instead of being merged into the 442nd's First Battalion. Henceforth, the unit would be known as the 100th/442nd Regimental Combat Team—the first infantry regiment in history consisting of all American men of Japanese ancestry, commanded primarily by Caucasian officers and sharing a lineage stretching all the way back to Camp Shelby.

The occasion was also a happy reunion. The men of the two units were glad to see one another; many were reunited with brothers and cousins, friends and acquaintances, some of whom had grown up together and hadn't seen each other since the attack on Pearl Harbor. The men were given a few days off; at night they exchanged stories from home, drank wine, and sang Hawaiian songs. Some finally made it to Rome, where the Italians—perplexed by the presence of Japanese Americans—figured they must be prisoners. The Italians couldn't imagine these soldiers fighting to the death as loyal Americans.

The new, young men of the 442nd were among the best-trained soldiers in the military, but they had never been in combat before and still had a lot to learn. The older and vastly more experienced men of the 100th tried to become their mentors, but there were some things the younger men could learn only on the battlefield.

Their first battle together was the battle of Belvedere, north of Rome. On June 26, 1944, just as the 442nd was weakening and beginning to lose men, the 100th seized the town and attacked the motorized German battalion. The 100th lost 4 men and had 7 wounded, while the enemy suffered 178 dead, 20 wounded, and 86 captured. The American battalion also captured and destroyed an impressive amount of enemy equipment and supplies: forty-eight vehicles, five tanks, three artillery pieces, one self-propelled howitzer, and two antitank guns.

On July 27, 1944, Lieutenant General Mark W. Clark, commander of the Fifth Army in charge of the Italian theater, awarded the 100th Infantry Battalion its first of three Presidential Unit Citations— the army's highest honor for "heroism against enemy forces under extremely difficult and hazardous conditions"—for its actions in the battles of Belvedere, Luciana, and Livorno. By this time the 100th had already received nine Distinguished Service Crosses, forty-four Silver Stars, thirty-one Bronze Stars, three Legion of Merit medals, fifteen battlefield commissions, and more than one thousand Purple Hearts.

Lieutenant General Clark said the 100th was one of the most valuable units in the Fifth Army, a "bright spot" in this campaign. He added, "You are always thinking of your country before yourselves. You have never complained through your long periods in the line. You have written a brilliant chapter in the history of the fighting men in America. You are always ready to close with the enemy, and you have always defeated him. The 34th Division is proud of you, the Fifth Army is proud of you, and the whole United States is proud of you."

Mike Masaoka, serving in the 442nd with three brothers, was an enlisted public relations officer with responsibilities to interview the Nisei GIs from the front and send their stories back to their hometowns on the West Coast. In the more than two thousand stories that Masaoka dispatched from the front while enlisted with the 100th/442nd, he quoted Nisei soldiers saying in their own words how they were willing to give their lives to prove that they and their families were Americans, and that they were fighting for their future as Americans. When asked by correspondents if the Nisei would fight the Japanese, Masaoka stressed that they were fighting against fascism and tyranny, regardless of race. He knew their sacrifices would be worth it only if their valor helped to rehabilitate the image of Japanese Americans in the public eye.

The 100th/442nd then proceeded to take several German strongholds over the next three weeks. By September 1944 they had become a major force in driving the Germans north to the Arno River. In the heavy fighting more than one fourth of the unit suffered casualties, which numbered 1,272. On September 30 the 100th/442nd joined in the campaign to retake the Vosges Mountains together with the Thirty-Sixth Infantry Division (the "Texas" Division) of the Seventh Army in northeastern France, commanded by Major General John E. Dahlquist.

According to Young Oak Kim, now a captain, Dahlquist was known for giving "totally wrong information and crazy orders." Dahlquist would ignore the opinions of his advisers, dismiss intelligence from the front, and often underestimate the strength of the enemy prior to sending in troops. He would demand that the men continue to advance, often before their positions could be consolidated and before they could ensure functioning supply lines and adequate artillery support.

• • •

He was personally a brave man but a dangerously ambitious man who sought personal glory and who cared very little for subordinates' lives. Much of the tremendous losses suffered by the entire 442nd can be attributed to his poor leadership. He violated every principle [of] leadership and tactics.

—Captain Young Oak Kim, male, Korean American, 100th/442nd Regimental Combat Team[244]

• • •

On October 14, 1944, the 100th/442nd began its attack on Bruyères in deplorable conditions—they were ordered to advance approximately six miles a day through ice storms and fog, dodging land mines and deadly "tree bursts" (when artillery rounds detonate in trees and rain shrapnel and branches and splinters of wood onto everything below). Dahlquist told them there was only a "token number of Germans" defending Hill A and blamed the American battalion's timidity as the reason they hadn't captured it. Captain Kim knew better from previous attempts, and in fact, they were showered with heavy artillery. Because Dahlquist's orders could have gotten them killed, Kim was forced to cut off all communication with headquarters. Still, they managed to secure the town five days later. The 100th/442nd captured over one hundred Germans and suffered only two wounded.

Although they had been promised two days' rest, the Nisei were instead ordered at midnight to take Hill C, with its sweeping views five miles behind German lines. In addition, they were ordered to give up the hill once its capture was secured, effectively nullifying the entire operation in order to liberate Biffontaine—a farm town of three hundred people completely controlled by Germans that lacked any true tactical advantage. (Hill C had to be retaken later at great cost.) Forced into nonstop combat for no reason, sleep deprived, and extremely low on food, medical supplies, and ammunition, the 100th was now cut off from the 442nd, isolated seven miles behind enemy lines on a hilltop beyond radio range, and at least a mile from artillery support. The 100th managed to escape, but Kim was among those who were seriously injured.

Dahlquist, meanwhile, had ordered into harm's way another regiment—the 141st Infantry Regiment, Thirty-Sixth Infantry Division—consisting mainly of soldiers from Texas. He made them advance four miles into enemy territory, even though he was warned that the unit could get cut off because it had no protection in the rear. Now 275 men of the Thirty-Sixth Division found themselves hopelessly pinned down, isolated from their unit and stranded on a ridge surrounded by 700 German soldiers with tanks and artillery on three sides. The stranded men had one radio, and their battery power was getting low as they repeatedly requested food, water, and plasma for the wounded. Adolf Hitler himself is reported to have heard about the trapped unit and ordered his men to block the rescue, no matter what losses occurred on the German side.

After ten days of battle the 100th/442nd was given only two days' rest before Dahlquist ordered them to rescue the trapped men, referred to as the Lost Battalion. At least two rescue attempts by other battalions had been made already, and needless to say, both had failed. And so, deep in the Vosges Mountains, the 100th/442nd undertook its bloodiest battle yet and one of the ten most ferocious battles in US Army history.

Moving out at two a.m. on October 27, 1944, in the freezing rain, young Nisei men picked their way over mines on narrow, muddy paths up the heavily forested hills. The steep, nearly impenetrable terrain was almost impossible to traverse. They held on to the backpack straps belonging to the man in front of them and followed white squares of toilet paper attached to their backs so they would not get separated in the pitch-black darkness. But in two days they managed to advance only a few hundred yards and found themselves trapped on a narrow ridge with sharp, vertical drops on either side. They were forced to execute their last resort: a banzai charge straight up the middle.

A banzai charge is a kind of military Hail Mary, horrific to watch and hear. The men would affix their bayonets and then charge, on command, sounding for all the world like a pack of screaming banshees. If it worked, they'd break through the line and possibly live to see another day; if it didn't, they would die with honor. In either case, the losses would be unimaginable because they'd be charging directly into enemy fire—the ultimate Go for Broke moment.

Chaplain Masao Yamada wrote in a letter to fellow chaplain George Aki, "Though we had been fighting for days on end, we were recalled to rescue the Lost Battalion. . . . The men are obedient and brave; they charge right into machine gun fire and are mowed down, but those who can get up, charge again and again in waves, like the waves beating on the shores. Our losses are heavy. . . . And now trench foot is setting in, cutting down our men along with the wounded and the dead. . . ."

· · ·

We just went hog wild crazy, and we were mad at everybody, and we were ready to kill anything that there was. And finally we made contact with the Lost Battalion. . . . But we lost 400 men trying to rescue [them]—what a terrible price we paid!

—Robert Ichigi **Kashiwagi**, male, Nisei, Woodland, California, incarcerated age 23, Merced Assembly Center, Granada (Amache) Relocation Center[245]

After four days of fierce fighting, . . . the cost has been high. I admire the courage and the discipline of our loyal men. They take their orders in stride without complaint and went into the volley of fire, with one spirit and one mind. Actually, those that saw the charge (our men call it the "banzai" charge) came home with a vivid and stirring account of our men unflinchingly charging on the double, falling under machine-gun fire, yet moving on as the ceaseless waves beat on a seashore.

I am spiritually low for once. My heart weeps with our men, especially with those who gave all. Never has any combat affected me so deeply as has this emergency mission. I am probably getting soft, but to me the price is too costly for our men. I feel this way because the burden is laid on the combat team when the rest of the 141st [Battalion, Thirty-Sixth Division] is not forced to take the same responsibility.

In spite of my personal lamentations, our men are facing their enemy with the courage that comes from the heart. When we complete this mission, which we will today or tomorrow, we will have written with our own blood another chapter in the story of our adventures in Democracy.

—Masao **Yamada**, America's first Japanese American chaplain, male, Nisei, Kauai, Hawaii, age 34 when Pearl Harbor was attacked[246]

· · ·

On October 30, through the human wreckage of "Suicide Hill," the 442nd finally reached the Lost Battalion; they saved the remaining 211 men and secured the ridge that had been the Lost Battalion's original objective. As soon as the 442nd had broken through the German line, forward artillary observer Second Lieutenant Erwin Blonder of the 131st field artillary, with Company A, radioed to division headquarters: "Patrol 442nd here. Tell them we love them." Reporters rushed to the Vosges front, and newspapers throughout America were carrying stories about the heroism of the Nisei soldiers. The message was getting out there that the gallant 100th/442nd was indeed fighting for freedom while their families were imprisoned in American concentration camps.

The members of the Lost Battalion never forgot their Japanese

American rescuers. In gratitude, the men of the Thirty-Sixth Division declared all members of the 100th/442nd to be honorary Texans. But the toll on the 100th/442nd RCT was catastrophic. War correspondent Lyn Crost reported the Nisei soldiers suffered approximately eight hundred casualties, four times the number of men they rescued.

• • •

I am absolutely certain all of us were well aware that we were being used for the rescue because we were expendable.
—The Honorable Daniel "Dan" Ken **Inouye**, male, Nisei, Honolulu, Hawaii, age 17 when Pearl Harbor was attacked[247]

My memories of France still show the bitterness burnt deeply into my soul. Later, Gordon Singles, while filling a Brigadier General's position at Fort Bragg, refused to publicly shake General Dahlquist's hand at a full dress review in the presence of the entire III Corps. Dahlquist was then a visiting 4-star General. [Singles] preferred remaining a Colonel than to shake Dahlquist's hand even though [Dahlquist] asked forgiveness. Years later after he retired, General Pence could not mention Dahlquist's name without his voice shaking with anger.
—Captain Young Oak Kim, male, Korean American, 100th/442nd Regimental Combat Team[248]

• • •

Decades later, in June 2000, Private Barney F. Hajiro and Private George T. Sakato were awarded individual Congressional Medals of Honor for their banzai attacks.

CONGRESSIONAL MEDAL OF HONOR CITATION
PRIVATE BARNEY F. HAJIRO

On 29 October 1944, in a wooded area in the vicinity of Biffontaine, France, Private Barney F. Hajiro initiated an attack up the slope of a hill referred to as "Suicide Hill" by running forward approximately 100 yards under fire. He then advanced ahead of his comrades about 10 yards, drawing fire and spotting camouflaged machine gun nests. He fearlessly met fire with fire and single-handedly destroyed two machine gun nests and killed two enemy snipers.

CONGRESSIONAL MEDAL OF HONOR CITATION
PRIVATE GEORGE T. SAKATO

Private George T. Sakato . . . made a one-man rush that encouraged his platoon to charge and destroy the enemy strongpoint. While his platoon was reorganizing, he proved to be the inspiration of his squad in halting a counter-attack on the left flank during which his squad leader was killed. Taking charge of the squad, he continued his relentless tactics, using an enemy rifle and P-38 pistol to stop an organized enemy attack. During this entire action, he killed 12 and wounded two, personally captured four and assisted his platoon in taking 34 prisoners.

After enduring sixteen brutal days of combat to rescue the Lost Battalion, the Nisei men were exhausted. A number of them were suffering from trench foot and other ailments. The surviving soldiers from the 100th/442nd were expecting to receive some time off for rest and recuperation—as the 211 Texans they had just saved were enjoying. But instead of allowing them time to recover, Dahlquist ordered them to spend nine more days driving Germans through the forest.

For its actions in the Vosges Mountains during the period of October 15–30, 1944, the 100th Infantry Battalion received its second of three Presidential Unit Citations. The 442nd RCT received four Presidential Unit Citations for its actions in rescuing the Lost Battalion during the period of October 27–30, 1944. These citations were specifically awarded within the regiment to Companies F and L of the Second Battalion, the entire Second Battalion, the entire Third Battalion, and the 232nd Combat Engineer Company.

Never before had army troops merited five Presidential Unit Citations in less than a month of combat.

• • •

When General Dahlquist called the regiment out for a retreat parade to commend us personally, he is reported to have said to the C.O., "Colonel, I asked that the entire regiment be present for this occasion. Where are the rest of your men?"

And Colonel Charles W. Pence [commanding officer of the 442nd], as bone-weary as any dogface in the outfit, replied, "Sir, you are looking at the entire regiment. Except for two men on guard duty at each company, this is all that is left of the 442nd Combat Team."

And there we were, cooks, medics, band and a handful of riflemen, a ragged lot at rigid attention, without a single company at even half its normal strength. One [company] had only 17 men and was commanded by a staff sergeant. My outfit, E Company, with a normal complement of 197 men, had exactly 40 soldiers able to march to the parade ground.

General Dahlquist looked at us for a long time. Twice he started to speak and choked on the overpowering feelings that took hold of him. And in the end, all he could manage was an emotional "Thank you, men. Thank you from the bottom of my heart." And the saddest retreat parade in the history of the 442nd was over.

—The Honorable Daniel "Dan" Ken **Inouye**, male, Nisei, Honolulu, Hawaii, age 17 when Pearl Harbor was attacked[249]

• • •

From mid-November 1944 to March 23, 1945, the 100th/442nd patrolled the Maritime Alps, engaging in regular skirmishes and ducking sniper fire. They called it the Champagne Campaign because they could take leaves in towns along the French Riviera. Their numbers were so depleted by then that they weren't regiment size, so all they could do was guard a twelve-mile stretch of the Italian-French border. More than two thousand of their regiment lay in hospitals in France, Italy, England, and the United States.

On March 25, what was left of the 100th/442nd returned to northern Italy, where over the next two months they would contribute to the first Allied victory over the Axis powers in the war. The Germans had spent nine months building the Gothic Line—an impregnable series of concrete fortifications, dug into the rock of the Apennine Mountains by two thousand Slovaks and fifteen thousand Italian slave laborers. With bunkers, tunnels, antitank ditches, and more than 2,300 gun nests, it was the most formidable military stronghold in the country, stretching between the east and west coasts, beginning a few miles north of Pisa and ending in Pesaro. After five months of bombing and shelling, the Allied forces had still not been able to breach it.

To break this impasse, Clark, now a four-star general, made a specific request to Supreme Allied Commander General Dwight D. Eisenhower that the 100th/442nd be sent to conduct a major attack on the west end of the line, diverting the Germans' attention away from preparations for the main assault to be made by Lieutenant General Lucian Truscott's Fifth Army. The British Eighth Army would attack to the east and then turn west, creating a massive pincer movement.

The 100th/442nd would face at least four divisions of enemy soldiers who were guarding the Gothic Line's western area. The Nisei soldiers would be climbing up into a mountain range—Mount Cerreta, Mount Folgorito, Mount Carchio, and Mount Belvedere—eluding minefields and artillery aimed at the mountain trails, and flushing out the enemy from hundreds of bunkers. The mission was for the 100th to make a frontal assault at the westernmost end of the enemy line by scaling the sheer mountain walls and gaining the Folgorito ridgeline, which rose abruptly three thousand feet from the coastal plain. The Third Battalion of the 442nd would attack from four miles to the east and then march west to converge with the 100th. According to war correspondent Lyn Crost, the goal was to create a "mini-pincer movement within the overall campaign."

The men of the 100th/442nd came together in Pisa. To minimize the likelihood that the Germans could spot them and identify them as US enemy soldiers, they removed the insignias from their helmets and uniforms. On the night of April 3, 1945, the 100th and the Third Battalion of the 442nd were trucked seventeen miles north toward Pietrasanta. The 100th stealthily moved eight miles west to a forward assembly area in the vicinity of Vallecchia. Meanwhile, the 442nd and the medic Jim Okubo were to hike four miles to Seravezza, and then another eight miles up, guided by Italian partisans, to the mountainside village of Azzano.

> The climb to Azzano was terrifying. Local guides led Okubo and the others up narrow trails carved into the hillsides in the dark. Switchbacks were especially treacherous, and unseen rocks on the path could become as deadly as a land mine. Most men carried enough K rations for three days, one pouch for a canteen, another to carry grenades, more grenades attached to a shoulder strap, their weapon, extra bandoliers of ammunition, spare socks stuffed inside their shirts, and toilet paper tucked into their helmet liners. Loaded down with equipment tightly strapped to their bodies, twenty-five men fell off the trail, sliding and rolling uncontrollably down the hill. Two had to be hospitalized from the injuries they suffered in their fall. None uttered a sound as they caromed off rocks. The Germans could not learn of a sneak attack.[*]

All during the next day, men from both the 100th and the 442nd hid from German observation. Absolute silence, utmost secrecy, and

---

[*] McGaugh, Scott. *Honor Before Glory: The Epic World War II Story of the Japanese American GIs Who Rescued the Lost Battalion.*

remaining undetected were critical to the mission's success. But the 442nd still had to cross one more valley and navigate trails toward Mount Folgorito and Mount Carchio with drop-offs of 15 to 150 feet. At the same time, Company A of the 100th Battalion began moving into place for a frontal assault on a mountain stronghold by climbing a vertical cliff face in full military gear. They proceeded for eight hours at a sixty-degree angle up to the top of the ridge in as close to absolute silence as possible. Their only advantage was in waging a surprise attack. If they made a sound that gave away their presence, their end was inevitable; they had to stifle their cries when they saw some of their fellow soldiers slip and fall soundlessly to their deaths. Even those soldiers did not cry out.

At dawn on April 5, having reached the Folgorito ridgeline, the Nisei teams needed only thirty-two minutes to drive the Germans out of their entrenchments and capture the stronghold. The Germans were caught completely by surprise. Company A, Second Platoon, had been assigned the task of making the frontal attack over a minefield. The men had advanced quietly and had traversed almost the length of a football field before one of the men stepped on a land mine, alerting the Germans to their presence. Although they reacted quickly and engaged in a furious battle, the Germans couldn't overcome the dedicated and accomplished Nisei teams. The 100th/442nd then focused on winning nine of the main fortified hills; within forty-eight hours they had taken them all.

Sadao Munemori, the Second Platoon squad leader from Company A, made a banzai charge that knocked out two machine gun nests. Without hesitating, he threw his body onto a grenade the second before it exploded, saving the lives of two of his men. For his brave and selfless sacrifice, he was posthumously awarded a Congressional Medal of Honor.

The same day, the Third Battalion also surprised the Germans by capturing Mount Folgorito to the south and Mount Carchio to the north. Two days later the 100th and the Third Battalion converged forces and overcame enemy resistance on Mount Cerreta. They had taken the western end of the Gothic Line.

Over the next two weeks, with the 100th/442nd hard on their heels, the Germans headed through Aulla on their last escape route into the Po Valley. During the battles that ensued, Second Lieutenant Daniel K. Inouye, just twenty years old, displayed bravery and heroics that earned the soldier, who would go on to serve the state of Hawaii as a congressman and a senator for forty-nine years, a Distinguished Service Cross and a Congressional Medal of Honor.

CONGRESSIONAL MEDAL OF HONOR CITATION
SECOND LIEUTENANT DANIEL K. INOUYE

> With complete disregard for his personal safety, Second Lieutenant Inouye crawled up the treacherous slope to within five yards of the nearest machine gun and hurled two grenades, destroying the emplacement. Before the enemy could retaliate, he stood up and neutralized a second machine gun nest. Although wounded by a sniper's bullet, he continued to engage other hostile positions at close range until an exploding grenade shattered his right arm. Despite the intense pain, he refused evacuation and continued to direct his platoon until enemy resistance was broken and his men were again deployed in defensive positions. In the attack, 25 enemy soldiers were killed and eight others captured. By his gallant, aggressive tactics and by his indomitable leadership, Second Lieutenant Inouye enabled his platoon to advance through formidable resistance and was instrumental in the capture of the ridge.

For its actions to break the Gothic Line in the vicinity of Seravezza, Carrara, and Fosdinovo, Italy, during the period of April 5–14, 1945, the 100th/442nd RCT (less the Second Battalion and the 522nd Field

Artillery Battalion, but including the 232nd Combat Engineer Company) received yet another Presidential Unit Citation.

The unit still had one assignment left: cut off the road to Aulla, the last line of German resistance in northern Italy. On April 25, Major Mitsuyoshi Fukuda led a special battalion called Task Force Fukuda (the first task force to be named after a Nisei) and took Aulla in a two-day campaign. During that battle, they fought the Bersaglieri—the Fascist members of an Italian infantry corps who were waging their own vicious war alongside Nazi Germany troops during the final Allied offensive.

Meanwhile, the men of the 522nd Field Artillery Battalion of the 100th/442nd had been sent on assignment as a roving battalion for the Allied forces marching into Germany. While the rest of the 100th/442nd was still engaged in the Italian campaign, the 522nd completed fifty-two assignments in Germany. They covered 1,100 miles—forty towns in sixty days—and fired more than fifteen thousand rounds. After demolishing the Germans in Alsace-Lorraine, France, the battalion headed south into Bavaria.

On April 29, 1945, the Nisei soldiers from the 552nd together with other US soldiers from the Fourth Armored Division, came upon some barracks encircled by barbed wire as they moved through the small town of Lager Lechfield, Germany. To their horror, they discovered it was Kaufering IV Hurlach, a subcamp of the Dachau slave labor camp. The soldiers from the 522nd could not believe their eyes. The inmates, more dead than alive, were confused to see Japanese faces and assumed the Nisei were Japanese soldiers. But once they understood that the Nisei soldiers were American, the captives knew they were saved.

• • •

The camp itself was almost completely burned down and near the entrance I found more than 200 almost completely charred bodies. The few uncharred bodies were emaciated skeletons, literally consisting of only skin and bones. The opening of two large, makeshift pits, carried out by a Health officer, revealed a huge number of corpses piled on top

*of one another, in five layers. The arms and legs of many of the corpses
had been broken, apparently to force them into the pit.*

—Captain John Barnett, testimony at the Dachau trials (upon
witnessing the Kaufering IV Hurlach camp, on April 30, 1945)[250]

*They were just skin and bones, and they looked so cold. Here I was
kneeling down. In my arms sat an inmate of Dachau, and all I could
do was hold him as he said, "Please help me." As his body went limp,
all I could do was cry. I had to think, What the heck am I doing here?
My family was still behind barbed wire in Wyoming . . . here I was in
Germany liberating people from camps.*

—Clarence "Cal" Satoru **Matsumura**, male, Nisei, Los Angeles,
California, incarcerated age 21, Pomona Assembly Center, Heart
Mountain Relocation Center[251]

*It is ironic that members of one persecuted minority were liberating
those of another minority.*

—Bonnie Gurewitsch, former archivist/librarian of the Museum of
Jewish Heritage, New York[252]

• • •

Three days later, on May 2, 1945, the 522nd stumbled across hundreds
of bodies in the snow, some shot, some dead, some barely alive, all victims of a death march through the mountains. The survivors were lifted to
shelter, and the soldiers tended to their needs as best they could. Finally
the Nisei soldiers came to the town of Waakirchen, Germany, where they
were greeted by the cheers of five thousand Dachau survivors.

The Nisei's experience at Dachau was classified, and so for many
years their role was not known or acknowledged. But the colors of the
442nd are now displayed in the United States Holocaust Memorial
Museum in Washington, DC.

As Dachau survivors were celebrating their liberation, all German
forces in Italy surrendered.

The war in Italy was over.

Germany surrendered on May 7, 1945, one week after Hitler's suicide.

On that same day, Mitsuyoshi Fukuda was promoted to the rank of major and became the first American of Japanese ancestry to be named a battalion commander. Exactly two months later he was named the commanding officer of the 100th Infantry Battalion. He also became the first Asian American to serve as the executive officer of the 442nd. He flew home as the last original member of the 100th Infantry Battalion (Separate) to leave Europe, included on a special plane reserved for high-ranking officers.

The war in Europe had finally ended.

Now Japan was fighting alone.

• • •

They bought an awful hunk of America with their blood . . . you're damn right those Nisei boys have a place in the American heart, now and forever. We cannot allow a single injustice to be done to the Nisei without defeating the purposes for which we fought.

—Major General Joseph "Vinegar Joe" Stilwell[253]

The 100th had proved that loyalty to the United States is not a matter of race or ancestry. And it had set an example for people of all nations who seek sanctuary here to fight for those values and concepts of government which have made the United States a refuge from the hunger and despair which haunts so much of the world.

—Eleanor Elizabeth Crost, known professionally as Lyn Crost, on the occasion of the fiftieth anniversary of the 100th Infantry Battalion's formation, *Hawaii Herald*, June 19, 1992[254]

• • •

The 100th/442nd RCT has been called the most decorated military unit for its size and length of service in all of US military history. At the time the segregated units were formed, the military could not have anticipated that "by concentrating Japanese Americans in the 100th and the 442nd, it had unwittingly created what amounted to elite fighting units."* The soldiers were generally older and better educated than the average troops and motivated by an uncommon sense of mission. As a result, they performed "more like the newly formed Rangers, modeled after the British Commandos, than like ordinary infantry outfits."†

In the late 1990s it came to light that some 100th/442nd recipients of the Distinguished Service Cross should have merited a Medal of Honor. The honors were finally awarded in 2000.

Ten years later, on October 5, 2010, President Barack Obama signed a bill in which the US Congress awarded its highest civilian award, the Congressional Gold Medal, to all of the Japanese Americans who served in the 100th Infantry Battalion (Separate), the 442nd Regimental Combat Team, and the Military Intelligence Service.

According to the records of the Go for Broke National Education Center, 14,140 awards have been given to the approximately eighteen thousand members of the 100th/442nd RCT and to the regiment as a whole, broken down as follows:

21 Medals of Honor
29 Distinguished Service Crosses
560 Silver Stars
4,000 Bronze Stars
9,486 Purple Hearts
7 Presidential Unit Citations
22 Legion of Merit medals
15 Soldier's Medals

• • •

I think it was my predecessor who said that Americanism is not a matter of race or creed, it is a matter of the heart. You fought for the

---

* Asahina, Robert. *Just Americans: How Japanese Americans Won a War at Home and Abroad: The Story of the 100th Battalion/442nd Regimental Combat Team in World War II.*
† Ibid.

free nations of the world along with the rest of us. . . . You are now on your way home. You fought not only the enemy, but you fought prejudice—and you have won. Keep up that fight, and we will continue to win—to make this great Republic stand for just what the Constitution says it stands for: the welfare of all the people all the time.

—President Harry S. Truman, addressing 500 Nisei troops after their
march down Constitution Avenue, Washington, DC, and pinning the
seventh Presidential Unit Citation on their 100th/442nd banners, July
15, 1946[255]

• • •

The estimated 33,000 Japanese Americans who served in the US military during World War II includes 142 Nisei women who volunteered for the Women's Army Corps (WAC). Other Nisei women volunteered to serve in the Army Nurse Corps and as military doctors, army personnel, and MIS linguists. In contrast to their male counterparts, who were placed in segregated units, the Nisei servicewomen numbered too few to form their own segregated unit in any capacity; they served wherever they were needed without regard to their race. Despite their small numbers, the contributions of the female Nisei service members, combined with those of the male Nisei military personnel, made possible the postwar future of all persons of Japanese ancestry in the United States.

The courage and relentless fighting spirit of all Nisei in service— and especially the "demonstration in blood" by the MIS and the 100th/442nd Regimental Combat Team—convinced many Americans that people of Japanese ancestry were willing to put their lives on the line to prove their loyalty and go into combat in defense of their country. In large part, the sacrifice of the Nisei military helped all those imprisoned in the camps to take a critical step on the road to freedom.

The road, however, was long and winding. Getting into the camps had been one trauma; getting out of them would be another.

LOYALTY

I am a citizen—
Let no slander
Slur my status.

In the other war,
I stood with countless others
Side by side
To fight the foe.
My arm was just as strong
My blood fell
As bright as theirs
In the defense of a new world
More precious far
Than any tie of land or race.

If in this holocaust
It be decreed
My loyalty be tested
By submission,
What is the difference
If the end be same?

My reason may be tested—
Not my heart.

O, what is loyalty
If it be something
That can bend
With every wind?
Steadfast I stand,

Staunchly I plant
The Stars and Stripes
Before my barracks door,
Crying defiance
To all wavering hearts.

I am a citizen—
I can take
The bad with good.

by Sada Murayama
Tulean Dispatch, *May 27, 1943*

—Sada (Hasegawa) **Murayama**, female, Issei, San Francisco, California, incarcerated age 41, Tule Lake Relocation Center[256]

PART FOUR

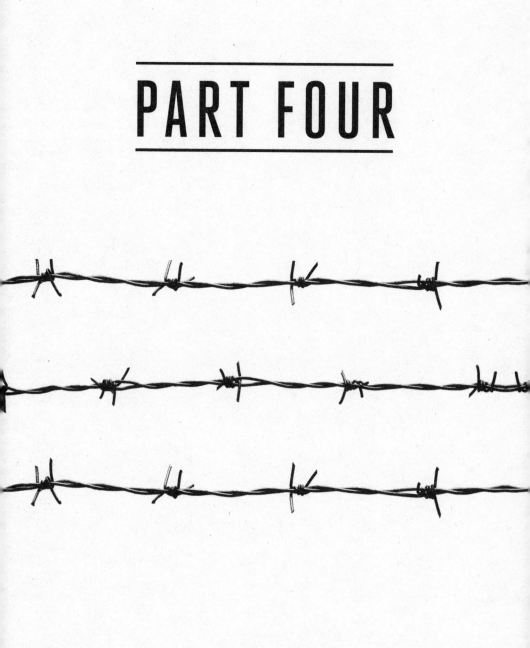

CHAPTER NINE

The Supreme Court's Loaded Weapon

Ancestry is not a crime.

> —Gordon Kiyoshi **Hirabayashi**, male, Nisei, Seattle, Washington,
> age 22 when Pearl Harbor was attacked, King County Jail, Tucson
> Federal Prison/Catalina Federal Honor Camp, McNeil Island
> Federal Penitentiary[257]

Firrst came President Roosevelt's Executive Order 9066, which proclaimed the necessity of preventing espionage and sabotage in the United States and authorized his military leaders to issue whatever orders they deemed necessary for that purpose. Because the executive order was written this way, it achieved the politically brilliant effect of protecting the president from being blamed for any decisions the military made on his behalf. Then the Western Defense Command issued a series of military orders that put all Japanese Americans under a curfew and subsequently prevented them from living on the West Coast by incarcerating them indefinitely like criminals in concentration camps. And as if that weren't enough, Congress passed Public Law 503, which made it a felony if the Japanese Americans did not obey any of these military orders.

On March 30, 1942, two days after he was arrested for refusing to obey the military curfew order, Minoru Yasui was released on bail. Less than a month later he was removed from his home in Hood River, Oregon, with a Thompson submachine gun pointed at him, and was locked up at the Portland Assembly Center. From there, he and his family were sent to the Minidoka concentration camp in Idaho, where he awaited trial of his test case on the constitutionality of the incarceration. On June 12, 1942, he was taken in handcuffs to Portland's district court to appear before Judge James Alger Fee.

There wasn't any question that he was guilty of violating the curfew order. Even so, Judge Fee ruled that the military curfew orders imposed against Japanese American citizens on the basis of their ancestry alone were "unconstitutional, illegal, and unenforceable." Nevertheless, the judge delivered a strangely mixed verdict, which would have a long tail of ramifications once Yasui's case reached the Supreme Court. Judge Fee concluded that even though DeWitt's curfew order could *not* be applied to American citizens, it could be applied to aliens.

In a bizarre distortion of facts and interpretation of the law, the judge ruled that despite being born in America, Yasui had in effect "repudiated his citizenship" by working for the Japanese consulate in Chicago before the outbreak of war. Consequently, Judge Fee reasoned that DeWitt's curfew order could apply to Yasui as a de facto enemy alien. The judge imposed a fine of $5,000, sentenced Yasui to one year in prison, and denied his release on bond pending his appeal. He was thrown into solitary confinement, where he languished for nine months at the Multnomah County Jail.

Similarly, Gordon Hirabayashi was in the King County Jail. He had been waiting for his trial since May 16, 1942, when he had turned himself in to the FBI instead of submitting himself to forced removal. Based on his conscientious objector status as a Quaker, he, too, was intending to be a constitutional test case. But at Hirabayashi's Seattle trial on October 20, 1942, the jury took only ten minutes to render a guilty verdict on two counts of violating the curfew and refusing to obey the exclusion order. Judge Lloyd D. Black sentenced Hirabayashi to two concurrent thirty-day jail terms. Because Hirabayashi said he would rather serve his sentence outside in a road camp than inside a jail cell and was willing to take a longer sentence to make that possible, Judge Black increased his sentence from sixty to ninety days so that Hirabayashi would qualify for a work camp. He served two months of his ninety-day concurrent sentences for both convictions at the

Dupont Road camp outside Tacoma, Washington, and was released on bail while his case was on appeal.

Finally, Fred Korematsu was with his family at the Tanforan Assembly Center, awaiting trial after he'd been released from San Francisco's Presidio stockade. It had been two and a half months since his arrest on May 30, 1942, for failing to report for evacuation. Korematsu hadn't intended to become a constitutional test case until he'd been approached at the Presidio for that purpose by Ernest Besig, director of the ACLU's San Francisco office. Korematsu had agreed, and on September 8, 1942, represented by Besig, he stood trial before Judge Adolphus St. Sure.

Not surprisingly, the judge found Korematsu guilty of violating military orders. But surprisingly, the judge sentenced him to five years' probation instead of imposing a prison term. Normally a defendant would be happy with probation instead of jail time, but in Korematsu's case, probation meant returning to incarceration—first at Tanforan, then at the Topaz Relocation Center. Moreover, Judge St. Sure's order of probation significantly compromised Korematsu's ability to appeal his case. Only cases decided definitively can be appealed, and there was some question as to whether probation counted as a final judgment eligible for appeal.

On February 19, 1943 (one year to the day after Executive Order 9066 had been signed), the attorneys representing Yasui, Hirabayashi, and Korematsu argued their cases before the Court of Appeals for the Ninth Circuit. However, on March 27, 1943, the Ninth Circuit did something unusual: Instead of ruling on the issues presented in each of the three cases, as would normally occur, it passed the cases directly on to the Supreme Court. This maneuver gave the Supreme Court the option to send the cases back to the Ninth Circuit to decide, or to rule on them itself without hearing oral arguments, or to hear all three cases, including oral arguments.

The Supreme Court responded that it would hear the *Yasui* and

Hirabayashi cases to determine if those men had been rightfully convicted. In Yasui's case, the Ninth Circuit passed along to the Supreme Court the issue of whether Yasui had renounced his citizenship by working for the Japanese consulate. In Hirabayashi's case, the Ninth Circuit asked the Supreme Court whether DeWitt's curfew and exclusion orders were constitutional and whether it was a crime not to obey these orders, as stated in Public Law 503. In Korematsu's case, the Supreme Court would only address the issue of whether he could appeal his sentence of probation, or to put it another way, whether his probation constituted an appealable judgment. The Supreme Court scheduled oral arguments on May 10 and 11, 1943.

With only about six weeks to prepare for a Supreme Court hearing, all of the attorneys were scrambling. Lawyers involved with the defense of both Hirabayashi and Korematsu were affiliated with the ACLU, but the board of the national ACLU had voted not to challenge the constitutionality of Executive Order 9066. However, the branch of the ACLU in Northern California continued with its constitutional defense of Hirabayashi's case—but only in regard to how the order discriminated against Japanese Americans, not that the order itself was unconstitutional.

On the government's side, two groups within the Justice Department were at loggerheads. One team, in the Alien Enemy Control Unit, was headed by Edward Ennis. Ironically, he and his deputy John Burling were among the Justice Department lawyers who had strenuously objected to a mass evacuation before Executive Order 9066 was ever issued. Now their job was to defend it. Ennis and Burling were at odds with the other Justice Department group, under the direction of Solicitor General Charles Fahy. There were also sharp disagreements between the two groups of attorneys at the War Department: one headed by Assistant Secretary of War John McCloy and the other by Philip Glick, the WRA solicitor. In reality, there were at least four different factions vying to determine the government's positions in the three cases, and the conflicts among them would become embittered.

The position of the Justice Department, both in its briefs and in Fahy's oral arguments, was that the curfew and the mass incarceration of Japanese Americans in the camps were justified by "military necessity." The government's rationale was based on two points. First, the government attorneys put forth unsubstantiated claims that the cultural practices of Japanese Americans (such as being Buddhist or maintaining Japanese-language schools) were indications that they had not assimilated to being American, and therefore it was likely that some were disloyal. On this point the government expected the court to accept as fact that evidence existed of Japanese American disloyalty, even though no such evidence was entered into the court record at any point in the proceedings.

The government's second point was that because the country was experiencing a war emergency, the administration did not have time to identify and separate the disloyal from the loyal. Therefore, the government took the position that time was of the essence, which also served to justify its loyalty screenings later, in a less pressured environment, when it was evaluating the Nisei men for military service.

But in order to make these arguments, the War Department had to cover up some big problems. Extensive historical research in the early 1980s by Peter Irons and Aiko Herzig-Yoshinaga shows that the government attorneys purposefully suppressed, altered, and destroyed important evidence in order to support their case for "military necessity" and to prevent the Supreme Court from reviewing evidence that contradicted the government's claims.

One major problem was that Colonel Bendetsen had drafted and bound a massive document under General DeWitt's name titled "Final Report, Japanese Evacuation from the West Coast, 1942" without consulting the Justice Department. DeWitt air-expressed the report from San Francisco to McCloy in Washington, DC, in April 1943 so that the War Department attorneys could use it in preparing their briefs for the

Supreme Court. The report specifically stated that the reason for evacuating all the Japanese Americans was their race—it was their racial characteristics that made it *impossible* to distinguish between a loyal and a disloyal person of Japanese descent. Prejudice, not time, had been the chief factor in DeWitt's decision to order the mass removal of 120,000 Japanese Americans.

When McCloy read DeWitt's report, he hit the roof. He knew these statements directly contradicted the position that the government intended to take with the Supreme Court. Alarmed that the final report was a dangerous document, McCloy then ordered all ten original copies to be recalled and destroyed. He further directed that DeWitt's report be rewritten in a way that supported the government's "time was of the essence" argument. McCloy deliberately concealed the knowledge of DeWitt's racist underlying rationale for the mass removal and sought to eradicate the existence of DeWitt's original report. Ennis had requested to see the report, but it was kept from him and the other Justice Department lawyers for another nine months until January 1944, when Ennis was finally given the revised version while the Justice Department team was preparing for the *Korematsu* case. Nine of the ten copies of the original final report were destroyed, but the tenth copy remained unaccounted for, leaving evidence of the government's behind-the-scenes misdeeds.

Meanwhile, military officials were leaking false information from the fraudulent DeWitt report to state officials in the western states who were preparing their amicus briefs in support of the mass evacuation. The lies would be replicated and perpetuated in the states' written presentations to the court.

• • •

So I found this document signed by Warrant Officer Theodore J. E. Smith saying that, "I have witnessed the destruction of galley proofs, memos, letters having to do with the first version of the final report." Okay, so since I knew the history behind the fact that there was an

*original version . . . I recognized this particular book that was sitting on
the corner of an archivist's desk that I was thumbing through. I looked
at it and said, "Ooh, this looks like the final, DeWitt's final report." . . .
And, oh, my goodness. This is one of the first versions. And this is the
one that they could not locate. There had been ten copies, messages and
cablegrams went back and forth between McCloy's office and the Western Defense Command saying, "Hey, we got nine copies back, where is
the tenth copy? We've got to find it." Well, apparently they never found
it. I never saw any documents saying, "Here is the tenth copy," or anything. It ended up in somebody's office in the War Department when
everything was moved over to the archives. It got mixed in with all the
papers that belonged to the War Department. Either the War Department downtown—in Washington or Western Defense Command. I
think it's the Western Defense Command, because they worked from
the notes to make the changes. So I recognized this as that one, the
tenth copy that was missing.*

—Aiko **Yoshinaga** (Herzig), female, Nisei, Los Angeles, California,
incarcerated age 17, Manzanar Relocation Center, Jerome Relocation
Center, Rohwer Relocation Center[258]

• • •

On top of this, DeWitt claimed in his final report that Japanese
Americans were engaged in illegal shore-to-ship signaling, to further strengthen his argument that enough Japanese Americans were
disloyal to justify their mass removal. However, the FBI, the ONI,
and the Federal Communications Commission (FCC) had reported
directly to Attorney General Francis Biddle that no evidence of such
Japanese American activity existed; the three agencies had all completely refuted DeWitt's claims. But the government's briefs to the
court did not reference any of the FBI, ONI, or FCC reports contain-
ing this information.

In fact, Biddle himself had transmitted to McCloy the January 1942
report by ONI's Lieutenant Commander Kenneth Ringle, in which

Ringle recommended that the issue of loyalty be handled not on the basis of citizenship or race, but on an individual basis. Ennis informed Solicitor General Fahy, his superior, that Ringle's report directly undermined DeWitt's claim that mass evacuation was necessary. Ennis went so far as to warn Fahy that he considered it a suppression of evidence not to advise the court of the Ringle report; in fact, not to advise the court of this information would constitute a breach of the government's ethical responsibilities. Despite these warnings by Ennis, the government did not provide Ringle's report to the Supreme Court nor represent its existence in its briefs.

• • •

I picked out the box [in the National Archives] that said Korematsu v. United States. . . . I found a memo. And it was written by a government Justice Department lawyer named Edward Ennis . . . to the solicitor general of the United States, Charles Fahy. . . . And in that memo . . . to [Fahy] who was preparing to argue the Korematsu case before the Supreme Court in 1944, Ennis said, "We are in possession of information that shows that the War Department's report on the internment is a lie. And we have an ethical obligation not to tell a lie to the Supreme Court, and we must decide whether to correct that record." And looking at that document, I still remember vividly thinking, "Oh, my God. This is amazing. This is like a smoking gun." Here's a lawyer for the government about to . . . [argue] before the Supreme Court saying, "We are telling lies to the Supreme Court." . . . The memo said, "This may approximate the suppression of evidence." As a lawyer, I realized this is dynamite.
—Peter H. Irons, civil rights attorney, legal scholar, and professor emeritus of political science at University of California, San Diego[259]

• • •

At the stroke of noon on Monday, May 10, 1943, the marshal of the Supreme Court announced, "The Honorable, the Chief Justice and the Associate Justices of the Supreme Court of the United States. Oyez! Oyez! Oyez! All persons having business before the Honorable, the Supreme Court of the United States, are admonished to draw near and give their attention, for the Court is now sitting. God save the United States and this Honorable Court!"

Nine Supreme Court justices walked through the red velvet curtains to take their places on the bench: Chief Justice Harlan Fiske Stone and his colleagues Justices Owen Josephus Roberts, Hugo Lafayette Black, Stanley Forman Reed, Felix Frankfurter, William Orville Douglas, Frank Murphy, Robert Houghwout Jackson, and Wiley Blount Rutledge.

The attorneys representing the US government took their seats at the counsel tables. On one side of the podium was the solicitor general of the Justice Department, Charles Fahy, the person representing the US government before the Supreme Court. Fahy was proud of his track record before the high court. By the time he'd been appointed as an assistant solicitor general in 1940, he had already won sixteen out of eighteen cases he had argued before the Supreme Court, and the court had partially upheld his arguments in the other two. His streak had continued since his appointment as solicitor general. On the other side of the podium sat the attorneys for Yasui, Hirabayashi, and Korematsu. It had been about a year since each of the three men had been arrested.

Before them stood plain tables with inkwells and goose quill pens, reminders of the historic significance of their high court appearance.

Hirabayashi's two attorneys, Frank Walters and Harold Evans, had just met for the first time a half hour before the court session was due to start. Walters stood in the chambers of the imposing building known as the Marble Palace to open the hearing; he had never argued a case in the Supreme Court before. He began, "May it please the Court," and not long into his argument, he was caught off guard by the justices' questioning.

The justices focused on the extent to which the judiciary should review the decisions of the military during wartime. Walters and Evans got so distracted by this line of questioning that they never got around to making the point that DeWitt's orders unlawfully discriminated against Japanese Americans as a class, in violation of due process and equal protection under the law.

The next day the court reconvened to hear the *Yasui* case. Earl Bernard, one of Yasui's lawyers, did not raise the unconstitutionality of the curfew at all. The whole reason Yasui had gotten himself arrested was to test the constitutional principle behind the curfew and ultimately the exclusion orders. Instead, Bernard belabored the point the government had already conceded in its briefs: Judge Fee had wrongly decided that Yasui had renounced his citizenship because of his employment with the Japanese consulate. Yasui's other counsel, A. L. Wirin, then attacked DeWitt and the Roberts Commission report (with Justice Roberts, the chair of the commission, sitting on the bench in front of him). Justice Black responded by raising questions similar to those posed to Hirabayashi's lawyers.

"To what extent," Black asked, "can we review the decision of a general selected to make those decisions?"

Wirin responded by referring to a prior Supreme Court decision, *Sterling v. Constantin*, in which the court outlined the circumstances that could trigger a review of a military leader's decision-making process. In further questioning, Justice Black showed his skepticism about Wirin's answer. Justice Douglas weighed in, commenting that even though "some individuals among those evacuated [were] loyal Americans," this fact did "not affect the soundness of the military judgment."

Fahy then took the podium to respond to the *Hirabayashi* and *Yasui* petitions, arguing that the executive and legislative branches shared enough constitutional power to override the due process rights of citizens during wartime. Calmly and eloquently, he proceeded to justify the government's actions and handled the justices' questions professionally. The lawyers for Yasui and Hirabayashi recognized how well the skilled solicitor general resonated with the justices; when the two-day session was over, they knew they had been outmatched. After-ward Wirin admitted to Besig, the attorney who had first contacted Korematsu, "The arguments in the Yasui and Hirabayashi cases went badly for us."

As the nine members of the Supreme Court gathered on Mon-day morning, May 17, for their closed-door conference on the *Yasui*, *Hirabayashi*, and *Korematsu* cases, they exchanged handshakes, observing a court tradition to begin each conference with this symbolic sign of fraternity. But beneath this veneer of camaraderie was a deeply divided court, with some members barely speaking to one another.

The most straightforward case was Korematsu's. In the oral argu-ments Burling, representing the government, had all but conceded that Korematsu's sentence of probation was a final judgment that could be appealed. And so, as anticipated, in a unanimous decision announced on June 1, 1943, the court sent Korematsu's case back to the Ninth Circuit for it to address the constitutionality of the mass removal. Because of the time it would take for the Ninth Circuit to revisit Korematsu's case, the government succeeded in delaying the Supreme Court's consideration of the merits of Korematsu's case for another year. For this reason, the Supreme Court decisions in Yasui's and Hirabayashi's cases became separated in history from Korematsu's case, even though the three men had started out their constitutional challenges at about the same time.

Chief Justice Stone's goal in considering the *Hirabayashi* and *Yasui* cases was to have the court present a united front in support of the president and the war effort. After all, FDR had appointed eight of the nine justices; Justice Roberts was the lone appointee by President Herbert Hoover, FDR's predecessor.

Since Judge Lloyd D. Black had given Hirabayashi concurrent sen-tences for violating the curfew and the exclusion order, the Supreme Court used the combined sentencing as a basis for considering only one of Hirabayashi's two convictions. Instead of ruling on the constitutionality of the mass removal, as Hirabayashi had intended, the court chose only to consider his curfew conviction. As a result, the court saw Hirabayashi's case and Yasui's case as addressing the same issue and treated them as companion cases. Stone said it was "unnecessary to consider the questions raised" by the exclusion orders.

The chief justice then exercised his prerogative to write the opinions for both cases. Over the next month Stone was able to sustain unanimous consensus in what became the court's opinions, which found that imposing a curfew was a reasonable executive power to give to the military so it could exercise restrictions on a race with whom the United States was at war.

Stone devoted the *Hirabayashi* opinion to setting forth the rationale for upholding the constitutionality of the curfew order:

- the military installations and weapons production on the West Coast were important to the war effort;
- there was a concentration of Japanese Americans who lived near these installations;
- individuals of Japanese descent felt a "solidarity" with their motherland;
- the military knew best about threats of war; and
- curfews were an "obvious protection" against sabotage and a "protective measure necessary to meet the threat of sabotage and espionage."

Without requiring any evidence, the court accepted the government's "time was of the essence" argument and the stereotypes put forward in DeWitt's report that people of Japanese ancestry were unassimilated and therefore suspect. In his *Hirabayashi* opinion, Stone wrote, "We cannot reject as unfounded the judgment of the military authorities and of Congress that there were disloyal members of that population, whose number and strength could not be precisely and quickly ascertained."

Stone's accompanying *Yasui* opinion was a scant three-page document, referring to the rationale and conclusions in the lengthier *Hiraba-yashi* opinion, and did not contain any concurring opinions nor dissents.

The Supreme Court ruled against Yasui and Hirabayashi, issuing opinions in both cases on June 21, 1943.

Although the two opinions were unanimous, Stone's task of holding together that consensus hadn't been easy. Justice Murphy had been so upset with Stone justifying racial discrimination, even during wartime, that he'd drafted a dissent in *Hirabayashi*; he was later persuaded to change it to a concurring opinion. Justice Douglas had been troubled by the habeas corpus issue and had raised the feasibility of holding separate habeas corpus hearings for each incarcerated person of Japanese ancestry. He ended up acknowledging the government's position that this sorting process would be time consuming, and agreeing with the War Department's contention that time was of the essence. The briefness of Justice Rutledge's concurrence does not reflect the doubts he had in these cases. He wrote to the chief justice, "I am now clear to go with you," but he also indicated, "I have had more anguish over this case than any I have decided, save possibly one death case in the [Court] of Appeals."

· · ·

In the checks-and-balances system of the United States, the judicial, legislative, and executive branches of the government jealously guard their respective prerogatives. But the Supreme Court seemingly abdicated its duty to defend and uphold the Constitution, deferring to the executive branch, saying "You're the specialists running the war, and who are we to tell you what to do?" or something to that effect. . . . I thought the raison d'etre for the Supreme Court was to uphold the Constitution. . . . President Roosevelt wanted a decision in favor of the government. He apparently passed the word to one of his appointees that it would be a good thing for the war effort if there was a unanimous decision. . . . Well, I thought—I guess the Constitution had gone to war, too!

—Gordon Kiyoshi **Hirabayashi**, male, Nisei, Seattle, Washington, age 22 when Pearl Harbor was attacked, King County Jail, Tucson Federal Prison/Catalina Federal Honor Camp, McNeil Island Federal Penitentiary[260]

. . .

It had been almost a year since Judge Michael Roche had held the hearing in July 1942 on Mitsuye Endo's habeas corpus petition, and the judge had yet to issue his decision. A judge is expected to rule quickly in a habeas corpus case, but Judge Roche was stalling. He'd been waiting for the Supreme Court to act on the three criminal conviction cases. In July 1943, twelve days after the Supreme Court's announcement of the *Yasui* and *Hirabayashi* decisions, Judge Roche denied Endo's petition without explanation.

Endo appealed to the Ninth Circuit, which—just as it had done with the *Yasui*, *Hirabayashi*, and *Korematsu* cases—asked the Supreme Court to address certain issues of law before the Ninth Circuit considered the case. The Supreme Court announced on March 27, 1944, that it had chosen to hear Endo's case, now referred to as *Ex parte Endo*, with oral arguments set for October 1944, at the beginning of the court's upcoming term.

By the time Endo's case would be heard by the Supreme Court, she would have been incarcerated at the Tule Lake Relocation Center for over two years. In an attempt to get Endo to abandon her case, WRA attorney Philip Glick offered her the opportunity to be released from camp. But in an act of commitment to the cause, Endo steadfastly refused Glick's offer so that the lawsuit could continue, even though it meant she would remain imprisoned.

. . .

During that time in camp, I was anxious to have my case settled because most of my friends had already gone out, been relocated, and I was anxious to get out too. . . . I could have left earlier, but [my attorney] needed me to be in camp.

—Mitsuye Maureen **Endo** (Tsutsumi), female, Nisei, Sacramento, California, incarcerated age 22, Sacramento Assembly Center, Tule Lake Relocation Center, Topaz Relocation Center[261]

• • •

On the same day the Supreme Court announced it would hear the *Endo* case in October 1944, it also announced that it would hear the *Korematsu* case in that same month. By then almost two and a half years would have elapsed since Korematsu's arrest.

Faced with the mounting pressure of having to defend the mass evacuation and detention at all costs, Solicitor General Fahy and Assistant Secretary of War McCloy continued to manipulate and suppress the evidence, as well as rely upon false representations in the preparation of the government's *Korematsu* brief. Justice Department attorneys Ennis and Burling attempted to include a section in the official brief that would describe the misrepresentations in DeWitt's final report or, at minimum, indicate to the court that the government had information in opposition to its rationale for the evacuation. In a dramatic showdown in which the presses printing the government's final brief were stopped twice as revisions were negotiated, Ennis and Burling were ultimately overruled in their quest to avoid suppression of evidence.

In his oral arguments before the court in the *Korematsu* hearing on October 11, 1944, Solicitor General Fahy said, "No person in any responsible position has ever taken a contrary position" to DeWitt's assertions—a bald-faced lie because he himself had seen the reports that contradicted DeWitt's claims.

On Monday, December 18, 1944, the Supreme Court, by a vote of six to three, affirmed Korematsu's conviction and upheld the exclusion orders as a constitutional exercise of wartime executive power.

In his majority opinion, Justice Black set forth words that have since become famous in constitutional law: "All legal restrictions which curtail the civil rights of a single racial group are immediately suspect. That is not to say that all such restrictions are unconstitutional. It is to say that courts must subject them to the most rigid scrutiny." However, Justice Black (a longtime close friend of DeWitt's) failed to apply any scrutiny whatsoever to the justification for the exclusion orders, accepting without question the judgment of military leaders.

In a position that struck at the heart of the reasoning behind the Constitutional separation of powers, Justice Frankfurter stated in his concurring opinion that it was not the role of the judicial branch to second-guess the executive and legislative branches in their exercise of their powers to wage war. Regarding the military's determination that it was necessary to remove and incarcerate Japanese Americans, Frankfurter emphatically stated, "That is their business, not ours."

The three dissenting opinions—by Justices Roberts, Murphy, and Jackson—in the *Korematsu* case reflected the deep divisions within the court on the many issues lurking beneath the unanimity of the *Hirabayashi* and *Yasui* decisions. Justice Roberts wrote, "I think the indisputable facts exhibit a clear violation of Constitutional rights." Justice Murphy opened his dissent by saying, "Such exclusion goes over 'the very brink of constitutional power' and falls into the ugly abyss of racism." He concluded with an emphatic objection to "this legalization of racism."

In the third dissent, Justice Jackson pointed out the illogical situation in which the exclusion orders had placed Korematsu as well as all other persons of Japanese ancestry: They were forbidden to remain in their homes, yet they were also forbidden to leave, such that the only way to avoid committing a crime was to submit to "indeterminate confinement in detention camps." He continued: "Here is an attempt to make an otherwise innocent act a crime merely because this prisoner is the son of parents as to whom he had no choice, and belongs to a race from which there is no way to resign." With words that have become prophetic, Justice Jackson concluded:

Once a judicial opinion rationalizes [a military order] to show that it conforms to the Constitution, or rather rationalizes the Constitution to show that the Constitution sanctions such an order, the Court for all time has validated the principle of racial discrimination in criminal procedure and of transplanting American citizens. The principle then lies about like **a loaded weapon** [emphasis added] ready for the hand of any authority that can bring forward a plausible claim of an urgent need.

But as eloquent as these three dissents were, they did not carry the day for Korematsu or the constitutional principles he was fighting for.

• • •

In 1944, in Detroit, I received a letter from Mr. Besig and he told me that we lost in the Supreme Court. And I just couldn't believe it. . . . It just seemed like the bottom dropped out. I just felt like, "Am I an American or not?" And how about all those other Japanese Americans; are they Japanese American? . . . When I found out I lost my decision, I thought I lost my country.

—Fred Toyosaburo **Korematsu**, male, Nisei, San Leandro, California, age 22 when Pearl Harbor was attacked, Presidio, Tanforan Assembly Center, Topaz Relocation Center[262]

CHAPTER TEN

Resettling into an Uncertain Future

The desert must have claimed its own
Now that the wayfarers are gone.
—Toyo **Suyemoto** (Kawakami), female, Nisei, Alameda County,
California, incarcerated age 26, Tanforan Assembly Center, Topaz
Relocation Center[263]

As the war continued, thousands of Nikkei families in camp were still missing their fathers and husbands. The Issei men who had been arrested right after the attack on Pearl Harbor had been languishing in DOJ or US Army internment camps for years. Considered disloyal without any opportunity to prove otherwise, they continued to exist in a legal limbo, separated from their families.

One of the imprisoned Issei was Jack Yasutake, father of the poet Mitsuye Yasutake Yamada. For over twenty years Yasutake had worked for the Immigration and Naturalization Service (INS) as a translator. The Stanford-educated community leader could quote Shakespeare and was attending a meeting of his poetry club, the Senryu Society, dedicated to a seventeen-syllable form of haiku, when the FBI arrested him on December 7, 1941. Finally, in March 1944, almost two and a half years later, he was called before an alien enemy special hearing board.

These boards usually consisted of a lawyer; representatives from the FBI, the US attorney general's office, and the INS; and three civilians from the local community. After hearing Yasutake's case, the board was faced with the decision of whether to intern him for the rest of the war in a DOJ or US Army internment camp, release him unconditionally, or put him on parole.

The board was unanimous in its decision: "We are entirely convinced that this man is not only entitled to his freedom, but that he is entitled to an immediate release." They said he was "an honorable type of man" who could now be reunited with his family at Minidoka. But Attorney General Francis Biddle refused to release him. Almost four months later, on July 1, 1944, the attorney general ruled that Yasutake could be "paroled." So even though Yasutake had never been found guilty of any crime, he was now considered an ex-convict.

More than a year earlier, in May 1943, WRA Director Dillon Myer had questioned Secretary of War Henry Stimson on how the War Department was continuing to justify the exclusion of Japanese Americans from the West Coast under the military exclusion orders. Myer believed that until the Japanese Americans were allowed to return to the West Coast, his plan for closing the camps and resettling the population would continue at a snail's pace.

Stimson wouldn't address the issue directly, but finally in May 1944 he conceded there was no longer a military justification (indeed if there ever had been) for considering the West Coast an area of military operations. Stimson, as the secretary of war, had the authority to lift the military exclusion orders, but not Executive Order 9066 itself, which was the right of the president.

Stimson broached the subject at the president's cabinet meeting on May 26, 1944. Attorney General Biddle recorded in his notes:

> The Secretary of War raised the question of whether it was appropriate for the War Department, at this time, to cancel the Japanese Exclusion Orders and let the Japs go home. War, Interior, and Justice had all agreed that this could be done without danger to defense considerations but doubted the wisdom of doing it at this time before the election.

Undersecretary of State Edward Stettinius Jr. put a fine point on it for the president: "The question appears to be largely a political one, the reaction in California, on which I am sure you will probably wish to reach your own decision."

FDR was preparing to be reelected, for an unprecedented fourth term, in the November 1944 election, and he knew that West Coast politicians and their constituents continued to vehemently oppose the Nikkei's return to their hometowns. Roosevelt was not about to antagonize voters in the key state of California; he was determined not to let the persistent "Japanese problem" jeopardize his chances for reelection. But Roosevelt's refusal to let the Japanese Americans out of the camps, even as the war was ending, and knowing that the government could not justify any claim of military necessity, resulted in the Japanese Americans spending an additional six months imprisoned.

Secretary of the Interior Harold Ickes kept up the pressure. In a letter he wrote to FDR on June 2, 1944, he stated, "The continued exclusion of American citizens of Japanese ancestry in the affected areas is clearly unconstitutional in the present circumstances" and "The continued retention of these innocent people in the relocation centers would be a blot upon the history of this country."

Like Myer and First Lady Eleanor Roosevelt, Ickes was especially concerned about the young Japanese Americans who were quickly "becoming a hopelessly maladjusted generation, apprehensive of the outside world and divorced from the possibility of associating [with]—or even seeing to any considerable extent—Americans of other races."

Once Myer had been able to remove background checks, job requirements, and other obstacles from the leave clearance program, the number of those seeking permanent leave had increased to 11,000 by the end of 1944. Nearly 35,000 had been released into communities across the country as seasonal workers or students. Many had been drafted. Seven out of every ten who left camp in 1943 and 1944 were between the ages of fifteen and thirty-five. But there were still at least 75,000 people in the concentration camps, mostly women of all ages, men older than fifty, and children and teenagers younger than seventeen. Myer now realized he had a different problem—many of the incarcerated just didn't want to leave. The older Issei had grown used to their grim but predictable life. They now saw the camps as safe havens from racist, all-White communities. Only one out of every six Issei had left camp. It had been more than two years since they had lived with White people, and now they were afraid of them.

On November 7, 1944, FDR was elected president to a historic fourth term. Once reelected, he finally allowed the War Department to lift the exclusion orders. But Roosevelt had not overestimated the hostility against Japanese Americans on the West Coast. As the War Department began plans to terminate the detention program, the American Legion in Hood River, Oregon, erased the names of the sixteen Nisei servicemen on their honor rolls (which they would not restore until April 1945).

Meanwhile, McCloy was working hard behind the scenes to shield FDR from the political fallout of the decision to end the incarceration. McCloy prevailed upon Chief Justice Stone to stall the announcement of the court's *Korematsu* and *Endo* decisions until the army was ready to publicly announce that Japanese Americans could leave the camps and return to the West Coast. The Western Defense Command of the War Department was told, off the record (most likely by Justice Frankfurter), that the court planned to announce both of its decisions on Monday, December 18, 1944. This tip enabled the army to arrange for their own announcement to be made the day before the Supreme Court announcements, unusual for a Sunday.

And so it was that on Sunday, December 17, 1944, Major General Henry C. Pratt, the Western Defense Command commanding general, issued Public Proclamation No. 21, declaring that the exclusion orders would be lifted effective midnight January 2, 1945.

Nearly three years after FDR had signed Executive Order 9066, the West Coast Japanese Americans could go home.

Twenty-four hours later, on December 18, in a brief opinion by Justice

Douglas, the Supreme Court ruled unanimously in *Ex parte Endo* that Mitsuye Endo was "entitled to an unconditional release by the War Relocation Authority." The court dodged the question of whether the detention of Endo and the other Japanese Americans was constitutional or not, but the *Endo* decision did conclude that the federal government could no longer detain loyal American citizens against their will.

• • •

I never imagined [my case] would go to the Supreme Court. In fact I thought it might be thrown out of court because of all that bad sentiment toward us. While all this was going on, it seemed like a dream. It just didn't seem like it was happening to me. . . . Do I have any regrets at all about the test case? No . . . because of the way it turned out.

—Mitsuye Maureen **Endo** (Tsutsumi), female, Nisei, Sacramento, California, incarcerated age 22, Sacramento Assembly Center, Tule Lake Relocation Center, Topaz Relocation Center[264]

• • •

Just as the Roosevelt administration had intended, the War Department's Sunday announcement overshadowed the Supreme Court's Monday announcements in the press. The Supreme Court had held back on issuing these decisions earlier in the fall to accommodate the White House. Although communication between the Supreme Court and the White House was rare, in this case it appeared that the court was giving the White House and the War Department a chance to make a preemptive strike; the War Department's announcement a day earlier was clearly designed to curtail the impact of the *Endo* Supreme Court decision. In effect, the court allowed the army to retain its control over the public's perception of its moral leadership, and the executive branch avoided the appearance that it was being told what to do by the judiciary.

On Tuesday, December 19, 1944, Myer announced that all relocation centers would close by January 2, 1946, at which time all incarcerees would be required to leave.

Myer's announcement came as a shock and precipitated yet another emotional uproar in the camps. The incarcerees debated various options at meetings that became turbulent. The situation grew so volatile that the incarcerees called for a WRA-approved All-Center Conference, which took place in Salt Lake City, Utah, from February 16 to February 22, 1945, with over thirty representatives from at least seven relocation centers. At that meeting the majority of the incarcerees rejected the idea that the camps would be closing and insisted that they remain open until the war with Japan was over. The Issei argued that the government had forced this imprisonment upon them, and now it was obligated to provide a roof over their heads, food on their plates, and medical care as they aged.

• • •

We were in Poston from '42–'45—three and a half years. My dad always said, "They put me in here—they're going to have to kick me out!" The camp was getting emptier and emptier. I remember my mom saying, "Well, when are we going to leave?" And my dad said, "When they close the place." And that's exactly what happened. . . . I think he felt that way because he was put there against his will and by G-d they'll have to kick him out. . . . He still had the property in Delano, but he didn't want to go back there because anti-Japanese feelings were so bad in California. His friends who went back early had difficulty with prejudice.
—Ellen Shizue **Yukawa** (Spink), female, Sansei, Kern County,
California, incarcerated age 9, Poston Relocation Center[265]

By the end of 1944 about 6,000 people remained at Manzanar and those, for the most part, were the aging and the [very] young. Whoever had prospects on the outside and the energy to go, were leaving, relocating or entering military service. No one could blame them. To most Nisei, anything looked better than remaining in the camps. [But] for many of their parents, just the opposite was true.
—Jeanne Toyo **Wakatsuki** (Houston), female, Nisei, Santa Monica,

California, incarcerated age 8, Manzanar Reception Center,
Manzanar Relocation Center[266]

. . .

Fears about what Japanese Americans would face if they returned
to California, Oregon, or Washington were well founded. The anti-
Japanese sentiments on the West Coast were stronger than ever, and
with the announcement that the government was closing the camps,
the post–Pearl Harbor racist aggression intensified. Adventurous souls
who were the first to leave wrote letters to friends still living at the
camps, describing how much their old neighborhoods had changed.
Black people had moved into Little Tokyo in Los Angeles, which was
now called Bronzeville, causing a different kind of racial tension when
the Japanese Americans returned to reclaim their lives. What had once
been so familiar and safe now seemed strange and threatening. White
merchants were boycotting fruits, flowers, and produce grown by Japanese Americans, so it was difficult to reestablish their farms and businesses. Some of the letters contained horrifying stories of arson, night
rider attacks, and drive-by shootings.

Myer was especially concerned about these incidents and called
the perpetrators "terrorists." He reported that one of the first moves
made by terrorists in California to scare off the returning incarcerees
occurred on January 8, 1945, when an attempt was made to dynamite
and burn the fruit packing shed of a returnee in Placer County. This
incident was followed by about thirty other attempts by terrorists to
frighten the Nikkei away from their homes. Most of these involved
shooting incidents in which shots were directed at the corners and
other portions of their houses with long-range rifles to try to frighten
the residents into leaving.

In a statement to the public, Interior Secretary Ickes said, "In the
absence of vigorous local law enforcement, a pattern of planned terrorism by hoodlums has developed. It is a matter of national concern
because this lawless minority, whose actions are condemned by the

decent citizens who make up an overwhelming majority of West Coast residents, seems determined to employ its Nazi storm trooper tactics against loyal Japanese Americans and law-abiding Japanese aliens in spite of the state laws and Constitutional safeguards designed to protect the lives and property of all of the people of this country."

Young Mary Masuda had left the Gila River camp ahead of the rest of her family to assess the condition of their farm in Fountain Valley, California. She found that strangers had moved into their home and had been farming their land. While she was staying with Caucasian friends, four men from the Native Sons of the Golden West threatened her with "bodily harm" if she did not leave the county. The WRA said it was prepared to turn over the names of her harassers to the authorities, but the local sheriff maintained that nothing had happened to her. So Mary went to the press, and Ickes got the local sheriff back on the case.

Mary bravely ignored the threats and returned to the farm with her mother and three brothers just out of the military, all honorably discharged. Tragically, Mary's other brother, Kazuo, was not joining them. A 442nd soldier, Staff Sergeant Masuda had been killed in battle and was awarded a posthumous Distinguished Service Cross. Mary's problems moving back to the family farm and the posthumous awarding of her brother's medal happened to coincide with the WRA and War Department's launch of a pro–Japanese American publicity push to combat terrorism and discrimination, and the Masuda family was factored into the campaign.

The government's publicists arranged for General Joseph Stilwell to present the medal to the family, in person, on the front steps of the Masuda farmhouse on December 8, 1945. But Kazuo's mother refused the medal in protest for having lost her son while being incarcerated by the country he'd been serving. Stilwell pinned the medal on Mary instead, who turned around and pinned it on her mother.

The event resulted in an avalanche of news coverage by newsreel and press photographers. After the medal ceremony at the Masuda home, Stilwell spoke at a United America Day rally at the Santa Ana Bowl, which he attended with Mary and her family. He was joined there by Hollywood actors, who also spoke, including a young army captain named Ronald Reagan.

General Stilwell stood up and said, "The amount of money, the color of one's skin do not make a measure of Americanism. A square deal all around: free speech; equality before the law; a fair field with no favor; obedience to the majority. An American not only believes in such things but is willing to fight for them. Who, after all, is the real American? The real American is the man who calls it a fair exchange to lay down his life in order that American ideals may go on living. And judging by such a test Sgt. Masuda was a better American than any of us here today."

And then Captain Ronald Reagan rose and said, "The blood that has soaked into the sand is all one color. America stands unique in the world, the only country not founded on race, but on a way—an ideal. Not in spite of, but because of our polyglot background, we have had all the strength in the world. That is the American way. Mr. and Mrs. Masuda, just as one member of the family of Americans, speaking to another member, I want to say for what your son Kazuo did—Thanks."

Three years later the Masuda family finally received Kazuo's remains from Europe, which triggered another round of racism. As she tried to arrange for her brother's burial at a local cemetery—the one he had chosen in the event of his death—Mary was told outright that any "desirable plots" (land with grass and trees) were "covered by a racial restrictive covenant and the burial of persons not of Caucasian ancestry [was not] permitted in the restricted area."

Mary reported this situation to the *Pacific Citizen*, the national newspaper of the JACL. The *Rafu Shimpo* also ran an article about the Masuda family's dilemma under the headline "With Gratitude to Kaz Masuda, the Hero of Fountain Valley." The coverage sparked a public outcry in support of a war hero having a place to rest in peace. The regional director of the JACL, Joe Grant Masaoka (Mike's brother), wrote to General Mark W. Clark, commander of the Fifth Army, saying it was "inconsistent for one to have given his life and then be denied a plot in a land he died to defend for final burial." General Clark called upon the cemetery's board of directors to reverse its decision, and Mary was offered a "desirable" plot for her brother.

But this refusal by private cemeteries to provide burial plots for the Nisei soldiers killed in action was common up and down the Pacific coast. The *Pacific Citizen* reported that families were finding it almost impossible to obtain plots for their deceased soldiers even in Chicago and Minnesota. The only alternative was cremation.

Gold Star families fared better with the Arlington National Cemetery. Private First Class Fumitake Nagato and Private First Class Saburo Tanamachi of the 100th/442nd RCT were the first two Japanese American soldiers to be buried there, on June 4, 1948. Every Memorial Day, the Washington, DC, chapter of the JACL and the Japanese American Veterans Association (JAVA) place a bouquet of flowers on the grave of every Japanese American soldier who fought in any war and on the graves of the Caucasian officers who commanded Nisei units. It's the longest-running annual service held at Arlington Cemetery by any independent organization in the country. According to JAVA, as of 2019, the number of graves has grown to ninety.

Meanwhile, other Japanese Americans had gone home and found it impossible to reclaim the farms that were legally theirs, or their farms had been so poorly cared for by the people who'd promised to look after them that the land was overgrown with weeds. Their equipment had been vandalized, and their belongings had been stolen from storage facilities. Like the Masudas, other returning incarcerees reported that strangers were squatting in their homes, and the homeowners were having a hard time getting these squatters out.

Jobs and housing generally were hard to find, in part because of discrimination. Educated and highly skilled workers were forced to take jobs as laborers, janitors, gardeners, and farmworkers. Many women worked as housekeepers just to have a room to live in; without any occupational skills, they invariably had to take the lowest-paying jobs. Children returning to school were ostracized and bullied; in some cases, the higher education of Japanese American high school students was being sabotaged.

• • •

Some [teachers] never gave Japanese American students more than a C, so they couldn't qualify for scholarships.

—Masaru "Mas" **Hashimoto**, male, Nisei, Watsonville, California, incarcerated age 6, Salinas Assembly Center, Poston Relocation Center[267]

My mother was very concerned about my sister and me starting school. The superintendent told her, "Don't worry. I've sent a note to the principal explaining that there are two little Japanese girls coming to school and I want everyone to welcome them." It was an upper-middle-class, very white school. We got on the school bus, and everyone was very patronizing, like, "You can sit in this seat." I just felt it was fake. We were singled out, and I felt very uncomfortable. Then there was a special assembly for us. I thought, I want to fall through the cracks. At recess time I never played with anyone. No one ever played with me. The teachers were very nice. There was no really anti-Japanese thing. Just that we were the only two Japanese in the school. There was one black boy who was very nice. The kids tried to be nice, except they didn't play with me. Maybe it was me because I was so super-shy I was unapproachable. That could have been it too. . . . I couldn't wait to move on.

—Emi "Amy" **Akiyama** (Berger), female, Sansei, Berkeley, California, incarcerated age 8, Tanforan Assembly Center, Topaz Relocation Center[268]

• • •

The worst shame of all was when families had to rely on welfare checks. Landlords wouldn't rent to Japanese. Many of them moved into trailer parks that had been quickly assembled around defense plants, now hiring in the postwar economy. But even if they could find a one-room apartment, they couldn't afford it, or if they could, they would soon learn that their relatives needed a place to live too (and were willing to sleep on the floor).

· · ·

The uncertain period of resettlement was not easy for my family. My older sisters worked at low paying jobs. For four years, we lived in a one bedroom apartment that housed five of us. Our two sons were immediately placed in public schools and the experience of being resettled persons was compounded with jeering remarks and fights.

—May Kikuko (Tominaga) **Ichida**, female, Nisei, San Francisco, California, incarcerated age 34, Manzanar Reception Center, Manzanar Relocation Center[269]

To me, the saddest thing that happened was when my father came out of internment, after being idle for four years. He had to resettle in Chicago, and he didn't have any money. No capital. No nothing, and even with his education. As you can imagine, a sixty-year-old man trying to get a white collar job—there was nothing available for him. My father kept looking for work, and he couldn't find anything. Finally he decided he would try opening some kind of office and do bookkeeping services and try to sell real estate and things like that. He never was able to get back on his feet in the real sense of the word.

—Chiye **Tomihiro**, female, Nisei, Portland, Oregon, incarcerated age 17, Portland Assembly Center, Minidoka Relocation Center[270]

The only work that we could find was servant-type labor as gardeners, houseboys, busboys, janitors, dishwashers, and so forth.

Mom worked in a fish cannery on Terminal Island until she was in her 70's. . . . My father was unable to work.

. . . My father and my mother died, very sad, and unfulfilled. . . . Their chance to achieve their dreams and goals had been crushed by [the] unconstitutional and illegal actions of the U.S. Government.

. . . And by the overreaction and paranoid inhuman creation of detention camps. In 1955 my father, feeling he was a failure and a burden on his children, died of a broken heart.

> —Masani "Mas" **Fukai**, male, Nisei, Gardena, California,
> incarcerated age 15, Tulare Assembly Center, Gila River Relocation
> Center[271]

The Usui family lived in the Seinan area, the southwest portion of the city of Los Angeles, from 1925 to the date of the evacuation. . . .

In 1938, my father and older brother, my mother and younger sister started a landscape nursery. . . . It was called Friend Club Nursery. We bought the property at a price of $10,000 and established an equity of approximately $4,500 by the time of the evacuation date. We had enough inventory to cover almost every available space with plants. . . .

I was attending UCLA at the time. . . . We had about two weeks [after the war began] to do something, either lease the property or sell everything: the land, the building, the tools and plants. There was no way we could meet the monthly mortgage payments if we closed. . . . We finally decided to sell. We advertised and let the people in the neighborhood know we were selling. Finally, after a few days, we had to leave. A lady had heard . . . that our property and business was for sale. . . . She offered us $1,000 for everything: the property, the building, and inventory. We took the offer because it was the best of a bad situation. . . .

I served [as a paratrooper] until February 1946 and was [honorably] discharged from the army at San Pedro, California. . . . After I reached home, my father asked me to go immediately to the nursery and try to buy it back. Still in my uniform, I hurriedly went to the nursery and asked if the owner would sell . . . the nursery back to us. The owner of the nursery . . . had bought it from the lady to whom we [had] sold it.

He said, "Yep, I'll sell you the nursery. Give me $13,000 for the land and $13,000 for the inventory."

"Impossible!" I exclaimed and went to the back of the property and kicked over a five-gallon can. The man wanted to know what I was doing, so I showed him some Japanese writings on the bottom of the can. "Can you see what's written here?" I said. "It says here this plant was planted from a seed on this day, was transplanted into a gallon can on this day, and finally into this five-gallon can on this date. My mother planted all these plants and the five-gallon cans and all the big trees in the back and now you want to sell them back to us at these outrageous prices?"

All he said was, "Well, that's the way the ball bounces."

I came home to tell my folks what happened. My father just broke down and cried.

Thereafter, my father never recovered . . . and it was all downhill. In 1953 he passed away. Even to this day when I recall this incident, tears come into my eyes.

—Mitsuo "Mits" **Usui**, male, Nisei, Los Angeles, California, incarcerated age 25, Santa Anita Assembly Center, Granada (Amache) Relocation Center[272]

• • •

The returning Japanese Americans did not have many friends, but they were grateful for the ones they did have. Walt and Milly Woodward, owners and editors of the *Bainbridge Review*, were the first newspaper publishers on the West Coast and the only ones in western Washington to condemn the forced removal of Japanese Americans. When the Japanese American islanders had been packing to leave for camp, the Woodwards had hired Paul Ohtaki, their young Nisei janitor, to serve as a *Bainbridge Review* camp correspondent so they could publish regular updates on the daily lives of the Japanese American Bainbridge families while they were incarcerated. In this way, the Woodwards intended for the incarcerees to be remembered as part of the island community, smoothing their reentry whenever they were released from camp.

However, in advance of their homecoming, Bainbridge resident Lambert Schuyler intensified his efforts to rally community opposition to the return of the Japanese American islanders. In his lengthy letter to the editors, which the Woodwards published, Schuyler referred to the exiled Nikkei islanders as "monkey-jawed and yellow-skinned" and as "smiling and inscrutable operators of truck farms and grocery stores." He added, "No amount of star-spangled valor on the part of conscripted Japs will change our minds," concluding that "they could never be trusted again." Schuyler attacked the Woodwards as "Jap lovers." He also published his views in a pamphlet titled *The Japs Must Not Come Back! A Practical Approach to the Racial Problem* and talked about it continually in town halls.

The Woodwards provided a model for the role and the power of the press. They covered Schuyler's anti-Japanese activities and offered their newspaper as a forum for the local residents to air their views, while maintaining their editorial position in support of the Nikkei. When the war ended, the Woodwards' daughter observed that "Bainbridge Islanders as a group rejected the racism that flowered in nearby communities." As a result, over half of those Japanese American families from Bainbridge Island did come home—a much higher rate of return than the rest of the northwest. David Guterson based his bestselling novel *Snow Falling on Cedars* upon the experiences of the Japanese American community leaving and returning to Bainbridge Island. He drew inspiration for the character of Arthur Chambers from Walt Woodward himself.

Some incarcerees were welcomed by the same group of White friends and neighbors who had bid them a sad farewell nearly three years earlier. Local civic and church groups set up temporary housing until the Japanese Americans could find places of their own.

A few friends had done a good job of looking after the incarcerees' property. When they had been ordered to leave the West Coast, Mary Oyama Mittwer and her husband, Fred Mittwer, realized that they would need to rent out their home in the Los Angeles area of Boyle Heights in order to afford the mortgage and sustain their ownership during their absence. The Mittwers had unsuccessfully interviewed a number of prospective tenants when a friend suggested to Oyama Mittwer, an established writer and community activist, that the Mittwers meet with Chester Himes, a Black writer, and his wife, Jean Lucinda Johnson.

Oyama Mittwer had not known any Black people, but said to herself, "OK, gal, you've always believed in democracy. Now's your chance to do your stuff," and agreed to meet Himes and Johnson. The couples immediately bonded. Himes and Johnson took care of the Mittwers' home until the Mittwers returned from camp. Through their enduring friendship, each family learned of the prejudices that the other family faced. In his book *If He Hollers Let Him Go*, Himes included a character based upon the Mittwers' young son, Ricky, singing "God Bless America" as his family is escorted away to camp.

The returning incarcerees in Los Angeles had another friend from the Black community in Roy Loggins, who owned a catering business. Those who sought refuge in the Senshin Buddhist Hostel were grateful for the chance to work for Loggins part-time and for the leftovers he would bring to them from his catering events for the Hollywood studios.

There were reports of people getting their old jobs back or landing new ones offered by employers who thought that giving in to irrational racist fears wasn't the American way. And from time to time, people came up to them on the street and apologized for the

way they had behaved in the days and weeks following the attack on
Pearl Harbor.

• • •

*Business is good. All our old customers have come back. People
drop in to say "hello."*

 —Haruyo (Takeuchi) **Hozaki**, female, Issei, Los Angeles, California,
 incarcerated age 46, and Kyuji **Hozaki**, male, Issei, Los Angeles,
 California, incarcerated age 45, Santa Anita Assembly Center,
 Rohwer Relocation Center[273]

*I was in Jerome from October 1942 to May 1944. My sisters were
already out. Two were working in Washington, DC, and they sent
for me. I stayed with a Caucasian couple who had done missionary
work in Africa. They had opened their home to rent rooms to Japanese
Americans. I would do light housework, and they let me eat with them.
There was no separation. It was really wonderful. They took me in as
a member of the family.*

 —Dollie Kimiko **Nagai** (Fukawa), female, Nisei, Fresno, California,
 incarcerated age 15, Fresno Assembly Center, Jerome Relocation
 Center[274]

*Coming home, I was boarding a bus on Olympic Boulevard. A lady
sitting in the front row of the bus saw me and said, "Damn Jap." Here I
was a proud American soldier, just coming back with my new uniform
and new paratrooper boots, with all my campaign medals and awards,
proudly displayed on my chest, and this? The bus driver upon hearing
this remark stopped the bus and said, "Lady, apologize to this American soldier, or get off my bus." She got off the bus.*

 —Mitsuo "Mits" **Usui**, male, Nisei, Los Angeles, California,
 incarcerated age 25, Santa Anita Assembly Center, Granada (Amache)
 Relocation Center[275]

My father, me, and my brother left camp and took the bus from Heart Mountain to Montana. We were on our way to Minnesota. My father's friend had settled there and said the people in Minnesota were very nice. My father wanted us to find a place, and then he'd have my mother and the three girls come out. On the bus we learned it was VJ day [Victory over Japan Day]. What bad luck . . . ! It was bedlam. People were looking at us, and we thought they were going to kill us. Some of them got hysterical. I was never so scared. My brother said, "Don't say anything. Just look down."

    —Lillian Reiko **Sugita** (Nakano), female, Sansei, Honolulu, Hawaii, incarcerated age 14, Jerome Relocation Center, Heart Mountain Relocation Center[276]

I had been discharged from [the hospital] and was on my way home for good. Naturally I wanted to look my spruced-up best and a day or so before the troopship left, I went to this barbershop in one of the towns ringing San Francisco—and got as far as the door.

"Are you Chinese?" the man said to me.

I looked past him at the three empty chairs—the other two barbers [were] watching us closely. "I'm an American."

"Are you Chinese?"

"I think what you want to know is where my father was born. My father was born in Japan. I am an American."

Deep in my gut I knew what was coming.

"Don't give me that American stuff," he said swiftly. "You're a Jap and we don't cut Jap hair."

I wanted to hit him. I could see myself—it was as though I were standing in front of a mirror. There I stood in full uniform, the new captain's bars bright on my shoulders, four rows of ribbons on my chest, the combat infantry badge, the distinguished unit citation—and a hook where my hand was supposed to be. And he didn't cut Jap hair.

To think that I had gone through the war to save his skin—and he
didn't cut Jap hair.

I said, "I'm sorry. I'm sorry for you and the likes of you."

And I went back to my ship.

—The Honorable Daniel "Dan" Ken **Inouye**, male, Nisei, Honolulu,
Hawaii, age 17 when Pearl Harbor was attacked[277]

• • •

On June 22, 1945, the Allies won the Battle of Okinawa, although in
Okinawa the official date is June 23—the day that Lieutenant General
Mitsuru Ushijima committed suicide. Both dates are commemorated
each year as memorial days for those who lost their lives in battle. The
end of the Allied Philippine offensive came on July 5, 1945.

Then at 8:15 a.m., August 6, 1945, the United States Army Air
Forces dropped an atomic bomb on the heavily populated Japanese
city of Hiroshima. Nagasaki was hit three days later.

Second Lieutenant Harry Katsuharu Fukuhara was working as a
linguist and interpreter for the MIS and was stationed in the Philippines at the time. His Issei mother, three brothers, and extended
family were all living in Hiroshima. Fukuhara had to process the news
for himself before delivering the news to the Japanese POWs being
held near Manila.

• • •

I told them that a new bomb called the atomic bomb, equivalent to
thousands of tons of TNT, had been dropped on Hiroshima on August
6, and that one single explosion had completely wiped out the entire
city of Hiroshima and that it had been erased from the surface of the
earth. I told them nothing living had survived and that all human
and animal life was non-existent. I further elaborated that no vege-
tation, plant life or tree would grow there and people would not be
able to live there for at least 100 years, due to radiation. When I told
them that, they were silent—either they did not believe me or else the

information was beyond their comprehension. I know that I did not want to believe it myself.

—Harry Katsuharu **Fukuhara**, male, Nisei, Los Angeles, California, incarcerated age 22, Tulare Assembly Center, Gila River Relocation Center[278]

. . .

A few weeks later Fukuhara was sent to Japan with the US occupying forces and was given permission to search for his family in the ruins. Miraculously, his mother and aunt had survived in an underground bomb shelter, along with two of his brothers. His older brother died of radiation sickness a few months after the blast.

. . .

My wife, also a U.S. citizen, and her family . . . received a telegram [at Jerome], supposedly from Japan, that her family was being called back to Japan . . . and the American government had no other choice but to send them back. Upon reaching there . . . they discovered that their family had been exchanged for the return of another family to the United States. Her father was killed by the atomic bomb at Hiroshima. Her mother and family were 20 miles from the bomb site. I am led to believe that this was not an isolated case.

—Masani "Mas" **Fukai**, male, Nisei, Gardena, California, incarcerated age 15, Tulare Assembly Center, Gila River Relocation Center[279]

. . .

On August 15, 1945, Emperor Hirohito of Japan announced Japan's surrender, and the formal surrender document was signed on board the USS *Missouri* in Tokyo Bay on September 2, 1945.

World War II had finally come to an end.

Only ten people had been convicted of spying for Japan.

All of them were White.

. . .

FROM THE LAST HIGH SCHOOL COMMENCEMENT ADDRESSES INSIDE POSTON

June 1, 1945

We, the Class of 1945, feel highly honored to be the first, the last, and only class ever to graduate from such a fine auditorium and to complete three years of high school in this Utopia isolated from the rest of the world.

To the teachers, who so unselfishly stayed together with us, to provide us with high ideals and a broader outlook on life, especially in times like the present, we cannot express in mere words just how we feel toward you and . . . your kind in the community. Your work will always be remembered as we depart and strive for a bigger and better goal in the outside world. Our intentions to get ahead will undoubtedly be based on your teaching. And to the parents who quietly and patiently encouraged us . . . when everything seemed so blue, we are very, very grateful.

Richard Shindo, Senior Class President
17 years old, Poston High School, Poston I

> —Richard Takeshi **Shindo**, male, Nisei, Los Angeles, California, incarcerated age 14, Poston Relocation Center[280]

. . . Three years ago this was only a barren desert. In this desert has sprouted a thriving community, blessed with a school far better than could be expected in this day of chaos and uncertainty. Before long Miles E. Cary High will be but a lingering memory which shall remain with us and be cherished forever. It is difficult to convey our thoughts on departing from the school we have come to love. But in a larger sense, it is a departure not only for us; everyone will soon be leaving to pursue his destiny.

We seniors are prepared to embark toward a new horizon. This graduation service is a symbol of our eagerness to challenge the future; the diplomas we will receive are our passports to the destination we so earnestly seek. The future belongs to those who prepare for it. Already we have spent years in preparation. We now look to the future—and success—with renewed confidence and determination. . . .

Hiroshi Kamei, Salutatorian
17 years old, Miles E. Cary High School, Poston II

—Hiroshi **Kamei**, male, Nisei, Westminster, California, incarcerated age 14, Poston Relocation Center[281]

Commencement promises the beginning of a bigger life—a life which holds greater responsibilities, new experiences, and a deeper significance in living. It is a time when mixed emotions rule each graduate as his head is held [high] with pride or bowed in serious contemplation of the future . . . as his eyes grow misty with tears of gladness or dim with a questioning, unresolved fear of the years to come. . . .

Can we ever forget our first year of school in Poston? Classes were held in unimpressive, black, tar-papered barracks. The rooms were crowded with students but empty of the barest essentials of a school. . . . We will always remember our first assembly, our first student body election and the first commencement exercises of Poston III. A hastily constructed outdoor stage was the setting of that great event. The one hundred and twenty-three graduating members did not wear the traditional cap and gown. . . . We see that fateful storm in August which destroyed half of the constructed adobe buildings. We hear the urgent call for volunteers to help complete our school. We remember the quick response of students, teachers and parents. Those willing, determined workers can justly say, "We helped build this—our school." We see rows of adobe buildings, some of them still incomplete. . . .

. . . Yes, indeed, we know that the year '43-'44 . . . holds many memorable events. That was the year the construction of this auditorium began, "Old Glory" was first raised to the sky, our first Kampus Karnival was held and our first "Campus Echoes" was published. And we mustn't forget that during that year our school received Arizona's accreditation and our school was officially named Parker Valley High School. The commencement exercises of the class of '44 were held here in this auditorium. We remember that as we looked up at a portion of the ceiling, we saw the stars twinkling at us from above. We remember those ninety-eight graduates as they, clad in caps and gowns, marched down the aisles with faces suddenly serious.

In reminiscing about our final year at Parker Valley High School, we can see . . . the great accomplishments we achieved in leadership, scholarship and citizenship. . . . The Prom, our Senior Ball, our class play, our Senior Day and our Banquet were the result of initiative, determination and diligence. . . .

Two and one half years ago, we, the members of the class of 1945, were attending schools in twenty-five different communities along the Pacific Coast. Tonight we are gathered here as one class. We represent such towns and cities as Los Angeles, Reedley, Visalia, Santa Barbara, Monterey and San Diego. As a result of the years spent together a deep understanding of one another has grown and lasting friendships have been formed. . . .

With the passing of the summer and winter of 1945 each of us will find himself in his former hometown or in an entirely new community. We may be in Chicago or New York, in Milwaukee or Kansas City, in San Diego or any other city. . . . Wherever we are we may encounter hardships and misunderstandings. As we try to solve our difficulties our lives may become a turmoil. During trying times such as these we will recall . . . happiness was attained only through real understanding between one another.

Misako Mayumi, Salutatorian
18 years old, Parker Valley High School, Poston III

—Misako "Micki" **Mayumi** (Honda), female, Nisei, Chula Vista, California, incarcerated age 15, Santa Anita Assembly Center, Poston Relocation Center[282]

The pioneering, adventurous life is the true life of any existence, a life that has the scope for diverse experiences, a life that will cut itself off from the old and the familiar to the new, a life willing to gamble the present for infinitely better possibilities. What I mean by the pioneering life is a life unwilling to linger at the wayside, but impatient to march along in progress.

Today, we are, in a sense, modern pioneers—those who go before, preparing the way for others. To better understand our future, we must review our past.

The Issei, in their prime of life, never had the opportunity from the beginning to realize the truly American way of life for themselves. It may be said that they have always been internees. Their very existence is being made miserable by the constant malicious abuses in the newspapers, compelled to protect themselves against unscrupulous attacks, and often their loyalty was strained to the breaking point by subjection to arduous trials.

They came to this country, not to escape religious or political conditions, but to find work in order to improve their economic status. Self respect was esteemed the highest by the Issei. Crime was no problem among them or their second generation children. And they paid their debts. Even during depression, they did not seek public relief or assistance. They were proud people, frugal, and met all financial obligations. They believed in mutual aid and assistance.

They made a record for themselves in the California vegetable market. They reclaimed useless sub-marginal lands and turned them into productive gardens. At the same time, they raised their standard of living.

When the Nisei followed, the Issei resolved that America would be the permanent place they would call home. The Nisei [were] confronted with many social obstacles for many years. True they took their place as accepted citizens in the high schools and colleges, but difficulties in finding their places in the civic society after graduation was cumulative. Consequently, they retreated into Little Tokyos.

Then—came December 7. Everyone knows too vividly the panorama of human grief that took place among the Japanese [as] a direct consequence of evacuation. We have come to know that it was not so much military necessity, as it was the result of the constant clamoring of the minority bigots of California, who urged the mass evacuation.

Isolated into a compressed racial community, the residents of three camps became almost completely separated from the American way of life. . . . Where there was a question of self-government in the centers, it was found that the Issei could best provide the authority, the stability, and the seasoned wisdom. The leadership of family and community was theirs; it was the tradition. But now, their spans of life are fast being spent. It is for us to assume the leadership. . . .

Fear grips our heart as we enter upon the society which had excluded us a few years ago. The society beyond the fence appears to be ambiguous, vast and foreboding. Accustomed to the protected life of the crowded centers, it is difficult to venture off into the unknown, and face more discrimination than our parents did as immigrants. Antagonism is apt to increase—not diminish—now that the European war is ended.

But reflect. Our forefathers, the Issei, journeyed across 5,000 miles of the largest ocean in the world to a land completely foreign. Undaunted by differences of language and custom, they carried on, *courageously. Their vision and spunk should be an inspiration to us who are only moving within the borders of our own native land—and have the linguistic and cultural advantage.*

There, then, is the open road to the future. Wherever we look in America, we find men pioneering the unknown ways: pioneering science, pioneering business, pioneering literature, pioneering religion and philosophy. A brave man asks for nothing more than a fighting chance against the odds. Our fighting chance is in relocation.

What will these camps produce? Out of them come great leaders and prophets. Faithful, patient men and women blazing the ways to overcome racial prejudice. Adversity will serve to intensify their great faith and make it stronger. The imperfections are but a challenge that we might more actively assume our obligations and responsibilities as Nisei citizens, Americans in a greater America.

We must accept that challenge.

Mollie Ohashi, Valedictorian
18 years old, Parker Valley High School, Poston III

—Molly Moriko **Ohashi** (Yamamoto), female, Nisei, Tulare County, California, incarcerated age 15, Poston Relocation Center[283]

• • •

Dillon Myer was stunned. The war had ended and there were still 45,000 people left in the camps, mostly elderly Issei, women with young children, and the infirm. They said they had nowhere to go, having lost their homes and their jobs. They were afraid of anti-Japanese violence. They were afraid of being tricked. But, family by family, the remaining incarcerees had to face the reality of living in a hostile world without any sure way of supporting themselves.

As the incarcerees left camp, they received a one-way bus ticket and twenty-five dollars. The government shipped the possessions that the incarcerees had accumulated in camp—including household furniture—to their new locations free of charge. To encourage the inmates to resettle in regions other than the West Coast throughout the United States, the WRA had set up regional offices around the country, and offered to meet the incarcerees upon arrival. The WRA would give them job training, loan assistance, and legal advice. But if the incarcerees didn't make plans, the WRA would be forced to send them back to wherever they had been living before they were taken.

Although WRA officials could not legally prevent anyone from going home to the Pacific states, they adopted policies designed to motivate the inmates to go elsewhere. In order to return to the West Coast, incarcerees were required to submit applications for financial assistance with detailed plans outlining their housing and employment options.The WRA field office then confirmed those plans before they approved the applications. Through this bureaucratic process, handled by letter and telegram between multiple levels of WRA and Department of the Interior approval, the WRA was able to deliberately slow down the incarcerees' rate of return. Even after they were home, the WRA took its time before it provided the approved resettlement assistance the people so desperately needed. Despite these barriers, approximately two thirds of the 120,000 inmates chose to return to the West Coast.

After an estimated federal cost of $250 million, the "evacuation" program was finally coming to an end. But for the remaining incarcerees, a new nightmare was just beginning.

• • •

There were still thousands of Japanese Americans in Camp, unable to move out. . . . Everything they had was gone. They were afraid to bring their families out to be free and independent again. Their savings had long been depleted. Without jobs or homes the return seemed a formidable task.

—Mary Tsuruko (Dakuzaku) **Tsukamoto**, female, Nisei, Florin, California, incarcerated age 27, Fresno Assembly Center, Jerome Relocation Center[284]

Those who did not choose to leave voluntarily would be scheduled for resettlement in weekly quotas. Once you were scheduled you could choose a place—a state, a city, a town—and the government would pay your way there. If you didn't choose, they'd send you back to the community you lived in before you were evacuated.

—Jeanne Toyo **Wakatsuki** (Houston), female, Nisei, Santa Monica, California, incarcerated age 8, Manzanar Reception Center, Manzanar Relocation Center[285]

We came back to Little Tokyo for a little while. . . . There just simply was no housing available. . . . So we wound up in these trailer courts in Long Beach, [California,] the Los Cerritos trailer camp. . . . I'm not talking about a few trailers, there were like hundreds and hundreds of 'em. And a lot of people lived in there, blacks, whites, everything. And these were like dingy little . . . I would say they're barely fit for human habitation . . . but a lot of Japanese Americans wound up in these trailer camps, not just in Long Beach but in Roger Young Village in Griffith Park, they were in Quonset huts . . . and then Sun Valley, they had a whole bunch of trailers over there.

. . . [My sisters] were working at the Queen of (Angels) Hospital, nurse's aides. . . . They did the grunge work. They emptied out the bedpans, they made the beds, they did . . . the dirty work.

. . . My father never, never found a job after that. [My] sisters were supporting [our] parents.

. . . I went to visit . . . my sisters during the weekend, and they had a little house in the back in the Echo Park area. And I heard the toilet flush. It was like, I can't describe the sound to you. It was like, "I'm back to civilization. I'm back among living people."

—Haruyuki "Jim" **Matsuoka**, male, Nisei, Los Angeles, California, incarcerated age 7, Manzanar Reception Center, Manzanar Relocation Center[286]

The day that we left Manzanar, my father said to me and my three brothers, "Never forget this place. It's important for you to remember it, and if at some point in your life you have an opportunity to do something about this, to make it right, it's your obligation to your family, to the community and to the country."

—John Yoshio **Tateishi**, male, Sansei, Los Angeles, California, incarcerated age 3, Manzanar Reception Center, Manzanar Relocation Center[287]

• • •

The number of people in each center dwindled down to the elderly and infirm without families. As Manzanar was closing, Reverend Shinjo Nagatomi and his family stayed to help anyone who lacked the resources to move out—Buddhists and Christians alike. The Nagatomis did not leave Manzanar until they made sure that the last incarcerees had support in their departure. One by one, the mess halls closed, the blocks closed, the barracks closed. Tule Lake was the last. At the end, those who hid under their beds had their bags packed for them and they were carried onto buses and trains. There was no one left to say good-bye.

• • •

Standing
On the wide desert,
Before the silent wind,
My body sank
Into nothingness

—Fumiko (Ito) **Ogawa**, female, Issei, Los Angeles, California, incarcerated age 39, Pomona Assembly Center, Heart Mountain Relocation Center[288]

• • •

By March 20, 1946, all the camps were empty.

PART FIVE

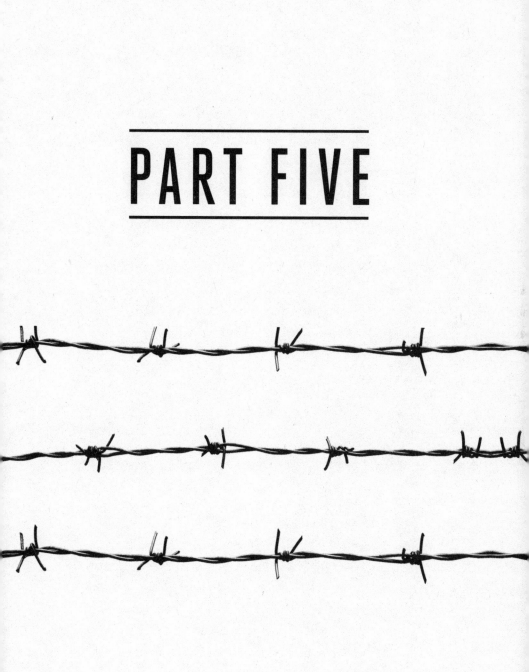

CHAPTER ELEVEN

Righting a Great Wrong

Sansei children, who experienced the Vietnam War, with its violent confrontations and protest marches, have asked questions about those early World War II years. Why did you let it happen? Why didn't you fight for your civil rights? Why did you go without protest to the concentration camps?

—Yoshiko **Uchida**, female, Nisei, Berkeley, California, incarcerated age 21, Tanforan Assembly Center, Topaz Relocation Center[289]

Michi Nishiura Weglyn, a costume designer in New York City, was sifting through documents in the Franklin D. Roosevelt Presidential Library in Hyde Park, New York. It was the 1960s, the era of anti–Vietnam War protests and the emerging civil rights movement, when citizens, including Asian Americans, were starting to explore social issues and confront actions taken by the US government. In this charged political environment, Weglyn became motivated to learn how and why she, an honors high school student in 1942, was deprived of her college dreams and ended up in the Turlock Assembly Center and the Gila River Relocation Center for three years with her family. During her seven-year hunt for information, she combed through dusty boxes in institutions like the New York Public Library and the National Archives in Washington, DC.

What she unearthed shocked her. A self-taught historical researcher, Weglyn was the first person to assemble irrefutable evidence that the government had had no "military necessity" for the incarceration and had blundered its way through decisions that had been motivated by racial prejudice. In 1976, to set the record straight, she published her findings in the groundbreaking national bestseller *Years of Infamy:*

The Untold Story of America's Concentration Camps. The book not only raised public awareness of the West Coast Nikkei incarceration, but it also brought other new and alarming information to light.

Weglyn detailed the US government's little-known wartime program that forcibly removed 2,264 men, women, and children of Japanese ancestry from thirteen Latin American countries and incarcerated them in the United States. Approximately 80 percent of these Japanese Latin Americans (JLA) were from Peru. After local authorities wrested the Latin American Nikkei from their homes, US troops took them into custody and transported them to Department of Justice internment camps in Texas at Crystal City, Kenedy, and Seagoville, and other DOJ camps throughout the country.

The US and Latin American governments justified their cooperation in the deportation and incarceration of Japanese Latin Americans as a way of keeping the Western hemisphere safe against Japan's military aggression. But by 1946 the federal government's true purpose was clear—it had exchanged nearly 900 JLA hostages for American POWs and US citizens who had been stranded in Japan after the Pearl Harbor attack.

After the war, some Latin American countries allowed their citizens to return, but the Peruvian government refused. Then the US government dealt the final blow: it classified the remaining Latin American detainees as illegal aliens. The Peruvian JLAs could not return to their home country, and now the country that had brought them here against their will was requiring them to leave. Some fought to stay in the US as undocumented aliens, but the federal government deported most of them to Japan. Many did not even speak Japanese or have any reason to be in Japan. Nevertheless, they were forced to live out their days in a land where they did not want to be.

• • •

The Republic of Peru found it a splendid opportunity for "cleansing" itself of its Japanese element and supplied eighty percent of those who were literally kidnapped. Men were picked up off the streets or seized in their homes by the local police, then turned over to American authorities and shipped to US concentration camps. It was an Orwellian nightmare, as all were first turned into "illegal aliens" before landing on American soil by the confiscation of their papers and passports. In the meantime . . . homes, businesses, farms, even family treasures, were confiscated. [And later,] when Peru refused reentry of its unwanted ethnics after the war, the State Department declared [the Japanese Peruvians] to be "illegally" in the United States [and] simply dump[ed] the one-time kidnap victims on a defeated, war-pulverized, starving Japan. Only because of the legal intervention of an outraged San Francisco lawyer were deportations halted and the final contingent of some 360 [Japanese Peruvian] deportees permitted to remain in the United States.

—Michiko "Michi" (**Nishiura**) Weglyn, female, Nisei, Brentwood, California, incarcerated age 15, Turlock Assembly Center, Gila River Relocation Center[290]

• • •

Years of Infamy became a touchstone for former incarcerees. In the postwar decades the Issei and in particular the Nisei adopted a range of social and psychological responses to the cumulative traumas of their exclusion, detention, and resettlement; their lives were forever divided between "before the war" and "after camp." A common "after camp" Nisei behavior was to focus on what they had to do to get themselves back on track, taking the attitude that they must put the past behind them and move on.

Having experienced the dangers of being Japanese, many Nisei distanced themselves from Japanese culture and whatever highlighted their Japanese identity; they just wanted to blend in. The 1969 book *Nisei: The Quiet Americans*, by former incarceree and JACL leader Bill Hosokawa, furthered the notion that second-generation Japanese Americans were a "model minority" that succeeded without "making waves."

But the image projected by the model minority masked the long-term negative effects of incarceration, especially upon the Nisei as children and teenagers. The incarcerees have been likened to rape survivors, innocent victims of traumatizing events who internalize anger, frustration, and feelings of helplessness into guilt, shame, and inferiority.

• • •

With profound remorse, I believed, as did numerous Japanese Americans, that somehow the stain of dishonor we collectively felt for the treachery of Pearl Harbor must be eradicated, however great the sacrifice, however little we were responsible for it. . . . In an inexplicable spirit of atonement and with great sadness, we went with our parents to concentration camps. . . . Curiosity led me into exhuming documents of this extraordinary chapter in our history. . . . Persuaded that the enormity of a bygone injustice has been only partially perceived, I have taken upon myself the task of piecing together what might be called the "forgotten" or ignored parts of the tapestry of those years.

—Michiko "Michi" (**Nishiura**) Weglyn, female, Nisei, Brentwood, California, incarcerated age 15, Turlock Assembly Center, Gila River Relocation Center[291]

After the war my growing understanding of those events, combined with my memories, produced in me a strange and gnawing sense of shame about my years spent behind barbed wire.

Indeed, I felt an uneasy sense of shame about being Japanese. On the first days of school when the teacher taking roll would inevitably mispronounce my Japanese name, I would not correct that mispronunciation. Instead, I myself assumed that mispronunciation, thinking that that made me that much less Japanese.

There was a teacher I remember who would casually refer to me as "that Jap boy." I remember the sting each time she called me that, but I bit my tongue and didn't complain.

The shadow cast by the camp experience reached far into the post-

war period of my boyhood and stayed in my head a long, long time.

—George Hosato **Takei**, male, Nisei, Los Angeles, California,
incarcerated age 5, Santa Anita Assembly Center, Rohwer Relocation
Center, Tule Lake Relocation Center[292]

*The most difficult problem for me to overcome . . . was the anger
and bitterness which has gradually surfaced over the past 39 years.
When the photographs of camp were shown at the Pasadena Art
Museum some years ago, I burst into tears and could not stop the tears
from flowing. All the pent-up emotion held back for so many years was
released. The numbness of the evacuation was finally lifted. Because
of the humiliation and shame, I could never tell my four children my
true feelings. . . . I did not want my children to [know the] feeling of
rejection by their fellow Americans. I wanted them to feel that in spite
of what was done to us, this was still the best place in the world to live.*

—Mary **Sakaguchi** (Oda), female, Nisei, Los Angeles, California,
incarcerated age 22, Manzanar Reception Center, Manzanar
Relocation Center[293]

*To this day, the incident I recall was the body search that I was sub-
jected to at Pinedale Assembly Center. At the age of 14, I still remember it being very degrading, very unfair, and I was very angry. I am
still very angry. I'm still very angry because when a Caucasian person would ask me about my interned years they would become very
defensve, and they did not see the violation of our rights, only as a
military necessity.*

*After that, I chose not to speak to most people about this issue. I just
tabled it; they could go ask somebody else.*

—Yasuko "Yas" **Kodani** (Morimoto), female, Nisei, Snoqualmie,
Washington, incarcerated age 14, Pinedale Assembly Center, Tule
Lake Relocation Center[294]

· · ·

The coping mechanisms adopted by Nisei parents in turn affected how they raised and related to their children, the third generation. The Sansei were growing up not knowing anything about the wartime experiences of their grandparents and parents, except perhaps for random comments of *shikata ga nai* ("it couldn't be helped") or focusing on some positive remembrance of a happy time. But their grandparents and parents weren't the only ones in silence: school textbooks and educational materials made no, or scant, mention of this episode in our history.

Karen Korematsu was sixteen years old before she knew anything about her father's wartime criminal conviction and Supreme Court case. As a junior at San Lorenzo High School in California, Karen heard her childhood friend Maya Okada mention the camps in a social studies class, along with a "famous Supreme Court case, *Korematsu v. United States.*" Karen had never heard anything about the camps, let alone a Supreme Court case bearing her family's name.

. . .

I'm thinking, well, what's this about? I knew Korematsu was an unusual Japanese name. . . . And all of a sudden I had, you know, thirty-five pairs of eyes kind of staring at me, and I'm thinking, oh, this has gotta be a black sheep of the family. . . . The thought never even occurred to me that it had anything to do with my father . . . because I thought I would have been told. . . . I could think of everyone else but my father. Because my father just didn't have, to me, that personality to do something that was against the law. . . . Certainly, if it was a famous Supreme Court case, I would have heard about it, or somebody would have said something by then.

—Karen Anne **Korematsu**, female, Sansei, daughter of Fred
Korematsu, and founder and executive director of the Fred T.
Korematsu Institute[295]

. . .

Karen hurried home. Her mother confirmed that the Supreme Court case was indeed her father's, and said she'd have to wait until her father got home from work to ask him about it. In her brief conversation with her father later that evening, he simply said that what had happened had taken place a long time ago and he'd done what he felt was right at the time. He admitted that he still had a criminal conviction, and Karen realized how painful it was for him to talk about the past. He had meant to tell her and her brother about it, but he thought they would be ashamed and might understand it better if he told them when they were older. Karen let the conversation drop. Her brother knew nothing about the Supreme Court case either until he heard about it in his high school history class. It seemed as though this secret knowledge was common-place when it came to the incarceration experience.

• • •

One day in 1971, Jeanne Wakatsuki Houston, a writer in Santa Cruz, California, had a visit from one of her nephews. A student at the University of California, Berkeley, he had heard his sociology profes-sor say the word "Manzanar" in class. It was the first time he had ever heard anyone mention it outside of his family.

"Aunty," he said, "You know I was born in Manzanar and I don't know anything about the place. Can you tell me about it?"

"Sure," I said, "but why don't you ask your folks?" I felt no hes-itancy in talking about the internment camp and wondered why he couldn't get information from them.

"I have, Aunty, but they seem reluctant to talk about it. Like I shouldn't be asking or there's some skeleton in the closet."

That's strange, I thought. I then began telling him about life in camp—about the schools, the outdoor movie theater, baseball games, judo pavilion, dances, and beautiful rock gardens. Whenever my fam-ily got together and we happened to talk about camp, we would joke about the lousy food, the dust storms or the communal showers, or we talked lightheartedly about recreational activities. I reiterated the same stories to my nephew in the same superficial way.

He looked at me intently, as if never seeing me before. "Aunty, you're telling me all these bizarre things. I mean, how did you feel about being locked up like that?"

For a moment I was stunned. He asked me a question no one had ever asked before, a question I had never dared to ask myself. Feel? How did I feel? For the first time I dropped the protective cover of humor and nonchalance. I allowed myself to "feel." I began to cry. I couldn't stop crying. He was shocked. What had he done to send me into hysterics? I was embarrassed, and when I gained control of myself, told him I would talk to him some other time. But now I understood his parents' reluctance to discuss too deeply the matter of the internment.

At the time, I was "aunty" to thirty-six nieces and nephews. Seven had been born in camp. I realized none knew about their birthplace, Manzanar. Since it seemed too painful to talk about it, perhaps I could write a memoir, a history—just for the family.

—Jeanne Toyo **Wakatsuki** (Houston), female, Nisei, Santa Monica, California, incarcerated age 8, Manzanar Reception Center, Manzanar Relocation Center[296]

· · ·

Together with her husband, writer James D. Houston, Jeanne began what was meant to be a memoir just for her family. That work became the Houstons' bestselling book, *Farewell to Manzanar*, published in 1973. Her story became a prime-time made-for-TV movie three years later, the first commercial film written, performed, photographed, and scored by Japanese Americans about the incarceration experience.

Then in 1979, Asian American literary pioneers Lawson Fusao Inada and Frank Chin republished John Okada's *No-No Boy*, one of the first Japanese American novels as well as one of the first works to bring to light the issues of racial identity and politics during the incarceration. Events such as the annual pilgrimage to the remains of the Manzanar camp, launched by former incarceree Sue Kunitomi

Embrey, became a way to spark discussions and connections within the Los Angeles Japanese American community. The pilgrimage that started in 1969 continues to this day, now as a forum for discussing the Japanese American wartime travesty as it relates to current events.

But political activism was new to Japanese Americans; lobbying against authority figures was antithetical to their ways. Still, some saw the importance of doing something about existing laws that could lead to another version of their incarceration. They were motivated to show the country and themselves that they were capable of having a powerful, unified voice and changing America for the better. One of their first successes was repealing Title II of the Internal Security Act of 1950.

Raymond Okamura and Edison Uno, both Nisei progressives and civil rights leaders, were concerned about Title II (also referred to as the Emergency Detention Act), which gave the attorney general of the United States the power to apprehend and detain any persons who the government thought might engage in acts of sabotage or espionage. The act also denied citizenship to Communists. The law had been enacted during the Cold War and was strangely reminiscent of Executive Order 9066. It even mentioned the "fifth columns" in World War II that "demonstrated the grave dangers and fatal effectiveness of such internal espionage and sabotage." President Harry S. Truman vetoed the act, calling it a "mockery of the Bill of Rights . . . the greatest danger to freedom of speech, press, and assembly since the Alien and Sedition Laws of 1798." But Congress overrode his veto.

In the late 1960s, Okamura, Uno, and others managed to overcome conservative objections within the JACL to wage a campaign for the repeal of Title II. Senator Daniel K. Inouye introduced a bill into the Ninety-First Congress to repeal the act, and President Richard M. Nixon signed the bill into law on September 25, 1971. The repeal of Title II was mostly symbolic, but the grassroots effort became proof of concept to the Japanese American community that it could tackle political issues.

And then came the campaign for the presidential pardon of Iva Toguri D'Aquino—so-called Tokyo Rose. D'Aquino, a Nisei, had been visiting Japan when the war broke out and had been unable to return to the United States. To support herself in Japan, she took a job translating scripts for broadcast on Radio Tokyo, which targeted Allied troops in the Pacific. Later she agreed to be a radio broadcaster for a propaganda show called *Zero Hour*. Allied prisoners of war were brought in to produce the show, and over time D'Aquino and the POWs conspired to sabotage the propaganda through innuendo, double entendre, and sarcasm. The troops in the Pacific theater listening to these and other propaganda broadcasts called any English-speaking woman broadcaster by the made-up name "Tokyo Rose."

After the war was over, Henry Brundidge, associate editor of *Cosmopolitan* magazine, and Clark Lee, a reporter from the International News Service, (both of the Hearst empire) approached D'Aquino to be interviewed as the real Tokyo Rose. Brundidge offered her the enormous sum of $2,000 on behalf of the magazine. Desperate to fund her return to the United States and naive about the possible consequences of being associated with the Tokyo Rose name, D'Aquino agreed to the interview. On September 3, 1945, Lee's story was published on the front page of the *Los Angeles Examiner*, identifying D'Aquino as the "one and only Tokyo Rose."

Two days later the military police of the US Eighth Army took her into custody. D'Aquino was never paid because Frances Whiting, chief editor of *Cosmopolitan*, refused to publish a feature about a "traitor." D'Aquino ended up spending a year in prison in Japan and was then brought by military escort to the US, where she was rearrested, tried, and convicted of treason for aiding the Japanese government during the war. She served six years of a ten-year sentence at the Federal Reformatory for Women in Alderson, West Virginia.

Okamura, Clifford Uyeda, and other JACL leaders believed that she'd been wrongly convicted, and formed a committee in April

1975 to campaign for a presidential pardon. On January 19, 1977, President Gerald Ford, on his last day in office, granted her a full and unconditional pardon, the first and only time a pardon for treason was ever given. The success of the campaign on behalf of D'Aquino added to the momentum of political activism in the Japanese American community.

Inspired by Michi Weglyn's research, more former incarcerees were ready to face their long-suppressed emotions and initiate their own forms of investigation and activism. Uno led a group within the JACL that wanted to move beyond wartime compliance as a show of loyalty and focus on the injustice of the incarceration itself. The delegates to the 1970, 1972, and 1974 national JACL conventions passed resolutions supporting the concept of "redress"—a term taken from the phrase in the First Amendment that says citizens have the right to petition their government for a "redress of grievances." Hence, the term "redress" was adopted as a less inflammatory word than "reparations." Japanese Americans across the country, not just within the JACL, wanted their wartime incarceration to be deemed unconstitutional. They wanted a formal apology from the federal government and payments of reparations or restitution to surviving incarcerees. But no matter what they wanted or what the effort was called, the resolutions were getting no real traction even within the JACL.

In 1976 members of the Seattle JACL chapter, together with other leaders across the country, seized the initiative to lobby President Ford to revoke Executive Order 9066. Even though the executive order had ended in practice, it had remained in force since the war years, and revoking it, while largely symbolic, was nevertheless important.

Ford agreed and signed Proclamation 4417, terminating Executive Order 9066 on the thirty-fourth anniversary of its signing by Roosevelt. At the proclamation signing ceremony, Ford said, "We now know what we should have known then—not only was the evacuation wrong, but Japanese-Americans were and are loyal Americans. . . . I call upon the

American people to . . . resolve that this kind of error shall never again be repeated."

Then in 1979 the ad hoc group within the Seattle JACL chapter known as the Seattle Evacuation Redress Committee (SERC) organized a Day of Remembrance—the first of many—as a way of bringing attention to their early redress efforts. The committee—which included Henry Miyatake, Mike Nakata, Ken Nakano, and Shosuke Sasaki—scheduled the commemoration for February 19, the date FDR issued Executive Order 9066 and a date seared onto the hearts of many Japanese Americans. SERC believed it was time to call for reparations to former incarcerees while they were still alive. The movement was gaining support in the Pacific Northwest, but some thought that the national JACL was dragging its feet on the issue.

As it seemed with all concerns facing the Japanese American community, there were vehement divisions of opinion over the wisdom of pursuing redress. The objections were many. Some felt that no amount of money could compensate for their loss and placing a dollar figure on their hardships would trivialize them.

· · ·

I felt that [reparations payments] would cheapen our sacrifice, to put out our hands and say, "Give us some money for what we went through."
  —William "Bill" Kumpai **Hosokawa**, male, Nisei, Seattle,
  Washington, incarcerated age 27, Puyallup Assembly Center, Heart
  Mountain Relocation Center[297]

· · ·

Others thought the Sansei redress advocates were being critical of the way the Nisei had conducted themselves during the war. The Sansei were perceived as being disrespectful and unappreciative of what the incarcerees had had to endure. Some were afraid that redress would "stir up the past" and generate a possible "White backlash" against them. And some objected to the appearance of seeking charity. Even though most educated and professional Nisei earned less than White Americans with equivalent credentials, some worried that a public perception of Japanese Americans prospering economically after the war would sink any real chance of them receiving reparation payments.

Some feared that the Japanese American Evacuation Claims Act of 1948 would be viewed as having already addressed the damages. But anyone who understood anything about the Evacuation Claims Act knew how preposterous it was. Reimbursements generated from the act didn't include lost wages or anticipated profits, personal injury, pain and suffering, or any cost pertaining to being forced to give up most everything they owned within such a short period of time that there had been no hope of selling their belongings and businesses for what they had actually been worth. Former inmates had been required to give sworn testimony and produce receipts and other proofs of their losses; claims had been limited to $2,500. Japanese Americans filed a total of 23,689 claims under the act, but by 1950 the Justice Department had authorized only 137 of them.

And lastly, some simply thought it was too late.

• • •

I felt JACL's insistence on individual monetary redress was futile, not only because most of the individuals who suffered financial loss would be dead and gone by the time Congress acted, but also because the demand might frustrate the movement's other goals.

—Mike Masaru **Masaoka**, male, Nisei, North Platte, Nebraska, age 26 when Pearl Harbor was attacked[298]

• • •

In 1978, Clifford Uyeda became the JACL's national president and made redress a priority for the organization. At the same time, the Seattle JACL chapter had forged ahead, developing its own plan for redress, including monetary compensation for each and every living former incarceree. Uyeda brought on board as redress chair John

Tateishi, who, as a Sansei, could speak to his childhood experiences in Manzanar. Ron Ikejiri from Gardena, California, became the JACL representative in Washington, DC. By January 1979, the JACL had surveyed its national membership and found that approximately 90 percent of its respondents supported some form of action and 87 percent supported some form of compensation.

Tateishi and a small group of other JACL redress leaders met with four Nikkei members of Congress in late January 1979 to assess their willingness to put forward redress legislation. Even though the politicians were of Japanese ancestry, their support was not a given. Senators Daniel K. Inouye and Spark Matsunaga, both decorated 100th/442nd veterans from Hawaii, did not represent constituents who had been incarcerated. Congressmen Norman Mineta and Robert Matsui, both from California, represented districts without large Asian American populations. They were also former incarcerees themselves, so they risked having people think they would personally benefit from redress legislation. Matsui had just been elected and did not yet have the tenure in office to have built up a bank of political capital. The four were acutely aware of the challenges ahead of them in getting their fellow members of Congress to support a bill for monetary compensation in an era of fiscal restraint and from a public that was largely unaware of and unsympathetic to the experiences of Japanese Americans.

To the great dismay of the JACL leaders, Inouye recommended that before they propose a bill for redress, they first seek to establish a congressional commission that would be charged with gathering information concerning the incarceration experience, produce a report on its findings, and recommend appropriate remedies. A seasoned and astute legislator, Inouye anticipated that his congressional colleagues, as well as the public, would need to be educated about the importance of the issue before they'd be receptive to any recommendations for redress. He felt that only the credibility of a blue-ribbon commission could make that possible.

At their meeting Inouye said, "You folks are going to have to convince the public before we can push legislation here." As Tateishi later summarized Inouye's thinking, "This would not be [Japanese Americans] asking for money. . . . We would be implementing actions recommended by an official body of the government to correct a past wrong."

Tateishi was in a difficult position. "In my heart of hearts," he confessed, "I did not want to go for a Commission." But the JACL redress leaders carefully considered Inouye's advice and came to agree with the senior senator's point of view. They realized that without creating more public awareness, any attempt to get a huge appropriations bill for former incarcerees in 1979 was unrealistic. But going with the commission approach would mean that any proposal for redress legislation would have to wait until a commission was formed and made its recommendations—a two-year delay, at best. Bracing for the anticipated backlash from the community, the JACL redress leaders agreed to support the commission approach.

The backlash came, swiftly and harshly. Recalling the JACL's wartime role in urging cooperation with the government, critics now accused the JACL of backsliding and once again of "selling out" the interests of the community, this time for not immediately pursuing a redress bill that included reparatory payments. Tateishi even started getting threats, and from fellow Japanese Americans, no less. But it was clear that the four Nikkei members of Congress would not proceed any other way.

• • •

There was no model we could work with because it was the only time in the history of the country that any group had attempted to seek redress from the United States Congress. Everybody said it was doomed to failure.

—John Yoshio **Tateishi**, male, Sansei, Los Angeles, California, incarcerated age 3, Manzanar Reception Center, Manzanar Relocation Center[299]

. . .

On August 2, 1979, under the leadership of Senators Inouye and Matsunaga, a bipartisan group of senators introduced the bill S. 1647 to form the commission. President Jimmy Carter signed the bill into law on July 31, 1980, establishing the Commission on Wartime Relocation and Internment of Civilians (CWRIC).

Members of the CWRIC were just the kind of distinguished group of delegates that Inouye had envisioned, and they represented a cross section of backgrounds. The appointees included Joan Z. Bernstein (chair), former general counsel of the US Department of Health and Human Services; Daniel E. Lungren (vice chair), Republican representative from California's Thirty-Fourth Congressional District; Dr. Arthur S. Flemming, chairman of the US Commission on Civil Rights and former secretary of the Department of Health, Education and Welfare under President Eisenhower; Father Robert F. Drinan, a Jesuit priest, former Democratic congressman from Massachusetts, and a law professor at Georgetown University; Edward W. Brooke, the first popularly elected Black US Senator; Hugh B. Mitchell, former Democratic US senator and congressman from Washington State; Father Ishmael V. Gromoff, a Russian Orthodox priest and one of the Aleuts who had been forcibly removed under Executive Order 9066; and Arthur J. Goldberg, former ambassador to the United Nations and former Supreme Court justice. The commission had only one Japanese American serving on it—former incarceree Judge William Marutani of the Philadelphia Court of Common Pleas. That the commission would have just one Japanese American as a commissioner was another strategic move by Senator Inouye, who recognized that the power of the commission's message would be the most effective coming from non–Japanese Americans.

Angus Macbeth, former chief of environmental enforcement at the Justice Department during the Carter administration, served as special counsel, overseeing the archival research necessary to compile a report on the causes, experiences, and impacts of the incarceration—a report that would be all the more important because the only existing official government account at the time was the 1943 DeWitt final report that had been unethically altered to justify its claim of "military necessity."

Put off—even outraged—by the JACL's commission approach, two other organizations that had formed within the Japanese American community became significant contributors to the redress cause: the National Coalition for Redress/Reparations (NCRR) and the National Council for Japanese American Redress (NCJAR). The three organizations differed in more than their strategic approaches for achieving redress; they were motivated by fundamentally different perspectives, experiences, and interpretations of what had happened during World War II.

The NCRR grew out of the community activism in Los Angeles's Little Tokyo. Progressive Nisei such as Bert and Lillian Sugita Nakano, Alan Nishio (who'd been born in Manzanar), and Jim Matsuoka joined with politically energized Sansei who saw no place for themselves in the JACL. NCRR members placed the Japanese American incarceration as one chapter in a long history of White elitism oppressing people of color. Finding common ground with other social justice organizations across the country, the NCRR took a broad, community-based-coalition approach, at one point growing to eight thousand members nationwide.

The NCJAR was spearheaded by William Minoru Hohri of Chicago. NCJAR supporters sharply criticized the JACL for what NCJAR perceived as a pattern of collaborating with the government. To them, the JACL glorified the contributions of the Nisei military, while the NCJAR considered the real World War II heroes to be the No-Nos, draft resisters, and others who stood up to injustice in nonmilitary ways. The NCJAR saw the commission approach as an easy out for the legislators and believed it was destined to fail. The NCJAR redress approach was based upon resistance and confrontation pursued through the judicial process. Hohri wanted the incarcerees to have their day in court.

On March 16, 1983, the NCJAR filed a class action lawsuit in the US District Court for the District of Columbia on behalf of the 120,000 persons of Japanese ancestry who had been affected by the wartime evacuation and incarceration. To represent the class at large, the NCJAR identified twenty-five Japanese Americans to serve as plaintiffs of diverse backgrounds. The suit listed twenty-two causes of action against the federal government, seeking $10,000 per cause of action per person, totaling $26.4 billion.

• • •

We are placing the issues of exclusion and detention squarely before the bar of justice and the bar of history.
  —William "Bill" Minoru **Hohri**, male, Nisei, Los Angeles, California, incarcerated age 14, Manzanar Reception Center, Manzanar Relocation Center[300]

You have to sometimes bring your community dragging and screaming behind you, but you better have strong convictions that what you're doing is right.
  —John Yoshio **Tateishi**, male, Sansei, Los Angeles, California, incarcerated age 3, Manzanar Reception Center, Manzanar Relocation Center[301]

• • •

When the commission announced it would be conducting hearings, Mike Masaoka and other JACL leaders figured the witnesses would be community leaders, veterans, and scholars of Japanese American studies presenting testimony in Washington, DC. NCRR pushed to hold hearings around the country, especially in areas where the majority of camp survivors were now relocated. And so, after the opening hearings in the Senate Caucus Room on July 14–16, 1981, the commission went on the road. Subsequent hearings were held in Los Angeles, Sacramento, and San Francisco in August 1981; then in Seattle, Anchorage, and Chicago in September 1981; again in Washington, DC, and New

York City in November 1981; and finally in Cambridge, Massachusetts, at Harvard University, in December 1981.

During the second set of hearings on Capitol Hill, the former incarcerees had their first opportunity to see the faces of two of those responsible for putting them in camp. In his appearance before the commission on November 3, Karl Bendetsen downplayed his role. Having proudly claimed earlier in his career that he was the "architect of the internment," Bendetsen now maintained that he had just been following orders. He steadfastly insisted in front of former incarcerees that their compulsory removal to the camps had been for their own good.

That same day it was especially astonishing to hear the testimony of John McCloy, then eighty-six years old. After the war McCloy went on to serve as the United States high commissioner in Germany, as chairman of the Chase Manhattan Bank, chairman of the board of the Ford Foundation, chairman of the Council on Foreign Relations, president of the World Bank, and a lawyer on Wall Street. McCloy not only defended the wartime decisions by President Roosevelt, Secretary of War Henry Stimson, and others, but he said he would do it again.

McCloy repeatedly insisted that the camps had been conducted in a "compassionate, benign way" and had "very pleasant conditions." He was visibly annoyed when many in the audience hissed, booed, and burst out in sarcastic laughter.

"I visited those camps. . . . I saw the solicitude," McCloy testified.

"That's not the point," Marutani said.

"I do not think that the Japanese-Americans were unduly subjected to distress," McCloy said.

Marutani is reported to have shouted, "What other Americans, Mr. McCloy, fought for this country while their parents, brothers and sisters were incarcerated?"

"I don't like the word 'incarcerated,'" McCloy replied.

"Well, all right, behind barbed wire fences," Marutani snapped.

McCloy reportedly raised his voice as well, replying, "It's impossible to make an equal distribution [of the suffering]. You can't do it."

As Marutani started to reply, McCloy interrupted him and continued, "I don't think the Japanese population was unduly subjected, considering all the exigencies to which a number did share in the way of retribution for the attack on Pearl Harbor."

Marutani had an icy expression on his face. McCloy had just implied that incarcerating the entire West Coast Japanese American population was an acceptable payback for Japan having bombed Pearl Harbor. The room went very quiet as Marutani asked the staff member recording the hearing to play back the audiotape of what McCloy had just said. It was a rare, completely unexpected request. The staffer fumbled with the equipment and rewound the recording of the hearing to replay McCloy's statement. Once again the audience heard McCloy say the word "retribution." McCloy immediately responded that he wanted to replace the word "retribution" with "consequences."

"The cat was out of the bag as far as I was concerned," Marutani later recalled. Forty years had gone by and McCloy had no regrets about his role in the incarceration.

As they prepared for the hearings scheduled in Los Angeles and in other cities around the country, the redress leaders realized it would be a tall order to get the Nisei, and especially the Japanese-speaking Issei, to do what they had never done before—open up and tell their stories to the public, and to congressionally appointed commissioners, no less. JACL staff leaders Ron Wakabayashi and Carole Hayashino organized mock hearings in Northern California so Nisei witnesses could have a trial run at giving their testimonies. The organizers convened a group of JACL chapter presidents to give five minutes of practice testimony.

• • •

We got Quentin Kopp, kind of a curmudgeonly member of the San Francisco Board of Supervisors, and a couple of judges to play commissioners, just to kind of do a walkthrough because there was not enough experience with commissions. So, we go and do this and the first chapter president goes up, and then he can't continue. He breaks down. Second guy. He breaks down. Third guy breaks down. Fourth guy. We didn't get one completed that day. No one finished.

—Ronald "Ron" Kaoru **Wakabayashi**, male, Sansei, former national director of the JACL[302]

• • •

At the end of that day, Wakabayashi told his wife, Jean, a psychiatric social worker, "I've not seen Niseis cry, I don't see them break down. It's not like they were sobbing, but no one could finish. And that scares me."

• • •

How could I as a 6-month-old child born in this country be declared by my own Government to be an enemy alien? How can my mother and father who were born in this country also be declared a potential enemy alien to their country? They did not go before a court of law, they did not know what charges were filed against them. They were just told, "You have three days to pack and be incarcerated." That is the fundamental issue here.

How can a nation founded on principles of individual rights suddenly deny the due process rights of an entire group of people? How can a government protect itself and its citizens from its own overzealousness? How do individuals remain so loyal to a nation that questions their loyalty so completely? And long after you have been imprisoned without cause, how do you convince friends, children, and even yourself that you did nothing wrong?

—The Honorable Robert "Bob" Takeo **Matsui**, male, Sansei, Sacramento, California, incarcerated age 6 months, Pinedale Assembly Center, Tule Lake Relocation Center[303]

• • •

Despite the acrimony that existed between the national organizations of the JACL and the NCRR, the local leaders of both organizations in the greater Los Angeles area worked together to encourage the former incarcerees to testify, and to convince them to practice in mock hearings. The LA leaders persuaded the commission to have one evening session so that working people could participate and arranged to have that session held in Little Tokyo Towers, a senior housing complex, so that the Issei living there could attend. The NCRR activists also had translators available at the Los Angeles and San Francisco hearings so the Issei could testify in Japanese.

The hearings were held in Los Angeles on August 4–6, 1981. It was standing room only.

The redress movement had one well-known Japanese American opponent who testified: S. I. Hayakawa, the seventy-five-year-old California senator. Before the commission in Los Angeles, he said, "I am proud to be a Japanese-American, but when a small but vocal group demand a cash indemnity of $25,000 for those who went to relocation camps, my flesh crawls with shame and embarrassment."

Hayakawa doubled down on previous statements he had made that "the wartime relocation was perhaps the best thing that could have happened to the Japanese Americans," maintaining that it forced their dispersal "to discover the rest of America."

He believed, "Against a background of almost 100 years of anti-Oriental agitation throughout California, it is easy to understand that the attack on Pearl Harbor aroused all the superstitious, racist fears that had been generated over the years, as well as the normal insanities of wartime."

Hayakawa's position justifying the government's wartime actions was particularly galling to former incarcerees. Redress leaders were quick to point out that Canadian-born Hayakawa had been teaching in Chicago during the war and had nothing to do with the internment program. It therefore had been easy for him to avoid incarceration. But Canada also had forcibly removed Japanese Canadians from its west coast to inland camps. Had he himself experienced incarceration, Hayakawa might have had a completely different perspective instead of calling redress "absurd." Nevertheless, Tateishi and other redress leaders found the silver lining in Hayakawa's attacks. Those who had been reluctant to support redress began to realize the depth and scope of John DeWitt's "military necessity" fiction; the support for redress grew as more Nisei galvanized around the importance of correcting the record.

The assembled audience was shocked when Lillian Baker, a White conservative author and vocal redress opponent, approached Jim Kawaminami, president of the 100th/442nd Veterans Association, while he was testifying and grabbed his arm in a wrestling match to take his notes away from him. As the security guards restrained Baker and escorted her and her colleague out of the hearing, the Japanese Americans in the audience stood to yell and heckle her. Baker, who denied that Japanese Americans were ever incarcerated against their will in concentration camps, also opposed designating Manzanar as a national historical site. She was the founder of the International Club for the Collection of Hatpins and Hatpin Holders and had served as the regional manager for S. I. Hayakawa's 1976 US Senate bid in California.

In the end, what happened at the commission hearings was simply remarkable. Often overcome with emotion, the former incarcerees bravely opened up about their pain and personal losses in heart-wrenching and eye-opening ways. The typically reticent Japanese Americans in the audience were uncharacteristically demonstrative: They cheered, booed, clapped, and jeered. The anger and grief suppressed over forty years burst forth. Many witnesses told stories that no one close to them, including their own children, had ever heard before. The entire hearing experience was stunningly cathartic, and their testimonies captured national attention.

• • •

While I did not directly experience the ordeal of the incarceration, except for being carried into Manzanar and Topaz to visit family members as an infant, I am certainly a product of those times. . . .

Gradually . . . people of my generation began to get a grasp of what had occurred. In our minds, the camps were simply a terrible wrong. Our parents were and are, simply incapable of the kind of wrongdoing that could warrant their wholesale incarceration as a people. Blaming the victim, we deprecated the Nisei on the basis of this understanding. Why didn't they resist this obvious wrong? Why did they cooperate? . . . We made ironclad arguments to belittle what in our perception, was the quiet acquiescence to a clear and monumental injustice. More blaming the victim.

The assumption that the Nisei did not make a principled stand for their rights as American citizens, has haunted a whole generation for four decades. . . .

This Commission has the benefit of hindsight. . . . There is no wartime hysteria now. . . . What went on before the barbed wire went up? . . . How early did the government study the feasibility of the incarceration? Why did the evacuation continue after the Battle of Midway, when the very last vestige of any potential invasion ceased to exist? How did it happen that the servicemen recruited from the concentration camps suffered 300% casualties, when 15% was considered high? As National Director of the Japanese American Citizens League, I would like to request that the records taken from JACL during the Second World War be returned by the Federal Government.

The Commission . . . needs to recommend compensation to communities, whose institutions for protection and services were destroyed by the uprooting that took place. It needs to recommend methods through which the real story of the concentration camps reaches the vast majority of Americans, to set the record straight and to educate the populous that their vigilance is required to maintain the human rights of all our citizenry.

—Ronald "Ron" Kaoru **Wakabayashi**, male, Sansei, former national director of the JACL[304]

In school we were taught glowingly of the tradition of America, the heritage of individual dignity and liberty.

For us, however, our American heritage is, in fact, the loss of freedom and liberty. Ours is a story of indignity and incarceration. Ours is a case of the failure of the American ideals. Because of this history those ideas of individual dignity and freedom are that much more precious to me.

. . . I have come to understand that as noble and as precious as our American ideals are, they can also be very fragile. Democracy can only be as good or as strong or as true as the people who make it so.

It is my belief that America today is strong enough and confident enough to recognize a grievous failure. I believe that it is honest enough to acknowledge that damage was done. And I would like to think that it is honorable enough to provide proper restitution for the injury done.

For in a larger sense, injury was done to those very ideals that we hold as fundamental to the American system. We, all of us as Americans, must strive to redeem those precepts that faltered years ago when I was a boy.

And in that role as an American, I urge restitution for the incarceration of American citizens of Japanese ancestry. . . . And in so doing, would move to strengthen the integrity of America.

 —George Hosato **Takei**, male, Nisei, Los Angeles, California,
  incarcerated age 5, Santa Anita Assembly Center, Rohwer Relocation
  Center, Tule Lake Relocation Center[305]

You wonder what I am. I'm one of the younger Niseis and I am a product of the camps. And what you're looking at in many ways is sort of a living cancer cell. And I'm going to multiply and really make this country sick, and the only cure for something like me is to really show me that you have a country that can live up to some of its promises . . . [and] behave as a nation of laws.

 —Haruyuki "Jim" **Matsuoka**, male, Nisei, Los Angeles, California,
  incarcerated age 7, Manzanar Reception Center, Manzanar
  Relocation Center[306]

• • •

The hearings were a real turning point for the Japanese American community. At the end of the Los Angeles hearings, Commissioner Hugh B. Mitchell said, "In some way the Japanese people have broken away from that earlier feeling in regard to words. Now they have the whole nation talking."

The firsthand accounts of the tragedy of the incarceration changed the dynamic for the redress campaign. Congressman Mineta said, "Talking about it became the first step along the path to political activism. It was only after talking about it that people could go on to the next step and actually do something about it."

For many Sansei, frustration with their parents and grandparents over why they hadn't fought back turned into a newfound appreciation of the meaning of *gaman*—to persevere.

Under the direction of special counsel Angus Macbeth, the commission spent a year and a half researching primary sources. Self-taught researcher Aiko Herzig-Yoshinaga took on the task of identifying, cataloging, and assessing hundreds of thousands of documents in the National Archives. The commission released its 467-page report, *Personal Justice Denied*, in February 1983. Its conclusions and recommendations were published four months later:

> Executive Order 9066 was not justified by military necessity, and the decisions which followed from it—detention, ending detention, and ending exclusion—were not driven by analysis of military conditions. The broad historical causes which shaped these decisions were race prejudice, war hysteria and a failure of political leadership. Widespread ignorance of Japanese Americans contributed to a policy conceived and executed in an atmosphere of fear and anger at Japan. A grave injustice was done to American citizens and resident aliens of Japanese ancestry who,

without individual review or any probative evidence against them, were excluded, removed and detained by the United States during World War II.

The commission unanimously recommended

(1) that Congress pass a joint resolution, to be signed by the president, offering a national apology;

(2) a presidential pardon for those convicted of violating the curfew or exclusion orders;

(3) that Congress direct executive agencies to which Japanese Americans may apply for restitution of losses;

(4) the establishment of an educational and humanitarian foundation; and

(5) individual compensation payments of $20,000 to each surviving incarceree.

The release of the commission's report and its subsequent recommendations made national news. As Senator Inouye had predicted, the commission approach was invaluable in creating public awareness of this period in US history, which in turn fostered a more favorable political environment in which to pursue redress legislation.

Predictably, there were those who denounced the findings. McCloy called the report "a shocking outrage" and sought to discredit it entirely.

But for former incarceree Mas Fukai, the commission findings and recommendations were significant: "It is not [that] it means so much to me, but it is what it will mean to my grandchildren. The history books will show what happened. And my grandchildren will now grow up in the mainstream of America without being stereotyped as enemies during time of war."

· · ·

We, as older Japanese Americans, have been criticized in the past by our young people—why we never fought or spoke up on this

unforgivable action. . . . If it happened to us, it could happen to anyone:
Germans, Irish, Italians, Catholics, Jews, English or Protestants. . . .

The United States government owes the Americans of Japanese ances-
try compensation for lost opportunities, lost property, lost security, and
lost self-esteem. But most of all, the government owes compensation for
the loss of regard for the principle of equal justice under the law for all
people upon which this country was founded. . . .

—Masani "Mas" **Fukai**, male, Nisei, Gardena, California,
incarcerated age 15, Tulare Assembly Center, Gila River Relocation
Center[307]

• • •

With the CWRIC recommendations in hand, Senators Inouye and
Matsunaga and Congressmen Mineta and Matsui now agreed—in the
spirit of the 100th/442nd—to go for broke. They would propose a bill
that would implement all of the commission's recommendations, including the provision of a one-time payment of $20,000 to each surviving
incarceree. In a strategic move, the bill was entitled the Civil Liberties Act. The passage of the bill would depend on it being understood
as an apple-pie cause, fundamental to the constitutional rights of all
Americans—as opposed to a liberal, civil rights, special-interest issue.

Senators and members of Congress vote for bills that are important
to their constituents, so the Nikkei congressional leaders needed their
colleagues to hear that the voters they represent would support redress.
The Japanese American community had to bring its political A game
to the fore to generate support for redress in states and congressional
districts across the country where there was little or no awareness of
the incarceration. But in the 1980s the Nikkei on the mainland were
not politically active, and the various organizations were neophytes in
the realm of federal legislative lobbying. And although the commission
hearings had brought new hope to the prospect of achieving redress,
the chances of it happening were still slim.

The supporters of the different redress initiatives brought by the

JACL, the NCRR, and the NCJAR made mutual accusations of one another that the actions of the other organizations were handicapping the redress cause. Certainly, their divisions were deep and rancorous, and would remain so. But there was one consideration they all shared—the reality that with the 1980 elections, the political environment in Washington was now operating under the Reagan era of fiscal restraint. The redress bill, in a Republican-controlled Senate, would remain stalled in Congress until 1986.

However, during this frustrating time, JACL leaders were able to make one key connection with the Reagan White House. On August 10, 1984, John Tateishi, Ron Ikejiri, and JACL leaders Floyd Mori and Frank Sato, who was the inspector general at the Veterans' Administration, met in the West Wing with John A. Svahn, Reagan's chief domestic policy adviser, to present their case for redress. They told the story of Reagan's appearance at an event nearly forty years earlier, when as a young army captain he honored the fallen 442nd soldier Kazuo Masuda of Orange County, California, at the Santa Ana Bowl alongside General Joseph Stilwell. Svahn later reported that President Reagan seemed to vaguely recall the 1945 memorial tribute, and described the president as "very interested but also noncommittal" on the issue. Svahn's colleagues in the White House were divided on redress, but Svahn himself became an advocate and continued to raise the subject with the president at his "Monday issues lunches."

But still hanging over the heads of the redress proponents were the wartime Supreme Court decisions in the cases of *Hirabayashi*, *Yasui*, and *Korematsu*. In the intervening decades, legal scholars by and large had discredited these rulings, yet they were still valid law and presented major legal as well as political obstacles in the redress path going forward. Members of Congress did not have the patience to be educated on the nuances and complexities of the Supreme Court's flawed reasoning in the three criminal conviction cases, let alone about the significance of the *Endo* habeas corpus decision. They—and the public—simply understood that the Supreme Court had upheld the constitutionality of the government's wartime actions. When Tateishi and the redress proponents tried to speak with members of Congress, they were repeatedly told that since the Supreme Court had already decided the constitutional issue, the politicians saw the matter as settled and had no motivation for considering the matter further. Without breaking through this seemingly intractable barrier, the redress effort would be symbolic at best.

Meanwhile, in the years since the Supreme Court had ruled against him, Min Yasui had kept thinking there must be some way to show conclusively that the incarceration process had been unconstitutional. Over the years, Los Angeles attorney and former JACL president Frank Chuman, a Nisei, had raised the idea with Yasui of using an arcane legal petition, the writ of coram nobis, to reopen the *Yasui*, *Hirabayashi*, and *Korematsu* trio of cases. In this rare legal proceeding, a person who has been convicted of a crime and who has already served his or her sentence can petition with the coram nobis writ to have the case reopened and the conviction set aside if "manifest injustice" can be proven. The writ directs the court to review its own judgment based on alleged errors of fact. In such an action, the normal statute of limitations does not apply. Still, Chuman had not been able to see a way for Yasui, Hirabayashi, and Korematsu to put forth evidence of "manifest injustice."

In another remarkable outcome of the commission hearings, however, historian and attorney Peter Irons described in his testimony the massive amount of documentation that he and Aiko Herzig-Yoshinaga had uncovered, revealing the War Department's stunning manipulation of evidence in the Supreme Court proceedings. After learning of Irons's and Herzig-Yoshinaga's discoveries, Chuman, Marutani, and Yasui conferred with one another. The three attorneys concurred that this documentation could be the evidence they needed in order to show "manifest injustice." Even better, Irons had personal experience in filing the writ of coram nobis, which he'd successfully used on his own behalf to vacate his conviction for failing to report for military service. Yasui, then a leader in the JACL's legislative redress campaign, jumped at the chance to pursue the coram nobis idea.

With this encouragement from Chuman, Marutani, and Yasui, Irons then called Hirabayashi, at that time a retired sociology professor. Hirabayashi said, "I've been waiting over forty years for this call."

But Irons needed Korematsu to be on board too. Irons and the group anticipated that Korematsu, a private person who had stayed out of the limelight since his conviction, would be a tougher sell. Over the years he had become weary—and wary—of the many phone calls he received from professors and others who were writing about his case and the World War II days. He never much cared to revisit his painful past. So when Irons called him and identified himself as a professor at the University of Massachusetts, Amherst, writing a book about the World War II Supreme Court incarceration cases, Korematsu figured nothing new would come of the conversation. Similar to Yasui and Hirabayashi, Korematsu felt wronged by the judicial system, but he didn't think there was a legal basis for doing anything about his criminal conviction and was at a loss for how to fund any legal action.

Irons explained that he had found some documents that Korematsu might like to see and asked to visit Korematsu in his San Leandro home. Cautious but ever polite, Korematsu said that Irons could call if he visited the Bay Area and then Korematsu "would see" if they could arrange to meet.

On January 12, 1982, Irons called Korematsu again to say he was in San Francisco and had already spoken with Ernest Besig, Korematsu's wartime attorney, which seemed to break the ice.

"Well, I might be able to see you tonight if you can come over," Korematsu said with some hesitance.

Irons immediately set off for the Korematsus' home.

For about half an hour, Irons led Korematsu through a sampling of the documents that he and Herzig-Yoshinaga had found, explaining how much the government had lied to the Supreme Court in his and the other cases by engineering a false and fraudulent record. Irons was nervous. Korematsu listened silently, puffing on his pipe. Irons said, as he had to Yasui and Hirabayashi, that he thought these documents showed enough "manifest injustice" to reopen all three cases.

After what seemed to Irons an eternity, Korematsu looked up and said, "They did me a great wrong. Are you a lawyer?"

"Yes, I am," Irons replied.

And then Korematsu asked, "Would you be my lawyer?"

Irons said he would be delighted to help. They both relaxed, then discussed the possible strategies, the work, and the time involved; of course, there was no way of knowing if this effort would succeed. But after consulting with his wife, Korematsu said yes. He was willing to pursue reopening his case. And Irons would undertake something that had never been attempted before.

With all three of the original litigants on board, Irons now needed a team in each of the three cities of the federal district courts where the original wartime cases had taken place. Through a series of connections, Irons assembled teams of passionate and dedicated volunteers under Dale Minami in San Francisco for Korematsu, Kathryn Bannai in Seattle for Hirabayashi, and Peggy Nagae in Portland for Yasui. Irons worked with the Korematsu team and helped coordinate the three teams. For the most part, the coram nobis team members were Sansei and recent law school graduates. The teams also had an unusually strong component of young women at a time when there were few women of color practicing as attorneys.

Lorraine Bannai, of the Korematsu team, tells the story that during her team's first meeting with Korematsu and his wife, Kathryn, in their living room, Korematsu whispered to Irons, "Hey, these look like high school kids."

Irons reassured him, "Oh, no, they're the best."

The teams rolled up their sleeves and bonded over the chance to bring the Supreme Court decisions to the attention of the public—to "retry the case in the court of public opinion" as much as to rectify past wrongs. For most of them, their own family members had been among the incarcerees, so the cause was personal as well. And they all had read the Supreme Court decisions in law school. When Minami first read about the *Korematsu* case as a law student at the University of California, Berkeley, School of Law, he thought, "We should do something about this." To Minami, "The *Korematsu* case was a case about power and it wasn't a case about justice and law."

Korematsu and his family had to wrap their heads around the teams' willingness to do a monumental amount of work pro bono, that is, as volunteers without any charge to the three petitioners. Karen Kai, on Korematsu's team, described the passion they all felt to be "involved in something much bigger than yourself." Fellow Korematsu team member Donald Tamaki recalled later, "And we weren't paid for it, but, to be honest with you, I would have paid to be on the team. . . . We were motivated by a sense of injustice of the case. And our desire to right a wrong."

Nevertheless, the legal team had to raise money to cover hard costs such as photocopying, telephone bills, postage, and travel to meet with the other teams at a time before email and videoconferencing. They didn't even have cell phones. Tamaki took on fund-raising, but part of the challenge was how to raise money while keeping the project confidential until the petitions were filed.

"We were concerned about people destroying documents in order to save their reputations," Tamaki explained later. "We were very much concerned that these documents would start disappearing, and we weren't even certain that we had all of them or not."

The team members appealed to their family and friends, saying, "We can't tell you what this case is about, but it's really, really important."

The checks came in from relatives and friends in small amounts— fifteen, twenty-five, fifty, one hundred, and two hundred dollars at a time—and others contributed valuable resources such as office space and photocopying. Somehow they managed the finances, as well as the logistical and organizational challenges of shaping the legal strategies and shepherding the thousands of pieces of evidence in support of the petitions and supporting documents. Irons, Herzig-Yoshinaga, and others they enlisted continued the research in the National Archives in Washington, DC.

The teams decided to file separate but coordinated coram nobis petitions in each of the respective cases, giving them "three bites of the apple." Based upon their analysis of the judges on the district courts in San Francisco, Portland, and Seattle, the group found the most liberal judges were in San Francisco, so they decided that Korematsu's team should file there first. And as they were polishing the documents to file, Tamaki arranged for press coverage.

"I think the most astounding thing to me was how ignorant the American press was," Tamaki reflects. "I even got questions like, 'Well, the internment—that happened in America?' And 'Isn't that about Japanese prisoners of war?' I had to inform them we were talking about America imprisoning its own citizens for no other reason than their national origin and racial ancestry."

After filing Korematsu's petition in San Francisco's US District Court for the Northern District of California on the morning of January 31, 1983, Minami, Irons, and Lorraine Bannai rushed off to announce the reopening of the famous case in a press conference. Waiting for them at the San Francisco Press Club were Korematsu, Hirabayashi, and Yasui. Although their names had been linked together for decades, the three men had not actually met one another before that momentous day. In a room packed with reporters, the trio had their first chance to briefly tell their stories. Irons described the shocking evidence upon which the coram nobis cases were based. Thanks to Tamaki's public relations acumen, the launch made national news. The other two teams filed their respective petitions soon thereafter.

The strategy of the legal team representing the government in all cases was to delay as long as possible. Just a few weeks after the petitions were filed, the CWRIC issued its *Personal Justice Denied* report, which described the *Korematsu* decision as having been "overruled in the court of history." Victor Stone, the Justice Department attorney leading the government team, managed to delay consideration of the Korematsu petition until after the CWRIC had issued its recommendations in June 1983.

Ironically, the CWRIC recommendation that the three men receive presidential pardons was something that Korematsu, Hirabayashi, and Yasui did not want. Rather than having the punishments for their convictions set aside by pardons, their coram nobis cases were seeking acknowledgment of a government cover-up and admission of the truth: They were never criminals to begin with.

"We should be the ones pardoning the government," Korematsu told Minami, his lead attorney.

Almost ten months after the team filed the Korematsu petition, Judge Marilyn Hall Patel held the long-anticipated hearing on November 10, 1983, in the District Court for the Northern District of California. In consideration of the case's historic implications, Judge Patel arranged for the hearing to be held in the courthouse's ceremonial courtroom. As news crews filmed the arrival of Fred and Kathryn Korematsu with the coram nobis team, over three hundred people, mostly elderly Nisei, crowded in to take their seats in the audience. The air was electric with emotion.

In his opening statement Minami explained the significance of the moment. Calling the *Korematsu* Supreme Court decision a "great civil rights disaster," he said, "For those Japanese Americans interned, for those ex-internees in the audience, for Fred Korematsu and for this court, this is the last opportunity to finally achieve justice denied forty years ago."

With permission from Judge Patel, Korematsu finally had a chance to speak for himself and on behalf of all those whose imprisonment he had protested.

In his soft voice he said, "As long as my record stands in federal court, any American citizen can be held in prison or concentration camps without a trial or a hearing. . . . I would like to see the government admit that they were wrong and do something about it so this will never happen again to any American citizen of any race, creed, or color."

Victor Stone had the unenviable position of following Korematsu at the podium. In his brief remarks he characterized the petition as a "symbolic matter." At the conclusion of all the presentations, a judge typically would end the hearing and issue an opinion at a later point. But Judge Patel surprised the audience by proceeding to read a prepared statement from the bench. She first described the government's positions in the case to be "tantamount to a confession of error," words that must have boded well to the Korematsu team. As a district court judge in the matter before her, Judge Patel did not have the ability to reverse a Supreme Court decision, and she pointed this out to the audience:

> *Korematsu* remains on the pages of our legal and political history. As a legal precedent it is now recognized as having very limited application. As historical precedent it stands as a constant caution that in times of war or declared military necessity our institutions must be vigilant in protecting constitutional guarantees. It stands as a caution that in times of international hostility our institutions, legislative, executive, and judicial, must be prepared to exercise the authority to protect all citizens from the petty fears and prejudices that are so easily aroused.

After a pause Judge Patel announced, "The petition for a writ of coram nobis is granted." Then she rose to return to her chambers without further comment.

The Korematsus, the coram nobis team, and the audience sat there in a few moments of stunned silence, processing what Judge Patel had just said. As Minami and Bannai were explaining to the Korematsus that Fred had won his case, and as the people began to absorb the meaning of Judge Patel's words, the emotions pent up for over forty years burst forth in tears and jubilation. Karen Kai remembered "seeing the judge pause and smile at the scene before leaving the courtroom, and people pressing to reach Fred to thank and congratulate him. He was smiling, of course, and people were crying, laughing, pressing to shake his hand and kiss his cheek."

Judge Patel later recalled that the hearing was a very emotional and heartwarming experience for her: "This was a case everyone reads in law school, and I never dreamed I would have the opportunity to revisit [it]."

Korematsu's wife, Kathryn, paid tribute to the legal team, saying, "You all just fulfilled his biggest dream to reopen his case. Who else would've done it but some crazy young people?"

• • •

What happened forty years ago involved my family and my personal life, and I had to do some real deep thinking in order to reopen this case again. . . . I am very happy I did, because this is important not only for Japanese American citizens but for all Americans who might get involved in similar conditions.

—Fred Toyosaburo **Korematsu**, male, Nisei, San Leandro,
California, age 22 when Pearl Harbor was attacked, Presidio,
Tanforan Assembly Center, Topaz Relocation Center[308]

• • •

The coram nobis teams suspected that the judges who had been assigned to the Yasui and Hirabayashi petitions were waiting for the outcome of the Korematsu hearing before proceeding. Sure enough, after the Patel ruling, Judge Robert C. Belloni set the hearing on Yasui's petition for January 16, 1984. Ten days later, on January 26, 1984, Judge Belloni vacated Yasui's conviction but declined to consider Yasui's coram nobis petition. Judge Belloni tersely refused to address the question of the government's wartime actions.

Yasui and his legal team continued to pursue an appeal, but on

November 12, 1986, Yasui died while waiting for his case to be heard in the Ninth Circuit Court of Appeals, which brought his case to an end. Of the three litigants—Yasui, Hirabayashi, and Korematsu—Yasui was the only attorney. He had deliberately broken the law to make himself a test case and spent the better part of his life building a constitutional case based on his wartime stand. He was disappointed that both his 1944 case and his coram nobis case had been given curt treatment by the courts. Yet he never gave up his belief in the Constitution and his commitment to constitutional principles.

On November 24, 2015, the Yasui family was invited to the White House by President Barack Obama to receive the Presidential Medal of Freedom on Yasui's behalf.

• • •

The overwhelming tragedy for the United States and all our people is that the highest court of our country failed to require [an] actual relationship between [the] wildest rumors based on outright racial prejudices and individual guilt or responsibility. . . .

Inasmuch as the government attorneys did not . . . contend that I had lost my United States citizenship, the U.S. Supreme Court remanded my case back to the U.S. District Court . . . for re-sentencing in accordance with the decision in the Hirabayashi *case. My release came through on August 17, 1943, because . . . having been confined for nine months, . . . it was considered that I had served my full time in jail. The $5,000.00 fine was suspended. . . . I was returned to the Minidoka WRA center under escort by a U.S. marshall from Portland, Oregon, to Idaho. . . . I was not handcuffed this time. I savored of being able to walk in the open air and to see the blue sky above. After having been confined to a six-by-eight foot cell for a long, long time, one is humbly grateful for small things. . . .*

My steadfast position in camp, even as it is today, is that the United States is still the best country in the world, despite all of its defects, injustices, warts and blemishes. It is incumbent upon us, as

*responsible members of our country, to point out those things that
are wrong and to work assiduously to correct such wrongs.*

    —Minoru "Min" **Yasui**, male, Nisei, Portland, Oregon, incarcerated
    age 24, Portland Assembly Center, Minidoka Relocation
    Center, Multnomah County Jail[309]

• • •

In the last of the three cases, Judge Donald Voorhees in Seattle scheduled a full hearing on the evidence in Hirabayashi's coram nobis petition
for May 18, 1984. In a manner similar to how Judge Patel had handled
the Korematsu petition, Judge Voorhees moved the hearing to the federal
courthouse's largest courtroom to accommodate the anticipated crowd.
One wrinkle for the coram nobis team was that the day before the hearing, the judge in the NCJAR class action suit had dismissed that case
because the statute of limitations had run out. In the hearing Judge Voorhees seemed cognizant of the differences between the two cases.

After more than forty years, Hirabayashi finally had the opportunity
to speak for himself. He asked Judge Voorhees if he could read out
loud an anonymous letter he had received, dated October 1982. Judge
Voorhees permitted him to do so. Hirabayashi read:

> Maybe our government did irrational things . . . so did your
> people when they attacked the Islands. . . . This was war and
> during such a confrontation one can expect bizarre solutions
> to problems. . . . Have you forgotten how the US Government
> helped Japan to reestablish itself as a world power? . . . Can't you
> find anything to be grateful for, or is your ambition cloistered in
> a desire to get even no matter what the consequences?

Then Hirabayashi continued in his own words:

> Your Honor, this is a letter written not forty years ago during
> the war but in the 1980s. Note: This letter characterizes me as

an Imperial Japanese subject, ungrateful for all the good things America has done for Japan. This view is representative of more people than I think America deserves, so a continued effort must be made to enlighten all Americans of the precious commodity that our Constitution is. . . . I cannot understand how our government continues in this day to defend violations of our Constitution and not acknowledge our petition in the interest of justice. . . . I have filed the petition to clear my name of the stigma of questionable loyalty to the United States.

Another highlight of the hearing for the Japanese American community was the appearance of seventy-six-year-old Edward Ennis as the Hirabayashi team's star witness. Under examination and cross-examination, the former Justice Department attorney relayed his objections to the War Department's suppression of evidence and its deception in altering DeWitt's final report. Ennis directly accused McCloy of personal deception in his testimony at the commission hearings.

Ennis testified, "This is a case where the government violated the Constitution, and they knew it."

Although both McCloy and Bendetsen had appeared before the commission during the hearings in Washington, DC, the government attorneys did not present either one to testify on the evidence as witnesses in the Hirabayashi hearing. Perhaps McCloy and Bendetsen were unwilling to perjure themselves, under oath, if they were forced to deny the charges leveled by Ennis in court.

On February 10, 1986, Judge Voorhees vacated Hirabayashi's conviction for violating the exclusion order, but oddly, he did not vacate the curfew conviction, on the basis that it rested upon a legal foundation different from that of the exclusion conviction. Both Hirabayashi and the government appealed to the Ninth Circuit.

A three-judge panel heard arguments on March 2, 1987. Judge Mary Schroeder of the Ninth Circuit ruled on September 24, 1987, that both of Hirabayashi's convictions should be vacated. In her opinion, she found that the coram nobis team had presented evidence that documented "historical judgments that the convictions were unjust" and had demonstrated that "there could have been no reasonable military assessment of an emergency at the time, that the orders were based upon racial stereotypes, and that [the] orders caused needless suffering and shame for thousands of American citizens." Judge Schroeder agreed with vacating Hirabayashi's exclusion conviction but reversed Judge Voorhees's finding as to his curfew conviction, ordering that the district court vacate Hirabayashi's curfew conviction as well.

Following additional appellate maneuvers by the government, Judge Voorhees vacated Hirabayashi's curfew conviction on January 12, 1988, bringing an end to Hirabayashi's legal journey, which had started as a test case in 1942, almost forty-six years earlier.

Judge Patel's decision in the Korematsu coram nobis case was a game changer for the redress cause. Tateishi and the redress leaders capitalized on the media coverage of the coram nobis cases, which provided much-needed energy to the legislative redress effort. He could now go back to members of Congress and see where, on principle, they might stand on the matter; they could no longer claim to be constrained by some earlier court decision.

•   •   •

There [were] members of Congress I went to see and said, "Do you remember the conversation we had once? . . . Well, let me tell you, the Korematsu case just got vacated. . . . Now it really comes down to your conscience. . . . If you're gonna vote no, at least do it honestly and don't hide behind these nonsense excuses. And there were, I know, at least ten or fifteen who [said] . . . well, no, that changes everything. . . . The decision by Patel was huge. Even though it may not have changed some members' minds, it broke down the defense they had and what it did was expose them for who they really were.

—John Yoshio **Tateishi**, male, Sansei, Los Angeles, California,

incarcerated age 3, Manzanar Reception Center, Manzanar
Relocation Center[310]

•   •   •

By late 1985, Tateishi was transitioning out of his JACL role and
Grayce Uyehara, a Nisei social worker from Philadelphia, had assumed
the lead in the redress campaign as executive director of the newly
formed JACL Legislative Education Committee. In addition, Masaoka
and Yasui (the year before he died) had brought on Grant Ujifusa as
strategy chair. As co-author of the long-running *Almanac of American Politics*, the bible of Washington politics, Ujifusa was considered
the ultimate Washington insider. He brought sophisticated knowledge
about the backgrounds of the legislators and an understanding of what
would motivate their votes.

The NCRR also developed an effective grassroots campaign. The
organization coordinated tens of thousands of letters of support and
generated media coverage of its rallies and events. Two NCRR delega-
tions fanned out in the congressional hallways and in July 1987 made
an impact as the largest group of Asian American citizens ever to visit
congressional offices. Korematsu was among the 127 NCRR members
of the 1987 delegation who visited 101 congressional offices.

And in the House of Representatives, before his colleagues on
the House Judiciary Subcommittee on Administrative Law and
Governmental Relations, Mineta was extremely effective in sharing
his experiences during the incarceration. His remarks were met with
applause.

•   •   •

*My father was not a traitor. He came to this country in 1902 and
he loved this country. . . . My mother was not a secret agent. She kept
house and raised her children to be what she was, a loyal American.
Who amongst us was the security risk? Was it my sister Aya, or perhaps Etsu, or Helen? Or maybe I was the one, a boy of 10½ who this
powerful nation [thought] was so dangerous I needed to be locked up*

without a trial, kept behind barbed wire, and guarded by troops in high guard towers armed with machine guns.

—The Honorable Norman "Norm" Yoshio **Mineta**, male, Nisei, San Jose, California, incarcerated age 10, Santa Anita Assembly Center, Heart Mountain Relocation Center[311]

· · ·

As one of four Japanese American legislators, Mineta worked closely with community advocates and lobbied his fellow members of Congress throughout the lengthy legislative process to gain support for H.R. 442—named after the 442nd Regimental Combat Team—which would implement the CWRIC recommendations. House Speaker Jim Wright suggested to Mineta that they introduce the bill on the House floor on September 17, 1987, the two hundredth anniversary of the signing of the Constitution. On that day, in an especially touching tribute to Mineta, Wright gave up his chair as Speaker of the House and insisted that Mineta sit in it instead so that he could serve as Speaker pro tem and preside over the vote for H.R. 442.

By then the JACL had nearly two hundred endorsements from cities, counties, states, churches, labor organizations, the US Conference of Mayors, the National Council of La Raza (the largest Latino advocacy organization in the US, now called UnidosUS), the American Bar Association, and the American Federation of Teachers. The wide spectrum of support was critical in having redress viewed not just as a piece of special-interest legislation, but as one affecting all Americans.

While the vote was underway, NCRR member and decorated 442nd veteran Rudy Tokiwa was sitting in the House balcony in the handicapped spectators' section, watching as Congressman Charles E. Bennett, a Democrat from Florida, entered the chamber. Earlier that summer during NCRR's hallway campaign, Tokiwa had been part of a group of Nisei vets who lobbied House and Senate vets. Tokiwa, who had been grievously and permanently disabled in the Lost Battalion rescue, took on Congressman Bennett's opposition of redress. Bennett was himself a disabled World War II vet who had served as a jungle fighter in New Guinea. During his later tour of duty in the Philippines, Bennett had contracted polio, and walked with the aid of a leg brace in addition to a cane or crutches for the rest of his life. As the second-ranking member of the House Armed Services Committee and the dean of the Florida congressional delegation, his vote was crucial.

During that July visit, Congressman Bennett had tried to get Tokiwa, along with other members of the NCRR, thrown out of his office. But Tokiwa refused to go; instead, he stayed behind to thank Bennett for his public service despite his injury during World War II, and then commiserated on having a similar injury and enduring the pain. Tokiwa's sincerity moved Bennett, and he reluctantly agreed to vote for H.R. 442. Nevertheless, between the July lobbying effort and this September day of the House vote, Bennett had reconsidered and reversed his opinion. Tokiwa was sitting in the gallery, wearing his army coat and hat, when Bennett walked with difficulty onto the House floor.

· · ·

And they announced for [Bennett] to go up to the podium, and that he has three minutes to talk against the redress bill. So he got up—and I was watching and as he [came] down the aisle between the seats, I saw him, he looked up and he stopped once and he stood there for a while, and all of a sudden he [came] to the end of the row, [maneuvered] down the stairs, [but] instead of taking a step up to the podium he went right out the door. And I was confused, I was sittin' up there— what the hell is he doing? He was supposed to talk for three minutes against the redress, and I couldn't understand it, until I looked at . . . you know, in the House there, they have all the congressmen's names and at the end of each row, there's a blue button, there's a red button. Red button, you're against; blue button, you're for. I see, I looked at his name and he's voted for the redress bill.

—Rudy Kazuo **Tokiwa**, male, Nisei, Salinas, California, incarcerated age 17, Salinas Assembly Center, Poston Relocation Center[312]

• • •

Bennett, to the surprise of many, was unable to vote against redress with Tokiwa there to remind him of the sacrifices of the 442nd. And because Bennett was head of the Florida delegation, he had told three other members to follow his vote, so the legislation gained four yea votes that it would not have had otherwise, if it hadn't been for Tokiwa and his service in the 442nd.

It was a day to celebrate the Constitution. H.R. 442 passed by a vote of 243 to 141.

Meanwhile, on the Senate side, Senator Matsunaga had been applying his legendary personal touch. He had the ability to connect with colleagues in many ways beyond being a decorated member of the 100th/442nd. Matsunaga was so well regarded by his Senate colleagues that by the time the bill S. 1009 was introduced in the spring of 1987, he had secured enough co-sponsors to guarantee the votes for passage out of the Senate; he even had enough votes to prevent a filibuster.

With passage of the redress bill looking promising, the looming question was whether President Reagan would sign the bill if it made it to his desk. Ujifusa had been working ahead to secure White House support. In October 1987, New Jersey governor Thomas Kean let Ujifusa know that he would be riding in a limousine with the president when the two of them would be making campaign appearances in New Jersey. At Ujifusa's behest, Kean reminded the president of the 1945 Masuda event. But Kean also heard from the president a common misperception about the Japanese American incarceration. Reagan said he'd been told that the Japanese Americans had been taken into "protective custody" and had gone into the camps voluntarily. Kean explained that, on the contrary, the Japanese Americans had been incarcerated against their will, and "the bill presented him with an opportunity to erase one of the few black marks in American history." Reagan then turned to his deputy chief of staff, Ken

Duberstein, and said, "Maybe we should take a re-look at this one."

Ujifusa arranged for Kean to send a follow-up letter of support to the president that included a letter from Ujifusa explaining how the "protective custody" narrative was an after-the-fact rationalization invented by journalists and government officials. Kean also enclosed photographs of armed soldiers with their guns trained on mostly women, children, and teenagers. In addition to Ujifusa's letter, Kean included a letter from June Masuda Goto, one of Kazuo Masuda's surviving sisters (Mary had died years before), to remind the president of her brother's story and the United America Day rally, where Reagan had thanked her parents for her brother's sacrifice.

On April 20, 1988, H.R. 442's companion bill S. 1009 passed the Senate with a vote of 69 to 27.

The two bills went to a conference committee to reconcile the House and Senate versions before the redress bill could be sent to the president for his signature. The legislative goal line was in sight, but it wasn't time yet to celebrate. There were signs that a presidential veto was likely. Both the Justice Department and the Office of Management and Budget had already taken positions that should the redress bill make it to his desk, President Reagan should veto it.

Anne Higgins, special assistant to President Reagan and director of correspondence, told Ujifusa they "were swamped by the negative mail . . . four or five or six to one, particularly from outraged veterans." Lillian Baker and her Americans for Historical Accuracy group, and groups of "Concerned Americans," placed opposition ads in California newspapers, as well as in the *New York Times* and the *Boston Globe*. Former California Senator S. I. Hayakawa wrote a handwritten note to the president's chief of staff, Howard Baker, to say Japanese Americans were "just rolling in prosperity." He continued, "They are a damn sight better off than whites, but they play on the widespread assumption that non-whites are all more-to-be-pitied than whites. Makes me damn sick to listen to those skillful hustlers. I crawl with embarrassment at their gimme/gimme attitude towards government."

On May 6, 1988, Grayce Uyehara sent out an urgent "action alert" from the JACL, requesting that the redress network write to the White House urging the president to sign H.R. 442 when it reached his desk. In her letter, Rose Ochi, a civil rights leader from Los Angeles, also reminded the president of his remarks at the 1945 Masuda event. For many from the redress organizations who had handwritten countless letters to lawmakers in support of the various redress bills over the long campaign, these became the most significant letters of all.

Senator Alan Simpson from Wyoming, a close friend of Reagan's as well as Congressman Mineta's, brought up redress to the president a number of times. Congressman Robert Matsui knew Duberstein; Matsui also asked Patrick Butler, the Washington vice president of the Times Mirror Company, to speak about the redress bill with Baker. Even Vice President George H. W. Bush took a pro-redress stance because of the importance of the issue in California during the 1988 presidential campaign.

Months passed, and in the summer of 1988, Duberstein and Joe Wright, director of the Office of Management and Budget, signaled to the House-Senate conference committee that if they could work out some of the fiscal impact issues in H.R. 442, "the president would look favorably on it and in all likelihood sign the legislation." Richard K. Willard, assistant attorney general for the DOJ's Civil Division, also confirmed with Ujifusa that he would not send his staff to the Hill to lobby against the bill, nor would he contact the president to recommend a veto.

On August 1, 1988, three days before the House was scheduled to vote on the conference committee's bill, the president sent a public letter to House Speaker Jim Wright, saying, "The enactment of H.R. 442 will close a sad chapter in American history in a way that reaffirms America's commitment to the preservation of liberty and justice for all. I urge the House of Representatives to act swiftly and favorably on the bill."

And with that expression of support from the president, Congress passed H.R. 442, the Civil Liberties Act of 1988, which provided a formal apology and a compensatory payment of $20,000 to each of the surviving incarcerees.

. . .

As a member of Congress who was both an observer of and a participant in the battle for redress, I know that the effect of this legislation on my colleagues was powerful. Representatives and senators—many of whom had little or no knowledge of what occurred in 1942 and had few, if any, constituents who were incarcerated—told me that the passage of redress was one of the most important votes they ever cast. . . . Conservative Republicans, such as Newt Gingrich and Henry Hyde, joined with liberal Democrats, such as Barney Frank and Ron Dellums, to support the legislation, because it was the right thing to do and because it affirmed their own belief in the Constitution.

—The Honorable Robert "Bob" Takeo **Matsui**, male, Sansei,
Sacramento, California, incarcerated age 6 months, Pinedale
Assembly Center, Tule Lake Relocation Center[313]

. . .

Because of the hot and humid August weather conditions in Washington, DC, the White House decided against holding the signing ceremony in the outdoor Rose Garden and scheduled it instead in the air-conditioned South Court Auditorium, in the Old Executive Office Building (now known as the Eisenhower Executive Office Building). Redress leaders were invited from across the country and flew in on short notice to witness the momentous occasion that they could hardly believe was happening.

The redress leaders from the SELANOCO (Southeast Los Angeles and North Orange County) chapter of the JACL—Gene Takamine, Hiroshi Kamei, Susan Kamei, Peter Ota, and Clarence Nishizu—had arrived on red-eye flights and were biding their time in the early morning in a downtown coffee shop.

Ota and Hiroshi Kamei exchanged memories of when they, as teenagers, learned that Pearl Harbor had been bombed. Kamei said he knew at that moment the life he and his family were living in California had ended forever. Asked if he could ever have imagined that, decades later, he would be invited by a president of the United States to be a guest of the White House to witness an apology for the wrongs committed by the US government, he gazed into the distance and his eyes filled with tears. The very idea left him speechless.

In the president's opening remarks at the August 10, 1988, ceremony, exactly four years to the day from that providential meeting of JACL leaders at the White House, President Reagan said that the Civil Liberties Act of 1988 would "right a grave wrong." With his actor's sense of timing and delivery, Reagan echoed the words he had delivered four decades earlier when he'd paid tribute to the valor of Staff Sergeant Kazuo Masuda and other Nisei servicemen killed in action: "Blood that has soaked into the sands of a beach is all of one color. America stands unique in the world, the only country not founded on race, but on a way—an ideal. Not in spite of, but because of our polyglot background, we have had all the strength in the world. That is the American way."

Before Reagan sat down to sign the bill, Congressman Mineta gestured for June Masuda Goto to come to the edge of the stage to greet the president.

"Mary?" Reagan said.

"No, Mr. President. My sister, Mary, passed away. I am here representing the family."

Reagan nodded and warmly shook her hand before taking his seat at the table to sign H.R. 442 into law.

After the ceremony, the redress leaders returned to Capitol Hill to continue the celebration at a reception hosted by Congressman Robert Matsui and his wife, Doris, who was later elected as her husband's successor after his death in 2005 and who still represents California's Sixth Congressional District to this day.

For Senator Spark Matsunaga and his fellow Nisei veterans, the passage of the Civil Liberties Act was what they had fought for as soldiers of the 100th/442nd.

• • •

To me, [the signing of the redress bill] was one of great gratification for hard work. And as one of Japanese ancestry, I felt that here was final recognition of our loyalty to the United States. Those of us who fought in the 100th Infantry Battalion, the 442nd Regimental Combat Team, and the Military Intelligence Service, we feel now that our efforts at the battlefront—giving up our lives and being wounded and maimed and disabled—all this was for a great cause, great ideals; that is, to remove the one big blot on the Constitution that has been there for over 45 years.

—The Honorable Spark Masayuki **Matsunaga**, male, Nisei, Kauai, Hawaii, age 25 when Pearl Harbor was attacked[314]

• • •

Redress supporters were elated, but the ultimate Washington insider's game was just starting. Congress hadn't yet provided the money, and getting the votes for appropriations would be just as hard as, if not harder than, passing the redress bill. Despite the feel-good moment of the signing ceremony, the Japanese American community was shocked to learn that the Reagan administration's proposed budget for fiscal year 1989, his last year in office, contained no redress funds. Redress supporters would need bills passed each year in order to keep the redress payments funded.

On top of that, they now had to confront the harsh reality of a ticking clock. Eligible redress recipients were dying at an estimated rate of about two hundred people per month, so getting the money into the hands of the most elderly former incarcerees was the top priority. Moreover, by law the payments needed to be made within a ten-year period. A new wave of skepticism swept through the community.

Senator Daniel Inouye was on the case. As an alternative to having to fight each year for appropriations, Inouye led the effort to make redress a federal entitlement program—a legally binding financial commitment from the government. When the time came for a full Senate vote, Inouye spoke with emotion on the Senate floor.

• • •

Mr. President [pro tempore of the Senate], the matter of redress for Japanese-Americans who were interned in the Federal Government internment camps during World War II has been before us and debated for over a decade. And my participation in these debates, as many have been aware, has been rather minimal. So it is most difficult for me to admit that I have been inhibited and reluctant to say much about this because of my ethnic background. I reached the conclusion that as a result of this reluctance to participate, I may have performed a great disservice to many of my fellow Americans with whom I served in the Army during World War II.

So, Mr. President, I believe the time has come for me to tell my colleagues what has been in my heart for all these many years.

Mr. President, I was a very young 18-year-old high school graduate when I volunteered and put on the uniform of my country. At that moment, because of wartime censorship in Hawaii and other restrictions, I was not made aware of the strange plight of my fellow Americans of Japanese ancestry who were then residing on the mainland United States. However, I was made aware of their unbelievable problems soon after I joined them in a training camp in Mississippi. I learned that over 120,000 Americans were given 48 hours to settle their accounts, businesses and they were required by law to leave their residences and be sent to barracks and makeshift camps in distant parts of the United States. History now shows that their only crime was that they were born of parents of Japanese ancestry. History also shows that there was no evidence of any fifth column sabotage activities carried out by any of these Americans of Japanese ancestry.

So when our special infantry regiment was being formed, I was aware that half of this regiment was made up of men from Hawaii and the other half from the mainland United States. Mr. President, all of our volunteers were of Japanese ancestry. These mainland men volunteered from behind barbed wire in these camps. They did not volunteer, as other Americans did, in free American communities. So to this day, I look back with awe and disbelief that these men who had been denied their civil rights, deprived of their worldly goods and humiliated with unjust incarceration would, nonetheless, stand up and take the oath to defend the country that was mistreating them without due process of law.

So, Mr. President, I have oftentimes asked myself the question: Would I have volunteered under these circumstances? In all honesty, I cannot give you a forthright answer. The men who volunteered from these camps were very reluctant to share their unfortunate internment experiences. They would just shrug their shoulders and mutter, "I suppose that is the way life is." But in a rare moment, one of them would open up and tell us about some episode in his camp. For example, I remember a story I heard on a cold night in the field. One of my mainland buddies told us about his experiences in the Manzanar camp where soldiers shot and killed 3 internees and wounded about 10 others because they were demonstrating for the release of a fellow internee who had been arrested for allegedly assaulting another internee.

Just because they were demonstrating, they were shot. According to the provisions of this bill, these three men who were killed would not receive any redress payments [because no payments will be made to heirs]. And then while we were training in Mississippi to prepare us for combat in Europe, word came to several of my buddies from California that their State had just begun to implement a strange law which authorized the seizure and resale of idle farm machinery. Obviously, idle farm machinery that was found in the State of California during that time was almost always those that the internees were forced to abandon. Needless to say, these California internees were not around to bid for them.

Further, we were at times told about the great losses that these young volunteers and their families had to incur. For example, it was commonplace for residences, farms and personal items to be sold for a fraction of their market value. In fact, one of those men in my squad sold his almost brand new 1941 Ford for $100. He had no choice. Although it was in good condition, that was all he could get from his neighbors. And now we are told that these losses have exceeded $6 billion.

Most of the Members of the Senate have been in this body for at least 10 years, and during that time we have given our vote and our support for other reparations programs.

Mr. President, redress and reparations are not unique in our history. For example, in 1980—that is less than a decade ago—we in the Senate appropriated funds to provide $10,000 to each of the 1,318 anti-Vietnam war demonstrators who were found to have been wrongly jailed for 1 weekend. They spent 2 days and 1 night and we paid $10,000; no fuss.

More recently, in 1986, we appropriated sums to give each American hostage $22,000 for his or her bitter experience in Iran. We were not the ones who incarcerated these hostages, but we felt that they were entitled to $22,000.

Mr. President, the internment of most of the families of those with whom I served in combat was for over 3 years. My mainland buddies were silent because they could not bring themselves to share their humiliation with those of us from Hawaii.

Mr. President, as a footnote, I should point out that during the 1 year of almost continuous and intensive combat in Europe, over 200 of those mainland volunteers from internment camps went through the ranks of my company; that is, Company E 2d Battalion, 442d. Of that number, all with the exception of about 20 were either seriously wounded or killed in action. That is a very high percentage of Purple Hearts, much higher than one would find in any other unit.

Incidentally, Mr. President, the regiment with which I was privileged *and honored to serve was the most decorated unit in World War II.*

That is about all I have to say, Mr. President. I hope my colleagues will support the action that will be made by the chairman of this committee to make this proper, and as my dear friend from New Hampshire said during the markup, it is the right thing to do.

—The Honorable Daniel "Dan" Ken **Inouye**, male, Nisei, Honolulu, Hawaii, age 17 when Pearl Harbor was attacked[315]

• • •

Inouye and the redress leaders were able to secure an agreement so there would be enough funding to pay all the redress recipients over a three-year period, but there was a compromise: The funding would not start until the 1991 fiscal year. The appropriation bill was signed by President George H. W. Bush, but the fact that more eligible incarcerees would not live to receive their payments made for a bittersweet conclusion to the ten-year quest for legislative redress.

At an emotional ceremony held in Washington, DC, on October 9, 1990, Attorney General Richard L. Thornburgh presented the nine oldest surviving incarcerees with their redress checks for $20,000, accompanied by a formal apology by President Bush. Other elderly former incarcerees received their checks at ceremonies that took place all around the country; the rest received their checks in the mail. Those checks were also accompanied by President Bush's letter on White House stationery:

A monetary sum and words alone cannot restore lost years or erase painful memories; neither can they fully convey our Nation's resolve to rectify injustice and to uphold the rights of individuals. We can never fully right the wrongs of the past. But we can take a clear stand for justice and recognize that serious injustices were done to Japanese Americans during World War II.

In enacting a law calling for restitution and offering a sincere apology, your fellow Americans have, in a very real sense, renewed their traditional commitment to the ideals of freedom, equality, and justice. You and your family have our best wishes for the future.

A total of 82,219 former incarcerees received these redress payments. Although the payments could not compensate for the losses suffered as a result of the incarceration, the government paid out more than $1.6 billion over ten years to verified survivors. The federal redress program made its final payments in 1993, but there are still lessons to be learned from the Japanese American incarceration about resulting abuses of power when our constitutional framework of checks and balances among the executive, legislative, and judicial branches is disrespected.

• • •

They returned as victims of an assault of tremendous magnitude.

They were scarred deeply and lived with this pain that took many years to overcome.

But the underlying grief was the heartache, a gnawing sense of great tragedy, that this happened in America. I feel an overwhelming sadness for my country.

At a Cultural Heritage School, I faced the fourth generation, the great grandchildren of dear Isseis I had known in my growing years at Florin. They asked this disturbing question, "Was my great grandpa really a criminal? Was he a Traitor? A Spy?"

I was shocked and realized that I could not rest until we could set the record straight and add a hopeful ending to this American tragedy.

How would you answer Americans who ask, "Did it really happen? Why hadn't I learned about it in school in the past thirty years? They must have been guilty of something for the government to imprison them for nearly three years."

If the Government responsible for the massive violation remains quiet, the episode will remain a haunting unfinished story. It will remain a frightening precedent set into American history, ready to engulf another unfortunate minority group at another time of crisis. . . .

All of our children, the future Americans of this land, are entitled to a legacy that can ring true to the promises which our Founding Fathers have established. The truth must now be told, the record cleared. The victims of this experience must be vindicated for the gross denial of personal justice.

For 44 years we have lived within the shadows of this humiliating lie. There was never a military necessity to exclude us! Yet we were presumed guilty and condemned.

All Americans were betrayed when the constitution was violated. . . .

I firmly believe, and I am determined to prove, Democracy can correct its own mistakes.

It is time to model that kind of honest responsible citizenship that will not falter.

We must make possible equal justice for all people. We must remain tireless in preserving America's honor and gain back dignity as a people who can all dream of a Nation that truly upholds the promise of Liberty, Equality, and Justice for All.

—Mary Tsuruko (Dakuzaku) **Tsukamoto**, female, Nisei, Florin, California, incarcerated age 27, Fresno Assembly Center, Jerome Relocation Center[316]

CHAPTER TWELVE

Allyship

First they came for the Communists, and I did not speak out—because I was not a Communist.

Then they came for the Socialists, and I did not speak out—because I was not a Socialist.

Then they came for the trade unionists, and I did not speak out—because I was not a trade unionist.

Then they came for the Jews, and I did not speak out—because I was not a Jew.

Then they came for me—and there was no one left to speak out for me.

—Martin Niemöller, Lutheran pastor and outspoken critic of Adolf Hitler, imprisoned during World War II[317]

Right after the first plane hit New York City's World Trade Center on the morning of September 11, 2001, President George W. Bush summoned Norman Mineta, his secretary of transportation, to the White House. Mineta, who as a child experienced the aftermath of the 1941 Pearl Harbor attack, was now dealing with the ramifications of another deadly attack on US soil. This shocking attack by Islamic extremists killed nearly three thousand people. For Mineta, the comparisons between Pearl Harbor and 9/11 were inescapable.

• • •

There's no question that right after September 11th they were saying, "Take all these Arab Americans and Muslims and put them in camp." I don't believe this—what am I hearing? . . . On September 12th, there was a Cabinet meeting with the members of the Democratic and Republican leadership. . . . And towards the end of the meeting, Congressman David Bonior from Michigan . . . said, "Mr. President, we have a very

large population of Arab Americans in Michigan, and they're very con-
cerned . . . about what they're hearing on radio, television, reading in
the paper about some of the security measures that might be taken relat-
ing to transportation." And the president said, "David, you're absolutely
correct. We are also concerned about this, and we want to make sure
that what happened to Norm in 1942 doesn't happen today."

    —The Honorable Norman "Norm" Yoshio **Mineta**, male, Nisei, San
    Jose, California, incarcerated age 10, Santa Anita Assembly Center,
    Heart Mountain Relocation Center[318]

• • •

Japanese Americans know what it is like to suffer the consequences
of government action based upon prejudice. So they strive for "allyship," meaning they act as allies of other groups and individuals who
are experiencing similar discrimination on the basis of their race. In
the years since 9/11, many members of the Japanese American community have acted in solidarity with Muslim Americans to protest and
defend against discrimination and to work for social justice.

In September 2017, President Donald Trump began issuing a series
of executive orders restricting travel to the United States from mostly
Muslim countries. Again parallels were raised between the president's
actions and the government's World War II incarceration of Japanese
Americans.

Congressman Mark Takano said, "How you react to the Muslim
ban today is how you would have reacted to the imprisonment of my
grandparents and parents 75 years ago."

The state of Hawaii's challenge to the second of the three executive orders ended up before the Supreme Court. The children of
Minoru Yasui, Gordon Hirabayashi, and Fred Korematsu, together
with national bar associations of color and civil rights organizations,
filed amicus briefs to remind the Supreme Court of the importance of
its role in checking executive power when it exerts claims of "military
necessity" or "national security."

Attorney Neal Katyal appeared before the Supreme Court on April 25, 2018, to argue that the Trump administration had exceeded its constitutional authority in issuing the travel bans. Katyal had a unique perspective of the similarities between this case and the *Korematsu* and other wartime Supreme Court decisions. On May 20, 2011, while he was Acting Solicitor General in President Barack Obama's administration, Katyal issued a rare "confession of error," in which he acknowledged the Solicitor General Office's mistakes in its handling of the *Yasui*, *Hirabayashi*, and *Korematsu* cases and in defending the government's actions in the incarceration.

On June 26, 2018, the Supreme Court upheld the Trump administration's third version of the travel ban, maintaining broad deference to executive power to restrict immigration on the premise of protecting national security. Although Chief Justice John Roberts in his majority opinion referred to the *Korematsu* case as having been overruled "in the court of history," Justice Sonia Sotomayor pointed out in her dissenting opinion that the court was following the same flawed logic of the 1944 court in not scrutinizing the motivations of the presidential actions.

The Japanese American Supreme Court cases also arose in the spring of 2019, when the Trump administration proposed that the 2020 census ask respondents if they were US citizens. In the public debate, those protesting this proposal raised how the government had used confidential census data to locate Japanese Americans for incarceration purposes. The ghost of the *Korematsu* case and the Japanese American incarceration lives on in controversy.

For this reason, Satsuki Ina, born in the Tule Lake camp, thinks it is important to speak for others and to "stop repeating history." In the summer of 2019, Ina and other Japanese Americans, Native Americans, and immigrant rights advocates protested the government's plans to temporarily house 1,400 migrant children without a parent or legal guardian in the Fort Sill, Oklahoma, army base. Fort Still is where, in 1894, the army held 342 Chiricahua Apache prisoners of war. The army facility also served as a detention facility for seven hundred Issei who were considered enemy aliens and ineligible for citizenship. Two of them were killed by guards.

At the Fort Sill protest Ina said, "This place represents pain and suffering for people of color. We are here today to be the allies that we needed during World War II when we were imprisoned."

The protest worked. On July 29, 2019, the government announced that its plans to house migrant children at Fort Sill were "on hold."

The coalition that assembled at Fort Sill continues its social justice advocacy as Tsuru for Solidarity. *Tsuru* is the Japanese word for "crane," a symbol of long life, happiness, and peace. Paper cranes folded in the traditional Japanese folk art of origami are expressions of hope for the future. The custom of presenting and hanging strands of origami cranes at places of trauma began more than sixty years ago at the site of the Children's Peace Monument in remembrance of the Hiroshima bombing victims, and strands of folded *tsuru* are offered today to show support for communities under attack. Tsuru for Solidarity supporters have folded and presented hundreds of thousands of origami cranes as part of their advocacy for immigrant children and other victims of state violence.

The power behind the symbolic offerings is the strength of many, even countless, individuals and communities coming together to fight against unconstitutional imprisonment, structural racism, and systemic bias that has resulted in the forced removal, exclusion, detention, and separation of families. As soon as bayonets and guns were pointed at them, the Issei and Nisei realized they were powerless to change the political dynamic. Too few people spoke up for them when they couldn't speak for themselves. What we can learn from the proponents of redress, organizers of Tsuru for Solidarity, and supporters of the Black Lives Matter movement is the critical necessity of creating awareness of the plights of others, and building understanding and empathy so that we can overcome our differences and work together toward a more equitable and just society. It is vitally important to join voices in the public discourse to stop prejudicial policies and practices, to prevent them from happening again, and to reconcile with our past.

The voices of the Issei and Nisei who experienced the wartime incarceration are falling silent with the passage of time. It is up to their descendants—the Sansei, Yonsei, and even Gosei, as well as future generations—along with their allies, to know their stories and hold the government accountable under the Constitution.

Tule Lake incarceree Joe Matsuzawa told his granddaughter Kara, "You need to speak up if you're a minority. People will always pick on the minority. Anyone can be incarcerated. . . . Never forget this event. It could happen to you, too."

EPILOGUE

MARION KONISHI'S VALEDICTORIAN ADDRESS

On May 21, 2016, Marion Tsuruko Konishi (Takehara), at the age of ninety-one, boarded a bus in Denver, Colorado, for a nearly four-hour journey to the fortieth annual Amache Pilgrimage at the Granada Relocation Center, also known as Camp Amache. The camp was named after Princess Amache, the daughter of Chief Ochinee (One-Eye), a medicine man of the Cheyenne, both of whom were victims of the Sand Creek Massacre. Konishi was making her first return trip to the camp of her incarceration since the end of the war. There she would read the valedictorian address that she had given on June 25, 1943, at the age of eighteen, upon her graduation from Amache Senior High School almost seventy-three years earlier. The same speech would be read on the floor of the US Senate just a few days later, on June 9, 2016, as a tribute to her by Senator Cory Gardner.

. . .

AMERICA, OUR HOPE IS IN YOU

One and a half years ago I knew only one America—an America that gave me an equal chance in the struggle for life, liberty, and the pursuit of happiness. If I were asked then—"What does America mean to you?"—I would answer without any hesitation and with all sincerity—"America means freedom, equality, security, and justice."

The other night while I was preparing for this speech, I asked myself this same question—"What does America mean to you?" I hesitated—I was not sure of my answer. I wondered if America still means and will mean freedom, equality, security, and justice when some of its citizens were segregated, discriminated against, and treated so unfairly. I knew I was not the only American seeking an answer.

Then I remembered that old saying—All the answers to the future will be found in the past for all men. So unmindful of the searchlights reflecting in my windows, I sat down and tried to recall all the things that were taught to me in my history, sociology, and American life classes. This is what I remembered:

America was born in Philadelphia on July 4, 1776, and for 167 years it has been held as the hope, the only hope, for the common man. America has guaranteed to each and all, native and foreign, the right to build a home, to earn a livelihood, to worship, think, speak, and act as he pleased—as a free man equal to every other man.

Every revolution within the last 167 years which had for its aim more freedom was based on her constitution. No cry from an oppressed people has ever gone unanswered by her. America froze, shoeless, in the snow at Valley Forge, and battled for her life at Gettysburg. She gave the world its greatest symbols of democracy: George Washington, who freed her from tyranny; Thomas Jefferson, who defined her democratic course; and Abraham Lincoln, who saved her and renewed her faith.

Sometimes America failed and suffered. Sometimes she made mistakes, great mistakes, but she always admitted them and tried to rectify all the injustice that flowed from them. I noticed that the major trend in American history has been towards equality and fair play for all. America hounded and harassed the Indians, then remembering that these were the first Americans, she gave them back their citizenship. She enslaved the Negroes, then again remembering Americanism, she wrote out the Emancipation Proclamation. She persecuted the German-Americans during the first World War, then recalling that America was born of those who came from every nation seeking liberty and justice, she repented. Her history is full of errors but with each mistake she has learned and has marched forward onward toward a goal of security and peace and a society of free men where the understanding that all men are created equal, an understanding that all men whatever their race, color, or religion be given an equal opportunity to serve themselves and each other according to their needs and abilities.

I was once again at my desk. True, I was just as much embittered as any other evacuee. But I had found in the past the answer to my question. I had also found my faith in America—faith in the America that is still alive in the hearts, minds, and consciences of true Americans today—faith in the American sportsmanship and attitude of fair play that will judge citizenship and patriotism on the basis of actions and achievements and not on the basis of physical characteristics.

Can we the graduating class of Amache Senior High School, still believe that America means freedom, equality, security, and justice? Do I believe this? Do my classmates believe this? Yes, with all our hearts, because in that faith, in that hope, is my future, our future, and the world's future.

—Marion Tsuruko **Konishi** (Takehara), female, Nisei, Los Angeles, California, incarcerated age 16, Santa Anita Assembly Center, Granada (Amache) Relocation Center[319]

PART SIX

Contributor Biographies

This section provides biographical information on the contributors of Japanese descent whose voices are featured in this book. Young Oak Kim, a Korean American, is included because he fought alongside Japanese Americans in the 100th/442nd Regimental Combat Team and had a close identity with the Japanese American community. I would have loved to write a complete biography for each contributor, and each life deserves a book unto itself. Despite extensive research and attempts to contact as many of the contributors and their families as possible, I recognize there might be important omissions or unintended inaccuracies. If you are familiar with any of these individuals and would like to make a correction or add something personal about them for future editions, please post it in the Facebook group for *When Can We Go Back to America?* or send a message to whencanwegobacktoamerica@gmail.com.

. . .

Hatsune "Helen" **Aihara** (Kitaji), female, Nisei, Santa Clara Valley, California, incarcerated age 29, Salinas Assembly Center, Poston Relocation Center. Helen was born in Monta Vista, California, on November 18, 1913, the eldest of four children, to Teikichi "George" Aihara and Torano "Tura" (Ishiwara) Aihara. Both of her parents were born in Gunma Prefecture, Japan, her mother in Maebashi and her father in Takasaki. Her father left Japan for Hawaii in 1899 and came to San Francisco in 1903. He worked as a day laborer in the orchards of Agnew, what is now Santa Clara. During the San Francisco earthquake of 1906, he witnessed the destruction of the Agnew State Mental Hospital, which killed over one hundred patients.

Helen's mother was well-educated, so she decided she would rather go to America as a picture bride than marry anyone in Japan. She sailed to Seattle to meet her husband; they were married in San Francisco in 1912. George was working at the McLeod Ranch when Helen was born. The family then moved to Cupertino, where George worked for Charles R. Bocks Sr., a wealthy landowner known as the cherry king of Santa Clara valley.

Helen lived in a mostly Caucasian world, and her mother wanted her to speak perfect English. The Bockses treated Helen and her siblings as if they were part of the family and Helen often played homemade games with the Bocks children. Helen was the first Japanese girl to attend Sunnyvale Grammar School and graduated from Sunnyvale's Fremont High School. The Aiharas attended the First Methodist Church that consisted almost entirely of Caucasian congregants.

During the Depression her family had very little cash, but they lived on the ranch for free and always had enough to eat, so they never felt truly poor. Her father saved enough money from growing tomatoes to buy a Ford Model T, in which Helen learned to drive. She had summer jobs picking prunes, cutting apricots, sorting pears, and also working in the Mariana Packing Company fruit cannery. After high school, she commuted to San Jose State College and majored in speech correction and elementary school education. She was one of only thirteen women elected in their senior year to a secret society for women called the Black Masque. They met secretly and had reunions on campus every year.

Helen served on the college advisory board at San Jose State and went to several Edward W. Hazen Foundation conferences on student guidance and counseling. She was also on the board of the YWCA. Through her YWCA connections, she became part of a small Bible study group, led by Stanford professor Harry Rathbun and his Mexican American wife, Emelia. While listening to classical music, the group discussed many forms of religion—including Buddhism—ethics, psychology, and the cultivation of human potential.

For three years Helen participated in a month-long retreat at the remote Salmon Lake Lodge in the Sierra Nevada of Northern California. The group was often referred to as the Pinks—the name for liberals—because the members discussed communal living, the fight for civil rights in the South, problems in countries like the Soviet Union, and their own philosophy of life.

Because public schools were not hiring Japanese Americans, Helen taught English privately to immigrants who were aspiring to US citizenship. Among the families she taught were Kunisaku and Kane Mineta, the parents of Norman Mineta. When Helen's mother died in 1937 at the age of forty-nine, a German family, the Hinze sisters, took Helen into their home.

As soon as the war broke out, FBI agents came to investigate Helen at San Jose State College based on a tip from a young Italian newspaper reporter at the *Mercury Herald* who had learned Helen was teaching English to his mother. But the president of the university managed to clear her from any FBI questioning. Helen had been continuing her education at Stanford University for her master's degree and secondary education teaching credential. But the mass incarceration prevented her from finishing the program, and she could not convince Stanford to let her transfer credits to an inland university.

At the Salinas Assembly Center, she started a nursery school, and at Poston she taught first grade. The Indian Service then hired her to teach at a boarding school for the Navajo Nation in Fort Defiance, Arizona. She traveled many miles through Navajo and Hopi lands with Dr. George Boyce, the superintendent of the Navajo and Hopi schools, and met Henry Chee Dodge, the last official head chief of the Navajo Nation and chairman of the Navajo Tribal Council during World War II. Helen developed a deep regard for Native Americans that lasted throughout her life.

After teaching for four months at Fort Defiance, Helen left to marry Robert Rokuro Kitaji in Chicago, where he was working in a motor factory. They moved briefly to Marsing, Idaho, near the Snake River, where they farmed until Robert was inducted into the army as a staff sergeant for the 442nd Regimental Combat Team, 232nd Combat Engineer Company.

Helen returned to Poston to join her father and gave birth to her first child. After the war they went to San Jose, where they lived temporarily with the Hinze sisters until Robert was discharged from the army. When he came home, he discovered the Kitaji farm property in Castroville had been destroyed and most of the buildings had been vandalized or burned. Robert rebuilt the home and farmed the land. They had three more children, and in 1953 they sold it all and moved to a small farm south of Salinas. After an unfortunate series of farming failures, they moved to North Salinas and Robert became a landscape gardener.

Helen returned to San Jose State University to refresh her education and then taught for the next nineteen years at Natividad Elementary School and the Mission Park Elementary School, receiving many honors for outstanding teaching. She was the first female president of the Salinas Valley JACL during the redress effort and president of the Salinas-Ichikikushikino Sister City Association (formerly Salinas-Kushikino). Later in life she was on the committee to restore the Castroville Japanese Language School building. The renovation was completed successfully in December 2009. Robert died in 1987, but she lived independently for the next twenty-eight years. She remained active with the Lincoln Avenue Presbyterian Church as well as Delta Kappa Gamma (a group for women educators), and traveled around the world.

Kyuji **Aizumi**, male, Issei, San Diego, California, incarcerated age 56, Fort Missoula Alien Detention Center, Santa Anita Assembly Center, Poston Relocation Center. Kyuji was born in Tono, Iwate Prefecture, Japan, on July 10, 1886. His mother's maiden name was Sakai. He graduated from Morioka Agricultural College in Tono, and he came to the United States by himself to study veterinary medicine. He ended up in San Diego, working in the fishing industry instead. He was a partner with Tokunosuke Abe in the Southern Commercial Company, a major Japanese-owned San Diego fish brokerage with ownership interests in many fishing boats. He was a founding member of Ocean View Church of Christ, wrote poetry, loved his garden, and polished interesting rocks to show their beauty.

George **Aki**, male, Nisei, Berkeley, California, incarcerated age 28, Tanforan Assembly Center, Topaz Relocation Center, Jerome Relocation Center. George was born in Livingston, California, on September 11, 1914, the second oldest of four children, to Kamesaburo Aki and Haru Aki. He grew up in

Fresno, California, where he became the first non-White civil servant in the city. His father was a medical doctor primarily for the Japanese community in the San Joaquin valley. He graduated with a philosophy degree from Fresno State College (now California State University, Fresno), but he was inspired to become a minister by Reverend Joseph K. Fukushima of the Fresno Independent Congregational Church, who would regularly denounce discrimination against the Japanese people.

George was a student at Berkeley's Pacific School of Religion in 1942 when he and his wife, Misaki (Iijima) Aki, were forcibly removed just days before his graduation. One of the guards at Tanforan had attended the same school but dropped out; the guard attended the graduation in George's place, received his diploma, and brought it back to him. George's ordination took place shortly afterward in the Tanforan mess hall, officiated by Reverend Robert Inglis of Oakland's Plymouth Congregational Church, together with other White clergy from nearby churches, and with over five hundred people attending.

George and his wife were then sent to Topaz but were granted a transfer to Jerome so they could be with George's parents. Their first child was stillborn. In 1943, George volunteered as a chaplain for the 100th/442nd Regimental Combat Team, and he was sent to the Army Chaplain School at Harvard University. On July 8, 1945, George was shipped off to Italy. He visited soldiers in hospitals, identified the dead from dog tags, looked for their graves, and fought racism and mistreatment from commanding officers toward Nisei troops. George was honorably discharged as a major in 1946 and returned to advocating for racial equality, a key aspect of his ministry. He served three churches in Fresno, Chicago, and Los Angeles before becoming the first Japanese American minister to serve a Caucasian church in San Luis Obispo, California.

In 1966 the Pacific School of Religion gave him an honorary doctorate of divinity degree. After retirement he spent a year in Japan teaching English at volunteer missionaries, served on the Rev. Martin Luther King Jr. High School Memorial Scholarship Fund Committee in San Luis Obispo, and regularly washed cars to raise money for charitable organizations. George raised more than $8,000 on his Habitat for Humanity walk to Tijuana, Mexico, in 1990.

George **Akimoto**, male, Nisei, Stockton, California, incarcerated age 20, Stockton Assembly Center, Rohwer Relocation Center. George was born in Stockton, California, on November 13, 1922, the younger of two children, to Kensuke Akimoto and Tatsumi (Yamada) Akimoto. The family's twenty-acre farm was taken care of by a neighbor while the family was incarcerated. At the Rohwer concentration camp, he created the cartoon character Lil Dan'l, which became the camp mascot and was featured in the camp journal, the *Rohwer Outpost*, and then later in his book, *Lil Dan'l: One Year in a Relocation Center* (1943). George had a notable career as a movie-poster and aviation artist.

Emi "Amy" **Akiyama** (Berger), female, Sansei (mother was Nisei; father was Issei), Berkeley, California, incarcerated age 8, Tanforan Assembly Center, Topaz Relocation Center. Amy was born in Berkeley, California, on February 24, 1933, the eldest of five siblings, to Ichiro Akiyama and Beni (Ogawa) Akiyama. Amy's father was born in 1899 in Yamaguchi Prefecture, Japan; he immigrated to Berkeley at the age of twenty-eight. Beni, her mother, was born in 1908 in San Francisco; Beni's grandfather was a samurai admiral.

At the time of the family's incarceration, Amy's father was working as a gardener and her mother was cleaning homes. After the war they returned to Berkeley, and her father found work as a caretaker for an estate in Oakland that was owned by a couple who were child psychologists; Beni was hired as their maid. Later her mother found work at the bookstore of the University of California, Berkeley, and she was employed there until she died in 1970 of a tragic and rare brain ailment called Creutzfeldt-Jakob disease.

After graduating from Berkeley High School, Amy attended the California College of the Arts and studied fine arts. She moved to New York City in 1956 to pursue painting and exhibited her work in a number of galleries. She met her husband, Jesse Berger, while they were both working for Weaver's, a company in Manhattan that specialized in typography, page design, and graphic illustrations for periodicals. The couple and their two children then moved to New Rochelle, New York, and Amy opened a clothing consignment shop with two friends; they also sold their own handmade children's crafts. After the store closed, she had a long career as art director of the Cuisenaire Company of America that produced educational materials for children.

Jesse and Amy eventually retired to Bearsville, New York, in the Catskill Mountains. She was a member of the JACL and would faithfully attend the annual Day of Remembrance observances, honoring her late parents, on February 19, the date Franklin D. Roosevelt signed Executive Order 9066.

Frank Nobuo **Bunya**, male, Nisei, Seattle, Washington, incarcerated age 16, Puyallup Assembly Center, Minidoka Relocation Center. Frank was born in Tacoma, Washington, in 1926, the youngest of five children, to Shinichiro Bunya and Shige (Nishida) Bunya; they were both from Okayama Prefecture, Japan. Although the family registration book was stolen, Frank's mother, Shige, could recite twelve generations of family names and claimed her family descended from samurai.

Shinichiro came to America first and then returned to Japan to marry Shige, who had the equivalent of a high school education, which was very rare for a Japanese woman in the nineteenth century. Shinichiro had been a teacher in Japan, but in the United States he worked as a tallyman at the sawmill in Fairfax, Washington (now a ghost town).

Frank's father died when Frank was only a year and a half old, so his mother raised five children on her own, with assistance from uncle Ed (Ichitaro Akagi). Shige also worked at a Seattle hotel and as a waitress. Frank attended Washington Grade School and Broadway High School and helped his mother at the hotel. One sister, Alice, died in her teens from tuberculosis. Frank eventually graduated from Hunt High School while in camp at Minidoka, where he was a dishwasher, waiter, fry cook, and mechanic's apprentice.

After Frank turned eighteen, he went to Spokane, Washington, and enlisted in the 100th/442nd Regimental Combat Team. He had tried to enlist at Minidoka, but he was only seventeen and his mother wouldn't give him permission. He served in the Second Battalion, Company H, reaching the rank of staff sergeant. He was on a ship to Italy when the war ended and was honorably discharged in 1946. He then signed up for an additional year of active duty at Fort Ord near Monterey, California.

Meanwhile, his brother and one of his sisters had moved to Chicago, so in 1947 he followed them there. He enrolled in the Industrial Training Institute to study drafting and mechanical design, and also studied auto mechanics at another trade school. By his own description, Frank was a "jack of all trades, master of none." Over the course of his working life, he had many jobs: He laid track for railroads; he was a typist, an assistant foreman, a farmworker who thinned lettuce and picked radishes and onions, and an auto mechanic for an English car distributor. He worked at an apple juice processing plant, ironed laundry, made sliding cardboard calculators, loaded ice into produce freight cars, and injected moldings at a plastic plant. He also loved playing football and was in a Chicago semipro league.

In 1952 Frank was hired by Palo Alto Engineering Company, which later became part of the Hewlett-Packard Company (HP). He helped design the first transformer used in HP computers and worked there for over thirty-five years. He met his wife, Esther (Nakatani) Bunya, at a dance held at San Jose State University. Frank was a gifted gardener and skilled woodworker and continued to remodel their home and yard after he retired. As a member of the 100th/442nd, he was awarded the 2011 Congressional Gold Medal and participated in the San Jose ceremony in 2012. He has lived with Esther in Los Altos, California, for over sixty years. In 2021, they marked their sixty-sixth anniversary.

Namiko "Nami" Aurora (Nakashima) **Diaz**, female, Nisei, Long Beach, California, incarcerated age 25, Santa Anita Assembly Center. Nami was born in Los Angeles, California, on September 5, 1916, the second oldest of seven children, to Carl Tsuruji Nakashima and Paula Carmona. Carmona was the former partner of Enrique Flores Magón, the anarchist who, along with his brother Ricardo, led the Mexican Liberal Party movement to the Mexican Revolution of 1910. Paula and Enrique had three children (one died in infancy), but Enrique later disowned Paula and their children.

Paula met Carl Nakashima, a Japanese national, while working at a hotel in Los Angeles. Because interracial marriages were against the law, they got married at sea off the coast of San Diego. After they married, they ran an ice cream shop called the Bon Ton at the Long Beach Pike until there was a shortage of sugar during World War I. They later bought some land in Long Beach that was intended for farming—but they discovered oil instead. Paula and Carl had seven children together, including Nami, who also had to confront the issue of entering into an interracial marriage. She and Mexican American Avery Diaz solved the problem by getting married in Tijuana, Mexico.

Nami was incarcerated at the Santa Anita Assembly Center, and her husband insisted on being incarcerated with her even though Mexican American men were under no obligation to be detained with wives of any amount of Japanese heritage. His presence there resulted in his being drafted by the navy directly from the assembly center, but the navy allowed Nami to leave early, since her husband was not of Japanese descent. The FBI, however, did check on her activities every month during the war. When the war was over, Avery became a longshoreman and organized a work gang consisting only of Japanese Americans.

Frank Seishi **Emi**, male, Nisei, Los Angeles, California, incarcerated age 26, Pomona Assembly Center, Heart Mountain Relocation Center, Leavenworth Penitentiary. Frank was born in Los Angeles, California, on September 23, 1916, the second of four children, to Yanusuke Emi and Tsune Emi. His father, a professor at Kyoto University, first went to Texas to start a community of Japanese farmers called Yamato Colony with a group of other professors. When that didn't work out, he went to Alabama, imported Japanese orange trees, and planted them on the land of a company where he was the foreman. But then he quit and traveled to all the southern states, before ending up in

Los Angeles and farming in El Monte. Meanwhile, his wife and two children were still in Japan. When they finally arrived in Seattle in 1915, the children stayed with their father at the Mt. Fuji Hotel, while their mother remained at the immigration office recovering from some form of parasite.

Finally, on New Year's Day 1916, they sailed by first class to Los Angeles, landing in San Pedro. Frank's father moved them around a lot, establishing farms and stores, and even opening a hotel in San Pedro. In the city of San Fernando, they added a fruit and vegetable section to the first open-air persimmon stand that they operated. Frank started out going to the San Fernando Grammar School, which had a mostly Latino student population, but he ended up at a Caucasian school called O'Melveny Grammar School, where he got into a lot of fights. He graduated from Long Beach Polytechnic High School and attended Los Angeles Junior College. Then his father was injured in a car accident, and he had to drop out of college to run his parents' produce business.

At Heart Mountain, Frank drove a truck and made tofu. He also became a civil rights activist and refused to answer questions twenty-seven and twenty-eight on the loyalty questionnaire. He formed the Heart Mountain Fair Play Committee—the only organized protest of the draft in the camps—with Kiyoshi Okamoto and five other incarcerees. They demanded their release and the restoration of their rights as American citizens. Frank was married with children, so he already had a military deferment. Even so, he was arrested for conspiracy to violate the Selective Training and Service Act and served eighteen months of a four-year sentence at the penitentiary in Leavenworth, Kansas. On one of his first days in prison, all of the Nisei, including Frank, who had a black belt in judo, gathered to demonstrate their expertise in martial arts. One of the smallest Nisei was pitted against a big White inmate; the Nisei flipped him easily. After that, the other prisoners kept their distance, so the Nisei were safe.

After the war Frank worked first at a produce market and then as a gardener. He took the civil service exam and was hired by the US Postal Service, and then worked for the California State unemployment office for ten years. He joined the redress movement and began giving talks on the role of civil disobedience in wartime. He was also a senior teacher of judo with an eighth-degree black belt and taught judo to children.

Mitsuye Maureen **Endo** (Tsutsumi), female, Nisei, Sacramento, California, incarcerated age 22, Sacramento Assembly Center, Tule Lake Relocation Center, Topaz Relocation Center. Mitsuye was born in Sacramento, California, on May 10, 1920, the second of four children, to Jinshiro Endo and Shima (Ota) Endo. She graduated from Sacramento Senior High School and attended secretarial school; her first job was as a typist for the California Department of Motor Vehicles. After the attack on Pearl Harbor, Mitsuye and all other Japanese American state employees were suspended from their jobs and threatened with dismissal by the California State Personnel Board.

While incarcerated, Mitsuye agreed to become a plaintiff in a habeas corpus petition to challenge the constitutionality of detention based solely upon race. She was considered an ideal petitioner. She had an all-American profile—she was a Christian who had never been to Japan, with a brother who had been drafted into the army before the Pearl Harbor bombing and was serving in the 442nd Regimental Combat Team. She was willing to remain in camp while her case wended its way through the courts. In December 1944 the Supreme Court ruled that she should be released from detention, prompting the closure of all camps.

In May 1945, Mitsuye resettled in Chicago and became a secretary for the Mayor's Committee on Race Relations. She married Kenneth Tsutsumi, whom she met in the Topaz War Relocation Center. They raised three children.

For the rest of her life, she said very little about her incarceration experience and her role in the Supreme Court case. Her daughter was in her twenties before she learned about her mother's pivotal role in Japanese American history. The only interview she granted was to John Tateishi, providing a brief oral history, which he included in his 1984 anthology *And Justice for All*.

Yoshihiko Fred **Fujikawa**, male, Nisei, Terminal Island, California, incarcerated age 32, Santa Anita Assembly Center, Jerome Relocation Center. Fred was born in San Francisco, California, on July 4, 1910, to Hikozo Fujikawa and Yu (Nomura) Fujikawa, who worked as migrant grape farmers. His mother was also a social activist who embroidered and wrote poetry. He had one younger sister, Gyo Fujikawa. They grew up in a fishing village on Terminal Island, near San Pedro, California, where their father worked in a fish cannery. Fred attended UCLA for two years, then transferred to University of California, Berkeley. In 1934 he graduated from Creighton University School of Medicine in Omaha, Nebraska—one of the first Japanese Americans to attend medical school—having paid his way by working at a fruit stand. His medical internship was at Los Angeles General Hospital.

Meanwhile, his sister, Gyo, had received a scholarship to Chouinard Art Institute (now California Institute of the Arts). She spent a year traveling in Japan, then came home to Los Angeles, where she worked on murals for department store displays. She was then hired by Walt Disney Studios to design a book based on the Disney movie *Fantasia*.

At the time of the attack on Pearl Harbor, Fred had been practicing medicine on Terminal Island for five years. The moment the reports were broadcast on the radio, Terminal Island was shut down.

Walt Disney himself was worried about Gyo, and to avoid her being incarcerated, he sent her to New York to work in a studio designing Disney books, posters for movies, and a composite of Disney characters for *McCall's* magazine. She also designed pharmaceutical advertisements. So while her brother and parents were incarcerated, she was free but feeling guilty about pursuing a career in commercial art.

At the Santa Anita Assembly Center, Fred was one of six doctors who took care of eighteen thousand people. Later he was one of eight doctors who took care of ten thousand people at Jerome. But he was allowed to leave camp early to work at a sanitorium in Missouri, treating patients with tuberculosis. His presence, however, triggered action in the Missouri legislature; some wanted to pass a bill prohibiting him from working in the state. Then Orland

K. Armstrong, a Republican who supported civil rights, spoke up and decried the prejudice; the bill was defeated. Fred's experience at the sanitorium led to his specialty in chest surgery for the next forty years. In the meantime, Gyo illustrated fifty children's books, forty-five of which she wrote and illustrated herself. Two of them, *Babies* and *Baby Animals*, have sold more than two million copies and are still in print. She also designed six US postage stamps—the thirty-two-cent yellow rose was issued in 1997.

Edward Kanta **Fujimoto**, male, Issei, San Francisco, California, incarcerated age 43, Fort Lincoln Internment Camp, Camp Livingston Internment Camp, Topaz Relocation Center. Edward was born in Chayamachi, Okayama Prefecture, Japan, on March 4, 1898, to Genpei Fujimoto and Tsuya (Miyake) Fujimoto. He was the younger brother of Koraku (Fujimoto) Yamane, his sister.

Edward stayed behind in Japan as a student when his parents migrated to San Francisco in 1910. They founded the Fujimoto Miso Company, the earliest known miso plant in America. Their son followed seven years later and eventually took over the company. He also became a talented player of the shakuhachi, the Japanese bamboo flute, and accompanied musicians in recitals featuring the koto, the Japanese floor harp.

Edward was trout fishing with friends at the foot of the Sierra Nevada when Pearl Harbor was bombed. He didn't know it had happened until he was stopped by soldiers at the San Francisco–Oakland Bay Bridge. He was immediately interned at Fort Lincoln in Bismarck, North Dakota, then Camp Livingston in Alexandria, Louisiana, before being reunited with his family at Topaz.

After the war he was fortunate enough to be able to resume his miso business in Salt Lake City, Utah, where he worked until his untimely death on June 7, 1956, at the age of fifty-eight. His boat capsized in the Snake River near Eagle Rock, eight miles southwest of American Falls, Idaho. He drowned, along with four others: Roy Masao Yamane, Satoru Harada, August Tokuo Hondo, and Joe Chotaro Miya. Koraku lost her younger son and only brother in that boat accident. A few weeks later, on August 18, 1956, Koraku also passed away.

Masani "Mas" **Fukai**, male, Nisei, Gardena, California, incarcerated age 15, Tulare Assembly Center, Gila River Relocation Center. Mas was born in Perry, California, on January 2, 1927, the youngest of four children, to Hatsutaro Fukai and Yoshi (Sugimoto) Fukai. He attended local schools and worked on the family farm until the family's incarceration. Mas was drafted into the 442nd Regimental Combat Team and served until 1947, attaining the rank of corporal. After his discharge he went back to Los Angeles, attended Los Angeles Trade Technical College, and ran his own auto body repair business for thirteen years. He continued his education at the California School of Insurance and became successful in the insurance industry.

While directing a sports league in Gardena for at-risk youths, he caught the attention of Los Angeles County supervisor Kenneth Hahn, who named him to a post on the county's Narcotics and Dangerous Drugs Commission. In 1974, Mas won a seat on the Gardena City Council. A year later Hahn appointed him as his assistant chief deputy to serve as a liaison with the growing Japanese American community in the Second Supervisorial District. Mas went on to serve as Hahn's chief of staff. Following his retirement from the county post in 1993, he continued to serve as a councilman in Gardena for five more years. A park in Gardena has been named after him.

Harry Katsuharu **Fukuhara**, male, Nisei, Los Angeles, California, incarcerated age 22, Tulare Assembly Center, Gila River Relocation Center. Harry was born in Seattle, Washington, on January 1, 1920, the third eldest of five children, to Harry Katsuji Fukuhara and Kinu (Sasaki) Fukuhara.

After Harry's father died of pleurisy in 1933, his mother took the family back to Hiroshima, Japan, where Harry graduated from high school. He then left his family to return to America. He paid his way through Glendale Junior College in Glendale, California, only to be incarcerated at Gila River Relocation Center six months later. In November 1942 he enlisted in the Military Intelligence Service Language School and trained at Camp Savage in Minnesota. His mission was to be an Allied translator and interpreter in the Pacific theater of operations.

Meanwhile, his three brothers in Japan had joined the Imperial Japanese Navy, so Harry and his brothers were on opposite sides of the war. It would be four years before he saw his family again. During that time he was able to show his superiors how his understanding of the Japanese people was key in getting Japanese soldiers to surrender and provide important information. He became a master sergeant and was awarded a Bronze Star with two Oak Leaf Clusters; he received a battlefield commission to second lieutenant. His mother, his aunt, and two of his brothers survived the atomic bombing of Hiroshima by taking refuge in an underground bomb shelter, but his older brother died of radiation sickness a few months later.

After the war Harry enrolled in the basic course of the Counter Intelligence Corps at Fort Holabird in Maryland and participated in counterintelligence operations in Japan and Indochina during the Cold War and the Korean War. In July 1972 he became chief of the 500th Military Intelligence Brigade's Foreign Liaison Detachment, whose work was highly respected throughout the intelligence community. He served nearly four decades in Japan as a US military intelligence officer, rising to the rank of colonel.

Harry earned a Legion of Merit medal, Meritorious Service Medal, Army Commendation Medal, and Combat Infantryman Badge. For his contributions to national intelligence, he was awarded the National Intelligence Distinguished Service Medal by the director of the Central Intelligence Agency, and the Department of the Army Decoration for Exceptional Civilian Service by the secretary of the army. In 1988 he was inducted into the US Army Military Intelligence Corps Hall of Fame. In 1990 he received the Order of the Rising Sun, Third Class, Gold Rays with Neck Ribbon, from the emperor of Japan and the President's Award for Distinguished Federal Civilian Service, signed by President George H. W. Bush.

His family's story is told in *Midnight in Broad Daylight: A Japanese Family Caught Between Two Worlds* by Pamela Rotner Sakamoto.

Grace **Harada**, female, Nisei, Pocatello, Idaho, age 20 when Pearl Harbor was attacked. Grace was born in Ucon, Idaho, on December 27, 1921, the younger of two girls. Her father worked for the railroad for over thirty years, but lost his job when the war broke out. No one would rent her family a home, so for a while they lived in their car. Her father died when she was nine months old. Her mother married her father's cousin, as her father had requested before he died, so she wouldn't be deported to Japan. With her second husband, Grace's mother had three sons and another daughter. Grace served in the Nisei squadron of the Women's Army Corps and trained at the Military Intelligence Service Language School. She was sent to Japan while her brother was serving in the 442nd Regimental Combat Team.

Masaru "Mas" **Hashimoto**, male, Nisei, Watsonville, California, incarcerated age 6, Salinas Assembly Center, Poston Relocation Center. Mas was born in Watsonville, California, on September 15, 1935, the youngest of six children, to Ikuta Hashimoto and Nami (Haraguchi) Hashimoto. At age ten he began working in the fields harvesting strawberries, raspberries, and lettuce. Following his college graduation, he earned his teaching credential and was drafted into the US Army in the 1950s. He worked in the chemical department, where everyone had top secret clearance for nuclear, chemical, and biological weapons. He completed a two-year stint and then returned to Watsonville, where he taught high school history for thirty-six years. He has been active in speaking to students about the civil rights issues of the incarceration. In 2020 he and his wife, Marcia, celebrated their fiftieth wedding anniversary.

Sato **Hashizume**, female, Nisei, Portland, Oregon, incarcerated age 11, Portland Assembly Center, Minidoka Relocation Center. Sato was born in Iida, Nagano Prefecture, Japan, on July 14, 1931, the youngest of five children, to Shiro Hashizume and Kanaye (Yazawa) Hashizume. She was born in Japan because her mother was visiting family there at the time. Sato was three when her mother died, and she was raised by her father in Portland, where he was the superintendent of an apartment building. The one possession she would not give up during the forced removal was her mother's piano, and at the last minute a woman from the YWCA stored it for her.

After leaving camp, the family went to Salt Lake City briefly, then back to Portland, where Sato graduated from high school. She got her BA at Oregon Health and Science University and became a visiting nurse and clinical instructor. She earned a master's degree in public health from the University of Minnesota and went to summer school at the University of Oslo; then she taught at the University of California, San Francisco, as an assistant professor. She ended up coordinating the home care program in the school of medicine and becoming a nurse practitioner. She was a member of Sigma Theta Tau, a nursing honor society. She retired after twenty-six years and then worked aboard the USS *Hope* in Sri Lanka. She later began touring high schools to share her story and wrote about her incarceration in an essay published in the anthology *From Our Side of the Fence: Growing Up in America's Concentration Camps*, edited by Brian Komei Dempster.

Kazuko (Ikeda) **Hayashi**, female, Issei, Salinas, California, incarcerated age 56, Salinas Assembly Center, Poston Relocation Center. Kazuko was born in the port city of Sakai, located then in the Hyogo Prefecture (now Osaka Prefecture), Japan, on March 24, 1886, the youngest of six children, to Noboru Ikeda and Kimio (Nagai) Ikeda. Her father was an only son; her mother was an only daughter.

As a young man, her father, Noboru, was a ronin, a samurai warrior who had lost his master either by death or by a fall from grace or power. To avoid the consequences of *ako hanshi*, which can mean the ultimate sacrifice of committing seppuku, or ritual suicide, he found a job as a priest at a Kampei Taisha, one of the most important shrines of the Shinto sect.

In order to be a priest at that shrine, Noboru had to live on a high mountain, but his wife did not want to live there. So Kazuko's mother chose a woman to be his concubine (*mekake*). Noboru eventually became a *guuji*, the highest-ranking priest in the Shinto shrine, and among the *guuji* rankings he was *shogoi*— the fifth. The rankings were bestowed by the emperor in an official letter called a *jirei* with a *kikuno gomon*, a sign of the chrysanthemum as a watermark.

Noboru died of a heart attack when Kazuko was eight years old. Everyone attended his funeral in costumes of Shintoism (*eboshi-shitatare*) and walked up the mountain to the graveyard, with the Shinto shrine musicians playing in the background. At the funeral Kazuko discovered that her father's concubine had a daughter close to her age. Her mother shared her father's inheritance with the concubine so that the daughter could get an education. Though they never met, Kazuko found out later that the daughter went on to graduate from a university for women and married a journalist. However, Kazuko only made it as far as middle school before she had to quit and work as her mother's maid.

Her mother had inherited wealth as a child from a sake-making business when both of her parents died in a cholera epidemic. But the money was running out and even though Kazuko's father had been a respected man (*erai-hito*), there was no pension to support his family. After Noboru's death Kimio fell in social status. For a while a Buddhist temple gave her a room in which she could sell family heirlooms and the valuable antiques (*kotto-butsu*) that had belonged to Kazuko's father, but gradually the family became impoverished and had to rely on wealthy friends.

Eventually they moved to Yokohama, near the coast, where Kazuko's brother worked for the customs office, as he could speak English. Her brother had attended Doshisha University in Kyoto, a college known for harboring hidden Christians. Kazuko was certain her mother did not practice Christianity, but her mother had selected this college for her brother to attend.

Tomozo, one of Kazuko's other brothers, was executive secretary of the American Friendship Society (*Bei-yu Kyokai*), founded in Tokyo by Kaneko Kentaro. Kazuko met her prospective husband, Giichi Minejima, through a mutual friend of Tomozo's. Giichi had been in America and had just returned to Japan to visit his very ill father, Rokuuyemon Minejima, a well-known member of a village council in Chiba. Kazuko was already considering marriage to a man from a family in Kanagawa Prefecture who owned a lacquer factory. But Tomozo convinced her to go to America with Giichi, and the procedure for matchmaking to Giichi began.

First came the *omiai*—the initial meeting—which went well, so the engagement was celebrated not long after that with an exchange of symbolic betrothal gifts (*yuino*). Rokuuyemon's concubine presented, on his behalf, the gift of a *montsuki*—a sheer lavender material with white underneath, with the leaves of the Tusuda plant as the family crest (*mon*). This Kazuko would sew into a formal kimono that would be her wedding attire.

Their wedding was held at Kinezuka Ryokan, a hotel owned by Rokuuyemon's best friend, who was responsible for the match. Kyutaro and Yona Abiko were also there, because Kyutaro and Giichi were involved in a farming community in the United States together, and they were also good friends. A few weeks later, Kazuko and Giichi set sail on the *Siberia Maru* for San Francisco, with the ultimate destination of Livingston, California.

Giichi Minejima was the first president of the Yamato Colony, a utopian Christian community of farms consisting of 3,200 acres. It was Kyutaro Abiko's dream, and he achieved it in Livingston. When Kazuko arrived there in 1909, all she saw was wilderness and oil lamps. No telephones. No electricity. Just a kerosene stove, so most everything was cooked over a fire pit. All of Giichi's books were in English, but she could read and speak only Japanese. She learned to work in the fields and grew asparagus and sweet potatoes. It was just three years after the 1906 San Francisco earthquake, so lumber was expensive. The community of the Yamato Colony built its own crude houses and most families each homesteaded thirty or forty acres; some homesteads were as large as hundreds of acres. The colony functioned like a co-op, with all its problems discussed as a group in Kazuko's living room with her husband, who was the village chief. Kazuko didn't know anything about business, but she took lessons in Japanese brush writing so she could keep up with the correspondence.

Then Giichi fell ill. Through donations from the community, he was transported by train to the university hospital in San Francisco. But two years after Kazuko had arrived in Livingston as a newlywed, Giichi died of throat cancer at the age of forty-three, leaving her five months pregnant with their only son, Riuzo. And then she also became ill and gave birth to her son a month early.

Kazuko was invited to stay with Nobutada Sato, whose wife was superintendent of nurses with the Red Cross, and she helped Kazuko take care of her infant. Then one day while Kazuko was walking with the baby outside on the grounds, she saw the house burst into flames and burn to the ground with all of her belongings and condolence money inside. Only things made of metal were spared, including the sword her father-in-law had given to Giichi if things didn't work out and he had no choice but to commit hara-kiri.

The community felt that she shouldn't remain in Livingston alone with a child because life there was too laborious. And so she and her son moved to San Francisco and stayed with Junzo Fukihira, a local bank president. Eventually they moved in with the Abikos, who treated her like a daughter. It was Yona Abiko who arranged her next marriage, to Shichibei Hayashi, born in Kokubu, Kagoshima Prefecture, Japan. In 1923, Shichibei was foreman of a ranch and the first to grow lettuce in Salinas successfully. He also grew cauliflower and used the landowner's packinghouse to get the produce to market.

It was Valentine's Day 1925, and the cauliflower was being packed for the first time. Shichibei had been working for eighteen hours straight. Kazuko heard the crash. Her second husband died in an auto collision with a train that was crossing the fields at night. He was thirty-nine years old. Once again Kazuko was left pregnant, this time with Osame, the last of her seven children. And then Riuzo, her only child with Giichi, died tragically in 1931, when Osame was six years old.

For the next seventeen years Kazuko raised the children by herself. She managed to pass on to them the Japanese culture she'd grown up with and loved, including music, art, and flower arranging. She owned a piano, and all four daughters had lessons. Shichibei's two older brothers took care of the farming until one of them died from an electric shock. To make money, Kazuko was a cook for thirty people in a farm labor camp. A Japanese man lent her a house on twenty acres of land, and her son Shuki, in his second year at the University of California, Berkeley, came home to help refurbish it.

Shortly thereafter the family had to prepare for incarceration. The sword given to Giichi by his father was buried in the backyard.

By that time, the Abikos had two more colonies—Cressey and Cortez— and to secure all three for the duration of the war, a corporation was formed and administered by a Caucasian man, who managed the farms in the Abikos' absence. The colonies, as a unit, became among the few communities to survive the war intact.

At Poston, one of Kazuko's daughters suffered sunstroke so severely she almost died, but by the end of 1943 all her children—Shuki Hayashi, Masa Aoki, Michi Kato, Yuki Fujimoto, Tadao "Beanie" Hayashi, and Osame Doi— had left camp. Her two sons, Shuki and Tadao, joined the 442nd Regimental Combat Team. The daughters went to universities; Masa and Michi were already in Chicago. Kazuko followed them there and found an apartment on Lake Michigan.

Meanwhile, Yuki and Osame ended up in Philadelphia. With the help of Yona Abiko—who had also moved to Philadelphia to stay with her Quaker friends and avoid incarceration—Yuki and Osame were both given scholarships to go to nursing school: Yuki at the Pennsylvania Hospital School of Nursing and Osame at the Lankenau Hospital School of Nursing. Osame was the school's first student of Japanese heritage.

On April 23, 1945, Kazuko's son Tadao was killed in action. Fellow 442nd RCT soldier Sadaichi Kubota credited Tadao with saving his life by taking a sniper's bullet intended for him during a scouting detail. It was just a week before the end of the war. Fifty-nine years later Sadaichi returned to the battlegrounds in Europe and found the knoll in Tendola, Italy, where Tadao had fallen. He set up a memorial with incense sticks, then kneeled, bowed his head in prayer, and saluted.

Kazuko lived in Chicago for five and a half years, then moved to Minneapolis and lived there until 1960. She finally settled in Sacramento to be near Shuki and Osame, and there she befriended the local pharmacist Harold Ouye. She attended the Parkview Presbyterian Church, but her lifelong membership was with the Lincoln Avenue Presbyterian Church in Salinas. She never did learn English.

Allan Minoru **Hida**, male, Nisei, Sacramento, California, incarcerated age 13, Sacramento Assembly Center, Tule Lake Relocation Center, Granada

(Amache) Relocation Center. Allan was born in Sacramento, California, on January 16, 1929, the elder of two boys, to Soichi "Howard" Hida and Hide (Hironaka) Hida. Due to his mother's marriage to an Issei and the Cable Act of 1922, Allan's mother lost her US citizenship but was able to regain it when the law was repealed in 1936. At the time of the mass removal, his father had to sell at a tremendous loss his prized 1914 Model T with a brass radiator, gas lights, klaxon horn, magneto system, and a hand crank. The family home was a duplex with four garages, legally owned in his mother's name. His father's former boss and friend agreed to watch over the house, collect the rent, pay the taxes, and pay the mortgage while Allan's family was incarcerated so his parents wouldn't lose it. At Tule Lake, Allan remembered ice-skating on the frozen sewage runoff.

The government wanted the families to go east, but his father looked at geography books and felt that an industrial city of hardworking people like Milwaukee, Wisconsin, might be best, so he left camp and found a job there working on cars. Allan eventually graduated from Lincoln High School, where he played clarinet in the marching band and was on the gymnastics team. He went on to attend the University of Wisconsin, letter in gymnastics, and graduate in 1951 with a degree in science education. It wasn't until then that his parents were able to purchase their own home in Wisconsin and give Allan a home base. Then he was drafted into the US Marine Corps and had to drop out of graduate school at the University of Illinois.

After basic training in San Diego, California, he was sent to chemical, biological, and radiological warfare school at Fort McClellan in Anniston, Alabama. This was followed by advanced infantry training at Camp Pendleton near Oceanside, California. He was assigned to the Third Tank Battalion, Third Marine Division, and lived in a five-man tent.

In 1953 he was sent to Nevada for six weeks to participate in an exercise in which a twenty-five-kiloton atomic bomb was attached to a one-hundred-foot steel tower and detonated. He was among the troops about 1,600 yards away from ground zero, which turned into a cone-shaped crater seventy-five to one hundred feet wide. After the detonation the troops in helicopters were to approach the crater from the back side, while Allan and his troops were to arrive by land. He saw what happened to military equipment when it was subjected to an atomic bomb. The steel tower had evaporated, and the turret on a tank had been ripped off and flung fifty to one hundred yards. Allan was serving as a radiation monitor, testing personnel. Many of the troops thought they didn't have any injuries because no one was bleeding and they didn't feel any actual pain. But in 1965, Allan developed a tumor on his thyroid gland; it would be another thirty-three years before he was declared disabled.

From Nevada, Allan returned to Camp Pendleton and extended his service for nine more months so he could go to Japan for the first time with the entire Third Marine Division—all 25,000 troops. He was stationed at the base of Mount Fuji, south of the city of Gotemba, Shizuoka Prefecture, and attended a mapping and photo interpreter school at Gifu. He left the Marine Corps in July 1954, after receiving the National Defense, United Nations, and Korean Service medals.

He met his wife at the First Methodist Church in Milwaukee, Wisconsin, where they both sang in the church choir. He went on to teach biology, photography, and one of the first ecology classes at several Milwaukee public schools, including Madison High School, where he was the science department chair, and then the career specialty program chair for twenty years. He was elected president of the Wisconsin Society of Science Teachers in 1977. After retiring in 1988, he helped social studies teachers throughout Wisconsin to teach the history of the incarceration in their classes.

For decades he was on the board of the JACL Milwaukee, Wisconsin, chapter and in 1991–92 served as Midwest District Governor. In 1998, he was honored with the National "JACLer of the Biennium" award. He also became a guide for *Uprooted!*, the permanent Japanese American exhibit at the California Museum, after he moved to Sacramento in 2005.

Gordon Kiyoshi **Hirabayashi**, male, Nisei, Seattle, Washington, age 22 when Pearl Harbor was attacked, King County Jail, Tucson Federal Prison/Catalina Federal Honor Camp, McNeil Island Federal Penitentiary. Gordon was born in the neighborhood of Sand Point in Seattle, Washington, on April 23, 1918, the eldest of five children, to Shungo Hirabayashi and Mitsuko Rhoda Hirabayashi from Nagano, Japan. His parents were committed to Christian principles, and in particular to the Mokyokai movement, which advocated pacifism and aligning one's beliefs with behavior. Because of his parents' influence, Gordon registered as a conscientious objector with the Selective Service in Seattle and joined the Quakers (the Religious Society of Friends). He was a senior at the University of Washington when Franklin D. Roosevelt signed Executive Order 9066.

Gordon decided to deliberately defy the curfew and the order to register for exclusion, or mass removal. He turned himself in to the FBI with the intent of becoming a test case to challenge the constitutionality of the government's actions. Ultimately, his criminal convictions for his failure to comply with the curfew and exclusion orders were unanimously upheld by the Supreme Court in *Hirabayashi v. United States*. He served time in federal prison not only for these criminal convictions, but also for refusing induction into the US Armed Forces.

After the war Gordon returned to the University of Washington, where he earned BA, MA, and PhD degrees in sociology. He was a sociology professor at the University of Alberta, Canada, and remained active in civil rights causes throughout his life. In 1987 the US Court of Appeals for the Ninth Circuit upheld the granting of his petition for coram nobis, finding that the Supreme Court decisions in his case and in the other two Japanese American cases, *Yasui v. United States* and *Korematsu v. United States*, were most likely materially affected by the government's misconduct in presenting to the Supreme Court false claims of Japanese American espionage; both of his criminal convictions were vacated.

He and Fred Korematsu were awarded the 2001 Roger N. Baldwin Medal of Liberty by the American Civil Liberties Union for lifetime contributions to the advancement of civil liberties. On May 29, 2012, President Barack Obama posthumously awarded Gordon the Presidential Medal of Freedom.

Tetsuzo "Ted" or "Tets" **Hirasaki**, male, Nisei, San Diego, California, incarcerated age 22, Santa Anita Assembly Center, Poston Relocation Center. Ted was born in San Diego, California, on September 6, 1920, the older brother of his sister, Yaeko. His parents were Chiyomatsu Hirasaki and Sumiyo (Kanazawa) Hirasaki. Ted's mother died when he was five; his sister was three. At the age of eight, he went to the children's section of the public library and met Clara Breed, the San Diego city librarian; she ignited his passion for books and they corresponded for years, especially during his incarceration. He once wrote that poverty and "man's inhumanity to man" are "directly tied to the growing numbers of people who . . . lack the key that opens doors—THE ABILITY TO READ." He graduated from San Diego High School in 1938, and his father trained him to be a barber in his barbershop. He then had to get reconstructive surgery on his right arm, which had developed a tubercular lesion. When the war broke out, his father was immediately arrested and sent to federal prison in Bismarck, North Dakota, and then New Mexico, while his children were sent to Santa Anita and Poston. In the fall of 1943 Ted volunteered to save the WRA vegetable crop at the Tule Lake Relocation Center. Although his arm was still a problem, he was allowed to participate in the crop effort. After the war he worked for Consolidated-Vultee Aircraft Corporation and, later, General Dynamics.

John Sohei **Hohri**, male, Nisei, Los Angeles, California, incarcerated age 17, Manzanar Reception Center, Manzanar Relocation Center. John was born in Los Angeles, California, on February 4, 1925, the fifth of six children, to Daisuke Hohri and Asa (Utsunomiya) Hohri. His parents were Protestant Christian missionaries who immigrated to the United States in 1922. In 1930 they contracted tuberculosis and were hospitalized at the Olive View Sanitarium in the San Fernando valley. During that time, at the age of five, John and his brother Bill (see his biography), age three, went to live at the Japanese Children's Home of Southern California, often referred to as the Shonien, which took in Japanese American orphans or children whose parents could not take care of them. The family was reunited after a three-year separation. John graduated from Ralph Waldo Emerson High School in Westwood, California. He was living with his family in North Hollywood when Pearl Harbor was attacked. Within hours the FBI picked up his father, a Christian minister who made his living at a nursery.

At the Manzanar Children's Village, the camp orphanage, John told stories to the children from *Les Misérables*, by Victor Hugo, and Homer's *The Odyssey*. He left camp to work in Milwaukee, Wisconsin, and served in the US Army. He spent his tour of duty in Japan and was awarded a World War II Victory Medal and an Army of Occupation Medal with Japan clasp. He graduated from the University of Chicago with a degree in philosophy and traveled to Paris on the GI Bill to study abstract painting with Fernand Léger. He returned to New York seven years later to begin a thirty-one-year career as the librarian and curator at the New York Yacht Club. As an artist, he created gold-leafed scrolls for the upper-rank competitors of the America's Cup. He loved book collecting and acquired more than thirty thousand volumes over his lifetime, with a special interest in children's books. The New York Yacht Club named the Sohei Hohri Rare Book Room in his honor.

William "Bill" Minoru **Hohri**, male, Nisei, Los Angeles, California, incarcerated age 14, Manzanar Reception Center, Manzanar Relocation Center. Bill was born in San Francisco, California, on March 13, 1927, the youngest of six children—and brother to John (see his biography for information common to both brothers)—to Daisuke Hohri and Asa (Utsunomiya) Hohri. When his family was sent to Manzanar, Bill was fourteen years old and in the tenth grade at North Hollywood High School. He ended up graduating in 1944 from Manzanar High, the makeshift camp school. Shortly thereafter he was given leave clearance to relocate to Madison, Wisconsin. In March 1945 he was returning to Manzanar to tell his parents not to come to Wisconsin because jobs were scarce, when he was stopped and jailed for traveling without a permit, even though the US government had lifted the exclusion order for Japanese Americans two months earlier. At gunpoint he was issued an exclusion order for individuals, which required him to leave the state by midnight.

Bill worked full-time to pay for his college tuition and graduated from the University of Chicago in 1949; he married Yuriko Katayama two years later. During their honeymoon in New Orleans, they became conscious of the segregation issue. Once the couple returned to Chicago, he found a job as a computer programmer but remained conscious of racial discrimination.

The couple became active members of the United Methodist Church (UMC), and Bill participated in civil rights marches and antiwar rallies against the Vietnam War. He was one of the few Japanese Americans who participated in the 1966 march in the Deep South organized by James Meredith, the first Black student admitted to the University of Mississippi. During the 1970s, Bill and Nelson Yuji Kitsuse worked through the UMC to support the national movement that secured a presidential pardon for Iva Toguri D'Aquino, who had been wrongly identified as Tokyo Rose.

He was an early backer of the JACL's redress initiative, but when the JACL changed its support from redress legislation to establishing a commission, Bill formed a new redress organization, the National Council for Japanese American Redress (NCJAR). He adapted Frank Fujii's *ichi-ni-san* barbed wire logo from Seattle's Day of Remembrance for the NCJAR masthead. The focus of the NCJAR became a class action lawsuit, which the Supreme Court eventually rejected. However, some observers believe that the suit may have contributed to the ultimate passage of the Civil Liberties Act of 1988.

Bill was also part of an informal group of writers who called themselves the Asian American Literary Arts Society. In the *Rafu Shimpo* newspaper, he wrote a regular column titled Rambler's Nemesis, and he published *Repairing America: An Account of the Movement for Japanese-American Redress* (1988), *Resistance: Challenging America's Wartime Internment of Japanese-Americans* (2001), and the novel *Manzanar Rites* (2002).

In his later years Bill continued to investigate whether the US government violated the Selective Training and Service Act of 1940 by drafting Japanese American males from the WRA relocation centers.

Masami **Honda**, male, Nisei, San Diego, California, incarcerated age 25, Santa Anita Assembly Center, Poston Relocation Center. Masami was born in San Diego, California, on August 9, 1917, the oldest of six children, to the farming family of Hachiro Honda and Fumino (Kobayama) Honda. His parents leased land to grow truck crops in Spring Valley, Lemon Grove, and the

Mission Valley neighborhood of San Diego. By the time Masami was in high school, his family was growing chrysanthemums in the Encanto area. The Hondas later started a landscape gardening business.

In the aftermath of the Pearl Harbor attack, Masami's father was one of the Issei community leaders arrested by the FBI and sent to the US Department of Justice internment camp in Crystal City, Texas. Masami became one of the young adult leaders who took responsibility for the Buddhist Temple of San Diego after the Issei leadership was arrested and before he, his mother, and his siblings were removed to the Santa Anita Assembly Center. In the removal process he was forced to sell all of the family's landscape gardening equipment.

At Poston, Masami was active on the camp council and represented, during the incarceration, the governing body of the Buddhist Temple of San Diego, which required working closely with an attorney who was managing the temple. His knowledge of legal matters made him invaluable to the revitalization of the temple community following the war.

After he left camp, Masami briefly visited Chicago and moved on to New York City, where he took a job at the Doubleday Book Shop. But the Buddhist temple members prevailed upon him to return to San Diego and help reestablish the temple. He went to San Diego for a few months, then returned to New York City. Not long after he came back, he got word that his mother had been hit by a car and died, compelling his immediate departure for San Diego. He joined his family living at the Frontier Homes Housing Project and decided to settle there permanently. Masami's presence in San Diego made it possible for his father to leave the Crystal City camp and reunite with his family. From the Frontier Homes Housing Project, Masami and his wife moved into a rental home in the North Park area of San Diego. With a loan from the San Diego JACL credit union, Masami was able to buy new landscaping equipment and resume his old landscaping business. He participated in the JACL and the gardeners' association in San Diego. His wife, Ruth Yaeko Honda, was a poet and was active in the Buddhist community.

In 1983, Masami moved into the newly opened Kiku Gardens, a senior citizen housing complex, as a charter resident, and was a manager for seventeen years.

Bebe Toshiko **Horiuchi** (Reschke), female, Nisei, Los Angeles, California, incarcerated age 10, Santa Anita Assembly Center, Rohwer Relocation Center. Bebe was born in Los Angeles on October 20, 1932, an only child, to Koryi G. Horiuchi and Ichiko Jane (Ando) Horiuchi. After her release from Rohwer, she joined the American Civil Liberties Union as a way of coping with the panic resulting from her imprisonment. She worked as a psychiatric social worker at an adult outpatient clinic in Hollywood, California. Bebe was part of the mental health professionals panel at the CWRIC hearings in Los Angeles. In her testimony she described how Japanese Americans tried to hide their "Japaneseness" to escape racism; they "suffered in silence and developed a poor self-image." She felt that being incarcerated "did a great deal to take away [her] feeling of self-esteem and made [her] more fearful in fighting back." Bebe testified that when one of her teachers in Detroit taught history and referred to "treacherous Japs," her fear rendered her speechless to confront him.

Robert Ritsuro **Hosokawa**, male, Nisei, Seattle, Washington, incarcerated age 24, Puyallup Assembly Center, Minidoka Relocation Center. Robert was born in Seattle, Washington, on September 15, 1918, to Setsugo Hosokawa and Kimiyo (Omura) Hosokawa. His older brother is William "Bill" Kumpai Hosokawa (see his biography). Robert graduated Phi Beta Kappa from Whitman College in 1940. Following his incarceration, he worked in Minneapolis, Minnesota, as a newspaper editor and public relations executive, before becoming a journalism professor at the University of Missouri and the University of Central Florida.

William "Bill" Kumpai **Hosokawa**, male, Nisei, Seattle, Washington, incarcerated age 27, Puyallup Assembly Center, Heart Mountain Relocation Center. Bill was born in Seattle, Washington, on January 30, 1915, to Setsugo Hosokawa and Kimiyo (Omura) Hosokawa. His younger brother is Robert Ritsuro Hosokawa (see his biography). Bill graduated with a degree in journalism from the University of Washington in 1937. Even in the days before Pearl Harbor, his adviser told him that no one in the country would hire a Japanese reporter, so he took a job at the Japanese consulate in Seattle. Then, in 1938, he traveled to Singapore to work at the *Singapore Herald* as an English-language editor and later to Shanghai to work for the *Shang-hai Times*, an English-language daily, and the *Far Eastern Review*, writing pro-Japanese articles. When the United States and Japan seemed to be on the brink of war, he went home to Seattle, where his wife had given birth to a son. Five weeks later Pearl Harbor was attacked, and he immediately became active in forming the Emergency Defense Council to help people of Japanese ancestry communicate with their local government.

During his incarceration, he was editor of the camp newspaper, the *Heart Mountain Sentinel*, and afterward worked as a copy editor at the *Des Moines Register*. In 1946 he joined the *Denver Post*, where he was a foreign corre-spondent for thirty-eight years. He was also a columnist for the *Pacific Cit-izen*. In 1984 he went to the *Rocky Mountain News*, where he worked until his retirement in 1992.

Bill wrote eleven books, including his 1969 controversial bestseller, *Nisei: The Quiet Americans*, and co-authored Mike Masaoka's autobiography, *They Call Me Moses Masaoka*. Initially, he was a critic of the campaign for redress because he thought that asking for money somehow "cheapened" the incarcer-ation experience. But after the release of the congressional commission's report, *Personal Justice Denied*, in which the causes for the concentration camps were described as "racial prejudice, wartime hysteria and a failure of political leader-ship," he changed his mind and then supported the redress effort.

He was a founder of the Japan America Society of Colorado and became the honorary consul general of Japan for Colorado, Utah, and New Mexico. He was also a recipient of the 2007 Civil Rights Award from the Anti-Defamation League. The Denver Botanic Gardens named its Japanese exhibit after him, calling it the Bill Hosokawa Bonsai Pavilion.

Haruyo (Takeuchi) **Hozaki**, female, Issei, Los Angeles, California, incar-cerated age 46, Santa Anita Assembly Center, Rohwer Relocation Center. Haruyo was born in the Kusatsu neighborhood of Hiroshima, Japan, on

March 23, 1896. As a master barber, she owned and operated a barbershop in Los Angeles with her husband, Kyuji. One of their sons, Private First Class Toshio Hozaki, received a Purple Heart for his actions in France in October 1944 and was killed in action with the 100th/442nd Regimental Combat Team in Italy on April 5, 1945. Their other son, Teruo, was also a private first class and served with the First Army in Germany.

Kyuji **Hozaki**, male, Issei, Los Angeles, California, incarcerated age 45, Santa Anita Assembly Center, Rohwer Relocation Center. Kyuji was born in the village of Nakatsu, Fukuoka Prefecture, Japan, on March 8, 1897. As a master barber, he owned and operated a barbershop in Los Angeles with his wife, Haruyo. They were among the few who managed to reestablish their business when they came home after their incarceration.

May Kikuko (Tominaga) **Ichida**, female, Nisei, San Francisco, California, incarcerated age 34, Manzanar Reception Center, Manzanar Relocation Center. May was born in El Monte, California, on February 15, 1908, the second of three children, to Kurahachi Tominaga and Chiyono (Tok) Tominaga. Her family moved to San Francisco when she was young. She joined the Salvation Army in the 1920s and entered the Salvation Army's officer training school, where she met Ainosuke Ichida, who had come from Japan in 1915. They were married in 1928 and traveled to Seattle for their first Salvation Army assignment. May and Ainosuke made a lasting impression in Seattle's Japantown, where they worked with young Nisei, many of whom were living in crowded group homes. They also ran the Salvation Army Fresh Air Camp on the Green River near Auburn, Washington, where these kids would go every summer. According to Bill Hosokawa, "The camp was on a dusty patch of land. Water was dipped out of a spring of doubtful quality and hauled to the kitchen in buckets by the larger boys. The sanitary facility was an outhouse built close to the riverbank, and on field days, the shack was used for wall-climbing contests."

At the time of the forced removal, May's husband was hospitalized at a tuberculosis sanitorium and she was working with orphans at the Salvation Army's Japanese Children's Home in San Francisco. They and their two children were incarcerated at Manzanar, where May worked at the Children's Village and also as general secretary of the Manzanar YWCA. After leaving camp, the family moved to Cleveland, Ohio, where she became minister to the Japanese-speaking Issei Christian congregation in nearby Euclid. She and her husband were program directors of the Salvation Army's Men's Social Service Center. They retired from the Salvation Army after forty years of service.

The Honorable Daniel "Dan" Ken **Inouye**, male, Nisei, Honolulu, Hawaii, age 17 when Pearl Harbor was attacked. Dan was born in Honolulu, Hawaii, on September 7, 1924, the eldest of four children, to Hyotaro Inouye and Kame (Imanaga) Inouye. He was raised in the Moiliili and McCully sections of Oahu with other Japanese families of modest circumstances. According to family folklore, Dan's grandfather left Japan to earn money in Hawaii to pay off his father's debt, incurred when a fire destroyed the Inouye family home and the homes of three neighbors.

After the Pearl Harbor attack, Dan served as a medical volunteer, giving first aid to civilians. He was never incarcerated. In 1943, while attending pre-med classes at the University of Hawai'i at Manoa, he enlisted in the 442nd Regimental Combat Team. He lost his right arm in battle and also his dream of becoming a surgeon. He was awarded a Distinguished Service Cross, a Bronze Star, a Purple Heart with Oak Leaf Cluster, and a Congressional Medal of Honor for actions in the vicinity of San Terenzo, Italy, in April 1945.

He graduated from the University of Hawai'i in 1950 with a degree in government and economics, and from the George Washington University Law School in 1952. When Hawaii became the fiftieth state of the United States in 1959, Dan became the first Japanese American to be elected to the House of Representatives, and in 1962 the first Japanese American to serve as a US senator. He served over nine consecutive terms and was one of the most powerful senators on the Watergate Committee and the Senate Rules Committee, and chaired the Iran-Contra committee, the Senate Select Committee on Intelligence, the Senate Appropriations Committee, the Senate Appropriations Subcommittee on Defense, and the Indian Affairs Committee.

Together with his fellow Hawaii senator Spark Matsunaga, Dan was a leader in the passage of the bill that established the Commission on Wartime Relocation and Internment of Civilians. The commission issued its 1983 findings in the report *Personal Justice Denied*, while Dan and Spark continued their push for redress legislation, which led to the enactment of the Civil Liberties Act of 1988.

Dan was awarded the Grand Cordon of the Order of the Rising Sun and the Grand Cordon of the Order of the Paulownia Flowers by the government of Japan, four awards from the Philippines, one from France, and one from Israel. He was married to his wife, Maggie Awamura Inouye, for fifty-seven years. After Maggie's death, he married Irene Hirano. His last word was "Aloha." He was the first Japanese American whose body lay in state in the US Capitol rotunda. President Barack Obama awarded him the Presidential Medal of Freedom posthumously in 2012.

Haru Michida **Isaki**, female, Nisei, San Francisco, California, incarcerated age 28, Tanforan Assembly Center, Topaz Relocation Center. Haru was born in San Francisco, California, on January 13, 1914, the second oldest of three children, to Yonetaro Isaki and Masa (Kobiki) Isaki. On the evening of December 10, 1941, two FBI agents took her father into custody. He'd been living in California for forty-one years and worked in his own dry-cleaning shop. She did not see him again for two years. She and her husband were married two days before their families were forcibly removed. She miscarried her first child in the harsh winter of 1942–43 but had a son in 1944, born on D-day, June 6. "Life in camp was full of ironies like this—almost as though we were being taunted," she said.

Margaret "Maggie" Tokuko **Ishino**, female, Nisei, San Diego, California, incarcerated age 17, Santa Anita Assembly Center, Poston Relocation Center.

Maggie was born in San Diego, California, on May 16, 1925, the second old-est of five children, to Tomota Ishino and Tei (Yoshizuka) Ishino. Her parents had a fruit and vegetable stand before the war. After the Pearl Harbor bomb-ing, FBI agents came to the family home while her mother was still in bed, having just given birth to a third child. They ripped off her covers, suspecting she was hiding something.

During her incarceration, Maggie was a frequent correspondent with Clara Breed, the San Diego librarian. Maggie's mother became very ill, so the responsi-bilities of housekeeping and caring for her younger sister and baby brother fell to her. As a teenager, she did all of her family's laundry, including her baby brother's diapers. She created a crib for him out of a pig's trough. At camp she worked as a waitress in the mess halls. She graduated from high school in Poston in 1943.

After the war her family didn't want to return to San Diego, so her father left for Seabrook Farms in New Jersey, while Maggie joined her older brother and his wife in Washington, DC. Thanks to the shorthand and typing courses she'd taken in junior high school and high school, she was able to get a job at the Department of Labor as well as the local Community Chest (now called the United Way) that collected funds from the community for the purpose of charitable giving. In DC she was able to see the 100th/442nd Regimental Combat Team parade down Constitution Avenue to the White House lawn on July 15, 1946.

Maggie spent several years on the East Coast and later returned to San Diego with her father and siblings. For two months the Ishinos stayed with the family of the midwife who had delivered the five Ishino children. Maggie eventually moved to Los Angeles and worked part-time for the Japanese Amer-ican newspaper *Rafu Shimpo*. In 2019, Maggie, at ninety-four years old, was still taking three buses twice a week to the newspaper offices to work on her column, Maggie's Meow. She has been a member of the Union Church of Los Angeles for over fifty years and was lifelong friends with Louise Ogawa, another one of Miss Breed's correspondents.

Monica Kazuko **Itoi** (Sone), female, Nisei, Seattle, Washington, incarcerated age 23, Puyallup Assembly Center, Minidoka Relocation Center. Monica was born in Seattle, Washington, on September 1, 1919, the second of four children, to Seizo Itoi and Benko (Nagashima) Itoi. In 1953 she was the first Nisei woman to publish an autobiography, *Nisei Daughter*. The book recounts her years growing up in the Carrollton Hotel, managed by her parents, on the Seattle waterfront during the 1920s and 1930s, with its burlesque house and taverns. She attended the Bailey Gatzert grammar school, whose students were mostly from Chinatown and Nihonmachi (Japantown) and which lost 45 percent of its student body when the Japanese Americans were incarcerated. Monica also attended Broadway High School, after which she completed a two-year secretarial course in one year but came down with tuberculosis. She lived in a sanatorium for nine months and wrote numerous letters to her friend and popular novelist Betty MacDonald, which figures into the beginning of her book. The bombing of Pearl Harbor prevented her from going to the University of Washington. After passing the so-called loyalty questionnaire, she was allowed to leave Minidoka early and relocate to the Chicago area, where she worked as a dental assistant and lived with a White Presbyterian minister and his family.

She graduated from Hanover College, a Presbyterian institution in Hanover, Indiana, and earned her master's degree in clinical psychology at Case Western Reserve University. She practiced as a clinical psychologist and social worker for thirty-eight years in Canton, Ohio, primarily for the Catholic Community League.

Bruce Teruo **Kaji**, male, Nisei, Los Angeles, California, incarcerated age 16, Manzanar Reception Center, Manzanar Relocation Center. Bruce was born in the Boyle Heights area of downtown Los Angeles, California, on May 9, 1926, the youngest of three children, with two older sisters. His parents were Umetaro Kaji and Katsu (Shimada) Kaji, from Fukuoka Prefecture on the island of Kyushu, Japan. His father graduated from Kumamoto University in Japan as a veterinarian. Umetaro wanted to marry his first cousin, but his parents rejected that proposal, so he signed up to do agricultural work in the United States. He couldn't be a veterinarian because he couldn't take the tests in English, so he worked on farms in Seattle. When he couldn't make enough money, he left for Los Angeles and became a railroad coach repairman for the Santa Fe railroad. His job fixing wheels and brakes demanded pounding metal and welding steel, which permanently impaired his hearing and affected his ability to communicate. But his income was stable, so he wrote to his sisters in Japan and asked them to find him a picture bride. They arranged a marriage to Katsu Shimada from Fukuoka Prefecture. When Katsu arrived, she also got a job with the Santa Fe railroad, changing sheets on the sleeper trains. In her spare time she socialized with other women in the Fukuoka Kenjinkai—a local group of individuals from the same prefecture.

One of the benefits from Bruce's father's job was a free ride once a year on the train to San Diego for the whole family. His parents were active members of the New Thought Japanese religion called Seicho-No-Ie, which believes in a monotheistic universal god and reveres nature, the family, and the ancestors. It was so new at the time that a group of Issei believers met at the Kaji home once a month; Bruce's family also attended the Evergreen Baptist Church on Sundays.

Bruce took up the trumpet and cornet at Hollenbeck Junior High and joined the school orchestra. He chose the nickname "Bruce" after Bruce Wayne—Batman's secret identity—a nickname that he later legalized. He attended Roosevelt High School and Chuo Gakuen, a Japanese-language and martial arts school. As a member of the Chuo Gakuen Boy Scouts, he was in their drum and bugle corps and marching band. The band competed, especially during Nisei Week, with other Japanese Boy Scout troops at the Nishi Hongwanji and the Koyasan Buddhist Temples; the temples had the latest equipment (piston bugles instead of regular bugles, tenor and bass drum sets instead of just regular drums) because their members were more affluent. Bruce later left Chuo Gakuen for Onodera Gakuen because Ray Onodera was his best friend. He and Ray also had a circle of Jewish friends; they were the only Japanese Americans in their Jewish sports club, the Wabash Saxons. And then, two days after Pearl Harbor was bombed, Bruce was fired from his part-time job selling evening newspapers on street corners after school.

At Manzanar, Bruce was the features editor for the *Campus Pepper* and a member of the camp orchestra. Bill Wakatsuki, an operatic singer and one of the leaders of the camp's music center, created a camp dance band with Bruce and some of the other camp musicians, called the Jive Bombers. (Bill Wakatsuki was the older brother of Jeanne Wakatsuki Houston, co-author of *Farewell to Manzanar*.) Bruce was also a member of the camp's boys' club called the Manza-Knights, which consisted mainly of boys from Boyle Heights and downtown East Los Angeles. Some of the other clubs at camp were the Yogores, the San Fernando Aces, and the Bel-Airs.

Bruce graduated from Manzanar High School with honors in 1944 and received a scholarship from the California Scholarship Federation, but he couldn't get it unless he was accepted into a college outside of California. He was accepted into Morningside College in Sioux City, Iowa, and registered as premed. He had worked in Manzanar's hospital and got a job at Methodist Hospital in Sioux City. But after only one semester he was drafted into the army, just a few months before the end of the war. He was sent for intensive training as a Japanese-language interpreter in the Military Intelligence Service. He then served in Japan and the Philippines with the 795th Military Police Battalion, and was sent to Luzon POW Camp #1 for the war crimes tribunal, where he translated testimony of Japanese prisoners of war. He was honorably discharged in 1947 and returned to Los Angeles.

Bruce switched from medicine to accounting, earning a degree at the University of Southern California. He briefly worked for the Reginald K. Wilson CPA firm as a bookkeeper, a job he obtained through his Jewish friends from high school, since most firms refused to hire Japanese Americans. The experience enabled him to apply for his CPA certification. And then, in 1950, he opened his own accounting firm with Kiyo Maruyama and landed Toyota as a client; the company was trying to sell cars in the United States at a time when "Made in Japan" was considered a derogatory term.

He was elected city treasurer in Gardena in 1960. Then he branched out as a real estate developer with his brother-in-law Taul Watanabe. In 1962 he became president of Merit Savings and Loan, one of the first chartered

Japanese American–owned banks, which became number one among all minority-owned associations in the United States. He established the Little Tokyo Redevelopment Association in 1963, and in the early 1970s Bruce was appointed to the board of the newly built Los Angeles County Martin Luther King Jr. Hospital.

But his personal dream was to create a museum dedicated to the story of Japanese Americans, and in 1985, with the help of Nisei World War II veterans, the Japanese American National Museum was incorporated, with Bruce as its founding president. He received the Order of the Rising Sun, Gold and Silver Rays, from the Japanese government in 1997. In 2011 he was honored with the Congressional Gold Medal, along with fellow members of the Military Intelligence Service and the 100th/442nd RCT. The Japanese American National Museum, which opened its doors in 1992, presented Bruce, at the age of ninety-one, with its Legacy Award in May 2017.

Hiroshi **Kamei**, male, Nisei, Westminster, California, incarcerated age 14, Poston Relocation Center. Hiroshi was born in Gardena, California, on October 1, 1927, the fifth of seven children, to Toranosuke Wada Kamei and Shizu Kamei from Wakayama, Japan. In 1930 his family moved to Orange County, California, where they grew mostly strawberries, tomatoes, and celery in Buena Park, Tustin, Orange, and Westminster. Hiroshi was a freshman at Huntington Beach Union High School when, on the night of December 7, 1941, several FBI agents came to search his home and interrogate his father. They did not arrest Toranosuke because he was not involved in any community associations.

The next day Franklin D. Roosevelt's Day of Infamy address was broadcast in a school assembly, and Hiroshi decided to drop out after winter break to avoid being a target of animosity. When the family received its notice to report to camp in May 1942, they had a five-acre crop of celery ready to harvest. But the market price for celery had fallen to less than the cost of the crate, so they left the celery crop standing in the field. A few weeks later, after the Japanese American farmers had been forcibly removed, the market price for celery soared to between four and five dollars a crate. While the Kameis were in camp, they were furious to learn that the people who had taken over their lease had profited from the Kameis' crop.

By this time in the process of mass removal, Poston was already open, so Hiroshi's family was told to go directly there. On May 17, 1942, as he waited to board the train to Poston, a Quaker volunteer gave him a peanut butter sandwich to take with him. It was the first time he'd ever been on a train or even outside Orange County. The family wouldn't get outside of Poston again until four months after they arrived, when Hiroshi, his parents, and his siblings were able to go on a work leave together for a month to top sugar beets in Rifle, Colorado. When they came back to Poston, Hiroshi returned to his part-time job as a "pearl diver," a coined phrase for a dishwasher in the mess hall.

He graduated from the Miles E. Cary High School at Poston II as its salutatorian in June 1945. He wanted to go to college and study engineering, but he couldn't find a school that would accept a student coming from an unaccredited camp high school. Georgia Day Robertson, his math teacher at camp, wrote on Hiroshi's behalf to a Quaker friend and former colleague who was the registrar of Iowa State College; the registrar agreed to admit Hiroshi if he passed an entrance exam. Hiroshi took the test and was accepted into the school. But he was there for only one semester before he was drafted into the army. He served in the army's Medical Corps and saw duty in occupied Japan until 1947.

After the war and his honorable discharge, he rejoined his family, who had returned to farming in Garden Grove, California. On the basis of his few college credits, he was admitted to the California Institute of Technology (Caltech) in Pasadena, California. He commuted between Pasadena and Garden Grove by bus and trolley so he could help with the farm on weekends. During the week he worked at the Athenaeum, Caltech's faculty club, to pay for his room and board. He met his wife, Tami Kurose, on a blind date while she was a student at Pasadena Junior College (now Pasadena City College). He graduated from Caltech with a bachelor of science degree in chemical engineering in 1951 and a master of science degree, also in chemical engineering, a year later.

He obtained his professional engineer license in mechanical engineering from the state's licensure board and worked in various management positions for North American Aviation and its successor companies, North American Rockwell, Rockwell International, and Boeing, for thirty-six years. He was a recognized industry expert in aerospace electronics heat transfer and thermal analysis.

Hiroshi was on the board of the Caltech Alumni Association and an officer of several Orange County and Southland historical and cultural organizations. He served three terms as president of the SELANOCO chapter of the JACL and was a recipient of the Japanese American Association's 1996 Community Service Award. He was also a member of the Kazuo Masuda Memorial VFW Post 3670, a founder and president of the Justice Stephen K. Tamura Scholarship Foundation, and a charter member of the Japanese American National Museum. He was recognized as a Nisei Week Pioneer in 1998 and received numerous awards for his leadership in the redress movement, which resulted in the passage of the Civil Liberties Act of 1988. For over forty years, Hiroshi and his wife, Tami, resided in the Peralta Hills area of Anaheim, near Santa Ana Canyon, one of the places where his family had farmed.

In 1981, Hiroshi testified in hearings before the Commission on Wartime Relocation and Internment of Civilians about the economic losses his family had incurred from having to abandon their crops, their farming investment in equipment, their Model A pickup, and all their other belongings at a fraction of their value. He also described how the incarceration had damaged the educational opportunities of his Nisei generation, and paid tribute in his testimony to the difference that his camp math teacher, Mrs. Robertson, had made in his life.

Wayne Masao **Kanemoto**, male, Nisei, San Jose, California, incarcerated age 24, Santa Anita Assembly Center, Gila River Relocation Center. Wayne was born in San Jose, California, on March 9, 1918, the youngest of four children, and the only son, to Shinichi Kanemoto and Kimi (Matsuura) Kanemoto. He graduated from San Jose State College and in absentia from Santa Clara Law School. He took the bar exam in Los Angeles under military escort and was sworn in to the California bar while incarcerated. In 1943 he volunteered for the 442nd Regimental Combat Team and was transferred to the Military Intelligence Service Language School at Camp Savage in Minnesota. He later served in the Tenth Air Force in India and Burma.

Wayne became the first Japanese American attorney and judge in Santa Clara County, California, and assisted in the first swearing-in ceremonies for Issei immigrants who finally became American citizens. He participated in the San Jose Human Relations Commission; the San Jose Sister Cities program with Okayama, Japan; and the creation of the Japanese Friendship Garden in a walled section of San Jose's Kelley Park. In 1962 he was appointed to the San Jose Municipal Court, becoming the first Nisei jurist in Northern California. He served as presiding judge, as president of the Conference of Santa Clara County Municipal Court Judges, and as president of the Santa Clara County Law Library Board. He retired from the bench in 1982 but continued to be active in the community as a member of the City of San Jose Commission on the Internment of Local Japanese Americans, which documents the history of the local Japanese American incarceration experience and commissioned a memorial monument by the noted sculptor Ruth Asawa, which is located outside of the Robert F. Peckham Federal Building in San Jose.

Robert Ichigi **Kashiwagi**, male, Nisei, Woodland, California, incarcerated age 23, Merced Assembly Center, Granada (Amache) Relocation Center. Robert was born in Hayward, California, on February 11, 1919, the second oldest of eight children, to Frank Haito Kashiwagi and Tatsu (Furusawa) Kashiwagi. His father was a foreman on a rice farm in Sacramento.

In 1941 his number came up for the draft, but he was rejected because he was suffering from a lung infection known as San Joaquin fever. He was convalescing in a sanatorium, still bedridden, when Executive Order 9066 was issued, but he was ordered home to prepare for the forced removal.

He remained bedridden for a year after arriving at the camp, receiving very little medical care. Nevertheless, he and his two brothers volunteered for the 442nd Regimental Combat Team in 1943. He became a scout in Company K, Third Battalion, and was wounded by shrapnel north of Rome. He then participated in the 1944 campaign to rescue the Lost Battalion, where he was hit by shrapnel twice and his company was obliterated—he was one of only seventeen soldiers still standing out of 186 men. Not long afterward, he was wounded by shrapnel again, in the hand and foot, and was finally honorably discharged in 1946.

When he came home, he discovered that his parents were destitute and living at Camp Kohler—the new name given to the former Sacramento Assembly Center—along with 234 other destitute Japanese American families. All of them were paying the US government room and board. He immediately took a job at the California Division of Highways so he could afford to move his parents into a home of their own, and he worked at that job for thirty-two years.

Shuzo Chris **Kato**, male, Nisei, Seattle, Washington, incarcerated age 16, Puyallup Assembly Center, Minidoka Relocation Center. Chris was born in Seattle, Washington, on December 8, 1926, the third eldest of six children, to Jenzo Kato and Hatsue (Sugino) Kato. At the time of the forced removal, he was a sophomore at Broadway High School. His parents owned a forty-five-room hotel with a tavern, restaurant, and pool hall in Seattle's Maynard Building and left behind "countless family heirlooms and treasures."

After his incarceration, Chris went to a small Kansas college for one year and then worked on a wheat harvesting crew in Kansas, Oklahoma, and South Dakota. He served in the US Army for two years and in 1947 became a sophomore in chemistry at the University of Washington. He graduated with a bachelor's degree and then worked for the National Bureau of Standards while studying part-time for a teaching certificate. In 1953 he was hired by the Seattle school district, where he taught for eighteen years until he acquired his administrator credentials. Then he was appointed the first Japanese American principal of a senior high school in Seattle. He retired as principal of Chief Sealth High School after thirty-six years in education. He also taught judo as a sensei for forty-three years, achieving a seventh-degree black belt.

Katsumi Thomas "Tom" **Kawaguchi**, male, Nisei, San Francisco, California, incarcerated age 21, Tanforan Assembly Center, Topaz Relocation Center. Tom was born in Tacoma, Washington, on January 25, 1921, the sixth of seven children, to Masai Frank Kawaguchi and Matsuki (Oiki) Kawaguchi from Kochi, Japan. Tom's mother was a picture bride. His father first came to Seattle in 1898 to get a job on the railroads but then enrolled in Elgin Watchmakers College outside of Chicago, Illinois. Masai also learned how to be a photographer. When he went back to Seattle, he opened his own watchmaking and photography shop. Then Masai decided to take his skills to San Francisco, where Tom was raised in a Jewish neighborhood from the age of three. All of Tom's friends were Jewish; he learned how to swear in Yiddish before he learned how to swear in Japanese. But his father had a stroke and had to close the business. The family moved to Japantown, where Tom's father was able to manage an apartment building as an invalid.

Tom attended San Francisco Junior College (now City College of San Francisco) for two years, then went to work for Mitsubishi as a business accountant at the docks, meeting Japanese ships, exchanging bills of lading, trading acceptances, and delivering them to the purser. The day of the attack on Pearl Harbor, Tom was in the library and emerged to the sound of newspaper boys shouting the headlines. He didn't know where Pearl Harbor was. The next day he was summoned for an interview by the FBI. A few days later he was fired from his job and met the FBI at his office so they could go through his desk.

Tom volunteered for the 442nd Regimental Combat Team and fought in three major campaigns in Italy and France. After the war, he reenlisted and had a twenty-year career in the US Army. He was a graduate of the Army Finance School and the Military Assistance Institute in Washington, DC, and his service took him through Europe, Asia, and the Pacific as a finance officer. He also served as a military adviser in Vietnam. He retired at the rank of major.

He then became a systems analyst and auditor for public agencies, and financial controller for the cities of Richmond and Pasadena. He once volunteered to work for the JACL as a messenger and met Mike Masaoka. He founded Go for Broke, now known as the National Japanese American Historical Society, whose mission is to archive the history of the 100th/442nd RCT.

Yoshisada **Kawai**, male, Issei, Seattle, Washington, incarcerated age 52, Puyallup Assembly Center, Minidoka Relocation Center. Yoshisada was born in the Mukaeda neighborhood in the village of Wada, Futami District (present-day Mukoueta, Miyoshi City), Hiroshima Prefecture, Japan, on March 4, 1889, the fourth son of a farmer and carpenter. He grew up in the countryside in Japan and had to walk almost two miles to school; there was no other transportation. In winter he walked through the snow in bamboo sandals (*zori*) with a cloak (*mantoe*) thrown over his shoulders. At home, there was no electricity, just oil lamps. Yoshisada's father expressed his belief in Buddhism in daily rituals. In the morning his father faced east and clapped his hands in gratitude, and in the evening he lit the oil lamp, made an offering of hot rice, then recited a Buddhist prayer (*okyo*) and rang a chime. Yoshisada remembered his mother saying, "If you disrespect rice grains, then you will become blind. . . . In other words, when we treat things with disrespect, then our eyes in our heart go blind, and we become heartless, ungrateful persons."

Yoshisada attended a new school built in Shiomachi, Hiroshima Prefecture, Japan. There he took advanced courses in liberal arts and graduated from high school. At seventeen years old, in the fall of 1906, he came to San Francisco in the cargo hold of a ship called *Korea Maru*. He was staying at the Mikado Hotel, probably in Stockton, California, when the owner found him a job in an apple-canning factory in Watsonville, California. The job only lasted for a short time; he became a migrant laborer, picking oranges, peaches, grapes, and pears.

At one point he went to San Bernardino to pick peaches but there wasn't a job when he got there. He snuck onto a train but was caught and thrown off in the middle of nowhere. He knocked on a random door, and an elderly Christian couple, the Commacks, answered. They invited him in for coffee and told him about a Japanese boardinghouse nearby. Yoshisada ended up working in their home as a schoolboy, listening to readings of the New Testament and singing hymns in order to learn English. Then he came down with pneumonia and the couple took care of him and paid his medical bills. Through the Commacks, he "came to know the power of love in the lonesome journey in the world." Soon after, Yoshisada decided it was time to move to Los Angeles. Before he left, Mrs. Commack gave him a small Bible that she signed "Mother Commack." He kept the Bible in his possession for the rest of his life.

In Los Angeles, he went to night school to work on his English and finished a course in bookkeeping. Later, he enrolled in the National Automotive School on Figueroa Street and became a professional automobile mechanic. But he couldn't get a job because he was Japanese and racism was rampant. So he became a chauffeur for a Caucasian family, and somehow he met and befriended Hal E. Roach, owner of Hal Roach Studios in Culver City. Roach was the producer of the *Our Gang* and *Laurel and Hardy* films and those starring actress ZaSu Pitts. Yoshisada began working for him exclusively, repairing company cars and cars owned by the actors. At the time, only a few other Japanese men were working for people in the movie business, including Toraichi Kono, who was Charlie Chaplin's bodyguard, manservant, and driver for thirty years; and Mr. Somen, who worked as a chauffeur for Harold Lloyd, one of the most influential comedians in silent films.

But after two years of working for Hal Roach, Yoshisada got sick again, this time with typhoid fever. His fever went as high as 107, and his lips burned black and purple. In his fever dreams he saw God embracing him in a blazing flame. The next day the fever broke and he began to get better—but it took another ten days.

Right before the war, his wife had a laundry business. When they were forced to leave for the assembly center, they had to sell the business for next to nothing. After the war, Yoshisada and his wife went to Chicago, where his wife worked in a clothing store and Yoshisada repaired radios, cut records for Japanese songs, and made fiberglass fishing poles.

They saved enough money to relocate to Seattle and bought a hotel, which he managed for twenty years. He wrote a book based on his diary called *A Walk of Morning Light (Komyo no Ayumi)*, and in November 1952, he was baptized by Reverend Noji in the Presbyterian Church. He came to believe his typhoid visions had been real, and he remembered a quote from a high Buddhist priest, "Dream is the expression of one's heart. The reality of the world is the world of confusion. And when we wake up from this confusion, we will be able to acknowledge the sight of the true life."

Charles **Kikuchi**, male, Nisei, San Francisco, California, incarcerated age 26, Tanforan Assembly Center, Gila River Relocation Center. Charles was born in Vallejo, California, on January 18, 1916, the oldest of seven children, to Nakajero Kikuchi and Shizue (Iwata) Kikuchi. His father was a barber. His parents placed him in a multiracial orphanage seventy miles north of San Francisco when he was eight years old; he grew up there until he was a teenager and old enough to work. He graduated from San Francisco State College in 1939 and entered the School of Social Welfare at the University of California with plans to become a social activist.

Due to his prewar anonymous publication of "A Young American with a Japanese Face," an essay included in the anthology *From Many Lands*, edited by Louis Adamic, literary figures such as William Saroyan and Carey McWilliams (the future editor of the *Nation*) encouraged him to write for publication from the perspective as a "new American."

During his incarceration he kept a diary as part of the Japanese American Evacuation and Resettlement Study under the direction of Dorothy Swaine Thomas. He later published his wartime writings in *The Kikuchi Diary: Chronicle from an American Concentration Camp*. After the war he resettled in Chicago and became an expert in the method of recording life stories. He eventually completed his master's degree at the New York School of Social Work and began a twenty-four-year career as a psychiatric social worker in Veterans' Administration hospitals, counseling Black veterans of the Vietnam War. He was participating in a peace march in the Soviet Union when he died in 1988 at the age of seventy-two.

Young Oak **Kim**, male, Korean American, 100th/442nd Regimental Combat Team. Young was born in Los Angeles, California, on January 26, 1919, the second oldest of six children, to Korean immigrants Soon Kwon Kim and Nora (Koh) Kim. He grew up in downtown Los Angeles amidst the Japanese, Chinese, Mexican, and Jewish émigré communities.

In January 1941 he enlisted in the US Army. When he was selected for the infantry officer candidate school at Fort Benning in Georgia, he was the only Asian American in his class. In February 1943, Young was assigned to lead the 100th Infantry Battalion. His commanding officer was aware of a potential conflict between Korean and Japanese soldiers and offered Young a transfer. But he declined the offer, believing that the unit would fight together as Americans. He and the members of his unit went on to develop a deep mutual respect for one another, and his leadership was considered a critical element of the 100th's military success.

In 1944, Young received his first Silver Star and Purple Heart for his actions near Santa Maria Oliveto, Italy. During the battle in Anzio, he volunteered, along with Private First Class Irving M. Akahoshi, to capture two German soldiers in order to obtain vital intelligence information. For his service, which contributed to the liberation of Rome from the Nazis, Young was awarded the Distinguished Service Cross.

Following his honorable discharge at the end of World War II, Young returned to Los Angeles and established a laundry business. When the Korean War broke out in 1950, he decided to reenlist, this time commanding a South Korean guerrilla unit in Korea. For his actions as part of the United Nations forces in Korea, he was awarded his second Silver Star and second Bronze Star. When Young was promoted to the rank of major, he became the first Asian American to command a regular US combat battalion in a war. He eventually served thirty years in the army, rising to the rank of colonel. When he retired, he was the most decorated Asian American in the US military.

After his retirement from the military, Young devoted his life to the service of others. He looked after the interests of Korean War orphans and supported numerous Asian American civic organizations; he served on the board of the Go for Broke National Education Center, which is dedicated to maintaining the legacy of Nisei veterans, and was director of the Los Angeles chapter of the United Way from 1978 to 1988.

In 2003 the Korean government posthumously awarded him the Korean Taeguk Cordon of the Order of Military Merit. And in 2009 the Los Angeles Unified School District named a new middle school in Koreatown the Young Oak Kim Academy in his honor. In June 2010, Edward T. Chang, professor of ethnic studies at the University of California, Riverside, founded the Young Oak Kim Center for Korean American Studies. A year later the center published *Unsung Hero: The Story of Colonel Young Oak Kim*—the English translation of Kim's biography by Woo Sung Han.

Chizuko "Chizu" **Kitano** (Iiyama), female, Nisei, Berkeley, California, incarcerated age 21, Santa Anita Assembly Center, Topaz Relocation Center. Chizu was born in San Francisco, California, on November 14, 1921, the fifth of seven children, to Motoji Kitano and Kou (Yuki) Kitano. Her family owned the Kitano Hotel in San Francisco's Chinatown. She entered the University of California, Berkeley, in 1938 as a psychology major and worked her way through school as a servant in a private home, after which she vowed never again to place herself in a demeaning environment. But she also worked at the World's Fair on Treasure Island and as an intern at Berkeley's art department for forty cents an hour. As soon as she found out she would be incarcerated, her college professors gave her extra assignments so that she could graduate early.

At Topaz she met a group of fellow incarcerees who had been politically active in a radical Japanese American organization in San Francisco called the

Nisei Young Democrats, and she learned about progressive politics. But she had to turn down a scholarship to Smith College because her father had just returned from a DOJ camp and her mother was ill.

After the war she and her new husband moved to New York, opened a dry-cleaning business, and joined the Japanese American Committee for Democracy and the American Labor Party, which led her to become one of the first incarcerees to speak publicly about her camp experience. She and her husband eventually resettled in Chicago, where they formed a branch of the Nisei Progressives.

Chizu earned her master's degree in human development from the University of Chicago and became a civil rights activist for such issues as employment discrimination against Black people, the abolition of nuclear weapons, and the integration of a White-only beach and other public facilities. She eventually moved back to California and was head of the Early Childhood Education Department at Contra Costa College. She also served on the Human Relations Commission in Richmond, California, and began working with the JACL's redress campaign—educating, lobbying, and grassroots organizing. In 1983 she co-founded, with Mei Nakano, the JACL Women's Concerns Committee. She continued to lobby on behalf of the National Coalition for Redress/Reparations to seek redress for as many people as possible, even after the Civil Liberties Act of 1988 was signed into law. In 1999, Chizu traveled to Washington, DC, to lobby on behalf of Japanese Latin Americans, who were explicitly excluded from the redress legislation.

Chizu worked with the National Japanese American Historical Society, which resulted in *Strength and Diversity: Japanese American Women, 1885–1990*, an exhibition that opened in the Oakland Museum and traveled across the country. In 2009 she and her husband were awarded the Dr. Clifford I. Uyeda Peace and Humanitarian Award from the Bay Area Day of Remembrance Consortium.

William Masayoshi **Kochiyama**, male, Nisei, Alameda County, California, incarcerated age 21, Tanforan Assembly Center, Topaz Relocation Center.

William was born in Washington, DC, on May 10, 1921, to Yutaka Kochiyama and Suye (Makita) Kochiyama. At Topaz he volunteered to serve with the 442nd Regimental Combat Team. After his honorable discharge in 1946, he married Mary Yuriko "Yuri" Nakahara (see her biography) and moved to New York, where he and Yuri became heavily involved in civil rights campaigns against racial discrimination. They had six children and lived in public housing for twelve years.

William eventually graduated from Long Island University with a degree in journalism and became a public relations officer at the Japan International Christian University Foundation, the advertising firm of Tamblyn & Brown, and the New Jersey Institute of Technology. In 1960 the family moved to Harlem; William and his wife joined the Congress of Racial Equality and the Harlem Parents Committee, where they organized boycotts to demand quality education for inner-city children.

William was a founder of the Asian Community Center and headed the media committee of the Concerned Japanese Americans group and later the East Coast Japanese Americans for Redress, which pressured the Commission on Wartime Relocation and Internment of Civilians to hold hearings in New York. Eleven hearings were then scheduled from July to December 1981 in ten cities, including New York. During his New York testimony, his wife, among others, marched into the courtroom with political art.

Yasuko "Yas" **Kodani** (Morimoto), female, Nisei, Snoqualmie, Washington, incarcerated age 14, Pinedale Assembly Center, Tule Lake Relocation Center. Yasuko was born in a logging camp in Snoqualmie, Washington, on October 23, 1927, the third oldest of six children, to Mangoro Kodani and Shizue (Hirata) Kodani. Her father was a farmer and her family lived in Bellevue, Washington. At Tule Lake no one in the family would answer questions number 27 and 28, so they were considered to be disloyal. After the war, Yas enrolled in the nursing program at the Los Angeles County General Hospital. The family, meanwhile, did not return to Bellevue because all of their farming equipment had been stolen; they relocated to Sacramento.

Yas married Noboru "Nob" Morimoto in 1950 just before he was called into the army. Nob began having heart trouble and to extend his life, Yas became a Reiki practitioner; she became skilled at administering many other healing alternatives. She taught classes in Reiki and line dancing. She ended up working for forty years at Stanford Hospital in the labor and delivery unit.

She traveled around the world, participating in everything from a sweat lodge ceremony in Sedona, Arizona, to meeting the spiritual leader Sai Baba in India. She preferred to travel alone, but she made an exception to be with a UFO group at Machu Picchu in southern Peru.

She made a point of taking ministers attending conferences in San Francisco to Finocchio's, a nightclub featuring female impersonators. For many years, she also served as a camp nurse at the Lake Sequoia Retreat, founded by the Central Valley YMCA. The family remembers her long relationship with a young man, blind and brain damaged in the Vietnam War.

She and Nob enjoyed camping, fishing, horse races, going to Reno, sumo wrestling, and the 49ers. (Nob and professional football star Randy Cross were childhood friends.) She made pickles, jams, dried apricots, umeboshi, and kazunoko, and gathered chestnuts in the mountains. In crafts, she made resin grapes, lamps, lighters, and ashtrays. She collected netsukes and fishing glass balls, and was addicted to Korean dramas. She took her son, Roger, and daughters, Joann, Carolyn, and Naomi—even when she was in a full body cast and confined to a wheelchair after having surgery for scoliosis—to the Beatles' last concert at Candlestick Park in 1966. She believed in karma.

Marion Tsuruko **Konishi** (Takehara), female, Nisei, Los Angeles, California, incarcerated age 16, Santa Anita Assembly Center, Granada (Amache) Relocation Center. Marion was born in Los Angeles, California, on May 7, 1925, the older of two children, to Tanigaro Konishi and Clara (Eiki) Konishi. Her father was descended from a samurai family and was the first in his family to come to the United States from Japan. He attended high school in Los Angeles and the University of California and he later owned a produce stand. Marion grew up in a Japanese neighborhood and was attending Dorsey High School, with students who were predominantly Caucasian, at the time she was incarcerated.

In 1943 she gave the valedictorian address at her graduation from Amache Senior High School. From camp her parents relocated to Cleveland, Ohio, where her father got a job in which he developed bombing maps. Marion received a scholarship to Simpson College in Indianola, Iowa, from the Methodist church and majored in biology. She was accepted to medical school, but she elected not to go; she married fellow Simpson graduate Kenneth Takehara, a veteran and former army medic with the 442nd Regimental Combat Team. Ken joined the army reserve after the war and was promoted to first lieutenant. Ken, who majored in biology at Simpson College, earned a master's degree at the University of Iowa. Marion became a medical technician at the University of Iowa hospital. Ken was offered a job as a medical laboratory director at Conemaugh Valley Memorial Hospital and they moved to Johnston, Pennsylvania. Marion obtained a master's degree in early childhood education and became an elementary school teacher.

On May 21, 2016, as part of the fortieth annual Amache Pilgrimage at the Granada Relocation Center, Marion made her first return trip to Camp Amache at the age of ninety-one to give the same valedictorian address that she had given at the age of eighteen, over seventy years earlier. In tribute to Marion, on June 9, 2016, Colorado senator Cory Gardner read her speech on the floor of the United States Senate and entered her speech into the Congressional Record.

Fred Toyosaburo **Korematsu**, male, Nisei, San Leandro, California, age 22 when Pearl Harbor was attacked, Presidio, Tanforan Assembly Center, Topaz Relocation Center. Fred was born in Oakland, California, on January 30, 1919, the third of four sons, to Kakusaburo Korematsu and Kotsui (Aoki) Korematsu, who ran a floral nursery business. After the Pearl Harbor attack, Fred lost his job as a shipyard welder and elected to be with his Italian American girlfriend rather than report to his designated assembly center. He was arrested on May 30, 1942, for failing to comply with the exclusion order. Ernest Besig, executive director of the ACLU of Northern California, approached him while he was in jail about the possibility of being a test case to challenge the constitutionality of Executive Order 9066.

On September 8, 1942, the federal district court in San Francisco found him guilty of violating the military orders, and he was placed on a five-year probation. He appealed his criminal conviction, and his case was eventually heard by the US Supreme Court in 1944. The case *Korematsu v. United States* upheld his conviction and found that his incarceration was justified by military necessity. Toward the end of the war, he worked as a welder in Salt Lake City and later moved to Detroit, where he met his wife, Kathryn. In late 1949 he returned to the Bay Area with his family and worked as a draftsman.

In 1983, Professor Peter Irons, a legal historian, and Aiko Herzig-Yoshinaga, a Nisei researcher, discovered key documents that the government had hidden from the Supreme Court in its 1944 presentation of the case. With these new documents, an all-volunteer legal team filed a petition called a writ of coram nobis to reopen Fred's forty-year-old case on the grounds that the Supreme Court had made its decision based on false information. On November 10, 1983, Judge Marilyn Hall Patel of the US District Court for the Northern District of California in San Francisco vacated his criminal conviction—but this ruling did not affect the outcome of the 1944 Supreme Court case.

Fred continued to advocate for civil rights in speaking engagements at colleges and law schools throughout the country, including the University of California, Berkeley; Stanford University; Georgetown University; the University of Michigan; Harvard University; and Yale University.

In the wake of the 9/11 attacks, he filed an amicus brief with the Supreme Court for two cases on behalf of Muslim inmates being held at Guantanamo Bay. He filed another amicus brief in 2004, citing similarities between the wrongful imprisonment of Japanese Americans during World War II and Muslims following 9/11. In 1999, Fred received the Presidential Medal of Freedom, the nation's highest civilian honor.

In 2010 the State of California designated January 30 as Fred Korematsu Day—the first day in the United States to be named after an Asian American. Learn more about Fred's legacy in advancing racial equity, social justice, and human rights through education from the Fred T. Korematsu Institute for Civil Rights and Education at korematsuinstitute.org/homepage.

Karen Anne **Korematsu**, female, Sansei. Karen was born in Oakland, California, on September 3, 1950, the older of two children, to Fred Toyosaburo Korematsu (see his biography) and Kathryn (Pearson) Korematsu. She is the founder and executive director of the Fred T. Korematsu Institute. In 2009, on the twenty-fifth anniversary of the vacating of her father's World War II conviction, she established the Fred T. Korematsu Institute for Civil Rights and Education as a community program with the Asian Law Caucus (ALC), now known as Asian Americans Advancing Justice-Asian Law Caucus in San Francisco. ALC provided key support to the coram nobis team that reopened *Korematsu v. United States* in 1983. In May 2013 Karen took over leadership of the institute and in July 2014 established it as an independent organization funded by community initiatives.

One of her significant accomplishments was working with Assembly member Warren Furutani to establish the "Fred Korematsu Day of Civil Liberties and the Constitution" for the State of California on January 30 in perpetuity. The first Fred Korematsu Day was observed on January 30, 2011.

Karen has been carrying on her father's legacy through education as a civil rights advocate, teacher workshop presenter, and speaker to K–12 public and private schools, universities, law schools, and organizations.

She has signed on to a number of amicus briefs, including for the cases of *Odah v. United States* in support of the Guantanamo Bay detainees regarding habeas corpus, *Turkman v. Ashcroft* in support of the rights of Muslim immigrants, *Hedges v. Obama* challenging provisions of the National Defense Authorization Act as potential infringement on constitutional rights, and *Trump v. Hawaii* challenging the travel bans imposed by the Trump administration.

Karen is a lead member of the national advisory board of the Fred T. Korematsu Center for Law and Equality at Seattle University School of Law and an adviser for the Fred T. Korematsu Chair in Law and Social Justice at the William S. Richardson School of Law, University of Hawai'i, Manoa. She currently sits on the national board of directors for the Asian Americans Advancing Justice in Washington, DC. Previously she served on the Marin Ballet Board of Directors and the ALC Board of Directors from 2000 to 2013.

Mitsuru "Mits" **Koshiyama**, male, Nisei, Santa Clara Valley, California, incarcerated age 18, Santa Anita Assembly Center, Heart Mountain Relocation Center, McNeil Island Federal Penitentiary. Mits was born in Mountain View, California, on August 7, 1924, the second son of four boys and three girls, to Tatsuhei Koshiyama and Tsutaye (Oka) Koshiyama. He was one of the sixty-three Nisei draft resisters and members of the Heart Mountain Fair Play Committee who were arrested in their fight to restore their civil rights in exchange for serving in the US military. It was the largest mass trial in Wyoming's history. In June 1944, Mits was convicted and sentenced to three years at McNeil Island Federal Penitentiary near Tacoma, Washington. After his release he returned to California, where his father was working as a gardener and his mother as a housekeeper. He started a wholesale flower business with his brother, growing and shipping chrysanthemums for more than thirty years. Eventually he was pardoned by President Harry S. Truman in December 1947.

Kaizo "K" George **Kubo**, male, Nisei, San Diego, California, incarcerated age 14, Santa Anita Assembly Center, Poston Relocation Center. Kaizo was born in San Diego, California, on February 28, 1928, the second youngest of five children, to Jinfaro Kubo and Tokino (Ohno) Kubo. Jinfaro came from Japan in steerage and found work packing fruit. Kaizo received an honorable mention (among 6,000 entries) for his essay "The Years Between," which he wrote while attending Parker Valley High School in Poston III for a *Scholastic* magazine literary contest.

After the war he became a house boy for the Lundstroms, an American family in Monticello, Indiana. According to Kaizo, Mrs. Lundstrom saved him from starvation. The Lundstroms enrolled him in New Trier High School in Winnetka, Illinois, for his senior year. Upon graduating, he returned to his family in the San Joaquin valley. But Kaizo hated working in the fields, so he traveled around the country, until he landed at McPherson College in McPherson, Kansas. He only got through one semester before going home again. He worked for two and a half years as a day laborer in Reedley, California. Then his father died.

In 1950 he attended Reedley Junior College, and under the mentorship of a young teacher named Ridgway Shinn, Kaizo became editor of the college literary magazine, vice president of the World Affairs Club, and toastmaster of the annual spring banquet. He was part of Reedley's delegation to Stanford's annual Model United Nations and he fell under the spell of the delegation from Pomona College in Claremont, California. He transferred to Pomona in his junior year with a full tuition scholarship of $650. His mother and sister covered the bulk of his financial gap; his mother contributed her earnings from her work in the onion fields and his sister shared her salary as a secretary in the psychology and philosophy department of Fresno State College. Kaizo added his own earnings from fruit-picking in the summer.

At Pomona's orientation, the students were asked their opinion of the José Clemente Orozco mural of Prometheus in Pomona's Frary Hall. That's how Kaizo first learned about the Greek hero who made humanity out of clay and stole fire—the symbol of knowledge—from the gods for the good of mankind. The orientation was also where Kaizo met a fellow student, the blind writer Ved Mehta, and the two became close friends. Mehta wrote about their friendship in the *New Yorker* and in one of his many books, *The Stolen Light*. Mehta was six years younger than Kaizo, but he remembered Kaizo as someone who "any thoughtful person would have been drawn to. . . . He had poise and dignity; he was sincere and cheerful, and had a persevering nature." According to Mehta, Kaizo had "an intense way of speaking, but he tended to use the passive voice and talk in the third person, as if he were speaking about someone else." Kaizo spoke to him about his immigrant parents, his mother living in poverty, and his desire for an education. He was driven both by intellectual pursuits as well as the motivation to help support his family; money was always a concern of his.

When Kaizo graduated cum laude from Pomona College in 1954 with a degree in history, his mother and sisters were thrilled. Even Mrs. Lundstrom wrote him a letter to reinforce her continued belief in him. Henry Cord Meyer, his mentor at Pomona, encouraged him to go straight for a doctorate, so he wouldn't have to deal with prejudice in the public and private high schools and could teach in a college instead. Meyer also pointed out that teaching high school would require yet another year of schooling in order to get a teaching credential. But all the doctoral programs that Kaizo applied to rejected him. His only acceptance was to get a master's at Claremont, where he was offered a full scholarship of $500 and a job as a resident assistant that included his room and board. Once again he was torn between his need to be employable as soon as possible and his desire to continue his education. He could not see how he could ask his mother to keep working in the onion fields so he could get another piece of paper and regretted his decision not to go for his teaching credentials. Meyer even helped him get into the doctorate program at the University of Wisconsin, which came with a teaching assistant fellowship of $1,000. But Kaizo turned it down, choosing to stay at Claremont to complete his master's so he could then immediately start studying for his teaching credential. But he couldn't bring himself to tell his mother about this turn of events; he didn't think she'd ever understand the need for a master's degree if it couldn't get him a job.

Moreover, Meyer was away for a year, which meant Kaizo had come under the supervision of John Howe Gleason, the one professor with whom Meyer was most at odds. Kaizo was struggling with a master's topic that was far too broad—the idea of progress in the eighteenth and nineteenth centuries—and Gleason was giving him no guidance.

Kaizo became utterly overwhelmed by the subject matter, but it was too late to do much about it.

He turned in his thesis after spring vacation, and Gleason told him that it had to be completely rewritten. Kaizo knew then it wasn't possible for him to finish by the deadline.

On May 2, 1955, the day his thesis was due, Kaizo climbed into bed wearing several layers of clothing, held two pillows against his chest, and fired into his abdomen twice with a small-caliber pistol.

A classmate ran toward the shots and heard his last words,

"I shot myself. . . . This is the way it should be."

He left behind a note for Professor Meyer, saying, "Forgive me," and a second note for Ridgway Shinn, his champion at Reedley College: "Mr. Shinn—I can't explain everything. Lately I've been so depressed—I've made many terrible mistakes. Forgive me. Kaizo."

The night before he died, several students had seen him standing before the Orozco mural, seemingly mesmerized. He was twenty-seven years old.

Michio "Mich" **Kunitani**, male, Nisei, Alameda County, California, incarcerated age 24, Tanforan Assembly Center, Poston Relocation Center. Mich was born in Los Angeles, California, on April 6, 1918, the eldest of three boys, to Michitoshi Kunitani and Tsuya (Takagi) Kunitani. The family lived in Boyle Heights, near Los Angeles's Little Tokyo. As a young person, he became involved in politics and supported President Franklin D. Roosevelt's New Deal. While visiting his paternal grandmother in Japan in 1936, he was troubled by Japan's militaristic society. That year Mich graduated from Roosevelt High School in Los Angeles and began his college studies that fall at the University of California, Berkeley. There he became active with the UC Young Democrats, and in his senior year, April 1940, he represented that club at the California Youth Legislature. He completed a bachelor of arts degree at University of California, Berkeley, and enrolled in a master's degree program.

Then, in February 1942, as president of the newly formed Oakland Nisei Young Democrats, he testified before the Tolan Committee that the Nisei generation was American not just by birth, but also by cultural and psychological identity and that the calls to evacuate the Japanese were racially motivated. In Tanforan, Mich worked for the Japanese American Evacuation and Resettlement Study to produce reports on the incarcerees' life in camp. In August, Mich and his wife, Ann Saito Kunitani, were transferred to the Poston Relocation Center. They left Poston in March 1943 and resettled in Cleveland, Ohio. Mich wrote a letter to First Lady Eleanor Roosevelt about the problems Japanese Americans were facing in resettlement, and she invited him to meet with her at the White House. Their meeting concentrated on the lack of support upon leaving the camps. The following year he addressed a meeting of the National Conference on Social Work. Mich enlisted in the US Army after the war ended in October 1946. Following his honorable discharge a year later, he worked for the California Department of Employment and SamTrans, a local commuter transport service.

Sueko "Sue" **Kunitomi** (Embrey), female, Nisei, Los Angeles, California, incarcerated age 19, Manzanar Reception Center, Manzanar Relocation Center. Sue was born in Los Angeles's Little Tokyo on January 6, 1923, the sixth of eight children, to Gonhichi Kunitomi and Komika (Kunitomi) Kunitomi from Okayama Prefecture, Japan. Her father and mother were from the same village in Japan and had the same last name. Sue attended Dai-ichi Gakuen, the Japanese-language school, every day after regular school and graduated from Lincoln High School in 1941. When she was fourteen years old, her father died in a truck accident. Her mother then went around the neighborhood, collecting the money still owed to her husband for his trucking services. She took out a loan and opened a grocery store, where Sue was working at the time of the attack on Pearl Harbor. Her mother was forced to sell the store at a loss to a Mexican American family.

Sue found work at the Manzanar camouflage net factory and then became managing editor of the biweekly camp newspaper, ironically named the *Manzanar Free Press*, where she had a column called Purely Personal. Three of her brothers served in the US Army, two of them with General Douglas MacArthur's occupation troops in Japan. Her younger brother, who was twelve years old at the time of his incarceration, volunteered for the army at the age of eighteen and became a casualty of the Korean War four years later.

She passed the government's loyalty questionnaire and was able to leave camp for Madison, Wisconsin, where she hoped to enroll at the University of Wisconsin. But she was rejected because, she was told, having her on campus would "endanger a war-related project then taking place at the school." So she took a job at a mail-order cheese factory instead. In 1944 she moved to Chicago and, aided by the American Friends Service Committee, found a job at the Newberry Library.

She returned to Los Angeles four years later to look after her mother and married a politically leftist Texan at a time when interracial marriages were not widely accepted. The camp experience had politicized her, and she joined a number of political groups, including the Democratic Club and the Nisei for Wallace group, which supported Henry Wallace for president on the Progressive Party ticket. The group later called itself the Nisei Progressives and helped elect Edward Roybal to the Los Angeles City Council. It was the 1950s, and her husband's political activities prompted frequent FBI visits to their home. Nonetheless, he was able to keep his teaching position at West Los Angeles College, where he taught for two decades.

Finally, by sharing childcare responsibilities with her husband, Sue was able to get a college education herself. She graduated in 1969 from California State University, Los Angeles, with a degree in English, then three years later from the University of Southern California with a master's degree in education. She found work as a teacher in an elementary school in the Los Angeles Unified School District and became active in United Teachers Los Angeles, the Asian Pacific American Labor Alliance, United Farm Workers, and the UCLA Labor Center, and worked at UCLA in the Asian American Studies Center in curriculum development. For ten years she served on the Los Angeles Commission on the Status of Women, and in 1980 she was selected as a delegate to the National Association of Commissions for Women Conference. She was also one of thirty-five US delegates to the United Nations Second World Conference on Women, which took place in Copenhagen on July 14–30, 1980.

In 1969 she was invited by Yonsei activist Warren Furutani to attend the Manzanar Pilgrimage for the first time since she was incarcerated, nearly twenty-seven years earlier. The pilgrimage was organized primarily by Sansei activists who were also involved in the civil rights movement in the Black community. For the first time, Sue spoke publicly about her camp experience with local reporters, and she was criticized for doing so by other incarcerees. Not long afterward she and Furutani co-chaired the Manzanar Committee, and she ended up chairing the annual pilgrimage for the next thirty-six years. She was in large part responsible for getting the site established as the Manzanar National Historic Site, which was signed into law by President George H. W. Bush. She served as the site's inaugural chair of the advisory commission and worked closely with the National Park Service in the site's development. She was the keynote speaker at the grand opening of the Manzanar National Historic Site's interpretive center in 2004. She is the author of *The Lost Years: 1942–46* and co-author, with Arthur A. Hansen and Betty Kulberg Mitson, of *The Manzanar Martyr: An Interview with Harry Y. Ueno.*

Yoshito "Yosh" **Kuromiya**, male, Nisei, Pasadena, California, incarcerated age 19, Pomona Assembly Center, Heart Mountain Relocation Center, Cheyenne County Jail, McNeil Island Federal Penitentiary. Yosh was born in Sierra Madre, California, on April 23, 1923, the fifth of six children, to Hisamitsu "James" Kuromiya and his picture bride, Hana (Tada) Kuromiya, both from Okayama Prefecture, Japan. His father worked for a family doing housework, gardening, and cooking. When he married Hana, his employers fixed up a chicken coop for them to live in. Eventually they moved to Monrovia, California, but they were evicted from their home because they were living in a redlined area, subject to a racially restrictive covenant against non-White persons residing there. They managed a small fruit stand and sold vegetables to local families.

Yosh had graduated from Monrovia-Arcadia-Duarte High School in 1941 and was studying art at Pasadena Junior College (now Pasadena City College) when World War II broke out. His older brother's engagement party was planned for "Pearl Harbor Sunday." Yosh continued to produce personal and communal art as a means of dealing with the hardships of camp life by creating landscapes and still-life drawings and portraits; he was part of the "Poster Shop Gang," designing and printing posters for wartime drives, dances, and fire safety at camp.

Yosh was also one of sixty-three members of the Heart Mountain Fair Play Committee who resisted the draft on the basis that the country was violating their civil rights. Yosh turned twenty-one in the Cheyenne County Jail in Sidney, Nebraska, alongside eighty-five other Japanese American draft resisters who were protesting their wartime imprisonment. Ironically, every Sunday a group of Caucasian Christians would visit the jail and sing hymns and read Bible verses. He was held for three years on McNeil Island near Tacoma, Washington. In 1947 all the draft resisters were pardoned by President Harry S. Truman. After his incarceration Yosh received his degree in landscape architecture at California State Polytechnic University, Pomona, and went on to have a career designing private gardens. In 2010 he was presented with an honorary degree from Pasadena City College.

Mike Masaru **Masaoka**, male, Nisei, North Platte, Nebraska, age 26 when Pearl Harbor was attacked. Mike was born in Fresno, California, on October 15, 1915, the fourth child of six sons and two daughters, to Ejiro Masaoka and Haruye (Goto) Masaoka. He grew up in Salt Lake City, Utah. His father died in a car accident when he was nine years old, leaving his mother to care for eight children on her own. He worked in his family's produce business while attending the University of Utah, where he became a master debater with a concentration in economics and politics; he graduated with honors in 1937.

In 1941 at the age of twenty-five, he became the leader of the American Loyalty League and the Progressive Citizens League; he continued to lead those organizations through World War II. That year Mike was named national secretary and field executive of the JACL. He was recruiting for the JACL in North Platte, Nebraska, when Pearl Harbor was attacked, and he was detained in a local jail. Utah senator Elbert D. Thomas was instrumental in securing Mike's release.

Mike was the first volunteer for the 442nd Regimental Combat Team and was awarded a Legion of Merit, a Bronze Star, and the Italian War Cross for Military Valor. After he was honorably discharged, the JACL appointed him its Washington representative, and he served as the national legislative director of the JACL's Anti-Discrimination Committee. He was widely criticized for encouraging compliance with the forced removal.

He established his own consulting firm after the war and represented a number of trade associations. He assisted in the passage of the Japanese American Evacuation Claims Act of 1948, which provided compensation to Japanese Americans for losses incurred during their incarceration. In 1950, Mike was named the JACL's Nisei of the Biennium.

Mike also lobbied for the Immigration and Nationality Act of 1952, which gave Japanese immigrants a pathway to naturalize as US citizens. He was a participant in Dr. Martin Luther King Jr.'s march on Washington, DC, in 1963 and helped form the Leadership Conference on Civil Rights. In 1968 the Emperor of Japan awarded him the Order of the Rising Sun, Gold Rays with Neck Ribbon. In 1970 the JACL created the Mike Masaoka Distinguished Public Service Award and the Mike M. Masaoka Fellowship Fund to develop leaders in public service.

The Emperor of Japan honored Mike again in 1983 with the Order of the Sacred Treasure, Gold and Silver Star. His memoir, *They Call Me Moses Masaoka*, written with Bill Hosokawa, was published in 1987.

Mike was the first Nisei to be elected president of the Japan America Society and became involved in many Nisei organizations, including the Go for Broke National Veterans Association (which later became the National Japanese American Memorial Foundation).

Kazuo **Masuda** [no relation to the fallen 442nd soldier of the same name], male, Nisei, Livingston, California, incarcerated age 33, Merced Assembly Center, Granada (Amache) Relocation Center. Kazuo was born in Livingston, California, on the farm in the Yamato Colony, the oldest of six children, to Yosuke Masuda and Kin (Kato) Masuda. He was actually born in January 1909, but the date was recorded as September 19, 1909, because his father thought he had to register the birth in San Francisco, so he waited until his next trip there.

Kazuo's mother was born in Nagoya, Japan. The headquarters for Canadian

Episcopal Missionaries was in her family's large home. When the missionaries left Japan, she went with them and then moved to San Francisco. Yosuke arrived in San Francisco in 1898. His parents met through a matchmaker in a refugee center after the San Francisco earthquake in 1906.

Kazuo graduated from Livingston High School in 1927 and then from the University of California, Berkeley, with a degree in business, in 1932. During the Depression he could only afford to go to college one semester a year. He was farming in Livingston at the time of their forced removal. He was married to Yayeko (Nagai) Masuda.

From camp his family moved to Cincinnati, Ohio, and lived in an area called Roselawn, the Jewish section of town. His family remembers that approximately 300 to 400 Japanese Americans resettled in Cincinnati and Dayton. Kazuo worked for the Drackett Company as a maintenance man and was a member of the Chemical Workers Union. Proctor and Gamble refused to hire him for any job even though he had a college degree. For years his family boycotted P&G products.

After the war, because of his asthma, he sold his share of the farm to his brother and eventually worked for the Winton Insurance Agency in Livingston.

The Honorable Robert "Bob" Takeo **Matsui**, male, Sansei, Sacramento, California, incarcerated age 6 months, Pinedale Assembly Center, Tule Lake Relocation Center. Bob was born in Sacramento, California, on September 17, 1941, the older brother of Barbara, to Yasuji Matsui and Alice (Nagata) Matsui. The Matsui family lost their produce business during the incarceration.

Bob was only six months old when they arrived at the Pinedale Assembly Center. As a baby he experienced a high fever and had an ear infection. Later he learned that he had suffered nerve damage, causing 20 percent hearing loss in each ear. His mother became pregnant again and contracted German measles. Meanwhile, his father had been sent to a Civilian Conservation Corps work camp in Weiser, Idaho, to harvest sugar beets; he had asked permission to come back to check on his family before the child was born, but permission was denied. So Bob's mother took advantage of the seasonal leave clearance to move to a farm camp in Caldwell, Idaho, that was built for migrant workers escaping the Dust Bowl and the Depression in 1939. There were no machine guns and barbed wire, but it was a "rural jail" with an 8:00 p.m. curfew. His mother gave birth in a two-room cottage in Caldwell to his sister, Barbara, who was born blind as a consequence of his mother having German measles during her pregnancy. Eventually his father was released and reunited with the family. But his mother had nightmares for the rest of her life.

After the war the family returned to Sacramento, where even as a child Bob could feel "a subtle message of shame that hung heavily over all Japanese-American homes." He remembers sitting down with his friend Eddie Takahashi on the porch in his backyard and Eddie saying, "I wish I wasn't Japanese." And Bob said, "Yeah, me too." He was eleven or twelve years old.

He graduated from C. K. McClatchy High School in 1959 and the University of California, Berkeley, in 1963 with a degree in political science. Bob remembered, after hearing John F. Kennedy's inaugural address, how Kennedy's words had inspired him to "look beyond ourselves, and look to our community, our state, and our nation to see how we can improve the lot of every American."

Three years later he received his JD from the University of California, Hastings College of the Law, in San Francisco and launched his private practice in Sacramento. At Berkeley, Bob met Doris Okada, another incarceree, who was born at the Poston concentration camp. They married in 1968.

Bob won a seat on the Sacramento City Council in 1971, at the age of twenty-nine, the first Japanese American to hold this position. He served as vice-mayor of Sacramento in 1977 and was on the city council until 1978. That year he was elected to the US House of Representatives for California's Fifth Congressional District, the office he held until his death at the end of his thirteenth term.

He served on the House Government Operations Committee, the Judiciary Committee, the Interstate and Foreign Commerce Committee (later named Energy and Commerce), the Ways and Means Committee, the Budget Committee, and the Select Committee on Narcotics Abuse and Control. Bob was on the influential Ways and Means Committee for most of his congressional career, and he used his knowledge of the tax code and the memory of his family's incarceration to help further social change, to protect vulnerable Americans, and to push for social equality. He championed the cause of Japanese American redress and supported children's issues and free trade policies.

In December 2002 fellow Californian and Democratic leader Nancy Pelosi tapped him to chair the Democratic Congressional Campaign Committee, which made him chief fund-raiser for the Democratic Party. But following the 2004 election cycle, his health deteriorated, and he lost a brief battle with pneumonia complicated by a rare blood disease on January 1, 2005. In that same year his wife, Doris Matsui, won a special election to succeed her husband as a representative in Congress, an office she holds to this day.

Clarence "Cal" Satoru **Matsumura**, male, Nisei, Los Angeles, California, incarcerated age 21, Pomona Assembly Center, Heart Mountain Relocation Center. Clarence was born in Bryan, Wyoming, on April 28, 1921, the middle boy of seven children, to Roy Rokuzaimon Matsumura and Takeko (Tomiye) Matsumura. Roy came to the United States in 1904 to help build the railroad over the Rockies and lived with his wife in a number of small railroad towns. Bryan, Wyoming, where Clarence was born, is a ghost town today, but for a short time it was a new town on the Black Forks River built to serve as the local headquarters of Union Pacific Railroad. But the town suffered a drought and the company feared the river wouldn't produce enough water to run the locomotives, so Union Pacific pulled up stakes and abandoned the town. But Roy continued to work for Union Pacific. He started out as a water boy and, thirty years later, he was section foreman.

Eventually, Roy moved the family to Los Angeles so his seven children could get a better education; Wyoming's rural schools didn't go past the eighth grade. He sunk his life savings into owning a grocery store in Hollywood. Cal graduated from John Marshall High School; some of his classmates were offspring of famous people in the movie business. He was a student at Los Angeles Trade Technical Junior College studying telecommunications and succeeded in getting a radio license. But after the attack on Pearl Harbor, his family lost everything. Ironically, they ended up back in Wyoming—but this time as inmates of Heart Mountain.

With his background in radio, Cal tried to enlist in the air force and then the navy. But these branches of service weren't open to Japanese Americans, and he wasn't interested in joining an all-Nisei army unit. So he left camp to work for the Great Northern Railroad and saved up enough money after six months to go to the University of Cincinnati and continue his studies in electronics. But being a student didn't prevent him from getting drafted; he was assigned to the all-Nisei unit anyway—the 442nd Regimental Combat Team's artillery attachment called the 522nd Field Artillery Battalion—as a radio repairman. Cal was shipped out to Italy on one of one hundred ships carrying supplies and reinforcements for the 100th/442nd RCT. So many of the harbors had been destroyed by bombs that army engineers had to build a temporary dock to receive the ship he was on. From there, Cal traveled by train to Marseilles, which took almost a week. He was one of the replacements for those who had fallen during the battle of the Lost Battalion and were now on the Franco-Italian border for the next four months.

Then on March 13, 1945, the 522nd Field Artillery Battalion was ordered to separate from the soldiers of the 100th/442nd RCT and become a roving artillery battalion to assist the Sixty-Third Division's assault on the Siegfried line between Eastern France and Germany. The battalion was the only unit of Japanese Americans to fight in Germany and in two months it was attached to four different divisions and covered over 1,100 miles in its push toward Berlin and Munich, firing more than 11,000 shells.

It was April 29 when Cal entered a "peaceful-looking town called Dachau." But then he smelled the decay of human flesh. Naked corpses were piled everywhere. He and his fellow men from the 522nd had come upon the surviving victims of the Kaufering IV Hurlach subcamp of the Dachau slave labor camp, and the Japanese Americans of the 522nd became their unlikely liberators.

Meanwhile, seventeen-year-old Solly Ganor was dying. A Jew, he was one of 15,000 prisoners of the Dachau's satellite labor camps who were sent on a forced Death March from Dachau to Tyrol, Austria. He knew that if he fell, he would be shot or the dogs would tear him apart. He had left on April 24, and by May 1 he and his father had marched thirty-seven miles. Only 6,000 prisoners were still alive. Then it started snowing heavily, and Solly fell to the ground. Because he was covered with snow, the Germans didn't see him. The next morning, May 2, Solly woke up to see Cal, holding out a chocolate bar, and then lifting him from the verge of death out of the snowbank. Cal was only twenty-four years old himself. He and other members of the 522nd had come upon Solly as a survivor of the Dachau Death March as they discovered bodies strewn through the stripped forest outside of Waakirchen, Germany.

Forty-seven years later, in 1992, Eric Saul and Lani Silver, director of San Francisco's Holocaust Oral History project, brought twenty-five liberators and their families to Israel to be honored by the Knesset. Miraculously, Eric tracked down Solly in Israel by phone and arranged a reunion with Cal, who had come all the way from California for the event. Cal was seventy-one years old; Solly was sixty-four. As he was reunited with Cal, Solly experienced a flood of tears, as if "the boy he had buried deep within [him] all those years had come out of hiding."

The Honorable Spark Masayuki **Matsunaga**, male, Nisei, Honolulu, Hawaii, age 25 when Pearl Harbor was attacked. Spark was born in Kukuiula on the island of Kauai, Hawaii, on October 8, 1916, the youngest of six children (including four stepsiblings), to Kingoro Matsunaga and Chiyono (Fukushima) Ikeda Matsunaga. His father ran away from a Japanese monastery at the age of nineteen and settled on Kauai, where he married a Japanese widow with four children and worked on a sugar plantation. One day a mountain of one-hundred-pound bags fell on him, and he vowed from his hospital bed that if lived through it, he would dedicate himself to a spiritual life. Thereafter his sons built him a Shinto temple in his backyard, and he became a Shinto priest.

Spark grew up on Kauai and in 1937 became a student at the University of

Hawai'i in Honolulu. He joined the ROTC program and graduated Phi Beta Kappa in 1941 with a degree in education. He volunteered for active service in June 1941 and was serving as an acting commander in the 299th Infantry Regiment of the Hawaii Army National Guard on the island of Molokai at the time of the attack on Pearl Harbor. By June 1942 he had responded to the recall of all soldiers of Japanese ancestry to Schofield Barracks and was serving as one of the original members of the 100th Infantry Battalion.

During basic training at Camp McCoy, he organized a petition for President Franklin D. Roosevelt to allow Japanese Americans to prove their loyalty in battle. A year later the 100th was in Italy, where he was wounded twice and awarded the Bronze Star and two Purple Hearts. He was then assigned to Fort Snelling in Minnesota, where he was a company commander at the Military Intelligence Service Language School for eight months, giving nearly eight hundred speeches at the request of the WRA about the bravery of the 100th/442nd Regimental Combat Team. After the war ended, he worked as a transition counselor for veterans leaving the military and as a surplus property officer at the War Assets Administration, certifying veterans to purchase surplus as priority buyers.

In May 1950 Spark was asked to testify before a congressional committee on Hawaii's statehood. Since Hawaii was the birthplace of the 100th, he said, "The granting of immediate statehood to Hawaii will mean the full and final recognition of the great sacrifices we made in answer to our country's call." A year later he graduated with distinction from Harvard Law School, then returned to Hawaii, where he worked as an assistant public prosecutor before going into private practice. In 1954 he was elected to serve in the Hawaii Territorial Legislature, and he helped to abolish the death penalty in 1957. As House majority leader in 1959, he also had a significant role in securing Hawaii's statehood.

Meanwhile, he continued his postgraduate studies at the Northwestern University Traffic Institute (now the Northwestern University Center for Public Safety) and the Lawyers' Post-Graduate Clinics of Chicago. In 1962 Spark was elected as a congressman in the newly minted state of Hawaii and became president of the incoming class. He was reelected six times, serving fourteen years, until he won a senate seat in 1976 and served for another fourteen years as a US senator. He was a leader in establishing the Commission on Wartime Relocation and Internment of Civilians to study Executive Order 9066.

Spark supported a wide range of interests, including arms control, renewable energy, legislation to create the US poet laureate position at the Library of Congress, and the joint exploration of space with the Russians. He also helped Iva Toguri D'Aquino, known erroneously as Tokyo Rose, to secure a pardon from President Gerald Ford. Finally, his dream of creating a peace academy came true with the 1984 passage of the United States Institute for Peace Act, which founded "an independent, nonprofit, national institute to serve the people and the Government . . . to promote international peace and the resolution of conflicts among the nations and peoples of the world without recourse to violence." He also cast a thumbs-up for the Clean Air Act, his last vote before succumbing to cancer on April 15, 1990, at the age of seventy-three.

Mary Haruko **Matsuno** (Makino), female, Nisei, Terminal Island, California, incarcerated age 14, Manzanar Reception Center, Manzanar Relocation Center. Mary was born in Burbank, California, on April 11, 1929, one of eight brothers and sisters, to Fukukuma Matsuno and Tamiko (Konomi) Matsuno. Her mother was hospitalized a few months before the attack on Pearl Harbor, and her father was a Terminal Island fisherman, so he was immediately arrested by the FBI and taken to the DOJ camp in Missoula, Montana. He was subsequently transferred to Bismarck, North Dakota; Crystal City, Texas; and Santa Fe, New Mexico. With her mother still unable to take care of the children, Mary and her siblings were put in the Shonien, or the Japanese Children's Home of Southern California. From there they were taken to the Children's Village at Manzanar. Mary convinced her older brother and sister, who were old enough to leave the Children's Village, to let her live with them in their block. The youngest sibling was six or seven months old. Mary's family left the camp in 1945 and went to Long Beach, California, where Mary worked as an office manager. In 1992 she organized a Manzanar Children's Village reunion together with her brothers and sisters. She married Toshio Arai Makino, who was an architect for over forty years.

Masako "Betty" (Fujisaki) **Matsuo**, female, Nisei, Stockton, California, incarcerated age 16, Stockton Assembly Center, Rohwer Relocation Center. Betty was born on Bacon Island, in California's Sacramento–San Joaquin River Delta, on May 29, 1925, one of four sisters, to Tomoso Fujisaki and Unoye Fujisaki, who were sharecroppers. After being raised on the delta islands, she moved to Stockton, California, and worked for John and Mabel Spaenhower so she could go to high school. The Spaenhowers became her guardians and foster parents and treated her like their own daughter. They tried all legal avenues to prevent her from being taken to camp, but nothing worked. They had to drive her to the Stockton Assembly Center and leave her weeping at the barbed wire. Betty was just a few months away from her graduation, and she had been accepted at Mills College.

At Rohwer she met and married George Matsuo. Her first daughter, Mikki, was born there. After the war they returned to San Francisco, where daughter Phyllis and son John were born, and she worked for the federal government. She became very active in the redress movement and retired to Yuba City, California, with frequent trips to Reno, Nevada, and Colusa, California.

Haruyuki "Jim" **Matsuoka**, male, Nisei, Los Angeles, California, incarcerated age 7, Manzanar Reception Center, Manzanar Relocation Center. Jim was born in Los Angeles, California, on July 27, 1935, the youngest of three children, with two older sisters, to Toichi Matsuoka and Hatsuyo (Sawada) Matsuoka, both from Hiroshima, Japan. He grew up in Little Tokyo. His father worked as a stock boy in a drugstore and his parents were members of the Nishi Hongwanji Buddhist Temple. After the war Jim's father discovered that his life savings was gone. It had been deposited at Sumitomo Bank in Los Angeles because the bank employed Japanese-speaking clerks, but years later, when Jim contacted the Justice Department to reclaim the money using his father's passbooks, he was told that it was too late; the money had already been repossessed and classified as abandoned.

Upon their release from Manzanar, the family was directed to a trailer park in Long Beach, where they lived for two years. They then made various moves to the Crenshaw and Virgil areas of Los Angeles, known as the J-Flats. Jim attended Foshay, Dorsey, and Belmont High Schools. He played football, and joined the Belmont glee club and the Hollywood Judo Dojo. He was given Belmont High School's highest award from its business department, but socialized with students at a continuation school who were getting a "last chance" before being permanently expelled.

Jim became involved in the club culture, which began with athletic clubs. The clubs eventually developed into groups that identified with ganglike territories and included members of Black, Japanese, and Mexican ancestry. Jim's club, the Black Juans, covered the J-Flats, Virgil, and Azusa territories and was all about cars and dance parties. Jim was considered a leader among the Black Juans and was nicknamed the General.

As violence ramped up between the east and west sides of Los Angeles, Jim joined the army to get away from the gangs. He served in the Signal Corps from 1958 to 1960, stationed first at Fort Huachuca in Arizona, where he was assigned as a driver in the motor pool at headquarters, and later at Fort MacArthur in San Pedro, California.

When he was honorably discharged, he went to work on an assembly line for the aerospace industry and became one of the first Asian Americans elected as shop steward (union representative) of United Aerospace Workers Local 887. He held this position for approximately ten years; his constituency was women and minority workers. His union role came to an end when the union members were considering whether to endorse as a presidential candidate either Eugene McCarthy, who wanted to end the war in Vietnam, or Lyndon B. Johnson, who as president had escalated it. When one of Jim's constituents said, "We ought to bomb them bastards just like we did in Hiroshima," Jim quit as steward and was subsequently laid off by the company.

While he was working in the aerospace industry, Jim had been attending college classes at night. He had enrolled at Los Angeles City College and transferred to California State University, Long Beach, where he received his bachelor's and master's degrees in social sciences. He was among the Asian American activists who came together in 1969 to form the group Oriental Concern. He also joined the Los Angeles Pioneer Project, whose purpose was to make life better for aging Issei. His activism continued with Asian Americans for Political Action, which opposed the war in Vietnam; the Anti-Eviction Task Force; and the Little Tokyo People's Rights Organization.

He organized the first Asian American studies class at California State University, Los Angeles, where he met Sue Embrey and became a key figure in forming the Manzanar Pilgrimage Committee. As a member of the Organization of Southland Asian American Organizations, he arranged its sponsorship of the first Manzanar Pilgrimage, which included delegates from UCLA; Occidental College; California State University, Long Beach; and California State University, Los Angeles. He was a founding member of the Los Angeles Community Coalition for Redress/Reparations and national treasurer for the National Coalition for Redress/Reparations. He ended up working with CSU Long Beach's Educational Opportunity Program for low-income students, taking care of the counseling and instructional programs. In 2019, at the age of eighty-three, Jim received the Sue Kunitomi Embrey Legacy Award.

Jack Shigeru **Matsuoka**, male, Nisei, Watsonville, California, incarcerated age 17, Salinas Assembly Center, Poston Relocation Center. Jack was born in Watsonville, California, on November 6, 1925, the older brother to a sister, Ruth, to Tonai Matsuoka and Tora (Matsukuma) Matsuoka. His father was in the laundry business and his mother was a midwife. He was an artist for the camp newspaper the *Poston Chronicle* and graduated from one of Poston's first high schools in 1943.

After his incarceration he relocated to Ohio and spent one semester at the Cleveland School of Art before he was drafted into the army. He joined the Military Intelligence Service (MIS) and went to the Military Intelligence Service Language School in Monterey, California. He was assigned to the Military Intelligence Corps in Japan and resided in occupied Tokyo from 1945 to 1961.

In 1956 he published a book of cartoons called *Rice-Paddy Daddy: The Adventures of G.I. "Bill" in Japan*. After his military service, he attended Hartnell College in Salinas, California, and then transferred to Keio and Sophia Universities in Japan, where he worked for the *Japan Times* and published political cartoons in the *Yomiuri Shimbun*. He then joined the *Manga Kyokai* as the only bilingual cartoonist on staff. He later moved to San Francisco and began working for the Marubeni-Iida Company, a trading house in the import-export business.

Jack became a professional cartoonist in 1969. He regularly published his comic strip, *Sensei*, in the newspaper *Hokubei Mainichi* during the 1960s and 1970s, and in other West Coast newspapers, such as the *San Jose Mercury News* and the *San Francisco Examiner*. *Sensei's* character was inspired by Koshin Ogui, a former minister at the Buddhist Church of San Francisco. Jack had a particular passion for caricatures of athletes and did cartoon work for the San Francisco Giants and the 49ers.

He was a member of the National Cartoonists Society and the Northern California Cartoonists Society; he won numerous awards and had many exhibitions of his work. In the 1970s he was the editorial cartoonist for the *Pacifica Tribune*, and in 1974 he published *Camp II, Block 211: Daily Life in an Internment Camp*, based on sketches from his Poston incarceration. In 2010 Mayor Luis Alejo honored him in his hometown of Watsonville, and when Alejo was elected to the California State Assembly in 2012, he honored Jack again at the state capitol for educating children about the incarceration of Japanese Americans during World War II.

For his service during the Korean War, he received a Congressional Gold Medal along with all the soldiers of the 100th/442nd Regimental Combat Team and the MIS.

Misako "Micki" **Mayumi** (Honda), female, Nisei, Chula Vista, California, incarcerated age 15, Santa Anita Assembly Center, Poston Relocation Center. Micki was born in Huntington Park, California, on April 27, 1927, the third of seven children, to Kiyoji Mayumi and Tamio Mayumi of Mie Prefecture, Japan. Her family farmed fruits and vegetable crops in Chula Vista.

Micki graduated as salutatorian from Parker Valley High School in the Poston III concentration camp in 1945. She was a member of the Girl Scouts, the Junior League, and the basketball team. She was also a reporter for the Poston school newspaper, the *Hi-Times*.

After the war Micki's family moved to Ogden, Utah, for four years to work in a vegetable cannery before returning to San Diego to resume farming. She went to sewing school in Los Angeles and then worked as a seamstress. Soon after, she worked as a secretary for the City of Los Angeles and then for the Los Angeles Unified School District while still attending college. Eventually she earned her bachelor's degree from the University of Redlands. Micki received several awards for her superior work ethic; she was a senior secretary for many years.

Micki married Harry K. Honda, the longtime editor (1952–82) of the *Pacific Citizen*, the newspaper of the JACL. She and Harry were dedicated to Japanese American civil rights causes such as redress and preserving cultural awareness within the community. They were founding members of the Downtown JACL chapter's 1,000 Club and the Japanese American National Museum. They were lifelong active parishioners at Maryknoll Catholic Church in Little Tokyo. For her many years of volunteer service at the Keiro Nursing Home in Boyle Heights, Micki was a recipient of their Kansha Award.

She was also very involved in numerous national and international Japanese American conventions and associations, with a special interest in Latin America, the *Rafu Shimpo*, Nisei festivals, historical societies, Poston reunions, veterans organizations, social service and community development groups, and the Seabrook Educational and Cultural Center.

Most of all, Micki cherished volunteering at her daughter's schools and showing her grandchildren her favorite places in Little Tokyo.

Kunisaku "Kay" **Mineta**, male, Issei, San Jose, California, incarcerated age 54, Santa Anita Assembly Center, Heart Mountain Relocation Center. Kay was born in the village of Shimizu, Sunto District, Shizuoka Prefecture, Japan, on October 3, 1888, the son of Shigetaro Mineta and Saku (Ono) Mineta. He left Japan in 1902 at age fourteen on a ship to meet his uncle in Salinas, California, but he mistakenly got off the ship in Seattle, Washington. It took him two years to work his way from Seattle to Salinas where he could finally connect with his uncle.

His uncle forced him, as a teenager, to become a first-grade student in elementary school in order to learn English. Then Kay started working for the Spreckels Sugar Company near Salinas. Around 1910 the company set up a sugar beet operation in San Martin, just south of San Jose, and the sugar company moved him to the San Martin location.

By early 1914, at age twenty-five, he was farming 140 acres of land that he had leased in partnership with an American citizen; this allowed him to farm the land despite the provisions of the California Alien Land Law, which forbade him from owning the land himself. That year his picture bride wife, Kane Watanabe, arrived from Yokohama, Kanagawa Prefecture, Japan, and they began their married life together.

Kay contracted influenza at the onset of the worldwide Spanish flu pandemic in 1917 and spent a number of months in the Santa Clara county hospital. As a result, he was not able to return to the strenuous work of farming, so he moved to San Jose and undertook a number of odd jobs, including work as an interpreter in the local court. Then in 1920 he was asked if he would like to go into the insurance business, and the Mineta Insurance Agency was launched in San Jose.

In 1928 he bought a parcel of land in the name of his attorney, J. B. Peckham, who held land titles for the benefit of foreigners such as Kay. On this parcel he built a Spanish-style stucco house, in which he and Kane raised five children, including his son Norman, who later became secretary of commerce under President Bill Clinton and secretary of transportation under President George W. Bush.

After Pearl Harbor was attacked, the state insurance commissioner suspended the licenses of all insurance agents of Japanese descent, shutting down the insurance agency that Kay had owned for more than twenty years. The family's savings accounts in the Yokohama Specie Bank were confiscated. In 1943 he was able to leave camp early and took a job in Chicago teaching Japanese to US Army soldiers at a University of Chicago army training program. After the war Kay, Kane, and their youngest son, Norman, returned to San Jose, and Kay reopened his insurance agency. In 1956, after Norman was discharged from his army service in the Korean War, his father welcomed him as a colleague in the Mineta Insurance Agency. Together they were actively involved as leaders in the San Jose community.

The Honorable Norman "Norm" Yoshio **Mineta**, male, Nisei, San Jose, California, incarcerated age 10, Santa Anita Assembly Center, Heart Mountain Relocation Center. Norm was born in San Jose, California, on November 12, 1931, the youngest of five children, to Kunisaku "Kay" Mineta and Kane (Watanabe) Mineta (see his father's biography above).

When the war was over, the Mineta family returned to San Jose, where Norm's father resumed his insurance business. The family was able to move back into their home because a local attorney had held it for them during the war. Norm attended San Jose High School, where he was elected student body president before graduating in 1949. He then graduated from the University of California, Berkeley, majoring in business. He participated in the ROTC program and then served as an intelligence officer with the US Army in Japan during the Korean War from 1953 to 1956. Following his military service, he returned to San Jose and worked for his father.

Norm became involved in the JACL and the local Japanese American Methodist church. He was appointed to the San Jose Human Relations Commission in 1962 and then to the municipal Housing Authority Board in 1966. He was elected to the San Jose City Council after serving briefly in an appointed position. Then, in 1971, he was elected mayor of San Jose, the first Asian Pacific American to serve as mayor in a major American city.

In 1974, Norm was elected to the US House of Representatives for

California's Thirteenth District, the first Democrat to win that district in thirty years and the first Japanese American from the mainland to be elected to Congress. Over his twenty-two years of service, he sponsored or co-sponsored 479 bills, including the Americans with Disabilities Act of 1990 and the Intermodal Surface Transportation Efficiency Act of 1991. He was appointed to the position of Democratic deputy whip of the Ninety-Seventh Congress and became a member of the Democratic Steering and Policy Committee. He also served as chair of the House Public Works and Transportation Committee (1992–94), the Aviation Subcommittee (1981–86), and the Surface Transportation Subcommittee (1989–91). In 1994 he co-founded the Congressional Asian Pacific American Caucus and served as its first chair.

Norm played a crucial leadership role in the passage of the Civil Liberties Act of 1988. As one of four Japanese American legislators, he worked closely with community advocates and lobbied his fellow members of Congress throughout the lengthy legislative process leading up to the vote on House bill H.R. 442 on September 17, 1987, a date he selected because it marked the two hundredth anniversary of the signing of the US Constitution.

Following his congressional service, Norm served as vice president of Lockheed Martin Corporation, an aeronautical engineering company, and chairman of the National Civil Aviation Review Commission. In 2000, at the end of his second term, President Bill Clinton appointed Norm as his secretary of commerce, making him the first Asian American to serve in a presidential cabinet. After President George W. Bush took office in 2001, Norm became his secretary of transportation. During the 9/11 attack, he ordered all civil aircraft over US airspace to land immediately after the third plane flew into the Pentagon. He then instructed all airlines to refrain from racial profiling against Middle Eastern or Muslim passengers. Over the next year the newly formed Transportation Security Administration (TSA) was placed under his department, and his team oversaw its mobilization before the TSA moved to the Department of Homeland Security in 2003. Norm served in President Bush's cabinet for over five years and resigned in 2006, having been the longest-serving secretary in the department's history.

After leaving the cabinet post, he became vice-chairman of Hill+Knowlton Strategies, a strategic global planning firm. In 2010 he joined L&L Energy as its vice-chairman.

In 2002 the San Jose Airport was renamed the Norman Y. Mineta San Jose International Airport, and San Jose State University named the Mineta Transportation Institute after him. California State Route 85 was also renamed in his honor. President Bush awarded him with the Presidential Medal of Freedom in 2006. A year later he was given the Grand Cordon of the Order of the Rising Sun by the government of Japan. He also received the Distinguished Medal of Honor for Lifetime Achievement and Public Service from the Japanese American National Museum in 2012. He has received two Immigrant Heritage Awards from the Angel Island Immigration Station Foundation: a Community Leadership Award in 2015 and a Visionary Award in 2017. Norm currently serves as the chairman of the board of trustees of the Japanese American National Museum in Los Angeles, California.

Chiyoko **Morita**, female, Nisei, Santa Clara County, California, incarcerated age 14, Salinas Assembly Center, Poston Relocation Center. Chiyoko was born in Gilroy, California, on September 8, 1928, the youngest of six children, to Kakuichi Morita and Nami (Sakai) Morita.

Mark Yutaka **Murakami**, male, Nisei, Multnomah County, Oregon, incarcerated age 32, Portland Assembly Center, Minidoka Relocation Center. Mark was born in Puuene on the island of Maui, Hawaii, on May 1, 1909, the third youngest of five children, to Shomatsu Murakami and Kinu (Yonemura) Murakami. Before the war, he worked in Honolulu at the territorial government Bureau of Conveyances.

On May 10, 1943, Mark left Minidoka to go to Camp Savage, Minnesota, where he worked on the Camp Savage staff for the Military Intelligence Service. He completed Military Intelligence Service Language School at Fort Snelling in 1944.

After the war, he returned to Hawaii and became an executive at the Island

Insurance Company. He was a member of Honpa Hongwanji Hawaii Betsuin and Kyodan (a Jodo Shinshu Buddhist temple), the United Japanese Society, Yamaguchi Kenjinkai (a community organization comprised of descendants from the Yamaguchi Prefecture on the island of Honshu in Japan), and Waki Cho Jin Kai (a club whose membership originated from the town of Waki in the Yamaguchi Prefecture of Japan). He also belonged to the Young Buddhist Association and Hui Aikane (a senior citizens club).

Sada (Hasegawa) **Murayama**, female, Issei, San Francisco, California, incarcerated age 41, Tule Lake Relocation Center. Sada was born in the city of Yokosuka in Kanagawa Prefecture, Japan, on July 12, 1901, the oldest of four children, to Tatsumo Hasegawa and Sono (Hanai) Hasegawa. She came to the United States at the age of six and grew up in Leavenworth, Washington, a town of about 1,200 people at the base of the Cascade mountains that also served as the regional location of the Great Northern Railway office. The railway facility had a railroad yard and a small sawmill that grew into the second largest sawmill in the state of Washington. Sada's father was the yard assistant foreman. Sada learned English quickly and soon became the Japanese community's translator so her father could communicate their needs to the Caucasian foreman.

The family stayed in Leavenworth until Sada was fifteen years old, when they moved to Seattle. She finished high school there and worked at a Frederick & Nelson department store before enrolling at the University of Washington. She majored in theater and was the leading lady in plays by Ibsen and Strindberg as part of the university's Free Theater Group. Then she met and fell in love with Takeshige Murayama, but he had to go back to Japan on family business for almost a year. Sada's mother didn't want her to marry Takeshige, but when he finally returned, Sada agreed to elope, on the condition that he wouldn't interfere with her work in the theater, even if they had children. She was nineteen years old when they married on June 19, 1920. Their first daughter, Constance Namiko Murayama, was born the following year. Sada left the university without even telling school officials, and the couple moved to San Francisco. Their second daughter, Joan Ikuka Murayama, was born on August 9, 1933, twelve and a half years later.

But Sada was unable to tolerate her husband, who expected her to conform to strict subservience. She found his attitudes to be suffocating and described feeling like "a plant growing until it breaks the pot in which it was confined." They decided to separate and Takeshige went back to Japan; they later divorced. At that time Constance was in her second year at the University of California, Berkeley, and Joan was six.

Sada's mother had been living with Sada since her father passed away in 1911, so throughout the thirties, Sada was the family's breadwinner. She worked at a number of department stores, including Gump's, and had raised the children as a single mother. At the time of the mass incarceration, they were all moved directly to the Tule Lake concentration camp. Sada accepted the law that forbid her to become an American citizen; she was born in Japan and that was that. She felt that she had no rights, aside from certain human rights, when her country was at war with the United States. She also accepted it in part because none of the Caucasians she knew treated her any differently from the way they treated anyone else. The PTA gave a going away party for her eight-year-old daughter; they gave her flowers and writing paper and pencils and urged her to write to them. When Sada was interviewed about it for a local newspaper, she said, "We will set an example for this country. We will make the desert bloom." Constance had graduated Phi Beta Kappa from Berkeley by then and after six months at camp, she left to get her master's degree in English and French literature at Smith College in Northampton, Massachusetts, where she had been offered a scholarship.

Tule Lake became a place for those loyal to Japan, so Sada, her mother, and Joan were transferred to Jerome. There Sada's theatrical skills were displayed in earnest. She organized the Little Nisei Theater and became its artistic manager; she selected the plays and directed almost all of its productions. She met and encouraged the future playwright Hiroshi Kashiwagi. Sada's influence in Nisei theater has been studied and written about in books and doctoral dissertations.

At both Tule Lake and Jerome, she was also asked to be director of the USO, a club for Nisei soldiers in basic training where Sada would recruit fifteen or more female "hostesses" to dance with the men. She wrote a patriotic USO column for the camp's newspaper every week. In 1944 she got leave clearance to work at the famous Stevens Hotel in Chicago (now the Hilton Chicago). She left her mother and daughter behind at camp to be looked after by Kenneth Yasuda, whom she had originally met at Tule Lake when they were both contributing to the *Tulean Dispatch*. Kenneth was a poet himself and a translator of Japanese poetry, and Sada encouraged him in his literary ambitions. Kenneth was also transferred to Jerome and would eventually marry Constance and become Sada's son-in-law.

Sada served as the executive house mother at the twenty-eight-story Stevens Hotel, which was considered the largest and most opulent hotel in the world when it opened in 1927. The hotel featured three thousand rooms, hand-painted frescoes, restaurants, shops, magnificent ballrooms and chandeliers, a bowling alley, a hospital, a special room for pets, and a miniature golf course called the Hi-Ho Golf Club on the roof. The hotel could produce 120 gallons of ice cream an hour.

In her role as executive house mother, Sada recruited young women from the camps to work as maids. She helped them make the beds and polish the silver. She eventually quit because she didn't like how the maids were being treated by management. After the war, Sada, her mother, and younger daughter went to New York City to live with her married brother who was an engineer. But she was barely getting by with her job at the Unitarian Services Committee, a human rights and social justice organization. She really wanted to go back to school. Then Kenneth Yasuda showed up. He had come to New York for graduate school in Japanese literature at Columbia University, and Knopf was about to publish his first book, *A Pepper-Pod: Classic Japanese Poems Together with Original Haiku*.

Kenneth made her an offer: Sada, her mother, and her daughter could live at his family's sixty-acre fruit ranch in California. A junior college was about ten miles away, and a bus could take Sada there. She could go to school, and during fruit season, she and her mother could work at the ranch wrapping fruit in tissue paper while being seated.

Sada agreed and after two years, she graduated from junior college and entered the University of California, Berkeley, as a junior, in her forties. During the summer she worked half-time at the university bookstore and half-time as a counselor for the students in the Honor Students Club. She received her bachelor's degree at forty-eight and went on to defy the thirty-five-year-old age limit to get into graduate school. Sada received her master's degree two years later in psychology and social work.

She then worked as a case worker in foster care for the Alameda County Welfare Department in Oakland for another fifteen years, with one year's leave of absence to travel around the world. When she retired, she went to live with Constance and Kenneth in Bloomington, Indiana, where he was a professor teaching in the East Asian Languages and Culture Department at Indiana University; Sada did volunteer work in geriatrics for the Bloomington Hospitality House.

Kimitomo "Kim" **Muromoto**, male, Nisei, King County, Washington, incarcerated age 19, Pinedale Assembly Center, Tule Lake Relocation Center. Kim was born in Bellevue, Washington, east of Lake Washington, on January 10, 1923, the middle boy of three children, to Gunsaburo Muromoto and Masu Muromoto. His parents, both of Okayama, Japan, were homesteaders and truck farmers in Hunts Point, Washington, and bought a farm in Clyde Hill in 1939. He went to Highland Grade School and attended Japanese-language school, but mostly he had to work on the family farm. On the morning of the attack on Pearl Harbor, he was headed to a holly farm to make wreaths. At the time his family was forcibly removed, the strawberry fields were ready to harvest. The Muromotos had to turn over the farm to a Caucasian friend, who harvested the crops and rented their house for the duration of the war. At Tule Lake Kim worked as a sweeper on a food truck and delivered food to different block kitchens. As soon as the opportunity presented itself, Kim applied for leave clearance and was sent to a Civilian Conservation Corps work camp in Weiser, Idaho, to harvest sugar beets.

In 1944 he was drafted into I Company, Third Battalion, 442nd Regimental

Combat Team, and was sent to France as one of the replacements for all the men who had been injured and killed during the rescue of the Lost Battalion. After he arrived, the company was sent to Italy to attack the Gothic Line. Kim was one of the men who had to climb the cliff face of Mount Folgorito.

In July 1946, Kim was in the group that received the Presidential Unit Citation and brought the regimental colors of the 100th/442nd RCT back to Washington, DC, to parade in front of President Harry S. Truman.

After the war he returned to the farm with his parents and eventually sold it. Kim then moved to South Bellevue, where he had a nursery for the next twenty-five years. He is married to Masako Muromoto; they had one son together and a son from her previous marriage.

Dollie Kimiko **Nagai** (Fukawa), female, Nisei, Fresno, California, incarcerated age 15, Fresno Assembly Center, Jerome Relocation Center. Dollie was born in Visalia, California, on May 15, 1927, the youngest of five girls, to Harry Nigoro Nagai and Shigeko (Yoshimatsu) Nagai. After the war she joined two of her sisters in Washington, DC, and graduated from Roosevelt High School. She attended Wilson Teachers College, earning a bachelor's degree in sociology. She eventually returned to California and worked for the Fresno County Welfare Department. She then went back to school for her master's degree in social work and became a medical and adoptions social worker for the Los Angeles County Department of Children and Family Services.

Mary Yuriko "Yuri" **Nakahara** (Kochiyama), female, Nisei, San Pedro, California, incarcerated age 21, Santa Anita Assembly Center, Jerome Relocation Center. Yuri was born in San Pedro, California, on May 19, 1921, to Seiichi Nakahara and Tsuma Tsuyako (Sawaguchi) Nakahara. She had a twin brother, Peter, and an older brother, Arthur. She grew up in an affluent, largely White neighborhood. She graduated from Compton Junior College in 1941. Within twenty-four hours of the bombing of Pearl Harbor, the FBI arrested her father, who had just had surgery for a stomach ulcer and was suffering complications from diabetes. He was detained for six weeks without medical care at the Terminal Island federal penitentiary and died the day after he was released.

Yuri, her mother, and her brothers were forcibly removed to the Santa Anita Assembly Center, where Yuri taught Sunday school and organized her students to write letters to Nisei soldiers. The group started out as a club of five high school girls who called themselves the Crusaders and met under the grandstands to write letters together. They began by writing to six soldiers, but by the time their membership grew to ninety Crusaders, they were writing to hundreds of Nisei soldiers. When Santa Anita closed and everyone moved to concentration camps, the Crusaders carried the idea with them and formed their own clubs at Poston, Topaz, Heart Mountain, Rohwer, and Jerome. From then on, especially around the holidays, the Crusaders were asked to write letters and postcards to more than three thousand active Nisei soldiers. Yuri would print excerpts of the letters they received back from the soldiers in her Jerome camp newspaper column, Nisei in Khaki. She met her future husband, Private William Kochiyama (see his biography), at the Jerome USO, an entertainment facility where Nisei troops from Camp Shelby (ten hours away by bus) would come to visit. Twice a month, women from Jerome and Rohwer were bussed to Camp Shelby for dances.

After the war Yuri moved to New York City, where she organized boycotts for better education in urban schools and became a passionate civil rights activist under her married name, Yuri Kochiyama. She participated in pro-tests sponsored by the Congress of Racial Equality, demanding jobs for Black and Puerto Rican workers, and was arrested, along with six hundred others, for blocking the entrance to a construction site. Malcolm X showed up at their hearing in Brooklyn on October 16, 1963, and she was immediately drawn to his call for Black liberation. In June 1964 she invited him (and he came) to one of her well-known weekend open houses to meet Japanese *hibakusha* (atomic bomb survivors).

On February 21, 1965, Yuri and her sixteen-year-old son were in the Audubon Ballroom, waiting to hear Malcolm X speak, when there was a burst of gunfire and she rushed to the stage. Yuri is shown in the famous *Life* magazine photograph kneeling beside the body of Malcolm X and cradling his head just after he was shot. After his assassination she became immersed in Black Power organizations and acted as a conduit between Asian American and civil rights movements.

When Ronald Reagan signed the Civil Liberties Act in 1988, Yuri leveraged that success to advocate for Black reparations.

Alice Natsuko **Nakamura** (Nishikawa), female, Nisei, Manteca, California, incarcerated age 17, Stockton Assembly Center, Rohwer Relocation Center. Alice was born in Acampo, California, on June 18, 1925, the fourth of seven children, to Sensuke "Sam" Nakamura and Waka (Nomura) Nakamura. After the war, she lived in Auburn, California, for forty-six years. She was a member of the Placer Buddhist Church in Penryn, California, and for over thirty years she worked as a psychiatric technician for Placer County.

George "Jobo" Ryoji **Nakamura**, male, Nisei, Berkeley, California, incarcerated age 35, Tule Lake Relocation Center. Jobo was born in Sacramento, California, on November 3, 1919, the oldest of three children, to Takichi Nakamura and Sikino (Yamasaki) Nakamura. His two younger sisters were Tami and Michiko. His Issei parents lost their ice cream parlor in Sacramento during the Depression, and his family worked in canneries and on farms in California to support themselves; later his father worked as a drug salesman. Because they had difficulty in making ends meet, his mother and sisters went back to Japan. The idea was that he and his father would stay in the United States and continue to work and build up savings.

Then World War II broke out. Jobo was a student at the University of California, Berkeley, when he and his father were incarcerated. At Tule Lake, Jobo served as editor for eleven issues of the *Tulean Dispatch* newspaper between August 1942 and July 1943. He published articles on camp life, short stories, and poetry. After the war he resettled in Chicago, earned a college degree, and began writing for the *Pacific Citizen* and the *Chicago Shimpo*. He later returned to California, where he became known as a travel writer and journalist for the San Francisco newspaper *Hokubei Mainichi*.

Jobo did not see his mother and sisters again until he visited them in Japan in 1952 for two months after a separation of seventeen years. He wrote about it for the travel magazine *Holiday*. His mother and sisters refused to come back with him to America, and he did not want to resettle in Japan. The postwar destruction of Japan was devastating. He was caught in a no-man's-land between two cultures. His heart "fluttered red, white and blue" at the sight of the American air base near Osaka, at a Japanese baseball game, and at the sound of "Auld Lang Syne" played by "an American-style jazz band" in Hiroshima and sung by a Tokyo cabaret singer named Keiko-san, whose voice sounded like "the tinkle of little bells." Jobo wrote, "But I had to remind myself that Keiko-san was not real. She was only my vague dream of a far-away land." Then he came back to the United States and to his job as a virus technician at the University of California, Berkeley. He found himself to be "far lonelier" than he had been before he left, especially when he was on his way home from his "workbench each evening" after having "a glum meal in the little hamburger stand patronized by impecunious college students and single, lonely men." Jobo could see ahead of him only "an estranged life in the United States." But he stayed and married Kazuko Nakamura in 1957, and they lived in Gardena, California.

May Kimiko **Nakamura** (Sasaki), female, Nisei, Seattle, Washington, incarcerated age 7, Puyallup Assembly Center, Minidoka Relocation Center. May was born in Seattle, Washington, on May 13, 1935, the youngest of five children, to Saiji "Henry" Nakamura and Yoshie (Mayeda) Nakamura. May was raised in Seattle's Japantown, where her family owned an apartment and the Nakamura Grocery Store. When they returned to Seattle after their incarceration, she continued her education at Bailey Gatzert Elementary School and Washington Junior High School. But her parents' properties were gone, so they found work as a hotel cook and a maid. Eventually they bought Nippon Kan Hall and ran it as a low-income hotel.

May was valedictorian at her graduation from Garfield High School and graduated cum laude from the University of Washington in 1957 with a bachelor's degree in education. She taught in the Highline School District and then in 1971 moved to the Seattle School District to teach in the Ethnic Cultural Heritage Program. She was promoted to administrator of staff development, while earning her master's degree in curriculum at Seattle University, and worked for the district for twenty-five years. She was active in the Seattle chapter of the JACL during the redress movement and became the chapter's president in 1987.

As a volunteer with the Nisei Veterans Committee (NVC), she developed the NVC Speaker's Bureau and was elected chairperson of the Education Outreach Program. She coordinated speaking engagements for veterans to tell the history of the incarceration and share their stories about the bravery of the Nisei soldiers and the Military Intelligence Service at public schools, universities, libraries, military bases, and other organizations.

After her retirement she took ukulele lessons and became a charter member of the Aloha Band, which played for many senior centers. The University of Washington gave her its Distinguished Alumnus Award in 2009.

Yoshio "Yosh" **Nakamura**, male, Nisei, El Monte, California, incarcerated age 17, Tulare Assembly Center, Gila River Relocation Center. Yosh was born in Rosemead, California, on June 30, 1925, the second of four children, to Kanesuke Nakamura and Kuni (Kawasaki) Nakamura. Yosh's mother died of breast cancer when he was almost six. The family moved to a farm in El Monte; Yosh was attending El Monte High School when Pearl Harbor was attacked. To prove his loyalty, he joined the 442nd Regimental Combat Team in 1943 and was called up as a replacement a year later. He was an ammunition carrier and participated in the battle to break the Gothic Line. For his actions he received a Bronze Star. All soldiers of the 100th/442nd RCT and the Military Intelligence Service received a Congressional Gold Medal on November 2, 2011.

While on a brief leave in Florence, Italy, he was able to visit the museums. He was drawn to watercolors, and the art he saw inspired him to become an artist himself. When he returned to the United States, he earned a bachelor's degree in fine arts from the University of Southern California in 1952. But no one would give him a teaching job because of his Japanese ancestry. He got a break and was hired to teach in the Whittier Union High School District after meeting the district supervisor, a trustee of his wife's alma mater, the University of Redlands.

He completed his master's degree and taught art at Whittier High School for the next eleven years. The Whittier chapter of the General Federation of Women's Clubs in the San Gabriel Valley District named him Teacher of the Year in 1960. Three years later he moved to the newly formed Rio Hondo College to become one of the school's first three instructors and its first fine arts department chair. He taught there for the next twenty-nine years, eventually becoming dean and vice president of community services and institutional development.

Recognized as an American treasure and hero by the Los Angeles County Board of Supervisors for his military service, he has also been active on Whittier's Art in Public Places Committee and the Cultural Arts Commission. His artwork is in more than 175 public, private, and corporate collections. Joe Vinatieri, the mayor of Whittier, called him a "Whittier icon." On November 22, 2016, he, along with four other veterans, were presented with the French Legion of Honor medal, which is bestowed on American veterans of World War I and II by the consulate general of France. The medal is given "in tribute to the French people's gratitude for those who risked and gave their lives defending liberty." On June 25, 2018, Yosh was one of eight veterans, all over ninety years old, who were honored in the senate chamber of the state capitol in Sacramento in a ceremony commemorating the seventy-fifth anniversary of the formation of the 100th/442nd RCT.

Theodore "Ted" Katsuyoshi **Nakashima**, male, Nisei, Seattle, Washington, incarcerated age 30, Puyallup Assembly Center, Tule Lake Relocation Center. Ted was born in Seattle, Washington, on August 19, 1911, the second youngest of four children, to Katsuharu Nakashima of samurai lineage from

Tottori, Japan, and Suzu (Toma) Nakashima. Suzu served for six years under Takeko Horikawa, official court taster for the Emperor Meiji, until her parents insisted she leave the court to marry. A fortune teller advised her not to marry a wealthy man but to marry "a poor man at a distance." Suzu was one of the first picture brides; she and Katsuharu married on the ship before it docked in Seattle in 1901. Katsuharu found work as a manager for the Asia Trading Company and then later worked for years as an editor and journalist for *Taihoku Nippon*, a Japanese-language newspaper.

Ted was an architectural draftsman at the University of Washington, working on a defense housing project design for the US Army Corps of Engineers, when the forced removal took place. He still had 391 defense homes to detail and was allowed to keep working on them at camp at the massively reduced pay of twenty dollars a month. He later returned to the field of architecture and apprenticed in the state of Washington to earn his credentials. He married Masako "Mako" Ida and had one daughter, Vicki Ida Nakashima. The family lived in Spokane, Bothell, and the Hood Canal community in the state of Washington.

Ted's brother, George, was considered a father of the craft movement and became one of the leading innovators of furniture design in the twentieth century. The emperor of Japan honored George with the Order of the Sacred Treasure in 1983. George's house, studio, workshop, and Conoid Studio in New Hope, Pennsylvania, are listed on the US National Register of Historic Places.

Richard "Dick" **Nishi**, male, Nisei, Yolo County, California, incarcerated age 21, Turlock Assembly Center, Gila River Relocation Center. Dick was born in Florin, California, on June 7, 1921, the second oldest of seven children, to Shizuo Nishi and Kikuyo (Asano) Nishi. His father was a ranch operator. After the war Dick worked as a civil engineer for Caltrans (California Department of Transportation) for thirty-seven years. He met his wife, Alice Shigezumi, who served as a trustee on the school board in Davis, California, and on the board of the Presbyterian Church USA. He was a member of the Area IV Agency on Aging, Yolo County Grand Jury, Davis Asians for Racial Equality

(DARE), the JACL, and the Davis Human Relations Commission.

In 1995 he received a Thong Hy Huynh Memorial Award for Lifetime Achievement from the City of Davis Human Relations Commission that honors community members whose actions exemplify the goals of diversity, community, social justice, and equal rights. The award is given annually in memory of the racially motivated stabbing death of seventeen-year-old Davis High School student Thong Hy Huynh on May 4, 1983.

The Nishi family owned 46.9 acres of land just outside Davis, California, which the family farmed for nearly fifty years. The property was sold for development in 2005 and the Nishi Gateway Housing Project was born. The plan to provide affordable housing, primarily for students at the University of California, Davis, consists of 700 rental units, with a total of 2,200 beds. The project was initially approved by Davis voters in 2018 but remained in litigation pertaining to its environmental impact until April 2, 2020, when the last appeal of the Yolo Supreme Court was withdrawn, paving the way for the project to move forward.

Elizabeth Aiko (Takahashi) **Nishikawa**, female, Nisei, Los Angeles, California, incarcerated age 31, Manzanar Reception Center, Manzanar Relocation Center. Elizabeth was born in Berkeley, California, on March 2, 1911, the seventh of twelve children, to Chiyokichi Takahashi and Shizuko (Higuchi) Takahashi. Her father was introduced to her mother at the Friends School, a Quaker school in Tokyo where she had been a student and a teacher. They were married in a Quaker meetinghouse in Tokyo before coming to Oakland in 1901, where her father had established a tailor shop. All their children were college graduates; five became optometrists and one a professor of plant pathology. Elizabeth lost a sister (Anna) in an auto accident and a brother (David), who was in the US Army Medical Corps, to the war.

Her father retired in 1926 and devoted the rest of his life to growing miniature Japanese gardens and trees. He won over sixty awards, including several first-place prizes at state fairs and garden shows. His gardens and trees were exhibited at the 1939 and 1940 Golden Gate International Expositions.

Her mother was a member of the University of California Mothers Club and the Friends Church.

Elizabeth went to Berkeley High School in Berkeley, California, and then attended and graduated from Whittier College. President Richard Nixon was one of her classmates. In 1936 she earned a master's degree from the Pacific School of Religion, Berkeley, and became a social worker. She married Philip Takeshi Nishikawa, a native of Hiroshima, Japan, a gardener and a Protestant minister. In Manzanar she organized the program to teach English as a second language. When the incarceration centers were closing down, she went on a speaking tour, with a Caucasian escort, to appeal for jobs and scholarships for the returning Japanese Americans. Although she was only four feet eight she had a caring heart and a powerful voice.

Rhoda Akiko **Nishimura** (Iyoya), female, Nisei, Berkeley, California, incarcerated age 15, Tanforan Assembly Center, Topaz Relocation Center. Rhoda was born in Los Angeles, California, on November 14, 1925, the eldest and only girl in a family with four brothers, to Masamoto Nishimura and Kimiko (Ishihara) Nishimura; one brother was disabled and died when he was six. Kimiko's parents divorced when she was young, and she chose to be with her father—which perhaps is why she ended up at a strict Shinto boarding school. She decided to become a Christian after attending a Christian friend's funeral and came upon a Salvation Army street corner meeting. But she couldn't be a Christian while still attending the Shinto school, so she left to become a secretary at Mitsubishi, one of the first women hired by the company. Then, at the age of twenty-one, she joined the Salvation Army, which sent her to a training school in San Francisco. She taught at the Salvation Army orphanage, and also learned how to play the guitar and the trumpet and put together a brass band.

Masamoto, Rhoda's father, was born in Tottori, Japan, but graduated from high school in Oakland, California. By that time he was working for *his* father, Kumaichiro Shinoda. They had different last names because her grandfather was adopted by the Shinoda family in order to carry on the Shinoda family name. Meanwhile, one of her Nishimura uncles didn't have any children, so her father was adopted to carry on the Nishimura family name. Consequently, Masamoto has the Nishimura name, but his seven other siblings (five brothers and two sisters) all have the last name of Shinoda.

After high school her father went to work for her grandfather's new family business, the San Lorenzo Nursery, but Masamoto left the job when he felt a calling to go into the ministry. He attended Northwest Nazarene College, a Bible college in Nampa, Idaho. On his way home from Idaho, he met a Free Methodist missionary and moved to Los Angeles to start his missionary work, which at the time focused on generating financial aid for victims of the 1923 earthquake in Japan. Rhoda's mother was doing the same thing for the Salvation Army, which is how she met Rhoda's father. He was also studying for his master's degree at the University of Southern California School of Religion.

Later Rhoda's father launched the Berkeley Free Methodist Church; he was minister there for seventeen years before the mass removal. His church attracted people in need, such as gamblers and women with children out of wedlock. He had a prison ministry at San Quentin, where he would lead a service for Japanese-speaking inmates once a month. Some were released to him on parole, and he would find jobs for them in the community; their first meal would often be at her father's house. In addition to assisting the church, her mother took *sumie* (ink painting) lessons from established artists Taro Yashima and Chiura Obata and became a gifted calligrapher.

Then the Depression hit and her father had to sell his gold fillings to buy shoes for her and her brothers. But the San Lorenzo Nursery, still owned by Rhoda's grandfather, was doing well and grew to become one of the most successful floral companies in the country, which is still true today. In fact, in 1929, at the height of the Depression, Kumaichiro Shinoda gifted a portion of his nursery property to the San Lorenzo Holiness Church, including a two-story former roadside inn that served as church and parsonage for thirty years. Another one of Shinoda's sons, the Reverend Daniel Shinoda, would eventually become pastor there.

Rhoda had been at Berkeley High School for just a year and a half before the war broke out. At Topaz she was vice president of the student body and graduated at the top of her class. The National Japanese American Student Relocation Council arranged for a scholarship for Rhoda to go to Vassar College. She was also able to get jobs at a lab in Albany, New York, and at the YWCA as a group leader for girls.

Her parents followed her from camp to New York, where her mother worked as a clerk in the records room of Mount Sinai Hospital and published a collection of writings called *Hato* (*The Doves*), which included the tanka poetry of Iku Umegaki Uchida, the mother of writer Yoshiko Uchida. Rhoda's father remained active in the church with other former incarcerees in New York City.

Rhoda graduated from Vassar in three years and two summer semesters. After the war the family returned to California, and she went to the University of California, Berkeley, for graduate work in biology. She then went to Chicago and became a parish worker at the Ellis Community Center, which served Japanese Americans; she also worked in the pathology department at the University of Chicago, where she received her master's degree in education. She then returned to Los Angeles, where her father was a minister at the Los Angeles Free Methodist Church. Her mother wrote two books, *Izumi no uta* (*Songs of a Spring*) and *Wakaba* (*Young Leaves*), and sold homemade *omochi* (pounded rice cakes), all to raise money for a building fund earmarked for senior citizens.

At this point, Rhoda was working full-time in the pathology department at UCLA and helped out at the West Adams Christian Church. She married Nicholas Mineo Iyoya, an ordained minister, and spent the rest of her life raising six children and working for the church, first at Long Beach, then New York, then San Francisco for nine years and Monterey for another nine. Her husband was then called to Iwakuni, Yamaguchi Prefecture, Japan, to become director of the Serendipity Community Center outside of a US naval base. Rhoda worked with the women and young people from the community and helped to bridge the cultural gap between the United States and Japan.

Then they received the news that their son John, nicknamed Bodie, had committed suicide at college. He'd gone to Vassar, Rhoda's alma mater, and wanted to teach art to children. In his memory, the Education Department at Vassar set up an annual exhibition of children's art from the Poughkeepsie elementary schools and awarded a prize to the Vassar student most closely emulated what John had stood for: bringing the love of art and children together. Both the show and the prize have continued to this day. In 2020, Vassar College held the thirty-fifth annual John Iyoya Children's Art Show at the Palmer Gallery, accompanied by the annual John Iyoya Prize.

Michiko "Michi" (**Nishiura**) Weglyn, female, Nisei, Brentwood, California, incarcerated age 15, Turlock Assembly Center, Gila River Relocation Center. Michi was born in Stockton, California, on November 29, 1926, the older of two daughters, to Tomojiro Nishiura and Misao (Yuwasa) Nishiura. Misao was a picture bride who arrived in America in 1922. Michi's parents established themselves as tenant farmers in the San Joaquin valley, growing cantaloupes, tomatoes, cucumbers, and apricots. An outstanding student at Liberty Union High School, Michi won an American Legion citizenship award in 1940 and first prize in a Rotary Club essay competition on the US Constitution.

During her family's three-year incarceration, Michi continued to be an exemplary student leader at Butte High School and graduated in 1944. She organized and led a Girl Scout troop, served as president of the Forensics League, and continued to win essay and oratorical contests. As Girls League president, she organized a daylong Girls League Convention at the concentration camp, attended by over five hundred girls from throughout Arizona.

Michi was accepted to Mount Holyoke College in Massachusetts with a full scholarship from the National Japanese American Student Relocation Council. At college she became interested in set and costume design but was forced to withdraw from school when she contracted tuberculosis in December 1945. She then joined her family in Bridgeton, New Jersey, where they'd resettled to work at Seabrook Farms, a frozen food plant that employed other Japanese Americans and Japanese Latin Americans. Michi continued taking classes, first at Barnard College in New York City in 1947 and then at the

New York Fashion Academy in 1948. During this time she met German Jewish national Walter Matthys Weglyn, who had escaped Nazi Germany as a teenager and lived in hiding in Holland for five years. They married in 1950.

By 1952, Michi was working as a costume designer in show business, designing costumes for the ice shows at the RKO Roxy Theatre, for productions at nightclubs such as the famed Copacabana, and later for television and musical variety shows starring Tony Bennett, Patti Page, Dinah Shore, and Perry Como.

When *The Perry Como Show* moved its production to Los Angeles in 1966, Michi briefly ran her own costume rental and manufacturing company, but in the political environment of the 1960s civil rights movement, she began turning her energies toward understanding the causes of the incarceration. She undertook seven years of research at the National Archives, the Franklin D. Roosevelt Presidential Library, and the New York Public Library, uncovering documents that refuted the federal government's claim that the incarceration of Japanese Americans was a "military necessity." Her research revealed other shocking aspects of the Roosevelt administration's wartime actions, including the government's detention of Japanese Latin Americans with the intent to use them as prisoners in exchange for POWs held by Japan.

She published her research in 1975 in her bestselling book *Years of Infamy: The Untold Story of America's Concentration Camps*, which received widespread critical acclaim and attracted national attention to the constitutional travesty of the wartime experience of Japanese Americans. Her book shed light on little-known aspects of the incarceration, such as the protests at Tule Lake and those who had renounced their US citizenship. Her work provided the spark for the movement within the Japanese American community to seek redress for wartime injustices.

Among the honors she received were honorary degrees from Mount Holyoke College, Hunter College, and California State Polytechnic University, Pomona, which in 2003 established the Michi and Walter Weglyn Endowed Chair of Multicultural Studies to continue the legacy of her substantial contribution to civil rights.

Kinya **Noguchi**, male, Nisei, Kent, Washington, incarcerated age 14, Pinedale Assembly Center, Tule Lake Relocation Center. Kinya was born in Kent, Washington, on November 16, 1927, the fourth of seven children, to Sampei Noguchi and Yasume (Tanaka) Noguchi. He served in the Korean War until his honorable discharge in 1954. Three years later he became Sacramento County's first Asian deputy sheriff and retired as a lieutenant after twenty-six years. Through the Veterans of Foreign Wars Post 8985, he and other veterans began visiting schools and educating students on the history of the Japanese American incarceration.

Fumiko (Ito) **Ogawa**, female, Issei, Los Angeles, California, incarcerated age 39, Pomona Assembly Center, Heart Mountain Relocation Center. Fumiko was born in Nagoya, Aichi Prefecture, Japan, on July 13, 1903, one of ten children. She nursed victims of the catastrophic 1923 earthquake while a student at Tokyo's prestigious St. Luke's College of Nursing. She married William Yukichi Ogawa in an arranged marriage on May 14, 1927, the same year she graduated from nursing school, in Nagoya, Japan.

William was born in the town of Shima, Mie Prefecture, Japan, on January 19, 1888. He completed his education, and in 1910, at the age of twenty-two, he left Japan for America. He spent a few years in Chicago, then traveled through Europe, and then returned to see other sites in the US, including the Grand Canyon, which may have triggered his interest in geology and paleontology. He supported himself by teaching in Japanese-language schools, then returned to Japan to marry Fumiko. He and Fumiko arrived in San Francisco in May 1928. Fumiko gave birth to their first child there. The couple moved to Los Angeles two years later and Fumiko had two more sons.

During the Depression years, William worked as a houseboy, a cook, and a babysitter. Fumiko, as a registered nurse, became the breadwinner of the family. She worked predominantly at the Japanese Hospital in Boyle Heights, Los Angeles, which was built with the pooled savings of five Japanese American physicians to serve a community of Japanese immigrants who were routinely denied care at public hospitals. (The Japanese Hospital has since been declared a historic-cultural monument by the Los Angeles City Council.) In early 1934, they both taught for two years in Compton, California. Then William bought a hotel on Stanford Avenue and managed it himself. He sold the hotel at a loss when they were forcibly removed.

After the war, Fumiko and William returned to Los Angeles, and William used their savings to buy the infamous Hotel Central at 310 Clay Street. He was eventually forced to sell the property to the Community Redevelopment Agency of the City of Los Angeles to pave the way for the 133-acre Bunker Hill urban renewal project. From then on, William decided to pursue his passions: fossil-hunting, photography, and oil painting under the tutelage of Taro Yashima. He organized fossil-hunting trips in Utah with his sons and in 1951, he established the Ogawa Memorial Earth Science Group and became a member of the Palaeontological Society of Japan. His interest in paleontology led to William's acquisition of an entire Allosaurus skeleton assembled by James R. Madsen Jr., a curator at the Natural History Museum of Utah, which William donated to the National Museum of Nature and Science in Tokyo, Japan. An Allosaurus and a Camptosaurus were also acquired by William at his own expense a year later and donated to the Bunka Center in Kagoshima, Kagoshima Prefecture, Japan. For these gifts, the Imperial Palace conferred the Kunsho medal or the Order of the Sacred Treasure with Gold and Silver Rays. He was honored at a testimonial dinner at the Biltmore Hotel in Los Angeles.

Upon returning from Heart Mountain, Fumiko would occasionally work for the Japanese Hospital and also she started writing poetry but only in Japanese calligraphy. She joined the *Nanka Totsukani* (Southern California) circle of tanka writers under the leadership of their mentor, Master Yoshihiko Tomari. It was through the poetry circle that Fumiko met Lucille M. Nixon, a translator of poems written originally in Japanese calligraphy. Lucille published one of Fumiko's tankas in the book *Sounds from the Unknown: A Collection of Japanese-American Tanka*, a collection she edited and translated with Tomoe Tana. The collection is unique in that each poem appears in three versions on the same page: the original Japanese calligraphy, the Romanized version of the Japanese language, and in English. The English translation of Fumiko's tanka in this collection is included in this book.

Japan's Imperial Palace New Year Poetry Party, the highest honor for tanka excellence, has taken place in Japan for more than a thousand years, but only since 1884 have commoners been able to enter. Out of 30,000 entries from all over the world, on December 26, 1956, fifteen award-winning poets were invited to the Imperial Poetry Party to be held at the Imperial Palace in Tokyo on January 11, 1957. Thirteen of the poets were Japanese living in Japan. Fumiko was a naturalized American citizen cited as the best Japanese national poet outside of Japan. An elementary education consultant with the Palo Alto school system, Lucille was the first American in history not of Japanese descent to receive an invitation.

The *Palo Alto Times* immediately called upon President Eisenhower, Senator Thomas Kuchel from California, and the US State Department to pay Fumiko and Lucille's way to be given this honor in person. The government offered to pay Lucille's way but not Fumiko's. Lucille had to insist that Fumiko receive the same aid, and the government officials finally agreed.

So Lucille and Fumiko attended the New Year Poetry Party at the Imperial Palace together. Both of them had the honor of hearing their thirty-one-syllable poems chanted in the form of a medieval-style chorus in the presence of Emperor Hirohito and Empress Kojun, staged according to century-old tradition of pageantry, by five Japanese poet laureates.

Fumiko was accomplished in various Japanese art forms. She played the koto, the thirteen-string Japanese floor harp; studied flower-arranging; and achieved a teacher's rank in conducting the Japanese tea ceremony. Each year she also enjoyed observing the traditional Japanese holiday customs on New Year's day, displaying dolls as part of the Girls' Day celebration on March 3, and displaying armor as part of the Boys' Day celebration on May 5.

Louise Yoshiko **Ogawa** (Watanabe), female, Nisei, San Diego, California, incarcerated age 18, Santa Anita Assembly Center, Poston Relocation Center. Louise was born in Rialto, California, on April 15, 1924, the only daughter, together with two stepchildren, to Zenichi Ogawa and Hisayo (Kawakami) Ogawa. As a teenager during the incarceration, she was a regular correspondent with San Diego librarian Clara Breed. During the summer of 1944, Louise left camp to take a job in Chicago. For two years she worked in the correspondence department of the publisher A. C. McClurg & Company. When her father returned to San Diego, she joined him there and became a clerk for the purchasing department of the City of San Diego. In 1947 she married Richard Watanabe, and together they raised a family in San Diego. Louise was reunited with Miss Breed and other friends from Poston at the 1991 Poston reunion.

Molly Moriko **Ohashi** (Yamamoto), female, Issei, Tulare County, California, incarcerated age 15, Poston Relocation Center. Molly was born in Olympia, Washington, on November 26, 1927, one of five children, to Ryotaro Ohashi and Sawa (Hamasaki) Ohashi. Her parents were farmers. She left camp to go to the Pennsylvania College of Women, where a scholarship was arranged for her by Anna Jane Goodwin, president of the YWCA on campus. The YWCA had asked the entire student body to vote for permission to accept her. The vote was unanimous—not a single dissenting vote. She graduated from the University of California, Los Angeles, on June 20, 1954, with a bachelor's degree in psychology.

Paul Tsutomu **Ohtaki**, male, Nisei, Bainbridge Island, Washington, incarcerated age 18, Owens Valley Reception Center, Manzanar Relocation Center. Paul was born in the Winslow neighborhood of Bainbridge Island, Washington, on September 29, 1924, the younger of two sons, to George Ohtaki and Lora Ohtaki. Paul was a high school student working as a janitor for the local newspaper *Bainbridge Review* when he and his family were ordered off the island. Walt Woodward, publisher of the *Bainbridge Review*, asked him to write a weekly column about the daily lives of Bainbridge Island Japanese Americans in camp, with the goal of easing their transition when they returned to Bainbridge Island after the war's end. In 2001, Paul compiled the stories of his connection with Woodward and their letters in an anthology called *It Was the Right Thing to Do!*

Paul enlisted in the Military Intelligence Service and served in the Pacific theater during the latter part of World War II. He met his wife, Katherine (Kitty), at Macalester College in Saint Paul, Minnesota. After graduating from Macalester, he and Kitty moved to San Francisco, where Paul started Diversified Business Forms, a printing business.

Miné **Okubo**, female, Nisei, Berkeley, California, incarcerated age 30, Tanforan Assembly Center, Topaz Relocation Center. Miné was born in Riverside, California, on June 27, 1912, one of seven children, to Tametsugu and Miyoko (Kato) Okubo. She graduated from Riverside Polytechnic High School and attended Riverside Junior College (now called Riverside City College). In 1933 she was awarded a fellowship by the University of California, Berkeley, where she graduated with a bachelor's degree in art and a master's degree in art and anthropology. She received Berkeley's Bertha Taussig Traveling Art Fellowship in 1938, which allowed her to paint, travel, and study in Europe for two years. In Paris she studied with the avant-garde painter Fernand Léger, but when the war broke out in 1939, she was forced to leave the country and give up the last six months of her fellowship. She barely got on board the last ship from Bordeaux, France, to the United States.

Back home, she was commissioned to create mosaic and fresco murals for the army at Fort Ord. She also painted murals at the Oakland Hospitality House with the Federal Art Project, in conjunction with the Works Progress Administration. She was then chosen to work at the second season of the Golden Gate International Exposition (May 25–September 29, 1940), as part of an exhibit called *Art in Action*, which allowed the public to view artists in the act of creating their paintings, sculptures, and frescoes. Miné's job was to explain to visitors Diego Rivera's live creation of a gigantic portable fresco while Rivera was painting on a scaffold below her. In 1940 and 1941 she had two solo exhibitions at the San Francisco Museum of Modern Art and was included in the museum's Sixty-First Annual Exhibition of Painting and Sculpture, where her work received the Anne Bremer Memorial Prize.

After the attack on Pearl Harbor, Miné's father was arrested and sent to an internment camp in Missoula, Montana. The rest of her family was forcibly removed and separated into different camps. Miné and her brother Toku ended up at the Tanforan horse stalls, where she and other incarcerated artists, such as Berkeley professor Chiura Obata, started the Tanforan Art School. The school later became the Topaz Art School when she relocated to the Topaz Relocation Center. Her oldest brother, Benji, a director of the Art Students League in Los Angeles, opened an art school at Heart Mountain. Most of Miné's other family members were sent to Poston.

Miné illustrated the *Topaz Times* and helped to create a literary and arts magazine called *Trek*. She drew over two thousand sketches using charcoal, watercolor, and pen and ink to document her incarceration. Several of them were featured in the *San Francisco Chronicle* and caught the attention of *Fortune* magazine, which then commissioned her and two other Nikkei artists to work on a Japan issue; Miné's camp sketches were published to widespread acclaim. The San Francisco Museum of Modern Art mounted an exhibition of her sketches in 1944. *Fortune* then offered her a job, assisted her in the leave clearance process, and found her a rent-controlled apartment in Greenwich Village, where she lived and worked for the rest of her life.

Miné's next show, in March 1945, opened in the offices of *Common Ground*, a pro-immigrant quarterly, and then was moved to the New School for Social Research before touring the West Coast. When it opened at the Seattle Art Museum, Miné appeared in *Time* magazine. She supported herself as a commercial artist and illustrator for newspapers, magazines, and books and was asked by American Export Lines to paint eight murals for four new ships. In 1946 Columbia University Press published *Citizen 13660*, a graphic novel of 206 drawings that tell the story of her incarceration in words and pictures. The first major retrospective of her work was shown at the Oakland Museum in 1972. She testified before Congress in 1981 and showed her artwork as proof of her experiences at Topaz. *Citizen 13660* was reissued in 1983 by University of Washington Press and won the 1984 American Book Award.

California's Department of Education, in 1987, selected her as one of twelve pioneers in the history of the state. In 1991 she was honored in Washington, DC, with a Lifetime Achievement Award from the Women's Caucus for Art.

Mabel Takako (Kawashima) **Ota**, female, Nisei, Holtville, California, incarcerated age 26, Poston Relocation Center. Mabel was born in San Diego, California, on September 13, 1916, the elder of two daughters of Suezo Kawashima and Iyo (Obonai) Kawashima. Her mother was born in the Ninohe District of the Fukuoka Prefecture. Her father was born in Fukuoka Prefecture on the northern shore of the Japanese island of Kyushu.

Mabel was raised in California's Imperial Valley. Her family lived in Calexico and her parents ran a small grocery store in Holtville. She graduated from UCLA in 1939 where she was a member of Chi Alpha Delta. The following year she married Fred Kaname Ota, who worked as a salesman at the Los Angeles Wholesale Produce Market. Mabel was a cashier in a retail market until she took a City of Los Angeles civil service exam, after which she worked as a clerk in the fingerprint and identification bureau of the Los Angeles Police Department. When the war broke out, she was transferred to the Jefferson Branch Library for a six-week assignment and then was terminated without cause.

When the WRA called for volunteers to go early to the Poston Relocation Center in Arizona to help prepare the camp for resettlement, the Otas volunteered, since they knew they would be sent there anyway. They sold their car to a young man who agreed to drive them to the camp, and took advantage of the opportunity to fill the car with their personal belongings instead of leaving them all behind.

In Poston, Fred was appointed general manager of community enterprises, responsible for opening stores, barbershops, beauty shops, or whatever was needed in a community; Mabel became head librarian and used discarded books to organize a public library. By the end of the year, Fred was offered a job in New York by the Quakers as assistant manager of Cooperative Distributors, a mail-order house. He left camp, but Mabel stayed behind because she was pregnant. After twenty-eight hours of labor, Mabel needed a cesarean section, but there was no anesthesiologist. The doctor ended up using forceps to deliver the baby, which scarred Mabel for life and caused irreversible brain damage to her daughter. No one was held responsible. Mabel had planned to join Fred as soon as possible after the birth, but she was told that she'd have to wait six months, until her daughter was stronger. Finally they met Fred in New York and settled in a fifth-floor apartment.

Just a few months later, in 1944, Mabel received a letter from her mother in Poston asking her to return because her father had been admitted to the hospital. She and Fred sold their furniture, sublet the apartment, and went back to Poston.

Before the war Mabel's father had been living a normal life, working six days a week at the grocery store and managing his diabetes through insulin injections and a careful diet. Now the camp doctor was saying that her father's diabetes was under control, but he was suffering from melancholia. The doctor arranged for her father to be sent to a Phoenix rest home, where he was given shock treatments. The melancholia was a misdiagnosis. His condition was actually a complication of diabetes, which had become exponentially worse by living on a camp diet of sugar and starch instead of the fresh vegetables he'd grown on his farm. Her father fell into a diabetic coma and died six weeks after he was transferred.

In order to support her daughter's lifelong care, Mabel returned to college and obtained her elementary school teaching credential. Later she became the first Asian American principal in California.

Harold Norio **Ouye**, male, Nisei, Sacramento, California, incarcerated age 35, Sacramento Assembly Center, Tule Lake Relocation Center, Heart Mountain Relocation Center. Harold was born in Florin, California, on March 13, 1907, the third of seven children, to Kenichi Nishimoto Ouye and Sada (Nakaye) Ouye. Sada was Kenichi's picture bride; they were both from the village of Yaga Hiroshima Prefecture, Japan. Kenichi's real last name was Nishimoto; he agreed to change his name to Ouye because a good friend did not have children and he wanted to help carry on the family name.

Harold graduated from Lodi High School and, in 1928, from the University of California School of Pharmacy in San Francisco. Four years later he opened the first Japanese drugstore in Sacramento's Old Japantown, called Nippon Drugs, which he had to sell when he was forced to evacuate. His wife, Grace Mitsuye Kawano, was pregnant when they were incarcerated at Tule Lake. He was put in charge of the pharmacy, and their first child, Sandy, was born there. After one year they were forced to move to Heart Mountain, where he worked for the camp pharmacist. He was recruited directly from camp by International Harvester for a job on the assembly line, making holes in connecting rods for Farmall tractors.

Harold and his family left for Chicago in 1944, and he passed the pharmacy exam, but he couldn't leave his job at International Harvester because the War Manpower Commission had put a freeze on employment in certain industries. In 1945 he and his family moved back to Sacramento, and he worked at McClellan Field repairing planes. No pharmacy in California would hire him.

Then in 1946 he and his brother Fred, who was also a pharmacist, became partners in a new drugstore called Ouye's Pharmacy in Sacramento's Japantown. Thirteen years later the city began redevelopment of the area, and the drugstore was moved to a different part of town. Harold worked as a pharmacist for more than forty years.

In his free time he played the banjo with the Sacramento Banjo Band. Harold N. Ouye Home Movies, a series of silent films about Sacramento's old Japantown and Japanese domestic life in California from 1950 to 1960, are part of the California Revealed collection at the Center for Sacramento History.

Mary **Sakaguchi** (Oda), female, Nisei, Los Angeles, California, incarcerated age 22, Manzanar Reception Center, Manzanar Relocation Center. Mary was born in Fresno, California, on March 15, 1920, the fifth of seven children, to Shiichiro Sakaguchi and Hisaji Sakaguchi. Her family lived in an apricot orchard they owned. Mary's parents were farmers, but her father sent all seven of his children to college. Her mother's family descended from samurai who were educated village leaders going back fifteen generations. Her Issei mother attended college herself, hoping to be a teacher. Mary graduated from North Hollywood High School in 1937 and UCLA in 1941. She was in her first year of medical school at the University of California, Berkeley, when her education was interrupted by the forced removal. The family farm and the house were rented to people who never paid because they knew they could not be evicted.

At Manzanar, three members of her family died within seven months of one another. Her eldest sister, Chico, worked as a reporter for the *Manzanar Free Press* and introduced Mary to her husband, James Oda. Chico died of an asthma attack from the severe dust storms at the age of twenty-six. Mary's father developed cancer of the nasal pharynx and died soon thereafter. A brother, Obo, who had been a practicing dentist, transferred to Manzanar from Gila River to be with his mother and sick father. Obo then fell ill himself with stomach cancer and died at age thirty-two—he was the third member of the family to die in 1944. Then Mary's younger sister, Lily, had a nervous breakdown, but she eventually completed her education at the University of Pennsylvania.

After the war Mary resumed her studies and graduated cum laude in January 1946 from the Women's Medical College of Pennsylvania (which would later merge into the Drexel University College of Medicine). Between her second and third years, her husband was drafted into the Military Intelligence Service as a linguist. She was pregnant during her last year of medical school and gave birth to a daughter a month after she graduated. She joined her husband in Minnesota, where he was teaching at the Military Intelligence Service Language School, and completed her residency there. She then followed him to Tokyo when he was assigned to work with the occupation forces. They returned to California with three small children and briefly ran an egg farm in Glendora.

Mary began her medical career in earnest at the Pacific State Hospital in

Pomona. Seven years later, in 1960, she joined her brother Sanbo, a surgeon, and her sister Lily, a lab technician, in Sanbo's San Fernando medical practice. She worked there for the next forty-nine years, delivering over thirty-five hundred babies. In 2003, Mary established the Eugene David Oda Endowed Scholarship Fund at Drexel University College of Medicine, named after her son who was killed in a tragic car accident. She also established two academic prizes at UCLA—one undergraduate, one graduate—for the study of the incarceration of Japanese Americans during World War II.

David Masao **Sakai**, male, Nisei, San Jose, California, incarcerated age 25, Santa Anita Assembly Center, Heart Mountain Relocation Center. David was born in San Juan Bautista, California, on March 24, 1917, one of nine children, to Tatsusaburo Sakai and Ei Sakai. He grew up in Salinas and graduated with a degree in business from San Jose State University. He met his wife, Ruth, at the Santa Anita Assembly Center. They were married in 1944 and lived in Logan, Utah, for fourteen years after their incarceration. He was very involved in community service and received the Outstanding Man of the Year award from the Junior Chamber of Commerce. In 1957 he returned to California with his family to work at the Carl N. Swenson Construction Company. He retired as a vice president and project manager after twenty-eight years. He was a supporter of Yu-Ai Kai (a nonprofit organization for senior citizens in the Japanese American community), the San Jose–Okayama Sister Cities program, the West Valley Presbyterian Church, and the West Valley chapter of the JACL. He was passionate about tending to his manicured garden.

Misao "Sadie" Marietta (Nishitani) **Sakamoto**, female, Issei, Seattle, Washington, incarcerated age 36, Puyallup Assembly Center, Minidoka Relocation Center. Misao was born in the village of Kaminagata, Saihaku District, Tottori Prefecture, Japan, on February 16, 1906, the third of nine children, to Denjiro Nishitani and Jin (Aoto) Nishitani. Denjiro left his wife and three children, including Misao, in Japan while he emigrated to the United States through Canada to secure a home for his family. James Dickson Trenholme,

president of Thorndyke-Trenholme Company, a shipping company, hired her
father as a groundskeeper, which enabled him to send for her mother, Jin, in
1909. Their firstborn son, Hiromu, their second son, Yuu, and Misao stayed
with relatives until her father could afford to pay their passage. Two years
later, Denjiro sent for Hiromu, who sailed by himself at the age of eleven.

With Trenholme's encouragement, Denjiro opened a nursery called
Oriental Gardens, a floral shop, and a landscaping business on leased land.
Then in 1919, he bought the land in the name of his first American child,
seven-year-old son George, who was born on the Trenholme estate. That year
Misao, now thirteen, sailed to Seattle with Yuu, now fifteen, where they were
finally reunited with their eldest brother, Hiromu.

Misao was attending Lincoln High School in Seattle, when Jimmie Yoshi-
nori Sakamoto, the boy she would eventually marry, was already having an
impact on the community as an "athletic immortal" and a natural community activist. At Franklin High School Jimmie led the football team to victory
over its rival Broadway High for the first time in its history, despite being a
halfback who weighed less than 130 pounds. At seventeen, he also sat for an
impromptu interview with representatives from a congressional committee
on immigration and naturalization that had come to the West Coast to hear
testimony about immigration legislation. Jimmie's sister had volunteered to
speak and Jimmie had tagged along, intending to listen. Instead he found
himself taking the place of an absent scheduled volunteer. He spoke of his
desire to become more like an American; he described even trying to enlist
in the US military during World War I but he was rebuffed because he was
in his early teens.

In 1923 Jimmie moved to New York City to live with his older sister and
began taking seminary classes at Princeton University. For three years he
worked as an editor for the English language section of the *Nichi Bei Shimbun* (Japanese-American News). During this time he married Frances Imai, a
Eurasian woman, and the couple had one daughter named Blossom. To make
extra money, Jimmie became the first Japanese American boxer—in three
different weight classes—to fight professionally in Madison Square Garden.

He took on more fights than would normally be allowed by registering under an alias.

In just a few years, those fights took their toll on his body. The retina of his left eye was damaged in a fight in Utica, New York, in 1926. Then a year later, another blow detached the retina of his other eye. Doctors were not advanced enough in surgical techniques to reattach retinas. Jimmie was twenty-four years old and going blind. Then Frances died. Jimmie left Blossom with Frances's parents and went home to Seattle to live with his own parents. There he trained himself to walk up and down stairs, turn corners, and navigate in and out of rooms blindfolded. Brave, stoic, and alone, Jimmie was learning to navigate without eyesight, when he soon found a partner in Misao Nishitani with the nickname "Sadie." They married shortly thereafter.

The Seattle Japanese American community that Jimmie had come home to in 1927 had changed significantly since he had left. Two competing athletic clubs—the Nippons and the Taiyos—were fiercely divided. Jimmie's childhood friend, George Ishihara, was president of the Taiyos, but instead of trying to unite the clubs, George wanted to reinvigorate the Seattle Progressive Citizens League, an existing organization of which he was the secretary. This group's original purpose was to fight anti-Japanese legislation, but Jimmie wanted to focus on the positive: Americanism. To do that effectively, he thought the community needed a voice.

With Sadie's help, Jimmie launched the weekly *The Japanese American Courier*, the first English language Japanese American newspaper, on January 1, 1928. Sadie served as the newspaper's bookkeeper and manager of its back office. She also helped to set the paper in type on an old linotype machine, as well as wrapped and mailed the papers to subscribers.

It wasn't long before the goals of the Seattle Progressive Citizens League, led by Clarence Arai, the first Japanese American attorney in Seattle who had been elected its president, had evolved into citizen movements in Oregon and California. Within a year of the *Courier*'s first publication, Jimmie called a meeting at its offices with Clarence Arai, George Ishihara, and Dr. Thomas T. Yatabe, founder of the Fresno American Loyalty League, at which

Clarence proposed a national organization called the Japanese American Citizens League. And so, the JACL was born with Clarence elected president pro tempore (meaning, *for a time*). But as Bill Hosokawa put it, the JACL was actually "fathered in some considerable part by the vision of sightless Jimmie Sakamoto. . . . Jimmie's devotion to the JACL was like that of a priest to his church."

And then four months later the stock market crashed, and the Depression began in earnest. Sadie became instrumental in keeping the bills at bay and the paper barely afloat. And just as it was finding its feet, the Northwest Japanese American community was hit again. The Japanese Commercial Bank in Seattle went bankrupt, along with virtually all of the Japanese American businesses in the region, including all of the paper's advertisers and personal subscribers. Lost were all of the *Courier's* money and the Sakamotos' personal funds. When some time passed and the paper could finally collect some payments, Jimmie and Sadie tried a new bank, the American Exchange Bank; two months later, that bank also collapsed. Sadie was forced to pay some bills three times. But the paper kept publishing and remained a beacon of hope for the entire community. It broadcast a radio program for the Issei and sponsored a cooking school in addition to local baseball, football, and basketball leagues for young Nisei.

And then in 1936, Jimmie was elected president of the JACL at its convention held in Seattle, nearly a decade after the paper was first published. He was "stunned" by the result and "overwhelmed by the honor." He served for two years during which his roles as newspaper publisher and leadership of the JACL became inextricable from one another and entwined with Jimmie's powerful drive to affect the destiny of the Nisei as Americans within the larger American identity. Sadie's support of Jimmie as he managed these responsibilities was so effective that some people forgot he was blind.

The paper survived for almost fifteen years until the Sakamotos had to shut it down to report to camp. They and their two daughters ended up at Minidoka, where a third daughter was born a year later.

In 1944 Sadie was able to take Marie and Marcia, her two older daughters, to St. Mary's College in South Bend, Indiana, where she worked as a maid and the children went to primary school. Jimmie stayed behind with one-year-old Denise and his parents, who were in their eighties. Eventually the whole family reunited in Seattle in 1946. And then, Father L. H. Tibesar, the Maryknoll priest who had converted the Sakamotos to Catholicism, got Jimmie a job at the St. Vincent de Paul Salvage Bureau. Over the next ten years Jimmie turned the bureau into one of the largest salvation operations in the world.

Every day Jimmie made his way to the bus alone early in the morning when the streets were uncrowded, but on December 3, 1955, his luck in negotiating the traffic independently ran out. Jimmie was hit by a car and died.

Sadie was a survivor and she carried on to support her family. She went back to school and studied to become a dental assistant, a compromise of her unrealized dream of becoming a registered nurse. She also continued her enduring love of gardening that began as a teenager at her father's nursery.

In the eulogy he offered about Jimmie, Bill Hosokawa described Sadie as the best thing that ever happened to him: "She was and is a woman of exceptional kindness, wisdom, patience, and courage. . . . As Jimmie's widow, she can take comfort in the knowledge that she was a tower of strength in Jimmie's darkest hours, that her companionship made Jimmie's life more full, more meaningful. She helped him gain his destiny as no other person could do."

Riichi **Satow**, male, Issei, Sacramento, California, incarcerated age 47, Pinedale Assembly Center, Poston Relocation Center. Riichi was born in Chiba Prefecture, Japan, on April 29, 1895, the third of six children. Riichi's father went to the United States to make enough money to reacquire his family's Japanese properties that he had gambled away. He worked as the foreman of a Japanese crew on a fruit ranch in Napa Valley, and eventually he was able to go home and buy back the land he had lost, then return to the US again. Riichi and his younger brother followed in his father's wake in 1912 and met him in Napa Valley. They all worked together for two years until his father came down with a recurring summer illness and his sons convinced him to go home to Japan for his health. Seven years later Riichi returned to Japan himself for the purpose of getting married to Chieko Oganuki, the woman his parents had chosen for him.

He and Chieko then sailed to the US and worked for nearly four years on a leased strawberry ranch in Sacramento. But Riichi wanted a more promising future, so they moved to San Francisco. Riichi got a job "type-picking" at the *Nichi Bei Shimbun* newspaper and learned English at night. They had three children by then and Chieko took on embroidery to make ends meet. Then Riichi fell ill with pneumonia and was told he had to leave San Francisco to get better, so he took his family back to Sacramento again. He was so successful growing strawberries there that he was able to buy his own farm in the name of a corporation he held with two other Japanese farmers.

He also became president of the Strawberry Growers' Association, which then merged with Otani Produce, Noji Farm Produce, and the Florin strawberry produce group in order to consolidate their distribution. Together they became the Strawberry Exchange, of which Riichi was also president when the war started. By that time he and Chieko had nine children and they had to abandon their home and their property in order to report to camp. After ten months in camp, Riichi found a job on a beet farm owned by a German-Russian family in Keenesburg, Colorado, and Riichi's family moved once more. They stayed a few years and then returned to Sacramento to their house, which was empty but still standing on fifteen acres of land. Their first harvest was of bushberries, boysenberries, and youngberries (a form of blackberry).

Riichi was Sacramento's minister representative of the Northern California Japanese Christian Church Federation for many years.

Ben Satoshi **Segawa**, male, Nisei, El Cajon, California, incarcerated age 11, Santa Anita Assembly Center, Poston Relocation Center. Ben was born in San Diego, California, on June 30, 1930, the sixth of ten children, to Kazuji Segawa and Misuye (Kai) Segawa. His family farmed forty acres of spinach, string beans, and beets in the South Bay area of San Diego County. While the Segawa family was incarcerated, a neighbor kept their farm running. Ben served in the US Air Force during the Korean War, after which he returned to farming, then took up real estate. He helped found the Japanese American Historical Society of San Diego and served as its first president. He used the reparations money given to him by the government to take his family to Washington, DC, so they could learn about democracy.

Sumiko "Sumi" **Seo** (Seki), female, Nisei, Los Angeles, California, incarcerated age 18, Santa Anita Assembly Center, Jerome Relocation Center. Sumi was born and raised on a farm in San Pedro, California, on November 22, 1924, the youngest of three children, to Midori Seo and Kazue (Takashi) Seo. Her father had established an abalone farm in 1913 and sharecropped the land near White Point and Palos Verdes (now the White Point Nature Preserve). This was her father's way of life until the Hearst newspapers accused Japanese Americans of spying on behalf of the Japanese government. The locals stoned the Japanese Americans at the White Point settlement, and the State of California passed a law prohibiting Japanese Americans from continuing to fish abalone.

In 1915, Tamiji Tagami helped develop the White Point Health Resort, which included sulfur-water baths and an Olympic-size swimming pool; it was popular with Japanese Americans because the seacoast reminded them of Japan and there were few places they were allowed to go for recreation. Sumi's father continued to farm in San Pedro. The first and only time she saw her father cry was when he was petting and saying good-bye to his horses as the family was being removed.

Her husband, Don Seki, lost an arm to German machine gun fire while rescuing the Lost Battalion as a member of the 100th/442nd Regimental Combat Team. When she returned to California after the war, she made buttonholes for fifty-five cents an hour; later she worked for Douglas Aircraft. She lived for fifteen years at Truman Boyd Manor, a federal housing project in Long Beach, where she became a community activist and got involved with the National Coalition for Redress/Reparations.

Richard Takeshi **Shindo**, male, Nisei, Los Angeles, California, incarcerated age 14, Poston Relocation Center. Richard was born in Los Angeles, California, on November 7, 1927, the oldest of four children, to Koryu "Thomas" Shindo and Mino (Okubo) Shindo. His mother was born in the port city of Niigata on the Japanese island of Honshu. His father was born in Kobuchizawa, Japan, where Richard's grandfather was the mayor. He encouraged Koryu to go to the United States so he wouldn't have to serve in the Japanese military. When Koryu arrived in Seattle, he chose to call himself "Thomas" and then settled in Los Angeles. He worked for a tailor and a grocer until 1918, when he became advertising director for the *Rafu Shimpo*; he ended up designing its masthead as well as notably encouraging the paper to sponsor photographic exhibitions in Little Tokyo.

Thomas was a member of the Japanese Pictorialists of California (JCPC), a Little Tokyo photographers organization formed in 1926; members shared darkrooms, critiques, and mentorships, and studied and exhibited together. Thomas published more photographs than any other Japanese American in the annual *Photograms of the Year*.

Richard would accompany his father on photo shoots to the mountains, Newport Beach, Lake Irvine, and other locations. On days off they'd go to Huntington Beach. At the *Rafu Shimpo* Thomas introduced Richard to his friend, Ansel Adams. The photographers in JCPC represented a modernist movement that was nearly extinguished when the bombing of Pearl Harbor made cameras contraband and most of their work was destroyed.

When Pearl Harbor was bombed, Richard was fourteen and attending Robert Louis Stevenson Junior High School. The entire student body was assembled in the auditorium for an important announcement by the principal James Hutt. He said to them all, "Our Japanese-*AMERICAN* students have *NOTHING* to do with the start of the war." It was a show of support for the Japanese American kids in school. Mr. Hutt wanted the other students to treat them fairly.

Richard's dream was to become an architect. In his drafting class he was the most skilled and his drafting teacher, Mr. Goldman, arranged for him and four of his classmates to go to the esteemed John H. Francis Polytechnic High School in Los Angeles. Richard's plan was to graduate from Polytechnic and then study architecture at the University of Southern California. But Richard's plan never came to pass. His dreams were derailed by his detention in a concentration camp.

After the war, his father worked as an assistant to photographer Shigemi Izuo in Denver, Colorado. When Izuo became ill with cancer, Thomas bought the studio. Meanwhile, after graduating from high school at Poston, Richard went to Cleveland, Ohio, to work in a warplant sewing collapsible water tanks. He eventually moved to Denver and was drafted into the army on January 31, 1946. He did basic training in Fort Lewis, Washington, after which he was sent to the US Army Engineering School at Fort Belvoir, Virginia. And then, as part of the 64th Engineer Topographic Battalion, he was stationed for a year and a half in Japan, where he met some of his relatives for the first time. The battalion worked out of the Isetan Department Store, third floor and up, in Shinjuku, a suburb of Tokyo.

Richard returned to the US in 1948 and was honorably discharged; he went back to Denver and met his future wife, Elene Kyoko Matsuda, shortly thereafter. He knew her family from before he was drafted—in fact, at twelve or thirteen years old he saw her perform in a tap-dancing troupe. He then went back to school on the GI Bill at the University of Denver and graduated with a bachelor of fine arts. Elene graduated from Colorado Women's College with an associate degree in 1953. She then worked as a stenographer for a Denver County Court judge.

In 1954 Richard's whole family moved back to Los Angeles, and Elene went with them. She lived with her aunt until she and Richard got married a year later at the Shatto Chapel in the First Congregational Church of Los Angeles. As a CalVet, Richard was eligible for another free year of schooling, so he attended the Chouinard Art Institute. He also helped his father when he launched his own studio on First Street in Boyle Heights.

Elene worked as a secretary for the comptroller of a medical group and later for a psychiatrist, while Richard was doing freelance work with an interest in food packaging design. Eventually, he joined Pafford and Associates, a surveying company, and surveyed the land for the Del Amo Fashion Square in Torrance, California; the Century Plaza Hotel in Century City; and Bunker Hill in Los Angeles. He and Elene loved to save quarters in a jar and gamble in Las Vegas; they are also big band aficionados and went to concerts with Johnny Mathis, King Cole Trio, Sammy Davis Jr., Ella Fitzgerald, and Kaye Ballard. They raised two children. In 2020 he and Elene celebrated their 65th wedding anniversary and at 93, Richard remains passionate about taking walks six times a week.

Aiko Grace **Shinoda** (Nakamura), female, Nisei, Los Angeles, California, incarcerated age 15, Manzanar Reception Center, Manzanar Relocation Center. Grace was born in Los Angeles, California, on February 18, 1927, the elder of two children, to Kiyoshi Shinoda and Hide (Watanabe) Shinoda. Her father, who died when she was six years old, was born in Tottori, Japan, and graduated from the University of California, Berkeley, as an electrical engineer. Her mother graduated from Woodbury University. They met at the Union Church of Los Angeles. Her maternal grandparents were Tomoichi Watanabe and Masano (Takenaka) Watanabe; her paternal grandparents were Kumaichiro Shinoda and Masuno (Nakashima) Shinoda. Paul Yashiro Shinoda was her uncle (see his biography); Teru Watanabe was her aunt (see her biography). Grace began drawing as a child. Art was a talent she shared with her brother, Lawrence, who became an automotive designer, best known for his design of the Chevrolet Corvette and the Ford Mustang, and for the use of graphics on vehicles.

Grace's family was released from camp to join Grace's uncle Paul and his family, who had chosen to leave California voluntarily and were working on a sugar beet and dairy farm in Grand Junction, Colorado. Grace and her family went to Grand Junction to help care for Grace's grandfather, who had suffered a stroke. In the spring of 1944, through the American Friends Service Committee, Grace was offered a scholarship to the University of Redlands to study sociology and education. She graduated with honors and went on to become the first Japanese American to be hired as a teacher in the Pasadena School District. She obtained two master's degrees from Whittier College— one in teaching fine arts, the other in counseling—and became active in her community of Whittier, California. She served as a trustee of the Whittier Public Library and was instrumental in getting a viewing platform installed at the Whittier Narrows Nature Center. She also started a native plant green- house project at La Serna High School through an Audubon YES! grant. She and her husband, Yosh Nakamura (see his biography), were recipients of the Whittier Area Audubon Society's Lifetime Achievement Award. She often spoke against anti-Muslim rhetoric during the 2016 presidential campaign.

"She saw history repeating itself," her husband said. "She warned to be suspicious of those who create a climate of fear."

Paul Yashiro **Shinoda**, male, Nisei, Gardena, California, age 28 when Pearl Harbor was attacked. Paul was born in Oakland, California, on April 29, 1913, the seventh of nine children, to Kumaichiro Shinoda and Masuno (Nakashima) Shinoda. Kumaichiro came to California in 1905 and, after a series of false starts, grew roses for profit on five acres in San Lorenzo. The business, K. Shinoda and Sons, flourished during the Spanish flu pandemic after World War I because so many flowers were needed for funerals. The roses were shipped by rail to Paul's brother Kiyoshi, who sold them at the flower market in Los Angeles. The company would later become the San Lorenzo Nursery Company, the largest floral operation in the United States.

Paul began as a student at Oregon State University, but he was turned away from his assigned dorm because it didn't allow students of Japanese descent. A year and a half later he left for the University of Illinois—the only school of horticulture in the country—where he studied for a year. Then his brother Kiyoshi died, and he ended up transferring to the University of California, Berkeley, and graduated in 1935. Four years later he bought five acres of land in Torrance, California, which grew to over nineteen acres, and built all the greenhouses himself from the ground up; in 1966 he moved the nursery to Santa Barbara.

Paul was never formally incarcerated; he opted instead for "voluntary evacuation" and boarded a train with his wife, his three children, his brother Daniel, and their elderly parents to find work temporarily out of the state. Their first stop was Blackfoot, Idaho, where a company had advertised for men to harvest sugar beets. They disembarked from the railway cars, and the farmers chose from 130 men, all standing in a lineup. The Shinoda family didn't get chosen because they clearly needed housing. Their next stop was a Farm Security Administration migratory labor camp in Grand Junction, Colorado, where Paul got a job as a farmhand for ninety dollars a month as well as a house with running water, a woodstove, and an outhouse. The grammar school was across the street. Paul did carpentry repairs on the farmer's house, cut hay and alfalfa, and harvested grain and potatoes. Kumaichiro had a stroke not long after they arrived, and Paul's sister-in-law, Hide (Watanabe) Shinoda, and her two children, Aiko Grace and Lawrence, were released from Manzanar to help care for him. When Kumaichiro died in December 1944, there were no flowers in town to prepare for the funeral, so Johnny Fukushima, one of Kumaichiro's employees, went all the way to California to get red roses shipped to Grand Junction from the San Lorenzo Nursery.

Paul was president of the Gardena chapter of the JACL, a member of the Santa Barbara Kiwanis Club, and a leader of the Torrance Boy Scouts, for which he received a council-level Silver Beaver Award for distinguished service. He also was active with the Gardena Valley Baptist Church and the Bethany Congregational Church in Santa Barbara. An avid fisherman, he took annual deep-sea fishing trips to Mexico and surf-fishing trips to Baja California. After his retirement, he compiled a memoir called "Recollections." He and his wife traveled around the world and for two decades; they spent every summer on the Alaskan Kenai Peninsula. Aiko Grace (Shinoda) Nakamura was his niece; Teru Watanabe was his sister-in-law; and John Yoshio Tateishi is his son-in-law. (See their individual biographies.)

Emiko "Emi" (Yada) **Somekawa**, female, Nisei, Portland, Oregon, incarcerated age 24, Portland Assembly Center, Tule Lake Relocation Center. Emi was born on her family's farm in Brooks, Oregon, on May 10, 1918, the second of five children, to Misao "Jim" Yada and Hatsuno (Fukai) Yada. She graduated from high school in Salem, Oregon. In 1939 she finished nursing school and became a registered nurse in Portland, specializing in labor and delivery; she was hired by Emanuel Hospital (now Legacy Emanuel Medical Center). Her husband, Arthur Somekawa, worked for his father at the Nichi Bei Fish Company. At the time of the bombing of Pearl Harbor, she was supervising the maternity ward and pregnant herself with her second child. Her neighbors were German and were considered "enemy aliens," but they were never incarcerated.

Emi and her husband were removed, along with their nine-month-old infant, to the Portland Assembly Center, where their second baby was born in a horse stall. The laundry was several blocks away, and all their clothes had to be washed on a washboard. Her father-in-law was an invalid, having suffered a stroke the year before, but when the family was transferred to Tule Lake, he was taken to Minidoka separately. Emi and her husband were now traveling with two babies (one a newborn, and both still on bottles and baby food). At Tule Lake she immediately began working in the camp hospital, which had eighty or ninety patients at any one time. After the war Emi was one of the few incarcerees who was able to return to her job at Emanuel Hospital in Portland. She was the first female president of the JACL in Puyallup, Washington.

Lillian Reiko **Sugita** (Nakano), female, Sansei, Honolulu, Hawaii, incarcerated age 14, Jerome Relocation Center, Heart Mountain Relocation Center. Lillian was born in Honolulu, Hawaii, on April 30, 1928, the oldest girl of four girls and one brother, to Saburo Sugita and Shizuno (Nakamura) Sugita. She grew up in Honolulu, where her family had a wholesale bakery business. As a child, she studied the shamisen, a traditional three-stringed Japanese instrument, and classical dance. Her father was arrested by the FBI right after the bombing of Pearl Harbor and was detained for a year on Sand Island, Hawaii. To be reunited with him, her mother agreed for the whole family to be sent to another camp on the mainland. They were incarcerated first at Jerome, then at Heart Mountain, and in 1945 the family returned to Honolulu. There Lillian reconnected with Bert Nakano, whom she knew at Jerome High School, and they married in 1949.

The couple then moved to Chicago, where she went to art school and studied the shamisen. In 1955, under the tutelage of Madame Kineya Shofuku of the prestigious Kineya School, Lillian received her *natori* (master's certificate) and a professional name, Kineya Fukuju. Lillian and her husband moved briefly to Japan in 1964 but returned to the United States and settled in Gardena, California. She was active with the Little Tokyo People's Rights Organization. She and Bert were founding members of the National Coalition for Redress/ Reparations. A lifelong arts advocate, she co-created the Sanmi Ensemble with her nephew Glenn Horiuchi, a pianist and composer of music on concentration camp themes and a frequent performer of the shamisen. She was given a Master Musician Fellowship by the Durfee Foundation in 2001.

Toyo **Suyemoto** (Kawakami), female, Nisei, Alameda County, California, incarcerated age 26, Tanforan Assembly Center, Topaz Relocation Center. Toyo was born in Oroville, California, on January 14, 1916, the oldest of nine children, to Tsutomu Suyemoto and Mitsu (Hyakusoku) Suyemoto. She grew up in Sacramento's Nihonmachi (Japantown). At the University of California, Berkeley, she majored in English and Latin, graduating in 1937. She became a well-known figure in the Nisei literary community during her college years. When her family received orders to leave for the Tanforan Assembly Center, Toyo and her husband separated, and she went to Tanforan with her infant son and parents.

At Topaz she worked at the camp library and taught English and Latin. Together with her friend, the artist Miné Okubo, she worked on *Trek* and *All Aboard*, the camp literary magazines.

After the war she moved to Cincinnati, Ohio, and found jobs at the University of Cincinnati libraries and the Cincinnati Art Museum. In 1958 her sixteen-year-old son died of complications from the respiratory condition he had contracted at camp. She later earned a master's degree in library science at the University of Michigan and became head of the social work library and assistant head of the education and psychology library at the Ohio State University. She published poems in several anthologies and in publications such as the *Yale Review* and *Common Ground*. The writer Lawson Fusao Inada wrote in the *Nation* that Toyo Suyemoto was "our major Camp Poet and Nikkei Poet Laureate."

Ben Toshihiro **Tagami**, male, Nisei, Los Angeles, California, incarcerated age 17, Fresno Assembly Center, Jerome Relocation Center. Ben was born in Fresno, California, on January 30, 1925, one of four children, to Toshio Tagami and Tsugu (Ichishita) Tagami. Toshio was from Hiroshima, Japan, and Tsugu was from Kumamoto, Japan. Ben's father immigrated from Japan to Mexico, and then illegally entered the United States from Guadalajara, Mexico, strapped underneath a car for fifty or sixty miles. Toshio started out as a shoe salesman, then ran his own produce stand and grew strawberries. He became an alcoholic and physically abused members of the family. Ben's mother, Tsugu, had a nervous breakdown right before the family was incarcerated.

Ben served as a rifleman and mortarman with the 100th/442nd Regimental Combat Team and was part of the forces that broke through the Gothic Line. When he came back from Europe, he went home to Fresno and won enough money in a craps game for his mother to buy the Asia Hotel, which she ran with his father. (The journalist Lyn Crost stayed there for a couple of months.) He then reenlisted in the army and was stationed in San Francisco, where he taught cooking and baking as a mess sergeant. He was then transferred to Japan, where he married and was placed in the army's hotel service and the Military Railway Service shortly thereafter. When he was honorably discharged, he came back to America and worked at fruit stands, wholesale markets, and Safeway. In 1949 his mother died tragically from surgical complications resulting from an auto accident.

On November 2, 2011, he was among the soldiers of the 100th/442nd

Regimental Combat Team and the Military Intelligence Service who were awarded a Congressional Gold Medal for their bravery during World War II. Ben continued to remain active in the 100th Infantry Battalion Veterans organization.

Kojin **Tahara**, male, San Francisco, California. Kojin was a student of the poet Ogiwara Seisensui (the pen name of Ogiwara Tokichi), who led the parent group of free-verse haiku in Japan that abandoned traditional haiku language. According to Lucille Nixon, "The characteristics of this free-style haiku are:

1. No season need be expressed.

2. Syllables are not limited.

3. Devotees are permitted free style in expression; they 'just pick up words to make a beautiful picture.'"

Kojin applied the free-verse haiku approach to the tanka form of Japan poetry that was popular in San Francisco. His tanka work appeared in *Sounds from the Unknown: A Collection of Japanese-American Tanka*, edited by Lucille M. Nixon and Tomoe Tana.

Larry Taneyoshi **Tajiri**, male, Nisei, Los Angeles, California, age 27 when Pearl Harbor was attacked. Larry was born in Los Angeles, California, on May 7, 1914, the oldest of seven children, to Ryukichi Tajiri and Fuyo (Kikuta) Tajiri. His father was a wholesale produce salesman and a farm group spokesman. Larry attended Maryknoll School and Los Angeles Polytechnic High School, where he was editor of the school paper, the *Poly Optimist*. He named himself Lawrence Stephen after two Catholic saints. At the age of eighteen, he became the chief English-language editor of the Los Angeles *Kashu Mainichi* newspaper, to which he added a weekly sports page and a weekly literary page. His daily column was called Village Vagaries. He completed one year at Los Angeles City College, but he couldn't afford to continue. He went on to serve as the English-language editor and columnist of the *Nichi Bei Shimbun* newspaper in San Francisco and made the same editorial changes by adding sports and literary content as well as his own column, Nisei USA. He was also active in organizing chapters of the Nisei Young Democrats in Oakland and San Francisco.

In early 1940, before the attack on Pearl Harbor, he and his journalist wife, Guyo Okagaki, moved to New York, where he worked as a correspondent for Japan's *Asahi Shimbun* newspaper chain. After the war broke out, *Asahi* closed its New York office and Larry lost his job. He and Guyo returned to San Francisco. Together with Isamu Noguchi, they formed the Nisei Writers and Artists Mobilization for Democracy, which tried to organize a mass demonstration to prevent the incarceration. But Executive Order 9066 put an end to that.

Right before the "voluntary evacuation" option was eliminated, Larry and Guyo accepted an offer from the JACL to move to Salt Lake City and relaunch the JACL newsletter as the *Pacific Citizen* to replace the West Coast Japanese newspapers that had been shut down. The JACL offices there became a newspaper bureau, and the paper was distributed—at first weekly, then biweekly—to the Japanese American population in the camps. The paper, which the couple published themselves, contained bulletins, news reports, and government announcements. Larry and Guyo wrote many columns of original material based on their own reporting. Guyo wrote a column for women in camp under the pen name Ann Nisei. Larry used the newspaper to voice criticism of the Heart Mountain draft resisters as well as concerns about the JACL, national policies, and civil rights. The *Pacific Citizen* gave him a platform to speak and write nationally for *Common Ground, Asia and the Americas*, the *New Leader*, and *NOW*.

When the war ended, Larry and Guyo added regional correspondents Roku Sugahara and John Reinecke and columnists Mike Masaoka, Koji Ariyoshi, and folk singer Woody Guthrie. Not long afterward Guyo stopped working for the paper and, facing criticism from the more conservative JACL members for his liberal views and management style, Larry had reached his saturation point. After the Immigration and Nationality Act of 1952 was passed, allowing Japanese immigrants to become naturalized citizens for the first time, he resigned, having made peace with his contribution to the cause.

He later joined the *Denver Post* as a drama critic and entertainment columnist. He wrote a book on poker, drawing from his personal experience, and continued to write a semiweekly column for the *Pacific Citizen*. An award-winning newspaper now based in Los Angeles, the *Pacific Citizen* celebrated its ninetieth anniversary in 2019. Since its website was launched in 2005, it has gotten close to 450,000 hits per month. It is the leading provider of Asian Pacific American news in the United States.

Fuji (Okamoto) **Takaichi**, female, Nisei, San Jose, California, incarcerated age 29, Santa Anita Assembly Center, Heart Mountain Relocation Center. Fuji was born in San Jose, California, on August 12, 1913, the eldest of three children, to George Shinkichi Okamoto and Misa (Seki) Okamoto. George and Misa met in America.

Misa's parents owned an inn in Hiroshima, where Misa met and befriended a Caucasian girl named Bessie Whitney whose father had made his money as a merchant during the US gold rush. When the Whitneys were getting ready to return to America, they offered to bring Misa with them and sponsor her education. Misa's family agreed and gave Misa her dowry to take with her, including a "jinrickshaw" (a human-powered, two-wheeled, doorless vehicle with a chair-like body and collapsible hood for one or two passengers that is pulled by a man between two poles).

George had come to America with his father and worked as a houseboy in San Francisco at the age of fourteen while his father found work on a farm in the San Joaquin valley. George considered his first real job to be as a messenger for an art supply store in San Francisco. He went on to manage several art supply stores in the city until he moved to San Jose, and in 1906 he bought an art supply store of his own. George did very well for himself. Fuji was raised by an English nanny, and George could buy expensive shoes, which he polished every day—a passion borne out of having to wear girls' shoes when he first came to America because his father was broke.

Fuji graduated from San Jose High School and completed two years of college at San Jose State University before dropping out when she learned that being Japanese would make it virtually impossible to get a teaching job even if she was able to earn an education credential. She worked instead for the county as a stenographer. She married Leroy Jindo Takaichi, a boy she'd grown up with. In 1913, Leroy's father, Peter Takaichi, had become a partner with Toshio Kimura in his National Printing Company, established in 1910, in San Jose's Japantown. The print shop was where the *Soko Shinbun*, a San Francisco Japanese American newspaper, as well as the *Japanese Press* (later called the *San Jose Press*) was produced. Peter took over the business in 1915. He and his wife, Yoye, lived in a cottage behind the print shop.

Fuji and Leroy lived across the street from the Mineta family. Norman Mineta taught Sunday school to Fuji's only daughter, Mari, at the Wesley United Methodist Church. George died before the attack on Pearl Harbor, when Misa had to sell everything in the store.

Fuji and Leroy left camp after only a few months so that Leroy could work in Cody, Wyoming, as a pressman for the *Cody Enterprise* newspaper. Then, in 1944, they moved to Saint Paul, Minnesota, where they lived until they could return to California a year later. Leroy and his brother Sammy went first to rebuild the cottage and reopen the National Printing Company, which they could do because the building was still owned by the family.

In 1966 Fuji served as president of the Alpha Chi (San Jose) chapter of the Delphian Study Club, which had broken off from the Delphian Society, the national organization, to become a women's book club that provided courses in the humanities. Members were required to purchase a complete set of books that were published by the Delphian Society in history, literature, drama, art, poetry, and music. Once a year the members would demonstrate their acquired knowledge by giving informal talks to the group.

George Hosato **Takei**, male, Nisei, Los Angeles, California, incarcerated age 5, Santa Anita Assembly Center, Rohwer Relocation Center, Tule Lake Relocation Center. George was born in Los Angeles, California, on April 20, 1937, the oldest of three children, to Takekuma "Norman" Takei, who was born in Yamanashi Prefecture, Japan, and Fumiko Emily (Nakamura) Takei, born in Sacramento, California. His father worked in real estate. His aunt and baby cousin were "found burnt in a ditch" after the bombing of Hiroshima.

After the war the family was destitute for five years until they could build up their lives enough to move out of Skid Row. George attended Mount Vernon Junior High School and Los Angeles High School and then entered the University of California, Berkeley, to study architecture. Then in 1956 he began acting and performing voice-over work. He transferred to UCLA and graduated with a bachelor's degree and master's degree in theater in 1960 and 1964 respectively. He also studied at the Shakespeare Institute in Stratford-upon-Avon, England; Sophia University in Tokyo; and the Desilu Workshop in Hollywood. In 1966 he debuted his famous role as Hikaru Sulu in *Star Trek*. He acted alongside such legendary figures as Cary Grant, Frank Sinatra, Richard Burton, Alec Guinness, and John Wayne.

In 2004 George received the Order of the Rising Sun, Gold Rays with Rosette from the emperor of Japan and a Lifetime Achievement Award from the San Diego Asian Film Festival. In 2008 he married Brad Altman in a ceremony that included close friends from George's *Star Trek* days. He was also given the LGBT Humanist Pride Award by the American Humanist Association in 2012, the 2013 National Leadership Award by the National Gay and Lesbian Task Force, the 2014 Vito Russo Award from GLAAD, the Distinguished Medal of Honor for Lifetime Achievement and Public Service from the Japanese American National Museum in 2015, and in 2016 an honorary doctorate of humane letters from California State University, Los Angeles. During this time, his musical, *Allegiance*, based on his personal experiences of the incarceration, premiered in San Diego on September 20, 2012 and played on Broadway from October 2015 to February 2016.

In 2019 he published a graphic memoir titled *They Called Us Enemy* to help educate young people about the Japanese American World War II incarceration experience. He is chairman emeritus of the Board of Governors of the Japanese American National Museum.

George **Taketa**, male, Nisei, King County, Washington, incarcerated age 13, Pinedale Assembly Center, Tule Lake Relocation Center, Heart Mountain Relocation Center. George was born in Orillia, Washington, on May 31, 1929, the second youngest of five children, to Kumajiro Taketa and Mitsuno (Shinohara) Taketa. He was in eighth grade when Pearl Harbor was attacked. In May 1945 he resettled in Cleveland, Ohio, where he finished high school. From 1951 to 1953 he served in the Korean War.

Minoru "Min" **Tamaki**, male, Nisei, San Francisco, California, incarcerated age 24, Tanforan Assembly Center, Topaz Relocation Center. Min was born in San Francisco, California, on December 23, 1918, the second oldest of five siblings, to Kameichi Tamaki and Tsuruyo Tamaki, both from families who were brewers of sake in Okinawa, Japan. Min's father came to Hawaii in 1906, leaving behind his wife and three-month-old daughter, Sadako. Kameichi labored on a sugar plantation before stowing away on a merchant ship bound for Eureka, California. He made his way to San Francisco, working day jobs. It would be another ten years before Kameichi could afford to send for his family, which he did in 1917. Then both he and his wife worked at the Menlo Park estate of William and California Colton Cluff. (William Cluff was the pioneer founder of William Cluff and Company, wholesale grocers, and their daughter California Josephine Cluff, married John D. Breuner of the John Breuner Company furniture store.) Kameichi was a skilled cook; Tsuruyo was the upstairs maid until she became pregnant with Min.

Kameichi went into the hotel business shortly after Min's birth, renting a space on Grant Avenue until the owner reclaimed the property and forced him to relocate temporarily to Pacific Avenue, a derelict part of the city known as the Barbary Coast, where rents were cheap. By 1922 he had saved enough money to purchase a six-flat Victorian house in Japantown. He called it the Fuji Hotel, and it served as temporary housing for Japanese migrant laborers, men waiting for picture brides, and, later, Black workers. But California's racist Alien Land Law prohibited immigrant Japanese from owning most kinds of real property. In order to get around the law, Kameichi hired a

White lawyer, Guy Calden, to buy the property in Calden's name and hold it in trust for Kameichi's firstborn children on American soil, which would be Min and his younger sister Shizu. In the early years Kameichi found tenants by meeting Japanese immigrants coming in to Angel Island and helping them through the immigration process.

Two years before Min graduated from Commerce High School, his father finally allowed him to forgo his usual summer job of helping him with the family business and join his friends who worked on Japanese American farms in the countryside, planting celery and drying apples. Min entered junior college in 1937 and, two years later, the School of Pharmacy at the University of California, San Francisco (UCSF). In 1939 his father died, so in order to cover his tuition, Min worked two jobs: one, sponsored by the National Youth Administration, included building classroom equipment in a woodshop for the UCSF School of Pharmacy, as well as setting up and cleaning the laboratory; the second was working in the Stanford Hospital pharmacy.

The Tamaki family was first incarcerated at Tanforan, but Min was permitted to leave in order to take the state pharmacy exam in San Francisco. He was given three hours on each of the three exam days, but he left the exam after only one hour so he could enjoy his freedom and go to Chinatown and bring chow mein back to his family. Later, when asked why he'd left early, he said, "I felt I had nothing to lose."

Most surprising to him, he passed the exam and received his pharmacy license, which was mailed to him at Topaz. While his family was in camp, long-time Black tenants Clara and Morris Raglan maintained the hotel and collected rents from the other tenants in exchange for residing at the hotel at no charge.

At Topaz, Min met and married his wife, Iyo. He was determined to leave camp, so he enrolled in a welding class while on his honeymoon in Salt Lake City. He knew that having a wartime essential-industry skill meant a possible job on the outside. He was offered a welding job in Chicago, which he used for leave clearance to get out of camp, but then he gave the welding job to another Nisei and sought a pharmacy position for himself. But no one was willing to hire a Japanese American.

Disheartened, he relocated to Philadelphia, where his wife's sister, Kay Yamashita, worked for the National Japanese American Student Relocation Council, sponsored by the Quakers. With his diploma and license in hand, Min sought work at the Philadelphia School of Pharmacy and Science and was hired by Dr. Joseph Whipple Eugene Harrisson, professor of pharmacology and director of that department at the school. Later, Harrisson became president and director of LaWall and Harrisson Laboratories.

Min worked for Professor Harrisson as a chemist until he received his draft notice. Harrison said he could get Min exempted from the draft because he was testing drugs necessary for the war effort, but Min declined. He wanted to be able to tell his children that he had served his country. In the army he worked as chief pharmacist at Cushing General Hospital in Framingham, Massachusetts, a psychiatric and surgical facility primarily for injured World War II veterans, and the largest military hospital on the East Coast. He was offered the same job at Cushing as a civilian when he was honorably discharged. He and Iyo returned to Oakland two years later, and he continued to work in the civil service as a pharmacist for the Veterans' Administration.

Ruth **Tanaka** (Gray), female, Nisei, Dinuba, California, incarcerated age 13, Poston Relocation Center. Ruth was born in Oakland, California, on January 6, 1929, the second oldest of four children, to Henry Ryuzo Tanaka and Toshiko (Suganuma) Tanaka. At the time of her incarceration, her father was a cleaner and dyer, and her mother was a student at the University of California. Her poem "Saga of a People" won fourth place out of six thousand entries in a *Scholastic* magazine literary contest. She wrote it as a junior at Parker Valley High School in the Poston Relocation Center.

John Yoshio **Tateishi**, male, Sansei, Los Angeles, California, incarcerated age 3, Manzanar Reception Center, Manzanar Relocation Center. John was born in Los Angeles, California, on August 21, 1939, the youngest of four boys, to Sam Shigetoshi Tateishi and Lillian Yuriko (Wada) Tateishi. He served in the US Army and graduated from the University of California, Berkeley. He received a master's degree in English literature at the University of California, Davis, and went on to teach at Barking College of the University of London and City College of San Francisco.

John gained national prominence in 1978 when, as chairman of the JACL's National Redress Committee, he launched a campaign to seek redress for Japanese Americans who had been incarcerated by the US government. He is credited with developing the legislative strategies that strengthened the grassroots campaign, which culminated in the Civil Liberties Act of 1988 ten years later. It was during his chairmanship that the idea of forming a commission to investigate the wartime removal and incarceration of Japanese Americans was first conceived.

After leaving the JACL, he founded Tateishi/Shinoda and Associates, a management and public affairs consulting firm in San Francisco, and continued working as a civil rights advocate. In 1999 he became the national executive director of the JACL. In 2001–2 he was a senior fellow at the UCLA School of Public Policy and Social Research, and in 2005 he became a founding trustee of the University of California, Merced. He is the author of *And Justice for All: An Oral History of the Japanese American Detention Camps* and *Redress: The Inside Story of the Successful Campaign for Japanese American Reparations.* He was also a contributing author to *Last Witnesses: Reflections on the Wartime Internment of Japanese Americans* by Erica Harth, which includes his essay, "Memories from Behind Barbed Wire."

Yukio **Tatsumi**, male, Nisei, Terminal Island, California, incarcerated age 22, Manzanar Reception Center, Manzanar Relocation Center. Yukio was born on Terminal Island, California, on August 23, 1920, the oldest of three children, to Kobei Tatsumi and Ohina (Hatashita) Tatsumi. His father was one of the original hard-hat abalone divers who was forced out of White Point on the Palos Verdes Peninsula and fished on Terminal Island instead. Later he managed the only Japanese-owned cannery as well as the White Point Hotel in San Pedro. When Kobei died in 1933, Ohina returned to Japan with Yukio, and he went to school in his father's hometown, Shimosato, Wakayama Prefecture. He graduated from a Japanese commercial high school, then went back to Terminal Island and finished his high school education at San Pedro High School. He graduated in 1940 and soon became a crewman on a fishing boat. He was also second baseman for the Terminal Island baseball team—the San Pedro Skippers—which became the premier Japanese American baseball team in California, crowned California state champions in 1941.

For a short time after the attack on Pearl Harbor, Yukio was asked to be an interpreter for the Issei fishermen who'd been arrested by the FBI and temporarily housed at Terminal Island's federal penitentiary. Then he, along with approximately one thousand other Terminal Islanders, was incarcerated at Manzanar. It was there he married his wife, Chiye Shintani, whom he had been dating before they were forcibly removed.

When he returned from camp, he took a job as a crewman on fishing boats in Fish Harbor, since Terminal Island as a community no longer existed. He left fishing in 1952 and worked as a supermarket produce clerk. But in the 1954 parade of boats at San Pedro's Fisherman's Fiesta, he was on the team that won the grand prize for the decoration of its boat, *Western Explorer*.

Two years later he bought the Oriental Food Market in Long Beach and operated it with his wife for twenty-six years. After he sold it, he went to work for the Japanese-owned California Rice Company as a sales adviser. In 1971 he and a group of friends from Terminal Island formed a club called the Terminal Islanders. Yukio was its president for twenty-seven years.

In 2013 he received a commendation from Harry H. Horinouchi, the Los Angeles consul general of Japan, and the following year he received from Consul General Horinouchi the Order of the Rising Sun, Gold and Silver Rays, conferred by the emperor of Japan. Three years later, at the age of ninety-five, Yukio met Prime Minister Shinzo Abe and his wife at their request.

Yukio was also a calligraphy artist. His calligraphic waka inscription on the Terminal Island Memorial monument reads, in translation:

Black Current off our shore
Fishes so plentiful

yet, hardships parents endured
we remember
and honor forever
our village no more

Yoshiye **Togasaki**, female, Nisei, Los Angeles, California, incarcerated age 38, Manzanar Reception Center, Manzanar Relocation Center, Tule Lake Relocation Center. Yoshiye was born in San Francisco, California, on January 3, 1904, the fifth of eight children, to devout Christians Kikumatsu Togasaki and Shige (Kushida) Togasaki. Her mother was educated at a university in Tokyo and was sent to America by the Women's Christian Temperance Union to work among single Japanese women. Yoshiye and her sister Mitsuye were sent to live with their grandmother in Tokyo because their mother had more children than she could handle. They stayed with their grandmother until she died five years later. Then they were sent to live with their father's parents in the country (Ibaraki Prefecture) for six months. They returned to the United States in 1910, when Yoshiye was six years old.

The Togasaki home was a gathering place for Japanese immigrants. Yoshiye's mother served the sick and the poor in the community. Her father was a lawyer who became the owner of an import-export business; he helped Japanese men start their own businesses and fight discrimination.

Yoshiye graduated from Lowell High School in 1921. She received her bachelor's degree in public health from the University of California, Berkeley, in 1929. In fact, all five of Yoshiye's sisters graduated from Berkeley and went on to have careers in medicine: Mitsuye, Chiye, Yaye, Teru, and Kazue (one of the first two women of Japanese ancestry to receive a medical degree in the United States). Yoshiye obtained her medical degree in 1935 from the Johns Hopkins University School of Medicine (the first medical school in the country to accept women on an equal basis with men), and in 1948 her master's degree from Harvard's School of Public Health. She was one of the beneficiaries of a gift to Johns Hopkins from five Quaker women who required the university to have a co-ed student body; if it didn't admit women, the university would have to return the money with compound interest.

Yoshiye went to Los Angeles General Hospital for her internship and had accepted a pediatric residency at Bellevue Hospital in New York City at the time she was incarcerated. The JACL needed chaperones for the ten young female volunteers who were going to Manzanar to work as secretaries, so Yoshiye and a nurse in her office volunteered to accompany them. At Manzanar they set up a medical unit and immediately established sterilization techniques in the kitchen. No one had been immunized, so whooping cough, scarlet fever, and measles were rampant throughout the camp. There was no running water and, in those days, no antibiotics or measles vaccine. She treated patients with tuberculosis and demanded they be segregated from the rest of the population. She read a report from Heart Mountain that described symptoms she recognized as the result of drinking untreated surface water from the Sierra Nevada, and she arranged for the camp to get a water filtration and chlorination system so the water would be safe for human consumption.

At one point Yoshiye became ill herself, and the WRA allowed her to transfer from Manzanar to Tule Lake; her sister Kazue, an obstetrician, was incarcerated there. Yoshiye was accompanied by two other sisters: Dr. Teru Togasaki who had been at Poston and Chiye (Togasaki) Yamanaka, a registered nurse who had been at Minidoka. Kazue and Tule Lake's chief medical officer, Dr. George Hashiba, performed a hysterectomy on her, and she returned to the pediatric ward five days later. She remained for six more months, until Hashiba thought the sisters' treatment demands for the patients were too disruptive and transferred them back to Manzanar. When they realized they could not be effective at camp, they left Manzanar to finish their residencies. Yoshiye went to Bellevue, Kazue went to Chicago for training in obstetrics, and Chiye went to work for the Chicago Department of Public Health. Then Chiye discovered that her husband had been imprisoned in Japan for refusing to observe the religious military orders for emperor worship, so she sailed to Hiroshima to work as a public health nurse with the Atomic Bomb Casualty Commission. Teru went to Kings County Hospital, in New York, then to

Honolulu for thirteen years, and finally back to San Francisco to practice with Kazue.

After Bellevue, Yoshiye volunteered for military service as a medical officer with the United Nations Relief and Rehabilitation Administration in southern Italy's displaced persons camp; she was in charge of six camps for central European refugees. Later she joined the California Department of Public Health; she was the first Japanese American woman to work in a public health laboratory in California.

In 1951 she became assistant health officer at the Contra Costa County Health Department and stayed for the next twenty-one years; she was promoted to chief of the Division of Preventive Medical Services and deputy health officer for Contra Costa County. Yoshiye was a committed activist in the American Civil Liberties Union, president of the Contra Costa chapter of the JACL, and a founding member of the Japanese Women Alumnae of UC Berkeley, which gave her the 1991 Outstanding Alumna award.

She received a plethora of community service awards, including one from the California Association of Mental Health, the Distinguished Woman of the Year award from the American Association of University Women, the 1989 Lifelong Achievement Award from the Concord Human Relations Commission, the Humanitarian of the Year Award at the 1990 Contra Costa County Dr. Martin Luther King Jr. Commemoration, and the 1993 Elizabeth Blackwell Medal from the American Medical Women's Association, its most prestigious honor.

Rudy Kazuo **Tokiwa**, male, Nisei, Salinas, California, incarcerated age 17, Salinas Assembly Center, Poston Relocation Center. Rudy was born in Coyote, California, on July 7, 1925, the youngest of five children, to Jisuke Tokiwa and Fusa (Yokote) Tokiwa. He grew up in Salinas. At the age of thirteen, he went to live with his older sister in Manchuria and Japan and attended school there. He returned to California around 1939 and graduated from Salinas High School. Rudy left the Poston concentration camp on June 15, 1943, to work in Cozad, Nebraska, which was suffering from a rural labor shortage, and then volunteered to serve in the US Army. He was sent to Camp Shelby, in Mississippi, to join Company K of the 442nd Regimental Combat Team as a battalion runner. For his valor in the rescue of the Lost Battalion, the liberation of Bruyères, and other heroic actions, including the single-handed capture of a group of German officers, Rudy was awarded a Bronze Star and a Purple Heart.

Rudy was active in programs for young adults and established a homestay program for Hawaii youths. He was also recognized for his lifetime work as a Little League umpire. He served as the western regional director of the Boy Scouts of America and helped to start the Boy Scouts of America troop at the San Jose Buddhist Church Betsuin. Rudy was the founding president of Go for Broke (now the National Japanese American Historical Society) and an early supporter of the Japanese American Memorial to Patriotism during World War II in Washington, DC. He extensively lobbied members of Congress for the passage of H.R. 442 and was instrumental in securing votes from recalcitrant members, especially veterans.

Chiye **Tomihiro**, female, Nisei, Portland, Oregon, incarcerated age 17, Portland Assembly Center, Minidoka Relocation Center. Chiye was born in Portland, Oregon, on December 20, 1924, an only child, to Senichi Tomihiro and Satoru Tomihiro. The Tomihiro family were good friends of the Yasui family; Minoru Yasui had offices in her father's building.

Chiye was forcibly removed one month before graduating from high school; it was a great disappointment that the Portland Assembly Center was so close to her high school but she was prevented from participating in her graduation ceremony. She left Minidoka in April 1943 to attend the University of Denver. Chiye attended one year of college there and then transferred to the University of Wisconsin where she graduated with a degree in business. After college she moved to Chicago, where her family had resettled after camp, and became an accountant.

Chiye was actively involved with the Chicago chapter of the JACL and in developing support for the passage of the Immigration and Nationality Act of

1952. She also was instrumental in getting President Gerald Ford to rescind Executive Order 9066 that sent persons of Japanese ancestry to detention centers in World War II. As witness chair for the hearings of the Commission on Wartime Relocation and Internment of Civilians held in Chicago, Chiye solicited former incarcerees to testify before the commission and helped prepare them to give their testimonies. She later served as redress chair and as president of the Chicago chapter of the JACL from 1977 to 1978.

After she retired, she taught a weekly ikebana (Japanese flower arranging) class; she and her friends drove to the Stratford Shakespeare Festival in Canada every year.

Jack Kiyoto **Tono**, male, Nisei, San Jose, California, incarcerated age 22, Santa Anita Assembly Center, Heart Mountain Relocation Center, McNeil Island Federal Penitentiary. Jack was born in Gilroy, California, on November 16, 1920, the eldest of twelve children, to Matsuhei Tono and Shiteyo (Kono) Tono. They were sharecropper farmers in California. Jack graduated from Gilroy High School and was working in a vegetable packinghouse for Durio Brothers when Pearl Harbor was attacked. He was one of sixty-three men at Heart Mountain who were found guilty for their refusal to register for the draft and take their physical. He was sentenced to three years in prison at the McNeil Island Federal Penitentiary in Washington's Puget Sound. The draft resisters were pardoned by President Harry S. Truman in 1947.

At the end of the war, Jack's family moved to Bristol, Pennsylvania, and Jack followed when he was released from prison. He worked on the family farm and then as a welder on the NS *Savannah* at New York Shipbuilding in Camden, New Jersey. At the time the ship was one of only four nuclear-powered, non-military vessels in the world. Jack was present when First Lady Mamie Eisenhower christened the ship in July 1959. Later Jack went to work for Strick Trailers.

He met his wife, Mary, in New York, where she was going to the Traphagen School of Fashion at 1680 Broadway. Jack and Mary were married at the New York Buddhist Church and then joined Jack's family in Bristol.

Jack, Mary, and their five children moved to Chicago when Strick Trailers offered Jack a position there. Eventually, Jack started his own welding business repairing semi-trailers. Mary worked at the Chicago Board of Education for many years. They attended the Midwest Buddhist Temple and were active members in many Chicago associations.

June Hisaye (Abe) **Toshiyuki**, female, Nisei, Fresno, California, incarcerated age 28, Fresno Assembly Center, Jerome Relocation Center. June was born in Salinas Valley, California, on August 27, 1914, the oldest of four children, to Kyugoro Abe and Tone (Shinozaki) Abe. They lived on a beet farm in Blanco, California, owned by Adam Thompson. June was the only Japanese student at the local school. Then the family moved to Salinas to work on the Yamamoto strawberry farm. There June went to school with mostly Japanese students in a one-room schoolhouse in Natividad, California. She went to Salinas Union High School for two years until her family moved again to Chualar, California, to raise lettuce. Chualar didn't have a high school, so June was one of twenty-nine students to graduate high school in Gonzales, California.

Soon her family moved to Fresno to help her mother's second cousin with his Japanese-Chinese restaurant. June met her relative's son, Michio Toshiyuki, who had just come home from the University of Southern California in Los Angeles. They married a year later, after he graduated. Not long after their honeymoon, June began taking care of Michio's mother, an invalid with a heart condition; she would care for her mother-in-law for nineteen years. June also assumed the care of her brother's two-year-old son, whose mother had been killed in a car accident. Eventually, June and Michio took in another one of June's motherless nephews when he was thirteen years old. In addition to the other family members they cared for, the couple had two daughters of their own. Because Michio was the eldest son, the responsibility to feed the entire extended family often fell to June.

Michio became a pharmacist and together he and June owned the West Fresno Drug Store. They were known for personally delivering medication to shut-ins after hours. Their store was one of the largest establishments in

Fresno's Nihonmachi, with a large toy section and a Japanese art department. On the night before they had to leave for the assembly center, June was boxing for storage items labeled "Made in Japan" and shipping drugs back to the wholesaler when she suffered an acute appendicitis attack. She needed emergency surgery and recovered in the assembly center.

June was a member of the JACL and served on the Fresno County Grand Jury and the Fresno County Joint Commission for the Aging. In 1982 she was awarded Mother of the Year by the Fresno County Women's Chamber of Commerce, in part due to a letter written by Gene Lujuano, a Mexican boy who worked at the store and lived with June and Michio after his family moved away in his last year of high school. She was a founding member of the United Japanese Congregational Church in West Fresno, which merged with the Christ United Methodist Church and moved to Clovis. She was also an active participant of the Lake Sequoia Retreat (a summer camp for Japanese American Christian youth) for fourteen years.

Mary Tsuruko (Dakuzaku) **Tsukamoto**, female, Nisei, Florin, California, incarcerated age 27, Fresno Assembly Center, Jerome Relocation Center. Mary was born in San Francisco, California, on January 17, 1915, the second of six children, to Chosei Taro Dakuzaku and Kame (Yoshinaga) Dakuzaku from Okinawa, Japan. Her father was seventeen when he came to the United States and opened the Capitol Laundry on Geary Street in San Francisco. The family moved to Florin in 1925 to grow strawberries; all the children had chores on the farm. Mary attended the segregated Florin East Grammar School and graduated from the integrated Elk Grove Junior High School. One of her Caucasian teachers, Mabel Barron, was able to get her a $150 scholarship so she could attend the College of the Pacific, Stockton, in 1933, but Mary had to drop out due to ill health and money problems. In 1936 she married Al Iwao Tsukamoto, a farmer, strawberry salesman, and son of another Florin market gardener, with whom she would spend the next six decades. They had a daughter a year later. She taught Sunday school at the local Methodist church and became executive secretary of the Florin chapter of the JACL. In 1940 she and her husband finally persuaded the school board to stop segregating the schools.

After the attack on Pearl Harbor, she opened a JACL office in Florin. She consulted with the army's Wartime Civil Control Administration, the Federal Reserve Bank, and the Farm Security Administration, so she could advise the Issei and Nisei residents on what had to be done in order to comply with Executive Order 9066. At the Fresno Assembly Center, she was a speech teacher and taught English as a second language. She continued to teach English and public speaking to Issei incarcerees at Jerome and became hopeful when religious groups donated Christmas gifts for the children. Eleanor Roosevelt sent her a personal greeting in response to her holiday letter. Mary befriended activist Yuri Kochiyama (see the biography of Mary Yuriko "Yuri" Nakahara [Kochiyama]), and together they built YWCA and USO chapters in camp. Mary and Yuri organized Nisei women to serve as hostesses to the Nisei soldiers of the 442nd Regimental Combat Team when they visited from Camp Shelby in Mississippi.

Mary and her daughter left camp in November 1943; she was suffering from rheumatoid arthritis aggravated by camp conditions. They reunited with Al and his side of the family in Kalamazoo, Michigan, where he was working in a bakery. They were there for two years before returning to Florin in 1945, only to discover that most of it had burned to the ground. Al went to work at the Sacramento Army Depot. Mary went to Sacramento State College (now California State University, Sacramento) and started her twenty-six-year teaching career as a substitute teacher. She was hired permanently three years later at the Florin East Grammar School.

Her leadership in the Japanese American redress movement began in the 1970s. In 1975, she was selected Sacramento County Teacher of the Year, and a tree on Redwood Highway was dedicated to her. Two years later, she became director of Jan Ken Po Gakko, a Japanese cultural heritage program for Yonsei (fourth-generation Japanese Americans), a position she held for five years (*jan ken po* is the Japanese equivalent of the rock-paper-scissors game, and *gakko* means "school").

She chaired the redress committee of the Florin JACL chapter and testified before a House subcommittee at the 1981 hearings in San Francisco for the Commission on Wartime Relocation and Internment of Civilians. In 1986 she was awarded the Nisei of the Biennium award from the JACL. The following year she published a memoir, *We the People: A Story of Internment in America*; she also helped the Smithsonian Institution in curating artifacts for its exhibition called *A More Perfect Union* on the incarceration of Japanese Americans, which opened on October 1, 1987. She is responsible for creating the Japanese American Archival Collection at California State University, Sacramento.

In 1992 she received a National Humanitarian Award and the Mary Tsukamoto Elementary School in Sacramento was named after her. She was named a Notable Californian by the California State Senate in 1997, making her the second person ever to receive this high honor. This was followed by the California Asian Pacific Sesquicentennial Award for a life of accomplishments in the Asian American community. On January 27, 1998, three weeks after she died, Congressman Robert Matsui paid tribute to her in prepared remarks on the floor of the US House of Representatives.

Takashi "Dwight" **Uchida**, male, Issei, Berkeley, California, incarcerated age 58, Fort Missoula Alien Detention Center, Tanforan Assembly Center, Topaz Relocation Center. Dwight was born in Kyoto, Japan, on April 12, 1884, to Katsu (Sakane) Uchida. He was a student at Doshisha University in Kyoto before he left Japan in 1903 at the age of nineteen to teach Japanese in Hawaii. He arrived in San Francisco three years later, shortly after the earthquake, and found work with the Furuya Company, operated by Masajiro Furuya, a prominent Japanese entrepreneur, which eventually went bankrupt during the Great Depression. For the remainder of his working life until his mandatory retirement two years prior to World War II, he was an assistant manager of the San Francisco branch of Mitsui Bussan, one of Japan's major import-export firms.

As a former executive of a Japanese firm, he was among the first group of

Japanese men to be arrested by the FBI following the attack on Pearl Harbor. He was interned as an enemy alien in Missoula, Montana, until he was reunited with his family in the Tanforan Assembly Center. After the war he resettled in Oakland, California, and was committed to rebuilding his life, even though he had lost all of his Mitsui retirement benefits. He occupied himself with odd jobs such as mending clothes at a dry cleaner's and working as a packer in the shipping department of a church board (a body that oversees the ministry of a church to ensure it is solvent and is satisfying its core mission).

Yoshiko **Uchida**, female, Nisei, Berkeley, California, incarcerated age 21, Tanforan Assembly Center, Topaz Relocation Center. Yoshiko was born in Alameda, California, on November 24, 1921, the second daughter to Takashi "Dwight" Uchida (see his biography) and Iku (Umegaki) Uchida. Her mother was the eldest daughter of a prefectural governor of Japan and immigrated to the United States to marry Yoshiko's father in 1916. Both were graduates of Doshisha University, one of the early Christian universities of Japan.

Yoshiko grew up in a Berkeley neighborhood that once allowed only White residents. Her father was an assistant manager at Mitsui Bussan in San Francisco, so her family could afford to travel, go to concerts, and pay for piano lessons. The Uchida family attended the Japanese Independent Congregational Church every Sunday. Yoshiko graduated from high school in two and a half years and enrolled at the University of California, Berkeley, at the age of sixteen; she majored in English, history, and philosophy. She became president of the Japanese Women's Student Club for a year and also active in the Northern California Conference for Nisei Christians.

Because her father was a community leader, he was immediately arrested by the FBI after the bombing of Pearl Harbor and held at the immigration detention quarters in San Francisco. He was then transferred for internment in Missoula, Montana. The rest of the family was able to put some of their possessions in storage or with Caucasian friends at the First Congregational Church of Berkeley before being incarcerated.

Yoshiko taught second grade at the Tanforan Assembly Center, where she received her college diploma, with honors, at the horse stall where she was living. Her father joined them a few weeks later after he had been "paroled." In May 1943 she received an acceptance letter and full scholarship to graduate school at Smith College in Northampton, Massachusetts, and was permitted to leave Topaz. Her older sister, Keiko, who had graduated from Mills College with a degree in child development, had been offered a job close to Smith at Mount Holyoke College in South Hadley, Massachusetts, so the two sisters traveled east together while their parents resettled in Salt Lake City, Utah.

Yoshiko graduated from Smith a year later with a master's degree in education, and the sisters ended up in New York City. There she worked secretarial jobs and took a class on writing for children at Columbia University. She was encouraged to submit her manuscript of Japanese folktales, adapted from her mother's stories, to a commercial publisher, and in 1949 *The Dancing Kettle and Other Japanese Folk Tales* was published by Harcourt, Brace and Company. This was the start of her forty-two-year career as a writer, publishing an adult memoir, a young adult autobiography, and scores of children's books, many of them using Japanese American incarceration camps as a backdrop.

She won the Commonwealth Club of California's Silver Medal for *Samurai of Gold Hill* and the Children's Book of the Year from the Child Study Association of America for *The Happiest Ending*. In 1951 she received a Ford Foundation Fellowship to study in Japan for two years. When she returned, she chose to live in Oakland, where her parents had already resettled. After they died, she moved into an apartment in Berkeley, where she lived alone, writing books, for the rest of her life. In an interview with Bill Hosokawa for *Reader's Digest*, she said, to be frugal, she would write her first drafts on the back of junk mail before creating revised manuscripts on a typewriter. In 1971 she published *Journey to Topaz*, a novel based on her incarceration experience, which became a standard text in California classrooms. Between 1949 and 1987, she published twenty-five books supporting the relationship between the East and West. In 1992, a year before she died, she published a middle grade book called *The Invisible Thread*, an autobiography of her childhood during World War II and her incarceration.

Ernest Nobumaro **Uno**, male, Nisei, Los Angeles, California, incarcerated age 17, Santa Anita Assembly Center, Granada (Amache) Relocation Center. Ernest was born in Salt Lake City, Utah, on February 9, 1925, the seventh of ten children, to George Kumemaro Uno and Riki (Kita) Uno. Keiki "Kay" (Uno) Kaneko was his younger sister (see her biography). His father was one of fourteen children born into a samurai military family that trained falcons in Sendai, Miyagi Prefecture, Japan; his mother was born and raised in Kanazawa, Ishikawa Prefecture, Japan. They both attended missionary schools, both learned some English, and were childhood sweethearts.

His father came to the United States in 1906 when he was nineteen years old. He was made foreman of a Great Northern Railway gang (a group of workers who specialize in replacing sections of track) because he could translate instructions to the immigrants working on the railroad ties. He then went to work for his older sister's wealthy husband, who had his own canning factory in San Francisco. George sent for Riki, and they married in 1911. They lived in Richmond, California. He learned flower arranging from an Italian florist whom he would greet every day in the Ferry Building on his daily commute to San Francisco. He wrote to the Church of Jesus Christ of Latter-day Saints offering to be its florist for the Mormon Tabernacle and was hired. George and Riki moved to Salt Lake City, and his flower arranging there won him many international awards from the United Floral Association.

But Utah's weather was too severe, so Ernest's parents moved to Los Angeles, where his father worked for the Pacific Rose Company until he came down with the flu. He was diagnosed with tuberculosis and pleurisy and was told that he had to get out of the flower business if he wanted to regain his health. As he needed a job outdoors in the sun, he became a salesman, traveling up and down the West Coast by train or car to small farm towns, and took orders for custom-made men's suits based on sample swatches of wool he would carry around with him. Between the ages of twelve and fourteen, Ernest traveled with his father as he went from farm to farm selling suits.

At the time of the bombing of Pearl Harbor, Ernest was in eleventh grade; the vice-principal suggested he drop out. By this time his father was an honorary member of a professional entomologist association in Southern California. He had a new job working for the Department of Food and Agriculture as a self-taught entomologist, studying the insects eating crops. Then the war broke out, and his father was arrested in February 1942; he was imprisoned for the next five and a half years.

Instead of finishing high school at Camp Amache, Ernest designed and created silk-screen freedom posters for the US Navy. Two of his brothers were in Minnesota at the Military Intelligence Service Language School. Ernest volunteered for the 442nd Regimental Combat Team against his parents' wishes, but he couldn't be inducted until he'd undergone a double hernia operation at the camp.

Once in basic training, he received word from his eldest sister, Hana, that his mother, his two younger brothers, Edison and Robert, and his youngest sister, Kay, had left Granada to join his father in Crystal City, Texas. She told him that their father had petitioned the government for deportation to Japan and planned to take their mother and the kids with him. Shortly thereafter he received a letter from his father written in English that said his loyalty was to the emperor of Japan and that he truly believed his destiny was to return to the land of his birth. He also said he would consider Ernest a hero if he died on the battlefield, instead of a "live coward" if he survived; not dying for his country would be a shame on the family.

After the war Ernest returned to California a "homeless civilian." Based on his years of military service, he was offered a high school diploma by the same school system he had left in eleventh grade, without having to take another year of classes. His father was finally released from camp in September 1947, two full years after World War II had ended, because he was considered so dangerous. One of Ernest's brothers, Buddy, was working as a pro-Japan journalist in Japan, and the US government was in possession of two letters written by two other brothers, Howard and Stanley, who were in the Military Intelligence Service, testifying against their own father. They wanted the federal government to know that they didn't share their father's pro-Japan views; consequently, the government continued to detain him. Meanwhile, as soon as Kay, Robert, and Edison told their father that they refused to go with him to Japan, he took his name off the repatriation list.

Ernest was reunited with his family in California, but his mother died of a heart attack soon after. The remaining family in Los Angeles was able to move into the same house where they had lived for eighteen years before they were forcibly removed. Ernest graduated from Whittier College in 1950 with a degree in group social work and eventually became a branch executive of an interracial YMCA. He wanted to progress within the YMCA and become an administrator, but in 1962 he was told he couldn't reach that level in California because he was a Nisei, even though his skills were exemplary. Then a Black friend who had become a YMCA executive in Honolulu gave him a job as a program director. Three years later he took a similar position on the mainland at the Ventura YMCA, thinking it would be good for his career to socialize almost exclusively with Caucasians. Ernest moved back to Hawaii ten years later when he took a job at the new Nuuanu YMCA. He worked for the YMCA organization for thirty years; he was also ordained as a deacon in the Episcopal Church and served as chaplain for the 442nd Veterans Club.

Keiko "Kay" **Uno** (Kaneko), female, Nisei, Los Angeles, California, incarcerated age 10, Santa Anita Assembly Center, Granada (Amache) Relocation Center. Kay was born in Los Angeles, California, on October 7, 1932, the youngest of ten children, to George Kumemaro Uno and Riki (Kita) Uno. Ernest Nobumaro Uno was her older brother (see his biography). Kay enrolled in Los Angeles City College after high school; her aspiration was to become a nurse. Her college adviser convinced her to get a bachelor's degree at the University of California, Berkeley, and then attend the University of California, San Francisco School of Nursing. After one semester and a summer, she was short one credit in fine arts, so she stayed in San Francisco and worked at the Macy's department store while earning the extra credit through a correspondence course. She entered nursing school the following semester and graduated in a class of eleven students.

She had met Edwin Tetsuo Kaneko of Kona, Hawaii, when she was sixteen. It was 1948 and her mother had just died. Mutual friends had told Ed to look up her family when he was visiting Los Angeles. At the time the Unos were living in a Quonset hut in Rodger Young Village, a housing project for veterans in Griffith Park. Ed enjoyed seeing her, and once he was back in Hawaii, he kept in touch with her by mail. He joined the army before graduating from high school and let her know he would be going to Korea by way of Osaka, Japan. He knew that her brother Buddy, the journalist, was living there, so Ed met up with him and took pictures of him and his family to send back to her.

When Ed was discharged in 1953, he finished high school on the GI Bill at the University of Hawaii and then wrote her to say he'd be going to college— either the University of California or Michigan State University. Kay wrote back to say she was engaged, then realized she had made a mistake. She broke her engagement, but Ed had already accepted Michigan State. He wrote to her every day, sometimes twice a day, and visited her over three summers. They got engaged over the phone, which Ed had prearranged with Kay's niece, sister-in-law, and housemother. Suddenly they were all standing by the phone with a tray holding Ed's picture, a ring, and a lei of Hawaiian flowers. Edwin and Kay finally married in 1955 and lived in Michigan while he completed his master's degree in civil engineering.

Kay's work as a home care registered nurse followed Ed's career path in the Department of Transportation. They went to Honolulu, Hawaii, where they built a house in Waipahu, and lived there until the government moved them to Berkeley so that Ed could get a second master's degree in aviation. Then he was sent to Washington, DC, where the couple lived for five years while he worked for the Federal Aviation Administration (FAA). Eventually he was overseeing the entire Pacific Rim, supervising over four hundred workers, and he and Kay were living in Guam. Kay was working for the Red Cross, attending to pregnant women, children, and orphans in refugee camps.

After Guam they lived for fourteen years on Oahu, where Ed was the FAA's top division chief for both the Pacific and West Coast regions. Then he was appointed FAA manager for all of Asia, and they moved to Tokyo for three years, based at the US embassy. In Tokyo Kay belonged to two organizations, the Foreign Nurses Association and the College Women's Association of Japan. After Ed retired, they bought a Kona coffee farm in Holualoa, Hawaii, and Ed became a master weaver of lauhala hats.

Kay also worked as a public health nurse and a health counselor in a high school program for abused children, runaways, drug addicts, and youth who had attempted suicide. She was president of the Hawaii Association for Family and Community Education, a founding member of the Japanese American National Museum, and a supporter of the American Association of University Women's GEM (Gaining Educational Momentum) Fund. She was married to Ed for sixty-three years and raised three children.

Mitsuo "Mits" **Usui**, male, Nisei, Los Angeles, California, incarcerated age 25, Santa Anita Assembly Center, Granada (Amache) Relocation Center. Mits was born in Los Angeles, California, on March 7, 1917, the second oldest of four children, to Ryunosuke Usui and Fusa (Hosaya) Usui. His father was active in the Episcopal Church and was interned, along with Germans, Italians, and Japanese Peruvians, at the Tuna Canyon Detention Station in Tujunga, California, a former Civilian Conservation Corps camp run by the Department of Justice. As a result, the family lost its landscape nursery business.

Mits was a member of the Military Intelligence Service; he was a liaison between Okinawan and US Army interpreters and served in the Battle of Okinawa. At one point he was stationed in the Philippines and translated newspapers in Korea. His most vivid memory of military service was trying to learn the Okinawan dialect as he interrogated civilians. He received the Combat Infantryman Badge, the Combat Parachutist Badge, the Asiatic-Pacific Campaign Medal, the Philippine Liberation Medal, and the Good Conduct Medal.

After the war he entered into a partnership with his brother in the landscape nursery business but decided to become a real estate broker instead. Mits was a member of the JACL and a founding member of the San Fernando Valley Japanese American Community Center.

Ronald "Ron" Kaoru **Wakabayashi**, male, Sansei. Ron was born in Reno, Nevada, on November 13, 1944, to Fred Shinsuke Wakabayashi and Kimiko Edith (Yamadera) Wakabayashi. His Issei father immigrated from Yamanashi Prefecture, Japan, and was incarcerated in the Rohwer Relocation Center. His Kibei-Nisei mother and her family were incarcerated at Topaz and Tule Lake. His parents married after they left their respective camps and resettled in Reno, Nevada. His siblings consist of a sister, two half sisters, and two half brothers.

After the exclusion order was lifted, the Wakabayashis returned to Los Angeles, resettling first in the South Central neighborhood and later in East Los Angeles, where Ron's father worked for a dry cleaner. Ron was from a Buddhist family, but he attended the Maryknoll School run by the Catholic Church. He grew up as part of the multiracial community on the east side of Los Angeles as well as in Little Tokyo.

He became involved with Asian American political issues as a college student during the late 1960s; in 1969, as the JACL youth director, he helped to organize the first pilgrimage to Manzanar. During the administration of Mayor Tom Bradley in Los Angeles, he served in Oriental Concern, the Asian American Drug Abuse Program, and other community social service organizations.

Ron became the national director of the JACL, based in San Francisco, from 1981 to 1988; he was heavily involved in the redress movement. After leaving the JACL's administration, he returned to Los Angeles and served as the executive director of both the Los Angeles City and the Los Angeles County Commission on Human Relations. In 1999 he was appointed the western regional director with the US Department of Justice, Community Relations Service, which involved working with Muslim, Arab, and Sikh communities in the states of Arizona, California, Hawaii, and Nevada, and the US territories of American Samoa, Guam, and the Northern Mariana Islands. He is working in retirement with Black communities, particularly with a project at Ohio State's Divided Communities Project.

Jeanne Toyo **Wakatsuki** (Houston), female, Nisei, Santa Monica, California, incarcerated age 8, Manzanar Reception Center, Manzanar Relocation Center. Jeanne was born in Inglewood, California, on September 26, 1934, the youngest of ten children, to Ko "George" Wakatsuki and Riku (Sugai) Wakatsuki. Her father was a fisherman and farmer, born in Hiroshima Prefecture, Japan. Her mother was born on a boat in a harbor in Kauai, Hawaii.

Jeanne's family moved to Ocean Park, a neighborhood in Santa Monica, when she was two years old. Her father became a commercial fisherman and her mother worked in a Long Beach fish cannery. After the attack on Pearl Harbor, her father was falsely accused by the FBI of supplying oil to enemy submarines based on photographs of him with barrels of fish bait. He was immediately taken away for nine months to a prison in Bismarck, North Dakota; her mother didn't know where he was or if she'd ever see him again. The family moved to Terminal Island, but the community there was the first to be forcibly removed. By April they were on a bus to Manzanar.

When Jeanne was eventually reunited with her father in Manzanar, he was a changed man. She later described "his dark . . . brooding presence" and said, "It seemed he didn't go outside for months. He sat in there, or paced, alone a great deal of the time." She also noted, "He didn't die there, but things finished for him there, whereas for me it was like a birthplace. The camp was where our lifelines intersected." He refused to leave the camp until October 1945.

The family returned to live in a Long Beach housing project for the poor. The year before Jeanne graduated from high school, they moved again to San Jose. She was the first in her family to go to college. Jeanne graduated with a bachelor's degree in sociology from San Jose State University. For two years she worked at Hillcrest Juvenile Hall, a detention center in San Mateo, California, as a group counselor for teenage girls. In 1957 she married James D. Houston, whom she had dated in college, and they moved to Santa

Cruz, where, together, they authored *Farewell to Manzanar*, an account of her childhood before, during, and after her family's incarceration, which has become a contemporary classic and a staple in school curricula.

Teru **Watanabe**, female, Nisei, Los Angeles, California, incarcerated age 28, Manzanar Reception Center, Manzanar Relocation Center. Teru was born in Los Angeles, California, on March 10, 1914, the youngest of six children, to Tomoichi Watanabe and Masano (Takenaka) Watanabe from Gifu, Japan. Her older siblings were Hide, Aiko, Shinko, Nozomo, and Toshihisa "Tom" Watanabe. Shortly before the start of World War II, Teru went to work as a clerk for the California State Board of Equalization, Sales Tax Division, in Los Angeles. She obtained permanent work status on November 26, 1941.

On March 4, 1942, she was handed a notice of suspension without pay and was told not to return. She was one of six Nisei employees who were terminated this way. On March 18, 1942, she was charged with being a spy for the government of Japan because she had access to government files. Shocked to be accused of treason without cause, she and the other terminated Nisei employees hired an attorney, despite being unemployed and without any income. The State of California never retracted its accusation that she was a Japanese spy, although the charges against her were never proven.

Her brother, Dr. Tom Watanabe, lost his medical practice and had to leave behind all new office equipment and furnishings. Her father was arrested on the night of the Pearl Harbor attack and held for two years in eight different Department of Justice internment camps before he was found to be innocent of any suspicious activity. He was released from prison to rejoin his family in Manzanar on December 13, 1943. At Manzanar, Teru worked as a dish wiper for sixteen dollars per month and helped register volunteers for the US Army.

Teru left Manzanar for Chicago on January 19, 1944, with twenty-five dollars from the WRA and a train ticket. She returned to Los Angeles in June 1953 and worked as a CPA. A strong advocate for redress, Teru testified at the hearings of the Commission on Wartime Relocation and Internment of Civilians held in Los Angeles on August 6, 1981.

Masao **Yamada**, male, Nisei, Kauai, Hawaii, age 34 when Pearl Harbor was attacked. Masao was born in Makaweli (now known as Kaumakani) on the island of Kauai, Hawaii, on April 10, 1907, the third of seven children, to Suehichi Yamada and Kiku Yamada. His father was a plantation carpenter. While attending the University of Hawai'i, Masao became a youth leader at the YMCA, and then applied for a job there after he graduated. When he discovered that the job had been given to a younger, less experienced Caucasian undergraduate at a much higher salary, he confronted Frank Atherton, president of the Honolulu YMCA, and told him that he was quitting because of YMCA's unacceptable prejudice. Atherton was a wealthy investor in sugar plantations. He was so impressed by Masao's candor that he paid for him to attend Auburn Theological Seminary in New York City.

Masao continued his training at Andover Newton Theological School outside of Boston, then returned to Hawaii to become ordained as a Christian minister in 1933. He was sent to Central Kona Union Church to minister to Japanese immigrants. Two years later he married Ai Mukaida and moved to Japan to learn to speak Japanese fluently. Within a year, however, Japan's military government classified him as a "pacifist" and told him to leave the country. He and his wife returned to Kauai. He was ministering at the Hanapepe Japanese Christian Church when the war broke out.

He immediately joined Kauai's Emergency Service Committee as a liaison between the community leaders, the military, and the local Japanese people. He was instrumental in getting the 442nd Regimental Combat Team activated, but when he learned that the battalion had only Caucasian chaplains, he convinced the military leadership that the soldiers would respond better to a Japanese American chaplain. At age thirty-seven he was commissioned as a captain in the US Army to serve as the army's first Nisei chaplain.

On May 31, 1943, he left his wife and three young sons to enroll in the Army Chaplain School at Harvard University. By the end of the summer, he had joined the Third Battalion of the 442nd RCT at Camp Shelby. His communication skills helped to resolve conflicts between the men from Hawaii and the men from the mainland who had just left their families in concentration camps.

He urged the commander to recruit a second Japanese American chaplain from the mainland to help with the rift between the two factions. That chaplain would be George Aki. Masao then visited Jerome Relocation Center to better understand the camp experience for himself, and he was so affected by the sadness there that he came back and delivered a sermon about discrimination. It made the Caucasian chaplains uncomfortable, and for a while he was excluded from tasks assigned to other chaplains. In fact, one of the White chaplains told him that America was for Anglo-Saxon Protestants and all Americans of Japanese ancestry should go back to Japan. Masao's response was to pray for him.

Masao worked alongside the medical detachment of the 100th/442nd RCT in numerous conflicts and suffered serious injuries, narrowly avoiding death, and then returned to the battlefield. He also had many close calls; one soldier said he was "walking hand in hand with God." If the men were crouched in foxholes for long periods, he would travel from hole to hole to reassure and encourage them. He also traveled many miles, visiting up to ten hospitals a day. His most excruciating spiritual test came during the rescue of the Lost Battalion—the 141st Infantry Regiment, Thirty-Sixth Infantry Division, from Texas—watching as the men of the Third Battalion of the 100th were decimated. He received the Legion of Merit, a Purple Heart with Oak Leaf Cluster, and the Italian War Cross for Military Valor. After the war he ministered at several Hawaiian churches and the Hawaii State Hospital.

Mitsuye (Yasutake) **Yamada**, female, Nisei, Seattle, Washington, incarcerated age 19, Puyallup Assembly Center, Minidoka Relocation Center. Mitsuye was born in Fukuoka Prefecture, Japan, while her mother was visiting there from the United States, on July 5, 1923, the third of four children, to Jack Kaichiro Yasutake and Hide (Shiraki) Yasutake. Her mother left Mitsuye in Japan with a neighbor's family for three and a half years. Eventually they were reunited, but Mitsuye was sent back to Japan again to live with her paternal grandparents for eighteen months at the age of nine. She spent the rest of her childhood in Seattle, Washington.

Her father had come to San Francisco at the age of sixteen. He found work in a private home where he was given room and board while he finished high school and learned English. He studied engineering and the arts at Stanford University and met his wife on a trip to Japan. When they returned to America, he had to drop out of college and work days and nights to support her. Just after their first son was born in 1920, he happened to meet an Immigration and Naturalization Service (INS) agent who was looking for a Japanese translator, and suddenly Jack had a job for $1,200 per year. It was a miracle. He loyally worked as a translator for the federal government for the next twenty-one years—until he was arrested as an enemy alien after the attack on Pearl Harbor.

Jack was the founder and president of the Senryu Society, a poetry club committed to the seventeen-syllable form; sometimes the club would meet in the Yasutake home. Mitsuye would hear the poems recited by her father as the men composed them on the spot; the poems were less like haiku and more like stories full of life, laughter, satire, and often crass humor. Then she'd watch as a calligrapher wrote the poems on sheets of paper and tack them to the wall. To Mitsuye, it was "a beautiful process," and it would shape her into the poet she would become.

Her father was meeting with his poetry club at a local restaurant when three FBI agents found him after the Pearl Harbor attack. They tore down the poems from the wall and took him to the same building where he went to work every day—the INS office. His twenty-one years of service as a translator seemed to have evaporated. It gave him no special treatment whatsoever; in fact, it made him even more vulnerable to being charged with espionage. He was then sent to a temporary detention center at Fort Lewis, near Tacoma, Washington, where Japanese, German, and Italian enemy aliens were held during the war. On March 30, 1943, the facility closed, and the Japanese and German prisoners were transferred to the Fort Missoula Alien Detention Center in Montana.

At the time of her family's incarceration, Mitsuye was about to graduate from Cleveland High School; her oldest brother, Seiichi, was recovering from tuberculosis; her middle brother, Toshio, was a student at the University of

Washington; and her youngest brother, Joe, was at home, just nine years old. Later, at Minidoka, Mitsuye kept a journal of stories about the people and scenes around her that would evolve into her only book.

By early 1943 Toshio had decided to volunteer as a medic for the 442nd Regimental Combat Team, and Mitsuye and Toshio were given permission to visit their father at his internment camp in Lordsburg, New Mexico, so that Toshio could see him before he left for basic training. Mitsuye barely recognized her father; he'd lost weight and looked older. But he still seemed to have an unflappable enthusiasm underneath it all. It would be another year before the government allowed him to reunite with their mother and little brother at another Department of Justice internment camp for families in Crystal City, Texas.

Meanwhile, the American Friends Service Committee became sponsors for Mitsuye and Seiichi, so eighteen months after arriving at Minidoka, they were allowed to leave camp and study at the University of Cincinnati. Soon their parents were allowed to join them, but Seiichi had moved to Boston by then because he'd been expelled from the college for being a pacifist. Seiichi refused to fight in the war, so his answers on the loyalty questionnaire made his loyalty suspect. Two years after the war ended, Mitsuye's father finally found a job as executive director of the Chicago Resettlers Committee, helping other incarcerees to restart their lives.

Mitsuye transferred to New York University, where in 1947 she earned her bachelor's degree in English literature. Six years later she received a master's degree from the University of Chicago—the year her father became an American citizen after having lived in the United States for forty-six years. He died of a brain hemorrhage twenty-three days later.

Mitsuye made her home in New York City and married Yoshikazu Yamada, a research chemist and watercolorist; in 1955 she became a US citizen. By 1961 she had four children, but she became ill and was misdiagnosed with incurable emphysema. In one of the many newspapers she was reading in bed, she came upon an article about the letter-writing campaigns of Amnesty International to release political prisoners, and it struck a chord. She began writing letters. A former political prisoner herself, she wrote a seemingly end-less number of letters to release other political prisoners around the world, which gave her life a new direction.

Soon after, she moved to Orange County, California, for her husband's work and was offered her first teaching job at Fullerton College. Then in 1968 she left to teach at Cypress College, where she remained for twenty-one years. She is known as one of the earliest Asian American women poets to explore issues of domestic violence and sexual infidelity, and she played a significant role in establishing an Asian American Studies program at the University of California, Irvine. After she retired, she continued teaching as a writer-in-residence at numerous colleges in California and served on the board of the California Council for the Humanities. She also acted as a resource scholar at the Multicultural Women's Institute at the University of Chicago. For decades she volunteered for Amnesty International, serving on its executive board, and traveling to South Korea and Japan as chair of its Committee on International Development. She was in Geneva, Switzerland, for the first Amnesty International Intersectional Meeting on Women and Human Rights.

Camp Notes and Other Poems—the book she wrote at Minidoka thirty years earlier—was finally published by Shameless Hussy Press in 1976. In 1981 PBS broadcast a documentary about her and the Chinese American poet Nellie Wong called *Mitsuye and Nellie: Asian American Poets*, produced by Academy Award recipients Allie Light and Irving Saraf, which took her back to Minidoka for the first time since the camp closed. While there, she found herself unexpectedly in tears. The same thing happened in 1992 when she was attending a photographic exhibition at UCLA's Wight Art Gallery that com-memorated the fiftieth anniversary of Executive Order 9066. Once again she found herself emotionally overwhelmed by the memory of her experience.

Mitsuye has received numerous awards in recognition of her contributions to teaching, women's issues, feminist art, and poetry. In 2009, at the age of eighty-six, she was awarded an honorary doctorate of humane letters by Sim-mons College. On September 3, 2019, at the age of ninety-five, she published a new collection of poems entitled *Full Circle: New and Selected Poems* with the Department of Asian American Studies at the University of California, Santa Barbara.

Helen Matsue **Yamahiro** (Murao), female, Nisei, Portland, Oregon, incarcerated age 16, Portland Assembly Center, Minidoka Relocation Center. Helen was born on March 11, 1926, in Portland, Oregon, the second of four children, to Kunzo Yamahiro and Mineko (Ichikawa) Yamahiro. Helen's parents died within three years of each other while she was in grammar school. Her older sister, Mary, suffered from tuberculosis and was hospitalized in a sanatorium for four years. As a result, Helen became responsible at a young age for taking care of herself and her two younger brothers. Due to the stigma of tuberculosis, no Japanese family would take them in permanently, so the three Yamashiro children became wards of the state. A week before the evacuation, Mary was meant to come home, but she suffered a relapse and died, leaving Helen to evacuate with her two younger brothers by themselves. Helen became so depressed that she nearly committed suicide at the age of sixteen. But she persevered, and they eventually resettled as a family unit in Madison, Wisconsin, living together as orphans on very little money. One of her brothers became an MD; the other earned a PhD. Helen received a scholarship to attend Madison Business College and eventually put herself through the University of Wisconsin and earned a master's degree.

She married Shig Murao from Seattle, Washington, who served in Company I of the 442nd Regimental Combat Team, and raised three children. Helen and Shig settled in Evanston, Illinois, and she taught in Evanston schools. In 1981 she testified before the Commission on the Relocation and Internment of Civilians in the hearings held in Chicago.

Hisaye **Yamamoto** (Desoto), female, Nisei, Oceanside, California, incarcerated age 20, Poston Relocation Center. Hisaye was born in Redondo Beach, California, on August 23, 1921, the oldest of five children (one died in infancy), to Kanzo Yamamoto and Sae Yamamoto from Kumamoto Prefecture, Japan.

While her parents were truck-farming fields of strawberries and tomatoes, she was reading voraciously. At fourteen she began submitting essays under the pseudonym Napoleon to Nisei newspapers and wrote a column for the *Kashu Mainichi*, a Japanese newspaper in Los Angeles. The talk among her peers was who would write the next Great American Nisei Novel. After she graduated from high school, she entered Compton Junior College mostly to study foreign languages—Latin, French, Spanish, and German—and graduated with an associate of arts degree. Her mother died on September 1, 1939, when she was eighteen. By 1940 her columns contained literary criticism and reviews of books by writers such as Thomas Wolfe and Richard Wright. After the bombing of Pearl Harbor, the Japanese American press on the West Coast ceased publication.

She rejoined her family members who were in Oceanside to board the train to Poston. There she waitressed in the mess hall, worked as a receptionist for the hospital, and wrote pieces for the camp newspaper, the *Poston Chronicle*. Her work included a serialized mystery, "Death Rides the Rails to Poston," which was later published in her first collection of short stories. She began writing short fiction and befriended writers at camp, such as Wakako Yamauchi and Chizuko Omori (who would go on to produce with her sister the award-winning documentary *Rabbit in the Moon*).

For a short time in 1944 Hisaye and her two younger brothers, Yuke and Jemo, were sent to Springfield, Massachusetts, where Hisaye worked as a cook for a wealthy widow, Mary Ida (Stephenson) Young, an herbalist who had created a liniment for horses—out of menthol, wormwood oil, and herbs from her kitchen—that eventually spawned the Absorbine Jr. brand of liniment for humans. But six weeks after they started working for her, Hisaye and her brothers got the news that their brother Johnny had died in Italy as a member of the 442nd Regimental Combat Team, so they returned to camp to be with their father.

Hisaye went back to Los Angeles in 1945 and stayed at the Evergreen Hostel in the Forsythe Building in Boyle Heights. After the Japanese American community had been forcibly removed, the Black population in Little

Tokyo increased by thousands and the new residents started calling the area Bronzeville. But gradually Little Tokyo reclaimed some of its prewar identity when Japanese Americans who owned buildings in the area were able to restart their businesses.

As the Japanese Americans were returning home from the camps, the *Los Angeles Tribune*, a Black weekly—the only Los Angeles newspaper to oppose Executive Order 9066—wanted a Nisei columnist who could serve both communities. Hisaye worked at the paper for three years as a reporter and columnist at thirty-five dollars per week. In one story she wrote about White neighbors intimidating a Black family named Short. Backlash to the article resulted in the Shorts getting killed in an arson fire. The event propelled Hisaye to get involved with a civil rights group called Fellowship of Reconciliation; she also helped to organize the Los Angeles chapter of the Congress of Racial Equality. Then she left the newspaper and traveled across the country on public transportation because she was afraid of flying.

In 1948 the publication of her story about sexual harassment, "The High-Heeled Shoes, a Memoir" in the *Partisan Review*, a highly respected journal, was a literary breakthrough for her career. Together with insurance funds from her brother's death, she was able to quit journalism and write full-time. That year she also adopted a five-month-old Sansei boy. Over the next two years she received a fellowship from the John Hay Whitney Foundation and her stories appeared in the *Kenyon Review*, *Harper's Bazaar*, the *Carleton Miscellany*, and *Arizona Quarterly*. Four of her stories were included in "Distinctive Short Stories," an annual list compiled by Martha Foley in *Story* magazine. In addition, Foley included "Yoneko's Earthquake" in *Best American Short Stories: 1952*.

Hisaye was a great admirer of the Catholic Worker Movement, as well as the church's teachings on social justice and its devotion to nonviolence, voluntary poverty, and assisting those in need. In 1953 she turned down a writing fellowship from Stanford University and volunteered to work and live with her son on a Catholic Worker rehabilitation farm on Staten Island instead. She met her husband, Anthony DeSoto, there and two years later they moved to Los Angeles, where she had four more children. During the time she was raising five children, she experienced some family tragedies, and the culmination of these experiences drove her to a nervous breakdown. She entered a mental health facility for a month to recover.

In 1986 she received the Before Columbus Foundation's American Book Award for Lifetime Achievement. *Seventeen Syllables and Other Stories*, her only collection of short stories, spanned forty years of writing. It was published in 1988 by Kitchen Table: Women of Color Press, and for it she received the Association for Asian American Studies' Book Award. Her short stories are considered master literary works, and she is often compared to Grace Paley, Katherine Mansfield, and Flannery O'Connor. In 2010 she received the Asian American Writers' Workshop's Lifetime Achievement Award.

Minoru "Min" **Yasui**, male, Nisei, Portland, Oregon, incarcerated age 24, Portland Assembly Center, Minidoka Relocation Center, Multnomah County Jail. Min was born in Hood River, Oregon, on October 19, 1916, the third of six sons and three daughters, to Masuo Yasui and Shidzuyo (Miyake) Yasui.

Masuo arrived from Japan in 1903, following his father, Shinataro Yasui, who had left the rice paddies of Okayama, Japan, in the late 1890s. Together, Shintaro, Masao, and all of Masuo's brothers worked on the railroad gangs. Min's parents went to Tacoma, Washington, in 1912 and settled in the "lush, fruit-growing valley" of Hood River, Oregon, "nestled in the Cascade Mountains, abutting the Columbia River gorge on the north and at the foot of Mt. Hood to the south." By 1940 seventy-five to one hundred families of Japanese ancestry made their home in the Hood River valley and owned their land.

Masuo and his older brother built an enterprise in fruit and vegetable farming "by grub-staking Japanese tenant farmers, helping them to acquire acreages of logged-over stump land, which they laboriously cleared by hand, with teams of horses and blowing stumps with dynamite." They planted orchards of apples, pears, and cherries. Strawberries were planted between the rows in the young orchards until the trees grew to fruit-bearing size.

Min showed early promise as a scholar. After graduating as salutatorian from high school, he attended the University of Oregon and served as an ROTC cadet. He was commissioned as a second lieutenant in the Army Reserve after his college graduation.

In 1939 he became the first Japanese American to graduate from the University of Oregon School of Law, and he passed the Oregon bar exam the same year. But he was unable to find work as a lawyer, so he got a job through one of his father's connections with the Japanese consulate in Chicago. And, as required of American citizens, he registered with the US State Department as a civilian agent of a foreign government. He was working at the consulate as a political analyst when Pearl Harbor was attacked.

Min resigned his consulate position the next day, and on January 19, 1942, he was ordered to report for active duty at Camp Vancouver in Washington, in keeping with his commission as a second lieutenant through the ROTC. Although he volunteered for duty "on not less than 8 subsequent and separate occasions," the commanding general would not accept his services, so he was never formally inducted into the US military forces.

Instead, that same month, he opened a law office in Portland, Oregon, to handle the legal issues that his fellow Japanese Americans were suddenly confronting after Issei men had been taken into custody by the FBI. Their families were "frantic with worry concerning the well-being and health of their husbands and fathers." Min became enraged when his own father was among the Issei leaders arrested as suspected enemy aliens, and in early February 1942 he attended his father's enemy alien hearing in Missoula, Montana. But he wasn't permitted to participate in any other enemy alien hearings, even as an attorney representing the incarcerated. The internees had been stripped of their right to counsel and their right to face the accusers who were acting as witnesses against them. In his father's case, the only material evidence against him were schoolwork drawings made by his children of the Panama Canal.

"Prove that you didn't intend to blow up the Panama Canal!" the officer demanded.

Min's father spent the rest of the war in Army and Department of Justice internment camps.

After the issuance of Executive Order 9066, and as curfew and travel restrictions were being implemented, Min recognized the unconstitutionality of these government actions and intentionally decided to make himself a test case. His criminal conviction was upheld by the US Supreme Court in 1943.

After the war Min moved to Chicago and worked in an ice plant at sixty cents per hour, then moved to Denver, where he studied for the Colorado bar exam by enrolling in the University of Denver College of Law and auditing law classes at the Northwestern School of Law. After taking the bar exam in 1945, he was told by the Board of Bar Examiners that he had the highest score of all the applicants, but because of his "bad moral character," as evidenced by his violation of the military curfew order, he was considered unfit to practice law. With the assistance of an ACLU lawyer, his case was appealed to the Colorado Supreme Court and the ruling was overturned.

Min established a legal practice in Denver's postwar Japantown and devoted decades of community service to the greater Denver area. He was recognized for his contributions to race relations by the Urban League of Metropolitan Denver, the Latin American Research and Service Agency, and Denver's Human Rights Commission. He actively practiced law in Oregon and Colorado for twenty-five years, until being named executive director of the Denver Commission on Community Relations by appointment of the mayor, a position he held for over fifteen years.

He remained a fervent advocate of the rights of the incarcerated Japanese Americans, serving as chairman of the JACL's National Committee for Redress, and continued to pursue his own legal battle until his death. Although an Oregon district court vacated his criminal conviction on a coram nobis petition, Min died before he had the chance for the higher appellate courts to consider the constitutionality of the government orders underlying his Supreme Court conviction.

In November 2015 he was posthumously awarded the Presidential Medal of Freedom by President Barack Obama. The centennial of his birth was celebrated in 2016. His daughter Holly has written, produced, and directed a documentary, *Never Give Up! Minoru Yasui and the Fight for Justice*, now available on DVD. Min is remembered today with a monthly Minoru Yasui Community Volunteer Award. The University of Oregon School of Law created the Minoru Yasui Endowment for Human and Civil Rights Law, which now honors the legacy of an Oregon School of Law graduate "of uncommon courage and principle." In 2016 the law school established the Minoru Yasui Fellowship, and in 2017, the Oregon Law Minoru Yasui Justice Award.

Aiko **Yoshinaga** (Herzig), female, Nisei, Los Angeles, California, incarcerated age 17, Manzanar Relocation Center, Jerome Relocation Center, Rohwer Relocation Center. Aiko was born in Sacramento, California, on August 5, 1924, the second youngest of five children, to Sanji Yoshinaga and Shigeru (Kinuwaki) Yoshinaga, immigrants from Kyushu, Japan. At the time of the incarceration, she was a senior honors student at Los Angeles High School, aspiring to attend college and become a dancer and a singer. Two months later her high school principal summoned her and fourteen other students of Japanese descent in her graduating class and told them: "You don't deserve to get your high school diplomas because your people bombed Pearl Harbor." Aiko immediately eloped with her boyfriend and went with him to the Manzanar Relocation Center, where she began her married life and gave birth to a daughter.

After the war she studied to become a stenographer and divorced her husband. With her daughter, Aiko joined her mother and four siblings in New York. There she married an army officer and moved to where he was stationed in Japan. When that marriage also ended in divorce, she returned to New York, worked as a clerk, attended night classes at George Washington High School, and received a general equivalency diploma.

In New York she became involved with Asian Americans for Action, an advocacy group that opposed racism, nuclear testing, and the war in Vietnam. She married Jack Herzig, a former American paratrooper, and moved to Washington, DC, in 1978. Aiko was interested in learning more about her family's incarceration, so she became a self-taught, skilled historical researcher and research associate for the Commission on Wartime Relocation and Internment of Civilians. Her work began in the National Archives. Her process of cataloging thousands of documents and discovering key pieces of information provided the foundation for the commission's conclusion in 1983 that the wartime incarceration was motivated by "race prejudice, war hysteria and the failure of political leadership." David Kawamoto, a past president of the JACL, told the *Los Angeles Times* in 2011 that Aiko's research role was indispensable.

"Through her own personal efforts," he said, "she found the evidence that our community needed to seek out redress."

Ellen Shizue **Yukawa** (Spink), female, Sansei, Kern County, California, incarcerated age 9, Poston Relocation Center. Ellen was born in Farmersville, California, on April 13, 1933 to Isamu Samuel Yukawa and Setsuko Phyllis (Kurihara) Yukawa. At the time she left camp, she had one sister, Sachiko Elayne. After leaving Poston in 1945, Ellen and her family moved to Monticello, New York, a town in the Catskill Mountains, to work for the Osborn family rather than returning right away to Delano, California, where the Yukawa family owned land. At Monticello High School, Ellen was an honor student, a class officer, and a classmate of Joanne Oppenheim; Ellen was the first Japanese girl Joanne had ever met.

Decades later, in preparation for their high school's fiftieth reunion, Joanne tried to find Ellen, who had moved back with her family to California at the end of her sophomore year. Joanne came upon Ellen's letters to Clara Breed, the San Diego librarian, on the website of the Japanese American National Museum. Joanne became the author of *Dear Miss Breed: True Stories of the Japanese American Incarceration During World War II and a Librarian Who Made a Difference.* She included Ellen's letters in the book.

Ellen married Roy Y. Nagatani and George James Spink.

ACKNOWLEDGMENTS

First and foremost, I would like to express my deepest appreciation and gratitude to my literary agent, Kathleen Anderson, for the opportunity to produce this book and without whom this book would not have been possible. Sincere thanks also go to Justin Chanda, Krista Vitola, Kendra Levin, Catherine Laudone, Greg Stadnyk, and Hilary Zarycky, as well as Jenica Nasworthy and her team of copyeditors: Bara MacNeill and Erica Stahler, at Simon & Schuster for their patience and support; to Karen Bunya for the backstory to her father's contribution, and to Jane Kenealy of the Japanese American Historical Society of San Diego for her assistance with contributor biographies.

I would like to acknowledge the scholarship of Robert Asahina, Roger Daniels, Arthur Hansen, Aiko Herzig-Yoshinaga, Lane Ryo Hirabayashi, Harry Kitano, Lon Kurashige, Peter Irons, Alice Yang Murray, Eric Muller, Brian Niiya, Greg Robinson, Michi Weglyn, Duncan Ryūken Williams, and all those whose research has made the information about and understanding of the incarceration experience accessible to the public.

I would also like to acknowledge the invaluable resources that have been made publicly available from organizations such as Densho: The Japanese American Legacy Project, the 100th Infantry Battalion Veterans Education Center, the Go for Broke National Education Center, and the National Archives and Records Administration.

To Brian Niiya, Linda Vo, and Duncan Ryūken Williams, I am in your debt for your suggestions and input. My students at the University of Southern California inspire me to develop compelling ways to share the experiences and lessons of the Japanese American incarceration. I remember Min Yasui fondly and remain grateful for his mentorship.

I warmly thank Secretary Norman Y. Mineta for his moving foreword and for being an inspiration to me over many years. And most of all, I pay tribute to my father, Hiroshi Kamei, with whom I share a special bond on this topic from our work together for the cause of redress. His example motivates me every day to work hard, strive for excellence, and contribute to the greater good.

ASSEMBLY CENTERS

In the spring of 1942, the Wartime Civil Control Administration (WCCA), an agency established as part of the US Army's Western Defense Command, hastily converted existing public facilities into temporary detention centers to house persons of Japanese ancestry—man, woman, and child (aliens and citizens alike)—who had been removed from California, Oregon, Washington, and parts of Arizona following the issuance of Executive Order 9066. The WCCA euphemistically referred to these places of detention as "assembly centers" or "reception centers." The detainees at these centers were transferred to the War Relocation Authority facilities known as "relocation centers" in the latter part of 1942.

Fresno Assembly Center, California. May 6, 1942–October 30, 1942. Peak population: 5,120.

Marysville (Arboga) Assembly Center, California. May 8, 1942–June 29, 1942. Peak population: 2,451.

Mayer Assembly Center, Arizona. May 7, 1942–June 2, 1942. Peak population: 245.

Merced Assembly Center, California. May 6, 1942–September 15, 1942. Peak population: 4,508.

Pinedale Assembly Center, California. May 7, 1942–July 23, 1942. Peak population: 4,792.

Pomona Assembly Center, California. May 7, 1942–August 24, 1942. Peak population: 5,434.

Portland Assembly Center, Oregon. May 2, 1942–September 10, 1942. Peak population: 3,676.

Puyallup Assembly Center (also known as Camp Harmony), Washington. April 28, 1942–September 12, 1942. Peak population: 7,390.

Sacramento Assembly Center, California. May 6, 1942–June 26, 1942. Peak population: 4,739.

Salinas Assembly Center, California. April 27, 1942–July 4, 1942. Peak population: 3,586.

Santa Anita Assembly Center, California. March 27, 1942–October 27, 1942. Peak population: 18,719.

Stockton Assembly Center, California. May 10, 1942–October 17, 1942. Peak population: 4,271.

Tanforan Assembly Center, California. April 28, 1942–October 13, 1942. Peak population: 7,816.

Tulare Assembly Center, California. April 20, 1942–September 4, 1942. Peak population: 4,978.

Turlock Assembly Center, California. April 30, 1942–August 12, 1942. Peak population: 3,661.

Two other facilities known as reception centers functioned as assembly centers during the forced evacuation and then became War Relocation Authority relocation centers:

Parker Dam Reception Center, Arizona. May 8, 1942–May 31, 1942. It became the Colorado River Relocation Center on June 1, 1942, which was also known as Poston. Many inmates went there directly from their homes. It is not known what the peak population was for the period in which it was serving as a reception center.

Manzanar Reception Center, California. March 21, 1942–June 1, 1942. Originally operating under the name Owens Valley Reception Center, it officially became Manzanar Relocation Center on June 2, 1942. Peak population as a reception center: 9,666.

WAR RELOCATION AUTHORITY CENTERS

The War Relocation Authority (WRA) built and administered these ten facilities for the long-term detention of persons of Japanese ancestry (including US citizens) living in California, Oregon, Washington, and parts of Arizona who were forcibly removed from their homes pursuant to Executive Order 9066. The facilities, which are commonly referred to as "camps," are listed here according to the official WRA center names. They are also often but inaccurately referred to as "internment camps" and are different from the facilities that the Department of Justice and US Army operated for the internment of enemy aliens.

Colorado River Relocation Center (also known as Poston), Arizona. June 2, 1942–November 28, 1945. Peak population: 17,814.

Gila River Relocation Center, Arizona. July 20, 1942–November 16, 1945. Peak population: 13,348.

Granada Relocation Center (also known as Camp Amache), Colorado. August 27, 1942–October 15, 1945. Peak population: 7,318.

Heart Mountain Relocation Center, Wyoming. August 12, 1942–November 10, 1945. Peak population: 10,767.

Jerome Relocation Center, Arkansas. October 6, 1942–June 30, 1944. Peak population: 8,497.

Manzanar Relocation Center, California. June 2, 1942–November 21, 1945. Peak population: 10,046.

Minidoka Relocation Center, Idaho. August 10, 1942–October 28, 1945. Peak population: 9,397.

Rohwer Relocation Center, Arkansas. September 18, 1942–November 30, 1945. Peak population: 8,475.

Topaz Relocation Center (also known as Central Utah), Utah. September 11, 1942–October 31, 1945. Peak population: 8,130.

Tule Lake Relocation Center/Tule Lake Segregation Center, California. May 27, 1942–March 20, 1946. Peak population: 18,789.

DEPARTMENT OF JUSTICE INTERNMENT CAMPS FOR ENEMY ALIENS

The Department of Justice (DOJ) maintained facilities collectively known as "internment camps" to hold enemy aliens (persons living in the US who were not US citizens but were citizens of countries in conflict with the US). These locations included those that were run by the Immigration and Naturalization Service (INS), which was then part of the DOJ. The individuals detained in DOJ internment camps included Issei men while they waited for hearings to determine their loyalty. The places of detention listed here are the main ones where persons of Japanese descent were held during World War II and its immediate aftermath. The population numbers listed here are the currently known estimates.

Crystal City Internment Center, Crystal City, Texas. November 2, 1942–January 1948. Peak population: 4,000 (people of Japanese ancestry from the United States and Latin America and their families; also German and Italian nationals and their families).

Fort Lincoln (Bismarck) Internment Camp, Bismarck, North Dakota. December 7, 1941–March 6, 1946. Peak population: 1,518 (Japanese and German nationals, and Japanese Americans who had chosen to give up their US citizenship).

Fort Missoula Alien Detention Center, Missoula, Montana. December 18, 1941–July 1, 1944. Peak population: 2,003 (nonmilitary Italian seamen; also Japanese nationals from the US and Hawaii).

Fort Stanton Internment Camp, Capitan, New Mexico. Exact dates of operation and population unknown. Population description: Mostly German seamen and German residents of the United States, and housing the small Japanese Segregation Camp #1 for "incorrigible agitators," who were eventually deported to Japan.

Kenedy Alien Detention Camp, Kenedy, Texas. April 1, 1942–September 25, 1945. Peak population: 2,000 (Germans, Italians, and Japanese Latin

Americans, and Japanese Americans until September 1944, when the incarcerees were transferred to other facilities and it became a German and Japanese POW camp).

Kooskia Internment Camp, thirty miles northeast of Kooskia, Idaho. May 1943–May 1945. Peak population: 256 (Japanese Americans, Japanese Mexicans, Japanese Peruvians, and Japanese Panamanians; also German nationals).

Santa Fe Internment Camp, Santa Fe, New Mexico. February 1942–September 1946. Peak population: 2,100 (Japanese immigrants from the United States, Alaska, Hawaii, Latin America, and the Pacific Islands, and transfers from Tule Lake as well as Japanese Americans who had given up their US citizenship; also German and Italian nationals).

Seagoville Enemy Alien Detention Station, Seagoville, Texas. April 12, 1942–June 30, 1945. Peak population: 343 (mostly women and children of Japanese ancestry from the United States and Latin America, also female Japanese American language teachers, and German, Italian, and Japanese residents of the United States being repatriated to their home countries).

Tuna Canyon Detention Station, Tujunga, California. December 16, 1941–October 1, 1943. Peak population: 2,000 (Japanese, German, and Italian nationals and Japanese Peruvians).

US ARMY INTERNMENT CAMPS FOR ENEMY ALIENS

The US Army established these and other facilities throughout the country to hold individuals that the FBI and the Department of Justice had determined should be detained. The detainees included those considered to be enemy aliens, such as Issei men living on the West Coast who were arrested after the Pearl Harbor attack, many within hours of the bombing. Most of these facilities were built on or near US military bases. The population numbers listed here are the currently known estimates.

Camp Blanding Internment Camp, Starke, Florida. Exact dates of operation unknown. Peak population: 343 (Japanese immigrants from the United States; also German and Italian nationals and German POWs).

Camp Forrest Internment Camp, Tullahoma, Tennessee. Exact dates of operation and peak population unknown. Population description: German and Italian nationals; 172 Japanese residents of Hawaii spent one month here, between stays at Camp McCoy and Camp Livingston; by June 1942, 190 Americans of Japanese ancestry were either repatriated to Japan or transferred to Camp Livingston.

Camp Livingston Internment Camp, Alexandria, Louisiana. June 8, 1942–September 25, 1946. Peak population: 1,123 (Americans of Japanese ancestry transferred from Fort Missoula, Fort Sill, and Camp Forrest; Japanese men from Latin America).

Camp McCoy Internment Camp, near Tomah, Wisconsin. Opened March 1, 1942; closing date unknown. Peak population: 293 (Japanese residents of Hawaii; German and Italian nationals; Japanese and German POWs late in the war).

Florence Internment Camp, Florence, Arizona. Exact dates of operation unknown. Peak population: 343 (persons of Japanese ancestry).

Fort Bliss Internment Camp, near El Paso, Texas. Exact dates of operation unknown. Peak population: 91 (Japanese residents of the United States and Hawaii; transfers from Santa Fe Internment Camp; German and Italian nationals).

Fort Howard Internment Camp, Baltimore County, Maryland. Exact dates of operation unknown. Peak population: 30 (Japanese and German residents of the United States and German POWs).

Fort Lewis Internment Camp, near Tacoma, Washington. 1942–March 30, 1943. Peak population: 42 (individuals of Japanese descent living in Alaska, Hawaii, and the United States; also German and Italian nationals).

Fort McDowell Internment Camp (previously known as Angel Island Immigration Station), Angel Island, California. 1940–1946. Served as port of arrival for internees from Hawaii. Peak population: 99 (Japanese, German, and Italian residents of Hawaii).

Fort Meade Internment Camp, Anne Arundel County, Maryland. Exact dates of operation unknown. Peak population: 384 (Japanese, German, and Italian residents of the United States).

Fort Richardson Internment Camp, near Anchorage, Alaska. Exact dates of operation unknown. Peak population: 17 (Japanese residents of Alaska, German residents of the United States).

Fort Sam Houston Enemy Alien Detention Station, San Antonio, Texas. Served as temporary holding facility while permanent internment camps were being constructed. February–December 1942. Peak population: 106 (persons of Japanese descent from Alaska and Hawaii; German and Italian residents of the United States).

Fort Sill Internment Camp, near Lawton, Oklahoma. Opening date unknown; closed June 24, 1942. Peak population: 707 (Japanese and German residents of the United States).

Griffith Park Internment Camp, Los Angeles, California. Opened December 14, 1941; redesignated as a POW Processing Station on July 14, 1942. Peak population: 77 (Japanese, German, and Italian residents of the United States transferred to Tuna Canyon Detention Station in Tujunga, California).

Honouliuli Internment Camp, near Waipahu, Oahu, Hawaii. February 1943–1945. Peak civilian population: 300 (American citizens of Japanese ancestry and European nationals). Separately, the camp also became the largest POW camp in Hawaii during the war, with more than 4,000 soldiers from Italy, Japan (Okinawa), Korea, and Taiwan.

Lordsburg Internment Camp, Lordsburg, New Mexico. June 15, 1942–1944. Peak population: 2,500 (Issei; Americans of Japanese ancestry transferred from other army and Department of Justice internment camps; German residents of the United States; German and Japanese POWs; convicted US Army soldiers).

Sand Island Internment Camp, Honolulu, Hawaii. December 1941– March 1, 1943. Peak population: 300 (US citizens and aliens of Japanese descent living in Hawaii; Italian and Korean POWs; Austrian, Finnish, German, Italian, Korean, and Norwegian residents of the United States).

Stringtown Internment Camp, Stringtown, Oklahoma. March 30, 1942–June 1943. Peak population: 176 (Japanese residents of the United States, German POWs).

TIME LINE

March 26, 1790

Congress enacts the Naturalization Act of 1790, which provides that only an alien who is a "free white person, who shall have resided within the limits and under the jurisdiction of the United States for a term of two years, may be admitted to become a citizen thereof."

July 14, 1870

The Naturalization Act of 1870 is enacted, revoking the citizenship of naturalized citizens of Chinese descent.

May 6, 1882

Congress enacts the Chinese Exclusion Act, which ends the immigration of Chinese laborers for ten years. This is the first in a series of acts that ban Chinese immigration until the Immigration and Nationality Act of 1952.

February 8, 1885

The first Japanese immigrants arrive in Honolulu aboard the SS *City of Tokio* to work as contract laborers on the sugarcane plantations of Hawaii.

1891

Japanese immigrants start arriving on the mainland of the United States for work primarily as agricultural laborers.

May 1892

Denis Kearney, founder of the anti-Chinese Workingmen's Party, holds mass meetings in San Francisco to protest Japanese immigration.

May 7, 1900

Labor groups in San Francisco gather to adopt a resolution supporting policies that exclude the Japanese. This represents the first large-scale anti-Japanese protest in California.

February 23, 1905

The *San Francisco Chronicle* runs the front-page headline JAPANESE INVASION: THE PROBLEM OF THE HOUR FOR UNITED STATES, which escalates racism toward the Japanese in the Bay Area.

May 14, 1905

The Japanese and Korean Exclusion League in San Francisco is founded to broadly attack the Asian immigrant labor force and to organize against Japanese immigration.

October 11, 1906

The San Francisco Board of Education passes a resolution that children of Chinese, Japanese, and Korean ancestry must attend a racially segregated public school.

1907–8

Pursuant to an exchange of diplomatic correspondence known as the Gentlemen's Agreement, Japan agrees to halt the migration of Japanese male laborers into the United States; in exchange, the United States agrees to allow wives and family members of Japanese already in the United States to immigrate.

1908

The Japanese and Korean Exclusion League changes its name to the Asiatic Exclusion League and continues its White supremacist activities to stop immigration from Japan, as well as from China, Korea, and India.

August 10, 1913

The 1913 Alien Land Law goes into effect in California, prohibiting "all aliens ineligible for citizenship" from owning land, the first legislation depriving the Japanese of substantial property rights. Subsequent acts prohibit aliens not eligible for citizenship from leasing land as well.

December 9, 1920

The 1920 Alien Land Law becomes effective in California, intending to close loopholes in the 1913 Alien Land Law. Subsequent amendments to the 1920 act and various 1923 Supreme Court decisions on the alien land laws of western states further curtail the ability of Japanese persons to have any real property interests.

July 19, 1921

In Turlock, California, a mob of White vigilantes drive Japanese laborers out of town at gunpoint. Other violent incidents against Japanese and other laborers erupt across California and in other western states.

November 13, 1922

In *Ozawa v. United States*, the US Supreme Court affirms the ban preventing Japanese immigrants from becoming naturalized US citizens, a ban that will remain in effect until 1952.

July 1, 1924

The Immigration Act of 1924, unofficially known as the Japanese Exclusion Act and signed into law by President Calvin Coolidge, becomes effective, ending all Japanese immigration to the United States.

September 1, 1939

World War II begins when Germany attacks Poland.

June 10, 1940

Italy enters the war.

March 17, 1941

The US Army establishes the Western Defense Command for the defense of Arizona, California, Idaho, Montana, Nevada, Oregon, Utah, and Washington. Lieutenant General John L. DeWitt becomes its first commander at its headquarters in the Presidio, San Francisco, California.

June 22, 1941

Germany invades the Soviet Union.

November 1, 1941

The US Army opens the Fourth Army Intelligence School in San Francisco, California, later renamed the Military Intelligence Service Language School (MISLS).

November 7, 1941

The Munson report, an intelligence report commissioned by President Franklin D. Roosevelt, concludes that the great majority of Japanese Americans are loyal to the United States and do not pose a threat to national security in the event of a war with Japan.

December 7, 1941

Japan bombs US ships and planes at the Pearl Harbor military base in Hawaii. Over 3,500 servicemen and civilians are wounded or killed. Martial law is declared in Hawaii.

The FBI begins arresting Japanese immigrants identified as community leaders: priests, Japanese-language teachers, newspaper publishers, and heads of organizations. Most of these men will be incarcerated for the duration of the war, separated from their families.

December 7, 1941–January 1942

Throughout the West Coast, the FBI conducts searches of thousands of

Japanese American homes for items considered to be contraband, including shortwave radios, cameras, and materials written in Japanese.

December 8, 1941

President Roosevelt addresses Congress, which affirms that the United States is at war with the Empire of Japan.

December 11, 1941

Army Chief of Staff General George C. Marshall declares the Western Defense Command to be a "theater of operations," thereby defining the Pacific coast as a war zone.

Nazi Germany and Italy declare war on the United States.

December 15, 1941

At a press conference, Secretary of the Navy Frank Knox blames the Pearl Harbor attack on "fifth column work" by persons of Japanese ancestry living in Hawaii, without any such evidence.

January 5, 1942

The War Department reclassifies all Japanese American males 4-C, or "enemy aliens ineligible for the draft." Commanders on the mainland have the option of discharging Nisei soldiers already in the military.

January 29, 1942

Attorney General Francis Biddle designates prohibited areas on the West Coast, from which all enemy aliens are to be excluded.

February 14, 1942

Lieutenant General DeWitt recommends to the War Department that all persons of Japanese descent should be removed from the West Coast.

February 19, 1942

President Roosevelt signs Executive Order 9066, authorizing military authorities to exclude civilians from any area without trial or hearing, setting in motion the incarceration of persons of Japanese ancestry.

February 20, 1942

Secretary of War Henry Stimson instructs Lieutenant General DeWitt to designate military areas from which Japanese and German enemy aliens and Japanese American citizens will be excluded, and to begin moving those populations.

February 25, 1942

The US Navy orders all Japanese Americans living on Terminal Island (approximately 500 families) in the Port of Los Angeles to leave within forty-eight hours.

March 1942

The Wartime Civil Control Administration begins opening seventeen assembly centers. Approximately 92,000 men, women, and children are detained in assembly centers until permanent concentration camps are completed.

March 2, 1942

Lieutenant General DeWitt issues Public Proclamation No. 1, establishing Military Areas Nos. 1 and 2, from which persons of Japanese ancestry are excluded from living and working in California, Oregon, Washington, and parts of Arizona.

March 18, 1942

President Roosevelt signs Executive Order 9102, establishing the War Relocation Authority (WRA), and appoints Milton S. Eisenhower as director.

March 22, 1942

The Wartime Civil Control Administration of the US Army's Western Defense Command opens as a temporary reception center in Manzanar, California; the first Japanese Americans to arrive help with the camp construction.

March 24, 1942

With only six days' notice, 227 Japanese American residents are forced to leave their homes on Bainbridge Island, Washington, under gunpoint, the first group to be subjected to a Western Defense Command exclusion order. By the end of October 1942, the US government will have issued 108 exclusion orders throughout the West Coast.

Lieutenant General DeWitt issues Public Proclamation No. 3, which imposes a curfew and travel restriction on all persons of Japanese ancestry in a military area.

March 27, 1942

"Voluntary" evacuation ends when Public Proclamation No. 4 forbids all Japanese from leaving Military Areas Nos. 1 and 2 until ordered. Persons of Japanese ancestry (citizens as well as aliens) start to receive orders to report to assembly centers.

March 28, 1942

Minoru Yasui walks into a Portland police station to surrender himself for arrest in order to test the curfew regulations in court.

May 16, 1942

Gordon Hirabayashi, a University of Washington student, refuses to register for evacuation and is jailed.

May 28, 1942

The 1,432 Nisei men of the Hawaii Army National Guard and other units gather at Schofield Barracks to join the newly formed Hawaiian Provisional

Infantry Battalion, which later becomes part of the 100th Infantry Battalion (Separate).

May 30, 1942

Fred Korematsu is arrested for violating Civilian Exclusion Order No. 34 by not reporting to the Tanforan Assembly Center.

May–October 1942

The WRA opens ten relocation centers and starts transferring incarcerees from assembly centers into these incarceration facilities known as "camps": Tule Lake, Colorado River (Poston), Manzanar, Gila River, Minidoka, Heart Mountain, Granada (Amache), Topaz, Rohwer, and Jerome.

June 1, 1942

After moving to Savage, Minnesota, the MISLS gathers its first class of two hundred students and eighteen instructors in cabins formerly used as state facilities for indigent elderly men.

June 3–6, 1942

The Allied victory at the Battle of Midway turns the advantage in the war to the United States.

June 12, 1942

The 100th Infantry Battalion (Separate) is activated.

July 12, 1942

Mitsuye Endo's attorney files a writ of habeas corpus in the federal district court in San Francisco on her behalf.

July 27, 1942

Camp guards shoot two Issei men to death at the Lordsburg, New Mexico, enemy alien internment camp for allegedly trying to escape. However, both men were too ill to walk from the train station to the camp gate prior to being shot.

November 19, 1942

Issei and Nisei workers at the Poston Relocation Center go on strike in protest of WRA wage and other administrative policies. After a strike of approximately one week, the WRA administration agrees to most of the demands, making the Poston strike one of the most successful examples of incarceree resistance to WRA control.

November 1942

At a conference in Salt Lake City, Utah, over Thanksgiving weekend, leaders of the Japanese American Citizens League (JACL) pass a resolution in support of reinstating the draft for American citizens of Japanese descent.

December 5–6, 1942

The Manzanar Riot erupts over deep divisions among factions within the camp population and with the camp administration. Two incarcerees die and many are injured as a result of soldiers firing into the crowd. Martial law is instituted in the camp, and publicity around the violence in the camp fuels anti-Japanese sentiment.

January 6, 1943

The 100th Infantry Battalion leaves Camp McCoy in Wisconsin for Camp Shelby in Mississippi.

January 28, 1943

The War Department announces plans to organize a segregated all-volunteer Nisei fighting unit. The volunteers are nearly 10,000 Nisei from Hawaii who have not been incarcerated and 1,200 Nisei from the mainland who have been incarcerated in WRA camps.

February 1, 1943

The 442nd Regimental Combat Team (RCT), made up of the 442nd Infantry Regiment, the 522nd Field Artillery Battalion, and the 232nd Combat Engineer Company, is activated.

February 1943

The WRA launches the distribution of the loyalty questionnaire at the concentration camps in an attempt to identify those who are loyal from those who are disloyal. Two questions, numbers twenty-seven and twenty-eight, ask the incarcerees whether they are willing to serve in the US Armed Forces and if they swear unqualified allegiance to the United States of America, thereby forswearing any form of allegiance to the Japanese emperor. The term "No-No Boys" is coined for those who answer no to both questions.

March 28, 1943

Thousands gather at Iolani Palace in Honolulu, Hawaii, at an aloha ceremony for the 442nd RCT as the soldiers depart for Camp Shelby in Mississippi.

April 15, 1943

In his testimony before the House Naval Affairs Committee, Lieutenant General DeWitt protests the return of Japanese American soldiers and their families to their homes on the West Coast. In an off-the-record news conference the next day, DeWitt says, "A Jap's a Jap. It makes no difference if he is a citizen or not."

May 10, 1943

The 442nd RCT begins basic training at Camp Shelby.

June 21, 1943

In *Hirabayashi v. United States* and *Yasui v. United States*, the Supreme Court holds that curfews against citizens in time of war are constitutional.

August 21, 1943

The 100th Infantry Battalion ships out for North Africa to join the Thirty-Fourth Division.

September 13, 1943

"Loyal" incarcerees from Tule Lake depart to other camps, and "disloyal" incarcerees from other camps start arriving at Tule Lake.

January 1944

The MISLS begins sending Japanese American graduates to the US Army to help intercept radio traffic from Japanese aircraft. Over the next six months, more than 100 Nisei and Kibei join this effort.

January 20, 1944

The War Department announces that it has restored the draft for Nisei men, including those incarcerated in the camps. Most of those who don't comply are charged and imprisoned in a federal penitentiary.

January 24, 1944

The 100th begins its engagement in the battle at Monte Cassino in Italy.

March 26, 1944

The Thirty-Fourth Division, together with the 100th Battalion and 200 Nisei replacements, lands at Anzio, Italy.

May 2, 1944

The 442nd RCT ships out for Naples, Italy, with a stop at Oran, Algeria. They arrive in Italy on May 28.

May 10, 1944

Sixty-three Heart Mountain draft resisters are indicted by a federal grand jury. On June 26 they are all found guilty and sentenced to jail terms.

June 2, 1944

The 100th captures Lanuvio, which clears the path to Rome.

June 5, 1944

Allied troops liberate Rome.

June 6, 1944

Allied forces invade Normandy, France, in an operation known as D-day, the largest seaborne invasion in history.

June 11, 1944

The 100th meets up with the 442nd at Civitavecchia, Italy.

June 26, 1944

The 442nd is assigned to the Fifth Army. The 100th becomes attached to the 442nd RCT as a replacement for its absent First Battalion, which remains at Camp Shelby to train other troop reserves. The 100th is permitted to maintain its signature designation within the unit, which is renamed the 100th/442nd RCT. The 100th/442nd sees its first day of combat together in Belvedere, Italy.

June 30, 1944

Jerome Relocation Center closes; it was the last to open and the first to close. Incarcerees that haven't already left for resettlement elsewhere are moved to Rohwer.

July 27, 1944

The 100th is awarded the Presidential Unit Citation, the highest army unit award, for action in Belvedere, Italy.

August 19–25, 1944

Allied forces compel German troops in Paris to surrender, liberating the city.

September 1944

The 442nd, less the 100th, reaches the Arno River in Italy near Florence.

October 14–15, 1944

The 100th/442nd RCT engages in the battle at Bruyères, France, in the Vosges Mountains.

October 20, 1944

More than 100,000 American soldiers land on Leyte Island in the Philippines in preparation for a major invasion by General Douglas MacArthur. The battle takes sixty-seven days to win.

October 24, 1944

Martial law in Hawaii ends, but curfews and blackouts remain in effect until July 1945.

October 25, 1944

The 100th/442nd RCT captures the village of Biffontaine in France.

October 27–30, 1944

The 100th/442nd RCT makes a landmark rescue of more than 200 members of the 141st Infantry Regiment, Thirty-Sixth Infantry Division, from Texas (the Lost Battalion) in the Vosges Mountains in France. The unit suffers several hundred casualties. The 100th earns its second Presidential Unit Citation for its action in Biffontaine and with the Lost Battalion. Presidential Unit Citations are also awarded to the Second and Third Battalions, the 232nd Combat Engineer Company, and F and L Companies of the 442nd.

November 13, 1944

The 100th/442nd RCT begins four months of the Champagne Campaign on the French Riviera.

November 29, 1944

The American Legion in Hood River, Oregon, removes sixteen Nisei names from the post's honor rolls. Public outcry causes the post to reverse its decision and restore all names in April 1945.

December 16, 1944–January 25, 1945

In the Battle of the Bulge (also called the Battle of the Ardennes)—the last major German offensive campaign on the western front—Germany launches an unsuccessful attempt to push the Allies back from German home territory. The Allies suffer some 75,000 casualties; Germany loses 120,000 men.

December 17, 1944

More than three years after the bombing of Pearl Harbor, the Western Defense Command of the War Department announces that the mass West Coast exclusion orders will be lifted (effective midnight January 2, 1945), allowing Japanese Americans to leave the WRA camps. The announcement is timed to preempt the Supreme Court announcement of its decision in the *Ex parte Endo* case.

December 18, 1944

The Supreme Court rules unanimously in *Ex parte Endo* that the federal government can no longer detain loyal American citizens against their will and that they should be granted unconditional release from their confinement. However, the court also states that the removal of Japanese Americans from the West Coast and their subsequent three-year detention without charges or trial amounts to legitimate government and military actions during wartime.

The Supreme Court also rules against Korematsu in *Korematsu v. United States*. The court upholds the constitutionality of Executive Order 9066, determining that the government was justified in singling out a group of people based on their ancestry and imprisoning them without trial or charges in a time of war.

February 19, 1945

Several Nisei soldiers from the Military Intelligence Service land with the US Marines on Iwo Jima, where one of the last battles in the Pacific is fought.

March 13, 1945

As part of a roving battalion, the men of the 522nd Field Artillery Battalion become the only Japanese Americans to fight in Germany when they assist the Sixty-Third Division's assault on the Siegfried Line between eastern France and Germany.

March 20, 1945

The 100th/442nd RCT, less the 522nd Field Artillery Battalion, leaves France for Italy to join the all–African American Ninety-Second Infantry Division.

April 1, 1945

The Battle of Okinawa begins.

April 5–6, 1945

The 100th/442nd RCT breaks through the Gothic Line in a surprise attack on Nazi mountainside positions in Italy.

April 6, 1945

The 100th/442nd RCT begins to drive the enemy up the Italian coast to Genoa and Turin.

April 12, 1945

President Roosevelt dies.

April 29, 1945

The 522nd Field Artillery Battalion helps to liberate Jewish prisoners of a Dachau subcamp.

April 30, 1945

Adolf Hitler commits suicide.

May 2, 1945

The 522nd Field Artillery Battalion saves victims of a death march outside of Waakirchen, Germany.

All German forces in Italy surrender. The war in Italy is over.

May 7, 1945

Germany surrenders.

May 8, 1945

The war in Europe is over.

August 6, 1945

The United States destroys the city of Hiroshima with an atomic bomb.

August 9, 1945

The United States drops a second atomic bomb on Nagasaki.

September 2, 1945

Japan signs formal surrender document. World War II ends.

September 4, 1945

The Western Defense Command proclaims that all military restrictions and exclusion orders against those of Japanese descent are rescinded.

March 20, 1946

Tule Lake Segregation Center closes, the last WRA facility to close.

July 15, 1946

President Harry S. Truman awards a seventh Presidential Unit Citation to the 100th/442nd RCT on the White House lawn.

August 15, 1946

The 100th/442nd RCT is officially deactivated.

August 1, 1947

The 100th/442nd RCT is officially reactivated as the only infantry unit in the Army Reserve. It has since served in the Korean War, the Vietnam War, Kuwait, and Iraq. The unit no longer consists solely of Japanese Americans.

December 24, 1947

President Truman pardons 1,523 World War II draft resisters, which includes all convicted Nisei draft resisters.

July 2, 1948

President Truman signs the Japanese American Evacuation Claims Act. Approximately $38 million is paid from this act, only a small fraction of the estimated loss in income and property.

December 24, 1952

The Immigration and Nationality Act of 1952 takes effect, allowing Japanese immigrants to become naturalized US citizens.

August 21, 1959

Hawaii becomes the fiftieth state to be admitted to the union of the United States of America.

July 31, 1980

President Jimmy Carter signs Public Law 96-317, establishing a congressional commission to study the World War II incarceration of Japanese Americans to determine its causes and effects.

July 14, 1981

The Commission on Wartime Relocation and Internment of Civilians (CWRIC) holds the first public hearing in Washington, DC. Similar hearings are held in ten locations throughout the year. Over 750 witnesses testify. The last hearing is at Harvard University on December 9, 1981.

February 24, 1983

The CWRIC publishes its report, *Personal Justice Denied*. The commission finds that the incarceration was not justified by military necessity, and that its causes were racial prejudice, war hysteria, and a failure of political leadership. The CWRIC concludes that a grave personal injustice was done.

June 16, 1983

The CRWIC issues its recommendations. The recommendations call for a presidential apology and a $20,000 reparation payment to each of the approximately 60,000 surviving persons excluded from their places of residence pursuant to Executive Order 9066.

1983–1988

The wartime convictions of Yasui, Hirabayashi, and Korematsu are vacated on the basis of newly discovered evidence that the US military lied to the Supreme Court in the original proceedings.

October 1, 1987

A More Perfect Union: Japanese Americans and the U.S. Constitution opens at the Smithsonian Institution's National Museum of American History in Washington, DC, in commemoration of the bicentennial of the Constitution.

August 10, 1988

President Ronald Reagan signs the Civil Liberties Act into law. The act acknowledges that the wartime incarceration of individuals of Japanese descent was unjust, and offers an apology and reparation payments of $20,000 to each surviving incarcerated person.

October 9, 1990

US Attorney General Richard Thornburgh presents the first nine redress payments to the oldest surviving incarcerees at a ceremony at the Department of Justice in Washington, DC. Senators Daniel Inouye and Daniel Akaka and Congressmen Norman Mineta and Robert Matsui are among those present.

April 30, 1992

The Japanese American National Museum opens in Los Angeles, California.

March 3, 1992

Public Law 102-248 establishes the Manzanar National Historic Site, making Manzanar the first former Japanese American concentration camp site to become a National Park Service (NPS) unit. Subsequently, Minidoka (2001), Tule Lake (2008)—as part of the World War II Valor in the Pacific National Monument—and Honouliuli (2015) become NPS units.

June 12, 1998

The federal government settles *Mochizuki, et al. v. United States*, a lawsuit brought on behalf of Japanese Latin American internees that results in a letter of apology and $5,000 in reparations to surviving internees.

September 1998

The California Civil Liberties Public Education Act is signed into law, creating a grant program for educational resources about the World War II incarceration that will award some $9 million in grants over a twelve-year period. The State of Washington introduces a similar program in 2000.

November 9, 2000

The Japanese American Memorial to Patriotism during World War II is dedicated in Washington, DC.

December 21, 2006

Public Law 109-441 authorizes the Japanese American Confinement Sites grant program, administered by the National Park Service. Up to $38 million in grants "for the purpose of identifying, researching, evaluating, interpreting, protecting, restoring, repairing, and acquiring" former sites is authorized. The first grants are awarded in 2009.

May 20, 2011

Acting Solicitor General Neal Katyal issues a "confession of error," acknowledging the mistakes made by the Solicitor General's Office in its handling of the wartime Japanese American Supreme Court cases and in defending the government's actions in the incarceration.

March 30, 2018

Karen Korematsu (the daughter of Fred Korematsu), Jay Hirabayashi (the son of Gordon Hirabayashi), Holly Yasui (the daughter of Minoru Yasui), and the Fred T. Korematsu Center for Law and Equality file an amicus brief with the Supreme Court in the *Trump v. Hawaii* case to protest the Trump administration's Muslim travel ban.

April 27, 2019

The Manzanar Committee celebrates the fiftieth annual pilgrimage to the Manzanar National Historic Site.

April 27, 2020

In *Isamu Carlos "Art" Shibayama v. United States*, the Inter-American Commission on Human Rights determined that the US government owes redress to three brothers—Art, Tak, and Ken Shibayama—for human rights violations perpetrated on them as children kidnapped from Peru and imprisoned at the Crystal City, Texas, detention facility during World War II.

GLOSSARY

100th Infantry Battalion: The US Army unit composed of second-generation Japanese Americans from Hawaii who were already serving in the US Army before the start of World War II and those who were draftees. Renowned for its valor and service record, the battalion later became attached to the 442nd Regimental Combat Team.

442nd Regimental Combat Team (RCT): The US Army unit composed almost exclusively of second-generation Japanese American volunteers and draftees from Hawaii and the mainland, including from WRA detention camps, who fought the Nazis in Italy, France, and Germany in World War II. The 442nd RCT, along with the 100th Infantry Battalion, is often referred to as the most decorated unit in US military history for its size and length of service.

A-B-C lists: Records assembled by the Federal Bureau of Investigation, the Office of Naval Intelligence, and other intelligence agencies on Issei men who were community leaders, categorizing them as suspected saboteurs based on their perceived cultural or civic connection to Japan. Those on the lists were generally arrested and detained after the Pearl Harbor bombing.

Alien Enemies Act of 1798: The first of four laws known as the Alien and Sedition Acts that authorizes the president to detain, relocate, or deport immigrants from countries considered to be hostile to the US. During World War II the act was used to justify incarcerating Japanese, German, and Italian citizens residing in the US, confiscating their property, and deporting them to their home country. Certain provisions of the act remain in force today.

Alien Land Laws: A series of laws enacted in several states, particularly those in the West, that prohibited Asians and other "aliens ineligible for citizenship" from owning property.

Allied forces: The countries that banded together to fight the Axis powers of Germany, Japan, and Italy in World War II. The major Allies were the United States, the United Kingdom, the Soviet Union, and France.

allyship: The process of building trust and accountability with other persons or organizations and working together in mutually supportive ways.

American Civil Liberties Union (ACLU): Established in 1920 with the mission to defend the rights contained in the US Constitution, the organization and its local branches had complicated and conflicting roles in challenging the curfew and exclusion orders, particularly in the *Korematsu* Supreme Court test case.

American Friends Service Committee (AFSC): A Religious Society of Friends (Quaker) organization that "promotes lasting peace with justice, as a practical expression of faith in action." The AFSC in Seattle supported the cause of Gordon Hirabayashi in challenging the constitutionality of the government's forced removal of Japanese Americans from the West Coast.

Americanization program: The WRA initiative to promote "American" values and activities among the incarcerees, such as through participation in flag salutes, in clubs and organizations with patriotic purposes, and in English classes for the Japanese-speaking Issei.

amicus curiae: Latin for "friend of the court"; a person or group that petitions a court for permission to submit a brief even though that person or group is not a party to the case; nevertheless, it has positions on the issues that it wishes the court to consider.

assembly center: One of fifteen detention camps in California, Washington, Oregon, and Arizona under the jurisdiction of the Wartime Civil Control Administration that temporarily housed persons of Japanese ancestry who were forcibly removed from the West Coast under Executive Order 9066.

assimilation: The process through which a minority group takes on the values, culture, and behaviors of the majority or dominant group. Assimilation can occur to a degree where a group or culture loses its distinctive attributes and resembles another group or culture.

avocation: A hobby or side activity.

Axis powers: The countries—Germany, Japan, and Italy—that formed an alliance and fought against the Allied forces in World War II.

baishakunin: The Japanese word that means "go-between," or a person who is a matchmaker, representing a family's interest in identifying a suitable marriage match and arranging for the details of the marriage with the *baishakunin* who is representing the other family.

banzai charge: The practice of Japanese soldiers to charge at the enemy in a last-ditch effort to win a battle or die in the attempt, adopted by the Japanese American soldiers in the 100th/442nd Regimental Combat Team in combat against the Germans.

battalion: In the US Army, a unit composed of four to six companies, typically under the command of a lieutenant colonel.

Bill of Rights: The first ten amendments to the US Constitution, ratified in 1791, which guarantee certain civil liberties, such as freedom of religion, speech, and the press; the right to assemble; the right to petition the government for redress of grievances; freedom from unreasonable searches and seizures; the right to due process of law; and the right to a speedy and public trial.

bipartisan: Having the agreement or cooperation of members of both the Republican and the Democratic Parties.

birthright citizenship: The legal right to US citizenship that includes, under the Fourteenth Amendment to the US Constitution and the Immigration and Nationality Act, the right of individuals born within and subject to the jurisdiction of the United States to be US citizens.

block council: A community governance organization formed by the residents who lived within a block (a cluster of barracks with their communal mess hall, bathroom and laundry facilities, and recreational building) in the WRA detention camps.

block manager: An individual who was selected by a WRA detention camp director (or elected, at Manzanar) to serve as the communications liaison between the camp administration and the block residents; to handle various administrative tasks, such as distributing supplies and incoming and outgoing mail; and to oversee maintenance of the buildings and grounds.

Buddhahead: The term that the Nisei soldiers from the US mainland used to refer to the Nisei soldiers from Hawaii.

Buddhism: One of the world's largest religions, established by Siddhartha

Gautama in the fifth century BC in India, practiced by a vast majority of the Japanese Americans who were incarcerated. The Buddhist incarcerees drew upon their faith as a source of strength and community during their incarceration but were also considered by the US government to be less loyal than Christian Japanese Americans because of their non-Christian beliefs.

Cable Act of 1922: Federal legislation that affirmed provisions of the Expatriation Act of 1907 and stripped US women of their citizenship when they married Issei men who were ineligible for citizenship.

camaraderie: The spirit of friendship and loyalty among members of a group.

camp: The term that the incarcerees commonly used to refer to the WRA relocation center in which they were detained during World War II.

catch-22: A dilemma; a difficult situation that cannot be changed.

Chinese Exclusion Act: The immigration law passed in 1882 that halted Chinese labor immigration into the United States and excluded Chinese nationals from being eligible for US citizenship; the first immigration law that excluded immigration on the basis of race.

Civil Control Station: One of ninety-seven locations set up by the Wartime Civil Control Administration of the Western Defense Command within the military-designated exclusion zone. Representatives of Japanese American families were ordered to report to designated Civil Control Stations to register for their forced removal, to receive instructions on what they were allowed to bring, and to be issued the identification tags that each person of Japanese ancestry was required to wear.

Civilian Exclusion Orders: A series of 108 orders issued by Lieutenant General John L. DeWitt as the head of the Western Defense Command that directed the exclusion of all persons of Japanese ancestry (aliens as well as citizens) from areas on the West Coast designated as military zones. The exclusion orders were posted on telephone poles, public buildings, and other high-visibility places in the community.

Civil Liberties Act of 1988 (H.R. 442): The federal act that implemented

the recommendations of the Commission on Wartime Relocation and Internment of Civilians, signed into law by President Ronald Reagan on August 10,
1988. The act provided an official apology and $20,000 token reparation pay-
ments to the surviving US citizens and legal resident aliens of Japanese ancestry who had been incarcerated by the US government during World War II.

**Commission on Wartime Relocation and Internment of Civilians
(CWRIC):** The nine-member bipartisan commission established by the
US Congress in 1980 to investigate the circumstances and impact of Executive Order 9066. In 1983 the commission issued its report, *Personal Justice
Denied*, and made recommendations to Congress that survivors of the wartime detention receive a public apology and individual reparation payments
of $20,000.

concentration camp: A place where a large group of people is imprisoned
for political reasons, often on the basis of race, religion, or some perceived
"undesirable" trait. This term is believed to have originated with the British
establishment of a camp system in South Africa during the Anglo-Boer War,
in which tens of thousands of Boers suffered under inhumane conditions.
President Franklin D. Roosevelt and members of his administration used
this term in referring to the places where persons of Japanese ancestry were
unconstitutionally imprisoned under armed guard in harsh circumstances.
This term is also associated with the camps maintained by the Nazis to detain
and torture political prisoners and those accused of "socially deviant" behavior, and is often used to refer to the Nazi slave labor camps and the Nazi exter-
mination or death camps in which millions of Jews were mistreated, tortured,
and executed.

coram nobis: Latin for "before us"; a writ, or petition, brought by a defendant
who was convicted and served a sentence and who later claims that errors of
fact that could have changed the outcome of the case were knowingly with-
held in the court proceedings, and that the defendant suffered a "manifest
injustice" as a result. Three Japanese Americans—Minoru Yasui, Gordon
Hirabayashi, and Fred Korematsu—successfully used the writ of coram nobis
in the 1980s to show that the US government in World War II knowingly

presented false charges of Japanese American disloyalty. This allowed them to have their criminal convictions for violating the US government's wartime curfew and exclusion orders vacated.

court-martial: A court consisting of military officers for the purpose of trying members of the military who are charged with violating military law.

Court of Appeals for the Ninth Circuit: One of thirteen federal courts of appeals. The Ninth Circuit hears cases on appeal from federal districts in the western United States.

curfew: A regulation that requires people to remain indoors for a specified time, such as at night until the following morning.

Dachau: The first camp established by the Nazis in 1933, with the initial purpose of detaining political prisoners but that evolved into a death camp where tens of thousands of Jews were executed or died from mistreatment, malnutrition, and disease. During World War II the camp's prisoners were used as slave labor to support Germany's war efforts. US military forces, including the 522nd Field Artillery Battalion of the 442nd Regimental Combat Team, liberated Dachau and its subcamps in late April 1945.

Daughters of the American Revolution (DAR): An organization founded in 1890 whose members are women who are lineal descendants of a patriot of the American Revolution. During World War II many DAR members expressed anti-Japanese sentiments, believing persons of Japanese ancestry to be enemies of US interests.

Denaturalization Act of 1944: The federal law that was passed to allow US citizens to renounce their citizenship, specifically American-born Nisei who were disaffected by their wartime imprisonment by the government.

Department of Justice (DOJ): The US government agency, established in 1870, that is responsible for the enforcement of federal law and the administration of justice in the United States. Its roles today also include defending US interests, ensuring public safety against foreign and domestic threats, providing federal leadership in preventing and controlling crime, seeking just punishment for those found guilty of unlawful behavior, and ensuring fair and impartial administration of justice for all Americans. The US attorney general directs the DOJ, is the chief lawyer for the federal government, and is a member of the presidential cabinet of the United States.

Department of War: The US government agency, established in 1789, that oversaw the US Army until 1947, when it became part of the Department of Defense.

deport: To remove a foreign national or alien from the United States.

double entendre: A word or phrase that can be interpreted in two ways, one of which is usually sarcastic or risqué.

dragnet: A systematic approach for apprehending an individual or individuals, often those believed to be criminals or violators of some law.

enemy alien: An individual who is a citizen of a country at war with the United States.

entitlement: A federal program that is guaranteed to be funded in the federal budget as a binding commitment of the US government. Senator Daniel K. Inouye led the successful legislative effort that made redress payments to surviving incarcerees an entitlement, guaranteeing the funding of these payments from 1991 to 1999, when the program ended.

evacuation: The removal of individuals from an area for their own safety, as in the event of a natural disaster. The term was used euphemistically by the US government to refer to the forced removal of persons of Japanese ancestry from the West Coast because of political and economic motivations.

Executive Order 9066: The executive order issued by President Franklin D. Roosevelt on February 19, 1942, that authorized the secretary of war and his designated military commanders to identify military areas from which persons might be excluded. This order was used as the basis for the forcible removal of persons of Japanese ancestry from the West Coast into detention centers in the interior of the United States for the duration of World War II.

expatriation: The act of leaving one's country of citizenship.

fait accompli: French for "accomplished fact"; something that is already determined.

Farm Security Administration: An agency created as part of the US

Department of Agriculture in 1937 as a New Deal program of President Franklin D. Roosevelt to aid farmers, sharecroppers, tenant farmers, and migrant workers affected by the Great Depression.

Fascist: A member of a political regime, headed by an autocratic or dictatorial leader, who adheres to a philosophy of exalting the nation over the individual and a philosophy of allegiance to a master race or group. The term was associated with the German Nazi and Italian regimes in World War II.

Fellowship of Reconciliation: A progressive pacifist group that supported Gordon Hirabayashi and other Japanese Americans who chose not to report to a WRA assembly center.

fifth column: A group of sympathizers living within a country at war who are secretly working for its enemies. This is the translation of the Spanish phrase *quinta columna*, used during the Spanish Civil War to refer to a hidden column or group of rebel supporters within Madrid who would aid four rebel columns that were advancing on the city in 1936.

foreign national: A person who is a citizen of any country other than the US.

gaman: The Japanese word that conveys the idea of persevering or enduring with dignity, patience, and strength.

Gentlemen's Agreement: A diplomatic understanding reached between Japan and the United States by which Japan agreed not to issue passports to Japanese male laborers seeking to emigrate to the US, and President Theodore Roosevelt negotiated with the City of San Francisco to rescind its order segregating Japanese students from White students in its schools.

Gila monster: A large venomous lizard found in the deserts of the southwestern United States and especially in the Gila River area.

Go for Broke: The slogan of the 100th/442nd Regimental Combat Team that comes from the Hawaiian pidgin phrase used in crap games to wager everything on a single roll, meaning "to go all in."

goose quill pen: A writing implement made from a feather of a goose (or other large bird); the feather shaft holds ink, which flows to the carved tip by capillary action. Goose quill pens were used for centuries, until the advent of the metal pen in the nineteenth century.

Gosei: The Japanese word that refers to the fifth generation of Japanese in the United States; an American-born child of a Yonsei.

Gothic Line: The Germans' last major line of defense along the summits of the northern Apennine Mountains in Italy. When the American troops, including those of the 100th/442nd Regimental Combat Team, breached the Germans' Gothic Line in the Po River valley to advance into Italy, the Germans surrendered, ending the bitterly fought Italian campaign of World War II.

greasewood: A desert plant of the southwestern United States.

Greco-Roman wrestling: A style of wrestling and one of the sports that the Nisei practiced while detained in the assembly and relocation centers.

habeas corpus: Latin for "you should have the body"; a writ, or petition, brought by a detained person to have the case of their detention or imprisonment presented before a court to determine if the detention or imprisonment is lawful.

hakujin: The Japanese word that means "White person" or "Caucasian."

Hawaii Territorial Guard (HTG): The defense force for the State of Hawaii composed initially of the members of the University of Hawaii's Reserve Officers' Training Corps. After the Japanese American members of the HTG were discharged following the attack on Pearl Harbor, the discharged guardsmen were allowed by the military governor of Hawaii to form the Varsity Victory Volunteers, many of whom went on to become members of the 100th/442nd Regimental Combat Team.

Heart Mountain Fair Play Committee: An organization of draft-age Nisei men at the Heart Mountain Relocation Center who took the position that the rights of the Japanese Americans should be clarified before they complied with the orders to report for their physical examinations required as part of the draft induction process. Sixty-three members of the committee were arrested, tried, and convicted of violating provisions of the Selective Training and Service Act and served prison sentences. Although they were pardoned in 1947 by President Harry S. Truman, they and other draft resisters were criticized and ostracized by many in the Japanese American community. A divide still exists as to whether the draft resisters were loyal and courageous in their position or disloyal because they did not comply with the draft as others did.

Honorary Texans: What the surviving members of the 141st Infantry Regiment, Thirty-Sixth Infantry Division (the Lost Battalion), called their rescuers from the 100th/442nd Regimental Combat Team.

immigration: The process of people from one country coming to another country to live.

Immigration Act of 1924: The federal law signed on May 24, 1924, by President Calvin Coolidge that established a race-based quota system for immigration into the United States and banned immigration from Asia, including Japan.

Immigration and Nationality Act of 1952: The federal act that reinstated the ability of Asians to immigrate to the US on a limited basis and made the Issei eligible for naturalization, so they could finally become citizens.

Immigration and Naturalization Service (INS): The agency of the Department of Justice that administered federal immigration laws and regulations from 1940 to 2003. Following the September 11 attacks of 2001, the INS became part of the Department of Homeland Security in 2003.

incarceration: The preferred term for describing the wartime imprisonment of persons of Japanese ancestry instead of the term "internment," which refers specifically to the detention of individuals who are not US citizens by the US Army or Department of Justice.

incarceree: A person who was under the jurisdiction of the WRA and detained in one or more of its assembly centers and/or relocation centers.

inkwell: A small container or jar used for holding ink when writing with a brush, quill pen, or fountain pen.

innuendo: A statement that puts someone or something down in an indirect way.

internment: The term that refers to the power of the US government to detain aliens who are citizens of countries at war or in conflict with the US; the commonly used but inaccurate term that refers to the US government's wartime imprisonment of persons of Japanese ancestry, two thirds of whom were US citizens and did not fall within the definition of those who could be interned.

internment centers: Often the term used for the WRA relocation centers, but precisely used to refer to the Department of Justice or US Army sites where foreign nationals designated as enemy aliens were interned during World War II.

inu: The Japanese word for "dog," used in a derogatory way to refer to a Japanese American who was suspected of informing federal officials about disloyal or suspicious activities of other Japanese Americans.

Issei: The Japanese word that refers to a first-generation immigrant from Japan to the United States.

Japanese American Citizens League (JACL): The oldest and largest Asian American US civil rights organization. It was founded by Nisei in 1929.

Japanese American Evacuation and Resettlement Study: An academic study led by Dorothy Swaine Thomas, a sociologist at the University of California, Berkeley, on the forced removal, detention, and resettlement of Japanese Americans during World War II. The project was the source of publications and produced voluminous materials and data used in subsequent studies.

Jim Crow: A derogatory term for a Black man; the laws that enforced racial segregation in the South, from the end of the Reconstruction after the Civil War in 1877 to the beginning of the civil rights movement in the 1950s.

judo: A martial art form that originated in Japan and is similar to wrestling.

Kabuki: A classical Japanese dramatic art form that combines music, dance, and mime with elaborate costuming, staging, and customs.

kendo: A Japanese martial art that is a form of swordsmanship and uses bamboo swords and protective gear.

Kibei: The Japanese word that refers to an American-born child of Issei immigrants who was sent to Japan for some duration and later returned to the United States.

kodomo no tame ni: A Japanese expression that means "for the sake of the children" and represents the values of Japanese parents to sacrifice for the benefit of their offspring.

koto: The Japanese thirteen-stringed floor harp.

Kotonk: The term that the Nisei soldiers from Hawaii used to refer to the Nisei soldiers from the US mainland. One version of the origin of the word is that it is the hollow sound of their heads when they hit the ground, meaning the head is empty.

Ku Klux Klan: The oldest of American White supremacist groups, infamous for violent attacks in hooded white robes against Black persons, and also Jews, immigrants, and members of the LGBTQ community. The Klan was founded in 1866 by ex–Confederate soldiers and other Southerners opposed to Reconstruction after the Civil War.

leave clearance: A process that allowed certain incarcerees to leave camp once they were judged not to pose a security risk. Permission was granted to leave for personal business, education, and employment. Obtaining school and work leaves was challenging. For approval to leave for college, applicants had to be admitted to a college outside of the West Coast exclusion area, show they could afford the college expenses, and provide a statement from a local official that the prospective student would be accepted in the college community. For approval to leave for employment, applicants had to submit proof of a job offer, proof of the prospective employer's sponsorship, and letters of reference from White persons, and then pass an FBI security check.

Lost Battalion: The nickname for the 211 members of the 141st Infantry Regiment, Thirty-Sixth Infantry Division, who were caught behind German lines in the Vosges Mountains and who were rescued by members of the 100th/442nd Regimental Combat Team, who are reported to have suffered more than eight hundred casualties in the course of the rescue.

loyalty: The feelings of identity and commitment that the Issei had to the United States as their country of choice and that the Nisei had to the US as the country of their birth; the principle that the US government equated with race, assuming the Issei and Nisei owed a higher allegiance to Japan as persons of Japanese ancestry, and presuming them to be incapable of loyalty to the US; the criteria by which the US government determined which incarcerees could obtain a release from the wartime detention centers.

loyalty hearing: A hearing conducted by various government entities over the course of the incarceration to determine whether there was reason to suspect an individual was disloyal to the United States, justifying continued detention. These cursory hearings did not allow the detainees to have access to legal advice or to challenge any evidence brought against them. Such hearings were conducted, for example, for the Issei community leaders who were arrested after the Pearl Harbor attack and for those who responded to the loyalty questionnaires, which were meant to determine their eligibility for release from the camps. The hearing boards were generally composed of representatives of the military intelligence agencies.

loyalty questionnaires: A series of questionnaires produced by the US Army and the WRA that all persons of Japanese ancestry seventeen years of age and older in the WRA camps were required to answer; part of the government's bungled attempt to determine both eligibility for military service and eligibility for release and resettlement in areas outside of the West Coast exclusion area.

machine gun nest: A protected or concealed post in which one or more machine guns are set up.

mainland: The term that residents in the state of Hawaii often use to refer to the continental United States.

Manzanar Children's Village: The orphanage established at the Manzanar Relocation Center that housed orphans and foster children of Japanese ancestry who were incarcerated with their Japanese American caregivers.

Manzanar Riot: A series of protests and violent events on December 5–6, 1942, triggered by the beating of Fred Tayama, a national leader of the JACL, and the arrest and detention of Harry Ueno, who led the Mess Hall Workers Union, at the Manzanar Relocation Center. Military police fired into a large, unruly crowd of incarcerees intent on freeing Ueno, killing two and wounding nine others. Some factors identified as leading up to the riot include tensions between camp administrators and the incarcerees, friction within factions of incarcerees, and conflict between the Issei/Kibei and the Nisei generations.

martial law: Control of a nation or state by the military in a time of emergency.

Maryknoll Home for Japanese Children: An orphanage in Los Angeles from which Colonel Karl Bendetsen of the US Army's Western Defense Command removed babies and young children with any Japanese heritage and sent them to the Manzanar Relocation Center for indefinite detention.

Meiji era: The forty-four-year reign from 1868 to 1912 of Emperor Mutsuhito, known as the Meiji Emperor, which ended the era of the daimyo lords and the samurai, and initiated a period of rapid industrialization and modernization in Japan.

Military Intelligence Service (MIS): The military unit that trained and graduated nearly six thousand soldiers, the majority of whom were Japanese Americans, who served as interrogators, interpreters, translators, radio announcers, and propaganda writers and were considered instrumental in winning the war against Japan. Because they served in mostly classified operations, their contributions to the war effort were not known until the information about their service was declassified in recent decades.

Military Intelligence Service Language School (MISLS): The unit of the Military Intelligence Service that was responsible for providing soldiers with intensive training in Japanese reading, writing, conversation, culture, military practices, and techniques in communications, interrogation, and interpretation so that these soldiers could serve in various linguistic capacities in the Pacific theater during World War II and in occupied Japan after the war. The MISLS began operations in the Presidio in San Francisco and later operated at Camp Savage and Fort Snelling, both in Minnesota.

military necessity: The US government's unfounded rationale for unconstitutionally incarcerating 120,000 persons of Japanese ancestry because they were considered to be a security threat based solely upon their race.

military police: The law enforcement unit within a military branch.

model minority: A controversial concept whereby a demographic group is perceived to be higher achieving than the population at large; a stereotype applied to Japanese American Nisei that presumed they attained postwar success because of their commitment to academic excellence, hard work, and assimilation, but that masked the hardships and disadvantages the incarcerees were never able to overcome after the war.

Munson report: An intelligence report commissioned by President Franklin D. Roosevelt and prepared by Curtis B. Munson in November 1941. The report concluded that the vast majority of Japanese Americans were loyal to the United States and did not pose a national security threat in the event of war with Japan.

National Association for the Advancement of Colored People (NAACP): The nation's premier and largest civil rights organization. Founded in 1909, the NAACP works to eliminate discrimination based on race.

National Coalition for Redress/Reparations (NCRR): The organization that made a commitment to the grassroots community in the campaign to achieve redress and reparations for the wartime incarceration of Japanese Americans, and contributed to the successful passage of the Civil Liberties Act of 1988. Founded in 1980, and known as Nikkei for Civil Rights and Redress since 2000, the organization continues to work in the community in support of similar campaigns against injustice, such as those for Muslim American and Arab American groups following the 9/11 attacks.

National Council for Japanese American Redress (NCJAR): The group that was organized in 1979 under the leadership of William Hohri and filed a class action lawsuit, suing the US government for $27 billion for injuries suffered by the former Japanese American incarcerees as a result of their wartime exclusion and detention. Their case was heard by the Supreme Court during the appellate process, but ultimately the US district court ruling that granted the government's motion to dismiss the case was upheld. The NCJAR class action lawsuit—along with the redress bill resulting in the passage of the Civil Liberties Act of 1988 and the reopening of the wartime Supreme Court cases of Minoru Yasui, Gordon Hirabayashi, and Fred Korematsu through coram nobis petitions—helped to bring awareness to the general public and elected officials about the injustices of the wartime incarceration.

National Japanese American Student Relocation Council (NJASRC): The organization that facilitated the placement of Nisei students into colleges that accepted Japanese Americans, mostly in the Midwest, where they were able to continue their education.

natsukashi-mi: The Japanese term for an emotional state of yearning or longing.

naturalization: The process by which an alien is granted US citizenship after fulfilling requirements established by Congress in the Immigration and Nationality Act.

Nihongo: The Japanese word for "Japanese language."

Nihonmachi: The Japanese word for "Japantown," areas where persons of Japanese ancestry formed communities, such as in Seattle, San Francisco, San Jose, and Los Angeles, where the heart of the Japanese American community is called Little Tokyo.

Nikkei: The Japanese word for "persons of Japanese heritage."

Ninth Service Command: The unit of the US Army Service Forces during World War II that had jurisdiction over operations in Arizona, California, Idaho, Montana, Nevada, Oregon, Utah, and Washington.

Nisei: The Japanese word that refers to an American-born child of Issei immigrants; the second generation of Japanese in the United States.

Nisei draft resister: One of approximately three hundred draft-eligible Japanese American men over the age of seventeen incarcerated in a WRA detention center who refused to comply with the Selective Training and Service Act of 1940 and were convicted for their failure to act in accordance with the US Army's draft requirements.

non-alien: The term used by the Western Defense Command in the exclusion orders to disingenuously refer to the Nisei, who were US citizens; this designation required the Nisei to leave the West Coast for inland detention centers.

No-No Boy: Any Nikkei male over the age of seventeen who answered no to questions twenty-seven and twenty-eight of the loyalty questionnaire. As a consequence, he was considered disloyal to the United States and rendered himself ineligible for release from the WRA camps.

obon: An annual Buddhist festival, traditionally observed in mid-August, that honors families' ancestors. Japanese American communities celebrate *obon* with odori folk dancing, carnivals with games, taiko drumming, food fairs, and lantern lighting.

Office of Indian Affairs (OIA): As defined on the Office of Indian Affairs website, this is the federal agency within the US Department of the Interior responsible for the interests of "American Indians, Indian tribes, and Alaska Natives"; renamed the Bureau of Indian Affairs in 1947.

Office of Naval Intelligence (ONI): The military intelligence agency of the US Navy.

origami: The Japanese art of paper folding.

picture bride: A young Japanese woman who was arranged to marry an Issei man through an exchange of photographs and family information prior to her arrival in the United States. Upon meeting their husbands when they arrived in the US, the picture brides were often shocked and dismayed to find their husbands were not as successful and attractive as they had been represented to be. Nevertheless, with their husbands, the picture brides raised children, the Nisei generation, who were born as US citizens.

pidgin: A form of speech used by residents in Hawaii that combines words from English, Hawaiian, Japanese, Portuguese, and Chinese.

platoon: A military unit composed of two or more squads of soldiers, usually commanded by a lieutenant or other junior officer.

Presidential Unit Citation: The award given to units of the US Armed Forces and cobelligerent nations for extraordinary heroism in action against an armed enemy occurring on or after December 7, 1941. The unit must display such gallantry, determination, and esprit de corps in accomplishing its mission under extremely difficult and hazardous conditions as to set it apart from and above other units participating in the same campaign.

project director: The person in charge of each of the ten WRA camps.

Public Law 503: The federal legislation that President Franklin D. Roosevelt signed into law on March 21, 1942, that made it a crime to violate the military orders authorized by Roosevelt's Executive Order 9066.

rabble-rouser: A person who agitates the emotions of others, typically for political reasons.

racially restrictive covenant (RRC): A provision in a real property deed or an agreement between a seller and a buyer of property that the property will not be sold or leased to someone who is a racial minority.

redress: The process referred to in the First Amendment, that citizens have the right "to petition the Government for a redress of grievances." Japanese Americans used the term "redress" to describe the legislative and judicial strategies employed in the 1980s to have their wartime incarceration found to be unconstitutional. The redress movement was successful in securing the passage of the Civil Liberties Act of 1988, which provided an apology and $20,000 individual token reparation payments to surviving incarcerees.

Religious Society of Friends (Quakers): The religious organization to which Gordon Hirabayashi belonged that believes in the divinity of each person.

relocation center: The term used by the War Relocation Authority for the ten detention facilities in Arkansas, Arizona, California, Colorado, Idaho, Utah, and Wyoming under its jurisdiction where persons of Japanese ancestry who were forcibly removed from the West Coast under Executive Order 9066 were imprisoned for the duration of World War II.

renunciant: American-born Nisei who chose to renounce or give up their US citizenship and went to Japan to live as World War II was ending.

reparations: The making of amends for a wrong that has been committed, which could include the payment of money to acknowledge the harm that resulted from the wrongful act.

repatriation: The act of returning to one's country of citizenship. Many Issei immigrants, not eligible for US citizenship, chose to return to Japan during World War II.

reprisal reserve: The concept that Congressman John D. Dingell Sr. proposed to President Franklin D. Roosevelt that the US government detain Japanese aliens in the United States in the event they were needed to be offered to Japan in exchange for the release of US POWs.

Reserve Officers' Training Corps (ROTC): The competitive leadership program in which college students train to become officers in the US Army, Navy, Marines, and Air Force concurrently with their academic studies; upon successful completion of their training, ROTC graduates are commissioned as officers.

resettlement: The process by which incarcerees left the wartime detention camps, initially to resume or pursue education or jobs, mostly in the Midwest; with the closing of the camps, the migration of the former incarcerees either to other parts of the country or back to the West Coast.

retribution: Punishment inflicted as vengeance for a wrong or perceived wrong. Incarcerating persons of Japanese ancestry on the sole basis of their race was justified by some as retribution for Japan's attack on Pearl Harbor.

Ringle report: The January 1942 report written by Lieutenant Commander Kenneth D. Ringle, an intelligence officer in the Office of Naval Intelligence, to the chief of naval operations on the "Japanese question." In this report Ringle maintained that the Japanese Americans were loyal and that the "Japanese problem" had been magnified out of proportion. He recommended that the loyalty of persons of Japanese ancestry be evaluated on an individual basis, and not on a wholesale racial basis, but his report was ignored and suppressed by senior members of the Roosevelt administration.

Roberts Commission: The commission appointed by President Franklin D. Roosevelt on December 18, 1941, to investigate the causes of Japan's attack on Pearl Harbor. The vague reference to "Japanese spies" in the commission's report, issued on January 23, 1942, contributed to the public hysteria and political will to forcibly remove all persons of Japanese ancestry from the West Coast.

Russo-Japanese War: The 1904–5 military conflict in which Japan defeated Russia, thwarting Russia's expansionist ambitions in East Asia. Because it was the first major victory of an Asian country over a European one in modern times, the results of this war contributed to the views of President Franklin D. Roosevelt and his contemporaries that Japan was an enemy nation to be feared and hated.

saboteur: Someone who purposefully undertakes actions intended to destroy or weaken an enemy.

sagebrush: An aromatic shrub found in the plains of the western United States.

Salvation Army's Japanese Children's Home: An orphanage in San Francisco from which Colonel Karl Bendetsen of the US Army's Western Defense

Command removed babies and young children with any Japanese heritage, in order to send them to the Manzanar Relocation Center for indefinite detention.

Sansei: The Japanese word that refers to the third generation of Japanese in the United States; an American-born child of a Nisei.

seasonal leave: Permission to temporarily leave camp that was granted to incarcerees who were deemed to be loyal, in order to harvest sugar beets in western states. Approximately ten thousand Japanese Americans incarcerated in US detention camps were granted seasonal leave, thereby saving the sugar beet harvest that was critical to the war effort.

Seinan: Japanese for "southwest"; the neighborhood located southwest of downtown Los Angeles, generally within the area of Western Avenue on the west, Vermont Avenue on the east, Twenty-Seventh Street on the north, and Exposition Boulevard on the south. Japanese American families began living in the area in the 1920s because racially restrictive covenants and ordinances prevented them from buying homes within the boundaries of the City of Los Angeles. When the Japanese American families were forcibly removed from the area during World War II, Black and other wartime workers moved into the neighborhood.

shamisen: The Japanese three-stringed fretless instrument similar to a banjo that is plucked with a plectrum.

shikata ga nai: A Japanese expression that means "it can't be helped" or "nothing can be done about it," representing the ability to be at peace with that which cannot be changed.

Shinto: Of or relating to the ancient religion of Shintoism, which was the state religion of Japan until 1945. Persons of Japanese ancestry who indicated on the wartime loyalty questionnaires and other government forms that they identified as being Shinto were presumed to be disloyal to the United States.

Shonien: An orphanage in Los Angeles from which Colonel Karl Bendetsen of the US Army's Western Defense Command removed babies and young children with any Japanese heritage, in order to send them to the Manzanar Relocation Center for indefinite detention.

short-term leave: Permission to leave camp for personal business for a day or other designated short time, granted to incarcerees who were deemed to be loyal.

shoyu: The Japanese word for "soy sauce."

solicitor general: The person who supervises the litigation of the US government in matters before the US Supreme Court and who argues the government's cases before the US Supreme Court.

student leave: Permission to leave camp that was granted through a bureaucratic process to approximately four thousand Nisei students to continue their education at colleges in the Midwest and on the East Coast.

sumo: A Japanese form of wrestling.

Supreme Court: The highest court in the United States, charged with interpreting the US Constitution; currently composed of a chief justice and eight associate justices.

tar paper: Heavy paper coated with tar that is used in construction to provide waterproofing. Tar paper was often the only material besides wooden boards used to construct the camp barracks.

Tolan Committee: The name by which the House Select Committee Investigating National Defense Migration is commonly known. Its chair, Congressman John H. Tolan, held committee hearings in the spring of 1942, at which the majority of witnesses called for the removal of persons of Japanese ancestry from the West Coast.

tree bursts: The detonation of artillery rounds in trees that rained deadly debris such as shrapnel, wood branches, and splinters onto everything below.

tsuru: The Japanese word for "crane." Cranes are a symbol of long life, happiness, peace, and hope.

umi no oya yori mo sodate no oya: The Japanese phrase meaning that the parents who raised you are more important to you than your biological parents. For the Issei, this meant that the United States, their adoptive country, was more important to them than Japan, the country of their birth.

Uncle Sam: The personification of the US government.

US Census Bureau: The federal agency mandated by the US Constitution to count the population of the United States every ten years to determine the number of seats that each state has in the House of Representatives. The census that is conducted collects demographic, economic, and other statistical data, which is also used to allocate state and federal resources and for research purposes.

Varsity Victory Volunteers (VVV): The group of Japanese American ROTC students who were dismissed from the Hawaii Territorial Guard and who were later given permission to volunteer as a labor battalion at Schofield Barracks on the island of Oahu. The contributions and example of the VVV laid the foundation for the ability of the Nisei to serve in the 442nd Regimental Combat Team and the Military Intelligence Service.

voluntary evacuation: The withdrawal of nearly five thousand persons of Japanese ancestry from portions of the states of Arizona, California, Oregon, and Washington designated by the US Army's Western Defense Command as military areas, in advance of the forced removal under the exclusion orders issued in the spring of 1942. These individuals moved to other parts of the United States and avoided incarceration in the assembly and relocation centers.

War Relocation Authority (WRA): The federal agency created to administer the ten WRA detention facilities in which approximately 120,000 persons of Japanese ancestry were imprisoned during World War II.

Western Defense Command: The unit established by the US Army on March 17, 1941, to defend the states of Arizona, California, Idaho, Montana, Nevada, Oregon, Utah, and Washington, including the Pacific coast. Lieutenant General John L. DeWitt served as its first commanding general. He advocated for and oversaw the forced removal of Japanese Americans from the West Coast. The Western Defense Command was disbanded on March 6, 1946.

Women's Army Corps (WAC): The branch of the US Army, established on July 1, 1943, in which approximately 150,000 women served worldwide during World War II in noncombat roles such as switchboard operators, radio operators, electricians, mechanics, draftspeople, postal clerks, drivers, stenographers, clerk typists, interpreters, and bakers. The WAC as a branch was disbanded in 1978, and the women serving were integrated with male military units.

Yellow Peril: The term that refers to the belief that many Americans had, beginning in the mid-nineteenth century, that Chinese immigrants, and subsequently Japanese immigrants, represented a threat to Western values. This fear manifested as anti-Asian propaganda, promoted especially by the Hearst media empire, that portrayed persons of Asian heritage as villainous, untrustworthy, heathen, and unfit for naturalization or citizenship. The racial prejudices stoked by Yellow Peril contributed to anti-Asian labor movements, discriminatory laws and policies, and the fear that Japan would imminently attack the United States.

Yonsei: The Japanese word that refers to the fourth generation of Japanese in the United States; an American-born child of a Sansei.

LIST OF ABBREVIATIONS

ACLU: American Civil Liberties Union
AAPI: Asian American Pacific Islander
CWRIC: Commission on Wartime Relocation and Internment of Civilians
DOJ: Department of Justice
FBI: Federal Bureau of Investigation
FCC: Federal Communications Commission
FDR: Franklin Delano Roosevelt
HTG: Hawaii Territorial Guard
INS: Immigration and Naturalization Service
JACL: Japanese American Citizens League
MIS: Military Intelligence Service
MISLS: Military Intelligence Service Language School
NAACP: National Association for the Advancement of Colored People
NCJAR: National Council for Japanese American Redress
NCRR: formerly National Coalition for Redress/Reparations; now Nikkei for
    Civil Rights and Redress
NJASRC: National Japanese American Student Relocation Council
OIA: Office of Indian Affairs
ONI: Office of Naval Intelligence
POW: prisoner of war
RCT: regimental combat team
ROTC: Reserve Officers' Training Corps
RRC: racially restrictive covenant
SELANOCO: Southeast Los Angeles and North Orange County (JACL chapter)
SERC: Seattle Evacuation Redress Committee
VVV: Varsity Victory Volunteers
WAC: Women's Army Corps
WCCA: Wartime Civil Control Administration
WRA: War Relocation Authority

YMCA: Young Men's Christian Association
YWCA: Young Women's Christian Association

CONTRIBUTOR NOTES

1. Emi "Amy" Akiyama (Berger): Ellen Levine, *A Fence Away from Freedom: Japanese Americans and World War II* (New York: G. P. Putnam's Sons, 1995).

2. Daniel "Dan" Ken Inouye: Geoffrey C. Ward and Ken Burns, *The War: An Intimate History, 1941–1945* (New York: Knopf, 2014).

3. Mitsuo "Mits" Usui: Mitsuo Usui, Hearing for the Commission on Wartime Relocation and Internment of Civilians, August 6, 1981, Los Angeles, CA.

4. Monica Kazuko Itoi (Sone): Monica Sone, *Nisei Daughter* (Boston: Little, Brown and Company, 1953).

5. Frank Seishi Emi: California State University, Northridge, Delmar T. Oviatt Library, Department of Asian American Studies and the Urban Archives Center, "Telling Our Stories: Japanese Americans in the San Fernando Valley Oral History Project, Transcript of Frank Emi Oral History Interview," November 8, 2004, Densho Digital Repository.

6. David Masao Sakai: Audrie Girdner and Anne Loftis, *The Great Betrayal: The Evacuation of the Japanese-Americans during World War II* (Toronto: The Macmillan Company, 1969).

7. Aiko Grace Shinoda (Nakamura): "Grace Shinoda Nakamura Interview," January 25, 2012, Densho Digital Repository.

8. Jeanne Toyo Wakatsuki (Houston): Jeanne Wakatsuki Houston and James D. Houston, *Farewell to Manzanar: A True Story of Japanese American Experience during and after the World War II Internment* (Boston: Houghton Mifflin, 1973).

9. Hisaye Yamamoto (Desoto): Richard Reeves, *Infamy: The Shocking Story of the Japanese American Internment in World War II* (New York: Henry Holt and Company, 2015).

10. Monica Kazuko Itoi (Sone): Monica Sone, *Nisei Daughter* (Boston: Little, Brown and Company, 1953).

11. Takashi "Dwight" Uchida: Yoshiko Uchida, *Desert Exile: The Uprooting*

of a Japanese American Family (Seattle, WA: University of Washington Press, 1982).

12. Kyuji Aizumi: Donald H. Estes and Matthew T. Estes. "Further and Further Away," *The San Diego Historical Society Quarterly*, vol. 39, no. 1–2 (Spring 1993).

13. Dollie Kimiko Nagai (Fukawa): Ellen Levine, *A Fence Away from Freedom: Japanese Americans and World War II* (New York: G. P. Putnam's Sons, 1995).

14. Monica Kazuko Itoi (Sone): Monica Sone, *Nisei Daughter* (Boston: Little, Brown and Company, 1953).

15. Minoru "Min" Tamaki: Minoru Tamaki, Hearing for the Commission on Wartime Relocation and Internment of Civilians, August 13, 1981, San Francisco, CA.

16. Katsumi Thomas "Tom" Kawaguchi: *The Great Depression*, Interview with Tom and Sadako Kawaguchi, Interviewer: Rick Tejada-Flores. March 12, 1992. Washington University Film and Media Archive, Henry Hampton Collection.

17. Ben Toshihiro Tagami: Ellen Levine, *A Fence Away from Freedom: Japanese Americans and World War II* (New York: G. P. Putnam's Sons, 1995).

18. Mary Sakaguchi (Oda): Mary Oda, US Senate Subcommittee on Civil Service, Post Office, and General Services of the Committee on Governmental Affairs Hearings on H.R. 442 and H.R. 2116, August 16, 1984, Los Angeles, CA.

19. Edward Kanta Fujimoto: "Grace F. Oshita Interview," June 4, 2008, Densho Digital Repository.

20. Yoshito "Yosh" Kuromiya: Ellen Levine, *A Fence Away from Freedom: Japanese Americans and World War II* (New York: G. P. Putnam's Sons, 1995).

21. Minoru "Min" Tamaki: Minoru Tamaki, Hearing for the Commission on Wartime Relocation and Internment of Civilians, August 13, 1981, San Francisco, CA.

22. Haruyuki "Jim" Matsuoka: Ellen Levine, *A Fence Away from Freedom: Japanese Americans and World War II* (New York: G. P. Putnam's Sons, 1995).

23. Monica Kazuko Itoi (Sone): Monica Sone, *Nisei Daughter* (Boston: Little, Brown and Company, 1953).

24. Yukio Tatsumi: Ellen Levine, *A Fence Away from Freedom: Japanese Americans and World War II* (New York: G. P. Putnam's Sons, 1995).

25. Monica Kazuko Itoi (Sone): Monica Sone, *Nisei Daughter* (Boston: Little, Brown and Company, 1953).

26. Mary Tsuruko (Dakuzaku) Tsukamoto: John Tateishi, *And Justice for All: An Oral History of the Japanese American Detention Camps* (Seattle, WA: University of Washington Press, 1999).

27. Mitsuru "Mits" Koshiyama: Ellen Levine, *A Fence Away from Freedom: Japanese Americans and World War II* (New York: G. P. Putnam's Sons, 1995).

28. Bruce Teruo Kaji: Bruce T. Kaji with Sharon Yamato, *Jive Bomber: A Sentimental Journey* (Gardena, CA: Kaji & Associates, 2010).

29. Monica Kazuko Itoi (Sone): Monica Sone, *Nisei Daughter* (Boston: Little, Brown and Company, 1953).

30. Frank Seishi Emi: California State University, Northridge, Delmar T. Oviatt Library, Department of Asian American Studies and the Urban Archives Center, "Telling Our Stories: Japanese Americans in the San Fernando Valley Oral History Project, Transcript of Frank Emi Oral History Interview," November 8, 2004, Densho Digital Repository.

31. Namiko "Nami" Aurora (Nakashima) Diaz: Ellen Levine, *A Fence Away from Freedom: Japanese Americans and World War II* (New York: G. P. Putnam's Sons, 1995).

32. Yoshiko Uchida: Yoshiko Uchida, *Desert Exile: The Uprooting of a Japanese American Family* (Seattle, WA: University of Washington Press, 1982).

33. Paul Yashiro Shinoda: John Tateishi, *And Justice for All: An Oral History of the Japanese American Detention Camps* (Seattle, WA: University of Washington Press, 1999).

34. Mitsuru "Mits" Koshiyama: Ellen Levine, *A Fence Away from Freedom: Japanese Americans and World War II* (New York: G. P. Putnam's Sons, 1995).

35. Monica Kazuko Itoi (Sone): Monica Sone, *Nisei Daughter* (Boston: Little, Brown and Company, 1953).

36. Allan Minoru Hida: Allan Hida, Hearing for the Commission on Wartime Relocation and Internment of Civilians, September 22, 1981, Chicago, IL.

37. Elizabeth Aiko (Takahashi) Nishikawa: Elizabeth Nishikawa, Hearing for the Commission on Wartime Relocation and Internment of Civilians, August 6, 1981, Los Angeles, CA.

38. Mike Masaru Masaoka: Mike M. Masaoka with Bill Hosokawa, *They Call Me Moses Masaoka: An American Saga* (New York: William Morrow and Company, 1987).

39. Monica Kazuko Itoi (Sone): Monica Sone, *Nisei Daughter* (Boston: Little, Brown and Company, 1953).

40. Larry Taneyoshi Tajiri: Larry Tajiri, "Racial Hysteria for Profit," *The New Leader*, May 20, 1944.

41. Mitsuru "Mits" Koshiyama: Ellen Levine, *A Fence Away from Freedom: Japanese Americans and World War II* (New York: G. P. Putnam's Sons, 1995).

42. Sueko "Sue" Kunitomi (Embrey): Sue Kunitomi Embrey, November 6, 2002, Densho Digital Repository.

43. Sueko "Sue" Kunitomi (Embrey): Ellen Levine, *A Fence Away from Freedom: Japanese Americans and World War II* (New York: G. P. Putnam's Sons, 1995).

44. Monica Kazuko Itoi (Sone): Monica Sone, *Nisei Daughter* (Boston: Little, Brown and Company, 1953).

45. Mike Masaru Masaoka: Mike M. Masaoka with Bill Hosokawa, *They Call Me Moses Masaoka: An American Saga* (New York: William Morrow and Company, 1987).

46. Ibid.

47. Mary Tsuruko (Dakuzaku) Tsukamoto: John Tateishi, *And Justice for All: An Oral History of the Japanese American Detention Camps* (Seattle, WA: University of Washington Press, 1999).

48. Mike Masaru Masaoka: Mike M. Masaoka with Bill Hosokawa, *They Call Me Moses Masaoka: An American Saga* (New York: William Morrow and Company, 1987).

49. Mary Tsuruko (Dakuzaku) Tsukamoto: John Tateishi, *And Justice for All: An Oral History of the Japanese American Detention Camps* (Seattle, WA: University of Washington Press, 1999).

50. Mike Masaru Masaoka: Mike M. Masaoka with Bill Hosokawa, *They Call Me Moses Masaoka: An American Saga* (New York: William Morrow and Company, 1987).

51. Yoshihiko Fred Fujikawa: The Commission on Wartime Relocation and Internment of Civilians, *Personal Justice Denied* (Seattle, WA: University of Washington Press, 1997).

52. Paul Tsutomu Ohtaki: Shizue Seigel, *In Good Conscience: Supporting Japanese Americans during the Internment* (San Mateo, CA: Asian American Curriculum Project, 2006).

53. Yoshio "Yosh" Nakamura: Yoshio Nakamura, Hearing for the Commission on Wartime Relocation and Internment of Civilians, August 6, 1981, Los Angeles, CA.

54. Monica Kazuko Itoi (Sone): Monica Sone, *Nisei Daughter* (Boston: Little, Brown and Company, 1953).

55. Allan Minoru Hida: Allan Hida, Hearing for the Commission on Wartime Relocation and Internment of Civilians, September 22, 1981, Chicago, IL.

56. Mitsuru "Mits" Koshiyama: Mitsuru Koshiyama, July 14, 2001, Los Angeles, CA, Densho Digital Repository.

57. Monica Kazuko Itoi (Sone): Monica Sone, *Nisei Daughter* (Boston: Little, Brown and Company, 1953).

58. Yoshiko Uchida: Yoshiko Uchida, *Desert Exile: The Uprooting of a Japanese American Family* (Seattle, WA: University of Washington Press, 1982).

59. Ernest Nobumaro Uno: Hawaii Nikkei History Editorial Board, "Ernest Uno," *Japanese Eyes, American Hearts: Personal Reflections of Hawaii's World War II Nisei Soldiers* (Honolulu, HI: University of Hawaii Press, 1998).

60. William "Bill" Kumpai Hosokawa: Richard Reeves, *Infamy: The Shocking Story of the Japanese American Internment in World War II* (New York: Henry Holt and Company, 2015).

61. Theodore "Ted" Katsuyoshi Nakashima: Ted Nakashima, "Concentration Camp: U.S. Style," *New Republic*, vol. 106, no. 24 (June 15, 1942).

62. Hiroshi Kamei: Hiroshi Kamei, Hearing for the Commission on Wartime Relocation and Internment of Civilians, August 6, 1981, Los Angeles, CA.

63. Keiko "Kay" Uno (Kaneko): Kay Uno Kaneko, June 9, 2010, Kona, HI, Densho Digital Repository.

64. Sueko "Sue" Kunitomi (Embrey): Diana Meyers Bahr, *The Unquiet Nisei: An Oral History of the Life of Sue Kunitomi Embrey* (New York: Palgrave Macmillan, 2007).

65. Sueko "Sue" Kunitomi (Embrey): Ellen Levine, *A Fence Away from Freedom: Japanese Americans and World War II* (New York: G. P. Putnam's Sons, 1995).

66. Mary Tsuruko (Dakuzaku) Tsukamoto: John Tateishi, *And Justice for All: An Oral History of the Japanese American Detention Camps* (Seattle, WA: University of Washington Press, 1999).

67. Ibid.

68. Sumiko "Sumi" Seo (Seki): Ellen Levine, *A Fence Away from Freedom: Japanese Americans and World War II* (New York: G. P. Putnam's Sons, 1995).

69. Mary Tsuruko (Dakuzaku) Tsukamoto: Mary Tsukamoto, US House of Representatives Subcommittee on Administrative Law and Governmental Relations of the Committee on the Judiciary, 99th Congress, 2nd Session, Hearings on H.R. 442 and H.R. 2415, April 28, 1986, Washington, DC.

70. Teru Watanabe: The Commission on Wartime Relocation and Internment of Civilians, *Personal Justice Denied* (Seattle, WA: University of Washington Press, 1997).

71. Minoru "Min" Yasui: Minoru Yasui, Hearing for the Commission on Wartime Relocation and Internment of Civilians, July 16, 1981, Washington, DC.

72. Gordon Kiyoshi Hirabayashi: Gordon K. Hirabayashi with James A. Hirabayashi and Lane Ryo Hirabayashi, *A Principled Stand: The Story of* Hirabayashi v. United States (Seattle, WA: University of Washington Press, 2013).

73. Gordon Kiyoshi Hirabayashi: Peter Irons, *Justice at War: The Story of the Japanese-American Internment Cases* (New York: Oxford University Press, 1983).

74. Fred Toyosaburo Korematsu: Peter Irons, *Justice at War: The Story of the Japanese-American Internment Cases* (New York: Oxford University Press, 1983).

75. Mike Masaru Masaoka: Mike M. Masaoka with Bill Hosokawa, *They Call Me Moses Masaoka: An American Saga* (New York: William Morrow and Company, 1987).

76. Ruth Tanaka (Gray): Ruth Tanaka, "Saga of the People," California Digital Libraries, University of California, Berkeley, Bancroft Library, Colorado River War Relocation Project Collection.

77. Mary Sakaguchi (Oda): Mary Oda, US Senate Subcommittee on Civil Service, Post Office, and General Services of the Committee on Governmental Affairs Hearings on H.R. 442 and H.R. 2116, August 16, 1984, Los Angeles, CA.

78. Masako "Betty" (Fujisaki) Matsuo: The Commission on Wartime Relocation and Internment of Civilians, *Personal Justice Denied* (Seattle, WA: University of Washington Press, 1997).

79. Mary Tsuruko (Dakuzaku) Tsukamoto: Mary Tsukamoto, US House of Representatives Subcommittee on Administrative Law and Governmental Relations of the Committee on the Judiciary, 99th Congress, 2nd Session, Hearings on H.R. 442 and H.R. 2415, April 28, 1986, Washington, DC.

80. Aiko Yoshinaga (Herzig): James L. Dickerson, *Inside America's Concentration Camps: Two Centuries of Internment and Torture* (Chicago: Chicago Review Press, 2010).

81. Riichi Satow: Michiyo Laing and the Issei Oral History Project, *Issei Christians: Selected Interviews from the Issei Oral History Project* (Sacramento, CA: Issei Oral History Project, Inc., 1977).

82. Bebe Toshiko Horiuchi (Reschke): Bebe Reschke, Hearing for the Commission on Wartime Relocation and Internment of Civilians, August 6, 1981, Los Angeles, CA.

83. Miné Okubo: Miné Okubo, *Citizen 13660* (New York: Columbia University Press, 1946).

84. Yoshiko Uchida: Yoshiko Uchida, *Desert Exile: The Uprooting of a Japanese American Family* (Seattle, WA: University of Washington Press, 1982).

85. Aiko Grace Shinoda (Nakamura): Grace Shinoda Nakamura Interview, January 25, 2012, Whittier, CA, Densho Digital Repository.

86. Monica Kazuko Itoi (Sone): Monica Sone, *Nisei Daughter* (Boston: Little, Brown and Company, 1953).

87. Mitsuye (Yasutake) Yamada: Mitsuye Yamada, *Camp Notes and Other Writings: Mitsuye Yamada* (New Brunswick, NJ: Rutgers University Press, 1998).

88. Kunisaku "Kay" Mineta: Carl M. Cannon, "Peril for Bloomberg; Due Process; Back in the Game," *RealClear Politics*, November 12, 2019.

89. Norman "Norm" Yoshio Mineta: Betty Cuniberti, "Internment: Personal Voices, Powerful Choices," *Los Angeles Times*, October 4, 1987.

90. Louise Yoshiko Ogawa (Watanabe): Letter to Clara Breed from Louise Ogawa, Poston, AZ, June 28, 1943. Japanese American National Museum (gift of Elizabeth Y. Yamada, 93.75.31DY).

91. Ben Satoshi Segawa: San Diego Historical Society, ReGenerations Project, September 1990.

92. Fuji (Okamoto) Takaichi: Audrie Girdner and Anne Loftis, *The Great Betrayal: The Evacuation of the Japanese-Americans during World War II* (Toronto: Macmillan, 1970).

93. Chizuko "Chizu" Kitano (Iiyama): Telling Their Stories Oral History Archive Project, "Chizu Iiyama," April 6, 2006.

94. Shuzo Chris Kato: Shuzo Chris Kato, Hearing for the Commission on Wartime Relocation and Internment of Civilians, September 9, 1981, Seattle, WA.

95. Mary Tsuruko (Dakuzaku) Tsukamoto: John Tateishi, *And Justice for All: An Oral History of the Japanese American Detention Camps* (Seattle, WA: University of Washington Press, 1999).

96. William Masayoshi Kochiyama: The Commission on Wartime Reloca-

tion and Internment of Civilians, *Personal Justice Denied* (Seattle, WA: University of Washington Press, 1997).

97. Ben Satoshi Segawa: Joanne Oppenheim, *Dear Miss Breed: True Stories of the Japanese American Incarceration during World War II and a Librarian Who Made a Difference* (New York: Scholastic, 2006).

98. Miné Okubo: Miné Okubo, *Citizen 13660* (New York: Columbia University Press, 1946).

99. Monica Kazuko Itoi (Sone): Monica Sone, *Nisei Daughter* (Boston: Little, Brown and Company, 1953).

100. Margaret "Maggie" Tokuko Ishino: Joanne Oppenheim, *Dear Miss Breed: True Stories of the Japanese American Incarceration during World War II and a Librarian Who Made a Difference* (New York: Scholastic, 2006).

101. George Hosato Takei: George Takei, US Senate Subcommittee on Civil Service, Post Office, and General Services Hearing, 98th Congress, 2nd Session, August 16, 1984, Los Angeles, CA.

102. Minoru "Min" Yasui: Minoru Yasui, Hearing for the Commission on Wartime Relocation and Internment of Civilians, July 16, 1981, Washington, DC.

103. Monica Kazuko Itoi (Sone): Monica Sone, *Nisei Daughter* (Boston: Little, Brown and Company, 1953).

104. Miné Okubo: Miné Okubo, *Citizen 13660* (New York: Columbia University Press, 1946).

105. Charles Kikuchi: Charles Kikuchi, *The Kikuchi Diary: Chronicle from an American Concentration Camp* (Chicago: University of Illinois Press, 1993).

106. Mary Tsuruko (Dakuzaku) Tsukamoto: John Tateishi, *And Justice for All: An Oral History of the Japanese American Detention Camps* (Seattle, WA: University of Washington Press, 1999).

107. Ibid.

108. Misao "Sadie" Marietta (Nishitani) Sakamoto: The Commission on Wartime Relocation and Internment of Civilians, *Personal Justice Denied* (Seattle, WA: University of Washington Press, 1997).

109. Haru Michida Isaki: The Commission on Wartime Relocation and Internment of Civilians, *Personal Justice Denied* (Seattle, WA: University of Washington Press, 1997).

110. Mary Tsuruko (Dakuzaku) Tsukamoto: Mary Tsukamoto, US House of Representatives Subcommittee on Administrative Law and Governmental Relations of the Committee on the Judiciary, 99th Congress, 2nd Session, Hearings on H.R. 442 and H.R. 2415, April 28, 1986, Washington, DC.

111. Miné Okubo: Miné Okubo, *Citizen 13660* (New York: Columbia University Press, 1946).

112. Emiko "Emi" (Yada) Somekawa: Emi Somekawa, Hearing for the Commission on Wartime Relocation and Internment of Civilians, September 10, 1981, Seattle, WA.

113. Minoru "Min" Yasui: Minoru Yasui, Hearing for the Commission on Wartime Relocation and Internment of Civilians, July 16, 1981, Washington, DC.

114. Sato Hashizume: Telling Their Stories, Oral History Archive Project, "Sato Hashizume," January 23, 2008.

115. Charles Kikuchi: Charles Kikuchi, *The Kikuchi Diary: Chronicle from an American Concentration Camp* (Chicago: University of Illinois Press, 1993).

116. Louise Yoshiko Ogawa (Watanabe): Letter to Clara Breed from Louise Ogawa, Arcadia, CA, July 15, 1942, Japanese American National Museum (gift of Elizabeth Y. Yamada, 93.75.31V).

117. Charles Kikuchi: Charles Kikuchi, *The Kikuchi Diary: Chronicle from an American Concentration Camp* (Chicago: University of Illinois Press, 1993).

118. Emi "Amy" Akiyama (Berger): Ellen Levine, *A Fence Away from Freedom: Japanese Americans and World War II* (New York: G. P. Putnam's Sons, 1995).

119. Charles Kikuchi: Charles Kikuchi, *The Kikuchi Diary: Chronicle from an American Concentration Camp* (Chicago: University of Illinois Press, 1993).

120. Harry Katsuharu Fukuhara: Shizue Seigel, *In Good Conscience: Supporting Japanese Americans during the Internment* (San Mateo, CA: Asian American Curriculum Project, 2006).

121. Louise Yoshiko Ogawa (Watanabe): Letter to Clara Breed from Louise Ogawa, Arcadia, CA, July 15, 1942, Japanese American National Museum (gift of Elizabeth Y. Yamada, 93.75.31V).

122. Miné Okubo: Miné Okubo, *Citizen 13660* (New York: Columbia University Press, 1946).

123. Haru Michida Isaki: Haru Isaki, Hearing for the Commission on Wartime Relocation and Internment of Civilians, September 9, 1981, Seattle, WA.

124. Mabel Takako (Kawashima) Ota: John Tateishi, *And Justice for All: An Oral History of the Japanese American Detention Camps* (Seattle, WA: University of Washington Press, 1999).

125. George Akimoto: Deborah Gesensway and Mindy Roseman, *Beyond Words: Images from America's Concentration Camps* (Ithaca, NY: Cornell University Press, 1988).

126. Charles Kikuchi: Charles Kikuchi, *The Kikuchi Diary: Chronicle from an American Concentration Camp* (Chicago: University of Illinois Press, 1993).

127. Monica Kazuko Itoi (Sone): Monica Sone, *Nisei Daughter* (Boston: Little, Brown and Company, 1953).

128. Miné Okubo: Miné Okubo, *Citizen 13660* (New York: Columbia University Press, 1946).

129. Ibid.

130. Yoshiko Uchida: Yoshiko Uchida, *Desert Exile: The Uprooting of a Japanese American Family* (Seattle, WA: University of Washington Press, 1982).

131. Tetsuzo "Ted" or "Tets" Hirasaki: Letter to Miss Clara Breed from Tetsuzo Hirasaki, Poston, Arizona, September 7, 1942, Japanese American National Museum (gift of Elizabeth Y. Yamada, 3.75.3EL).

132. Minoru "Min" Yasui: Minoru Yasui, Hearing for the Commission on Wartime Relocation and Internment of Civilians, July 16, 1981, Washington, DC.

133. Elizabeth Aiko (Takahashi) Nishikawa: Elizabeth Nishikawa, "Thoughts on *Farewell to Manzanar*," *Los Angeles Times*, March 27, 1976.

134. Masami Honda: Ruth Okimoto, "Sharing a Desert Home: Life on the Colorado River Indian Reservation, Poston, Arizona, 1942–1945," *News from Native California*, 2001.

135. Miné Okubo: Miné Okubo, *Citizen 13660* (New York: Columbia University Press, 1946).

136. Yoshiko Uchida: Yoshiko Uchida, *Desert Exile: The Uprooting of a Japanese American Family* (Seattle, WA: University of Washington Press, 1982).

137. Mary Yuriko "Yuri" Nakahara (Kochiyama): Martin W. Sandler, *Imprisoned: The Betrayal of Japanese Americans in World War II* (New York: Bloomsbury USA Childrens, 2013).

138. Chiyoko Morita: Chiyoko Morita, "My First Few Days in Poston," *Jr. Red Cross*, vols. 1–2, The Huntington Library, Art Museum, and Botanical Gardens.

139. Louise Yoshiko Ogawa (Watanabe): Letter to Clara Breed from Louise Ogawa, Poston, AZ, August 27, 1942 (gift of Elizabeth Y. Yamada, 93.75.31IO).

140. Jeanne Toyo Wakatsuki (Houston): Jeanne Wakatsuki Houston and James D. Houston. *Farewell to Manzanar: A True Story of Japanese American Experience during and after the World War II Internment* (Boston: Houghton Mifflin, 1973).

141. Sumiko "Sumi" Seo (Seki): Ellen Levine, *A Fence Away from Freedom: Japanese Americans and World War II* (New York: G. P. Putnam's Sons, 1995).

142. Michio "Mich" Kunitani: Audrie Girdner and Anne Loftis, *The Great Betrayal: The Evacuation of the Japanese-Americans during World War II* (Toronto: The Macmillan Company, 1969).

143. Miné Okubo: Miné Okubo, *Citizen 13660* (New York: Columbia University Press, 1946).

144. Dollie Kimiko Nagai (Fukawa): Ellen Levine, *A Fence Away from Freedom: Japanese Americans and World War II* (New York: G. P. Putnam's Sons, 1995).

145. Yoshiko Uchida: Yoshiko Uchida, *Desert Exile: The Uprooting of a Japanese American Family* (Seattle, WA: University of Washington Press, 1982).

146. Jeanne Toyo Wakatsuki (Houston): Jeanne Wakatsuki Houston and James D. Houston, *Farewell to Manzanar: A True Story of Japanese American Experience during and after the World War II Internment* (Boston: Houghton Mifflin, 1973).

147. Toyo Suyemoto (Kawakami): Toyo Suyemoto and Susan B. Richardson, *I Call to Remembrance: Toyo Suyemoto's Years of Internment* (New Brunswick, NJ: Rutgers University Press, 2007).

148. Sumiko "Sumi" Seo (Seki): Ellen Levine, *A Fence Away from Freedom: Japanese Americans and World War II* (New York: G. P. Putnam's Sons, 1995).

149. Shuzo Chris Kato: Shuzo Chris Kato, Hearing for the Commission on Wartime Relocation and Internment of Civilians, September 9, 1981, Seattle, WA.

150. Louise Yoshiko Ogawa (Watanabe): Letter to Clara Breed from Louise Ogawa, Poston, AZ, August 27, 1942 (gift of Elizabeth Y. Yamada, 93.75.31IO).

151. Monica Kazuko Itoi (Sone): Monica Sone, *Nisei Daughter* (Boston: Little, Brown and Company, 1953).

152. Sueko "Sue" Kunitomi (Embrey): "Sue Kunitomi Embrey," November 6, 2002, Densho Digital Repository.

153. Mitsuye (Yasutake) Yamada: Mitsuye Yamada, *Camp Notes and Other Writings: Mitsuye Yamada* (New Brunswick, NJ: Rutgers University Press, 1998).

154. Toyo Suyemoto (Kawakami): Toyo Suyemoto and Susan B. Richardson, *I Call to Remembrance: Toyo Suyemoto's Years of Internment* (New Brunswick, NJ: Rutgers University Press, 2007).

155. Miné Okubo: Miné Okubo, *Citizen 13660* (New York: Columbia University Press, 1946).

156. Chizuko "Chizu" Kitano (Iiyama): Telling Their Stories Oral History Archive Project. "Chizu Iiyama," April 6, 2006.

157. Chiyoko Morita: Chiyoko Morita, "My First Few Days in Poston," *Jr.*

Red Cross, vols. 1–2, The Huntington Library, Art Museum, and Botanical Gardens.

158. Kyuji Aizumi: Kyuji Aizumi, Excerpt from "Further and Further Away" in the *Journal of San Diego History* 39, nos. 1–2 (Spring 1993).

159. Mitsuru "Mits" Koshiyama: Mitsuru Koshiyama, July 14, 2001, Los Angeles, CA, Densho Digital Repository.

160. Yoshito "Yosh" Kuromiya: "The Winters of Heart Mountain," undated essay, Densho Digital Repository.

161. Emiko "Emi" (Yada) Somekawa: John Tateishi, *And Justice for All: An Oral History of the Japanese American Detention Camps* (Seattle, WA: University of Washington Press, 1999).

162. Mabel Takako Ota: Mabel Ota, Hearing for the Commission on Wartime Relocation and Internment of Civilians, August 6, 1981, Los Angeles, CA.

163. Masako "Betty" (Fujisaki) Matsuo: The Commission on Wartime Relocation and Internment of Civilians, *Personal Justice Denied* (Seattle, WA: University of Washington Press, 1997).

164. John Sohei Hohri: Ellen Levine, *A Fence Away from Freedom: Japanese Americans and World War II* (New York: G. P. Putnam's Sons, 1995).

165. Lillian Reiko Sugita (Nakano): Ellen Levine, *A Fence Away from Freedom: Japanese Americans and World War II* (New York: G. P. Putnam's Sons, 1995).

166. Helen Matsue Yamahiro (Murao): John Tateishi, *And Justice for All: An Oral History of the Japanese American Detention Camps* (Seattle, WA: University of Washington Press, 1999).

167. Jeanne Toyo Wakatsuki (Houston): Jeanne Wakatsuki Houston and James D. Houston, *Farewell to Manzanar: A True Story of Japanese American Experience during and after the World War II Internment* (Boston: Houghton Mifflin, 1973).

168. Robert Ritsuro Hosokawa: Robert Hosokawa, "An American with a Japanese Face," undated essay, Japanese American Evacuation and Resettlement Study, University of California, Berkeley, Bancroft Library.

169. Jeanne Toyo Wakatsuki (Houston): Jeanne Wakatsuki Houston and

James D. Houston, *Farewell to Manzanar: A True Story of Japanese American Experience during and after the World War II Internment* (Boston: Houghton Mifflin, 1973).

170. Louise Yoshiko Ogawa (Watanabe): Letter to Clara Breed from Louise Ogawa, Poston, AZ, June 28, 1943, Japanese American National Museum (gift of Elizabeth Y. Yamada, 93.75.31DY).

171. Masaru "Mas" Hashimoto: 50 Objects/Stories: The American Japanese Incarceration. Object 4 Interview: "A Boy's Best Friend," November 4, 2018, https://www.youtube.com/watch?v=sppLJmtIoBg&t=52s.

172. Ruth Tanaka (Gray): Ruth Tanaka, "Mary," California Digital Libraries, University of California, Berkeley, Bancroft Library, Colorado River War Relocation Project Collection.

173. Mike Masaru Masaoka: Mike M. Masaoka with Bill Hosokawa, *They Call Me Moses Masaoka: An American Saga* (New York: William Morrow and Company, 1987).

174. William "Bill" Kumpai Hosokawa: Bill Hosokawa, *Nisei: The Quiet Americans* (Boulder, CO: University Press of Colorado, 2002).

175. Sada (Hasegawa) Murayama: Audrie Girdner and Anne Loftis, *The Great Betrayal: The Evacuation of the Japanese-Americans during World War II* (Toronto: Macmillan, 1970).

176. Elizabeth Aiko (Takahashi) Nishikawa: Elizabeth Nishikawa, Hearing for the Commission on Wartime Relocation and Internment of Civilians, August 6, 1981, Los Angeles, CA.

177. William "Bill" Kumpai Hosokawa: Bill Hosokawa, *Nisei: The Quiet Americans* (Boulder, CO: University Press of Colorado, 2002).

178. Miné Okubo: The Commission on Wartime Relocation and Internment of Civilians, *Personal Justice Denied* (Seattle, WA: University of Washington Press, 1997).

179. Kojin Tahara: Lucille M. Nixon and Tomoe Tana, *Sounds from the Unknown: A Collection of Japanese-American Tanka.* (Athens, OH: Swallow Press/Ohio University Press, 1963).

180. Marion Tsuruko Konishi (Takehara): Marion Konishi, "America, Our

Hope Is Anew [*sic*]." Valedictorian Address. Amache Senior High School Graduation, June 25, 1943. *Congressional Record*, vol. 162, S3694 9JN (June 9, 2016).

181. Tetsuzo "Ted" or "Tets" Hirasaki: Letter to Clara Breed from Tetsuzo (Ted) Hirasaki, Poston, Arizona, June 10, 1944, Japanese American National Museum (gift of Elizabeth Y. Yamada, 93.75.31GG).

182. Hatsune "Helen" Aihara (Kitaji): Audrie Girdner and Anne Loftis, *The Great Betrayal: The Evacuation of the Japanese-Americans during World War II* (Toronto: The Macmillan Company, 1969).

183. Ibid.

184. Toyo Suyemoto (Kawakami): Toyo Suyemoto and Susan B. Richardson, *I Call to Remembrance: Toyo Suyemoto's Years of Internment* (New Brunswick, NJ: Rutgers University Press, 2007).

185. Rhoda Akiko Nishimura (Iyoya): June Hisaye Toshiyuki and the Nisei Christian Oral History Project, *Nisei Christian Journey: Its Promise & Fulfillment* (Sunnyvale, CA: Nisei Christian Oral History Project for the Japanese Presbyterian Conference and the Northern California Japanese Christian Church Federation, 1988).

186. Toyo Suyemoto (Kawakami): Toyo Suyemoto, "Another Spring" in Erica Harth, ed., *Last Witnesses: Reflections on the Wartime Internment of Japanese Americans* (New York: Palgrave, 2001).

187. Mike Masaru Masaoka: Mike M. Masaoka with Bill Hosokawa, *They Call Me Moses Masaoka: An American Saga* (New York: William Morrow and Company, 1987).

188. May Kimiko Nakamura (Sasaki): May K. Sasaki Interview, October 28, 1997, Seattle, WA, Densho Digital Repository.

189. John Yoshio Tateishi: The Commission on Wartime Relocation and Internment of Civilians, *Personal Justice Denied* (Seattle, WA: University of Washington Press, 1997).

190. Jeanne Toyo Wakatsuki (Houston): Jeanne Wakatsuki Houston and James D. Houston, *Farewell to Manzanar: A True Story of Japanese American Experience during and after the World War II Internment* (Boston: Houghton Mifflin, 1973).

191. Ibid.

192. June Hisaye (Abe) Toshiyuki: June Hisaye Toshiyuki and the Nisei Christian Oral History Project, *Nisei Christian Journey: Its Promise & Fulfillment, Volume 1* (Sunnyvale, CA: Nisei Christian Oral History Project for the Japanese Presbyterian Conference and the Northern California Japanese Christian Church Federation, 1988).

193. Mary Haruko (Matsuno) Makino: Ellen Levine, *A Fence Away from Freedom: Japanese Americans and World War II* (New York: G. P. Putnam's Sons, 1995).

194. Jack Shigeru Matsuoka: Deborah Gesensway and Mindy Roseman, *Beyond Words: Images from America's Concentration Camps* (Ithaca, NY: Cornell University Press, 1988).

195. John Yoshio Tateishi: The Commission on Wartime Relocation and Internment of Civilians, *Personal Justice Denied* (Seattle, WA: University of Washington Press, 1997).

196. Alice Natsuko Nakamura (Nishikawa): Alice Nakamura, "Rohwer Center High School Commencement," July 30, 1943, National Archives and Records Administration, War Relocation Authority Collection, Washington, DC.

197. Mike Masaru Masaoka: Mike Masaoka with Bill Hosokawa, *They Call Me Moses Masaoka: An American Saga* (New York: William Morrow and Company, 1987).

198. Eugene V. Rostow: Eugene V. Rostow, "Our Worst Wartime Mistake," *Harper's Magazine*, September 1945.

199. Monica Kazuko Itoi (Sone): Monica Sone, *Nisei Daughter* (Boston: Little, Brown and Company, 1953).

200. Toyo Suyemoto (Kawakami): Toyo Suyemoto and Susan B. Richardson, *I Call to Remembrance: Toyo Suyemoto's Years of Internment* (New Brunswick, NJ: Rutgers University Press, 2007).

201. Kazuko (Ikeda) Hayashi: Michiyo Laing and the Issei Oral History Project, *Issei Christians: Selected Interviews from the Issei Oral History Project* (Sacramento, CA: Issei Oral History Project, Inc., 1977).

202. George "Jobo" Ryoji Nakamura: George Nakamura. "May 15, 1943:

The Outlook" in "A Nisei Diary," *A Tule Lake Interlude, The Tulean Dispatch*, May 27, 1943.

203. George Taketa: George Taketa, Hearing for the Commission on Wartime Relocation and Internment of Civilians, September 22, 1981, Chicago, IL.

204. Lillian Reiko Sugita (Nakano): Ellen Levine, *A Fence Away from Freedom: Japanese Americans and World War II* (New York: G. P. Putnam's Sons, 1995).

205. Kazuo Masuda: Audrie Girdner and Anne Loftis, *The Great Betrayal: The Evacuation of the Japanese-Americans during World War II* (Toronto: The Macmillan Company, 1969).

206. Sueko "Sue" Kunitomi (Embrey): Ellen Levine, *A Fence Away from Freedom: Japanese Americans and World War II* (New York: G. P. Putnam's Sons, 1995).

207. Robert Ritsuro Hosokawa: Robert Hosokawa, "An American with a Japanese Face," undated essay, Japanese American Evacuation and Resettlement Study, University of California, Berkeley, Bancroft Library.

208. Frank Nobuo Bunya: Audrie Girdner and Anne Loftis, *The Great Betrayal: The Evacuation of the Japanese-Americans during World War II* (Toronto: The Macmillan Company, 1969).

209. Sumiko "Sumi" Seo (Seki): Ellen Levine, *A Fence Away from Freedom: Japanese Americans and World War II* (New York: G. P. Putnam's Sons, 1995).

210. Louise Yoshiko Ogawa (Watanabe): Letter to Clara Breed from Louise Ogawa, Poston, AZ, September 3, 1943, Japanese American National Museum (gift of Elizabeth Y. Yamada, 93.75.31AE).

211. Richard "Dick" Nishi: The Commission on Wartime Relocation and Internment of Civilians, *Personal Justice Denied* (Seattle, WA: University of Washington Press, 1997).

212. George Aki: John F. Wukovits, *Internment of Japanese Americans* (Detroit, MI: Lucent Press, 2012).

213. Kaizo "K" George Kubo: Kaizo George Kubo, "The Years Between," National Archives and Records Administration, Records of the War Relocation Authority, Washington, DC.

214. Jeanne Toyo Wakatsuki (Houston): Jeanne Wakatsuki Houston and James D. Houston, *Farewell to Manzanar: A True Story of Japanese American Experience during and after the World War II Internment* (Boston: Houghton Mifflin, 1973).

215. Yoshiye Togasaki: John Tateishi, *And Justice for All: An Oral History of the Japanese American Detention Camps* (Seattle, WA: University of Washington Press, 1999).

216. Kinya Noguchi: Kinya Noguchi, Hearing for the Commission on Wartime Relocation and Internment of Civilians, August 11, 1981, San Francisco, CA.

217. Sueko "Sue" Kunitomi (Embrey): Sue Kunitomi Embrey, November 6, 2002, Densho Digital Repository.

218. Ibid.

219. Bruce Teruo Kaji: "Bruce T. Kaji," July 28, 2010, Densho Digital Repository.

220. Jeanne Toyo Wakatsuki (Houston): Jeanne Wakatsuki Houston and James D. Houston, *Farewell to Manzanar: A True Story of Japanese American Experience during and after the World War II Internment* (Boston: Houghton Mifflin, 1973).

221. Mary Tsuruko (Dakuzaku) Tsukamoto: John Tateishi, *And Justice for All: An Oral History of the Japanese American Detention Camps* (Seattle, WA: University of Washington Press, 1999).

222. Helen Matsue Yamahiro (Murao): John Tateishi, *And Justice for All: An Oral History of the Japanese American Detention Camps* (Seattle, WA: University of Washington Press, 1999).

223. William "Bill" Kumpai Hosokawa: Richard Reeves, *Infamy: The Shocking Story of the Japanese American Internment in World War II* (New York: Henry Holt and Company, 2015).

224. Mark Yutaka Murakami: The Commission on Wartime Relocation and Internment of Civilians, *Personal Justice Denied* (Seattle, WA: University of Washington Press, 1997).

225. Mike Masaru Masaoka: Audrie Girdner and Anne Loftis, *The Great*

Betrayal: The Evacuation of the Japanese-Americans during World War II (Toronto: The Macmillan Company, 1969).

226. Ibid.

227. Miné Okubo: Miné Okubo, *Citizen 13660* (New York: Columbia University Press, 1946).

228. Ibid.

229. Mary Sakaguchi (Oda): Mary Oda, US Senate Subcommittee on Civil Service, Post Office, and General Services of the Committee on Governmental Affairs, Hearings on H.R. 442 and H.R. 2116, August 16, 1984, Los Angeles, CA.

230. Harold Norio Ouye: The Commission on Wartime Relocation and Internment of Civilians, *Personal Justice Denied* (Seattle, WA: University of Washington Press, 1997).

231. Kimitomo "Kim" Muromoto: Robert Asahina, *Just Americans: How Japanese Americans Won a War at Home and Abroad: The Story of the 100th Battalion/442nd Regimental Combat Team in World War II* (New York: Gotham Books, 2006).

232. Wayne Masao Kanemoto: Audrie Girdner and Anne Loftis, *The Great Betrayal: The Evacuation of the Japanese-Americans during World War II* (Toronto: The Macmillan Company 1969).

233. Grace Harada: Brenda L. Moore, *Serving Our Country: Japanese American Women in the Military during World War II* (New Brunswick, NJ: Rutgers University Press, 2003).

234. Katsumi Thomas "Tom" Kawaguchi: John Tateishi, *And Justice for All: An Oral History of the Japanese American Detention Camps* (Seattle, WA: University of Washington Press, 1999).

235. Mitsuo "Mits" Usui: Mitsuo Usui, Hearing for the Commission on Wartime Relocation and Internment of Civilians, August 6, 1981, Los Angeles, CA.

236. Miné Okubo: Miné Okubo, *Citizen 13660* (New York: Columbia University Press, 1946).

237. Daniel "Dan" Ken Inouye: Daniel K. Inouye with Lawrence Elliot, *Journey to Washington* (Englewood Cliffs, NJ: Prentice-Hall, Inc., 1967).

238. Yoshisada Kawai: Michiyo Laing and the Issei Oral History Project, *Issei Christians: Selected Interviews from the Issei Oral History Project* (Sacramento, CA: Issei Oral History Project, Inc., 1977).

239. Yoshito "Yosh" Kuromiya: Susie Ling, "The Kuromiyas of Monrovia: A Family of Unsung Heroes," *Rafu Shimpo*, September 20, 2016.

240. Jack Kiyoto Tono: Jack Kiyoto Tono, US House of Representatives, Hearings before the Subcommittee on Administrative Law and Governmental Relations of the Committee on the Judiciary, 99th Congress, 2nd Session on H.R. 442 and H.R. 2415, April 28, 1986, Washington, DC.

241. Ibid.

242. Spark Masayuki Matsunaga: Senator Spark Masayuki Matsunaga, "This I Believe," Inter-American Defense College Address, Fort McNair, Washington, DC, March 11, 1964, *Congressional Record*, 88th Congress, 2nd Session, vol. 110, part 4, March 4, 1964–March 18, 1964.

243. Daniel "Dan" Ken Inouye: Dorothy Matsuo, *Boyhood to War: History and Anecdotes of the 442nd Regimental Combat Team* (Honolulu, HI: Mutual Publishing Company, 1992).

244. Captain Young Oak Kim: Young Oak Kim, "Keynote Address," Puka Puka Parades, July–August 1982, vol. 36, no. 3, 100th Infantry Battalion Veterans Education Center.

245. Robert Ichigi Kashiwagi: Ken Burns, dir., *The War: An Intimate History*, "Robert Kashiwagi." PBS, 2007. DVD. Written by Geoffrey C. Ward. Produced by Ken Burns and Lynn Novick.

246. Masao Yamada: Hawaii Nikkei History Editorial Board, *Japanese Eyes, American Heart: Personal Reflections of Hawaii's World War II Nisei Soldiers* (Honolulu, HI: Tendai Educational Foundation, 1998).

247. Daniel "Dan" Ken Inouye: Brian Niiya, ed., *Japanese American History: An A-to-Z Reference from 1868 to the Present* (Los Angeles: Facts on File, 1993).

248. Captain Young Oak Kim: Young Oak Kim, "Keynote Address," Puka Puka Parades, July–August 1982, vol. 36, no. 3, 100th Infantry Battalion Veterans Education Center.

249. Daniel "Dan" Ken Inouye: Daniel K. Inouye with Lawrence Elliot, *Journey to Washington* (Englewood Cliffs, NJ: Prentice-Hall, Inc., 1967).

250. Captain John Barnett: United States Holocaust Memorial Museum, "Capt. John Barnett Testifies to the Authenticity of Photos Taken When His Troops Overran the Dachau Concentration Camp at the Trial of Former Camp Personnel and Prisoners from Dachau," November 24, 1945, National Archives and Records Administration.

251. Clarence "Cal" Satoru Matsumura: Ellen Levine, *A Fence Away from Freedom: Japanese Americans and World War II* (New York: G. P. Putnam's Sons, 1995).

252. Bonnie Gurewitsch: Ben Tamashiro, "The Liberation of Dachau: The Story of the 522," *Hawaii Herald*, May 16, 1986.

253. Major General Joseph "Vinegar Joe" Stilwell: The Commission on Wartime Relocation and Internment of Civilians, *Personal Justice Denied* (Seattle, WA: University of Washington Press, 1997).

254. Eleanor Elizabeth Crost: Lyn Crost, *Honor by Fire: Japanese Americans at War in Europe and the Pacific* (Novato, CA: Presidio Press, 1994).

255. President Harry S. Truman: Harry S. Truman, "Remarks upon Presenting a Citation to a Nisei Regiment," July 15, 1946, Harry S. Truman Library and Museum.

256. Sada (Hasegawa) Murayama: *Tulean Dispatch*, May 27, 1943.

257. Gordon Kiyoshi Hirabayashi: Roger Daniels, *The Japanese American Cases: The Rule of Law in Time of War* (Lawrence, KS: University Press of Kansas, 2013).

258. Aiko Yoshinaga (Herzig): Aiko Yoshinaga-Herzig, Densho Visual History Collection, September 11, 1997, Densho Digital Repository.

259. Peter H. Irons: Peter Irons, Densho Visual History Collection, October 27, 2000, Densho Digital Repository.

260. Gordon Kiyoshi Hirabayashi: Gordon K. Hirabayashi with James A. Hirabayashi and Lane Ryo Hirabayashi, *A Principled Stand: The Story of Hirabayashi v. United States* (Seattle, WA: University of Washington Press, 2013).

261. Mitsuye Maureen Endo (Tsutsumi): John Tateishi, *And Justice for All: An Oral History of the Japanese American Detention Camps* (Seattle, WA: University of Washington Press, 1999).

262. Fred Toyosaburo Korematsu: Lorraine K. Bannai, *Enduring Conviction: Fred Korematsu and His Quest for Justice*. (Seattle, WA: University of Washington Press, 2015).

263. Toyo Suyemoto (Kawakami): Toyo Suyemoto, "Camp Memories: Rough and Broken Shards" in Roger Daniels, Sandra C. Taylor, and Harry H. L. Kitano, eds., *Japanese Americans: From Relocation to Redress* (Seattle, WA: University of Washington Press, 1991).

264. Mitsuye Maureen Endo (Tsutsumi): John Tateishi, *And Justice for All: An Oral History of the Japanese American Detention Camps* (Seattle, WA: University of Washington Press, 1999).

265. Ellen Shizue Yukawa (Spink): Joanne Oppenheim, *Dear Miss Breed: True Stories of the Japanese American Incarceration during World War II and a Librarian Who Made a Difference* (New York: Scholastic, 2006).

266. Jeanne Toyo Wakatsuki (Houston): Jeanne Wakatsuki Houston and James D. Houston, *Farewell to Manzanar: A True Story of Japanese American Experience during and after the World War II Internment* (Boston: Houghton Mifflin Company, 1973).

267. Masaru "Mas" Hashimoto: Jan Janes, "Internment Camp Survivor Views Prejudice, Racism and Civil Rights through a Seven-Decade Lens," Gavilan College, December 8, 2017.

268. Emi "Amy" Akiyama (Berger): Ellen Levine, *A Fence Away from Freedom: Japanese Americans and World War II* (New York: G. P. Putnam's Sons, 1995).

269. May Kikuko (Tominaga) Ichida: The Commission on Wartime Relocation and Internment of Civilians, *Personal Justice Denied* (Seattle, WA: University of Washington Press, 1997).

270. Chiye Tomihiro: John Tateishi, *And Justice for All: An Oral History of the Japanese American Detention Camps* (Seattle, WA: University of Washington Press, 1999).

271. Masani "Mas" Fukai: Mas Fukai, Hearings before the US Senate Subcommittee on Civil Service, Post Office, and General Services, 98th Congress, 2nd Session on S. 2116, August 16, 1984, Los Angeles, CA.

272. Mitsuo "Mits" Usui: Mitsuo Usui, Hearing for the Commission on Wartime Relocation and Internment of Civilians, August 6, 1981, Los Angeles, CA.

273. Haruyo (Takeuchi) Hozaki: Audrie Girdner and Anne Loftis, *The Great Betrayal: The Evacuation of the Japanese-Americans during World War II* (Toronto: The Macmillan Company, 1969).

274. Dollie Kimiko Nagai (Fukawa): Ellen Levine, *A Fence Away from Freedom: Japanese Americans and World War II* (New York: G. P. Putnam's Sons, 1995).

275. Mitsuo "Mits" Usui: Commission on Wartime Relocation and Internment of Civilians, *Personal Justice Denied* (Seattle, WA: University of Washington Press, 1997).

276. Lillian Reiko Sugita (Nakano): Ellen Levine, *A Fence Away from Freedom: Japanese Americans and World War II* (New York: G. P. Putnam's Sons, 1995).

277. Daniel "Dan" Ken Inouye: Daniel K. Inouye with Lawrence Elliot. *Journey to Washington* (Englewood Cliffs, NJ: Prentice-Hall, Inc., 1967).

278. Harry Katsuharu Fukuhara: Harry K. Fukuhara, "Military Occupation of Japan," *Discover Nikkei*, May 2, 2006.

279. Masani "Mas" Fukai: Mas Fukai, Hearings before the US Senate Subcommittee on Civil Service, Post Office, and General Services, 98th Congress, 2nd Session on S. 2116, August 16, 1984, Los Angeles, CA.

280. Richard Takeshi Shindo: Richard Shindo, commencement speech, Poston High School, Poston I, National Archives and Records Administration, Records of the War Relocation Authority, Washington, DC.

281. Hiroshi Kamei: Hiroshi Kamei, salutatory address, Miles E. Cary High School, Poston II, National Archives and Records Administration, Records of the War Relocation Authority, Washington, DC.

282. Misako "Micki" Mayumi (Honda): Misako Mayumi, "Remembrance,"

salutatory address, Parker Valley High School, Poston III, National Archives and Records Administration, Records of the War Relocation Authority, Washington, DC.

283. Molly Moriko Ohashi (Yamamoto): Mollie Moriko Ohashi, "Modern Pioneers," valedictorian address, Parker Valley High School, Poston III, National Archives and Records Administration, Records of the War Relocation Authority, Washington, DC.

284. Mary Tsuruko (Dakuzaku) Tsukamoto: Mary Tsukamoto, US House of Representatives Subcommittee on Administrative Law and Governmental Relations of the Committee on the Judiciary, 99th Congress, 2nd Session, Hearings on H.R. 442 and H.R. 2415, April 28, 1986, Washington, DC.

285. Jeanne Toyo Wakatsuki (Houston): Jeanne Wakatsuki Houston and James D. Houston, *Farewell to Manzanar: A True Story of Japanese American Experience during and after the World War II Internment* (Boston: Houghton Mifflin, 1973).

286. Haruyuki "Jim" Matsuoka: Jim Matsuoka Interview, May 24, 2010, Los Angeles, CA, Densho Digital Repository.

287. John Yoshio Tateishi: P.C. Staff, "San Diego JACL Reflects, Remembers on 30th Anniversary of Redress," *Pacific Citizen*, October 12, 2018.

288. Fumiko (Ito) Ogawa: Fumiko F. Ogawa in Lucille M. Nixon and Tomoe Tana, *Sounds from the Unknown: A Collection of Japanese-American Tanka.* (Athens, OH: Swallow Press/Ohio University Press, 1963).

289. Yoshiko Uchida: Yoshiko Uchida, *Desert Exile: The Uprooting of a Japanese American Family* (Seattle, WA: University of Washington Press, 1982).

290. Michiko "Michi" (Nishiura) Weglyn: Frank Chin Papers, Special Research Collections, UC Santa Barbara Library, untitled commencement address by Michi Weglyn, California State Polytechnic University, Pomona, June 12, 1993.

291. Michiko "Michi" (Nishiura) Weglyn: Michi Nishiura Weglyn, *Years of Infamy: The Untold Story of America's Concentration Camps* (Seattle, WA: University of Washington Press, 1976).

292. George Hosato Takei: George Takei, Hearings before the US Senate

Subcommittee on Civil Service, Post Office, and General Services, 98th Congress, 2nd Session on S. 2116, August 16, 1984, Los Angeles, CA.

293. Mary Sakaguchi (Oda): Mary Oda, Hearing for the Commission on Wartime Relocation and Internment of Civilians, August 4, 1981, Los Angeles, CA.

294. Yasuko "Yas" Kodani (Morimoto): Yasuko Morimoto, Hearing for the Commission on Wartime Relocation and Internment of Civilians, August 13, 1981, San Francisco, CA.

295. Karen Anne Korematsu: Lorraine K. Bannai, *Enduring Conviction: Fred Korematsu and His Quest for Justice* (Seattle, WA: University of Washington Press, 2015).

296. Jeanne Toyo Wakatsuki (Houston): Jeanne Wakatsuki Houston, "Autobiographical Essay," *Contemporary Authors Online*, Gale Literature, 2017.

297. William "Bill" Kumpai Hosokawa: Bill Hosokawa, Densho Visual History Collection, July 13, 2001, Densho Digital Repository.

298. Mike Masaru Masaoka: Alice Yang Murray, *Historical Memories of the Japanese American Internment and the Struggle for Redress* (Stanford, CA: Stanford University Press, 2008).

299. John Yoshio Tateishi: P.C. Staff, "Plenary Reveals Maneuvers That Helped Redress Succeed," *Pacific Citizen*, August 16, 2019.

300. William "Bill" Minoru Hohri: William Hohri, "Redress as a Movement Towards Enfranchisement," in *Japanese Americans: From Relocation to Redress*, Roger Daniels, Sandra C. Taylor, and Harry H.L. Kitano, eds. (Seattle, WA: University of Washington Press, 1991).

301. John Yoshio Tateishi: Bilal Qureshi, "From Wrong to Right: A US Apology for Japanese Internment," *All Things Considered*, NPR, August 9, 2013.

302. Ronald "Ron" Kaoru Wakabayashi: P.C. Staff, "Plenary Reveals Maneuvers That Helped Redress Succeed," *Pacific Citizen*, August 16, 2019.

303. Robert "Bob" Takeo Matsui: Mitchell T. Maki, Harry H.L. Kitano, and S. Megan Berthold, *Achieving the Impossible Dream: How Japanese Americans Obtained Redress* (Urbana, IL: University of Illinois Press, 1999).

304. Ronald "Ron" Kaoru Wakabayashi: Ron Wakabayashi, Hearing for the Commission on the Wartime Relocation and Internment of Civilians,

September 10, 1981, Seattle, WA, Densho Digital Repository.

305. George Hosato Takei: George Takei, Hearings before the US Senate Subcommittee on Civil Service, Post Office, and General Services, 98th Congress, 2nd Session on S. 2116, August 16, 1984, Los Angeles, CA.

306. Haruyuki "Jim" Matsuoka: Jim Matsuoka, Hearing for the Commission on Wartime Relocation and Internment of Civilians, August 6, 1981, Los Angeles, CA.

307. Masani "Mas" Fukai: Mas Fukai, Hearings before the US Senate Subcommittee on Civil Service, Post Office, and General Services, 98th Congress, 2nd Session on S. 2116, August 16, 1984, Los Angeles, CA.

308. Fred Toyosaburo Korematsu: *Los Angeles Times*, "Conviction of Man Who Evaded WWII Internment Is Overturned," November 11, 1983.

309. Minoru "Min" Yasui: Minoru Yasui, Hearing for the Commission on Wartime Relocation and Internment of Civilians, July 16, 1981, Washington, DC.

310. John Yoshio Tateishi: Lorraine K. Bannai, *Enduring Conviction: Fred Korematsu and His Quest for Justice* (Seattle, WA: University of Washington Press, 2015).

311. Norman "Norm" Yoshio Mineta: Calvin Naito and Esther Scott. "Against All Odds: The Japanese Americans' Campaign for Redress," Harvard University John F. Kennedy School of Government Case Program, C16-90-1006.0, January 1, 1990.

312. Rudy Kazuo Tokiwa: Rudy Tokiwa, September 13, 1997, Los Angeles, CA, Densho Digital Repository.

313. Robert "Bob" Takeo Matsui: Mitchell T. Maki, Harry H.L. Kitano, and S. Megan Berthold, *Achieving the Impossible Dream: How Japanese Americans Obtained Redress* (Urbana, IL: University of Illinois Press, 1999).

314. Spark Masayuki Matsunaga: Karleen Chinen and Reizo Watanabe, "The US Senator Spark Matsunaga," *Hawaii Herald*, October 7, 1988.

315. Daniel "Dan" Ken Inouye: Senator Daniel K. Inouye, *Congressional Record*, 101st Congress, 1st Session, vol. 135, no. 128, September 29, 1989, S 12218-19.

316. Mary Tsuruko (Dakuzaku) Tsukamoto: Mary Tsukamoto, Hearings before the House of Representatives Sub Subcommittee on Administrative Law and Governmental Relations of the Committee on the Judiciary, 99th Congress, 2nd Session on H.R. 442 and H.R. 2415, April 28, 1986, Washington, DC.

317. Martin Niemöller: Pastor Martin Niemoller, Holocaust Memorial Day Trust, "First They Came."*

318. Norman "Norm" Yoshio Mineta: Norman Mineta, "A Cabinet Meeting the Day after 9/11," April 9, 2015, Densho Digital Repository.

319. Marion Tsuruko Konishi (Takehara): Marion Konishi, "America, Our Hope Is Anew [sic]." Valedictorian address, Amache Senior High School graduation, June 25, 1943, *Congressional Record*, 114th Congress, 2nd Session, vol. 162, no. 91, S3694 9JN, June 9, 2016.

---

* Niemöller's famous quote can't be dated because it was never published as a printed document. The pastor used the quote as an oral narrative in many variations from 1946 to 1979. However, his first invocation of the quote was in January 1946.

CHAPTER SOURCES

Introduction

Breed, Clara. "All but Blind." *Library Journal*, vol. 68, February 1, 1943, p. 120.

Author's Note

Asahina, Robert. *Just Americans: How Japanese Americans Won a War at Home and Abroad: The Story of the 100th Battalion/442nd Regimental Combat Team in World War II*. New York: Gotham Books, 2006, pp. 263–264.

Daniels, Roger. "The Forced Migration of West Coast Japanese Americans, 1942–1946: A Quantitative Note." In *Japanese Americans: From Relocation to Redress*, edited by Roger Daniels, Sandra C. Taylor, and Harry H.L. Kitano. Seattle, WA: University of Washington Press, 1991, p. 74.

Farivar, Masood. "Hate Crimes Targeting Asian Americans Spiked by 150% in Major US Cities." *Voice of America*, March 2, 2021. https://www.voanews.com/usa/race-america/hate-crimes-targeting-asian-americans-spiked-150-major-us-cities.

Ikeda, Tom. "Internment 101." *Densho Blog*. March 19, 2010. https://densho.org/internment-101.

Irons, Peter. "Be Careful What You Call a Concentration Camp." *The San Francisco Chronicle*, July 20, 2019. https://www.sfchronicle.com/opinion/article/Be-careful-what-you-call-a-concentration-camp-14103290.php.

Japanese American National Museum. "Terminology and the Japanese American Experience." 2009. http://www.mediajanm.org/projects/ec/pdf/EC-Terminology.pdf.

Mak, Stephen. "Japanese American Latin Americans." *Densho Encyclopedia*. http://encyclopedia.densho.org/Japanese_Latin_Americans.

Matsui, Doris. "Matsui Testimony at House Judiciary Hearing on Anti-Asian Discrimination and Violence." March 18, 2021. https://matsui.house.gov/news/documentsingle.aspx?DocumentID=2066.

Nakamura, Kelli Y. "Alien Enemies Act of 1798." *Densho Encyclopedia*.

https://www.encyclopedia.densho.org/Alien_Enemies_Act_of_1798.

Robinson, Greg. *A Tragedy of Democracy: Japanese Confinement in North America*. New York: Columbia University Press, 2009, p. viii.

US Department of the Interior. *Evacuated People: A Quantitative Description*. Washington, DC: US Government Printing Office, 1946. http://npshistory.com/publications/incarceration/evacuated-people.pdf.

Van Heyningen, Elizabeth. *The Concentration Camps of the Anglo-Boer War: A Social History*. Johannesburg, South Africa: Jacana Media, 2013.

Chapter One

Associated Press. "Knox Statement on Hawaii," *New York Times*, December 16, 1941. https://timesmachine.nytimes.com/timesmachine/1941/12/16/105411071.html?pageNumber=1.

Bailey, Thomas A. "California, Japan, and the Alien Land Legislation of 1931." *Pacific Historical Review*, no. 1, March 1932, pp. 36–59. doi:10.2307/3633745.

Bannai, Lorraine K. *Enduring Conviction: Fred Korematsu and His Quest for Justice*. Seattle, WA: University of Washington Press, 2015, p. 20.

Barbash, Fred. "After Pearl Harbor: How a Government Official's Baseless Claim Helped Lead to the Internment of Japanese Americans." *The Washington Post*, December 12, 2016. https://www.washingtonpost.com/news/morning-mix/wp/2016/12/12/the-week-after-pearl-harbor-a-government-officials-ignominius-big-lie-and-the-internment-of-japanese-americans/?utm_term=.46ea8362da88.

Bever, Lindsey. "'AIRRAID ON PEARL HARBOR X THIS IS NO DRILL,' Urgent 1941 Radiogram Warns." *The Washington Post*, December 7, 2015. https://www.washingtonpost.com/news/post-nation/wp/2015/12/07/urgent-1941-radiogram-warns-airraid-on-pearl-harbor-x-this-is-no-drill.

Bosworth, Allan R. *America's Concentration Camps*. New York: Bantam Books, Inc., 1967, p. 34.

California State University, Sacramento, Florin Japanese American Citizens

League. "Oral History Interview with Allen Hida." July 28, 2000. https://
californiarevealed.org/islandora/object/cavpp%3A22602.

Cannon, Carl M. "Peril for Bloomberg; Due Process; Back in the Game."
RealClear Politics, November 12, 2019. https://www.realclearpolitics
.com/articles/2019/11/12/peril_for_bloomberg_due_process_back_in_the
_game___141717.html.

Carter, John Franklin. "Memorandum on C.B. Munson's Report 'Japanese on
the West Coast,'" November 7, 1941. Densho Digital Repository. http://
ddr.densho.org/ddr-densho-67-11.

Carter, John Franklin. "Summary of Report on Program for Loyal West Coast
Japanese," December 1941. Densho Digital Repository. https://encyclopedia
.densho.org/sources/en-denshopd-i67-00008-1.

Civil Liberties Public Education Fund. "List of Detention Camps, Temporary Detention Centers, and Department of Justice Internment Camps."
http://www.momomedia.com/CLPEF/camps.html.

Commission on Wartime Relocation and Internment of Civilians. *Personal
Justice Denied. Part 1 (December, 1982): Report of the Commission on
Wartime Relocation and Internment of Civilians*. Washington, DC: US
Government Printing Office, pp. 43, 47, 53–54, 68. https://www.archives
.gov/files/research/japanese-americans/justice-denied/chapter-2.pdf.

Cuniberti, Betty. "Internment: Personal Voices, Powerful Choices." *Los
Angeles Times*, October 4, 1987. https://www.latimes.com/archives/la
-xpm-1987-10-04-vw-33126-story.html.

Daniels, Roger. *Prisoners without Trial: Japanese Americans in World War II*.
New York: Hill and Wang, 1993, pp. 17–18.

De Nevers, Klancy Clark. *The Colonel and the Pacifist: Karl Bendetsen, Perry
Saito and the Incarceration of Japanese Americans during World War II*.
Salt Lake City, UT: University of Utah Press, 2004, p. 73.

Densho Digital Repository. "Sumi Okamoto Interview," Segment 11. April 26, 2006,
Spokane, WA. http://ddr.densho.org/interviews/ddr-densho-1000-192-11.

Densho Encyclopedia. "Tachibana Case." https://encyclopedia.densho.org
/Tachibana_case.

Duus, Peter. "Imperialism without Colonies: The Vision of a Greater East Asia Co-Prosperity Sphere." *Diplomacy and Statecraft*, March 1996, vol. 7, no. 1, pp. 54–72. https://www.tandfonline.com/doi/abs /10.1080/09592299608405994.

Encyclopaedia Britannica. "Pearl Harbor Attack: Japanese-United States History." *Encyclopædia Britannica*, November 1, 2018. https://www .britannica.com/event/Pearl-Harbor-attack.

Hayashi, Brian Masaru. *Democratizing the Enemy: The Japanese American Internment*. Princeton, NJ: Princeton University Press, 2004, pp. 32, 81–84.

Hoffecker, Lilian Takahashi. "Terminal Island, California." *Densho Encyclopedia*. https://encyclopedia.densho.org/Terminal_Island,_California.

Irons, Peter. *Justice at War: The Story of the Japanese American Internment Cases*. New York: Oxford University Press, 1983, pp. 21–22, 24.

Kashima, Tetsuden. "Custodial Detention/A-B-C list." *Densho Encyclopedia*. http://encyclopedia.densho.org/Custodial_detention_/_A-B-C_list.

Krebs, A.V. "Bitter Harvest." *The Washington Post*, February 2, 1992. https:// www.washingtonpost.com/archive/opinions/1992/02/02/bitter-harvest /c8389b23-884d-43bd-ad34-bf7b11077135.

Kumamoto, Junji. "Testimony of Junji Kumamoto." US Senate Committee on Governmental Affairs, "Recommendations of the Commission on Wartime Internment and Relocation of Citizens," Hearings on S. 2116. Washington, DC: US Government Printing Office, August 16, 1984, p. 173.

Leinberger, Lisa. "Musician Retires after 70 Years." *The Spokesman-Review*, November 1, 2007. https://www.spokesman.com/stories/2007/nov/01 /musician-retires-after-70-years.

Lewis, Danny. "75 Years Ago, the Secretary of the Navy Falsely Blamed Japanese-Americans for Pearl Harbor: The Baseless Accusation Sparked the Road to the Infamous Internment Camps." *Smithsonian Magazine*, December 15, 2016. https://www.smithsonianmag.com/smart-news/75 -years-ago-secretary-navy-blamed-japanese-americans-pearl-harbor -180961417.

Los Angeles Conservancy. "Japanese-American History at Terminal Island." https://www.laconservancy.org/node/1020.

Maffeo, Captain Steven E. *US Navy Codebreakers, Linguists, and Intelligence Officers against Japan, 1910–1941: A Biographical Dictionary.* Lanham, MD: Rowman & Littlefield, 2015, p. 324.

Muller, Eric L. *An American Inquisition: The Hunt for Japanese-American Disloyalty in World War II.* Chapel Hill, NC: The University of North Carolina Press, 2007, pp. 15–16.

Murray, Alice Yang. *What Did the Internment of Japanese Americans Mean?* Boston: Bedford/St. Martin's, 2000, p. 6.

National Archives and Records Administration. "The Day of Infamy." *Prologue Magazine*, vol. 48, no. 4 (Winter 2016). https://www.archives.gov /publications/prologue/2016/winter/pearl-harbor.

National Archives and Records Administration. "World War II Enemy Alien Control Program Overview: Brief Overview of the World War II Enemy Alien Control Program." https://archives.gov/research/immigration/enemy -aliens-overview.

National Park Service. "Pearl Harbor National Memorial, Hawai'i, Civilian Casualties." https://www.nps.gov/valr/Learn/historyculture/civilian -casualties.htm.

Niiya, Brian. "California Joint Immigration Committee." *Densho Encyclopedia*. https://California_Joint_Immigration_Committee.

Niiya, Brian. "Francis Biddle." *Densho Encyclopedia*. https://encyclopedia. densho.org/Francis_Biddle.

Niiya, Brian. "Frank Knox." *Densho Encyclopedia*. https://encyclopedia .densho.org/Frank_Knox.

Niiya, Brian. "Henry Stimson." *Densho Encyclopedia*. https://encyclopedia .densho.org/Henry_Stimson.

Niiya, Brian. "Kenneth Ringle." *Densho Encyclopedia*. https://encyclopedia .densho.org/Kenneth_Ringle.

Niiya, Brian. "Munson Report." *Densho Encyclopedia*. https://encyclopedia .densho.org/Munson_Report.

Oda, Mary. "Testimony of Dr. Mary Oda." US Senate, 98th Congress, 2nd Session, "Recommendations of the Commission on Wartime Internment and Relocation of Citizens," Hearings before the Subcommittee on Civil Service, Post Office, and General Services of the Committee on Governmental Affairs, on S. 2116. Washington, DC: US Government Printing Office, August 16, 1984. https://books.google.com.

Okihiro, Gary Y., ed. *Encyclopedia of Japanese American Internment*. Santa Barbara, CA: Greenwood, 2013, p. xv.

O'Sullivan, Christopher D. Unpublished biography of Frank Knox.

Pearl Harbor Warbirds. "Pearl Harbor Aircraft: An Overview." https://pearl-harborwarbirds.com/pearl-harbor-aircraft-an-overview.

Ringle, Ken. "What Did You Do before the War, Dad?" *The Washington Post*, December 6, 1981. https://www.washingtonpost.com/archive/lifestyle/magazine/1981/12/06/what-did-you-do-before-the-war-dad/a80178d5 -82e6-4145-be4c-4e14691bdb6b.

Robinson, Greg. *By Order of the President: FDR and the Internment of Japanese Americans*. Cambridge, MA: Harvard University Press, 2001, pp. 59, 62, 65–69, 74, 80–81.

Robinson, Greg. "John Franklin Carter." *Densho Encyclopedia*. https://encyclopedia.densho.org/John_Franklin_Carter.

Robinson, Greg. *A Tragedy of Democracy: Japanese Confinement in North America*. New York: Columbia University Press, 2009, pp. 55, 59-61, 65, 72.

Ross, Stewart Halsey. *How Roosevelt Failed America in World War II*. Jefferson, NC: McFarland & Company, Inc., 2006, pp. 76, 83.

Summers, Anthony, and Robbyn Swan. *A Matter of Honor: Pearl Harbor: Betrayal, Blame, and a Family's Quest for Justice*. New York: HarperCollins, 2016, p. 254.

Tateishi, John. *And Justice for All: An Oral History of the Japanese American Detention Camps*. Seattle, WA: University of Washington Press, 1999, pp. 33–34.

Taylor, Frank J. "The People Nobody Wants." *The Saturday Evening Post*, May 9, 1942, p. 66. https://www.saturdayeveningpost.com/2017/05/people -nobody-wants.

TenBroek, Jacobus, Edward N. Barnhart, and Floyd W. Matson. *Prejudice, War and the Constitution: Causes and Consequences of the Evacuation of the Japanese Americans in World War II*. Berkeley, CA: University of California Press, 1954, pp. 66–67, 78.

Uchida, Yoshiko. *Desert Exile: The Uprooting of a Japanese American Family*. Seattle, WA: University of Washington Press, 1982, pp. 49–50.

US Congress. Report of the Subcommittee on Japanese War Relocation Centers, May 7, 1943, Presidential Proclamation 2525. https://www.oldmagazinearticles.com/Proclamation-Number-2525-pdf.

Wald, Sarah D. *The Nature of California: Race, Citizenship, and Farming since the Dust Bowl*. Seattle, WA: University of Washington Press, 2016, pp. 77–78.

Wallace, Nina. "Of Spies and G-Men: How the US Government Turned Japanese Americans into Enemies of the State." *Densho Blog*. September 29, 2017. https://densho.org/of-spies-and-gmen.

Weglyn, Michi. *Years of Infamy: The Untold Story of America's Concentration Camps*, 3rd ed. Seattle, WA: University of Washington Press, 2003, pp. 55–56.

Williams, Duncan Ryūken. *American Sutra: A Story of Faith and Freedom in the Second World War*. Cambridge, MA: The Belknap Press of Harvard University Press, 2019, pp. 15–16.

Chapter Two

Anderson, Emily. "Anti-Japanese Exclusion Movement." *Densho Encyclopedia*. http://encyclopedia.densho.org/Anti-Japanese_exclusion_movement.

Chuman, Frank F. *The Bamboo People: The Law and Japanese-Americans*. Del Mar, CA: Publisher's Inc., 1976, pp. 8, 15, 102, 111–112.

Commission on Wartime Relocation and Internment of Civilians. *Personal Justice Denied. Part 1 (December, 1982): Report of the Commission on Wartime Relocation and Internment of Civilians*. Washington, DC: US Government Printing Office, pp. 30, 70–72. https://www.archives.gov/files/research/japanese-americans/justice-denied/chapter-2.pdf.

Daniels, Roger. "The Decision for Mass Evacuation." In *What Did the Internment of Japanese Americans Mean?* edited by Alice Yang Murray. Boston: Bedford/St. Martin's, 2000, p. 39.

Dickerson, James L. *Inside America's Concentration Camps: Two Centuries of Internment and Torture.* Chicago: Chicago Review Press, 2010, p. 68.

Din, Grant. "The Angel Island Story of Kane Mineta, Norman Mineta's Mother." *Discover Nikkei*, April 13, 2018. http://www.discovernikkei.org /en/journal/2018/4/13/kane-mineta.

Girdner, Audrie, and Anne Loftis. *The Great Betrayal: The Evacuation of the Japanese-Americans during World War II.* Toronto: The Macmillan Company, 1969, p. 31.

Irons, Peter. *Justice at War: The Story of the Japanese-American Internment Cases.* New York: Oxford University Press, 1983, p. 40.

Kurashige, Lon. *Two Faces of Exclusion: The Untold History of Anti-Asian Racism in the United States.* Chapel Hill, NC: The University of North Carolina Press, 2016, pp. 40–41.

Ling, Huping, and Allan W. Austin, eds. *Asian American History and Culture: An Encyclopedia.* New York: Routledge, 2010, pp. 380, 382, 407–408.

Loving v. Virginia, 388 US 1 (1967). https://supreme.justia.com/cases /federal/us/388/1.

Lyon, Cherstin M. "Alien Land Laws." *Densho Encyclopedia.* https:// encyclopedia.densho.org/Alien_land_laws.

Lyon, Cherstin M. "Cable Act." *Densho Encyclopedia.* https://encyclopedia .densho.org/Cable_Act.

Murray, Alice Yang. *Historical Memories of the Japanese American Internment and the Struggle for Redress.* Stanford, CA: Stanford University Press, 2008, p. 22.

Ngai, Mae M. *Impossible Subjects: Illegal Aliens and the Making of Modern America.* Princeton, NJ: Princeton University Press, 2004, pp. 3, 7, 37.

Niiya, Brian. "Munson Report." *Densho Encyclopedia.* https://encyclopedia .densho.org/Munson_Report.

Niiya, Brian. "Roberts Commission Report." *Densho Encyclopedia.* https://

encyclopedia.densho.org/Roberts_Commission_report.

Nordyke, Eleanor C., and Y. Scott Matsumoto. "The Japanese in Hawaii: A Historical and Demographic Perspective." Honolulu: East-West Center, 1977, pp. 162–174. https://evols.library.manoa.hawaii.edu/bitstream /10524/528/2/JL11174.pdf.

Otsuka, Julie. *The Buddha in the Attic*. New York: Alfred A. Knopf, 2011, p. 18.

Pluralism Project. *Organized Labor*. Harvard University, February 20, 1909. http://pluralism.org/document/the-asiatic-exclusion-league.

Robinson, Greg. "Native Sons of the Golden West/Native Daughters of the Golden West." *Densho Encyclopedia*. https://encyclopedia.densho.org /Native_Sons_of_the_Golden_West/Native_Daughters_of_the_Golden _West.

Robinson, Greg. "Restrictive Covenants." *Densho Encyclopedia*. http:// encyclopedia.densho.org/Restrictive_covenants.

Robinson, Greg. *A Tragedy of Democracy: Japanese Confinement in North America*. New York: Columbia University Press, 2009, pp. 7, 22, 52, 80–81.

Rosenfeld, Alan. "German and Italian Detainees." *Densho Encyclopedia*. https://encyclopedia.densho.org/German_and_Italian_detainees.

Takaki, Ronald. *Strangers from a Different Shore: A History of Asian Americans*. Boston: Little, Brown, 1998, pp. 218–219, 222–223.

Tolan, John. *The Rising Sun: The Decline and Fall of the Japanese Empire 1936–1945*. New York: Random House, 1970, p. 452.

Williams, Duncan Ryūken. *American Sutra: A Story of Faith and Freedom in the Second World War*. Cambridge, MA: The Belknap Press of Harvard University Press, 2019, p. 3.

Wilson, Robert A., and Bill Hosokawa. *East to America: A History of the Japanese in the United States*. New York: William Morrow & Company, Inc., 1980, pp. 55–56, 162.

Wu, Frank H. *Yellow: Race in America: Beyond Black and White*. New York: Basic Books, 2002, p. 97.

Zia, Helen. *Asian American Dreams: The Emergence of an American People*. New York: Farrar, Straus and Giroux, 2000, p. 42.

Chapter Three

Armed Forces History Museum. "US Army's Youngest General—Mark W. Clark." April 8, 2015. https://armedforcesmuseum.com/u-s-armys -youngest-general-mark-w-clark.

Arrington, Leonard J. *The Price of Prejudice: The Japanese-American Relocation Center in Utah during World War II.* Utah State University Faculty Honor Lectures, no. 25. (1962). Reprint, 2nd ed., 1977, Delta, UT: Topaz Museum, 1997. http://digital.lib.usu.edu/cdm/compoundobject /collection/Topaz/id/8175.

Bannai, Lorraine K. *Enduring Conviction: Fred Korematsu and His Quest for Justice.* Seattle, WA: University of Washington Press, 2015, pp. 33, 36, 49, 51, 74.

Biddle, Francis. *In Brief Authority.* Garden City, NY: Doubleday & Company, Inc., 1962, p. 219.

Bird, Kai. *The Chairman: John J. McCloy and the Making of the American Establishment.* New York: Simon & Schuster, 1992, pp. 149, 152, 158.

Blankenship, Anne. "Bainbridge Island, Washington." *Densho Encyclopedia.* https://encyclopedia.densho.org/Bainbridge_Island_Washington/.

Broom, Leonard, and Ruth Riemer. *Removal and Return: The Socio-Economic Effects of the War on Japanese Americans.* Berkeley, CA: University of California Press, 1949, pp. 155–156, 163–165.

Commission on Wartime Relocation and Internment of Civilians. *Personal Justice Denied.* Seattle, WA: University of Washington Press, 1997.

Commission on Wartime Relocation and Internment of Civilians. *Personal Justice Denied. Part 1 (December, 1982): Report of the Commission on Wartime Relocation and Internment of Civilians.* Washington, DC: US Government Printing Office, pp. 64, 108–110, 155. https://www .archives.gov/files/research/japanese-americans/justice-denied/chapter -2.pdf.

Conn, Stetson, Rose C. Engelman, and Byron Fairchild. *United States Army in World War II: Guarding the United States and Its Outposts.* The Western Hemisphere Series, vol. 2. Washington, DC: Office of the Chief of Military History, Department of the Army, 1962, pp. 33, 121–122, 126. https://history.army.mil/books/wwii/Guard-US/ch2.htm.

Cooper, Michael L. *Fighting for Honor: Japanese Americans and World War II*. New York: Clarion Books, 2000, p. 93.

Daniels, Roger. *The Decision to Relocate the Japanese Americans*. New York: J.B. Lippincott Company, 1975, pp. 32, 54, 77.

Daniels, Roger. *The Japanese American Cases: The Rule of Law in Time of War*. Lawrence, KS: University Press of Kansas, 2013, pp. 12, 29–30.

Daniels, Roger. *Prisoners without Trial: Japanese Americans in World War II*. New York: Hill and Wang, 1993, p. 49.

Daniels, Roger, Sandra C. Taylor, and Harry H.L. Kitano, eds. *Japanese Americans: From Relocation to Redress*. Seattle, WA: University of Washington Press, 1991, pp. 6–9 (note 6).

De Nevers, Klancy Clark. *The Colonel and the Pacifist: Karl Bendetsen, Perry Saito and the Incarceration of Japanese Americans during World War II*. Salt Lake City, UT: University of Utah Press, 2004, pp. 73, 120–122, 126.

De Nevers, Klancy Clark. "Karl Bendetsen." *Densho Encyclopedia*. https:// encyclopedia.densho.org/Karl_Bendetsen/.

Densho Digital Repository. "Exclusion Orders." https://ddr.densho.org/browse /topics/188.

Densho Encyclopedia. "Instructions to All Persons of Japanese Ancestry," posted in Seattle, WA, April 24, 1942. https://encyclopedia.densho.org /sources/en-denshopd-p25-00049-1/.

Densho Encyclopedia. "Western Defense Command." https://encyclopedia .densho.org/Western_Defense_Command/.

Dickerson, James L. *Inside America's Concentration Camps: Two Centuries of Internment and Torture*. Chicago: Chicago Review Press, 2010, pp. 68, 87.

Diltz, Colin. "How Bainbridge Island Japanese Were Registered, Forced from Their Homes during World War II," *Seattle Times*, originally published December 6, 2016; updated February 21, 2017. https://www .seattletimes.com/seattle-news/how-bainbridge-island-japanese-were -registered-forced-from-their-homes-during-world-war-ii-in-1942/.

Eisenhower, Milton S. *The President Is Calling*. Garden City, NY: Doubleday & Company, Inc., 1974, pp. 12, 72, 95, 118.

Eisenhower, M. S. "Letter to Hon. Claude R. Wickard, April 1, 1942." War Relocation Authority, Japanese American Evacuation and Resettlement Records, University of California, Berkeley Bancroft Library. http:// digitalassets.lib.berkeley.edu/jarda/ucb/text/cubanc6714_box025c01 _0002_3.pdf.

Eisenhower, M. S. "Letter to James Rowe, Jr., March 30, 1942." War Relocation Authority, Japanese American Evacuation and Resettlement Records, University of California, Berkeley Bancroft Library. http://digitalassets.lib.berkeley.edu/jarda/ucb/text/cubanc6714_box025c01_0002_3. pdf.

Fry, Amelia, and Miriam Feingold Stein, interviewers. "Japanese-American Relocation Reviewed: Volume 1, Decision and Exodus." Interviews of James H. Rowe and Edward Ennis. The Earl Warren Oral History Project. Berkeley, CA: University of California, 1976. http://texts.cdlib.org /view?docId=ft667nb2x8&doc.view=entire_text.

Goodwin, Doris Kearns. *No Ordinary Time*. New York: Simon & Schuster, 1994, p. 322.

Hall, Kermit L., and John J. Patrick. *The Pursuit of Justice: Supreme Court Decisions That Shaped America*. New York: Oxford University Press, 2006, p.106.

Hatamiya, Leslie T. *Righting a Wrong: Japanese Americans and the Passage of the Civil Liberties Act of 1988*. Stanford, CA: Stanford University Press, 1993, p. 23.

Hayashida, Francis. "Testimony of Fumiko Hayashida, Bainbridge Island Japanese American Community." US House of Representatives Sub-committee on National Parks of the Committee on Resources. Hearings on H.R. 5817, the Bainbridge Island Japanese American Monument Act of 2006, Washington, DC, September 28, 2006, p. 2. https://natural resources.house.gov/uploadedfiles/hayashidatestimony09.28.06.pdf.

Hirabayashi, Gordon K. *A Principled Stand: The Story of Hirabayashi v. United*

States. Seattle, WA: University of Washington Press, 2013, pp. 55, 134.

Hoffecker, Lilian Takahashi. "Terminal Island, California." *Densho Encyclopedia*. https://encyclopedia.densho.org/Terminal_Island,_California/.

Houston, Jeanne Wakatsuki, and James Houston. *Farewell to Manzanar: A True Story of Japanese American Experience during and after the World War II Internment*. Boston: Houghton Mifflin Company, 1973, pp. 10–11.

Irons, Peter. *Justice at War: The Story of the Japanese-American Internment Cases*. New York: Oxford University Press, 1983, pp. 26, 38–39, 58, 60–61, 63, 72–73, 91–93.

Lippmann, Walter. "The Fifth Column on the Coast." *The Washington Post*, February 12, 1942. https://encyclopedia.densho.org/sources/en-denshopd-i67-00001-1/.

Lyon, Cherstin M. "Gordon Hirabayashi." *Densho Encyclopedia*. http://encyclopedia.densho.org/Gordon_Hirabayashi/.

Masaoka, Mike M., with Bill Hosokawa. *They Call Me Moses Masaoka: An American Saga*. New York: William Morrow and Company, 1987, pp. 85, 97, 99–100, 109, 114.

Murray, Alice Yang. *What Did the Internment of Japanese Americans Mean?* Boston: Bedford/St. Martin's, 2000, pp. 7–9.

Muyskens, John, and Aaron Steckelberg. "Incarceration by Executive Order." *The Washington Post*, February 19, 2017. https://www.washingtonpost.com/graphics/national/incarceration-executive-order/.

National Archives and Records Administration. "Records of the War Relocation Authority." https://www.archives.gov/research/guide-fed-records/groups/210.html.

National Archives Catalog. "An Act of March 21, 1942, Public Law 77–503, 56 STAT 173 to Provide a Penalty for Violation of Restrictions or Orders with Respect to Persons Entering, Remaining in, Leaving or Committing Any Act in Military Areas or Zones," March 21, 1942. https://catalog.archives.gov/id/5730387.

Newsweek. "US Internment of Japanese-Americans in WWII," March 9, 1942.

https://www.scribd.com/document/208962626/U-S-Internment-of-Japanese-Americans-in-WWII.

Ng, Wendy. *Japanese American Internment during World War II: A History and Reference Guide*. Santa Barbara, CA: Greenwood, 2001, p. 25.

Niiya, Brian. "Civilian Exclusion Orders." *Densho Encyclopedia*. https://encyclopedia.densho.org/Civilian_exclusion_orders/.

Niiya, Brian. "Harold Ickes." *Densho Encyclopedia*. http://encyclopedia.densho.org/Harold_Ickes/.

Niiya, Brian. "John DeWitt." *Densho Encyclopedia*. https://encyclopedia.densho.org/John_DeWitt/.

Niiya, Brian. "Mark W. Clark." *Densho Encyclopedia*. https://www.encyclopedia.densho.org/Mark_W_Clark/.

Niiya, Brian. "Milton Eisenhower." *Densho Encyclopedia*. https://encyclopedia.densho.org/Milton_Eisenhower/.

Niiya, Brian. "Public Law 503." *Densho Encyclopedia*. https://encyclopedia.densho.org/Public_Law_503/.

Niiya, Brian. "Voluntary Evacuation." *Densho Encyclopedia*. https://encyclopedia.densho.org/Voluntary_evacuation/.

Ono, Gary T. "Camp Pets: Doggone it!—Part 1& 2." *Discover Nikkei*. August 21 and 29, 2012. http://www.discovernikkei.org/en/journal/2012/8/21/camp-pets-1/; http://www.discovernikkei.org/en/journal/2012/8/28/camp-pets-2/.

Oppenheim, Joanne. *Dear Miss Breed: True Stories of the Japanese American Incarceration during World War II and a Librarian Who Made a Difference*. New York: Scholastic, 2006, p. 49.

Perrett, Geoffrey. *Days of Sadness, Years of Triumph: The American People 1939–1945*, New York: Coward, McCann & Geoghegan Inc., 1973, pp. 216–217.

Pittsburgh Post-Gazette. "Wake Up, General Tells San Francisco: Few Bombs Might Be a Good Thing, Coast Civilians Hear." vol. 58, no. 169, December 10, 1941. https://www.newspapers.com/image/89884499.

Prewitt, Kenneth. "Email to Bureau of the Census staff," March 24, 2000,

cited in "Census Confidentiality and Privacy: 1790–2002." https://www
.census.gov/prod/2003pubs/conmono2.pdf#17.

Reeves, Richard. *Infamy: The Shocking Story of the Japanese American Internment in World War II*. New York: Henry Holt, 2015, p. 70.

Robinson, Greg. *By Order of the President: FDR and the Internment of Japanese Americans*. Cambridge, MA: Harvard University Press, 2001, pp. 68–69, 83, 85–86, 91–93, 105–107, 117, 123–125, 153–154, 244.

Robinson, Greg. *A Tragedy of Democracy: Japanese Confinement in North America*. New York: Columbia University Press, 2009, pp. 68–69, 74, 91–93, 105–107, 218, 220.

Robinson, Greg. "War Relocation Authority." *Densho Encyclopedia*. https://encyclopedia.densho.org/War_Relocation_Authority/.

Rosenfeld, Alan. "German and Italian Detainees." *Densho Encyclopedia*. https://encyclopedia.densho.org/German_and_Italian_detainees/.

Seigel, Shizue. *In Good Conscience: Supporting Japanese Americans during the Internment*. San Mateo, CA: Asian American Curriculum Project, 2006, pp. 9–10.

Shaffer, Robert. "Tolan Committee." *Densho Encyclopedia*. https://encyclopedia.densho.org/Tolan_Committee/.

Smith, Cary Stacy, and Li-Ching Hung. *The Patriot Act: Issues and Controversies*. Springfield, IL: Charles C Thomas Publisher, Ltd., 2010, p. 76.

Smith, Jean Edward. *FDR*. New York: Random House, 2007, pp. 551–552, (note 46).

Smithsonian Institution, National Museum of American History. *A More Perfect Union*. "*Store Closing Sign*." Photograph by Clem Albers, courtesy of Records of the War Relocation Authority, National Archives, April 11, 1942. http://amhistory.si.edu/perfectunion/collection/image.asp?ID=257.

Tateishi, John. *And Justice for All: An Oral History of the Japanese American Detention Camps*. Seattle, WA: University of Washington Press, 1999, p. 71.

Trueman, Chris N. "General Mark Clark." *History Learning Site*. https://

www.historylearningsite.co.uk/world-war-two/military-commanders-of
-world-war-two/general-mark-clark/.

Tsukamoto, Mary. "Testimony of Mary Tsukamoto." Hearings before the
House of Representatives Sub-Subcommittee on Administrative Law
and Governmental Relations of the Committee on the Judiciary. 99th
Congress, 2nd Session on H.R. 442 and H.R. 2415, Washington, DC,
April 28, 1986, Part I, pp. 720–732. https://books.google.com.

University of Notre Dame. *Fresh Writing*, vol. 15, "Can We Forgive Dr.
Seuss?" https://freshwriting.nd.edu/volumes/2015/essays/can-we-forgive
-dr-seuss.

Unrau, Harlan D. *The Evacuation and Relocation of Persons of Japanese
Ancestry during World War II: A Historical Study of the Manzanar
Relocation Center*. Historic Resource Study/Special History Study, vol. 1,
Department of the Interior, National Park Service, 1996, p. 18.

US Army Quartermaster Corps and Quartermaster School. "Major General John
L. DeWitt." http://www.quartermaster.army.mil/bios/previous-qm-generals
/quartermaster_general_bio-dewitt.html.

Varner, Natasha. "Sold, Damaged, Stolen, Gone: Japanese American Property Loss During WWII." *Densho Blog*. April 4, 2017. https://densho.org
/sold-damaged-stolen-gone-japanese-american-property-loss-wwii/.

Virtual Museum of the City of San Francisco. "Appendix to Chapter III. Final
Recommendation of the Commanding General, Western Defense Command and Fourth Army, Submitted to the Secretary of War." http://www.
sfmuseum.org/war/dewitt4.html.

Walker, Alan. "A Slap's a Slap: General John L. DeWitt and Four Little
Words." *The Text Message*, National Archives, November 22, 2013.
https://text-message.blogs.archives.gov/?s=DeWitt.

Washington University in Saint Louis School of Law. "Legal English: Legal
Fiction," December 14, 2012. https://onlinelaw.wustl.edu/blog/legal-english
-legal-fiction.

Watanabe, Teresa. "In 1943, Census Bureau Released Japanese Americans'
Individual Data." *Los Angeles Times*, March 31, 2007. https://www

.latimes.com/archives/la-xpm-2007-mar-31-na-census31-story.html.

Western Defense Command and Fourth Army. "Action of Congressional Committee on Handling Enemy Aliens on the West Coast," January 31, 1942. Headquarters War Department Memoranda. Office of the Commanding General, War Department, RG 338-2-7. 014.31 Aliens. *Densho Encyclopedia.* http://encyclopedia.densho.org/media/encyc-psms/en-denshopd-i67-00081-1.pdf.

Western Defense Command and Fourth Army. "Civilian Exclusion Order No. 1," March 24, 1942. Presidio of San Francisco, California, War Relocation Authority, Japanese American Evacuation and Resettlement Records, University of California, Berkeley Bancroft Library. http://digitalassets.lib.berkeley.edu/jarda/ucb/text/cubanc6714_b016b01_0001_1.pdf.

Western Defense Command and Fourth Army. "Civilian Exclusion Order No. 2," March 30, 1942. Presidio of San Francisco, California, War Relocation Authority, Japanese American Evacuation and Resettlement Records, University of California, Berkeley Bancroft Library. http://digitalassets.lib.berkeley.edu/jarda/ucb/text/cubanc6714_b016b01_0001_1.pdf.

Western Defense Command and Fourth Army. *Final Report: Japanese Evacuation from the West Coast*, 1942. Presidio of San Francisco, California. Chapters 1–2. Washington, DC: US Government Printing Office, 1943. https://archive.org/details/japaneseevacuati00dewi; https://archive.org/details/01130040R.nlm.nih.gov/page/n3.

Western Defense Command and Fourth Army. "Public Proclamation No. 1," March 2, 1942. University of Washington Library. Seattle, WA. https://digitalcollections.lib.washington.edu/digital/collection/pioneerlife/id/15297.

Western Defense Command and Fourth Army. "Public Proclamation No. 2," March 16, 1942. FRASER, Federal Reserve Bank of St. Louis Digital Library. St. Louis, MO. https://fraser.stlouisfed.org/files/docs/historical/eccles/038_17_0002.pdf.

Western Defense Command and Fourth Army. "Public Proclamation No. 3," March 24, 1942. California State University, Dominguez Hills Japanese American Digitization Project. Dominguez Hills, CA. https://cdm16855 .contentdm.oclc.org/digital/collection/p16855coll4/id/12197. .

Williams, Duncan Ryūken. *American Sutra: A Story of Faith and Freedom in the Second World War*. Cambridge, MA: The Belknap Press of Harvard University Press, 2019, pp. 3, 81–82.

Yenne, Bill. "Fear Itself: The General Who Panicked the West Coast." *World War II Magazine*, July 11, 2017. https://www.historynet.com/fear-itself -the-general-panicked-west-coast.htm.

Yenne, Bill. *Panic on the Pacific: How America Prepared for a West Coast Invasion*. New York: Regnery History, 2016.

Zia, Helen. *Asian American Dreams: The Emergence of an American People*. New York: Farrar, Straus and Giroux, 2000, p. 42.

Chapter Four

Azusa Street Mission Foundation, Inc. "Assembly Centers in Little Tokyo." https://312azusa.com/historictimeline/assembly-centers-in-little-tokyo/.

Bendetsen, Karl. "Memo to Colonels Hass and Evans. Subject: Separation of Families, March 31, 1942." War Relocation Authority, Japanese American Evacuation and Resettlement Records, University of California, Berkeley Bancroft Library. http://digitalassets.lib.berkeley.edu/jarda/ucb /text/cubanc6714_box025c01_0002_3.pdf.

Bosworth, Allan R. *America's Concentration Camps*. New York: Bantam Books, Inc., 1967, p. 114.

Burton, Jeffery F., Mary M. Farrell, Florence B. Lord, and Richard W. Lord, eds. *Confinement and Ethnicity: An Overview of World War II Japanese American Relocation Sites*. The Scott and Laurie Oki Series in Asian American Studies. Seattle, WA: University of Washington Press, 2002. https://www.nps.gov/articles/historyinternment.htm; https://www.nps.gov/parkhistory/online_books/anthropology74/ce3e.htm.

Cannon, Carl M. "Peril for Bloomberg; Due Process; Back in the Game."

RealClear Politics, November 12, 2019. https://www.realclearpolitics
.com/articles/2019/11/12/peril_for_bloomberg_due_process_back_in
_the_game___141717.html.

Commission on Wartime Relocation and Internment of Civilians. *Personal Justice Denied. Part 1 (December, 1982): Report of the Commission on Wartime Relocation and Internment of Civilians.* Washington, DC: US Government Printing Office, pp. 127, 136, 137, 139, 140, 143, 145–147, 149. https://www.archives.gov/files/research/japanese-americans/justice-denied/chapter-2.pdf.

Cuniberti, Betty. "Internment: Personal Voices, Powerful Choices." *Los Angeles Times*, October 4, 1987. https://www.latimes.com/archives/la-xpm-1987-10-04-vw-33126-story.html.

Daniels, Roger. "The Decision for Mass Evacuation." In *What Did the Internment of Japanese Americans Mean?* edited by Alice Yang Murray. Boston: Bedford/St. Martin's, 2000, p. 60.

De Nevers, Klancy Clark. "Karl Bendetsen." *Densho Encyclopedia.* https://encyclopedia.densho.org/Karl_Bendetsen/.

Densho Digital Repository. "Puyallup Camp Harmony News – Letter Collection." http://ddr.densho.org/ddr-densho-194/.

Densho Encyclopedia. "Parker Dam (detention facility)." https://encyclopedia.densho.org/Parker_Dam_(detention_facility).

DeWitt, John Lesesne. *Final Report, Japanese Evacuation from the West Coast, 1942.* Washington, DC: US Government Printing Office, 1943, p. 151. US National Library of Medicine Digital Collections. https://collections.nlm.nih.gov/catalog/nlm:nlmuid-01130040R-bk.

Fiset, Louis. "The Assembly Centers: An Introduction." *Discover Nikkei*, September 16, 2008. http://www.discovernikkei.org/en/journal/2008/9/16/enduring-communities/.

Fiset, Louis. *Camp Harmony: Seattle's Japanese Americans and the Puyallup Assembly Center.* Urbana and Chicago, IL: University of Illinois Press, 2009, p. 99.

Fiset, Louis. "Medical Care in Camp." *Densho Encyclopedia.* https://

encyclopedia.densho.org/Medical_care_in_camp/.

Fiset, Louis. "Puyallup (Detention Facility)." *Densho Encyclopedia*. https:// encyclopedia.densho.org/Puyallup_(detention_facility)/.

Fresno Bee. "To Preserve Rights, by 'M.S.' Del Rey, California." Editorial Page, April 18, 1942. https://www.newspapers.com/newspage/25802770/.

Fuchs, Chris. "Norman Mineta's American Story Helped the U.S. Apologize for Incarceration and Lead after 9/11." NBC Asian America, May 14, 2019. https://www.nbcnews.com/news/asian-america/norman-mineta -s-american-story-helped-u-s-apologize-incarceration-n1005406.

Gesensway, Deborah, and Mindy Roseman. *Beyond Words: Images from America's Concentration Camps.* Ithaca, NY: Cornell University Press, p. 100.

Girdner, Audrie, and Anne Loftis. *The Great Betrayal: The Evacuation of the Japanese-Americans during World War II.* Toronto: The Macmillan Company, 1969, pp. 141, 155, 159–165, 171–173, 196–198, 162–165, 211, 213.

Higa, Karen M. *The View from Within: Japanese American Art from the Internment Camps, 1942–1945.* Los Angeles: Japanese American National Museum, UCLA Wight Art Gallery, and UCLA Asian American Studies Center, 1992, pp. 21–22.

Hudson, Berkley. "Reparations Awaken Painful Recollections." *Los Angeles Times*, August 18, 1988. http://articles.latimes.com/1988-08-18/news/ga -840_1_santa-anita/2.

Hudson, Berkley. "A Troublesome Melting Pot Documented by Photographers." *Visual Communication Quarterly*, vol. 20, no. 2 (2013), pp. 62–63. https://doi.org/10.1080/15551393.2013.805046.

Ichida, May. "Testimony of May Ichida." Hearing for the Commission on Wartime Relocation and Internment of Civilians, September 22, 1981, Chicago, IL. Northeastern Illinois University, Japanese-American Redress Collection. http://collections.carli.illinois.edu/cdm/compoundobject/collection /nei_japan/id/1720/rec/1.

Irwin, Catherine. "Manzanar Children's Village." *Densho Encyclopedia*. https://encyclopedia.densho.org/Manzanar_Children's_Village/.

Kaji, Bruce T., with Sharon Yamato. *Jive Bomber: A Sentimental Journey.* Gardena, CA: Kaji & Associates, 2010, p. 44.

Leighton, Alexander H. *The Governing of Men: General Principles and Recommendations Based on Experience at a Japanese Relocation Camp.* Princeton, NJ: Princeton University Press, 1945, pp. 71–72.

Levine, Ellen. *A Fence Away from Freedom: Japanese Americans and World War II.* New York: G. P. Putnam's Sons, 1995, pp. 85–86.

Lindley, Ernest K. "Problems of Japanese Migration." *Newsweek*, Washington Tides. April 6, 1942, p. 26. https://www.scribd.com/document/208962626/U-S-Internment-of-Japanese-Americans-in-WWII.

Linke, Konrad. "Assembly Centers." *Densho Encyclopedia.* https://encyclopedia.densho.org/Assembly_centers/.

Linke, Konrad. "Santa Anita (Detention Facility)." *Densho Encyclopedia.* https://encyclopedia.densho.org/Santa_Anita_(detention_facility)/.

Linke, Konrad. "Tulare (Detention Facility)." *Densho Encyclopedia.* https://encyclopedia.densho.org/Tulare_(detention_facility)/.

Los Angeles Times. "Santa Anita Gates Open to 1000 Japs." April 4, 1942.

Mizuno, Takeya. "Newspapers in Camp." *Densho Encyclopedia.* https://encyclopedia.densho.org/Newspapers_in_camp/.

Murray, Alice Yang. *Historical Memories of the Japanese American Internment and the Struggle for Redress.* Stanford, CA: Stanford University Press, 2008, p. 61.

Niiya, Brian. "Santa Anita Pacemaker (newspaper)." *Densho Encyclopedia.* https://encyclopedia.densho.org/Santa_Anita_Pacemaker_(newspaper)/.

Niiya, Brian. "Voluntary Evacuation." *Densho Encyclopedia.* https://encyclopedia.densho.org/Voluntary_evacuation/.

Niiya, Brian. "'What an Ungodly Place to Meet': Tales from Camp Toilets." Densho Blog. June 14, 2018. https://www.densho.org/toilets-tales/.

Nisei Christian Oral History Project. *Nisei Christian Journey: Its Promise & Fulfillment, Vol. II*, 1992, p. 102. https://calisphere.org/item/ark:/13030/ft609nb331/.

Oda, Mary. "Testimony of Dr. Mary Oda." US Senate Subcommittee on Civil

Service, Post Office, and General Services of the Committee on Governmental Affairs. Hearings on H.R. 442 and H.R. 2116. Recommendations of the Commission on Wartime Internment and Relocation of Citizens. August 16,1984, Los Angeles, CA, pp. 97–99.

Oppenheim, Joanne. *Dear Miss Breed: True Stories of the Japanese American Incarceration during World War II and a Librarian Who Made a Difference*. New York: Scholastic, 2006, pp. 58, 66, 85, 87, 102.

Ota, Peter. "Testimony of Peter Ota." Commission on Wartime Relocation and Internment of Civilians Hearing. August 6, 1981, Los Angeles, CA. https://www.archives.gov/research/japanese-americans/hearings. CWRIC Los Angeles Hearings Video Collection, Nikkei for Civil Rights and Redress and Visual Communications. Reissued in 2018 on DVD as *Speak Out for Justice*.

Reeves, Richard. *Infamy: The Shocking Story of the Japanese American Internment in World War II*. New York: Henry Holt, 2015, p. 84.

Robinson, Greg. *A Tragedy of Democracy: Japanese Confinement in North America*. New York: Columbia University Press, 2009, pp. 126, 129–131.

Robinson, Greg. "War Relocation Authority." *Densho Encyclopedia*. https://encyclopedia.densho.org/War_Relocation_Authority/.

Sandler, Martin W. *Imprisoned: The Betrayal of Japanese Americans during World War II*. New York: Bloomsbury USA Childrens, 2013, p. 60.

San Francisco News. "S.F. Japanese Exodus Starts," April 7, 1942. The Virtual Museum of the City of San Francisco. http://www.sfmuseum.org/hist8/evac11.html.

Smith, Cary Stacy, and Li-Ching Hung. *The Patriot Act: Issues and Controversies*. Springfield: Charles C Thomas, Publisher, Ltd., 2010, p. 86.

Smithsonian Institution, National Museum of American History. *A More Perfect Union*. "Removal Process: Japanese Americans and the US Constitution." Colonel Karl Bendetsen: "One Drop of Japanese Blood." http://amhistory.si.edu/perfectunion/non-flash/removal_process.html.

Spickard, Paul R. "Injustice Compounded: Amerasians and Non-Japanese Americans in World War II Concentration Camps." *Journal of American*

Ethnic History, vol. 5, no. 2, Spring, 1986, pp. 5–22. The Immigration and Ethnic History Society. University of Illinois Press. https://www.jstor .org/stable/27500450.

Suyemoto, Toyo, and Susan B. Richardson, eds. *I Call to Remembrance: Toyo Suyemoto's Years of Internment*. New Brunswick, NJ: Rutgers University Press, 2007, pp. 51–52.

Tateishi, John. *And Justice for All: An Oral History of the Japanese American Detention Camps*. Seattle, WA: University of Washington Press, 1999, p. xxvii.

Tawa, Renee. "Childhood Lost: The Orphans of Manzanar." *Los Angeles Times*, March 11, 1997. http://articles.latimes.com/1997-03-11/news/mn -37002_1_manzanar-orphans.

US Department of the Interior. *Evacuated People: A Quantitative Description*. Washington, DC: US Government Printing Office, 1946. http:// npshistory.com/publications/incarceration/evacuated-people.pdf.

Weglyn, Michi Nishiura. *Years of Infamy: The Untold Story of America's Concentration Camps*. Seattle, WA: University of Washington Press, 1976, pp. 81, 89.

Western Defense Command and Fourth Army Wartime Civil Control Administration. "Center Regulations," July 18, 1942. University of Washington Library, Seattle, WA. https://digitalcollections.lib.washington.edu/digital /collection/pioneerlife/id/13343.

Williams, Duncan Ryūken. *American Sutra: A Story of Faith and Freedom in the Second World War*. Cambridge, MA: The Belknap Press of Harvard University Press, 2019, pp. 80, 102–103.

Chapter Five

Alinder, Jasmine. "Dorothea Lange." *Densho Encyclopedia*. http://encyclopedia .densho.org/Dorothea_Lange/.

Alinder, Jasmine. *Moving Images: Photography and the Japanese American Incarceration*. Champaign, IL: University of Illinois Press, 2010, pp. 30–102.

Amache.org. Overview. http://amache.org/overview/.

Anaheim Public Library and Muzeo Museum and Cultural Center. "I Am an American: Japanese Incarceration in a Time of Fear." August 25–November 3, 2019. https://muzeo.org/exhibition/i-am-an-american.

Arbuckle, Alex Q. "1943: Life at Manzanar." *Mashable*. https://mashable.com/2015/09/30/manzanar-internment-camp/#x.S_0QbMFmqT.

Arrington, Leonard J. "The Price of Prejudice: The Japanese-American Relocation Center in Utah during World War II." Utah State University Faculty Honor Lectures, no. 25, 1962, pp. 13, 31. Reprint, 2nd ed., Delta, UT: Topaz Museum, 1997. https://digitalcommons.usu.edu/honor_lectures/23.

Bearden, Russell E. "Jerome Relocation Center." *The Encyclopedia of Arkansas History & Culture*. June 13, 2018. http://www.encyclopediaofarkansas.net/encyclopedia/entry-detail.aspx?entryID=2399.

Bearden, Russell E. "Life inside Arkansas' Japanese-American Relocation Centers." *Arkansas Historical Quarterly*, vol. 48, no. 2, Summer 1989. Arkansas Historical Association, p. 170. https://www.jstor.org/stable/40030791.

Bernstein, Alison R. *American Indians and World War II: Toward a New Era in Indian Affairs*. Norman, OK: University of Oklahoma Press, 1991, pp. 82–85.

Bichell, Rae Ellen. "Remembering Japanese Internment in the Mountain West," 91.5 KRCC Morning Edition, February 21, 2018. https://www.cpr.org/2018/02/21/remembering-japanese-internment-in-the-mountain-west/.

Burton, J., M. Farrell, F. Lord, and R. Lord, eds. *Confinement and Ethnicity: An Overview of World War II Japanese American Relocation Sites*. The Scott and Laurie Oki Series in Asian American Studies. Seattle, WA: University of Washington Press, 2002, Chapter 10. Poston Relocation Center. https://parkhistory/online_books/anthropology74/ce10.htm.

Chapman, Stephanie, Jessica Keener, Nicole Sobota, and Courtney Whitmore. "Prisoners at Home: Everyday Life in Japanese Internment

Camps." Digital Public Library of America, July 2015. https://dp.la /exhibitions/japanese-internment.

Clark, Bonnie. "Amache (Granada)." *Densho Encyclopedia.* https://encyclopedia .densho.org/Amache_(Granada)/.

Cockrell, Cathy. "How Japanese Americans Preserved Traditions behind Barbed Wire." *Berkeley News,* June 10, 2010. University of California. http://news.berkeley.edu/2010/06/10/muramoto/.

Colorado State Archives. "Amache, Colorado, Granada Relocation Center." https://web.archive.org/web/20081004043059/http://www.colorado.gov dpa/doit/archives/wwcod/granada5.htm.

Commission on Wartime Relocation and Internment of Civilians. *Personal Justice Denied.* Seattle, WA: University of Washington Press, 1997.

Commission on Wartime Relocation and Internment of Civilians. *Personal Justice Denied. Part 1 (December, 1982): Report of the Commission on Wartime Relocation and Internment of Civilians.* Washington, DC: US Government Printing Office, pp. 151, 156, 158, 164–171, 176–177. https://www.archives.gov/files/research/japanese-americans/justice -denied/chapter-2.pdf.

Cornell University Blog Service. "Japanese American Relocation Centers Records: A Student Digital Exhibition," October 2014. "Missing Fathers" by Adam Bergere on "An Analysis of a Family with the Father in the Internment Camp, December, 12, 1942." http://blogs.cornell .edu/japaneseamericanrelocationrecordsarchive/aas-2130-fall-2014/family -dynamics/an-analysis-of-a-family-with-the-farther-in-the-internment -camp-12121942/.

Cornell University Blog Service. "Japanese American Relocation Centers Records: A Student Digital Exhibition," October 2014. Rowena Chen and Christopher Hayes on watercolor painting "Behind the Curtain– Annoyed Husband and Wife." http://blogs.cornell.edu/japanese americanrelocationrecordsarchive/gene-sogiokas-watercolor-paintings /behind-the-curtain-annoyed-husband-and-wife/.

Cuniberti, Betty. "Internment: Personal Voices, Powerful Choices." *Los*

Angeles Times, October 4, 1987. https://www.latimes.com/archives/la-xpm
-1987-10-04-vw-33126-story.html.

Davenport, John C. *The Internment of Japanese Americans during World War II: Detention of American Citizens*. Langhorne, PA: Chelsea House Publishers, 2010, p. 40.

Densho Digital Repository. "Mas Hashimoto Interview." July 20, 2008. https://ddr.densho.org/narrators/334/.

Densho Digital Repository. "Student Leave." http://ddr.densho.org/browse /topics/102/.

Densho Digital Repository. "Work and Jobs." http://ddr.densho.org/browse /topics/76/.

Drinnon, Richard. *Keeper of Concentration Camps: Dillon S. Myer and American Racism*. Berkeley and Los Angeles, CA: University of California Press, 1987, p. 44.

Dusselier, Jane E. *Artifacts of Loss: Crafting Survival in Japanese American Concentration Camps*. New Brunswick, NJ: Rutgers University Press, 2008, pp. 5–6, 135–137.

Dusselier, Jane. "Arts and Crafts in Camp." *Densho Encyclopedia*. https:// encyclopedia.densho.org/Arts_and_crafts_in_camp/.

Eaton, Allan H. *Beauty behind Barbed Wire: The Arts of the Japanese in Our War Relocation Camps*. New York: Harper & Brothers, 1952, pp. 42, 44–45, 184–185.

Eisenhower, M. S. "Letter to Elbert D. Thomas, Senator Utah, April 23, 1942." War Relocation Authority, Japanese American Evacuation and Resettlement Records, University of California, Berkeley Bancroft Library. http://digitalassets.lib.berkeley.edu/jarda/ucb/text/cubanc6714 _box025c01_0002_3.pdf.

Farzan, Antonia Noori. "ASU Collection of Japanese Internment Camp Newsletters Recalls a Low Point in American Life." *Phoenix New Times*, November 17, 2017. https://www.phoenixnewtimes.com/news/asu -collection-of-japanese-internment-camp-newsletters-recalls-a-low-point -in-american-life-9893407.

Fiset, Louis. "Puyallup (Detention Facility)." *Densho Encyclopedia*. https:// encyclopedia.densho.org/Puyallup_(detention_facility)/.

Fujita-Rony, Thomas. "Poston (Colorado River)." *Densho Encyclopedia*. https://encyclopedia.densho.org/Poston_(Colorado_River)/.

Gesensway, Deborah, and Mindy Roseman. *Beyond Words: Images from America's Concentration Camps*. Ithaca, NY: Cornell University Press, p. 100.

Gingold, Naomi. "Japanese Americans Weren't the Only US Citizens Housed in Camps." Public Radio International, October 18, 2017. https://www .pri.org/stories/2017-10-18/japanese-americans-werent-only-us-citizens -kept-camps.

Girdner, Audrie, and Anne Loftis. *The Great Betrayal: The Evacuation of the Japanese-Americans during World War II*. Toronto: The Macmillan Company, 1969, pp. 211, 213, 241.

Gordon, Linda, and Gary Y. Okihiro, eds. *Impounded: Dorothea Lange and the Censored Images of Japanese American Internment*. New York: W.W. Norton, 2006, p. 138.

Grant, Kimi Cunningham. *Silver Like Dust: One Family's Story of America's Japanese Internment*. New York: Pegasus, 2012, pp. 215, 217.

Hirasuna, Delphine, and Terry Heffernan. *The Art of Gaman: Arts and Crafts from the Japanese American Internment Camps 1942–1946*. Berkeley, CA: Ten Speed Press, 2005, dedication page.

Hosokawa, Bill. *Nisei: The Quiet Americans*. Revised Edition. Boulder, CO: University Press of Colorado, 2002, p. 352.

Huefner, Michael. "Topaz." *Densho Encyclopedia*. https://encyclopedia .densho.org/Topaz/.

Imai, Shiho. "Dillon Myer." *Densho Encyclopedia*. https://encyclopedia.densho .org/Dillon_Myer/.

Japanese American Veterans Association. "Minidoka Relocation Center, Idaho." http://www.javadc.org/minidoka_relocation_center.htm.

Japanese American Veterans Association. "Rohwer Relocation Center, Arkansas." http://www.javadc.org/rohwer_relocation_center.htm.

Jensen, Gwenn M. "Dysentery, Dust, and Determination: Health Care in the World War II Japanese American Detention Camps." *Discover Nikkei.* Enduring Communities. http://www.discovernikkei.org/en/journal /2008/6/21/enduring-communities/.

Kauffman, Eric. "Climate and Topography." *Atlas of the Biodiversity of California.* Sacramento, CA: California Department of Fish and Game, 2003. https://www.coastal.ca.gov/coastalvoices/resources/Biodiversity_Atlas _Climate_and_Topography.pdf

Leighton, Alexander H. *The Governing of Men: General Principles and Recommendations Based on Experience at a Japanese Relocation Camp.* Princeton, NJ: Princeton University Press, 1945, p. 63.

Leong, Karen. "Gila River." *Densho Encyclopedia.* https://encyclopedia .densho.org/Gila_River/.

Lillquist, Karl. *Imprisoned in the Desert: The Geography of World War II– Era Japanese American Relocation Centers in the Western United States.* Ellensburg, WA: Central Washington University, 2007, pp. 435, 496.

Lynn, Charles R. "Jerome Relocation Center Final Report, June 30, 1944," War Relocation Authority. Japanese American Evacuation and Resettlement Records, University of California, Berkeley Bancroft Library, p. 12. https://oac.cdlib.org/ark:/13030/k6dr32nb6/?brand=oac4.

Mastropolo, Frank. "An Internment Camp within an Internment Camp." ABC News, February 19, 2008. http://ww2f.com/threads/secret-emerges -from-wwii-internment-camp.12655/.

Matsumoto, Mieko. "Heart Mountain." *Densho Encyclopedia.* https:// encyclopedia.densho.org/Heart_Mountain/.

Matsumoto, Nancy. "Ansel Adams." *Densho Encyclopedia.* https:// encyclopedia.densho.org/Ansel_Adams/.

Minidoka Irrigator, vol. III, no. 4, March 20, 1943, http://ddr.densho.org /media/ddr-densho-119/ddr-densho-119-32-mezzanine-cd3181b4d8 .pdf; vol. III, no. 11, May 8, 1943, http://ddr.densho.org/media/ddr-densho -119/ddr-densho-119-39-mezzanine-011c1c8b49.pdf; vol. III, no. 32, October 2, 1943, http://encyclopedia.densho.org/media/ddr-densho-119

/ddr-densho-119-59-mezzanine-b6fa5fc820.pdf; vol. II [sic], no. 51, February 12, 1944, http://encyclopedia.densho.org/media/ddr-densho-119 /ddr-densho-119-76-mezzanine-22c4546690.pdf.

Moss, Dori Felice. "Strangers in Their Own Land: A Cultural History of Japanese American Internment Camps in Arkansas, 1942–1945." M.A. thesis: Georgia State University, 2007. https://scholarworks.gsu.edu /communication_theses/32.

Muller, Eric L. *Colors of Confinement: Rare Kodachrome Photographs of Japanese American Incarceration in World War II*. Chapel Hill, NC: The University of North Carolina Press, 2012.

Myer, Dillon S. "Letter to Secretary of War Henry Stimson, March 11, 1943, with attachment, Secretary of War to Dillon S. Myer, May 10, 1943." Papers of Dillon S. Myer, War Relocation Authority, The Incarceration of Japanese-Americans during World War II Collection, Harry S. Truman Presidential Library and Museum. https://www.trumanlibrary.gov/library /research-files/letter-dillon-s-myer-secretary-war-march-11-1943 -attachment-secretary-war?documentid=NA&pagenumber=1.

Myer, Dillon S. Oral History Interview, July 7, 1970. Interviewer: Helen S. Pryor, Berkeley, CA. University of California, Bancroft Library, Berkeley Regional Oral History Office. Harry S. Truman Presidential Library and Museum. Chapters IX–XIII. https://www.trumanlibrary.org/oralhist/myerds3.htm.

Myer, Dillon S. *Uprooted Americans: The Japanese Americans and the War Relocation Authority during World War II*. Tucson, AZ: University of Arizona Press, 1971, pp. 146, 198.

Myer, Dillon S. "Work of the War Relocation Authority: An Anniversary Statement by Dillon S. Myer," 1943. War Relocation Authority. http://www .mansell.com/eo9066/1943/43-03/TL10.html.

Nagata, Donna. "Psychological Effects of Camp." *Densho Encyclopedia*. http://encyclopedia.densho.org/Psychological_effects_of_camp/.

National Archives and Records Administration. "Toranosuke Kamei file." War Relocation Authority Collection, Record Group Number 210, Washington, DC.

National Park Service. "Japanese Americans at Manzanar." February 28, 2015. https://www.nps.gov/manz/learn/historyculture/japanese-americans -at-manzanar.htm.

National Park Service. Minidoka National Historic Site, Idaho. "Families, Food, and Dining." May 1943. https://www.nps.gov/miin/learn/history culture/families-food-and-dining.htm.

National Park Service. "Minidoka National Historic Site, ID, WA." https:// www.nps.gov/miin/index.htm.

Niiya, Brian. "Block Councils." *Densho Encyclopedia*. https://encyclopedia .densho.org/Block_councils/.

Niiya, Brian. "Community Councils." *Densho Encyclopedia*. https://encyclopedia .densho.org/Community_councils/.

Niiya, Brian. "Jerome." *Densho Encyclopedia*. https://encyclopedia.densho .org/Jerome/.

Niiya, Brian. "Milton Eisenhower." *Densho Encyclopedia*. https://encyclopedia .densho.org/Milton_Eisenhower/.

Nubile, James, and Joe Fox, directors. *Passing Poston: An American Story*. 2008. Documentary. Fly on the Wall Productions, Inc. iTunes.

Okimoto, Ruth Y. *Sharing a Desert Home: Life on the Colorado River Indian Reservation, Poston, Arizona 1942–1945*. Berkeley, CA: News from Native California, 2001, pp. 10–12, 14, 16.

Okubo, Miné. *Citizen 13660*. New York: Columbia University Press, 1946, p. 207.

O'Neill, William L. *A Democracy at War: America's Fight at Home and Abroad in World War II*. New York: The Free Press, 1993, p. 233.

Ono, Gary T. "Story behind the Name—Amache." *Discover Nikkei*, February 4, 2014. http://www.discovernikkei.org/en/journal/2014/2/4/story -behind-the-name/.

Prucha, Francis Paul. *The Great Father: The United States Government and the American Indians, Volume 1*. Lincoln, NE: University of Nebraska Press, 1995, p. 1,030.

Rafferty-Osaki, Terumi. "Sports and Recreation in Camp." *Densho Encyclo-*

pedia. https://encyclopedia.densho.org/Sports_and_recreation_in_camp/.

Rao, Mallika. "These Crafts Made by Japanese-American Prisoners Will Renew Your Faith in Human Ingenuity." *Huffington Post*, August 15, 2014. https://www.huffingtonpost.com/2014/08/15/art-of-gaman-arts-crafts -japanese-interment-camps_n_5655381.html.

Robinson, Greg. "John Collier." *Densho Encyclopedia*. http://encyclopedia .densho.org/John_Collier/.

Robinson, Greg. *A Tragedy of Democracy: Japanese Confinement in North America*. New York: Columbia University Press, 2009, pp. 142–143, 154– 156, 158, 160, 162.

Rogers, Vance. "Memo from Vance Rogers to Fryer–April 21, 1942." California State University, Sacramento. Department of Special Collections and University Archives. http://cdn.calisphere.org/data/28722/8v /bk0013c8x8v/files/bk0013c8x8v-FID1.pdf.

Rohwer Heritage Site. "Rohwer: Japanese American Relocation Center." http://rohwer.astate.edu/.

Spicer, Edward H. "Attitude of Local Indians." October 18, 1942. Notes, Observations, and Conversations, War Relocation Authority, Japanese American Evacuation and Resettlement Records, University of California, Berkeley Bancroft Library. http://digitalassets.lib.berkeley.edu/jarda/ucb/text /cubanc_35_1_01247939ta.pdf.

Staff. "Gila Zoo." *Gila News-Courier*, Rivers, AZ, September 12, 1942, p. 5. https://www.loc.gov.

Staff. *Official Daily Press* bulletin, Poston, AZ, October 8, 1942, p. 3. https:// www.loc.gov.

Takei, Barbara. "Tule Lake." *Densho Encyclopedia*. https://encyclopedia.densho .org/Tule_Lake/.

Taketa, George. "Testimony of George Taketa." Commission on Wartime Relocation and Internment of Civilians Hearing. September 22, 1981, Chicago, IL. Northeastern Illinois University, Japanese-American Redress Collection. http://collections.carli.illinois.edu/cdm/search/collection/nei_japan /searchterm/George%20Taketa/order/nosort.

Uchida, Yoshiko. *Desert Exile: The Uprooting of a Japanese American Family*. Seattle, WA: University of Washington Press, 1982, p. 115.

Varner, Natasha. "These Images of Japanese American Incarceration Were Embargoed for Almost 30 Years." *Densho Blog*. Public Radio International, April 30, 2016. https://www.pri.org/stories/2016-04-29/these-images-japanese-american-internment-were-embargoed-almost-30-years.

Wakatsuki, Hanako. "Minidoka." *Densho Encyclopedia*. https://encyclopedia.densho.org/Minidoka/.

Watanabe, Teresa. "Celebrating a Shared History." *Los Angeles Times*, February 19, 2008. https://www.latimes.com/local/la-me-poston19feb19-story.html.

Weiss, Rachel. "77 Years Ago, the U.S. Interned Thousands of Japanese-Americans." *Newsday*, February 19, 2019. https://www.newsday.com/news/nation/japanese-americans-reflect-on-internment-camps-75-years-later-1.13012943.

What Snake Is That? "Arkansas." http://www.whatsnakeisthat.com/category/region/southeast/arkansas/.

Whitaker, E. B. "Letter to Mr. Milton Eisenhower," April 27, 1942. War Relocation Authority, Japanese American Evacuation and Resettlement Records, University of California, Berkeley Bancroft Library. www.oac.cdlib.org/ark:/28722/bk0013c8x8v/FID1.

Wilson, John P. *Peoples of the Middle Gila: A Documentary History of the Pimas and Maricopas, 1500–1945*. Sacaton, AZ: Gila River Indian Community, 2014, p. 268.

Yamato, Sharon. "Toyo Miyatake." *Densho Encyclopedia*. https://encyclopedia.densho.org/Toyo_Miyatake/.

Zimmerman, William. "Letter to Hon. Jerry Voorhis," April 3, 1942. Office of Indian Affairs, War Relocation Authority, Japanese American Evacuation and Resettlement Records, University of California, Berkeley Bancroft Library. www.oac.cdlib.org/ark:/28722/bk0013c8x8v/FID1.

Chapter Six

Appropedia. "Ethanol from Organic Sugarbeets versus Refined Cane Sugar."

https://www.appropedia.org/Ethanol_from_organic_sugar_beets_versus
_refined_cane_sugar.

Austin, Allan V. "National Japanese American Student Relocation Council." *Densho Encyclopedia*. http://encyclopedia.densho.org/National_Japanese
_American_Student_Relocation_Council/.

Beck, Julie. "Two Boy Scouts Met in an Internment Camp, and Grew Up to Work in Congress." *The Atlantic,* May 17, 2019. https://www.theatlantic
.com/family/archive/2019/05/congressmen-norm-mineta-alan-simpson
-friendship-japanese-internment-camp/589603/.

Buck, Stephanie. "During the Internment, Japanese American Teens Created This Heartbreaking Scrapbook about Camp Life." *Timeline*, February 17, 2017. https://timeline.com/japanese-internment-scrapbook
-d3c0dd95d30f.

Commission on Wartime Relocation and Internment of Civilians. *Personal Justice Denied. Part 1 (December, 1982): Report of the Commission on Wartime Relocation and Internment of Civilians.* Washington, DC: US Government Printing Office, pp. 172–173, 181, 186, 188–189. https://www
.archives.gov/files/research/japanese-americans/justice-denied/chapter
-6.pdf; https://www.archives.gov/files/research/japanese-americans/justice
-denied/chapter-7.pdf

Cuniberti, Betty. "Internment: Personal Voices, Powerful Choices," *Los Angeles Times*, October 4, 1987. https://www.latimes.com/archives/la-xpm
-1987-10-04-vw-33126-story.html.

Daniels, Roger. *Prisoners without Trial: Japanese Americans in World War II.* New York: Hill and Wang, 1993, pp. 73–74.

Densho Blog. "Love and Caring: Fred Hoshiyama, YMCA Leader." September 10, 2010. https://densho.org/love-and-caring-fred-hoshiyama
-ymca/.

Densho Digital Repository. "Bruce T. Kaji Interview I." Interviewer: Martha Nakagawa. Segment 11. July 28, 2010, Los Angeles, CA. http://ddr
.densho.org/media/ddr-densho-1000/ddr-densho-1000-289-transcript
-76f2303633.htm.

Densho Digital Repository. "Henry Miyatake Interview II." Interviewer: Tom Ikeda, Segment 17. September 23, 1999, Seattle, WA. http://ddr.densho .org/interviews/ddr-densho-1000-54-17/.

Densho Digital Repository. "Kats Kunitsugu—Paul Tsuneishi Interview." Interviewers: Frank Abe and Frank Chin, Segment 1. August 22, 1995, Los Angeles, CA. http://ddr.densho.org/media/ddr-densho-122/ddr-densho -122-17-transcript-c3528ffd28.htm.

Eisenhower, M. S. "To: John J. McCloy, Assistant Secretary of War," April 13, 1942. War Relocation Authority, Japanese American Evacuation and Resettlement Records, University of California, Berkeley Bancroft Library. www.oac.cdlib.org/ark:/28722/bk0013c8x8v/FID1.

Encyclopaedia Britannica. "Battle of Midway: World War II." *Encyclopædia Britannica*. https://www.britannica.com/event/Battle-of-Midway.

Gammage, Jeff. "Born in an Internment Camp for Japanese Americans, She Fears Muslims Face a Similar Fate Today." *The Inquirer*, February 5, 2017. http://media.philly.com/storage/special_projects/Born_in_internment_camp _for_Japanese_Americans_she_fears_Muslims_face_similar_fate.html.

Goodwin, Doris Kearns. *No Ordinary Time: Franklin and Eleanor Roosevelt: The Home Front in World War II*. New York: W.W. Norton, 2006, pp. 428–429.

Hirabayashi, Lane Ryo. "The Impact of Incarceration on the Education of Nisei Schoolchildren." In *Japanese Americans: From Relocation to Redress*, edited by Roger Daniels, Sandra C. Taylor, and Harry H.L. Kitano. Seattle, WA: University of Washington Press, 1991, pp. 46–49.

Howard, John. *Concentration Camps on the Home Front: Japanese Americans in the House of Jim Crow*. Chicago: The University of Chicago Press, 2008, p. 152.

Irons, Peter. *Justice at War: The Story of the Japanese-American Internment Cases*. New York: Oxford University Press, 1983, pp. 100–103, 144.

James, Thomas. *Exile Within: The Schooling of Japanese Americans, 1942–1945*. Cambridge, MA: Harvard University Press, 1987, pp. 50, 52, 59, 74–75, 116–118.

Kamei, Hiroshi. "Testimony of Hiroshi Kamei." Commission on Wartime Relocation and Internment of Civilians Hearing. August 6, 1981, Los Angeles, CA. https://www.archives.gov/research/japanese-americans/hearings. CWRIC Los Angeles Hearings Video Collection, Nikkei for Civil Rights and Redress and Visual Communications. Reissued in 2018 on DVD as *Speak Out for Justice*.

Lyon, Cherstin M. "Habeas Corpus." *Densho Encyclopedia*. http://encyclopedia .densho.org/Habeas_corpus/.

Masaoka, Mike M., with Bill Hosokawa. *They Call Me Moses Masaoka: An American Saga*. New York: William Morrow and Company, 1987, pp. 101, 123–126, 189.

Moore, Brenda L. *Serving Our Country: Japanese American Women in the Military during World War II*. New Brunswick, NJ: Rutgers University Press, 2003, p. 15.

Mori, Darryl. "From Beets to the Battlefield: How WWII Farm Laborers Helped the War Effort," *Discover Nikkei*, November 18, 2016. http:// www.discovernikkei.org/en/journal/2016/11/18/from-beets-to-battlefield/.

Muller, Eric L. *An American Inquisition: The Hunt for Japanese-American Disloyalty in World War II*. Chapel Hill, NC: The University of North Carolina Press, 2007, pp. 31–32.

Murray, Alice Yang. *Historical Memories of the Japanese American Internment and the Struggle for Redress*. Stanford, CA: Stanford University Press, 2008, p. 272.

Myer, Dillon S. Oral History Interview, July 7, 1970. Interviewer: Helen S. Pryor. Berkeley, California. University of California, Bancroft Library, Berkeley Regional Oral History Office. Harry S. Truman Presidential Library and Museum. Chapters IX–XIII. https://www.trumanlibrary.gov /library/oral-histories/myerds3.

Myer, Dillon S. "Work of the War Relocation Authority: An Anniversary Statement by Dillon S. Myer." War Relocation Authority, 1943. http://www .mansell.com/eo9066/1943/43-03/TL10.html.

National Constitution Center. "Interactive Constitution—The Suspension

Clause. https://constitutioncenter.org/interactive-constitution/interpretation/article-i/clauses/763.

Niiya, Brian. "Mitsuye Endo." *Densho Encyclopedia*. http://encyclopedia.densho.org/Mitsuye_Endo/.

Okimoto, Ruth Y. *Sharing a Desert Home: Life on the Colorado River Indian Reservation, Poston, Arizona 1942–1945*. Berkeley, CA: News from Native California, 2001, pp. 11–12.

Okubo, Miné. *Citizen 13660*. New York: Columbia University Press, 1946, p. 207.

Oppenheim, Joanne. *Dear Miss Breed: True Stories of the Japanese American Incarceration during World War II and a Librarian Who Made a Difference*. New York: Scholastic, 2006, pp. 163–164.

PBS. "Norman Mineta and His Legacy: An American Story." May 20, 2019. https://www.pbs.org/show/norman-mineta-and-his-legacy-american-story/.

Rafferty-Osaki, Terumi. "Sports and Recreation in Camp." *Densho Encyclopedia*. https://encyclopedia.densho.org/Sports_and_recreation_in_camp/.

Robinson, Greg. *A Tragedy of Democracy: Japanese Confinement in North America*. New York: Columbia University Press, 2009, pp. 162, 211.

Sekerak, Eleanor Gerard. "A Teacher at Topaz." In *Japanese Americans: From Relocation to Redress*, edited by Roger Daniels, Sandra C. Taylor, and Harry H.L. Kitano. Seattle, WA: University of Washington Press, 1991, p. 41.

Smithsonian Institution, National Museum of American History. *A More Perfect Union*. *"Ramblings."* The Topaz High School Yearbook, 1945. http://amhistory.si.edu/perfectunion/collection/image.asp?ID=524.

Smithsonian Institution, National Museum of American History. "War Relocation Authority, Citizen's Short-Term Leave," May 2, 1943. http://americanhistory.si.edu/collections/search/object/nmah_1295207.

Tateishi, John. *And Justice for All: An Oral History of the Japanese American Detention Camps*. Seattle, WA: University of Washington Press, 1999, pp. 60–61.

University of Massachusetts Boston, Joseph P. Healy Library. "Interview with

Chiye Tomihiro." November 12, 2011, Chicago, IL. https://openarchives
.umb.edu/digital/collection/p15774coll5/id/99/.

US Department of the Interior. *Evacuated People: A Quantitative Description*. Washington, DC: US Government Printing Office, 1946. http://npshistory.com/publications/incarceration/evacuated-people.pdf.

Varner, Natasha. "What 'Back to School' Looked Like in World War II Concentration Camps." *Densho Blog*. August 22, 2016. https://densho.org/back-to-school/.

Wallace, Nina. "This Isn't the First Time White Supremacists Have Tried to Cancel Birthright Citizenship." *Densho Blog*. November 2, 2018. https://densho.org/birthright-citizenship-japanese.americans/.

War Relocation Authority. *Gila News-Courier*, Rivers, AZ, September 12, 1942. Library of Congress. https://www.loc.gov/resource/sn87062084/1942-10-08/ed-1/?sp=3&r=-1.162,-0.482,3.324,1.72,0.

War Relocation Authority. *Poston Press Bulletin* (Poston 2), Poston, AZ, October 8, 1942. Library of Congress. https://www.loc.gov/resource/sn87062084/1942-10-08/ed-1/?sp=3&r=-1.162,-0.482,3.324,1.72,0.

Weglyn, Michi Nishiura. *Years of Infamy: The Untold Story of America's Concentration Camps*. Seattle, WA: University of Washington Press, 1976, pp. 98–99.

Wilbur, Theodore. "American Friends Service Committee Efforts to Aid Japanese American Citizens during World War II." M.A. thesis, Boise State University, 2009. https://core.ac.uk/download/pdf/61714281.pdf.

Williams, Duncan Ryūken. *American Sutra: A Story of Faith and Freedom in the Second World War*. Cambridge, MA: The Belknap Press of Harvard University Press, 2019, pp. 140–144.

Chapter Seven

Chan, Jeffrey Paul, Frank Chin, Lawson Fusao Inada, and Shawn Wong, eds. *The Big Aiiieeeee!: An Anthology of Chinese American and Japanese American Literature*. New York: Plume, 1991, p. 381.

Christgau, John. "Collins versus the World: The Fight to Restore Citizenship to Japanese American Renunciants of World War II." *Pacific Historical Review*, vol. 54, no. 1. Oakland, CA: University of California Press, 1985, pp. 1–31. https://www.jstor.org/stable/3638863.

Commission on Wartime Relocation and Internment of Civilians. *Personal Justice Denied. Part 1 (December, 1982): Report of the Commission on Wartime Relocation and Internment of Civilians.* Washington, DC: US Government Printing Office, pp. 178, 187–191, 214–216, 256. https://www.archives.gov/files/research/japanese-americans/justice-denied/chapter-6.pdf; https://www.archives.gov/files/research/japanese-americans/justice-denied/chapter-7.pdf; https://www.archives.gov/files/research/japanese-americans/justice-denied/chapter-8.pdf; https://www.archives.gov/files/research/japanese-americans/justice-denied/chapter-10.pdf.

Crost, Lyn. "Hawaii's Legendary Battalion." *Hawaii Herald*, June 19, 1992. 100th Infantry Battalion Veterans Education Center. http://www.100thbattalion.org/archives/newspaper-articles/hawaii-herald/hawaiis-legendary-battalion/.

Crost, Lyn. *Honor by Fire: Japanese Americans at War in Europe and the Pacific.* Novato, CA: Presidio Press, 1994, pp. 10, 15.

DeCarlo, Peter J. "Military Intelligence Service Language School (MISLS)." MNOpedia, May 13, 2015. http://www.mnopedia.org/group/military-intelligence-service-language-school-misls.

Densho Digital Repository. "The So-Called 'Loyalty Questionnaire' (Page 4 of 4)." http://ddr.densho.org/ddr-densho-72-4-master-ce4cc2edc9/.

Densho Digital Repository. "Student Leave." http://ddr.densho.org/browse/topics/102/.

Densho Digital Repository. "Work and Jobs." http://ddr.densho.org/browse/topics/76/.

Densho Encyclopedia. "Wakayama Case." http://encyclopedia.densho.org/Wakayama_case/.

Drinnon, Richard. *Keeper of Concentration Camps: Dillon S. Myer and American Racism.* Berkeley, CA: University of California Press, 1987, p. 44.

Encyclopaedia Britannica. "Battle of Guadalcanal: World War II." December

15, 2016. https://www.britannica.com/event/Battle-of-Guadalcanal.

Endo, Ellen. "Unsolved Murder in Manzanar." *Rafu Shimpo*, July 22, 2013. https://www.rafu.com/2013/07/unsolved-murder-in-manzanar/.

Girdner, Audrie, and Anne Loftis. *The Great Betrayal: The Evacuation of the Japanese Americans during World War II*. Toronto: Macmillan, 1970, p. 241.

Goodwin, Doris Kearns. *No Ordinary Time: Franklin and Eleanor Roosevelt: The Home Front in World War II*. New York: Simon & Schuster, 1994, pp. 427–431.

Hansen, Arthur A. "Harry Ueno." *Densho Encyclopedia*. https://encyclopedia .densho.org/Harry_Ueno/.

Hansen, Arthur A., ed. *Japanese American World War II Evacuation Oral History Project: Resisters*. California State University, Fullerton. Munich, Germany: K.G. Saur Verlag, 1995. http://texts.cdlib.org.

Hansen, Arthur A., and David A. Hacker. "The Manzanar Riot: An Ethnic Perspective." *Amerasia Journal*, vol. 2, no. 2, 1974. UCLA Asian American Studies Center Press, pp. 112–157. https://doi.org/10.17953 /amer.2.2.1kl24477mkk70q51.

Hawaii Nikkei History Editorial Board. "100th Infantry Battalion (Separate) the Purple Heart Battalion." In *Japanese Eyes, American Hearts: Personal Reflections of Hawaii's World War II Nisei Soldiers*. Honolulu, HI: University of Hawaii Press, 1998, p. 397.

Irons, Peter. *Justice at War: The Story of the Japanese-American Internment Cases*. New York: Oxford University Press, 1983, pp. 114–116.

Kuromiya, Yosh. "Only in (Japanese) America." Densho Digital Repository. https://ddr.densho.org/ddr-densho-122-548/.

Leighton, Alexander H. *The Governing of Men: General Principles and Recommendations Based on Experience at a Japanese Relocation Camp*. Princeton, NJ: Princeton University Press, 1945, p. 263.

Longmont Times-Call. "Longmont Sisters Work to Ensure Father's Experiences during World War II Internment Prison Aren't Forgotten." *Longmont Times-Call*, March 17, 2012. https://www.timescall.com

/2012/03/17/longmont-sisters-work-to-ensure-fathers-experiences-during
-world-war-ii-internment-prison-arent-forgotten/.

Lyon, Cherstin. "Japanese American Citizens League." *Densho Encyclopedia*.
https://encyclopedia.densho.org/Japanese_American_Citizens_League/.

Lyon, Cherstin. "Loyalty Questionnaire." *Densho Encyclopedia*. https://
encyclopedia.densho.org/Loyalty_questionnaire/.

Lyon, Cherstin. "Segregation." *Densho Encyclopedia*. https://encyclopedia
.densho.org/Segregation/.

Marrin, Albert. *Uprooted: The Japanese American Experience during World
War II*. New York: Alfred A. Knopf, 2016, pp. 119–120.

Masaoka, Mike M., with Bill Hosokawa. *They Call Me Moses Masaoka: An
American Saga*. New York: William Morrow and Company, 1987, pp.
120–125, 127, 130.

McNaughton, James C. *Nisei Linguists: Japanese Americans in the Military
Intelligence Service during World War II*. Center of Military History
(CMH Pub 70-99-1). Washington, DC: Department of the Army, 2006,
pp. 379–380.

Military Intelligence Service Veterans Club of Hawaii. *MIS: America's Secret
Weapon: Japanese Americans in the Military Intelligence Service in World
War II*. http://www.misveteranshawaii.com/japanese-in-hawaii-the-build
up-to-war/.

Muller, Eric L. *An American Inquisition: The Hunt for Japanese-American
Disloyalty in World War II*. Chapel Hill, NC: The University of North
Carolina Press, 2007, pp. 32–33, 36, 38.

Muller, Eric L. "Draft Resistance." *Densho Encyclopedia*. https://encyclope-
dia.densho.org/Draft_resistance/.

Muller, Eric L. *Free to Die for Their Country: The Story of the Japanese
American Draft Resisters in World War II*. Chicago: The University of
Chicago Press, 2003, pp. 184–192.

Muller, Eric L. "Heart Mountain Fair Play Committee." *Densho Encyclopedia*.
https://encyclopedia.densho.org/Heart_Mountain_Fair_Play_Committee/.

Muller, Eric L. "A Penny for Their Thoughts: Draft Resistance at the

Poston Relocation Center." University of North Carolina School of Law, Carolina Law Scholarship Repository, 2005, p. 134. https://scholarship.law.unc.edu/cgi/viewcontent.cgi?article=1277&context=faculty_publications.

Murray, Alice Yang. *Historical Memories of the Japanese American Internment and the Struggle for Redress*. Stanford, CA: Stanford University Press, 2008, pp. 88, 426–429.

Murray, Alice Yang. *What Did the Internment of Japanese Americans Mean?* Boston: Bedford/St. Martin's, 2000, pp. 14–15, 17.

Myer, Dillon S. "Letter to the Secretary of War, March 11, 1943, with Attachment, Secretary of War to Dillon S. Myer, May 10, 1943." War Relocation Authority. Papers of Dillon S. Myer, the War Relocation Authority, the Incarceration of Japanese-Americans during World War II Collection, Harry S. Truman Presidential Library and Museum. https://www.trumanlibrary.gov/library/research-files/letter-dillon-s-myer-secretary-war-march-11-1943-attachment-secretary-war?documentid=NA&pagenumber=1.

Myer, Dillon S. Oral History Interview, July 7, 1970. Interviewer: Helen S. Pryor. Berkeley, California. University of California, Bancroft Library, Berkeley Regional Oral History Office. Harry S. Truman Presidential Library and Museum. Chapters IX–XIII. https://www.trumanlibrary.gov/library/oral-histories/myerds3.

Myer, Dillon S. "Work of the War Relocation Authority: An Anniversary Statement by Dillon S. Myer." War Relocation Authority, 1943. http://www.mansell.com/eo9066/1943/43-03/TL10.html.

Nakamura, Kelli. "Military Intelligence Service." *Densho Encyclopedia*. https://encyclopedia.densho.org/Military_Intelligence_Service/.

Nakamura, Kelli. "Military Intelligence Service Language School." *Densho Encyclopedia*. https://encyclopedia.densho.org/Military_Intelligence_Service_Language_School/.

National Archives and Records Administration. "World War II Army Enlistment Records, 1998." https://aad.archives.gov/aad/series-description.jsp?s=3360&cat=WR26&bc=,sl,fd.

Niiya, Brian. "Fred Tayama." *Densho Encyclopedia.* https://encyclopedia. densho.org/Fred_Tayama/.

Niiya, Brian. "Japanese Americans in Military during World War II." *Densho Encyclopedia.* http://encyclopedia.densho.org/Japanese_Americans_in_ military_during_World_War_II/.

Niiya, Brian. "Manzanar Riot/Uprising." *Densho Encyclopedia.* http:// encyclopedia.densho.org/Manzanar_riot/uprising/.

Niiya, Brian. "No-No Boys." *Densho Encyclopedia.* https://encyclopedia.densho .org/No-no_boys/.

Odo, Franklin. "100th Infantry Battalion." *Densho Encyclopedia.* https:// encyclopedia.densho.org/100th_Infantry_Battalion/.

Paltzer, Seth. "The Dogs of War: The US Army's Use of Canines in WWII." National Museum of the United States Army, June 2, 2016. http:// armyhistory.org/the-dogs-of-war-the-u-s-armys-use-of-canines-in-wwii/.

Robinson, Greg. *A Tragedy of Democracy: Japanese Confinement in North America.* New York: Columbia University Press, 2009, pp. 185–186, 194– 195, 206–207, 211, 214.

Roosevelt, Franklin D. Letter to "My Dear Mr. Secretary," February 1, 1943. Text of letter reinstating Selective Service for Nisei. Densho Digital Repository. https://ddr.densho.org/media/ddr-csujad-19/ddr-csujad-19-57 -mezzanine-64550b8115.pdf.

Selective Service Classifications for WWI, WWII, and PWWII through 1976. http://cufon.org/CRG/memo/74911231.html.

Selective Service Questionnaire. "Statement of United States Citizen of Japanese Ancestry." DSS form 304A, January 23, 1943. http://www .mansell.com/eo9066/1943/43-01/SelSrvcQ.html.

Smithsonian Institution, National Museum of American History. A More Perfect Union. *Loyalty: The Questionnaire.* http://amhistory.si.edu /perfectunion/non-flash/loyalty_questionnaire.html.

Spicer, Edward H., Asael T. Hansen, Katherine Luomala, and Mavin K. Opler. *Impounded People: Japanese-Americans in the Relocation Centers.*

United States War Relocation Authority. Washington, DC: US Government Printing Office, 1946, p. 13.

Takei, Barbara. "Tule Lake." *Densho Encyclopedia*. https://encyclopedia.densho .org/Tule_Lake/.

Tamura, Eileen H. *In Defense of Justice: Joseph Kurihara and the Japanese American Struggle for Equality*. Urbana, Chicago, and Springfield, IL: University of Illinois Press, 2013, pp. 54–58.

Tateishi, John. *And Justice for All: An Oral History of the Japanese American Detention Camps*. Seattle, WA: University of Washington Press, 1999, pp. 170, 173.

UCLA Newsroom. "Center Shatters Myth of 'Quiet' Japanese Americans Imprisoned in Camps." September 15, 2015. http://newsroom.ucla.edu/stories /center-shatters-myth-of-quiet-japanese-americans-imprisoned-in-camps.

United States v. Masaaki Kuwabara, 56 F. Supp. 716 (N.D. Cal. 1944). https:// law.justia.com/cases/federal/district-courts/FSupp/56/716/1441113/.

Wakida, Patricia, and Brian Niiya. "Violet Kazue de Cristoforo." *Densho Encyclopedia*. http://encyclopedia.densho.org/Violet_Kazue_de_Cristoforo/.

Chapter Eight

36th Division Association. "36th Division in World War II: Lost Battalion." Texas Military Forces Museum. http://www.texasmilitaryforcesmuseum .org/36division/archives/lostbat/lostbat.htm.

100th Infantry Battalion Veterans Education Center. "Italy: The First Four Months." http://www.100thbattalion.org/history/battalion-history/european -campaigns/italy/.

100th Infantry Battalion Veterans Education Center. "Jack Johnson." http:// www.100thbattalion.org/history/veterans/officers/jack-johnson/.

100th Infantry Battalion Veterans Education Center. "Masao Yamada." http:// www.100thbattalion.org/history/veterans/chaplains/masao-yamada/.

100th Infantry Battalion Veterans Education Center. "Mitsuyoshi Fukuda." http:// www.100thbattalion.org/history/veterans/officers/mitsuyoshi-fukuda/2/.

100th Infantry Battalion Veterans Education Center. "Timeline: 1940–1946." http://www.100thbattalion.org/learn/timeline/.

442nd Regimental Combat Team. *The Story of the 442nd Combat Team Composed of 442nd Infantry Regiment, 522nd Field Artillery Battalion, 232nd Combat Engineer Company.* Pamphlet, 1979. Mitsuye Yamada Papers, Special Collections and Archives, the University of California, Irvine Libraries. http://content.cdlib.org.

442nd Regimental Combat Team. "What Was the 442nd Regimental Combat Team?" http://www.the442.org/442ndfacts.html.

Aki, George. "My 30 Months (1944–1946)." Memoir manuscript. George Aki Collection. Veterans History Project, American Folklife Center, Library of Congress, p. 10. https://memory.loc.gov/diglib/vhp/story/loc.natlib .afc2001001.11135/.

Army Historical Foundation. "232nd Combat Engineer Company (Nisei), 442d Regimental Combat Team." National Museum of the United States Army. https://armyhistory.org/232d-engineer-combat-company-nisei-442d -regimental-combat-team.

Asahina, Robert. *Just Americans: How Japanese Americans Won a War at Home and Abroad: The Story of the 100th Battalion/442nd Regimental Combat Team in World War II.* New York: Gotham Books, 2006, pp. 58–60, 64, 157–159,163, 190–192, 201, 220.

British Broadcasting Corporation. *On This Day: 5 June.* "1944: Celebrations As Rome Is Liberated." http://news.bbc.co.uk/onthisday/hi/dates/stories /june/5/newsid_3547000/3547329.stm.

Bullock, Alan, Baron Bullock, John Lukacs, and Wilfrid F. Knapp. "Adolf Hitler: Dictator of Germany." *Encyclopædia Britannica.* https://www.britannica .com/biography/Adolf-Hitler.

Center of Military History. "Presidential Unit Citations (ARMY) Awarded to: 100th Battalion & 442nd Regimental Combat Team." Department of the Army. https://history.army.mil/html/topics/apam/puc.html#232engco.

Chang, Thelma. *"I Can Never Forget": Men of the 100th/442nd.* Honolulu, HI: Sigi Productions, Inc., 1991, p. 51.

Clark, General Mark W., and Martin Blumenson. *Calculated Risk*. New York: Enigma, 2007, p. 220.

Congressional Medal of Honor Society. "Barney F. Hajiro Citation." http://www.cmohs.org/recipient-detail/2766/hajiro-barney-f.php.

Congressional Medal of Honor Society. "Daniel K. Inouye Citation." http://www.cmohs.org/recipient-detail/2799/inouye-daniel-k.php.

Congressional Medal of Honor Society. "George T. Sakato Citation." http://www.cmohs.org/recipient-detail/2980/sakato-george-t.php.

Crost, Lyn. "Hawaii's Legendary Battalion." *Hawaii Herald*, June 19, 1992. 100th Infantry Battalion Veterans Education Center. http://www.100thbattalion.org/archives/newspaper-articles/hawaii-herald/hawaiis-legendary-battalion/.

Crost, Lyn. *Honor by Fire: Japanese Americans at War in Europe and the Pacific*. Novato: Presidio Press, 1994, pp. 10, 15, 61, 63, 69–70, 72, 79–81, 105–107, 113, 115–116, 141–143, 146–147, 149, 155, 174–179,185, 197, 239, 251, 301.

Discover Nikkei. "Henry S. 'Hank' Yoshitake." http://www.discovernikkei.org/en/resources/military/644/.

Duus, Masayo Umezawa. *Unlikely Liberators: The Men of the 100th and 442nd*. Translated by Peter Duus. Honolulu, HI: University of Hawaii Press, 2006, pp. 100, 120–124, 127.

Fuchs, Lawrence H. *Hawaii Pono: A Social History*. New York: Harcourt, Brace & World Inc., 1961, p. 306.

Go for Broke National Education Center. "442nd Regimental Combat Team." Accessed September 1, 2019. http://www.goforbroke.org/learn/history/military_units/442nd.php.

Go for Broke National Education Center. "522nd Field Artillery Battalion." Accessed September 1, 2019. http://www.goforbroke.org/learn/history/military_units/522nd.php.

Go for Broke National Education Center. "Anzio Campaign (January 22–May 24, 1944), the 100th Infantry Battalion (March 26–May 1944)." Accessed September 1, 2019. http://www.goforbroke.org/learn/history/combat

_history/world_war_2/european_theater/anzio_campaign.php.

Go for Broke National Education Center. "Central Europe Campaign (March 22–May 11, 1945), the 522nd Field Artillery Battalion and the Dachau Subcamps (March 9–May 11, 1945)." Accessed September 1, 2019. http://www.goforbroke.org/learn/history/combat_history/world_war_2 /european_theater/central_europe_campaign.php.

Go for Broke National Education Center. "Deployment to Africa (September 1943)." Accessed September 1, 2019. http://www.goforbroke.org/learn /history/combat_history/world_war_2/european_theater/deployment _to_africa.php.

Go for Broke National Education Center. "Hall of Honor Statistics." Accessed December 15, 2019. http://www.goforbroke.org/learn/history/hall_of _honor/awards_stats.php.

Go for Broke National Education Center. "Naples-Foggia Campaign (September 9, 1943–January 21, 1944), the 100th Infantry Battalion (Separate), (September 22, 1943–January 1944)." Accessed September 1, 2019. http:// www.goforbroke.org/learn/history/combat_history/world_war_2/european _theater/naples-foggia_campaign.php.

Go for Broke National Education Center. "North Apennines (September 10, 1944–April 4, 1945) and Po Valley (April 5, 1945–May 8, 1945) Campaigns, the 100th/442nd (less the 522nd Field Artillery Battalion) at the Gothic Line, March 25–May 1945)." Accessed September 1, 2019. http://www.goforbroke.org/learn/history/combat_history/world_war_2 /european_theater/north_apennines_campaigns.php.

Go for Broke National Education Center. "Rhineland Campaign-Vosges (September 15–November 21, 1944), the 100th/442nd RCT at Bruyeres, Belmont and Biffontaine (September 29–October 1944)." Accessed September 1, 2019. http://www.goforbroke.org/learn/history/combat_history /world_war_2/european_theater/rhineland_vosges.php.

Go for Broke National Education Center. "Rome-Arno Campaign (January 22–September 9, 1944), the 100th and the 442nd at Belvedere (June– September 1944)." Accessed September 1, 2019. http://www.goforbroke

.org/learn/history/combat_history/world_war_2/european_theater/rome
-arno_belvedere.php.

Go for Broke National Education Center. "Rome-Arno Campaign (January 22–September 9, 1944), the 100th at Cassino (January 24–February 11, 1944)." Accessed September 1, 2019. http://www.goforbroke.org/learn /history/combat_history/world_war_2/european_theater/rome-arno _cassino.php.

Grammarist.com. "Go for Broke." Accessed November 15, 2019. https:// grammarist.com/idiom/go-for-broke/.

Grubb, Abbie Salyers. "522nd Field Artillery Battalion." *Densho Encyclopedia*. https://encyclopedia.densho.org/522nd_Field_Artillery_Battalion/.

Grubb, Abbie Salyers. "Rescue of the Lost Battalion." *Densho Encyclopedia*. https://encyclopedia.densho.org/Rescue_of_the_Lost_Battalion/.

Haines, Lieutenant Marshall. Extract from a letter to Vernon McCann of the *Auburn (Calif.) Journal*, published in *The Pacific Citizen*, September 9, 1944. Online Archive of California. http://www.oac.cdlib.org.

Hall of Valor Project. "Irving M. Akahoshi." *Military Times*. Accessed November 24, 2019. https://valor.militarytimes.com/hero/21834.

Hall of Valor Project. "Young Oak Kim." *Military Times*. Accessed November 24, 2019. https://valor.militarytimes.com/hero/23053.

Hanley, James M. *A Matter of Honor: A Mémoire*. Springfield, MA: Vantage Press, 1995, pp. 51, 54, 61, 83.

Hatamiya, Leslie T. *Righting a Wrong: Japanese Americans and the Passage of the Civil Liberties Act of 1988*. Stanford, CA: Stanford University Press, 1993, p. 23.

Hawaii Nikkei History Editorial Board. "100th Infantry Battalion (Separate) the Purple Heart Battalion." In *Japanese Eyes, American Hearts: Personal Reflections of Hawaii's World War II Nisei Soldiers*. Honolulu, HI: University of Hawaii Press, 1998, p. 4.

Heart Mountain Film. "The Legacy of Heart Mountain—Dachau Liberation." September 7, 2015. https://www.youtube.com/watch?v=Kkp7l83MG48.

Higgins, Michael. "Trapped Texas Division Battalion in Vosges Forest

Relieved [*sic*] Today, 65 Years Ago." Japanese American Veterans Association, October 30, 2009. https://javadc.org/Press%20release%2010-30-09%20Trapped%20Texas%20Inf%20Div%20Battalion%20in%20Vosges%20Forests%20Relieved%2065%20Years%20Ago.htm.

Hirose, Stacey Yukari. "Japanese American Women and the Women's Army Corp, 1935–1950." M.A. thesis: University of California, Los Angeles, 1993, p. 26.

Historical Album Committee of the 522nd Field Artillery Battalion, 442nd Regimental Combat Team. *Fire for Effect: A Unit History of the 522nd Field Artillery Battalion.* Honolulu, HI: Fisher Printing Co., 1998, p. 12.

Huan, Woo Sung. *UnSung Hero: The Col. Young Oak Kim Story.* Translated by Edward T. Chang. Riverside, CA: Young Oak Kim Center for Korean American Studies, 2011, p. 74.

Japanese American Veterans Association. "The Japanese American Experience during World War II and Its Legacy." Accessed September 1, 2019. https://java.wildapricot.org/Nisei-Legacy.

Kim, Young Oak. "Keynote Address," Puka Puka Parades. July–August 1982, vol. 36, no. 3, 100th Infantry Battalion Veterans Educational Center. https://www.100thbattalion.org/archives/puka-puka-parades/european-campaigns/keynote-address-by-young-o-kim/

Learning Network. "May 7, 1945, Nazi Germany Surrenders in World War II." *New York Times,* May 7, 2012. https://learning.blogs.nytimes.com/2012/05/07/may-7-1945-nazi-germany-surrenders-in-world-war-ii/.

Lee, Jesse. "An Awe-Inspiring Chapter of America's History." The White House, President Barack Obama, Archives, October 5, 2010. https://obamawhitehouse.archives.gov/blog/2010/10/05/awe-inspiring-chapter-americas-history.

Masaoka, Mike M., with Bill Hosokawa. *They Call Me Moses Masaoka: An American Saga.* New York: William Morrow and Company, 1987, pp. 138, 144, 164–165, 175.

Matsuo, Dorothy. *Boyhood to War: History and Anecdotes of the 442nd Regi-*

mental Combat Team. Honolulu, HI: Mutual Publishing Company, 1992, pp. 44, 73, 125, 131, 202–203.

McDuff, Landon. "Remember the Alamo!-Anzio!: The Brave and Controversial Texas Army National Guard in WWII." New Hampshire State Elks Association. http://www.nh-elks.org/Doc/Mil_History.pdf.

McGaugh, Scott. *Honor before Glory: The Epic World War II Story of the Japanese American GIs Who Rescued the Lost Battalion*. Boston: Da Capo Press, 2016, pp. 198–200.

Moore, Brenda L. *Serving Our Country: Japanese American Women in the Military during World War II*. New Brunswick, NJ: Rutgers University Press, 2003, pp. 10–21.

Morita, Colonel Hiroaki. "The Nation's Most Decorated Military Unit, the 100th/442nd Regimental Combat Team." USAWC Military Studies Program Paper. Carlisle, PA: US Army War College, 1992. http://www.dtic.mil/dtic/tr/fulltext/u2/a249877.pdf.

Niiya, Brian. "Congressional Medal of Honor Recipients." *Densho Encyclopedia*. http://encyclopedia.densho.org/Congressional_Medal_of_Honor_recipients/.

Niiya, Brian. "Japanese Americans in Military during World War II." *Densho Encyclopedia*. https://encyclopedia.densho.org/Japanese_Americans_in_military_during_World_War_II/.

Nisei Veterans Legacy. *522 Liberates Dachau Prisoners*. Accessed August 19, 2019. https://www.nvlchawaii.org/522-liberates-dachau-prisoners.

Nisei Veterans Legacy. *Formation of 100th Infantry Battalion and 442nd Regimental Combat Team*. Accessed November 12, 2019. https://www.nvlchawaii.org/formation-100th-infantry-battalion-and-442nd-regimental-combat-team.

Odo, Franklin. "100th Infantry Battalion." *Densho Encyclopedia*. https://encyclopedia.densho.org/100th_Infantry_Battalion/.

Odo, Franklin. "442nd Regimental Combat Team." *Densho Encyclopedia*. https://encyclopedia.densho.org/442nd_Regimental_Combat_Team/.

O'Neill, Sgt. James P. "The Battle of Belvedere." *Yank Magazine: The Army*

Weekly, vol. 3, no. 10, August 25, 1944. http://www.100thbattalion.org /archives/puka-puka-parades/european-campaigns/italian-campaign/the -battle-of-belvedere.

Popa, Thomas A. "Po Valley: US Army Campaigns of World War II." Center of Military History (CMH Pub 72–33). Washington, DC: Department of the Army, 1995. https://history.army.mil/brochures/po/72-33.htm.

Robinson, Greg. *A Tragedy of Democracy: Japanese Confinement in North America*. New York: Columbia University Press, 2009, p. 209.

Saito, Marie. "Japanese American Women in Military." *Densho Encyclopedia*. http://encyclopedia.densho.org/Japanese_American_women_in_military/.

Schultz, Duane. "American Samurai." October 5, 2011. Historynet.com. https://www.historynet.com/american-samurai.htm.

Sexton, Ryan, and Judy Weightman, directors. "From Hawai'i to the Holocaust: A Shared Moment in History." The Hawaii Holocaust Project. https://resourceguide.densho.org/From%20Hawaii%20to%20the%20 Holocaust:%20A%20Shared%20Moment%20in%20History%20(film)/.

Shirey, Orville C. *Americans: The Story of the 442nd Combat Team*. Washington, D.C.: Infantry Journal Press, 1946, p. 20–21, 33.

Smithsonian Institution. "The Congressional Gold Medal." https://cgm .smithsonian.org/honors/congressional-gold-medal.html.

Steidl, Franz. *Lost Battalions: Going for Broke in the Vosges, Autumn 1944*. Novato, CA: Presidio Press, 1997, pp. 45, 48–49, 54, 57.

Sterner, C. Douglas. *Go for Broke: The Nisei Warriors of World War II Who Conquered Germany, Japan, and American Bigotry*. Clearfield, UT: American Legacy Historical Press, 2008, pp. 31–39, 64–66, 87.

Tanaka, Chester. *Go for Broke: A Pictorial History of the Japanese-American 100th Infantry Battalion and the 442nd Regimental Combat Team*. Novato, CA: Presidio Press, 1997, pp. 51, 80, 84, 88–89, 119.

Tanamachi, Sandra. "Marty Higgins at Age 90: Reflections of a Friend." Japanese American Veterans Association. September 2006, vol. 56, no. 8. https://www.nvcfoundation.org/newsletter/2006/9/marty-higgins-at-age -90-reflections-of-a-friend.

United States Holocaust Memorial Museum. "The 4th Infantry Division." *Holocaust Encyclopedia*. Accessed March 4, 2020. https://encyclopedia .ushmm.org/content/en/article/the-4th-infantry-division.

United States Holocaust Memorial Museum. "Capt. John Barnett Testifies to the Authenticity of Photos Taken When His Troops Overran the Dachau Concentration Camp at the Trial of Former Camp Personnel and Prisoners from Dachau." November 24, 1945. National Archives and Records Administration. https://collections.ushmm.org/search/catalog/pa1046003.

US Army Center of Military History. "Presidential Unit Citations (Army) Awarded to 100th Battalion and the 442nd Regimental Combat Team." https://history.army.mil/html/topics/apam/puc.html.

US Army Veteran Medals. "US Army Service, Campaign Medals and Foreign Awards Information." https://veteranmedals.army.mil/awardg&d.nsf /MedalsInformation.xsp.

Yenne, Bill. *Rising Sons: The Japanese American GIs Who Fought for the United States in World War II*. New York: Thomas Dunne Books, 2007, pp. 104, 181.

Chapter Nine

Asakawa, Gil. "Minoru Yasui." *Densho Encyclopedia*. https://encyclopedia .densho.org/Minoru_Yasui/.

Bannai, Lorraine K. *Enduring Conviction: Fred Korematsu and His Quest for Justice*. Seattle, WA: University of Washington Press, 2015, pp. 72, 83, 84, 94–95, 145–148.

Daniels, Roger. *The Japanese American Cases: The Rule of Law in Time of War*. Lawrence, KS: University Press of Kansas, 2013, pp. 56–58.

Densho Digital Repository. "Aiko Yoshinaga Herzig Interview." Interviewers: Larry Hashima and Glen Kitayama. Segment 7. September 11, 1997, University of California, Los Angeles. https://ddr.densho.org/media /ddr-densho-1000/ddr-densho-1000-16-transcript-35b7dd8cfa.htm.

Ex parte Endo, 323 US 283, 304 (1944). Accessed August 6, 2019. https:// supreme.justia.com/cases/federal/us/323/283/.

Feldman, Noah. *Scorpions: The Battles and Triumphs of FDR's Great Supreme Court Justices.* New York: Twelve, 2010, pp. 239–242.

Hirabayashi v. United States, 320 US 81, 99 (1943). Accessed August 6, 2019. https://supreme.justia.com/cases/federal/us/320/81/.

Hirabayashi, Gordon K. *A Principled Stand: The Story of* Hirabayashi v. United States. Seattle, WA: University of Washington Press, 2013, p. 133.

Imai, Shiho. *"Korematsu v. United States." Densho Encyclopedia.* https://encyclopedia.densho.org/Korematsu_v._United_States/.

Irons, Peter. "Fancy Dancing in the Marble Palace." University of Minnesota Law School, University of Minnesota Digital Conservancy, 1986. http://hdl.handle.net/11299/164753.

Irons, Peter. *Justice at War: The Story of the Japanese-American Internment Cases.* New York: Oxford University Press, 1983, pp. 91–93, 105, 150–151, 186, 195–197, 206–210, 219, 220–223, 226–271, 278–292.

Irons, Peter. *Justice Delayed: The Record of the Japanese American Internment Cases.* Middleton, CT: Wesleyan University Press, 1989, pp. 5–6, 296.

Korematsu v. United States, 323 US 214, 216, 225–226, 233, 242–243, 246 (1944). Accessed August 6, 2019. https://www.oyez.org/cases/1940-1955/323us214.

Pitzer, Andrea. "In the Wake of Pearl Harbor, a Secret Intel Report Could've Stopped the Internment Camps." Zocalo Public Square, January 18, 2017. https://www.zocalopublicsquare.org/2017/01/18/wake-pearl-harbor-secret-intel-report-couldve-stopped-internment-camps/chronicles/who-we-were/.

Ringle, Lieutenant Commander K. D. "Ringle Report on Japanese Internment." January 20, 1942. Naval History and Heritage Command. https://www.history.navy.mil/research/library/online-reading-room/title-list-alphabetically/r/ringle-report-on-japanese-internment.html.

Robinson, Greg. "Ex Parte Endo." *Densho Encyclopedia.* https://encyclopedia.densho.org/Ex_parte_Endo/.

Robinson, Greg. *A Tragedy of Democracy: Japanese Confinement in North*

America. New York: Columbia University Press, 2009, pp. 220–223.

Sterling v. Constantin, 287 US 378 (1932). Accessed December 2, 2019, https://supreme.justia.com/cases/federal/us/287/378/.

Supreme Court of the United States. "The Court and Its Procedures." Accessed December 8, 2019. https://www.supremecourt.gov/about/procedures.aspx.

US Department of Justice. "Office of the Solicitor General." Accessed December 8, 2019. https://www.justice.gov/osg.

US Department of Justice. "Solicitor General Charles Fahy." Accessed December 8, 2019. https://www.justice.gov/osg/bio/charles-fahy.

Yasui v. United States, 320 US 115 (1943). Accessed August 6, 2019. https://supreme.justia.com/cases/federal/us/320/115/.

Chapter Ten

Asaka, Megan. "Resettlement." *Densho Encyclopedia*. https://encyclopedia.densho.org/Resettlement/.

Atomic Heritage Foundation. "Hiroshima and Nagasaki Bombing Timeline." April 26, 2016. https://www.atomicheritage.org/history/hiroshima-and-nagasaki-bombing-timeline.

Bainbridge Public Library. "Lambert Schuyler: Local History." Accessed November 30, 2019. http://www.bainbridgepubliclibrary.org/lambert-schuyler.aspx.

Bainbridge Public Library. "Mary Woodward: Local History." Accessed November 30, 2019. http://www.bainbridgepubliclibrary.org/Mary-Woodward.aspx.

Ball, Howard. "Judicial Parsimony and Military Necessity Disinterred: A Reexamination of the Japanese Exclusion Cases, 1943–1944." In *Japanese Americans: From Relocation to Redress*, edited by Roger Daniels, Sandra C. Taylor, and Harry H.L. Kitano. Seattle, WA: University of Washington Press, 1991, p. 184.

Berg, Tom. "Family's Love of Country Overcame Injustices." *The Orange County Register*, May 27, 2014. https://www.ocregister.com/2014/05/27/familys-love-of-country-overcame-injustices/.

Bird, Kai. *The Chairman: John J. McCloy and the Making of the American Establishment.* New York: Simon & Schuster, 1992, p. 170.

Chandler, David P., Robert Cribb, and Li Narangoa, eds. *End of Empire: 100 Days in 1945 That Changed Asia and the World.* NIAS Asia Insights. Book 8. Copenhagen, Denmark: NIAS Press, 2016, pp. 73, 168.

Commission on Wartime Relocation and Internment of Civilians. *Personal Justice Denied.* Seattle, WA: University of Washington Press, 1997.

Commission on Wartime Relocation and Internment of Civilians. *Personal Justice Denied. Part 1 (December, 1982): Report of the Commission on Wartime Relocation and Internment of Civilians.* Washington, DC: US Government Printing Office, pp. 204, 224, 228, 240–241. https://www.archives .gov/files/research/japanese-americans/justice-denied/chapter-6.pdf.

Congressional Medal of Honor Society. "Kazuo Masuda Citation." http://cgm .smithsonianapa.org/stories/kazuo-masuda.html.

Davis, Daniel S. *Behind Barbed Wire: The Imprisonment of Japanese Americans during World War II.* New York: E. P. Dutton, 1982, p. 27.

Densho Digital Repository. "As General Stilwell Honored a Nisei Hero." *Pacific Citizen*, vol. 21, no. 24, December 15, 1945, p. 1. https://ddr.densho .org/media/ddr-pc-17/ddr-pc-17-50-mezzanine-51de48646b.pdf.

Densho Digital Repository. "Cemetery Offers Desired Plot for Burial of Nisei GI." *Pacific Citizen*, vol. 27, no. 22, November 27, 1948, p. 1. https://ddr .densho.org/media/ddr-pc-20/ddr-pc-20-47-mezzanine-2257b43865.pdf.

Densho Digital Repository. "General Stilwell Pins DSC on Sister of Nisei Hero in Ceremony at Masuda Ranch: 'Vinegar Joe' Participates in Americans United Rally in Santa Ana: Film Stars Pay Tribute to Combat Record of Japanese American Troops." *Pacific Citizen,* vol. 21, no. 24, December 15, 1945, p. 2. https://ddr.densho.org/media/ddr-pc-17/ddr-pc -17-50-mezzanine-51de48646b.pdf.

Densho Digital Repository. "Home Town Cemetery Bars Burial of Nisei War Hero." *Pacific Citizen,* vol. 27, no. 21, November 20, 1948, p. 1. https://ddr .densho.org/media/ddr-pc-20/ddr-pc-20-46-mezzanine-6f7a8e0a91.pdf.

Densho Digital Repository. "Ickes Blasts Terror Raids on Coast Evacuees: Says Hoodlums Seek Economic Beachhead on Properties of Japanese American Group." *Pacific Citizen*, vol. 20, no. 20, May 9, 1945, p. 3. https://ddr.densho.org/media/ddr-pc-17/ddr-pc-17-20-mezzanine-661c3aea03.pdf.

Densho Digital Repository. "Sheriff Elliot Says No Overt Acts Reported in County." *Pacific Citizen*, vol. 20, no. 20, May 9, 1945, p. 3. https://ddr.densho.org/media/ddr-pc-17/ddr-pc-17-20-mezzanine-661c3aea03.pdf.

Densho Digital Repository. "WRA Acts to Protect Nisei Girl on Coast." *Pacific Citizen*, vol. 20, no. 20, May 9, 1945, p. 3. https://ddr.densho.org/media/ddr-pc-17/ddr-pc-17-20-mezzanine-661c3aea03.pdf.

Fukuhara, Harry. "Military Occupation of Japan." *Discover Nikkei*, May 2, 2005. http://www.discovernikkei.org/en/journal/2005/5/2/military-occupation/.

Girdner, Audrie, and Anne Loftis. *The Great Betrayal: The Evacuation of the Japanese-Americans during World War II*. Toronto: The Macmillan Company, 1969, pp. 412–413.

Glass, Andrew. "US Rescinds Internment of Japanese-Americans, Dec. 17, 1944." *Politico*, December 16, 2016. https://www.politico.com/story/2016/12/us-rescinds-internment-of-japanese-americans-dec-17-1944-232630.

Hansen, Arthur A., ed. *Japanese American World War II Evacuation Oral History Project*. Interview with Ikuko Amatatsu Watanabe, July 24, 1974. California State University, Fullerton. Munich, Germany: K.G. Saur Verlag, 1995. http://www.oac.cdlib.org.

Hatamiya, Leslie T. *Righting a Wrong: Japanese Americans and the Passage of the Civil Liberties Act of 1988*. Stanford, CA: Stanford University Press, 1993, p. 24.

Hayashi, Brian Masaru. "All Center Conference." *Densho Encyclopedia*. http://encyclopedia.densho.org/All_Center_Conference/.

Hayashi, Brian Masaru. *Democratizing the Enemy: The Japanese American Internment*. Princeton, NJ: Princeton University Press, 2004, pp. 89, 197.

History.com Editors. "Battle of Okinawa." A&E Television Networks. *History*. October 29, 2009. https://www.history.com/topics/world-war-ii/battle-of-okinawa.

History.com Editors. "Japan Surrenders: 1945." A&E Television Networks. *History.* February 9, 2010. https://www.history.com/this-day-in-history /japan-surrenders.

History.com Editors. "United States Invades Luzon in Philippines." A&E Television Networks. *History.* November 9, 2009. https://www.history .com/this-day-in-history/united-states-invades-luzon-in-philippines.

Ickes, Harold, Secretary of the Interior. "Letter to 'My Dear Mr. President,' June 2, 1944." *Densho Encyclopedia.* http://encyclopedia.densho.org /media/encyc-psms/en-denshopd-i67-00087-1.pdf.

Irons, Peter. *Justice at War: The Story of the Japanese-American Internment Cases.* New York: Oxford University Press, 1983, pp. 277, 344.

Japanese American Veterans Association. *JAVA Advocate,* Summer 2018. https://java.wildapricot.org/resources/Documents/Advocate%20Summer %202018%20v2.pdf.

Kaji, Bruce T., with Sharon Yamato. *Jive Bomber: A Sentimental Journey.* Gardena, CA: Kaji & Associates, 2010, p. 74.

Kamei, Hiroshi. "Salutatory Address." Miles E. Cary High School, Poston II. Online Archive of California, University of California, Berkeley Bancroft Library. http://content.cdlib.org/ark:/13030/k6rb7bmj/FID1.

LeMay, Michael C. *Guarding the Gates: Immigration and National Security.* Westport, CT: Praeger Security International, 2006, p. 143.

Los Angeles Times. "Stilwell Salutes Nisei Hero's Family." December 9, 1945.

Mayumi, Misako. "Remembrance." Parker Valley High School, Poston III. Online Archive of California, University of California, Berkeley Bancroft Library. http://content.cdlib.org/ark:/13030/k6rb7bmj/FID1.

Myer, Dillon S. "Oral History Interview, July 7, 1970." Interviewer: Helen S. Pryor. Berkeley, California. University of California, Bancroft Library, Berkeley Regional Oral History Office. Harry S. Truman Presidential Library and Museum. Chapters IX–XIII. https://www.trumanlibrary.gov /library/oral-histories/myerds3.

National Archives and Records Administration. "Toranosuke Kamei File."

War Relocation Authority Collection, Record Group Number 210, Washington, DC.

Niedowski, Erika. "Prisoners of Their Heritage." *The Baltimore Sun*, December 6, 2004. https://www.baltimoresun.com/news/bal-te.camp06 dec06-story.html.

Niiya, Brian. "Kazuo Masuda." *Densho Encyclopedia*. https://encyclopedia .densho.org/Kazuo_Masuda/.

Niiya, Brian. "Return to West Coast." *Densho Encyclopedia*. https://encyclopedia .densho.org/Return_to_West_Coast/.

Ohashi, Mollie. "Modern Pioneers." Parker Valley High School, Poston III. Online Archive of California, University of California, Berkeley Bancroft Library. http://content.cdlib.org/ark:/13030/k6rb7bmj/FID1.

Pacific Citizen. "Memorial Day Ceremony at Arlington Cemetery Honors Japanese American Veterans." June 10, 2016. https://www.pacificcitizen.org /memorial-day-ceremony-at-arlington-cemetery-honors-japanese-american -veterans/.

Quinn, Ruth. "Torn Between Two Countries—Colonel Harry K. Fukuhara." *The US Army*, May 9, 2014. https://www.army.mil/article/125716/torn _between_two_countries_colonel_harry_k_fukuhara.

Robinson, Greg. *By Order of the President: FDR and the Internment of Japanese Americans*. Cambridge, MA: Harvard University Press, 2001, p. 250.

Robinson, Greg. "Ex Parte Endo." *Densho Encyclopedia*. https://encyclope-dia.densho.org/Ex_parte_Endo/.

Robinson, Greg. "The Great Unknown and the Unknown Great: Poet, Writer Mary Oyama Mittwer Championed Literary and Intellectural Exchanges." *Nichi Bei*, December 20, 2012. https://www.nichibei.org/2012/12/the -great-unknown-and-the-unknown-great-poet-writer-mary-oyama-mittwer -championed-literary-and-intellectual-exchanges/.

Robinson, Greg. *A Tragedy of Democracy: Japanese Confinement in North America*. New York: Columbia University Press, 2009, pp. 250, 252.

Schuyler, Lambert. *The Japs Must Not Come Back! A Practical Approach to the Racial Problem*. Winslow, WA: Heron House, 1944. https://oac.cdlib.org/ark:/13030/kt4489r763/?order=4&brand=oac4.

Seigel, Shizue. *In Good Conscience: Supporting Japanese Americans during the Internment*. San Mateo, CA: Asian American Curriculum Project, 2006, p. 2.

Shindo, Richard. "We, the Class of 1945." Poston High School. Online Archive of California, University of California, Berkeley Bancroft Library. http://content.cdlib.org/ark:/13030/k6rb7bmj/FID1.

Smith, Robert Ross. *The War in the Pacific: Triumph in the Philippines*. Center of Military History (CMH-Pub-5-10-1). Washington, DC: Department of the Army, 1963. https://history.army.mil/html/books/005/5-10-1/CMH_Pub_5-10-1.pdf.

Speidel, Jennifer. "After Internment: Seattle's Debate over Japanese Americans' Right to Return Home." Seattle Civil Rights & Labor History Project, University of Washington, 2005. http://depts.washington.edu/civilr/after_internment.htm.

Tamura, Linda. "Hood River Incident." *Densho Encyclopedia*. https://encyclopedia.densho.org/Hood_River_incident/.

US Department of the Interior and War Relocation Authority. *WRA: A Story of Human Conservation*. US Government Printing Office, 1946, p. 135. https://archive.org/details/wrastoryofhumanc00unit.

Weglyn, Michi Nishiura, *Years of Infamy: The Untold Story of America's Concentration Camps*. Seattle, WA: University of Washington Press, 1976, pp. 219–220.

Western Defense Command and Fourth Army. "Public Proclamation No. 21." December 17, 1944. California State University, Dominguez Hills. CSU Japanese American Digitization Project. https://calisphere.org.

Wilkinson, Sook, and Victor Jew, eds. *Asian Americans in Michigan: Voices from the Midwest*. Detroit, MI: Wayne State University Press, 2015, p. 240.

Williams, Duncan Ryūken. *American Sutra: A Story of Faith and Freedom in the Second World War*. Cambridge, MA: The Belknap Press of Harvard University Press, 2019, p. 228.

Williams, Duncan Ryūken. "The Karma of Becoming American." *Densho Encyclopedia*, July 4, 2020. https://densho.org/the-karma-of-becoming-american/.

Woodward, Mary. *In Defense of Our Neighbors: The Walt and Milly Woodward Story*. Bainbridge Island, WA: Fenwick Publishing Group, Inc., 2008, pp. 63–65, 100–115, 118, 142.

Chapter Eleven

100th Infantry Battalion Veterans Education Center. "Sparky Matsunaga." Accessed July 12, 2019. http://www.100thbattalion.org/history/veterans-in-public-service/sparky-matsunaga/.

Asakawa, Gil. "Bill Hosokawa." *Densho Encyclopedia*. http://encyclopedia.densho.org/Bill_Hosokawa.

Associated Press. "Hayakawa Denounces Claims of Nisei for Internment Pay." *New York Times*, August 5, 1981. https://www.nytimes.com/1981/08/05/us/hayakawa-denounces-claims-of-nisei-for-internment-pay.html.

Bannai, Lorraine K. *Enduring Conviction: Fred Korematsu and His Quest for Justice*. Seattle, WA: University of Washington Press, 2015, pp. 126–127, 137, 139, 150–152, 154–158, 160–161, 168, 186–188, 191.

Biographical Directory. "Matsunaga, Spark Masayuki (1916–1990)." US Congress. Accessed November 19, 2019. https://bioguideretro.congress.gov/Home/MemberDetails?memIndex=m000250.

Bird, Kai. *The Chairman: John J. McCloy and the Making of the American Establishment*. New York: Simon & Schuster, 1992, p. 659.

Broom, Leonard, and Ruth Riemer. *Removal and Return: The Socio-Economic Effects of the War on Japanese Americans*. Berkeley, CA: University of California Press, 1949, pp. 198–204.

Chan, Jeffrey Paul, Frank Chin, Lawson Fusao Inada, and Shawn Wong, eds. *The Big Aiiieeeee!: An Anthology of Chinese American and Japanese American Literature*. New York: Plume, 1991.

Civil Liberties Act of 1988. Public Law 100-383. Washington, DC: US Government Publishing Office. https://www.govinfo.gov/content/pkg/STATUTE-102/pdf/STATUTE-102-Pg903.pdf.

Commission on the Wartime Relocation and Internment of Civilians Los Angeles Hearings Video Collection, Nikkei for Civil Rights and Redress and Visual Communications. Reissued in 2018 on DVD as *Speak Out for Justice*.

Commission on Wartime Relocation and Internment of Civilians. *Personal Justice Denied*. Seattle, WA: University of Washington Press, 1997.

Commission on Wartime Relocation and Internment of Civilians. *Personal Justice Denied. Part 1 (December, 1982): Report of the Commission on Wartime Relocation and Internment of Civilians*. Washington, DC: US Government Printing Office, pp. 238, 297–301, 459. https://www.archives .gov/files/research/japanese-americans/justice-denied/chapter-8.pdf.

Commission on Wartime Relocation and Internment of Civilians. *Personal Justice Denied. Part 2 (June, 1983): Recommendations; Report of the Commission on Wartime Relocation and Internment of Civilians*. Washington, DC: US Government Printing Office. https://www.archives.gov/files/research /japanese-americans/justice-denied/part-2-recommendations.pdf.

Congressional Record, 101st Congress, 1st Session, vol. 135, no. 128, September 29, 1989, S 12218-19, Remarks, Senator Daniel K. Inouye. https://webarchive.loc.gov/congressional-record/20160517151609/http:// thomas.loc.gov/cgi-bin/query/F?r101:1:./temp/~r101dChu4s:e254271:.

Daniels, Roger. *The Japanese American Cases: The Rule of Law in Time of War*. Lawrence, KS: University Press of Kansas, 2013, pp. 167–168, 171– 172, 174–178, 182, 184–186.

Daniels, Roger, Sandra C. Taylor, and Harry H.L. Kitano, eds. *Japanese Americans: From Relocation to Redress*. Seattle, WA: University of Washington Press, 1991, p. 4.

Daniloff, Brittany Alicia. "Through Innocent Eyes: Childhood and the Japanese American Incarceration Experience." M.A. thesis: San Diego State University, 2016. https://sdsu-dspace.calstate.edu/bitstream/handle /10211.3/173725/Daniloff_sdsu_0220N_11424.pdf?sequence=1.

Densho Digital Repository. "Grant Ujifusa Interview II." Segments 8–12. March 2, 2002, Seattle, WA. http://ddr.densho.org/interviews/ddr-densho -1000-133-1/.

Densho Digital Repository. "Harry Kawahara Interview." Segment 18. September 20, 2011, Los Angeles, CA. http://ddr.densho.org/narrators/610/.

Densho Digital Repository. "Jim Matsuoka Interview." Segments 38–39. May 24, 2010, Los Angeles, CA. http://ddr.densho.org/narrators/484/.

Densho Digital Repository. "Norman Mineta Interview." July 4, 2008, Denver, CO. https://psms.densho.org/psms/media/sources/1/1643/en-denshovh-mnorman-01-0007-1.htm.

Densho Encyclopedia. "Written Apology Which Accompanied Reparations Checks." October 1990. https://encyclopedia.densho.org/sources/en-ddr-densho-153-20-1.

Duus, Masayo. *Tokyo Rose, Orphan of the Pacific*. Japan: Kodansha International, 1979, pp. 25, 32, 53.

Embrey, Sue Kunitomi. "From Manzanar to the Present: A Personal Journey." In *Last Witnesses: Reflections on the Wartime Internment of Japanese Americans*, edited by Erica Harth. New York: Palgrave, 2001, p. 180.

Felzenberg, Alvin S. *Governor Tom Kean: From the New Jersey Statehouse to the 9-11 Commission*. New Brunswick, NJ: Rutgers University Press, 2006, pp. 309–311.

Ford, Gerald R. "Proclamation 4417, Confirming the Termination of the Executive Order Authorizing Japanese-American Internment during World War II." February 19, 1976. https://www.fordlibrarymuseum.gov/library/speeches/760111p.htm.

Friedman, Max Paul. "The US Internment of Families from Latin America in World War II." *DEP: Deportate, Esuli e Profughe*, September 9, 2008. https://www.unive.it/pag/fileadmin/user_upload/dipartimenti/DSLCC/documenti/DEP/numeri/n9/04_Dep009Friedman-saggio.pdf.

Goto, June Masuda. "Letter to Ronald Reagan," December 19, 1987. ID 544222, Ronald Reagan Library.

Hatamiya, Leslie T. *Righting a Wrong: Japanese Americans and the Passage of the Civil Liberties Act of 1988*. Stanford, CA: Stanford University Press, 1993, pp. 43, 45, 82–83, 85–86, 88, 91–92, 99, 109, 133, 142–143, 145, 151–153, 158–164, 177, 201.

Hayakawa, S. I. "Testimony of S. I. Hayakawa." Commission on Wartime Relocation and Internment of Civilians Hearing. August 4, 1981, Los Angeles, CA. https://www.archives.gov/research/japanese-americans/hearings. CWRIC Los Angeles Hearings Video Collection, Nikkei for Civil Rights and Redress and Visual Communications. Reissued in 2018 on DVD as *Speak Out for Justice.*

Hayashi, Brian Masaru. *Democratizing the Enemy: The Japanese American Internment.* Princeton, NJ: Princeton University Press, 2004, pp. 197, 211.

Higgins, Anne. "Letter to Mr. Hiroshi Kamei." June 15, 1998, the White House, Washington, DC. Personal collection of Susan H. Kamei.

Hirabayashi, Gordon K. *A Principled Stand: The Story of* Hirabayashi v. United States. Seattle, WA: University of Washington Press, 2013, pp. 182, 186–188.

Hirabayashi v. United States, 627 F. Supp. 1145, 1457–1458 (W.D. Wash. 1986). https://www.courtlistener.com/opinion/1974210/hirabayashi-v-united -states/?q=Hirabayashi%20627%20F.%20Supp&type=o&order_by= score%20desc&stat_Precedential=on.

Hirabayashi v. United States, 828 F.2d 591, 593 (9th Cir. 1987). https:// casetext.com/case/hirabayashi-v-us.

Hohri, William. "Redress As a Movement Towards Enfranchisement." In *Japanese Americans: From Relocation to Redress*, edited by Roger Daniels, Sandra C. Taylor, and Harry H.L. Kitano. Seattle, WA: University of Washington Press, 1991, pp. 196–197, 199.

Honda, Harry. "Reagan Signs Redress Bill." *Pacific Citizen*, August 19–26, 1988, p. 1. http://ddr.densho.org/media/ddr-pc-60/ddr-pc-60-29-mezzanine -45fedc9398.pdf.

Hosokawa, Bill. *Nisei: The Quiet Americans*, revised ed. Boulder, CO: University Press of Colorado, 2002, pp. 473–474, 495–497.

Ibata, David. "History Her Way." *Chicago Tribune*, December 23, 1993. https://www.chicagotribune.com/news/ct-xpm-1993-12-23-9312230141 -story.html.

Internal Security Act of 1950, US Statutes at Large, 81st Congress, 2nd Session, Chapter 1024, pp. 987–1031. https://www.loc.gov/law/help/statutes-at-large/81st-congress/session-2/c81s2ch1024.pdf.

Irons, Peter, ed. *Justice Delayed: The Record of the Japanese American Internment Cases*. Middleton, OH: Wesleyan University Press, 1989, pp. 18, 24–26, 29–30.

Ishizuka, Karen L. *Lost & Found: Reclaiming the Japanese American Incarceration*. Urbana and Chicago: University of Illinois Press, 2006, p. 5.

Isumi, Masumi. "Repeal of Title II of the Internal Security Act of 1950 ('Emergency Detention Act')." *Densho Encyclopedia*. https://encyclopedia.densho.org/Repeal_of_Title_II_of_the_Internal_Security_Act_of_1950_(%22Emergency_Detention_Act%22)/.

Kamei, Susan H. Personal conversation with Hiroshi Kamei. Washington, DC, August 10, 1988.

Kean, Thomas H. "Letter to Ronald Reagan," February 6, 1987. ID 54222, Ronald Reagan Library.

Komai, Chris. "The Unseen Price of Redress." *Discover Nikkei*, February 19, 2016. https://www.discovernikkei.org/en/journal/2016/2/19/unseen-price-of-redress/.

Korematsu v. United States, 584 F. Supp. 1406, 1420 (N.D. Cal. 1984). https://law.justia.com/cases/federal/district-courts/FSupp/584/1406/2270281/.

Lee, Erika. "The WWII Incarceration of Japanese Americans Stretched beyond U.S. Borders." *Time*, December 4, 2019. https://time.com/5743555/wwii-incarceration-japanese-latin-americans/.

Ling, Huping, and Allan W. Austin, eds. *Asian American History and Culture: An Encyclopedia*. New York: Routledge, 2010, pp. 422–423.

Mak, Stephen. "Japanese Latin Americans." *Densho Encyclopedia*. http://encyclopedia.densho.org/Japanese_Latin_Americans/.

Maki, Mitchell T., and Darcie Iki, interviewers. "Appointing John Tateishi As National JACL Redress Chair: Clifford Uyeda." *Discover Nikkei*, July 1–2, 1998. http://www.discovernikkei.org/en/interviews/clips/973/

Maki, Mitchell T., Harry H.L. Kitano, and S. Megan Berthold. *Achieving the Impossible Dream: How Japanese Americans Obtained Redress*. Urbana,

Chicago and Springfield: University of Illinois Press, 1999, pp. x, 66, 190, 193–197, 200.

Manzanar Committee. "Alan Nishio: More Than 40 Years of Activism, Leadership and Mentorship." Accessed September 15, 2019. https://manzanar committee.org/2017/03/31/nishio-alm-2017ske/.

Michaelson, Judith. "Hearings a Catharsis for Internees: 'Quiet Americans' Break Silence." *Los Angeles Times*, August 7, 1981, Metro, Part II, pp. 1, 2, 5. https://www.newspapers.com/image/387293800.

Miller, Judith. "Wartime Internment of Japanese Was 'Grave Injustice,' Panel Says." *New York Times*, February 25, 1983, Section A, p. 1. https://www.nytimes.com/1983/02/25/us/wartime-internment-of-japanese-was -grave-injustice-panel-says.html.

Minami, Dale. "*Coram Nobis* and Redress." In *Japanese Americans: From Relocation to Redress*, edited by Roger Daniels, Sandra C. Taylor, and Harry H.L. Kitano. Seattle, WA: University of Washington Press, 1991, pp. 200–201.

Minami, Dale. "Japanese-American Redress." *Berkeley Journal of African-American Law & Policy*, vol. 6, no. 1, article 4 (2004). https://scholarship .law.berkeley.edu/bjalp/vol6/iss1/4/.

Miyoshi, Nobu, MSW. "Identity Crisis of the Sansei and the Concentration Camp." Sansei Legacy Project, Legacies of Camp Conference, March 13–15, 1998. San Francisco, CA. The Civil Liberties Public Education Fund. http://www.momomedia.com/CLPEF/sansei/identity.htm.

Molotsky, Irvin. "Senate Votes to Compensate Japanese-American Internees." *New York Times*, April 21, 1988. http://www.nytimes.com/1988/04/21/us /senate-votes-to-compensate-japanese-american-internees.html.

Murray, Alice Yang. *Historical Memories of the Japanese American Internment and the Struggle for Redress*. Stanford, CA: Stanford University Press, 2008, pp. 2–4, 164, 207–212, 233–237, 250–256, 287–299, 304–305, 313–329, 349–351, 366–379.

Nagano, Steve. "CWRIC Day of Rembrance [*sic*] Short." *Speak Out for Justice*, recordings of the August 1981 CWRIC Los Angeles hearings. Filmed by

CHAPTER SOURCES · 677

Nikkei for Civil Rights and Redress and Visual Communications. YouTube, July 14, 2017. https://www.youtube.com/watch?v=7ICyd9XvNYY.

Nagata, Donna. "Psychological Effects of Camp." *Densho Encyclopedia.* https://encyclopedia.densho.org/Psychological_effects_of_camp/.

Naito, Calvin, and Esther Scott. "Against All Odds: The Japanese Americans' Campaign for Redress." Harvard University John F. Kennedy School of Government Case Program. C16-90-1006.0, January 1, 1990, pp. 8, 10–11, 25. https://case.hks.harvard.edu/against-all-odds-the-campaign-in-congress-for-japanese-american-redress/.

Nakagawa, Martha. "Sue Kunitomi Embrey." *Densho Encyclopedia.* https://encyclopedia.densho.org/Sue_Kunitomi_Embrey/.

Nakamura, Kelli Y. "Spark Matsunaga." *Densho Encylopedia.* https://encyclopedia.densho.org/Spark_Matsunaga/.

Nash, Phil Tajitsu. Award announcement for *Years of Infamy: The Untold Story of America's Concentration Camps*, by Michi Weglyn. Anisfield-Wolf Book Awards, 1977 Nonfiction. https://www.anisfield-wolf.org/winners/years-of-infamy-the-untold-story-of-americas-concentration-camps/.

National Archives and Records Administration. "Commission on Wartime Relocation and Internment of Civilians Public Hearings and Testimonies." Accessed August 29, 2019. https://www.archives.gov/research/japanese-americans/hearings.

National Archives and Records Administration. "Records of Rights: First Amendment Rights: Internal Security Act of 1950." David M. Rubenstein Gallery. Accessed December 15, 2019. http://recordsofrights.org/events/82/internal-security-act.

New York Times. "Ex-Aide Calls Japanese Internment 'Humane.'" November 4, 1981. http://www.nytimes.com/1981/11/04/us/ex-aide-calls-japanese-internment-humane.html.

New York Times. "World War II Internment Is Defended." November 3, 1981. https://www.nytimes.com/1981/11/03/us/world-war-ii-internment-is-defended.html.

Niiya, Brian. "Farewell to Manzanar." *Densho Encyclopedia*. http://encyclopedia.densho.org/Farewell_to_Manzanar_(book)/.

Niiya, Brian. "No-No Boy." *Densho Encyclopedia*. http://encyclopedia.densho.org/No-no_boys/.

Niiya, Brian. "Seattle Evacuation Redress Committee." *Densho Encyclopedia*. http://encyclopedia.densho.org/Seattle_Evacuation_Redress_Committee/.

Oishi, Gene. "The Anxiety of Being a Japanese-American." *New York Times Magazine*, April 28, 1985. https://www.nytimes.com/1985/04/28/magazine/the-anxiety-of-being-a-japanese-american.html?pagewanted=all.

Okada, John. *No-No Boy*. Seattle, WA: University of Washington Press, 1976.

P.C. Staff. "Plenary Reveals Maneuvers That Helped Redress Succeed." *Pacific Citizen*, August 16, 2019. https://www.pacificcitizen.org/plenary-reveals-maneuvers-that-helped-redress-succeed/.

P.C. Staff. "San Diego JACL Reflects, Remembers on 30th Anniversary of Redress." *Pacific Citizen*, October 12, 2018. https://www/pacificcitizen.org/san-diego-jacl-reflects-remembers-on-30th-anniversary-of-redress/.

Pippert, Wesley G. "A Onetime Occupant of an Internment Camp Today Dramatically . . ." UPI, November 3, 1981. http://www.upi.com/Archives/1981/11/03/A-onetime-occupant-of-an-internment-camp-today-dramatically/6561373611600/.

Pippert, Wesley G. "We Were All Victims." UPI, November 3, 1981. https://www.upi.com/Archives/1981/11/03/We-were-all-victims/6352373611600/.

Pryor, Dick. "*Korematsu v. United States*: 'Decided on a Foundation of Fraud,'" *KGOU Sunday Radio Matinee*, February 20, 2020. https://www.kgou.org/post/korematsu-v-united-states-decided-foundation-fraud.

Reagan, Ronald. President Reagan's Remarks and Signing Ceremony for the Japanese-American Internment Compensation Bill (HR442) in the OEOB in Washington, DC, on August 10, 1988. Ronald Reagan Presidential Library. https://www.youtube.com/watch?v=kcaQRhcBXKY.

Robinson, Greg. "Japanese American Evacuation Claims Act." *Densho Encyclopedia*. http://encyclopedia.densho.org/Japanese_American_Evacuation_Claims_Act/.

Robinson, Greg. *A Tragedy of Democracy: Japanese Confinement in North America*. New York: Columbia University Press, 2009, pp. 171–172, 289–293, 296–299.

Sakamoto, Louise. "JACL and the Campaign for Redress." *Rafu Shimpo*, July 2, 2019. https://www.rafu.com/2019/07/jacl-and-the-campaign-for-redress/.

Smithsonian Institution. National Museum of American History, Behring Center. "Righting a Wrong: Japanese Americans and World War II—Redress Payments." https://americanhistory.si.edu/righting-wrong-japanese-americans-and-world-war-ii/redress-payments.

Stewart, Jocelyn Y. "Sue Kunitomi Embrey, 83; Former Internee Pushed for Historic Status of Manzanar." *Los Angeles Times*, May 16, 2006. http://articles.latimes.com/2006/may/16/local/me-embrey16.

Svahn, John A. *"There Must Be a Pony in Here Somewhere": Twenty Years with Ronald Reagan: A Memoir*. Minneapolis, MN: Langdon Street Press, 2011, pp. 275–279.

Tamashiro, Ben. "Spark Masayuki Matsunaga." *Puka Puka Parades*, May 1990. http://www.100thbattalion.org/archives/puka-puka-parades/veterans/officers/spark-masayuki-matsunaga/.

Tateishi, John. "For the Record: Dan." *Pacific Citizen*, January 18–31, 2013. https://pacificcitizen.org/wp-content/uploads/archives-menu/Vol.156_%2301_Jan_18_2013.pdf.

Tateishi, John. "The Japanese American Citizens League and the Struggle for Redress." In *Japanese Americans: From Relocation to Redress*, edited by Roger Daniels, Sandra C. Taylor, and Harry H.L. Kitano. Seattle, WA: University of Washington Press, 1991, pp. 192, 194–195.

Tateishi, John. *Redress: The Inside Story of the Successful Campaign for Japanese American Reparations*. Berkeley, CA: Heyday, 2020, pp. 331–332.

Ujifusa, Grant. "Grant Ujifusa's Keynote Speech at JAVA Quarterly Lunch in October 2013." Japanese American Veterans Association, October 12, 2013. http://javadc.org/event/grant-ujifusa-keynote-speech-at-java-quarterly-lunch-in-october-2013/.

Ujifusa, Grant. "Letter to Governor Tom Kean," November 24, 1987, ID 544222, Ronald Reagan Presidential Library. https://www.grantujifusa .org/pdfs/Three%20Letters.pdf.

Ujifusa, Grant. "With Gratitude to Kaz Masuda, the Hero of Fountain Valley." *Rafu Shimpo,* March 1, 2012. https://www.rafu.com/2012/03/with-gratitude-to-kaz-masuda-the-hero-of-fountain-valley/.

Unidos US. https://unidosus.org/about-us/.

US Congresswoman Doris Matsui. Accessed August 19, 2019. https://matsui .house.gov/.

Uyehara, Grayce. "Dear JACL Friends." Japanese American Citizens League Legislative Education Committee, August 25, 1988. Personal collection of Susan H. Kamei.

Uyehara, Grayce. "Immediate and Urgent Action to Obtain Presidential Signature on the Japanese American and Aleuts Redress Bill," Action Alert #9. Japanese American Citizens League Legislative Education Committee, May 6, 1988. Personal collection of Susan H. Kamei.

Wakida, Patricia. "No-No Boy (book)." *Densho Encyclopedia.* https:// encyclopedia.densho.org/No-No_Boy_(book)/.

Watanabe, Teresa. "Manzanar Pilgrimage Takes on Broad Themes of Democracy, Civil Rights." *Los Angeles Times*, April 27, 2019. https://www .latimes.com/local/lanow/la-me-ln-manzanar-50th-annual-pilgrimage -20190427-story.html.

Weglyn, Michi Nishiura. *Years of Infamy: The Untold Story of America's Concentration Camps.* Seattle, WA: University of Washington Press, 1976, p. 273.

Woodrum, Eric. "An Assessment of Japanese American Assimilation, Pluralism, and Subordination." *American Journal of Sociology.* vol. 87, no. 1, 1981. University of Chicago Press, pp. 157–169. https://www.jstor.org/stable /2778543?seq=1#page_scan_tab_contents.

Yamato, Sharon. "Civil Liberties Act of 1988." *Densho Encyclopedia.* https:// encyclopedia.densho.org/Civil_Liberties_Act_of_1988/.

Yang, Alice. "Redress Movement." *Densho Encyclopedia*. https://encyclopedia
.densho.org/Redress_movement/.

Yasui, Holly, and Will Doolittle. "Never Give Up! Minoru Yasui and the Fight
for Justice." Minoru Yasui Film, 2018. https://www.minoruyasuifilm.org/.

Yogi, Stan. "Peter Irons." *Densho Encyclopedia*. http://encyclopedia.densho
.org/Peter_Irons/.

Chapter Twelve

Brief of Karen Korematsu, Jay Hirabayashi, Holly Yasui, the Fred T. Korematsu Center for Law and Equality, Civil Rights Organizations, and National
Bar Associations of Color as *Amici Curiae* in Support of Respondents,
Trump v. Hawaii, 138 S. Ct. 2392, 585 US __ (2018). Accessed August
28, 2019. https://supreme.justia.com/cases/federal/us/585/17-965/#tab
-opinion-3920355.

Chordas, Peter. "60 Years after Sadako Sasaki's Death, the Story behind Hiroshima's Paper Cranes Is Still Unfolding." *The Japan Times*, August 1, 2018.
https://www.japantimes.co.jp/community/2018/08/01/issues/60-years
-sadakos-death-story-behind-hiroshimas-paper-cranes-still-unfolding/.

Densho Education. "A Cabinet Meeting the Day after 9/11—Norman
Mineta." April 9, 2015. https://www.youtube.com/watch?v=VH7rGPX
GicM.

Duke Law News. "Panel Considers Travel Ban Ruling and Parallels with
Korematsu." September 6, 2018. https://law.dusselier.edu/news/panel
-considers-travel-ban-ruling-and-parallels-korematsu/.

Fares, Melissa. "75 Years Later, Japanese Americans Recall Pain of Internment Camps." Reuters, February 17, 2017. https://www.reuters.com
/article/us-usa-japanese-anniversary/75-years-later-japanese-americans
-recall-pain-of-internment-camps-idUSKBN15W2E2.

Federal Register. Executive Order 13769 of January 27, 2017: Protecting the Nation from Foreign Terrorist Entry into the United States.
82 Federal Register 8977. https://www.federalregister.gov/documents

/2017/02/01/2017-02281/protecting-the-nation-from-foreign-terrorist
-entry-into-the-united-states.

Federal Register. Executive Order 13780 of March 6, 2017: Protecting
the Nation from Foreign Terrorist Entry into the United States. 82
Federal Register 13209. https://www.federalregister.gov/documents
/2017/03/09/2017-04837/protecting-the-nation-from-foreign-terrorist
-entry-into-the-united-states.

Federal Register. Proclamation 9645 of September 24, 2017: Enhanc-
ing Vetting Capabilities and Processes for Detecting Attempted Entry
into the United States by Terrorists or Other Public-Safety Threats."
82 Federal Register 45161. https://www.federalregister.gov/documents
/2017/09/27/2017-20899/enhancing-vetting-capabilities-and-processes
-for-detecting-attempted-entry-into-the-united-states-by.

Fenwick, Ben. "'Stop Repeating History': Plan to Keep Migrant Children at
Former Internment Camp Draws Outrage." *New York Times*, June 22,
2019. https://www.nytimes.com/2019/06/22/us/fort-sill-protests-japanese
-internment.html.

Grossman, Ron. "Flashback: When Japanese-Americans Were Sent to
Internment Camps." *Chicago Tribune*, February 9, 2017. https://www
.chicagotribune.com/opinion/commentary/ct-japanese-internment
-camps-war-trump-roosevelt-flashback-perspec-0212-jm-20170208-story
.html.

Hayoun, Massoud. "Muslim Ban: Japanese and Muslim Americans Join Forces:
Japanese Americans Remember Discrimination They Endured during
WWII and Say They Will Defend Muslim Americans." *Al Jazeera*, February 1, 2017. https://www.aljazeera.com/indepth/features/2017/02/muslim
-ban-japanese-muslim-americans-join-forces-170201055155362.html.

Hayoun, Massoud. "US: Remembering Japanese Internment Camps 75
Years On." *Al Jazeera*, February 19, 2017. https://www.aljazeera.com
/indepth/features/2017/02/remembering-japanese-internment-camps-75
-years-170213095548604.html.

History.com Editors. "9/11 Attacks." A&E Television Networks. *History*. Accessed September 5, 2019. https://www.history.com/topics/21st-century /9-11-attacks.

Hosokawa, Robert R. "We Knew We Weren't the Enemy." *Christian Science Monitor*, July 28, 2004. https://www.csmonitor.com/2004/0728/p09s01 -coop.html.

Kang, Jerry. "Thinking through Internment: 12/7 and 9/11." *Amerasia Journal*, vol. 27, no. 3, 2001, pp. 41–50. https://doi.org/10.17953/ amer.27.3.03274p4758752710.

Katyal, Neal. "Confession of Error: The Solicitor General's Mistakes during the Japanese-America Internment Cases." The White House, President Barack Obama, May 20, 2011. https://obamawhitehouse .archives.gov/blog/2011/05/20/confession-error-solicitor-generals -mistakes-during-japanese-american-internment-cas.

Katyal, Neal Kumar. "*Trump v. Hawaii*: How the Supreme Court Simultaneously Overturned and Revived *Korematsu*." *The Yale Law Journal*, vol. 128, January 30, 2019. https://www.yalelawjournal.org/forum /trump-v-hawaii#:~:text=abstract.,of%20Japanese%20Americans%20 in%20Korematsu.

Knight, Karen. "Recollections of Internment Camp Remain with Octogenarian." *Cape May County Herald*, March 15, 2018. https://www .capemaycountyherald.com/news/article_0acdf71a-285e-11e8-a1a3 -339e29c0995f.html.

Marcuse, Harold. "The Origin and Reception of Martin Niemoller's Quotation, 'First they came for the Communists . . .'" In *Remembering for the Future: Armenia, Auschwitz, and Beyond*, edited by Michael Berenbaum, Richard Libowitz, and Marcia Sachs Littell. Saint Paul, MN: Paragon House, 2016, pp. 173–199.

Matsuzawa, Kara. "Internment Camps." Interview of Joe Matsuzawa.

Merriam-Webster.com Dictionary. "Definition of 'Allyship.'" https://www .merriam-webster.com/dictionary/allyship.

Rafu Shimpo. "Plan to House Children at Ft. Sill Placed on Hold." July 29, 2019. https://www.rafu.com/2019/07/plan-to-house-children-at-ft-sill-placed -on-hold/.

Sawhney, Pia. "Then and Now: From Internment Camps to Muslim Bans: A Conversation with Pia Sawhney." Medium, October 17, 2017. https:// medium.com/@PiaS/then-and-now-191e73cd2b1a.

Stone, Geoffrey R. "It Can Happen Here: The 75th Anniversary of the Japanese Internment: Part I." *Huffington Post*, November 19, 2017. https:// www.huffingtonpost.com/entry/5a10b5e2e4b0e6450602eb9c.

Stone, Geoffrey R. "It Can Happen Here: The 75th Anniversary of the Japanese Internment: Part II." *Huffington Post*, November 19, 2017. https://www .huffingtonpost.com/entry/it-can-happen-here-the-75th-anniversary -of-the-japanese_us_5a121186e4b023121e0e9439.

Stone, Geoffrey R. "It Can Happen Here: The 75th Anniversary of the Japanese Internment: Part III." *Huffington Post*, November 21, 2017. https://www .huffingtonpost.com/entry/it-can-happen-here-the-75th-anniversary -of-the-japanese_us_5a135f12e4b05ec0ae8444e2.

Stop Repeating History. Accessed December 19, 2019. https://www.stop repeatinghistory.org/.

Trump v. Hawaii, 138 S. Ct. 2392, 585 US __ (2018). https://www.supremecourt .gov/opinions/17pdf/17-965_h315.pdf.

Appendices

Arakawa, Adele. "Amache HS Valedictorian Returning after More Than 70 Years." 9News, May 24, 2016. https://www.9news.com/article/news /local/amache-hs-valedictorian-returning-after-more-than-70-years/73 -205371370/.

Army.mil. "D-Day." Accessed August 19, 2019. https://www.army.mil/d-day/.

Buchwach, Buck. "Reactivation of 442nd Marked by Historic Ceremony." *Honolulu Advertiser*, August 1, 1947. https://www.newspapers.com/clip /15924716/the_honolulu_advertiser/.

Burton, Jeffery F., Mary M. Farrell, Florence B. Lord, and Richard W. Lord.

"Confinement and Ethnicity: An Overview of World War II Japanese American Relocation Sites, Chapter 1: Sites of Shame: An Introduction." Western Archeological and Conservation Center, National Park Service, US Department of the Interior, *Publications in Anthropology,* 74, 1999 (rev. July 2000). https://www.nps.gov/museum/exhibits/manz/Map_of_Camps.pdf.

Burton, Jeffery F., Mary M. Farrell, Florence B. Lord, and Richard W. Lord. "Confinement and Ethnicity: An Overview of World War II Japanese American Relocation Sites, Chapter 17: Department of Justice and US Army Facilities." Western Archeological and Conservation Center, National Park Service, US Department of the Interior, *Publications in Anthropology,* 74, 1999 (rev. July 2000). https://www.nps.gov/parkhistory/online_books/anthropology74/index.htm.

Congressional Record. House of Representatives, vol. 162, no. 91, June 9, 2016. https://www.congress.gov/114/crec/2016/06/09/CREC-2016-06-09.pdf.

C-SPAN. "Tribute to Marion Konishi." November 23, 2016. https://www.c-span.org/video/?c4632285/tribute-marion-konishi.

Densho Encyclopedia. "Sites of Incarceration." https://encyclopedia.densho.org/Sites_of_incarceration/.

Densho. "Sites of Shame." https://densho.org/sitesofshame/facilities.xml.

Densho. "Timeline: Important Moments in Japanese American History before, during, and after World War II Mass Incarceration." https://densho.org/timeline/.

Go for Broke National Education Center. "Timeline." http://www.goforbroke.org/learn/history/timeline/index.php.

Hatamiya, Leslie T. *Righting a Wrong: Japanese Americans and the Passage of the Civil Liberties Act of 1988.* Palo Alto, CA: Stanford University Press, 1993, p. 96.

Inter-American Commission on Human Rights. "Isamu Carlos Shibayama, Kenichi Javier Shibayama, and Takeshi Jorge Shibayama, United States of America." Report No. 26/20, Case 12.545 Merits Report, April 27, 2020. https://jlacampaignforjustice.files.wordpress.com/2020/07/20-04-28-iachr-published-report.pdf.

Masumoto, Marie. "Tuna Canyon Detention Facility." *Densho Encyclopedia*. https://encyclopedia.densho.org/Tuna_Canyon_(detention_facility).

Takehara, Marion Konishi. "America, Our Hope Is Anew [*sic*]." Valedictorian Address. Amache Senior High School Graduation, June 25, 1943. 162 Cong. Rec. S3694 9JN, June 9, 2016 (statement of Senator Cory Gardner).

Tuna Canyon Detention Station Coalition. *Only the Oaks Remain: The Story of Tuna Canyon Detention Station*. Pacoima, CA: Tuna Canyon Detention Station Coalition, San Fernando Valley Japanese American Community Center, 2018.

Veterans of Foreign Wars Youth Group. "The Kazuo Masuda Family Story." http://www.vfwyouthgroup.org/forms/kazuo1.pdf.

EXCERPT PERMISSIONS

RESOURCES

Further resources for this book are available on the Simon & Schuster website. You can find the full Bibliography, the Contributor Biography Sources, and a Teacher's Guide under the "Resources and Downloads" tab at www.simonandschuster.net/books/When-Can-We-Go-Back-to -America/Susan-H-Kamei/9781481401449.

INDEX

ABOUT SUSAN H. KAMEI

Susan H. Kamei volunteered as national deputy legal counsel and as a member of the legislative strategy team for the Japanese American Citizens League (JACL) in the successful passage of federal legislation that provided redress to persons of Japanese ancestry for their incarceration during World War II. She and her father, Hiroshi Kamei, have been recognized for their contributions to the redress effort. She teaches a course at the University of Southern California on the legal ramifications of the Japanese American wartime incarceration and the relevance of those constitutional issues today. Her career in law, business, and academia and her contributions to the community were recognized with the Woman of Courage Award in 2000 from the Friends of the Los Angeles City Commission on the Status of Women. She received her JD from the Georgetown University Law Center in Washington, DC, and her BA from the University of California, Irvine.